Preferred Argument Structure

Studies in Discourse and Grammar

Studies in Discourse and Grammar is a monograph series providing a forum for research on grammar as it emerges from and is accounted for by discourse contexts. The assumption underlying the series is that corpora reflecting language as it is actually used are necessary, not only for the verification of grammatical analyses, but also for understanding how the regularities we think of as grammar emerge from communicative needs.

Research in discourse and grammar draws upon both spoken and written corpora, and it is typically, though not necessarily, quantitative. Monographs in the series propose explanations for grammatical regularities in terms of recurrent discourse patterns, which reflect communicative needs, both informational and socio-cultural.

Volume 14

Preferred Argument Structure: Grammar as architecture for function
Edited by John W. Du Bois, Lorraine E. Kumpf and William J. Ashby

Preferred Argument Structure

Grammar as architecture for function

Edited by

John W. Du Bois

University of California, Santa Barbara

Lorraine E. Kumpf

California State University, Long Beach

William J. Ashby

University of California, Santa Barbara

John Benjamins Publishing Company

Amsterdam / Philadelphia

The paper used in this publication meets the minimum requirements of American National Standard for Information Sciences – Permanence of Paper for Printed Library Materials, ANSI Z39.48-1984.

Library of Congress Cataloging-in-Publication Data

Preferred argument structure : grammar as architecture for function / edited by
John W. Du Bois, Lorraine E. Kumpf, and William J. Ashby.
p. cm. (Studies in Discourse and Grammar, ISSN 0928–8929 ; v. 14)
Includes bibliographical references and indexes.
1. Grammar, Comparative and general. I. Du Bois, John W. II.
Kumpf, Lorraine Edith, 1948- III. Ashby, William J. IV. Series.

P151 .P74 2003
415-dc21 2002033024
ISBN 90 272 2624 5 (Eur.) / 1 58811 369 8 (US) (Hb; alk. paper)

John Benjamins Publishing Co. · P.O. Box 36224 · 1020 ME Amsterdam · The Netherlands
John Benjamins North America · P.O. Box 27519 · Philadelphia PA 19118-0519 · USA

Table of contents

Preface VII

Abbreviations IX

Introduction 1
John W. Du Bois, Lorraine E. Kumpf and William J. Ashby

Argument structure: Grammar in use 11
John W. Du Bois

Preferred Argument Structure across time and space: A comparative diachronic analysis of French and Spanish 61
William J. Ashby and Paola Bentivoglio

The lexicon in interaction: Developmental origins of Preferred Argument Structure in Korean 81
Patricia M. Clancy

Genre and Preferred Argument Structure: Sources of argument structure in classroom discourse 109
Lorraine E. Kumpf

Issues in the comparative argument structure analysis in Mayan narratives 131
Nora C. England and Laura Martin

New light on information pressure: Information conduits, "escape valves", and role alignment stretching 159
Mark Durie

Beyond Preferred Argument Structure: Sentences, pronouns, and given referents in Nepali 197
Carol Genetti and Laura D. Crain

Multiple constraints on reference form: Null, pronominal, and full reference in Mapudungun 225
Jennifer E. Arnold

Argument splits in Finnish grammar and discourse 247
Marja-Liisa Helasvuo

Core arguments and the inversion of the nominal hierarchy in Roviana 273
Simon H. Corston-Oliver

Preferred Argument Structure in early Inuktitut spontaneous speech data 301
Shanley E. M. Allen and Heike Schröder

The role of Preferred Argument Structure for understanding aphasic sentence planning 339
Susan E. Kohn and Ana Cragnolino

Nominal information flow in the talk of two boys with autism 353
Elizabeth G. Weber

Tracking the deer: Nominal reference, parallelism and Preferred Argument Structure in Itzaj Maya narrative genres 385
Charles Andrew Hofling

Narrator virtuosity and the strategic exploitation of Preferred Argument Structure in Mocho: Repetition and constructed speech in Mocho narrative 411
Laura Martin

Preferred Argument Structure Bibliography 437

Name index 447

Language index 449

Subject index 451

Preface

Since the time of the earliest work on the theory of Preferred Argument Structure some years ago, there has emerged not only a new set of researchers but also a new generation of ideas. The chance to explore and debate new approaches to discourse and grammar, with the focus that a specific shared topic like Preferred Argument Structure could provide, brought a group of researchers together at the University of California, Santa Barbara in the spring of 1995, at the invitation of the editors of this volume. The motivation was not so much reconfirmation of prior results as building from a common starting point toward new explorations and discoveries, as signaled by the conference's irreverently prophetic title: *Preferred Argument Structure: The Next Generation.* (This has metamorphosed into a more dignified and theoretically informative title for the present publication.) In seeking to develop, challenge, and extend the theory of Preferred Argument Structure, we were especially fortunate to have those three days of intense interaction in Santa Barbara: trying out ideas, debating the consequences, taking away new questions. Since then we have made good use of the stimulation of other perspectives, as the peaceful confrontation of ideas continues to inform the thinking of each of us, a process now come to fruition in the present volume. (Two of the papers in this volume, by Arnold and by Allen and Schroder, were not originally presented at the conference.) It can be said that all the papers in this book are marked by an eagerness to push the original model in new directions. Indeed, the best promise of this work lies in what may yet be realized through new perspectives like those presented here.

We are grateful for the generous support we have received for this project from the Interdisciplinary Humanities Center, Division of Arts and Humanities in the College of Letters and Science, Office of Research, Department of Linguistics, Department of French and Italian, and College of Creative Studies, all of the University of California, Santa Barbara; and from the College of Liberal Arts at California State University, Long Beach. We appreciate the authors for their contributions and their patience. Finally, we thank Sandy Thompson who, as series editor, has been such a steadfast supporter of this project all along the way.

John W. Du Bois
Lorraine E. Kumpf
William J. Ashby
Santa Barbara and Long Beach

Preface

Since the time of the earliest work on the theory of Preferred Argument Structure some years ago, there has emerged a growing body of research [illegible] a new generation of researchers has come to explore in new approaches to discourse and grammar, with the recognition that specific shared principles like Preferred Argument Structure could provide. This brought a group of researchers together at the University of California, Santa Barbara, in the summer of 1997, at the invitation of the editors of this volume. The motivation was not so much to summarize the prior results as bringing more recent investigations together toward new assessments and discoveries, as signaled by the conference's tentative title *Preferred Argument Structure: The Next Generation*. Following the conference, this has moved into a more diversified and theoretically informed title for the present publication. In seeking to develop, challenge, and extend the theory of Preferred Argument Structure, we were especially fortunate to have the knowledge of [illegible] at Santa Barbara bringing our ideas to bear on the consequences, taking up new questions. Since then we have made use of the stimulation of other perspectives, as the present confrontation of ideas continues to inform the thinking of many of us, and these now come to fruition in the present volume. Two of the papers in this volume, by Arnold and by Allen and Schröder, were not originally presented at the conference. It can be said that all the papers in this book are marked by an eagerness to push the original model in new directions. Indeed, the clear promise of this work lies in what may yet be realized through new perspectives like those presented here.

We are grateful for the generous support we have received for this project from the Interdisciplinary Humanities Center, Division of Arts and Humanities in the College of Letters and Science, Office of Research, Department of Linguistics, Department of French and Italian, and College of Creative Studies, all of the University of California, Santa Barbara; and from the College of Liberal Arts at California State University, Long Beach. We appreciate the authors for their contributions and their patience. Finally, we thank Sandy Thompson who, as series editor, has been such a steadfast supporter of this project all along the way.

John W. Du Bois
Lorraine E. Kumpf
William J. Ashby
Santa Barbara and Long Beach

Abbreviations

A	Transitive Subject
O	Transitive Object
S	Intransitive Subject (all)
Se	Intransitive Subject, Equative or Copular
Sx	Intransitive Subject, Existential
Si	Intransitive Subject, Other
Su	Subject, Transitive and Intransitive
Sa	Intransitive Subject with A properties
So	Intransitive Subject with O properties
I	Indirect Object
Obl	Oblique

Authors who have used other abbreviations for individual languages have listed them in an endnote.

Introduction

John W. Du Bois, Lorraine E. Kumpf and William J. Ashby

To understand grammar, find out how it is used. That is the guiding premise of a line of research today which aims to *describe* grammar in functional context, discovering its recurrent patterns of use, and to *explain* grammar, showing how fixed structures crystallize out of dynamic configurations of form and function in discourse. In this volume the elusive connection between structure and function is explored through a focus on a single unified grammatical problem: argument structure. Widely recognized as central to the organization of grammar, argument structure now appears to be equally important for organizing language use. The two faces of grammar — as structure and as use — are likely to be fully understood only when the issue of their relation to each other has been effectively clarified. How do structure and function interact, and what does their interaction tell us about the nature of language? Argument structure can be seen as key to this relation, poised as it is at the nexus of lexicon and syntax, as well as of structure and function.

As it happens, the grammatical territory explored in this volume represents something of a hot topic right now. It is likely to remain so. Argument structure has in recent years generated a level of interest and activity that impacts a far wider swath of work on grammar. The spreading influence within the clause of the structure of its arguments has naturally drawn the attentions of linguistic researchers from a variety of theoretical outlooks, from descriptive to formal to functional.

In this volume, we get an idea of what is to be learned about argument structure through taking grammar's function in context as pivotal. The questions raised here are posed against the backdrop of one specific claim about the relation of grammar and use, the hypothesis known as Preferred Argument Structure (Du Bois, 1987a). As such, the book represents a response to an idea — a concerted probing by diverse scholars of the implications of argument structure for grammar and use. The contributors are too diverse to be captured under any one label, but they share certain principles that guide the enterprise of understanding grammar. First is a commitment to asking how grammar serves its users' goals. We ask not just what the structure of arguments is, but what argument structure can do for language use. The most reliable place to look for evidence of grammar-users' goals is in discourse.

Moreover, discourse is where the speaker's immediate communicative intention is simultaneously subjected to any and all constraints from the multiple systems of language, from phonetics to syntax, grammar to pragmatics. In this complex environment, where the multiple forces and functions of language come together to shape the current utterance, we often find a kind of competition between the various factors that would shape the structure of the current utterance. And the means of resolving these competitions, if routinized in a consistent way, has the potential to impact the organization of grammar itself, through complex processes of grammaticization (Du Bois, 1985). In this light, identifying the complex configurations of grammatical structures and functions in discourse becomes an integral part of understanding grammar in use. And to the extent that the patterning of structure and function in discourse may influence the system of grammar, it becomes essential both to document the discourse configurations and to theorize the means of their potential influence on grammar. In this view, discourse — conceived as language in use — has an important role to play as the locus for processes of grammaticization, and ultimately in grounding a theoretical understanding of grammar.

While the authors in this volume begin with Preferred Argument Structure as their common point of departure, each moves beyond it in some way to explore new paths and directions. Diversity is ensured by the varied experiences and perspectives brought to bear on the topic, born of work with diverse languages, disciplines, theories, and methods. If anything, the common topic and commonalities in approach bring out more clearly the subtle but telling differences in perspectives, methodologies, and ultimate goals. It is hoped that this rich mosaic of ideas might encourage the reader to read between the authors, as it were, and to imagine still other dimensions waiting to be explored.

A word on the arrangement of the papers is in order. Given the many conceptual and methodological threads that interweave these papers, a division into separate topics did not seem the most useful way to organize the book for the reader. The sequence of chapters was chosen rather with an eye to facilitating a gradual progression into the theory and its consequences, from the more basic issues to those which elaborate on them, situate them, or depart from them in some new direction. No doubt other arrangements would have served as well, but we hope this one works. Even so, as with any complex subject there will necessarily be some topics that come up before their background is fully laid out. Moreover, since each paper was written independently and designed to stand on its own, inevitably some readers will encounter a particular paper without benefit of having read the others. Hence we have left intact the brief recapitulations of Preferred Argument Structure that most of the authors include near the beginning of their papers. These capsule summaries all come out a little different anyway, as each author selects a formulation that best reflects their own perspective on Preferred Argument

Structure — and in so doing usefully signals just which point of departure they will choose for introducing their own work. To further facilitate independent access to the papers, each retains its own separate list of references. A full bibliography of Preferred Argument Structure is provided at the end of the volume, listing works that refer specifically to the theory.

In "Argument Structure: Grammar in Use", Du Bois considers what role argument structure should play in our thinking about grammar, if we take seriously the proposition that it represents a central principle for organizing language use. He begins by recounting some of the history of how argument structure has taken on such a pivotal role in a wide range of present-day approaches to grammar, especially those in the vanguard of the shift to lexical, functional, and constructional visions of grammar. The sources that have fed into current thinking about argument structure are evidently quite broad, and show surprisingly deep historical roots. Focusing next on research on discourse and grammar, Du Bois outlines a brief statement of the Preferred Argument Structure hypothesis and its implications, asking whether it can be considered a universal. He then introduces the metaphor of "grammar as architecture for function", exploring how it frames the question of the structure-function relation. Finally, Du Bois sketches out a series of conclusions, as well as issues raised by Preferred Argument Structure which point beyond it toward questions for future research.

In the next paper, William Ashby and Paula Bentivoglio raise the question of what happens when we follow "Preferred Argument Structure across Time and Space", as they present a diachronic analysis of two historical stages in two Romance languages. Based on a comparison of medieval texts with modern counterparts in French and Spanish, Ashby and Bentivoglio ask whether a simple pattern in discourse can be sufficiently stable to remain recognizable over a period of seven centuries. They face various methodological challenges, for example in comparing modern spoken language to a time for which strictly oral material is not available — though the epic poetry they adduce may be as close as one can get — and in comparing grammar diachronically across systems whose grammatical details have changed. The clarity of the answer they are able to extract has important implications for the question of the generalizability of Preferred Argument Structure across diachronically changing grammatical systems, across certain genre differences, and ultimately for its universality.

In the next paper Patricia Clancy delves within the broad grammatical generalizations implicit in Preferred Argument Structure to get at the specifics of "The Lexicon in Interaction", detailing the "Developmental Origins of Preferred Argument Structure in Korean". Based on her analysis of extensive recordings of mother-child interactions in Korean, Clancy asks whether the Preferred Argument Structure patterns which have been repeatedly identified for adult speech will extend into early childhood. She finds that children recurrently engage in certain verbal activities that require them to focus attention, jointly with their caregivers, on a referent in the here-and-now. Moreover, the structure of semantic relations expressed tends to be predictable, frequently involving an identifiable human agent acting upon a succession of inanimate patients. Consequently the children are able to invoke predictable verbal strategies, using specific high-frequency verbs to successfully manage the communicative interaction. In pointing to the role of child-adult collaborative interactional frameworks in affording recurrent patterning of discourse and grammar, Clancy's work gives us a means of grounding Vygotskian theoretical notions of collaborative learning, via the detailed documentation of interactional patterns of use, which centrally integrate grammatical resources undergoing acquisition. Clancy brings out the implications of her findings for the nature of mental representations, with provocative conclusions about what aspects are and are not mentally represented, and about how discourse patterns may shape knowledge of grammar.

In "Genre and Preferred Argument Structure", Lorraine Kumpf explores the sources of argument structure patterning within one specific context, that of classroom science teaching. Kumpf shows how the teacher's task of establishing joint attention toward the scientific subject matter motivates the exploitation of a small repertoire of high-frequency argument structure strategies. Low content transitive verbs like 'have' are used repeatedly to present to the students the key scientific concepts being taught — even if the concept is not strictly new information in the usual sense of being introduced for the first time. Kumpf's work points to a larger issue concerning the cognitive work associated with the 'free' argument roles of Preferred Argument Structure. They apparently facilitate cognitively complex processing in general, regardless of whether new information is involved. Though the genre sampled is quite specific, the implications which emerge from the study are broad. The question arises, whether the functions of grammar must be relativized to particular genres and contexts of use, or whether grammar provides general-purpose resources whose functioning cuts across all contexts.

Nora England and Laura Martin turn a spotlight on method in their "Issues in Comparative Argument Structure Analysis in Mayan Narratives", probing such seemingly innocent questions as what constitutes a lexical mention, a new mention, or a clause. Every language differs in its grammar — certainly at the surface where the action takes place in Preferred Argument Structure — and the implications of such analytical issues for theories of argument structure are potentially confounding, with consequences for practices of categorizing, coding, counting, and comparing. Embarking on a comparison across languages could lead to the derailing of universal claims for Preferred Argument Structure, and England and Martin do not shy away from documenting significant divergences even between the various Mayan relatives of Sakapultek, as well as between genres within a given language. In some languages (e.g. Mam) the unusual discourse patterns could be argued to reflect particular grammatical configurations (e.g. of agreement morphology), but the precise explanation remains elusive. The findings England and Martin bring to bear on the issue of inter-grammar comparison have profound implications for what it means to establish a discourse-and-grammar universal.

Mark Durie undertakes to throw "New Light on Information Pressure" in his paper subtitled "Information Conduits, Escape Valves, and Role Alignment Stretching". He considers how putatively universal discourse patterns such as Preferred Argument Structure can grammaticize differently in different languages, resulting in the typological diversity of argument configurations that characterize the ergative-absolutive, nominative-accusative, and actor-undergoer language types. Based on data from Acehnese, a representative of the relatively rare actor-undergoer type (comparable to yet distinct from the active-stative type), he argues the need for a finer-grained accounting of the grammatical and semantic grid that frames research on correlations between discourse and grammar. In particular, the intransitive subject category (S) should be exploded to reveal crucial internal complexity, along semantic-grammatical lines. In Acehnese discourse, S's in Undergoer role turn out to pattern somewhat differently from S's in Actor role, leaning toward the pattern for O (Object) Undergoers. This discourse alignment partly mirrors the grammatical alignment of Acehnese, where Undergoers are marked as distinct from Actors regardless of whether the predication is transitive or intransitive. If Preferred Argument Structure patterns can be "tuned" differently in different languages, argues Durie, we must recognize a reciprocal shaping between discourse and grammar, whereby discourse patterns are grammaticized into discrete structural alignments which in turn influence the patterns of discourse. Along the way Durie introduces some valuable methodological tools for researching hierarchies of discourse-grammar patterning, including a concept of "referential density" for quantifying the effects of variable information pressure.

Taking their inquiry "Beyond Preferred Argument Structure", Carol Genetti and Laura Crain pursue the role of "Sentences, Pronouns, and Given Referents in Nepali". They identify certain distinctive Nepali discourse patterns which, while broadly compatible with the standard clause-based framing of Preferred Argument Structure, are better understood in terms of the sentence as the unit of generalization. Following up on some often-overlooked claims about the distribution of overt versus zero mentions in discourse and grammar (Du Bois, 1987b), Genetti and Crain argue that in Nepali the preference for one overt mention extends up to the sentence level, and motivates the frequent use of overt mentions for given referents. Nepali sentences exhibit complex structures including clause chains and complements, so the contrast between clause and sentence is significant. The authors also single out pronouns as playing a more prominent role in discourse than in some other languages for which Preferred Argument Structure has been identified. Marking a three-way discrimination between lexical, pronominal, and zero reference forms, they are able to document split distribution of referential forms in discourse: lexical nouns follow a more ergative-absolutive distribution in discourse, while pronouns follow a more nominative-accusative pattern. This discourse pattern matches the grammatical pattern of split ergativity exhibited by languages like Yidiny (Dixon, 1979; Silverstein, 1976), a finding which carries profound implications for grammaticization. Once again the explanatory power of competing motivations tests out against the typological distribution of split grammatical systems. Finally, Genetti and Crain argue for the co-existence of universal discourse-and-grammar correlations with language-specific, fine-tuned patterns linking local grammatical structures to local discourse patterns.

In her paper on "Multiple Constraints on Reference Form: Null, Pronominal, and Full Reference in Mapudungun", Jennifer Arnold explores how various factors interact to influence the choice of referential form in discourse. Into the standard discussion of Preferred Argument Structure, with its simplification of information flow factors into a binary opposition of new vs. not new, Arnold introduces the complexity of several additional factors, especially the continuous scalar approach of Accessibility Theory (Ariel, 1990, 2001) and the orientation to prior clause structure and argument hierarchies of Centering Theory (Grosz et al., 1995). Using statistical techniques characteristic of psycholinguistic research, she is able to substantiate the One Lexical Argument Constraint, to argue that it is not reducible to accessibility effects, and to identify effects of grammatical parallelism across adjacent clauses. Arnold's findings suggest that the marriage of Preferred Argument Structure with Accessibility Theory is a natural and indeed a fruitful one.

Marja-Liisa Helasvuo examines the relation between "Argument Splits in Finnish Grammar and Discourse", with a specific focus on identifying discourse patterns differentiating categories based on 'inherent lexical content' (Silverstein, 1976), such as between personal pronouns and other referential forms. Documenting the distribution of case marking, word order, and other grammatical phenomena in conversation, Helasvuo finds reason to raise doubts about certain longstanding assumptions about Finnish grammar. Where standard accounts represent Finnish as a classic free word order language, Helasvuo finds instead a strong tendency to converge on a limited array of recurrent patterns, typically subject-verb-object. Once the animacy status of referents is taken into account, for some referent types (e.g. human pronominal) the order becomes virtually fixed. Interestingly, while Finnish cannot be said to exhibit a true accusative-ergative split, it is nevertheless true that evidence supporting a nominative configuration is easiest to find for first and second person pronouns, but scarcer or absent for the domain of lexical nouns. The virtual neutralization of distinctive nominative-accusative treatment represents a collapse of the motivation for accusativity in the third person, which is at least consonant with cross-linguistic tendencies in the configuration of accusative-ergative splits.

In "Core Arguments and the Inversion of the Nominal Hierarchy", Simon Corston-Oliver identifies certain grammatical patterns in the marking of arguments in Roviana, an ergative language, which appear highly unusual when compared to generalizations about ergative languages as described in the typological literature. In some cases the expected pattern, based on a claimed universal hierarchy of noun phrase types (Dixon, 1979; Dixon, 1994; Silverstein, 1976), appears reversed in Roviana. Counter to universal prediction it is absolutives that are marked in Roviana, while ergatives are unmarked. Corston-Oliver accounts for this unusual pattern by showing how the discourse distribution of referring forms in Roviana motivates specific historical developments in the grammaticization of the modern system of argument marking. First, he shows that the absolutive role (S, O) synchronically constitutes the primary locus in Roviana for introducing new information into core roles, a grammar-pragmatics correlation predicted by Preferred Argument Structure. Then he argues that the absolutive marker derives historically from a new information marker, which was eventually extended analogically to all absolutives. In general, Corston-Oliver's work implies that the recognition of atypical grammatical patterns in ergative languages need not preclude the possibility of cogent and indeed general explanations, if the interaction of local historical developments with universal patterns of discourse is properly understood.

The examination of ergative languages continues in "Preferred Argument Structure in Early Inuktitut Spontaneous Speech Data", by Shanley E. M. Allen and Heike Schröder. The focus here is on young children in the early stages of learning an ergative language, one of the Inuit family spoken in northern Canada. Inuktitut's typological similarities with Sakapultek and the other Mayan languages described in this volume extend beyond ergativity to include details of the head-marking pattern (Nichols, 1986) of morphological information registered on the verb: both subject and object arguments are obligatorily cross-referenced via verbal affixes that index the person and number of the argument. Following the methodology and analytical categories developed by Clancy (Clancy, 1993) for the analysis of referential pragmatics in child discourse, Allen and Schröder probe what children do with the grammatical organization of full noun phrases and new information when the grammar they are learning is ergative. They are able to show that Inuktitut children follow the constraints of Preferred Argument Structure from the early stages of learning. Confirming the results first documented by Clancy (Clancy, 1993) for Preferred Argument Structure in Korean, an accusative language, Allen and Schröder's demonstration that the constraints are equally followed in an ergative language rounds out the picture in an important way (see also Duranti and Ochs, 1989). This work increases one's curiosity about the pragmatic-grammatical patterning of child discourse in languages of the as yet unexamined active and agentive types (not to mention other ergative languages including Mayan).

Susan E. Kohn and Ana Cragnolino explore "The Role of Preferred Argument Structure for Understanding Aphasic Sentence Planning", asking whether the proposed constraints are preserved even in individuals with agrammatic aphasia, a condition which significantly disrupts the production of grammatical utterances. They show that aphasic speakers produce sentences which are largely comparable to those of normal speakers in following the One Lexical Argument Constraint and the Non-Lexical A Constraint. When violations do occur, the pattern argues for the primacy of the latter over the former constraint. Increase in violations correlates with increase in the production of grammatically anomalous utterances, suggesting a close link between Preferred Argument Structure and grammar. Of course, since the findings reported here treat only transitive sentences, it remains to be seen how they will extend to intransitives. Kohn and Cragnolino's experimental methodology introduces some useful innovations. Among lexical nouns they distinguish between general and specific, and suggest that general nouns ('man', 'woman') may pattern like pronouns. And, whereas the original constraints of Preferred Argument Structure were based entirely on patterning in extended discourse, Kohn and Cragnolino's experimental model establishes their applicability even in the production of individual sentences in isolation, both for normals and aphasics. They conclude that the constraints may be part of the cognitive system for early planning of sentence production, and sufficiently robust to remain in place even under the neurological trauma of aphasia.

In a further probe of the status of discourse processing under difficult cognitive conditions, Elizabeth Weber examines "Nominal Information Flow in the Talk of Two Boys with Autism". Autism has long been attributed to a lack of a theory of mind. Given that a systematic awareness of other's minds is a presumed prerequisite for the appropriate management of information flow in discourse (Chafe, 1987, 1994; Clark, 1996), persons with autism should be expected to show significant disruptions in patterns of use of nominal reference forms, reflecting problems in maintaining awareness of which information can be appropriately considered as already activated in others' minds vs. which information must be considered as new to the addressee. Weber asks whether such disruptions can be verified in the naturally occurring, self-directed discourse of autistic children engaged in play, and if so, whether this will distort the patterns predicted by Preferred Argument Structure. She does find certain anomalies in aspects of the discourse, such as a disproportionate attention to inanimate rather than animate referents. What is more interesting, however, is what is not disrupted. Weber argues that the children's natural discourse mostly does not show, for example, inappropriate frequencies of use of pronouns vs. lexical nouns, of a sort that might be found in an experimental context. Rather, the frequencies seem consistent with the standard pattern for Preferred Argument Structure in spontaneous discourse among normal speakers. She argues that for the children in her study, the predictions of the theory of mind deficit are not fully borne out. Finally, Weber makes a case for looking at language use in its natural context of spoken interaction, lest the full range of any speaker's competences be overlooked.

For the finale we turn to the role of the individual engaged in aesthetic performance, with two papers on spoken narrative in Mayan languages. In "Tracking the Deer" Charles Hofling presents a detailed case study of "Nominal Reference, Parallelism and Preferred Argument Structure in Itzaj Maya Narrative Genres". Comparing a personal narrative and a mythic narrative which are united by their common topic of deer hunting (and their common speaker), Hofling follows the precise grammatical trajectory of various referents as they are first introduced and subsequently tracked through discourse. He finds interesting differences between the genres regarding the tracking of referents, reflecting partly their differing proportions of various kinds of topical referents (e.g. first versus third person). Sharper differences distinguish animate and inanimate referents, again tied to differences in topicality. Yet choice of referential form is influenced by more subtle factors of cultural and rhetorical prominence as well, including the Mayan aesthetic of structural parallelism. Reversing the equation, Hofling observes that the narrator's choice of referential form can be used to signal shifts in perspective, both personal and cultural.

The role of the individual speaker is preeminent in Laura Martin's paper on "Narrator Virtuosity and the Strategic Exploitation of Preferred Argument Structure", subtitled "Repetition and Constructed Speech in Mocho Narrative". Observing that a statistical abstract of the narrative would reveal little but the by now expected patterns of Preferred Argument Structure, Martin argues for a closer moment-by-moment inspection of the narrative trajectory, one that attends to the culturally situated rhetorical expectations in force at any given moment. She shows how a skilled speaker's decision about which referential form to use and which argument position to put it in may be sensitive to locally invoked cultural frames. The pervasive deployment of characteristically Mayan rhetorical frameworks such as structural parallelism and reported speech leads to local patterns in the form and configuration of arguments, which may depart from expected norms for European languages and genres to the extent that these privilege information management above all. Given that such individual strategic choices do not appear to disrupt the broader statistical tendencies to Preferred Argument Structure, the paradox of local choice and global pattern in discourse remains an issue well worth exploring.

It is fitting to close the volume with attention to the words of the individual speaker, who is after all the final agent of discourse. It is the speaker who, confronted by a specific context, and using a specific grammar, ultimately makes the decisions about which verb, argument structure, grammatical role, and referential form are to be employed in the accomplishment of immediate verbal intentions. We find here a role for speaker expressivity and even virtuosity. And yet the individual acts add up to a larger picture as well, seen from a height as it were, which, while necessarily blurring the uniqueness of each utterance act, tells us something new about the total ecology of language use. Taken together, the aggregate of individual speaker choices gives discourse its characteristic pattern. And discourse pattern sets the agenda for grammaticization. In the end the repertoire of grammatical architectures can be seen to evolve so as to elegantly subserve the prevailing patterns of function, while leaving room for the individual's creative act.

References

Ariel, Mira. 1990. *Accessing Noun-Phrase Antecedents.* London: Routledge.

Ariel, Mira. 2001. "Accessibility theory: An overview". In Ted Sanders, Joost Schilperoord and Wilbert Spooren (eds), *Text Representation: Linguistic and Psycholinguistic Aspects.* Amsterdam and Philadelphia: Benjamins, 29–87.

Chafe, Wallace L. 1987. "Cognitive constraints on information flow". In Russell S. Tomlin (ed.), *Coherence and Grounding in Discourse.* Amsterdam and Philadelphia: Benjamins, 21–51.

Chafe, Wallace L. 1994. *Discourse, Consciousness, and Time: The Flow and Displacement of Conscious Experience in Speaking and Writing.* Chicago: University of Chicago Press.

Clancy, Patricia M. 1993. "Preferred Argument Structure in Korean acquisition". In Eve V. Clark (ed.), *The Proceedings of the Twenty-Fifth Annual Child Language Research Forum.* Stanford: CSLI Publications, 307–14.

Clark, Herbert H. 1996. *Using Language.* Cambridge: Cambridge University Press.

Dixon, Robert M. W. 1979. "Ergativity". *Language* 55: 59–128.

Dixon, Robert M. W.. 1994. *Ergativity.* Cambridge: Cambridge University Press.

Du Bois, John W. 1985. "Competing motivations". In John Haiman (ed.), *Iconicity in Syntax.* Amsterdam and Philadelphia: Benjamins, 343–65.

Du Bois, John W.. 1987a. "The discourse basis of ergativity". *Language* 63: 805–55.

Du Bois, John W.. 1987b. "Absolutive zero: Paradigm adaptivity in Sacapultec Maya". *Lingua* 71: 203–22.

Duranti, Alessandro and Ochs, Elinor. 1989. *Acquisition of Genitive Agents in Samoan.* (*Papers & Reports on Child Language Development,* 28). Stanford University.

Grosz, Barbara, Joshi, Aravind and Weinstein, Scott. 1995. "Centering: A framework for modeling the local coherence of discourse". *Computational Linguistics* 21: 203–25.

Nichols, Johanna. 1986. "Head-marking and dependent-marking grammar". *Language* 62: 56–119.

Silverstein, Michael. 1976. "Hierarchy of features and ergativity". In Robert M. W. Dixon (ed.), *Grammatical Categories in Australian Languages.* Canberra: Australian Institute of Aboriginal Studies: 112–71.

Argument structure

Grammar in use

John W. Du Bois
University of California, Santa Barbara

Grammar in use

Language can be seen as responsive, in some degree, to the demands that are placed on it by its users. The question is how far this responsiveness goes. Is grammar implicated, or only the more malleable layers of lexical inventories? Clearly all grammars display some plasticity, as evidenced in the changes they continually undergo. But are these changes to be viewed as superficial or deep? Does the continual reconfiguration of the grammatical systems that organize form and meaning reflect anything profound about language?

On one view, the grammar of any language evolves so as to serve its users' goals, whether to conceptualize, communicate, or collaborate. Within discourse, considered as the domain of language use, the functions most often implemented will play the greatest role, it is claimed, in shaping how grammars come to be as they are. From the speaker's perspective, on the other hand, grammatical structures represent available resources, ready to mediate whatever actions are regularly undertaken with language. But this view raises a host of further questions. Among the more specific issues brought into focus is to what extent a given grammatical structure, such as a construction, a clause type, or a verb's argument structure, can be said to subserve a well-defined function in the domain of language use. And if a functional role is to be recognized for grammatical structures, there remains the question of what kinds of function may be realized. There is as yet little agreement among linguists as to how to go about answering such questions. Differing views of the nature of grammar motivate different paths toward apprehending the functions of specific linguistic structures.

Argument structure in particular has attracted attention from diverse perspectives. How noun phrases relate to their verbs virtually demands a multidimensional and even multidisciplinary approach, one capable of bringing together aspects of semantics, syntax, morphology, typology, diachrony, acquisition, cognition, and, some would urge, pragmatics. An uttered noun phrase token filling an argument role of a given verb exhibits properties along multiple dimensions: grammatically it is, say, a transitive subject, semantically a human experiencer, morphologically a pronoun, pragmatically given information. Of these dimensions, it was semantic structure that was the first to be taken seriously as a potential influence on — or even determinant of — argument structure, and it has remained the factor most consistently attended to. The attraction of the semantic approach stems partly, no doubt, from the fact that the meanings expressed by a particular verb, and by each co-argument within the verb's overall argument configuration, appear immediately accessible to intuition, even within the isolated constructed sentences that have supplied the primary source of data for much of the argument structure debate. Moreover, the verb word seems to concisely identify and isolate an event, which can then be systematically characterized through semantic analysis in terms of a small set of basic semantic features or entailments — just those aspects of the event's structure (or the verb's meaning) which are demonstrably relevant to the grammatical behavior of the argument structure it defines. Certainly such semantic analysis has achieved remarkable successes recently, and in some form is likely to constitute an indispensable dimension of any full explanation of argument structure phenomena. But the expectation that event semantics by itself could supply the entire basis for understanding argument structure begins to seem illusory to the extent that it overlooks significant contributions from other, more elusive, factors. The incompleteness of the semantic explanation becomes evident to the degree that one takes seriously the problem posed by grammar in use, and in particular, by how argument structures are used to do the full range of things that speakers need to do.

The dimension of the argument structure equation which has been most erratically attended to, though never entirely lost sight of, is pragmatics — specifically, discourse pragmatics. For many, an excursion into the referential-pragmatic and cognitive processes of introducing new information and tracking it through extended discourse would seem a distraction, the last thing that would come to mind as a way of resolving the challenges of argument structure. Argument structure already makes intense demands of its adherents, requiring simultaneous attention to a web of interrelated factors, including: semantic structure and conceptual structure, at the levels of both word and clause; semantic roles and grammatical relations, possibly at several degrees of abstraction; principles for linking or mapping between the domains of meaning and grammar; and questions of the role of morphology, lexicon, constructions, syntax, semantics, typology, universals, and learning in all of this. Apparently all these influences zero in on the one lexical category that lies at the heart of the matter: the verb. Conversely, a broad range of effects can be said to radiate out from the verbal center. With such a complex array of factors to attend to, all concentrated upon the narrow scope of a predicative word, a call to add discourse pragmatics to the picture may seem like a diversion from the more pressing concerns of syntactic description and semantic explanation. It is not immediately obvious how discourse pragmatic influences are to be integrated into the semantic and event-based explanations that currently yield such promising results. This reaction is the more understandable if we accept the commonplace view that discourse is several degrees removed in scale from the lexical level where argument structures are represented, and even from the clausal level where they spread their influence. But the assumption that discourse properly treats units larger than the sentence — and so by implication should leave the sentence with its clausal and lexical contents alone — is not well motivated. To understand what discourse pragmatics could possibly say about argument structure we need to address, if briefly, the scope of discourse research.

What does discourse imply? For many it denotes just more of the same: a larger stretch of speech extending beyond the sentence, which is to say, beyond the traditional scope of grammatical analysis. On such a view the proper domain of discourse begins where syntax ends, at the sentence boundary. Discourse research should look outside the sentence, while the sentence and its insides are left to syntax. But why, aside from the historical precedence of traditional syntax in this domain, should discourse limit itself to the outside of a sentence? To the contrary, some of the most interesting results are to be found by looking through the other end of the telescope — by bringing discourse analysis inside the clause. Within the narrow grammatical frame articulated by a verb and its dependent arguments may be discovered structural tendencies that respond not only to grammar and meaning, as has long been recognized, but also to the specific demands of discourse pragmatics. The noun phrase that is characterized by its grammatical category and by its syntactic and semantic relation to its verb is also, significantly, the carrier of information statuses such as accessibility or topicality, and pragmatic relations such as anaphora and contrast. It is only by pursuing the concerns of discourse inside the traditional territory of the grammarian that the powerful interaction of competing forces, and their systematic resolution through the processes of grammaticization, can be recognized as a foundation for the structural organization of the clause. On this view discourse is not a matter of size but of use. The utterances that comprise a discourse are taken as acts of language use regardless of their cumulative size relative to a sentence. Any natural discourse however brief represents a complex event fully invested with form and meaning at all linguistic levels, including morphology, lexicon, syntax, and phonology (including prosody); and bearing a totality of meaning in its semantic, pragmatic, and interactional dimensions. Out of this potentially overwhelming complexity it is nevertheless possible to abstract certain reliable organizing patterns, and speakers no less then linguists do this. It could be said that the business of grammar is to achieve a functional abstraction: to partial out a set of generalized architectural frames through which the enactment of function is organized.

In this light, the patterning of discourse has something to tell us about things inside the sentence, down to the level of verbal argument structures with their organizational influence across the clause. At a time when theories of argument structure have already undertaken to address the structural implications of interactions across domains of words, constructions, grammatical relations, semantic relations, lexicosemantic content, and conceptual construals of events and roles, there is still the possibility, indeed the necessity, to add the facts of discourse pragmatics to the equation. Discourse research has always dealt with interactions among diverse domains, and so can be expected to contribute a unifying perspective. Discourse-and-grammar studies regularly identify correlations between layered patterns in grammatical structure, semantic structure, and discourse-pragmatic structure, and seek to explain them through a strategic perspective on the grammaticization of language in use. Moreover, the discourse-functional approach has consistently embraced the typological diversity of languages, recognizing in the seeming variability of, for example, systems of grammatical relations (e.g. nominative-accusative vs. ergative-absolutive vs. actor-undergoer) a deeply revealing array of alternative resolutions of common, fundamental, and even universal motivations which compete for the effective organization of linguistic structure. Studies in typology have long provided grist for the mill of functional explanation, as other people's languages allow one to tease apart the factors that are already entwined, perhaps inextricably, in one's own language. Paradoxically, it is only by stepping up to the challenge of integrating across the multiple functional layers of language, and across the typologically diverse array of solutions to common grammaticization problems, that the most fundamental commonalities of language can be grasped.

The idea that discourse pragmatics constitutes a dimension of argument structure which parallels those of semantics and grammar, and in certain ways maps onto, interacts with, and even shapes them, will of necessity return as a theme in the narrative that follows. But we are getting ahead of ourselves. In this paper I first examine the idea of argument structure in light of the various roles it has played in the development of modern linguistics, particularly in its increasingly important role as a central organizing principle of language — a focus for the interaction of meaning, grammar, lexicon, and function. Argument structure is now core for several approaches to language, which makes it interesting to ask why it has become so important. The reality of this history demands that the larger share of attention go to developments in the grammatical characterization of argument structure, along with the semantically based explanations proposed for it. But the history also reveals an undeniable, if fragile, thread of pragmatic insight and analysis. The pragmatic observations of one generation seem continually to drift out of focus for the next, perhaps for lack of a framework to integrate them into the more highly valued grammatical and semantic analyses. It could be said that linguists have always been aware that certain pragmatic factors (for example topicality) played some kind of role relative to certain aspects of argument structure (for example subject selection), but they have never quite known what to do about it. Nevertheless they have apparently felt compelled, at irregular intervals, to record their observations of the pragmatic correlates of argument structure. I will present just a few selected highlights from this checkered history, as I ask where, if at all, discourse pragmatics fits into the argument structure picture. Among the specific phenomena I will foreground are what I call co-argument effects, which includes competition between alternative candidates for selection to the argument roles of a clause. I try to show that in addition to the previously recognized semantic co-argument effects, there are also pragmatic ones. The cognitive-pragmatic perspective also challenges the assumption that a verb's syntactic valence can be assumed to be a fixed target for argument linking. Next I bring up one of argument structure's perennially neglected problems, that of ergativity, especially split ergativity. Here I try to show that ergativity is not just a problem, it's part of the solution. Typological research on ergativity has prompted linguists to distinguish A, S, and O (transitive subject, intransitive subject, and direct object, respectively), which turns out to be a necessary precondition for uncovering certain covert patterns of grammar in use, with large consequences for understanding argument structure. With this background in place, I introduce the central hypothesis of this volume, that of Preferred Argument Structure, which concerns the relation between argument structure and certain patterns of grammar and pragmatics in discourse. I do not attempt to give a full explication of the theory here, since I have covered that territory elsewhere (Du Bois 1987a, 2003a), and further developments are well represented in the other papers of this volume. But I do discuss the significance of the model with respect to a number of the current issues in argument structure research. Next, I present a brief consideration of argument structure as an exemplar of *grammar as architecture for function*, a concept which provides the subtitle for this volume. Finally, I close with a survey of some of the applications of the Preferred Argument Structure approach to various current trends in argument structure research, and consider its implications for future work.

Argument structure

I turn now to the idea of argument structure as it has developed in modern linguistics, with a focus on the uses that linguists have found for it in their efforts to understand grammar and meaning. Modern linguistics first took on the notion of argument from philosophy, where it had long served as a conceptual tool for the logical analysis of abstract predication, with roots that go back at least to Frege. For Frege argument structure was an instrument for the formulation of 'pure thought' (1879 [1960]), and any application to the grammars of particular languages was a secondary consideration. But the few remarks that Frege did venture regarding natural language present a surprisingly modern perspective, prefiguring issues that remain relevant for the understanding of argument structure and grammatical relations to this day:

> The speaker usually intends the subject to be taken as the principal argument; the next in importance often appears as the object. Language has the liberty of arbitrarily presenting one or another part of the proposition as the principal argument by a choice between … words, e.g. between … 'give' and 'receive' … (Frege 1879 [1960]: 14–15)

In this passage Frege recognizes a hierarchy of arguments, differentiated along a scale of 'importance', where subject ranks above object. He observes that lexical alternatives within the same semantic domain provide alternative argument structures for different assignments of argument salience, as when verbs like 'give' and 'receive' define different subject selections. He goes on to point out that "this liberty is restricted by lack of words" (1879 [1960]: 14–15), which is to say that lexical gaps may occur in a language's repertoire of available argument structures. Frege even speculates on the pragmatic role of argument selection in the cognitive processing of extended discourse (to put it in modern terms):

> In language the place occupied by the subject in the word-order has the significance of a *specially important* place; it is where we put what we want the hearer to attend to specially. … This may, e.g., have the purpose of indicating a relation between this judgment and others, and thus making it easier for the hearer to grasp the whole sequence of thought. All such aspects of language are merely results of the reciprocal action of speaker and hearer; e.g. the speaker takes account of what the hearer expects, and tries to set him upon the right track before actually uttering the judgment. (1879 [1960]: 3)

As a capsule description of the pragmatics of argument selection (argument salience, attention management, argument reselection across clauses in sequence, discourse coherence marking, processing facilitation, speaker management of hearer expectations), this passage prefigures numerous issues which remain relevant today. But having gone thus far, Frege quickly distanced himself from the project of describing natural language, and reiterated instead his sole criterion for formalizing logic: "In my formalized language there is nothing that corresponds; only that part of judgments which affects the *possible inferences* is taken into consideration" (1879 [1960]: 3). One can only imagine what might have happened had Frege traveled farther along the road not taken.

Once linguists appropriated the concept of the argument to their purposes, their intrinsic concern with language led them to pursue further the relation of argument structure to the organization of linguistic expression. Though at first argument structure represented little more than a way to describe propositional meanings in logical terms, with no detailed connection to linguistic form, over time it inspired goals more ambitious and more indigenous to the study of language. Richard Montague's insistence that the evident structure of a natural language like English be taken seriously as the means through which meanings are more or less directly expressed appealed to the linguist's respect for form. Montague's ideas became particularly influential among formal semanticists, where his emphasis on function-argument structure as "the basic semantic glue by which meanings are combined" (Partee 1996:21) had a lasting impact on modern understandings of the role of grammar in meaning. For linguists argument structure came to be recognized as an indispensable element of grammar, influencing general theories of grammar and meaning as well as descriptions of particular grammatical and semantic phenomena among the world's languages. The concept is slanted now more towards structure, now more towards meaning. But its most important role, as often as not, has been to reconcile the two. Argument structure succinctly poses the problem of an articulate mapping between certain meaning relations on the one hand and certain grammatical relations on the other. Its import lies at the cross-roads: argument structure is where meaning meets grammar, and lexicon meets syntax. And if Frege was right, pragmatic function may be present at the cross-roads too, whether or not it is yet fully acknowledged and integrated into argument structure analyses.

Argument structure effectively organizes relations among the central grammatical components of a predication. Because of its ties to the lexical repertoire of verb meanings in a given language, argument structure has been recognized as suffused with meaning, always implicitly and often explicitly. Conversely, to the extent that meanings have been invoked as characterizing or even determining the structure of clauses, these meanings are admitted to be relatively abstract and even grammaticized in character, expressing a pale sort of semantics whose generality nevertheless affords it a wide application. Argument structure implies an organizing framework that establishes combinatorial relations between elements in at least two parallel dimensions, and again establishes a further set of relations between these dimensions. Along the combinatorial dimensions, (1) grammatically, nouns relate to verbs as subject, object etc. (however the terms of these relations may be specified for a given language type); and (2) semantically (and/or conceptually), entity concepts relate to event concepts, as agent, patient, etc. (or proto-agent and proto-patient — again, however these roles may be characterized). And between these two levels, there arises a systematic mapping between the set of co-present semantic (or thematic) relations and the set of co-present grammatical relations. The mapping process (or principles) have been characterized variously as alignment, linking, argument selection, or similar terms. Lexical specificity enters the picture as each member of the repertoire of verbs (or other argument-taking category of predicator) must be mapped individually in accordance with certain general principles, whose precise formulation remains an ongoing challenge. In one prominent formulation:

> Argument functions are directly mapped onto semantic or thematic roles in lexical predicate-argument structures. They provide a uniform way of designating the participants in the events, actions, and situations which are depicted by various subclasses of lexical predicators (Bresnan and Mchombo 1987:757).

The idea that argument structures and grammatical relations bear a motivated relation to something beyond themselves goes back quite a ways, as Frege's comments indicate. Grammatical relations and argument structures have been seen variously as linked to the domains of logic, semantics, and pragmatics, in proposals that would assign values such as agency, volitionality, empathy, and topicality, to name a few. For many, the strongest extra-grammatical connections to a verb's argument structure derive from its meaning. The semantic connection is consistent enough that well-defined rules of correlation can be specified, and verb semantics can be said to partly determine syntactic structure:

> The most striking illustration of the role of meaning in the determination of syntax is the tendency for arguments bearing certain semantic roles to be associated with particular syntactic expressions. … we call the regularities in the association of arguments bearing certain semantic roles to particular syntactic expressions *linking regularities*, and the rules that effect such associations *linking rules*. To the extent that the semantic role of an argument is determined by the meaning of the verb selecting it, the existence of linking regularities supports the idea that verb meaning is a factor in determining the syntactic structure of sentences. The striking similarities in the linking regularities across languages strongly suggest that they are part of the architecture of language. (Levin and Rappaport Hovav 1995:1)

The robustness of such cross-linguistic parallels in patterns of argument linking (or argument selection) is a useful indicator of their power to shape grammar. That this should earn argument structure principles a place in the "architecture of language" is a theme worth returning to (see my discussion below, in a somewhat different sense, of the grammar of argument structure as "architecture for function").

But the widespread recognition that a connection must be identified between argument structure and meaning (or other extra-grammatical function) does not imply agreement as to how this is to be achieved. Conceptions of argument structure vary widely, even among practitioners of the same theory. This is to be expected, according to Bresnan.

> The reason for this is that argument structure has two faces, semantic and syntactic. On the semantic side, argument structure represents the core participants in events (states, processes) designated by a single predicator.

> From this point of view it appears as a type of representation of event structure. On the syntactic side, argument structure represents the minimal information needed to characterize the syntactic dependents of an argument-taking head. From this point of view it appears as a type of syntactic subcategorization or valence register. Thus argument structure is an interface between the semantics and syntax of predicators (which we may take to be verbs in the general case) … (Bresnan 2001: 304)

Nevertheless argument structure is for Bresnan "fundamentally a lexical syntactic construct, not a semantic one", in that it encodes the quantity, type, and hierarchical organization of arguments, as a prelude to mapping them onto syntactic structures (2001: 304). Given the complexity of the interrelated domains, it is natural that different conclusions may be drawn. For example, Goldberg starts from many of the same premises but emphasizes more the multi-dimensionality of argument structure, concluding that a 'hybrid' definition is needed that can accommodate the two domains interacting: "the argument structure of a clause is defined as the surface syntactic form together with the overall event-interpretation of a clause" (forthcoming). Given her interest in pushing beyond the usual scope of argument structure to encompass larger constructions, Goldberg (1995) includes not only the traditional transitive and ditransitive, but also resultative and clausal complement constructions as characterized by argument structures. It is noteworthy that she also recognizes a significant role for the pragmatic correlates of argument structures (Goldberg, forthcoming).

We can agree that argument structure is multifaceted — with *at least* two faces — and that it stands in the middle of things, as an aspect of words (and constructions) which crucially mediates the process of meaning expression. Yet this mediation is not likely to be a simple one, so that its full explication will likely require attention to multiple levels of interacting structures and functions, organized via processes of grammaticization into specific coherent grammars capable of effectively organizing all the necessary aspects of meaningful expression.

Data

At this point it is useful to look at some actual instances of argument structures in use. Most of the examples I will present in this paper are taken from an extensive body of recordings of spoken discourse (Du Bois 2000, 2003b).[1] Due to space limitations, most excerpts are quite short — too short to properly represent the larger discourse context, unfortunately, but adequate to make the preliminary observations required here. Most of the cited examples are exactly one line long, where each line represents a single intonation unit (Chafe 1980, 1994, Du Bois et al. 1992). In syntactic terms, most of these intonation units correspond to a single clause. The first set of examples presented is limited to clauses in which all the argument positions are filled by pronouns. (Sentences containing full noun phrases raise additional issues, which we will encounter soon enough.) While pronoun-only clauses may not be the most frequent type of transitive clause in most genres of spontaneous speech, they are reasonably common. (Personal pronouns are also useful in that they provide, in a language like English, a useful indicator of grammatical role, by displaying their morphological case overtly.) Consider the following:[2]

(1) ALINA: I *grab* her again, ⟨SBC:CUZ 447⟩
(2) LORI: He *kissed* her, ⟨SBC:HOWARDS⟩
(3) BRAD: And so you would *hit* that, ⟨SBC:TAPEDECK⟩

These clauses contain what are thought of as canonical transitive verbs (*hit, grab, kiss*). Each of these clauses describes an event in which an agent performs an action which affects a patient.[3] The agent is realized in transitive subject (A) role, expressed by pre-verbal position with a pronoun in nominative case (*I, he*). The patient is in direct object (O) role, marked by post-verbal position, with a pronoun in accusative case (*her*). (Of course not all pronouns in English show the morphological case contrasts, e.g. *you, that.*) The presence of two argument noun phrases in a transitive clause raises the question as to which is to be realized in which role; that is, which referring expression will bear the grammatical relation of subject to the verb, and which the object? One commonplace notion holds that it is the agent of the action that will (proto-)typically be selected as subject: the grabber, the kisser, the hitter. Conversely the patient will be selected as object: the grabee, kissee, hittee. Of course, this simple scenario leans heavily on the presumption that in any two-argument clause (or two-entity event) there will be one and only one agent (or agent-like entity), and one and only one patient (or patient-like entity), and that each will be clearly recognizable as such — and verbalized accordingly.

In contrast is the intransitive clause, with its single argument:

(4) REBECCA: .. (H) she *moved* again, ⟨SBC:JURY 164⟩
(5) JOANNE: ... he *plays* hard, ⟨SBC:DEADLY 930⟩
(6) JOANNE: (H) she was f=rantically *running around*, ⟨SBC:DEADLY 1318⟩

Here the sole argument is realized grammatically as intransitive subject (S), expressed in English through pre-verbal position with nominative case (*she, he*). In the above examples, the verb expresses an action (*move, play, run*) which the subject referent controls and instigates — as player, mover, runner. But there are many one-argument predicates where the subject does not fit the actor-instigator-controller model:

(7) PAM: # She's *sleeping*. ⟨SBC:RAGING⟩
(8) LINDSEY: ... Oh you've *grow=n*. ⟨SBC:VETMORN 472⟩

(9) CAROLYN: We *lucked out*, ⟨SBC:RAGING 1289⟩

(10) JENNIFER: So he *sucks.* ⟨SBC:RISK 776⟩

(11) LINDSEY: or if he starts *vomiting*, ⟨SBC:VETMORN 64⟩

(12) PHIL: (H) It *broke.* ⟨SBC:ATOMS⟩

Verbs like *sleep, grow, luck out, suck, vomit,* and *break* do not denote (at least in the uses exemplified here) actions controlled by their subject referents; rather the subject referent undergoes an experience, event, or state of some kind, broadly speaking. Grammatical subject status is nevertheless confirmed by pre-verbal position and nominative case pronouns (*she, we, he*), showing that in English these formal features are governed not by semantic but by grammatical relations. Moreover, in a nominative-accusative language like English, they serve to overtly mark the grammatical alignment of all intransitive subjects (S) with transitive subjects (A). Lest this be taken for granted, there is nothing inevitable about this grammatical alignment, as is demonstrated by the fact that in other languages, the diversity of semantic relations motivates the differentiation of intransitives into grammatically distinct classes, expressed in so-called split intransitivity (Durie 1988, Merlan 1985, Mithun 1991). The grammatical heterogeneity of intransitive verbs has sometimes been argued to motivate a grammatical division into covert categories such as the so-called unaccusative vs. unergative verbs (Bresnan 2001, Dowty 1991, Levin and Rappaport Hovav 1995, Perlmutter 1978), a phenomenon which others would prefer to ground in semantic rather than syntactic explanation (Van Valin 1990).

The fact is, even two-argument predications often fail to fit the model of an agent performing an action that affects a patient, as has long been recognized (Dowty 1991, Fillmore 1968, Hopper and Thompson 1980, Jespersen 1924, Thompson and Hopper 2001). This is evident in verbs such as *doubt, hear, notice, love, miss:*

(13) NATHAN: .. (TSK) I *doubt* it. ⟨SBC:ZERO⟩

(14) CAROLYN: And we all *heard* it, ⟨SBC:RAGING⟩

(15) DORIS: did you *notice* em? ⟨SBC:RETIREMENT⟩

(16) DORIS: ... and I *love* you, ⟨SBC:RETIREMENT⟩

(17) JILL: (TSK) I *miss* you too. ⟨SBC:CUTIEPIE⟩

Although these verbs typically take a human referent as their subject (*I, we, you*), the semantic relation of this argument to the verb is not that of agent, but rather experiencer of a psychological state, whether cognitive or affective. As for the direct object, its role is not patient but stimulus, as the entity which evokes the state experienced.

The efficacy of a putative agent is clouded still further when a proposition is negated, questioned, or otherwise distanced from the domain of realis assertion.

Compare the following pairs of utterances:

(18) MARILYN: they *eat* it, ⟨SBC:CONCEPT⟩

(19) JOANNE: They won't *eat* it. ⟨SBC:DEADLY⟩

(20) REBECCA: … (TSK) And she *saw* it, ⟨SBC:JURY 113⟩

(21) JEFF: .. (H) she didn't *see* me. ⟨SBC:CUTIEPIE 969⟩

(22) JILL: .. that would *bother* me. ⟨SBC:CUTIEPIE⟩

(23) LYNNE: And that doesn't *bother* em a bit, ⟨SBC:BLACKSMITH⟩

(24) HAROLD: You *saw* that, ⟨SBC:LAMBADA⟩

(25) RANDY: … Did you *see* that? ⟨SBC:RUNWAY⟩

Whatever role we might wish to attribute to the subject of the positive predications above (*eat, see, bother*), the question arises as to whether that same role (e.g. eater, seer, pest) should still apply when the verb is negated (*not eat, not see, not bother*) or questioned (*did you see…?*). Do we need to recognize thematic relations of non-eater, non-seer, non-pest? It is hard to justify an analysis of 'agent affecting patient' when nothing happened and nobody was affected. The variability is only multiplied further if we consider the full range of actual clause tokens as realized in discourse. We might hope to escape these concerns by avoiding the full complexity of actual clause tokens with their problematic modality inflections, and restricting our analysis (and our accountability) to the domain of main verb types in the lexicon. But such a theoretical constriction would only sidestep the problem temporarily. Arguably, the effects of modality arise even within the lexicon, unavoidably impacting the problem of argument selection. As suggested by the work of Koenig and Davis (2001), an essential step toward the solution of this quandary may be to first factor out features of modality and negation, and then ground the argument selection process on those thematic relations which remain.

This is only one example of the kind of complexity which attends the process of argument selection. If we follow a single grammatical relation in isolation (e.g. subject) across a range of lexical verbs, the diversity of semantic relations that it encodes seems difficult to delimit or characterize. This has motivated many linguists to enlarge the view to encompass the full set of syntagmatic co-arguments within a given argument structure, so as to gain some leverage in considering how the several grammatical relations within a clause may interact and even compete, e.g. for subject selection. Challenges remain, however, in deciding how thematic roles should map onto grammatical roles. For example, consider:

(26) LINDA: and she *admired* him, ⟨SBC:HOWARDS 182⟩

(27) MARY: … And then of course he *adores* me. ⟨SBC:TREE 630⟩

The argument which is to be selected as subject of a verb like *admire* or *adore* is not the agent of effective action, but the experiencer of a psychological state. Nor is its object (*him, me*) necessarily affected as a patient — indeed the object referent may be quite unaware of the infatuation. Rather, the object is interpreted as the stimulus which causes the experiencer's state. The event concepts lexicalized in verbs like *admire* and *adore* can be said to involve two arguments, with the experiencer argument realized, in English, as the subject, and the stimulus realized as the object. (Again, this is not to be taken for granted, since other languages will map roles differently in the same domains of cognitive-affective predication.)

But one and the same scene can apparently be given two diametrically opposed treatments in terms of argument structure (Fillmore 1977a, 1977b, Grimshaw 1990). Compare the verbs *fear* and *scare:*

(28) DANNY: ... Because they *feared* **God**, ⟨SBC:VISION⟩

(29) MARY: ... did I *scare* **you kids**? ⟨SBC:TREE⟩

Here the depicted scenes could each be said to include an experiencer and a stimulus (or, better, to accommodate such an interpretation). But *fear* puts the experiencer in subject role and the stimulus in object role, while *scare* reverses the equation to place stimulus in subject and experiencer in object role. To encounter such a sharp grammatical divergence between two verbs so closely allied in meaning was originally taken by some to constitute an argument for the arbitrariness, and hence syntacticity, of argument selection. More recently many scholars have drawn the opposite conclusion, discerning subtle semantic divergences capable of motivating distinct argument structures (Dor 2000, Grimshaw 1990, Levin and Rappaport Hovav 1995).

These challenges to the simplest conceptions of subject and object selection are well known, and have occasioned many alternative formulations of the criteria for realization of argument structures, as well as of individual grammatical relations. One alternative holds, for example, that it is topic rather than agent that is the most prominent correlate of the subject category, while others attempt a combination of pragmatic and semantic criteria, proposing that subject is a grammaticization of topic and agent together (Chafe 1994, Comrie 1988, Givón 1979, Li and Thompson 1976). Attempts to motivate or explain the grammar of argument selection have typically invoked proposals for mapping functions in one domain (e.g. thematic relations) to functions in another (e.g. grammatical relations). While it has often been noted that discourse pragmatic factors seem to be involved along with the semantic ones, how to incorporate these effects has been less clear.

At this point it will be useful to examine one early proposal about argument selection in more detail.

Two questions

Fillmore's early work[4] on argument selection (initiated under the rubric of case grammar) defines an influential starting point for much subsequent research in the field (see historical discussions in Ackerman and Moore 2001, Davis 2001, Dowty 1991, Goldberg 1995: 101ff). While the particular rules and mechanisms he proposed have been partly superceded by later developments, and specific selection criteria have come and gone, what remains salient are the questions posed. The question most often addressed by researchers asks, concerning the participant roles in a given event, "which is to become the subject and which is to become the object?" (Fillmore 1977b: 73). So stated, the problem is variously spoken of in terms of argument linking, argument selection, and so on. What is often overlooked is that for Fillmore, this was actually the second half of a two-part question:

> The new question for the theory of cases is this: What do we need to know about the various participant roles in a situation in order to know which of these roles or which combinations of them can be put into perspective, and then, for those which have been put into perspective, which is to become the subject and which is to become the object? (1977b: 73)

For Fillmore the question of how to rank participants in the "situation" (which subsumes the event, and more) in order to link them to particular syntactic functions depends on the prior question of which participant roles will be selected for inclusion in the clause nucleus. The problem of argument selection thus requires addressing (at least) two questions, which we may label participant inclusion and participant ranking. While both questions appeared in the widely-read "The case for case reopened", the second apparently eclipsed the first, to judge by its uptake in later research. Actually, Fillmore explored the inclusion question in far greater depth in an often overlooked paper from the same year (1977a).[5] Here he posed the question of how "entities in a scene" are chosen for the clause nucleus (subject, object, indirect object), asking "What enters the nucleus?" With an answer to this question one can then go on to ask, "What determines the ranking of terms in a nucleus?" (1977a: 94).[6] But to focus only on ranking (or linking), taking the inclusion problem for granted, is to underestimate the scope of the problem of accounting for argument selection.

The inclusion problem is best understood with reference to what Fillmore called the *scene*, of which one illustration would be the commercial *event* of buying and selling (1977b: 72). Fillmore saw the scene/event as key to the grounding of meaning, proposing the axiom, "MEANINGS ARE RELATIVIZED TO SCENES" (1977b: 59). In relating the meaning of a given verb or noun to the scene through which it derives its conceptual framing, Fillmore's move prefigures the current interest in events and event structures as determinants of verb meanings and argument structures (Dowty 1991, Levin and Rappaport Hovav 1995, Levin 1999, Rappaport Hovav and Levin 2001, Talmy 1988). But Fillmore's scenes were broader, and less dependent on individual verbs. Moreover, he was careful to emphasize that the scene did not of itself necessarily determine argument selection, for the simple reason that speakers are in many cases able to choose among alternative verbalizations available for a given scene (cf. Frege 1879 [1960]).[7] For some scenes at least, multiple verbs provide for the expression of alternative perspectives, with a corresponding difference in subject selection. An oft-cited example is the commercial event, in which verbs like *buy*, *sell*, or *spend* offer alternative perspectives with correspondingly distinct argument selection patterns. Consider the following examples, taken from three different conversations:

(30) JAMIE: … They never *buy* **clothes.** ⟨SBC:LAMBADA⟩

(31) JIM: he may have *sold* **the rights.** ⟨SBC:NOTIONS⟩

(32) KATHY: You don't have to *spend* **money** on **goodies.** ⟨SBC:RAGING⟩

Participants in the commercial event include the buyer (expressed in example (30) as *they*, in example (32) as *you*); the seller (*he*); the goods (*clothes, the rights, goodies*); and the money (*money*). But speakers don't have to include all of these participants in the nucleus of every clause — and indeed, for some combinations they can't. For example, there are said to be two agents in the prototype commercial event, the buyer and the seller. But for any given verb, only one of these agents is included in the nucleus, and hence eligible for selection as subject. In the prototype of the commercial event scene,

> …two different individuals are agentively involved… any verb identifying any particular aspect of the commercial event will constrain us to bring one or more of the entities in the event INTO PERSPECTIVE, the manifestation of this choice for English being the selection of grammatical functions corresponding to the notions of underlying subject and direct object. For example, if I wish to take the perspective of the seller and the goods, I will use the verb *sell.* Should I wish to take the perspective of the buyer and the money, I will use the verb *spend.* … And so on. (Fillmore 1977b: 72–73)

Languages allow speakers to chose among alternative perspectives on a scene or event. To the extent that the different perspectives are realized by different lexical verbs, the pattern of argument selection may vary accordingly. Hence it becomes important to acknowledge that the set of event participants that is to be selected for inclusion among the core arguments is not a given, nor, consequently, is the identity of the role that will be linked to the subject function (or the object). In recognizing a role for speaker choice, Fillmore acknowledged an aspect of discourse pragmatics. Given the fact that what happens in the argument inclusion process will delimit from the outset which participants will form the set of candidates for argument linking, it becomes difficult to escape the need for referential pragmatics in argument selection. Perhaps this explains why, among those who prefer to maintain a purely semantic basis for argument selection (e.g. Dowty 1991), Fillmore's inclusion question has so often been passed over in favor of an exclusive focus on the ranking (or linking) question.

Writing at the same time as Fillmore, Chafe offers a similar picture of the linguistic representation of events, though with more emphasis on the cognitive process of verbalizing an actual event (not just an abstract or prototype event): "Propositionalizing includes (1) the factoring out of objects from the event or situation that the [experiential] chunk embraces, and (2) the assignment of roles to these objects within the event or situation" (Chafe 1977:226–227). More recently, the role of perspective-taking in language has attained its most elaborate development in the work of Langacker (1987, 1991, 1995) and his associates working on Cognitive Grammar, under the heading of *construal*.

Fillmore's second question — "which is to become the subject and which is to become the object?" — led to his proposal of a hierarchical procedure to determine argument selection by way of participant ranking: "What determines the ranking of terms in a nucleus?" (1977a:94). The procedure is largely based on evaluating argument candidates with respect to pairs of features, with each feature pair potentially contributing to deciding which candidate outranks the other. The seven features, listed in rank order, are as follows (based on Fillmore 1977a:102):

active	outranks	inactive
causal	outranks	noncausal
experiencer	outranks	non-experiencer
changed	outranks	nonchanged
complete/individuated	outranks	part
figure	outranks	ground
definite	outranks	indefinite

This is intended as a hierarchical procedure, with the paired criteria to be evaluated in the sequence listed, until a definitive ranking is reached when the hierarchy of nuclear roles has been filled (first subject, then object). This model has influenced a number of later authors, including Gawron (1983), Foley and Van Valin (1984), and Dowty (1991) (see discussion in Davis 2001:57ff)). To this we could add Hopper and Thompson (1980), whose proposal that transitivity is a scalar property at the level of the clause (rather than the verb) invokes a number of these same factors (see also Keenan 1976).

Fillmore called this the *saliency hierarchy*. Notably it includes as determinants of argument selection both semantic features (active, causal, experiencer, changed, complete/individuated) and pragmatic features (figure, definite). It also foregrounds what we might call co-argument effects. Co-arguments are defined as members of the set of arguments of a common predicator. Co-argument effects are when the form or function of one co-argument depends on the form or function of another co-argument. The most obvious co-argument effect involves competition, as when various participant roles compete for subject selection based on a hierarchy like that presented above. A given participant role may be selected for subject in one clause but not in another, depending on which other co-arguments appear in the same clause and how they rank on the applicable evaluating criteria. Co-argument effects had figured in Fillmore's earliest work on argument selection: "For most *combinations of cases* there is a 'preferred' or 'unmarked' subject choice; for some there is no actual choice — the subject is uniquely determined" (1968: 33, emphasis added). The significance of Fillmore's two questions comes together in co-argument effects. First, inclusion determines the membership of the co-argument set. Then ranking evaluates the co-arguments relative to each other to determine which is to be linked to a given target function. Note that the common predicator serves a crucial role as the unifying force that brings a set of nouns together as co-arguments, a fact which takes on expanded significance once complex predicates are considered.

Terminology

Given the number of different researchers operating in the area of argument structure and argument selection, the terminology is often quite variable, to the point of causing occasional uncertainty between researchers about whether they are referring to the same issue. It is probably inevitable that terminological variation will always be present, and even useful as an index of theoretical diversity in a complex research domain. Still it may be useful to have some general terms for conceiving the various issues that different researchers have put on the table. I propose to treat *argument selection* as a cover term for a complex process subsuming several logically distinct components. (Whether these components constitute separate principles, constraints, procedures, or stages, or are best treated in some more unified way, is another matter. For convenience I will speak of them as processes, though nothing immediately depends on this.) At least four issues have been more or less frequently recognized, albeit under various labels. To the four terms I will add a fifth, yielding, as candidates for the components of argument selection, the processes of argument *inclusion*, *ranking*, *linking*, *targeting*, and *realization*. To be sure, different labels are favored by different researchers, for whom they reflect different conceptions of the issues, so that these five terms are not necessarily conceived of as representing a co-existing set of processes which form part of a larger phenomenon of argument selection. For many researchers, in fact, one or another of these terms (for example *linking*) represents the preferred way of referring to the whole problem, rather than a part of it. By treating them as a set of processes to be conceptually distinguished, within a larger rubric of argument selection, I am taking more than a terminological stance. I am suggesting that there is a unified problem of argument selection, more complex than has usually been recognized, which is characterized by the interaction of multiple aspects or processes like those labeled above.

I will leave the discussion of argument realization to a later section. Of the remaining four, inclusion and targeting could be seen as the starting and ending points of argument selection, respectively, though they are more often taken for granted than recognized and problematized. *Inclusion* specifies which of the possible participant roles in the scene or event source domain will be verbalized within the relevant grammatical set or unit, for example as co-arguments of a single predicator. Although inclusion depends partly on pragmatic aspects of perspective-taking, its partial sensitivity to speaker prerogative (among other factors) should not detract from its critical role in defining the candidates for linking. At the opposite end of the process, *targeting* specifies what set of functions are available as endpoints for linking. One version of this would be to specify the valence of a given verb as intransitive, transitive, or ditransitive (or of a predicator as one-, two- or three-place). Bridging the gap between inclusion and the target is *linking*, which is that part of the argument selection process that finally associates an included participant role with a target function. For most people the link would be to a syntactic function like subject or object. For some, linking would also include a subsidiary process of *ranking*, placing arguments along a hierarchy according to some established criteria. For example, arguments may be ranked along a hierarchy of thematic roles ranging from agent to beneficiary to experiencer and so on down. There may also be a corresponding ranking of target functions. (But ranking, as such, may turn out to be dispensable, as several recent approaches would have it.)

In the end, argument selection probably involves a highly complex interaction of at least inclusion, linking, targeting, and realization. In addition to these four (or five) processes, it may be necessary to recognize multiple tiers, cycles, or recursions of some of them. For example, if there is a funneling of fine-grained verb-specific participant roles down to a few broad generalized proto-roles (Dowty 1991, Foley and Van Valin 1977), this could be considered to constitute an additional cycle or intermediate level of targeting and linking. No great significance should be attached to the order of listing, and in fact there is no need to assume an ordered sequence, since they could represent constraints applying simultaneously, for example. Moreover, while it is important to recognize the five terms as representing distinct issues or aspects of argument selection, this does not necessarily mean that they can be separated in reality as distinct processes or phenomena. What is more interesting, actually, is to consider the possible linkages and interactions between them. For example, can targeting affect inclusion, or inclusion targeting? On another level, it should be noted that argument selection need not be thought of as entirely synchronic. Diachronic processes of grammaticization presumably participate in specifying at least the set of available structural targets in a given language, and probably shape much more of the selection process.

It may be noticed that the one term I have not attempted to define, not even as provisionally as the above terms are defined, is the one that appears in my title, that of argument structure. This term may be the most elusive of all of them. Its variable usage often reflects deep differences in assumptions about what structure is and what role it plays in language. Some approaches take argument structure's fundamentals as given in more or less fixed form by logic, semantics, conception, or syntax. As such it should provide a fixed target for local lexical processes of argument selection. But what if there are no fixed targets? If the target changes due to interactions among component processes, argument selection must be aiming at a moving target. For example, variable processes of inclusion and targeting introduce contingency into the outcome of linking, which interacts with the fluidity of the grammar itself in responding to forces of grammaticization. So there is reason to be cautious about taking even the syntactic frame of argument structure too quickly for granted, or assuming prematurely that we know just what kind of thing argument structure is.[8] From the perspective of grammar in use, then, we can view argument structures as contingent products of grammaticization, responsive to a variety of complex functional demands on them, as mediated through complex processes of selection. And yet the label of argument *structure* remains justified, because in the end the grammaticization process results in a population of verbs with their argument structures, constituting, for the speakers of any given language, a repertoire of stable and predictable architectural frameworks for linguistic function.

Ergativity

Ergative languages present an interesting test case for models of argument selection, but most linguists seem only to have taken up the challenge, if at all, after first establishing their main theoretical commitments on the basis of the more familiar accusative languages. Early on, Fillmore proposed that his subject selection principles be considered universal, "given certain qualifications for the interpretation of ergative systems" (Fillmore 1977b: 61). Dowty acknowledged that the problem of "argument selection in ergative languages" (Dowty 1991: 581) was important for his proto-role model, but his outline of an analysis for ergativity does little more than revive the old "inverse" model, which "means in effect treating the transitive 'Patient' as a grammatical subject and the transitive 'Agent' as analogous to an object" (1991: 582). Argument selection principles use the same proto-agent and proto-patient roles as in accusative languages, but "merely REVERSE the syntactic association" with subject and object (1991: 582). But this move depends on an unrealistic image of "pure" ergativity, in which every relevant structure and function is the mirror image of its counterpart in an accusative language. If only ergativity was so simple. One reason it's not is split ergativity (Silverstein 1976), which does not admit of any simple reversal but rather displays a complex interaction of the forces that motivate both ergative and accusative languages (Du Bois 1985, 1987a). Dowty sidesteps this most challenging type of ergativity (1991: 581–582). Subsequent treatments of argument structure have tended to deal with ergativity only after their foundational theoretical assumptions have been set in place (Ackerman and Moore 2001: 1, fn. 1), by which time it is typically too late to respond with sufficient flexibility to the deeper challenges of ergativity.

Argument selection proposals have overwhelmingly assumed the primacy of the syntactic subject, thereby taking for granted that there is one fixed target for argument linking at the top of the syntactic hierarchy, and that this grammatical relation can be applied indiscriminately to transitive or intransitive clauses. Against the background of such assumptions, ergativity looks like a spoiler. The claimed universality of grammatical relations, though buttressed by efforts like Keenan (1976) for the subject relation, faces a perennial challenge in the stubbornly distinctive structure of ergative languages. According to the traditional textbook characterization of ergativity, the subject of an intransitive verb is marked grammatically like the object of a transitive verb (these two arguments together comprising the absolutive category), while the subject of a transitive verb is marked differently (comprising the ergative category). But this way of describing the phenomenon tends to make ergative languages sound aberrant, as if they would split up a perfectly good category like subject and lump half its contents with some other category. To counter this, Dixon found it necessary to deconstruct the traditional category of subject, so as to arrive at a set of categories sufficiently neutral for the description of Dyirbal (Dixon 1972: 128), and ultimately for the placement of ergative and accusative (and other) language types on an equal footing within a cross-linguistically viable typological scheme (Dixon 1979: 59, 1987, 1994). In his three-way opposition, Dixon distinguished between transitive subject (A), intransitive subject (S), and direct object (O). Comrie invoked similar categories of A, S, and P (1978: 332). The terms A, S, and O have since become widely used, though not necessarily with Dixon's assumption that they represent universal deep structure syntactic-semantic primitives (Dixon 1994: 6, Du Bois 1987a: 807, fn. 1). (For a critical perspective, see Chafe and Mithun 1999.) The typological neutrality of the terms represents an important starting point for attempts to understand ergativity, deflating the terminological presumption that the grammatical relations of accusative languages (e.g. subject and object) are more natural than those of ergative languages. (It should be noted that Preferred Argument Structure research uses the terms A, S, and O for the analysis of *surface* structure roles, not deep roles as Dixon proposed.)

While ergative languages may not be as common as accusative ones, they are spoken all over the globe and are not going away anytime soon. In this light, there is something to be valued in a model of grammatical relations which is capable of embracing the morphosyntax of ergative languages, rather than effacing it or treating it as a kind of distorted version of an accusative language. Here Silverstein's (1976, 1981, 1993) work on grammatical relations has been pivotal. Silverstein acknowledged the profound typological divergences between ergative and accusative languages in their systems of grammatical relations, but responded by building a framework which could give a unified treatment to this diversity by taking account of systematic interactions among multiple factors in semantic, pragmatic, and grammatical dimensions. The result is a model which not only addresses broad typological contrasts between different systems of grammatical relations, but is equally adept at treating diversity within a single language in the internal organization of its grammatical relations, as occurs notably in split ergativity. Silverstein's treatment been quite influential (Dixon 1979), for example strongly influencing Role and Reference Grammar (Foley and Van Valin 1984, Van Valin 1993, Van Valin and LaPolla 1997), one of the few theories of grammar to devote serious and consistent attention to ergative languages at a foundational level of theory construction.

Given Silverstein's goal to account for, among other things, complex mixtures of accusative and ergative patterning within a language's system of grammatical relations, it is interesting that his model prominently incorporates a discourse-pragmatic dimension. As one of four key factors in his model, Silverstein specified "reference-maintenance relations of arguments of predicates (as expressed by noun phrases in non-linked clausal structures across discourse-level structures)" (1976: 230). The other three dimensions distinguished are "inherent referential content of noun phrases;" case relation (Agent-of, Patient-of, etc.); and clause-linkage type (1976: 229–230). But in his oft-quoted summarizing statement, it was agency alone that ended up with the starring role: "This hierarchy expresses the semantic naturalness for a lexically-specified noun phrase to function as agent of a true transitive verb, and inversely the naturalness of functioning as patient of such" (1976: 113). This emphasis may partly explain why subsequent treatments tended to overlook the discourse pragmatic dimension in Silverstein's model, leading to a slimmed-down restatement as a linear implicational scale of "animacy" (Dixon 1979) or "agency". But Silverstein's multidimensional scale does not fit happily into its one-dimensional linearization, as Durie points out:

> Thus, for example, the relative position of third person nominals above kin terms and human nouns in the hierarchy cannot be derived from a 'potentiality of agency' explanation, and points to something pragmatic like 'topicality', rather than something as semantic as 'agency' or 'animacy': it is by no means obvious that an expression like *aunt* is less animate or agentive than third person pronouns like *she*. However third person pronouns *would* seem likely candidates to have higher topic continuity in discourse than kin terms or animate nouns, irrespective of 'animacy' or 'agency'. (Durie 1994b: 498)

Even the true animacy categories on the scale may owe their position partly to a proclivity for high or low topic continuity, since "animate nominal expressions have greater continuity than inanimates, and … names or kin terms have greater topic continuity than expressions [involving] common nouns" (Durie 1994b: 498). (See studies in Givón 1983.) If anything, a one-dimensional reduction of Silverstein's scale might better be labeled the "topicality hierarchy" (Du Bois 1987a, Mallinson and Blake 1982). While Silverstein's work has been influential, the larger implications for argument structure research of his analysis of split ergativity remain to be fully explored. Even now, revisiting the famous "agency" hierarchy in its original form as a complex feature matrix could provoke important insights via its framework for understanding complex interactions such as those between agency, topicality, and grammatical relations.

What is the significance of ergativity for argument structure? Ergativity problematizes some of the most fundamental assumptions on which discussions of argument selection and linking have been built. For example, linking models have tended to uncritically accept a foundational role for syntactic categories like subject and object, taking them as putative universal targets for argument linking. But Dixon's replacement of the traditional subject-object distinction with the more neutral A-S-O distinction has turned out to be a key factor in typologists' advances in understanding systems of grammatical relations which depart from the familiar accusative mold. Based partly on typological research on such languages, Foley and Van Valin (1984: 32) state that they find no compelling reason to recognize grammatical relations like subject and direct object as universals. To simply assume an undifferentiated "subject" concept as a supposed universal argument linking target seriously underestimates the problem, as research by Fox (1987) and others suggests. The three-term A-S-O distinction affords an additional advantage, allowing researchers to foreground the question of what links S with O in ergative languages to motivate the absolutive category. But it equally problematizes the organization of grammatical relations in accusative languages, posing the question of what links S with A to motivate the nominative category. To turn the tables and seek, if only as a theoretical exercise, to motivate the coherence of the subject (S, A) category as a viable, and possibly preferred, target of agent (or topic) linking may help explain the widespread presence of subject-based phenomena in ergative languages, as opposed to simply taking such phenomena for granted as natural consequences of the supposed universality of subjects. Conversely, to motivate the absolutive (S, O) category as an alternative target of linking (perhaps partly motivated by proto-patient features, as effectively argued by Keenan [1984]; see also Mithun [1991]) may help explain the presence of ergative-absolutive grammatical patterning in accusative languages.

On another level, ergative and active-agentive languages offer invaluable yet relatively unexplored sites for research at the lexical level, regarding the properties of individual verbs and classes of verbs. Given the view that "morphology may be as much of a determinant of eventual linguistic form as syntax is" (Börjars and Vincent 2000), it becomes interesting to probe how differences in available morphosyntactic categories (e.g. ergative and absolutive, or actor and undergoer) may interact with the semantics of scenes and events to grammaticize argument structure behaviors. Much could be gained from a systematic survey of argument structure in the verbal lexicon of even one ergative or active-agentive language, on the scale of (Levin 1993) but addressing also the semantic, pragmatic and grammaticization factors discussed by Mithun (1991) and Durie (1994b). But there is no need to wait for such a study in order to begin learning from ergativity. Ergativity should not be seen as a chore to be handled when (and if) one finds the time to get around to it, but as already providing an indispensable early clue to the framing of the argument selection problem. To open argument structure research up to typological insight, a useful minimal starting point would be to distinguish consistently between S and A, for example in problematizing the target for argument selection.

The functional correlates of ergative-absolutive grammar figure prominently in my own earlier work on Preferred Argument Structure (Du Bois 1985, 1987a, 1987b). In the next section, I give a sketch of what this theory is about.

Preferred Argument Structure

Preferred Argument Structure has something to say about argument structure per se, but given its grounding in discourse data and functional theory, it takes some careful reflection to see just how it relates to other lines of research on the topic. Here I will present just the basic outlines of the model, which is described more fully elsewhere (see the papers in this volume, and Du Bois 1987a, 2003a). My main purpose is to convey how this approach to argument structure differs markedly from others, yet still bears consequences for aspects of the grammar of argument structure that are of interest to all researchers on the topic. I will begin by presenting some illustrations of what it means to say that there is a Preferred Argument Structure in a given language, such as English. I will follow this with some of the cross-linguistic evidence suggesting that the Preferred Argument Structure which I initially identified in Sakapultek Maya can be considered a discourse universal. Finally, I will briefly point out some of the implications for argument structure-related issues including verb classes, constructions, and the grammaticization of argument structure.

On the face of it, Preferred Argument Structure is a very simple matter. It represents a hypothesis that in spontaneous discourse, certain configurations of arguments are systematically preferred over other grammatically possible alternatives. Because it makes claims about actual instances of grammar in use, it can be considered a model of argument realization (Butt and King 2000a: 1), or what we might call argument token selection. The model singles out certain argument realizations in certain argument positions as preferred, while defining others as dispreferred. But because the dispreferred argument realizations still generally yield grammatical sentences, it can be difficult for linguists used to seeing the grammaticality divide as the defining limit of language to appreciate, at first, what the fuss is all about.

What are the specific preferences for argument configurations? There is a grammatical and a pragmatic dimension to the phenomenon, which can be described in two pairs of soft constraints, one pair for each of the two dimensions. In the grammatical dimension, the first constraint limits the quantity of full lexical noun phrases that may appear among a predicator's core arguments to not more than one. The second constraint limits which grammatical roles the single lexical argument may appear in, specifically excluding it from the A role. These grammatical constraints are paralleled in the pragmatic dimension. Here, the quantity constraint limits to not more than one the number of new information noun phrases that may be realized among the core co-arguments of a predicator. The role constraint limits where the one new argument may appear, again excluding it from the A role. Since all four are soft constraints, they can be violated without producing ungrammaticality; and yet in spontaneous language use, overwhelmingly they are not. The four constraints are summarized in Table 1.

Table 1. Preferred Argument Structure constraints

	Grammar	**Pragmatics**
Quantity	*Avoid more than one lexical core argument*	*Avoid more than one new core argument*
Role	*Avoid lexical A*	*Avoid new A*

The claim is that, when attested spontaneous language use is systematically investigated, there will be consistent statistical tendencies marked by the predominance of certain grammatical configurations of argument realization, and the relative scarcity of others. Since the most obvious effect of the proposed constraints is on the use of multi-place predicates, let us look first at transitive clauses. For English two-place verbs like *break, name,* or *miss,* the prevailing grammatical configuration of argument realization is illustrated in the following examples:

(33) DARRYL: you just damn near *broke* **the damn needle there?** 〈SBC:DEATH〉

(34) KEN: he *named* like **half a dozen viruses,** 〈SBC:DEADLY 476〉

(35) PAMELA: (H) ... but I still *miss* **my grandmother.** ⟨SBC:DEATH⟩

In each of these clauses, one argument is realized with a lexical noun phrase, and one is realized with a pronoun. But what is relatively rare among argument realizations is a transitive clause containing two full lexical arguments. Even when the verb's argument structure makes two slots available, speakers tend strongly to avoid filling each of them with a lexical noun phrase.

Note that the quantity constraint on lexical core arguments represents only an upper bound. There is no *minimum* number of lexical arguments per clause. This is evident from the numerous examples cited earlier showing no lexical core arguments at all, only pronouns in all argument positions:

(36) BRAD: And so you would *hit* that, ⟨SBC:TAPEDECK⟩

(37) LINDA: and she *admired* him, ⟨SBC:HOWARDS 182⟩

(38) JILL: .. that would *bother* me. ⟨SBC:CUTIEPIE⟩

The tendency to avoid more than one lexical core argument appears to be consistent across languages, in spontaneous spoken discourse. In no language is it an absolute avoidance, however. Table 2 summarizes studies of five languages which show that clauses with either zero or one lexical core argument are common, while clauses with two are relatively rare.

Table 2. Lexical argument quantity: Frequency of clauses by quantity of lexical arguments[9]

Quantity:	0		1		2		Total	
Language	N	%	N	%	N	%	N	%
Hebrew	261	(50)	252	(48)	9	(2)	522	(100)
Sakapultek	211	(46)	240	(53)	5	(1)	456	(100)
Papago	430	(57)	307	(40)	22	(3)	759	(100)
English	252	(47)	241	(45)	39	(7)	535	(100)
Gooniyandi	2318	(62)	1305	(35)	114	(3)	3737	(100)

There is a second constraint on the grammatical configuration of lexical argument realization in two-place predicates. The constraint we have already seen (as evidenced in Table 2) readily 'allows' one lexical core argument per clause. However, while a transitive clause in principle provides two alternative argument positions for the one allowed lexical argument, speakers do not appear to treat the two argument slots equally as potential sites for lexical argument realization. Rather, as illustrated in examples (33)–(35) above, they avoid realizing the one lexical argument in subject (A) position, preferring direct object (O) position instead. Does this mean that speakers avoid the *subject* role when realizing lexical noun phrases? Not at all. Subject position welcomes lexical nouns (Assayag 1999), as long as the predicate is one-place — that is, if the subject is S rather than A.

(39) REBECCA: (H)= **The .. jury** … *sits* here. ⟨SBC:JURY⟩

(40) ALINA: (H) **@The @Black @guy** *@laughed.* ⟨SBC:CUZ⟩

(41) LARRY: this .. **this wall** is eventually gonna *come out.* ⟨SBC:FURNACE⟩

More generally, any one-place predicate, verbal or not, will freely accept a lexical subject. For example, a predicate adjective construction takes just one argument, so its subject (S) is unconstrained:

(42) PETE: … **the rainy season** *was all off,* ⟨SBC:CONCEPT⟩

(43) JOANNE: **The bowl** *was about yea big,* ⟨SBC:DEADLY⟩

(44) SHARON: .. **this kid** *is bad behaved,* ⟨SBC:RAGING⟩

And, in a precise parallel to the predicate adjective, the predicate nominal construction provides exactly one argument position, an (unconstrained) S:

(45) REBECCA: **your case in Oakland** *will be a felony.* ⟨SBC:JURY⟩

(46) CAROLYN: **Sweets** *are not the thing.* ⟨SBC:RAGING⟩

Here the post-copular noun phrases (which are almost always lexical, e.g. *a felony, the thing,* but rarely *him*) is not an argument at all, of course, but instead functions predicatively. Given its functional role as a non-argument, the predicate noun phrases are not governed by Preferred Argument Structure, and speakers do not treat them as subject to the relevant constraints.

As with the previous constraint, there is no minimum implied here. Although S allows a lexical argument, pronominal realizations are also common:

(47) REBECCA: .. (H) <u>she</u> *moved* again, ⟨SBC:JURY 164⟩

(48) PAM: # <u>She</u>'s *sleeping.* ⟨SBC:RAGING⟩

(49) PHIL: (H) <u>It</u> *broke.* ⟨SBC:ATOMS⟩

Similarly, the O role is allowed to be lexical, but is obviously not required to be so, as illustrated in examples (36)–(38) above.

The free occurrence of lexical argument realizations in S and O, combined with their relative avoidance in A, is the basis for the role constraint on lexical argument realizations, "Avoid lexical A". Table 3 summarizes evidence supporting this constraint from eight languages.

If we look at ditransitives, with their three structural opportunities for lexical argument realization, we nevertheless find that the same quantity and role constraints are observed as for transitives (Schuetze-Coburn 1987). Even with a three-place verb like *send* or *pass,* still only one of the three arguments is typically realized lexically:

Table 3. Lexical argument role: Syntactic role of lexical core arguments[10]

Role:	A		S		O		Total	
Language	**N**	**%**	**N**	**%**	**N**	**%**	**N**	**%**
Hebrew	18	(8)	103	(44)	111	(48)	232	(100)
Sakapultek	11	(5)	126	(58)	81	(37)	218	(100)
Papago	37	(10)	169	(47)	152	(42)	358	(99)
English	21	(8)	90	(35)	146	(57)	257	(100)
Spanish	35	(6)	215	(36)	341	(58)	591	(100)
French	32	(5)	290	(45)	324	(50)	646	(100)
BrPortuguese		(8)		(39)		(53)		(100)
Japanese	48	(7)	320	(48)	293	(44)	661	(100)

(50) JIM: … he's gonna *send* me **those forms,** ⟨SBC:BANK⟩

(51) NATHAN: … Will you *pass* me **some of that tea** please. ⟨SBC:ZERO⟩

Again, as with transitives, lexical mentions are avoided in A, while they freely appear in O. As for the third argument position, the indirect object (I) is typically realized with a reduced form, as illustrated in the above examples.

The grammatical realization of arguments in a clause does not take place in a functional vacuum. It is tied to cognitive and pragmatic factors like information management, which influence the realization of arguments as lexical or pronominal, with consequences as described in the previous two constraints. Corresponding to the grammatical contrast between lexical noun phrase and pronoun is the pragmatic contrast whereby the fuller form tends to be used for referents that are less cognitively accessible (Ariel 1990, 2001, Chafe 1987, 1994), while the reduced forms are used for more accessible referents. In the sentence below, the O role lexical noun phrase *cake with rum in it* represents the first mention of cake, while the A role pronominal *he* indexes a referent mentioned several times in the immediately preceding discourse:

(52) JOANNE: (H) He doesn't even *eat* **ca=ke with r=um in it.**
⟨SBC:DEADLY 1072⟩

Not all definite forms are alike when it comes to the degree of accessibility of an argument realization. For example, a referent referred to by a definite lexical noun phrase will tend to be less cognitively accessible than one referred to by a definite pronoun:

(53) DARRYL: you just damn near *broke* **the damn needle there?**
⟨SBC:DEATH⟩

Here the definite pronoun *you* refers to a discourse participant immediately present in the situational context. The definite lexical noun phrase *the damn needle there*, on the other hand, though situationally present, refers to something not previously mentioned or made salient in any way. As a first mention in the discourse, it is relatively less accessible and thus requires a more substantial lexical realization, even though it is also identifiable (after the fact, as it were) in the situational context.

The motivation for a particular referential form often becomes evident once the prior discourse context is consulted. Consider example (31), repeated here:

(54) JIM: he may have *sold* **the rights.**

While *the rights* represents a first mention in the discourse, pronominal *he* tracks a referent that was mentioned in the previous clause:

(55) JIM: he may never *see* **a penny** of it.
he may have *sold* **the rights.**

Note that the referent of *he* appears in A role in each of the two successive clauses, regardless of its shift from "experiencer" (or perhaps recipient) of *see* to agent of *sell.*

In the pragmatic dimension, then, the general pattern for two-place predicates is that only one core argument typically carries new information, and this argument is not the A. For ditransitives, the pattern is similar to that noted earlier, with any new (or low-accessible) information typically realized in O role, while only high-accessible information appears in the other roles (A and I). As for one-place predicates, once again they are the least constrained, because the quantity constraint on new arguments does not affect them. This gives them special importance as a site for the introduction of new information. The S role freely realizes new information, as in the following example, where *this new wave of people* represents a first mention in the discourse:

(56) ALINA: .. **this new wa=ve of people** *comes in.* ⟨SBC:CUZ⟩

In sum, the cognitively demanding task of introducing new or low-accessible information into the discourse is strongly avoided in A role, but is freely carried out in S or O roles. Counts supporting the quantity constraint on new arguments are presented in Table 4, while evidence for the role constraint is given in Table 5. Again, there is no lower limit on the amount of new or low-accessible information that is introduced in a clause's argument positions. All roles may be filled with non-new information, as is clear from the first column of Table 4, and illustrated in examples (36)–(38) and (47)–(49) above.

Preferred Argument Structure has been investigated in numerous studies extending across a typologically and genetically diverse array of languages (see the other papers, and the bibliography, of this volume). I will mention here only a few studies on specific aspects of the topic. A comparative and historical perspective was developed in a series of articles on Spanish and French by Ashby and Bentivoglio

Table 4. New argument quantity: Frequency of clause types by quantity of new core arguments[11]

Quantity:	0		1		2		Total	
Language	N	%	N	%	N	%	N	%
Sakapultek	336	(73)	122	(27)	0	(0)	458	(100)
English	463	(87)	72	(13)	0	(0)	535	(100)

Table 5. New argument role: Syntactic role of new core arguments[12]

Role:	A		S		O		Total	
Language	N	%	N	%	N	%	N	%
Hebrew	6	(6)	40	(43)	47	(51)	93	(100)
Sakapultek	6	(6)	58	(55)	42	(40)	106	(101)
English	0	(0)	15	(21)	57	(79)	72	(100)
Spanish	2	(1)	56	(28)	142	(71)	200	(100)
French	0	(0)	75	(34)	143	(66)	218	(100)

(Ashby and Bentivoglio 1993, Ashby and Bentivoglio 1997, Bentivoglio 1994). Theory and method for studying the acquisition of argument structure were developed by Clancy in several papers on Korean (1993, 1995, 1996, 1997), leading to investigations of acquisition in several additional languages (Allen 2000, Bentivoglio 1998, Brown 1998, Guerriero et al. 2001, Narasimhan, Budwig, and Murty, forthcoming). Second language acquisition was documented by Kumpf (1992). While the primary context claimed for Preferred Argument Structure is spontaneous spoken language, evidence that at least some written language genres follow the constraints was presented for Brazilian Portuguese by Brito (1996). Implications for the syntax of complex sentences were explored in studies of relativization in English conversation (Fox 1987, Fox and Thompson 1990)[13] and quantifier floating in Japanese (Downing 1993). The connection to intonation units and clauses was explored in Japanese by Matsumoto (2000, forthcoming). Arguments for the internal differentiation of the intransitive S category were given by Durie based on Acehnese (1988), and a finer-grained breakdown of S was also explored by Dutra (1987), Bentivoglio (1990), and Fox (1995). In computational linguistics, Preferred Argument Structure has been used in conjunction with a decision tree model of machine learning to parse Wall Street Journal articles, via the "fine-grained taxonomy of grammatical relations" of A, S, and O (Corston-Oliver 2000:1). On the critical side, a more skeptical approach to the categories A, S, and O as tools for linguistic analysis is urged by Chafe and Mithun (1999). The discourse alignment of S with A in English, rather than with O, is argued by Kärkkäinen (1996); see also

(O'Dowd 1990). Probably the most critical assessment of Preferred Argument Structure is that of Herring (1989). (For a rebuttal, see Durie, this volume, p. 162 fn. 4.)

Significance

On one level, Preferred Argument Structure is simply a description of a statistical preference for certain patterns in the realization of argument tokens in discourse. But the description is meant to support a broader significance as well. From a functional perspective, Preferred Argument Structure can be seen to carry implications for, among other things, strategies for information management, the discourse basis of ergativity, discourse profiles of verb classes and constructions, argument realization, and the grammaticization of the system of argument structure.

One task that all speakers must confront is that of managing the flow of information in discourse (Chafe 1980, 1987, 1994, Du Bois 1980, 1985), whereby speakers introduce new information, track old information, and so on. As a consequence, all languages provide resources for information management. Among these resources may be counted certain aspects of grammar. What Preferred Argument Structure shows in some detail is how particular cognitive-pragmatic functions are regularly associated with certain syntactic roles, to the exclusion of others. From the perspective of grammar in use, argument structures are resources for speakers to exploit, for cognitive-pragmatic as well as semantic functions. Among the things that a speaker may know about the verb *come in*, for example, is that its S role provides a reliably usable slot for introducing a new human protagonist into a discourse. Likewise, the O role of the verb *meet* may serve a similar function (Du Bois 2003a). While each of these verbs obviously functions to describe a particular kind of event semantics, this is not inconsistent with the claim that on at least some occasions their use is partly, or even primarily, motivated by their cognitive-pragmatic contributions. What these and other functionally comparable verbs have in common may be less their semantics than their distinctive absolutive argument configuration, with its capacity to evade limiting cognitive-pragmatic constraints, and to contribute to strategies for information management.

From a typological perspective, one long-standing question is why there are ergative languages in the world — or even just why there are ergative subsystems in some grammars. One way of specifying this issue, as noted earlier, is to ask what motivates linking S with O. This should be recognized as a prime test for any proposed theory of argument linking, but most theories have either not addressed the issue at all, or have had little of substance to say about it. At the very least, Preferred Argument Structure introduces a new type of empirical finding, which establishes a certain distributional and functional commonality between S and O, in contrast with A (and in contrast with the pairing of S with A). The cross-linguistic evidence cited above cuts across the ergative-absolutive and nominative-accusative language types to support the claim that the absolutive (S, O) role set constitutes the universally preferred locus for the introduction of new information. These empirical findings present an implicit challenge to most theories of argument selection, whether they explicitly claim to explain S-O linking or not. As I have argued elsewhere (Du Bois 1987a), the Preferred Argument Structure pattern of functional alignment provides part of an explanation for ergative-absolutive grammatical alignment. But it remains to be shown in some detail how this broad pragmatic motivation is to be integrated with the local lexicosemantic aspects of a verb-by-verb account of argument linking in split-ergative or active-agentive languages (Durie 1994b, Mithun 1991, Silverstein 1976, Van Valin 1990).

One interesting point about the constraints described is that they are not enforced by a rule of grammar. In most languages, violating them usually produces no penalty of ungrammaticality. Certainly, the statistical preference in spontaneous language use is clear, such that it is rare for a transitive clause to have both argument positions filled lexically, or to have a lexical A. But it is not impossible:

(57) WALT: ... **My wife** would *write* **a check for ten dollars,** ⟨SBC:FEAR⟩

(58) JOANNE: and **a lot of the kids** *mentioned* **Ana.** ⟨SBC:DEADLY⟩

It seems that when there is legitimate occasion to produce a two-place predicate with both arguments lexically realized, the result is not stigmatized as ungrammatical. The absence of perceived ungrammaticality would seem to preclude the postulation of any categorial rule of grammar. (For some linguists this fact alone might seem to vitiate the constraints' relevance for grammar, but I would urge against such a hasty conclusion.) Nevertheless speakers tend strongly to avoid such argument realizations. One way to characterize this avoidance is to frame it in terms of soft constraints, representing strong but not inviolable statistical preferences. (Compare the use of violable constraints in Optimality Theory.) Moving beyond a merely descriptive generalization, we could try to show that the rarity, but not impossibility, of such clauses is explained by the fact that they push, but do not necessarily break, the limits of routine on-line cognitive processing capacity. Another approach would take a closer look at the kinds of noun phrases that tend to appear in A role (e.g. *my wife, a lot of the kids*) to try to show that they are just those which are relatively high on the scale of accessibility (Ariel 1990, 2001), and so make relatively low demands on cognitive processing resources. The constraints would be redefined in such a way that the observed A role noun phrases are not problematic after all, once reference is made to scalar values for accessibility. Both of these lines of inquiry (which are not mutually exclusive) seem worth pursuing further.

The Preferred Argument Structure constraints as stated seem to be generalizations about syntactic roles like A, S, and O. But they can also be understood as implying generalizations about the discourse profiles of verb classes or predicate classes, taken in a broad sense, and this could provide a clue to their present significance and future potential for development. The broadest division of predicates into classes would presumably be into intransitive, transitive, and ditransitive verbs, or one-, two-, and three-place predicates. Preferred Argument Structure shows that each predicate class at this level has its own distinct grammatical-pragmatic ecology, or discourse profile, as it were. Ditransitive verbs, for example, require that two of their argument positions be more or less strictly contained in order that the third may be pragmatically "open". Here it becomes useful to extend the notion of co-argument effects (see above) to include pragmatic factors, as well as semantic. The presence of new information in one argument slot of a predicator affects other co-argument slots of that predicator by precluding their use for realizing new information. In this respect one can interpret the development from intransitive to transitive to ditransitive verbs (Tomasello 1992) as a gradual growth in complexity. Grammatical complexity-building must take cognitive-pragmatic co-argument effects into account if it is to succeed. The complexity of a transitive or ditransitive verb, modest as it is, is achieved at the cost of constraining all but one argument position to express only accessible information. The perspective of complexity-building can be extended to causatives and more complex syntactic constructions at various levels.

Preferred Argument Structure lends itself well to a constructional approach to argument structure, of the sort advanced by Goldberg (1995, forthcoming). Goldberg proposes that argument structures are best understood as constructions which have a reality independent of individual verbs. Argument structure constructions may assign semantic (and presumably pragmatic) values to each of their argument positions, in addition to bearing meaning as a whole. They combine with semantically compatible verbs in well-defined ways to form particular verb-argument configurations. Part of the motivation for this analysis lies in the grammatical versatility which many verbs in English exhibit:

> Most verbs readily appear in more than one argument structure pattern. … Slight differences in meaning are clearly one factor that distinguishes between alternate argument structure patterns. … Less studied is the role of pragmatics in differentiating argument structure possibilities. (Goldberg forthcoming)

The idea that argument structures have a reality independent of the specific verb (see also Fillmore 1968:27, García Velasco and Hengeveld 2002, Hengeveld forthcoming) seems quite compatible with the kinds of pragmatic-grammatical correlations we have been describing. From this perspective, Preferred Argument Structure can be seen as setting general constraints on which cognitive-pragmatic configurations can be linked to which argument structure constructions. Each high level argument structure construction (at the generalized level of valence types, for example) can be seen as having a pragmatic configuration associated with its argument positions as part of its value. To the extent that a given lexical verb, like *break* or *give*, can be used in more than one such argument structure construction, it will inherit the cognitive-pragmatic properties associated with that construction, thus allowing it, for example, to play different roles in strategies for information management depending on its argument structure.

As an empirical generalization about discourse data, Preferred Argument Structure identifies what we might call the "discourse profile" of verb classes at the broadest level of valence classes. The discourse profile of a grammatical type (such as the transitive or intransitive verb) represents the full array of systematically co-occurring elements in natural discourse, whether these be lexical, morphological, prosodic, syntactic, semantic, or pragmatic. The most consequential co-occurrences are those which statistically predominate in the "token aggregate", the mass of experienced linguistic form-meaning combinations (Du Bois 1987a). But if we take seriously the notion of verb classes or verb clusters (Goldberg 1995: 135), there is good reason to pursue a finer-grained discourse profile of particular subsets of transitive or intransitive verbs than that currently offered by the broad-brush version of Preferred Argument Structure. (On the differentiation of sub-categories within S, for example, see papers in this volume and Durie (1994a), Fox (1995), and Bentivoglio (1990). At this level we are talking about potentially very specific discourse profiles providing more detailed information, even down to the level of individual verbs, such as about particular types of complements and their discourse-pragmatic correlates (Thompson 2002).

Finally we might ask: Is the term Preferred Argument Structure justified? Or should it rather be called Preferred Argument Token Realization (or some such). Butt and King make a case for the importance of going beyond argument structure to describe *argument realization*, by which they mean that "the precise surface realization of any given argument must be accounted for" (Butt and King 2000a: 5). The constraints we have described undoubtedly pertain to argument realization in this sense, though perhaps not in the way Butt and King intended. The constraints can also be seen as governing argument tokens rather than just argument types, at least at one level of interpretation. However, I maintain that the original Preferred Argument Structure label remains appropriate, although like any label it cannot be expected to provide an adequate capsule description of the theory and methodology associated with it. To be sure, from a traditional argument structure perspective the four constraints appear merely to govern the preferred morphological and pragmatic realization of noun phrase tokens in various argument roles. If we hew to the static conception of argument structure as being provided with one fixed valence target for argument linking (e.g. as given by syntax), then the preferences defined by the four constraints may indeed appear grammatically inconsequential. If argument structures are assumed to be already in place, how their individual noun phrases are to be realized would seem a kind of afterthought — a "late" rule, a surface enhancement, a matter of cognitive style or speech production (which some would dismiss as performance) that ends in the local choice of a lexical noun or a pronoun in a particular morphological case form. But this makes sense only if we take argument structures for granted, as given either a priori or by some supposedly autonomous source like logic, syntax, or event metaphysics (Davis 2001, Dowty 1991, Levin 1999). From a more dynamic linguistic perspective, the functional demands of discourse preference may influence the "target" of argument structure itself, through such pragmatically driven processes as perspective and construal (Chafe 1977, Fillmore 1977a, Langacker 1995), with immediate consequences for event demarcation and argument inclusion (Carlson 1998). Taken together the four constraints amount to an effective preference, in some sense, for certain argument structure types. In fact, there is just one valence or argument structure target that turns out to be fully unconstrained in both grammatical (morphological) and cognitive-pragmatic dimensions: the one-place predicate. Other available argument structure types (transitive, ditransitive) are subject to various limitations in grammar and cognitive pragmatics. The preference identified by Preferred Argument Structure for one-place argument structures as the fundamental unconstrained architectural framework for linguistic function has large consequences throughout the grammar (Du Bois 1987a: 830–832), which are just beginning to be explored (Cumming 1994, Thompson and Hopper 2001). In addition, there are consequences for complex syntax, as when the "open" absolutive (versus "closed" A) freely accommodates grammatical expansion processes that build complexity, such as relative clause formation (Fox 1987, Fox and Thompson 1990). Over time such factors may influence the grammar of argument structure at the level of individual verbs, verb classes, and beyond, via general processes of grammaticization. Here the concept of discourse profile becomes especially important. Discourse profiles set the agenda for subsequent grammaticization. They represent the deeper regularities of discourse which activate or guide the grammaticization forces that in turn reshape the grammar of argument structure in the domain of types, affecting even typological systems of grammatical relations like the ergative or accusative.

One problem with emphasizing the role of new information introduction as a pragmatic correlate of syntactic roles, and a motivation for absolutive alignment, is that in spoken discourse, new information is not as common as is typically imagined. Speakers actually spend a lot of time continuing topics that have already been introduced. Thus they can speak for some time without introducing a new noun phrase. A close look at the counts in Table 5, for example, reveals that even though the S role freely allows new information, in general the majority of arguments in S express given (or accessible) information. Typically, given/accessible arguments are far more common than new ones in spoken discourse, and more evenly distributed. Still, if we keep focused on which aspects of the discourse distribution are likely to have the greatest impact on the grammaticization of argument structures, the conclusion must be drawn that what matters most is not the undifferentiated proliferation of unmarked elements (such as pronouns or given information) across all structural contexts, but rather the more limited and specialized distribution of marked categories — such as new information noun phrases — which show a well-defined avoidance of specific argument positions. Here we touch on the sensitive question of how pragmatic function can be said to relate to syntactic structure. Because the issue is an interesting one for theories of the functional motivation and grammaticization of argument structure, it is worth pursuing further, once we have explored one particular version of the popular linguistic metaphor of grammar as architecture.

Architecture for function

The Bauhaus slogan held that "form follows function", but let's not exaggerate how close it follows. There is a degree of connection between form and function but also, of necessity, a degree of independence. The design of any edifice cannot fully determine in advance exactly which functions will be performed in it, if it is to remain useable. A homely analogy is in order here. The stereotypical modern house contains a living room, a kitchen, some number of bedrooms, one or more bathrooms. In the kitchen are found certain features specialized for cooking (stove, oven, sink), while a different set of features typifies the bathroom (toilet, shower), and other rooms have their distinguishing affordances as well. We have no hesitation in saying that each of these rooms is adapted (by intentional design in this case) to the functions realized in it. Cooking takes place in the kitchen, sleeping in the bedroom, bathing in the bathroom. Yet the exact form of each activity is not fully determined by the facilitating structures. There is no way to predict in advance every action that will take place in the kitchen, and the architect who tries too closely to adapt the form to its ostensive function would create nothing but a straightjacket. But how does this homely stereotype correspond to reality? If we were to empirically monitor the time devoted to various activities performed in each room, we might well encounter some unbecoming facts — that in many kitchens, for example, the single commonest activity is conversation. Does this mean that the kitchen can no longer be considered as adapted to cooking? Turning things around, if it turns out that conversation is prominent all over the house but cooking occurs almost exclusively in the kitchen, we restore some sense to the meaning of architectural adaptation. Certain marked activities, like cooking, make considerable demands on supporting structures and hence influence their adaptation disproportionately. Other activities like conversing are not so particular about their requirements even though, or perhaps because, they are widespread. Likewise in grammar, a marked function that generates intensive demands on cognitive resources, such as the introduction of new information, will motivate locally specialized grammatical configurations, even if it turns out to be numerically overshadowed by a function more pervasive, yet unmarked and territorially indiscriminate, such as the tracking of previously introduced referents.

Consider the relation between form and function for the absolutive category (including the equivalent S/O role set in accusative languages). Although the absolutive can be shown to be the primary locus in spontaneous discourse for introducing new information among core arguments, it still does not reliably signal new information as such. It simply accommodates it. Thus it contrasts with the A role, which does not freely accommodate new information. As the cross-linguistic evidence on the distribution of new information among A, S, and O shows, A is strongly avoided for new information, while S and O are not. But neither do S and O show a correlation with new information that approaches anywhere near totality. In fact, for many languages and genres the commonest sort of referential form in S and O roles may be reduced forms (pronoun, cross-reference, zero), expressing given or high-accessible information. (In A role, of course, given information is even more frequent.) Does this mean that absolutive doesn't have a functional connection with new information? Only if we think that linguistic function must always be the (Saussurean) "sign function", as opposed to what I call the "structure function" (Du Bois 2003a). The structure function does not signal, but simply provides structural facilitation for, a given function. New information represents a cognitively demanding processing task, so it is useful to be able to predict where it will happen — if it happens. The absolutive category can be seen as reserving a structural locus for this cognitive-pragmatic processing. If on occasion the locus isn't needed for such demands, still there was no harm in being prepared. (And the co-existing event-semantic functions of the argument structure are still usefully implemented.) In general, argument structures can be seen as providing a predictable locus for unpredictable work. As noted earlier, accessible information is pervasive everywhere in the clause, and (like conversation in the house) can be taken as a more or less predictable default. But its very distributional promiscuity means that it does not exert the kind of *localized* and *specialized* functional pressures that new information generates. New information, being both costly in processing resources and localized in occurrence, exerts disproportionate selectional pressure on argument structures. This selectional pressure has implications for the grammatical evolution, through general processes of grammaticization, of the linkage between structure functions and the various constructions and verb classes.

When I speak of *grammar as architecture for function* I do not wish to invoke the grand scale implied in the usual talk about architecture of language, mind, or brain. Such metaphors tend to envision fixed structures and large centralized processing units (e.g. syntax) with pipelines channeling their output to (or input from) the next large component (e.g. logical form) in the assembly line. In comparison, my architectural frames are of modest scale, each covering no more than a single local grammatical structure (argument structure, construction, etc.), and they are rapidly reconfigurable. To employ a particular verb in discourse is to invoke via its argument structure a simple functional architecture, providing a local framework for linguistic action: for example, facilitating the introduction of new information or its subsequent tracking through the discourse, at the same time as semantic reference is made to an event or relation. But when these simple multi-functional architectural units are multiplied many times over the combined effect can be powerful. Variable populations of reconfigurable verbal and constructional resources are central to the process of building grammatical complexity from the bottom up, within a total ecology of grammar.

The grammar of argument structure constitutes architecture for function, inasmuch as it facilitates the enactment of multiple functions simultaneously. It provides the stability and generality needed for accommodating partly unpredictable high-demand cognitive tasks, like new information introduction, while at the same time and with the same structures fulfilling the expressive functions of predicative semantics. Rather than conceiving argument selection in terms of one-way causal effects linking taken-for-granted referents to assumed fixed targets, a more apt model might be one of co-selection between referents and argument structures, within an ecology of grammatical structures and functional demands like event verbalization and information management. Co-selection leads to co-evolution, as argument structures evolve to handle the semantics of event structures of the sort now widely attributed to them, but also simultaneously manage the distribution of cognitive attention for discourse-pragmatic functions. That there is so little conflict in actual language use between at once satisfying the semantic and cognitive-pragmatic demands calls for some sort of explanation. In part it is because of the strong discourse correlations that tend to make cross-domain pairings like agent and topic, or absolutive and new information, roughly compatible. But this can only work if there is a vast lexical conspiracy of co-evolving verbs, verb classes, and constructions that can *guarantee* their compatibility, for the most frequent patterns of demanding use.

On this understanding the grammar of any language provides speakers with, among other things, a large repertoire of low-level architectural frameworks for the organization of semantic and cognitive-pragmatic function in discourse. In addition to compatibility with verb-specific meaning, argument structures provide, in the cognitive-pragmatic dimension, a predictable locus for unpredictable work. The array of distinctive architectures, though reasonably stable over time, is highly susceptible to reconfiguration along new lines, through complex processes of grammaticization. Populations of verbs and constructions may be seen as organized into collectives based on similarity. Membership in these collectives may be restructured over time, as different groups compete to recruit new members based on similarities in semantic or discourse-pragmatic function, or more often, both. While the implications of conceiving grammar as architecture for function can only be hinted at here (see the papers in this volume), the idea may nevertheless provide a useful key for thinking about the nature of the connection between grammatical structure, semantics, and cognitive-pragmatic function.

Conclusions

Argument structure defines for itself so pivotal a locus in the organization of language that its influence is felt broadly. Because it impinges on so many linguistic domains, it attracts the attention of diverse researchers in language and cognition, who bring to the topic a variety of distinct concepts, methods, models, questions, and theoretical preoccupations. Still, the fans don't always talk to each other. As successful as it has been, argument structure research still suffers from a division into separate spheres, where each group tends to pursue its favored problems and explanatory agendas with little awareness of the others. It will take a substantial investment of labor and insight, as well as communication and collaboration across specializations and disciplines, to work out the full scope of argument structure's contribution to language. While it is too early to draw any definite conclusions regarding the precise role of argument structure in organizing grammar and use, I can offer my preliminary observations on why a collaborative effort to understand argument structure is likely to be worthwhile, and how the most valuable results are likely to be obtained.

This paper raises three closely linked questions. Why is argument structure important? Which aspects of recent approaches can be usefully combined to forge an integrated framework for understanding argument structure? Where does the perspective of pragmatics and *grammar in use* fit into the argument structure picture? I suggest that the importance of argument structure stems from its position at the crossroads — of meaning and pragmatics, lexicon and grammar, system and use. We could go so far as to say that argument structure creates this intersection and is created by it. Argument structure would not be what it is if it did not have to manage relations across disparate domains, forging compromises between systems with partly divergent and partly convergent demands, which are yoked together because grammar in use is useless unless it can meet all the demands simultaneously. In natural language it is not enough to come up with separate solutions for the problems of semantic expression, of referential pragmatics, of cognitive processing and speech production. There must be one integrated solution for all of these problems at once — though it need not be a simple one.

Argument structure is the focal point of this integration. Argument structure represents the most fundamental level at which relations are established between an event and the differentiated participants in that event. This brings with it the respective demands of verbalizing events and tracking participants. Prototypically, the event is an unrepeatable phenomenal moment, evoking issues of causality, aspect, time, manner, and such. In contrast, the event's participants have a stable identity which allows them to be tracked (or not) across successive predications, and hence treated as identifiable or not, given or new, and so on. Discourse, which is to say grammar in use, is where all these functions are realized at once. Discourse thus represents the critical environment for the evolution of argument structure and its integrative functions. Foley and Van Valin observe that "discourse, clause structure, and verb semantics are all intimately interwoven" (1984:373). The challenge is to understand just how the multiple functions of argument structure interweave across the domains of semantics, pragmatics, grammar, lexicon, cognition, and interaction to grammaticize into a verb-based repertoire of architectures for function.

Here it is useful to recall Fillmore's two questions for argument selection (1977b:73). The second question calls for an account of how each participant role in the set of co-arguments is linked (e.g. via ranking) to a particular grammatical role. But the prior question requires an account of how the initial co-argument set itself is selected from among the full range of participant roles present in the scene or event. If both the quantity and identity of arguments that are to be included in a particular event verbalization are contingent on cognitive-pragmatic factors like perspectivization and construal (Chafe 1977, 1994, Langacker 1987, 1991, 1995), as well as on language-specific grammatical encoding preferences (Slobin 1996, Talmy 1985, Talmy 2000), then valence can no longer be taken as a given, nor can the grammatical roles that constitute the syntactic target for linking. If correct, this is a major consequence, implying that argument linking is aiming at a moving target. A complete account will thus need to recognize the interaction of event-centered semantic factors and cognition-centered pragmatic factors, as verbalizable events are carved out — with the aid of linguistic argument structures — from the flux of human experience (Hopper 1997, Thompson and Hopper 2001). To clarify what kinds of factors are at stake under the broad rubric of argument selection, I have proposed to distinguish the processes of argument inclusion, ranking, linking, targeting, and realization. Cognitive-pragmatic factors like perspectivization and information management have their most obvious and direct impact on the "initial" and "final" processes of inclusion and realization, respectively, but may well participate in most or all of the processes, if only indirectly. For example, the quantity constraints of Preferred Argument Structure could be seen as inhibiting any argument selection processes that would tend to result in new information arguments being selected for each of two core grammatical roles. And the co-argument effects exhibited in semantically-based argument ranking or linking processes are paralleled by pragmatic co-argument effects, for example, when introduction of a new referent in one argument role precludes its introduction in another.

The contingency of argument structure fits well with the current view of the lexicon as more dynamic, constructed, and creative than was previously thought (Bresnan 2001, Butt and King 2000b, Davis 2001, Hopper 1997, Langacker 1987, 1991, Levin and Rappaport Hovav 1995, Pustejovsky 1995, Talmy 1985, 2000, Thompson and Hopper 2001). Researchers from a variety of points of view are asking how words are built up in accordance with cognitive, semantic, and pragmatic principles, reflecting a perspective that could be called lexical constructivism. One crucial move has been that of Goldberg (1995), whose constructional approach to argument structure effectively frees argument structures from verbs. Once the various argument structures are recognized as independent constructions in their own right, there can be greater flexibility in combining them with verbs — for example, to produce transitive and ditransitive versions of the same verb. Among the factors motivating the choice of one argument structure construction over another for a particular verb is likely to be pragmatics (Goldberg 2001). Here Preferred Argument Structure can play a significant role, via the concept of discourse profiles. The Preferred Argument Structure model makes definite predictions about the grammatical and pragmatic configuration of argument realizations in any argument structure construction. The empirical basis for these predictions lies in the various discourse profiles documented for intransitive, transitive, and ditransitive argument structures. The constructional account is well designed to be extended to more specific, fine-grained constructions, including those tied to individual verbs or verb classes. Thus an important direction for future Preferred Argument Structure research will be to develop, for each such construction, the correspondingly more detailed discourse profiles of pragmatic and grammatical correlates.

One research avenue opened up by lexical constructivism concerns complex predicates (Ackerman and Webelhuth 1998, Alsina et al. 1997, Durie 1997, Evans 1997, Hopper 1997, Thompson and Hopper 2001). This includes multi-verb constructions which are said to function more or less like a single predicate, and thus may have, under some interpretations, a single (complex) argument structure. As the constructional approach to argument structure (Goldberg 1995) extends to such complex predicates (as well as to other complex constructions), Preferred Argument Structure will extend naturally into the same territory. As structural complexity increases, Preferred Argument Structure has two roles to play. In its current form it sets definite limits on the quantity and role of new information that may be realized in any argument structure. From this perspective, complexity-building begins already with the transition from intransitive to transitive, inasmuch as the latter represents the first level of complexity at which an argument position must be pragmatically constrained (i.e. the "closed" A role). As referential-semantic complexity within a single argument structure continues to increase (through ditransitives, complex predicates, and so on), the overall cognitive processing limits are predicted to remain constant, which in turn predicts that additional argument positions must be constrained (e.g. the indirect object). But the empirical determination of the Preferred Argument Structure and discourse profiles for complex predicates remains to be determined by future research. This then represents the second role for Preferred Argument Structure research: to document the discourse profiles of complex predicates, including detailed pragmatic and grammatical realizations for all argument positions.

I have made a point of foregrounding the issues raised by ergativity, especially the question of what motivates linking S with O to form the absolutive category, while setting A apart as the ergative. This may seem a minority linguistic type, to be dealt with when convenient. However, ergativity should not be seen as a problem to be "handled", but as a gift. The gift comes to us from typological research, which makes us aware of systematic facts about the world's languages and the diverse ways they resolve the multiplex demands of language use. The fact is, I would not likely have discovered Preferred Argument Structure in my own native language, even though it is there. Being confronted with the ergative structure of Sakapultek Maya (Du Bois 1981) — and working from a theoretical stance that seeks functional explanations for grammatical structures — led me to ask what could motivate a grammatical system that has remained stable throughout four millennia of change in the Mayan language family (Du Bois 1987b). Typology contributes not only instructive problems but also some of the tools for solving them, and here Dixon's (1972) deconstruction of the subject into A, S, and O is pivotal. Argument structure research would stand to gain considerably from giving up loose talk of "subject" selection in favor of a consistent discrimination between S and A — except, of course, where subject (S=A) has been explicitly justified as such. Equipped with such tools, the further gift of split ergativity (Silverstein 1976) is likely to yield profound consequences for the understanding of argument structure — with implications for all language types.

How does the pragmatics of *grammar in use* fit into the argument structure picture? The history of argument structure research is ambiguous on this question, reflecting a certain ambivalence among practitioners toward the influence of pragmatic factors on argument structure. Frege's observations which began this chapter are impressive in the amount of pragmatic insight they pack into a few sentences, and his specific analysis of co-argument effects in the salience competition for subject versus object selection (1879 [1960]: 14–15) closely prefigures several modern analyses (Fillmore 1977b, Langacker 1995: 20). Yet he chooses to set this aside in favor of a logical conception of argument structure as an instrument for "pure thought". The same tension seems to arise again and again, though not always with the same outcome. Fillmore (1977a, 1977b) recognizes a role for pragmatic factors and embraces them in his model of argument selection. In contrast, Dowty (1991:564) recognizes pragmatic factors, such as topicality for subjects, but chooses to set them aside as not pertinent to argument structure, placing the entire explanatory burden instead on event entailments and semantic proto-roles (cf. Davis 2001:126–127). More recently the broad interest in lexical constructivism has opened up a more dynamic view of argument structure as responsive to multiple factors, which makes it natural to include pragmatic determinants among them. Especially the constructional approach of Goldberg (1995, forthcoming) is congenial to pragmatic factors, allowing for the more or less direct translation of Preferred Argument Structure patterns into properties of individual argument structure constructions. The flexibility of complex predicate formation also tends to open up argument structures to multiple potential influences, which would naturally extend to cognitive-pragmatic factors. Linguists have repeatedly recognized some kind of role for pragmatic influences on argument selection, but have not always agreed on the best way to account for the relationship. It seems that combining Preferred Argument Structure with a constructional approach to complexity may help clarify how pragmatic and semantic factors interact in a theory of argument structure.

It is often assumed that a lexical word (e.g. a verb) and its semantic meaning are more basic than how the word is used in context (e.g. how a given verb may be used to manage the pragmatics of information flow in discourse). On this assumption it would seem logical, in accounting for argument selection, to address the more basic matter first, or even exclusively. Other linguists see no harm in considering pragmatic effects on argument realization, as long as this is reserved for a suitably late stage, after the semantics of verbs or events has been consulted to determine the argument structure. But this is to mistake the linguist's problem for the speaker's problem. Linguists like to begin with a form, and ask in what ways it can be used. For example, a verb makes a typical starting point for the linguist's inquiry. Speakers, on the other hand, start with something to say, and ask what forms will help them say it. And in the actual act of speaking, there is not only an event to be verbalized, but also information to be managed. In many discourse contexts this is likely to include a *prior commitment* to a continuing topic. Thus it often happens that, perhaps surprisingly, the subject argument may very well have been chosen already in the previous clause, before the question of choosing a verb for the current clause even comes up. In this sense it is risky to take for granted the standard assumptions of the linguist's verb-first approach, if we are to take into consideration the speaker's observable practices in managing extended discourse. Actually, at this stage of our knowledge about verbs' semantic and pragmatic functions it cannot be said with certainty which, if either, has consistent priority over the other. To understand argument structure, then, it would seem judicious to include both discourse pragmatics and event semantics in the picture, and to attend particularly to their complex interactions in grammar in use. In the end, argument structure may best be understood as standing in the middle, mediating the competing demands of the local lexicosemantics of event description and the global pragmatics of cognitive processing and coherence.

From a cognitive and functional perspective, argument structure can be seen as a structure of expectations triggered by a form. Among other things, argument structure provides a predictable locus for unpredictable work, such as the introduction of new information in a clause. Against this background, where does Preferred Argument Structure fit in? Preferred Argument Structure is neither a syntactic structure nor a discourse structure, but a preference in discourse for a certain grammatical configuration of argument realizations. But even a preference can contribute to the organization of expectations, for example, regarding where in the clause the heaviest cognitive processing demands will occur. There is now extensive cross-linguistic evidence suggesting that the Preferred Argument Structure patterning of arguments in discourse is deeply systematic, stable, and consistent across typologically diverse languages. And yet these discourse patterns are not reducible to any grammatical rule, but must be recognized in their own right. Taken as fundamental universals of the patterning of grammar in use, they have profound implications for the grammaticization of argument structure and of the system of grammatical relations.

Argument structure is now recognized as a key locus for theoretical integration across multiple dimensions of language. Semantics and syntax, lexicon and grammar, are already brought together, and I have argued here for the key role of pragmatics and language use in the argument structure equation. As argument structure research opens up further to the theoretical and empirical potential of lexical constructivism, complex predicates, constructions, acquisition, typology, grammaticization, and other new developments, it will become still more important to address argument structure in its fullest context of function, which is to say, in natural discourse. The implications are just beginning to unfold of understanding argument structure as grammar in use — architecture for function.

Notes

1. As with most of the examples in this chapter, the data here are taken from the Santa Barbara Corpus of Spoken American English (Du Bois 2000, 2003b). The most salient transcription conventions are three dots for a pause, (H) for in-breath, (TSK) for a click, @ for a laugh, = following a lengthened segment, and [ ] to mark the beginning and end of simultaneous speech. For additional symbols and conventions, see page ix. Some transcriptions have been slightly simplified in details of their prosodic and interactional transcription for the sake of clarity. For example, where an excerpted utterance overlaps with an utterance that is not included in the cited excerpt, the square brackets that normally mark simultaneous speech are left out, to avoid confusion. And some details of vocal quality, etc., have been left out where not relevant to the immediate point. In general, speaker names are pseudonyms. For each Santa Barbara Corpus

example, the title of the discourse from which it was drawn is cited in parentheses (followed, in some cases, by the line number in the transcript). The full transcriptions, along with their corresponding audio, can be consulted in (Du Bois 2000, 2003b).

2. To highlight the distribution of pronominal and lexical arguments, which are important for Preferred Argument Structure, I adopt the following conventions (for spoken discourse examples only). Pronouns are underlined; full lexical noun phrases are boldfaced; and verbs are italicized. These notations are intended only as highlighting, not as linguistic analysis — especially for verbs, where the complexities of modals, particles, complex verbs, copular predicates, and so on far exceed what can readily be represented by a simple notation like italics. Please note that all of these highlighting notations (underline, boldface, italics) represent morphosyntax only; none is intended to indicate a particular prosodic stress or accent.

3. Labels for thematic roles (agent, patient, experiencer, theme, stimulus, and so on) are used here for descriptive convenience (as seems to be common practice nowadays — cf. Ackerman and Moore 2001, Davis 2001), without committing to a position that these categories operate as such in processes of argument selection.

4. Most of the papers by Fillmore cited in the present paper have been collected in one volume (Fillmore 2002).

5. One could say that the research program laid out in that paper is now coming to fruition in research on frame semantics (Fillmore and Baker 2001), which demonstrates significant relations between lexical semantics and argument structure, via their grounding in relation to the larger "scene"-level construct of the semantic frame.

6. The latter question was more fully developed as follows:

> When two or more elements from a scene get realized in the associated sentence as members of the nucleus, are there general principles that determine which of these is the subject, or first term, and which is the object, or second term? (Fillmore 1977a: 94)

7. Fillmore's scenes and frames also have a broader application than events as currently conceived, in that they can account for the conceptual relations of nouns and other categories, not just verbs (1977a, 2002).

8. In this light I will sometimes speak of a noun phrase as being selected for a particular "argument role" where others might speak of a syntactic function like subject or object. This usage seems compatible especially with Goldberg's (1995) approach to argument structures as constructions (see below).

9. Adapted from Du Bois (2003a: 62, Table 2.1). Sources for the languages cited are as follows: Hebrew (Smith 1996); Sakapultek (Du Bois 1987a); Papago (Payne 1987); English (Kumagai 2000); Gooniyandi (McGregor 1999). For further details see Du Bois (2003a: 62, fn. 7).

10. Adapted from Du Bois (2003a: 63, Table 2.2). Sources for the languages cited are as in the note for Table 2, plus the following: Spanish (Ashby and Bentivoglio 1993); French (Ashby and Bentivoglio 1993); Brazilian Portuguese (Dutra 1987); Japanese (Matsumoto 1997). For further details see Du Bois (2003a: 63, fn. 8).

11. Adapted from Du Bois (2003a: 69, Table 2.4). Sources are as for Table 2. For further details see Du Bois (2003a: 69, fn. 13).

12. Adapted from Du Bois (2003a: 70, Table 2.5). Sources are as for Table 3. For further details see Du Bois (2003a: 70, fn. 14).

13. Durie reports that relativization in Acehnese generally confirms Fox's (1987) proposal of a universally preferred absolutive pivot for relativization (Durie 1994b: 527, fn. 18).

References

Ackerman, Farrell, and Webelhuth, Gert. 1998. *A Theory of Predicates.* Stanford, CA: CSLI Publications.

Ackerman, Farrell, and Moore, John. 2001. *Proto-Properties and Grammatical Encoding: A Correspondence Theory of Argument Selection.* Stanford: CSLI Publications.

Allen, Shanley E.M. 2000. "A discourse pragmatic explanation for argument representation in child Inuktitut". *Linguistics* 38: 483–521.

Alsina, Alex, Bresnan, Joan, and Sells, Peter (eds). 1997. *Complex Predicates.* Stanford, CA: CSLI Publications.

Ariel, Mira. 1990. *Accessing Noun-Phrase Antecedents.* London: Routledge.

Ariel, Mira. 2001. "Accessibility theory: An overview". In T. Sanders, J. Schilperoord and W. Spooren (eds), *Text Representation: Linguistic and Psycholinguistic Aspects.* Amsterdam: Benjamins, 29–87.

Ashby, William J., and Bentivoglio, Paola. 1993. "Preferred Argument Structure in spoken French and Spanish". *Language Variation and Change* 5: 61–76.

Ashby, William J., and Bentivoglio, Paola. 1997. "Strategies for introducing new referents into discourse: A comparative analysis of French and Spanish presentational structures". In R.M. Hammond and M.B. MacDonald (eds), *Linguistic Studies in Honor of Bohdan Saciuk.* West Lafayette, IN: Learning Systems Incorporated, 9–25.

Assayag, Nurit. 1999. *Subject Selection in Discourse: Cognitive Constraints and Genre Effect.* Unpublished M.A. thesis, Linguistics Department. Tel Aviv: Tel Aviv University.

Bentivoglio, Paola. 1990. Los sujetos del tipo 'S' en el español hablado en Caracas. In *Actas del X Congreso Internacional de la ALFAL, Campinas 1990.* Campinas: UNICAMP: Universidade Estadual de Campinas, Brazil.

Bentivoglio, Paola. 1994. "Spanish Preferred Argument Structure across time and space". *Revista de Documentaçao de Estudos em Lingüística Teórica e Aplicada (DELTA)* 10: 227–293.

Bentivoglio, Paola. 1998. "The late acquisition of Preferred Argument Structure in Venezuelan spoken Spanish". In B. Caron (ed.), *Proceedings of the XVIth International Congress of Linguists.* Amsterdam: Elsevier.

Börjars, Kersti, and Vincent, Nigel. 2000. "Multiple case and the 'wimpiness' of Morphology". In M. Butt and T.H. King (eds), *Argument Realization.* Stanford, CA: CSLI Publications, 15–40.

Bresnan, Joan. 2001. *Lexical-Functional Syntax.* Oxford: Blackwell.

Bresnan, Joan, and Mchombo, Sam A. 1987. "Topic, pronoun, and agreement in Chichewa". *Language* 63: 741–782.

Brito, Célia Maria Coélho. 1996. *A Transitividade Verbal na Língua Portuguesa: Uma Investigaçao de Base Funcionalista.* São Paulo: Araraquara.

Brown, Penelope. 1998. "Early Tzeltal verbs: Argument structure and argument representation". *Proceedings of the Annual Child Language Research Forum* 29: 129–140.

Butt, Miriam, and King, Tracy Holloway. 2000a. "Introduction". In M. Butt and T.H. King (eds), *Argument Realization.* Stanford, CA: CSLI Publications, 1–13.

Butt, Miriam, and King, Tracy Holloway. 2000b. *Argument Realization.* Stanford, CA: CSLI Publications.

Carlson, Greg N. 1998. "Thematic roles and the individuation of events". In S. Rothstein (ed.), *Events and Grammar.* Dordrecht: Kluwer, 35–51.

Chafe, Wallace L. 1977. "The recall and verbalization of past experience". In R.W. Cole (ed.), *Current Issues in Linguistic Theory.* Bloomington: Indiana University Press, 215–246.

Chafe, Wallace L. 1980. "The deployment of consciousness in the production of a narrative". In W.L. Chafe (ed.), *The Pear Stories: Cognitive, Cultural, and Linguistic Aspects of Narrative Production.* Norwood, NJ: Ablex, 9–50.

Chafe, Wallace L. 1987. "Cognitive constraints on information flow". In R.S. Tomlin (ed.), *Coherence and Grounding in Discourse.* Amsterdam: Benjamins, 21–51.

Chafe, Wallace L. 1994. *Discourse, Consciousness, and Time: The Flow and Displacement of Conscious Experience in Speaking and Writing.* Chicago: University of Chicago Press.

Chafe, Wallace L., and Mithun, Marianne. 1999. "What are S, A, and O?" *Studies in Language* 23: 569–596.

Clancy, Patricia M. 1993. "Preferred argument structure in Korean acquisition". In E.V. Clark (ed.), *The Proceedings of the Twenty-Fifth Annual Child Language Research Forum.* Stanford: CSLI Publications, 307–314.

Clancy, Patricia M. 1995. "Subject and object in Korean acquisition: Surface expression and casemarking". In S. Kuno et al. (eds), *Harvard Studies in Korean Linguistics.* Cambridge, MA, 3–17.

Clancy, Patricia M. 1996. "Referential strategies and the co-construction of argument structure in Korean acquisition". In B. Fox (ed.), *Studies in Anaphora.* Amsterdam: Benjamins, 33–68.

Clancy, Patricia M. 1997. "Discourse motivations of referential choice in Korean acquisition". In H.-m. Sohn and J. Haig (eds), *Japanese/Korean Linguistics.* Stanford: CSLI Publications, 639–659.

Comrie, Bernard. 1978. "Ergativity". In W.P. Lehmann (ed.), *Syntactic Typology: Studies in the Phenomenology of Language.* Austin, TX: University of Texas Press, 329–374.

Comrie, Bernard. 1988. "Topics, grammaticalized topics, and subjects". *Preeedings of the Fourteenth Annual Meeting: General Session and Parassession on Grammaticalization.* Berkeley: Berkeley Linguistics Society, 265–279.

Corston-Oliver, Simon H. 2000. "Using decision trees to select the grammatical relation of a noun phrase". Paper presented at *Sigdial workshop: Theme Session on Principles for Dialogue System Evaluation. ACL-2000: The 38th Annual Meeting of the Association for Computational Linguistics,* Hong Kong.

Cumming, Susanna. 1994. "Functional categories in the lexicon: Referent introduction in Indonesian novels". *Text* 14: 465–494.

Davis, Anthony R. 2001. *Linking by Types in the Hierarchical Lexicon.* Stanford: CSLI Publications.

Dixon, Robert M.W. 1972. *The Dyirbal Language of North Queensland.* Cambridge: Cambridge University Press.

Dixon, Robert M.W. 1979. "Ergativity". *Language* 55: 59–128.

Dixon, Robert M.W. (ed.) 1987. *Studies in Ergativity.* Amsterdam: North-Holland.

Dixon, Robert M.W. 1994. *Ergativity.* Cambridge: Cambridge University Press.

Dor, Daniel. 2000. "From the autonomy of syntax to the autonomy of linguistic semantics: Notes on the correspondence between the transparency problem and the relationship problem". *Pragmatics and Cognition* 8: 325–356.

Downing, Pamela. 1993. "Pragmatic and semantic constraints on numeral quantifier position in Japanese". *Journal of Linguistics* 29: 65–93.

Dowty, David. 1991. "Thematic proto-roles and argument selection". *Language* 67: 547–619.

Du Bois, John W. 1980. "Beyond definiteness: The trace of identity in discourse". In W.L. Chafe (ed.), *The Pear Stories: Cognitive, Cultural, and Linguistic Aspects of Narrative Production.* Norwood, NJ: Ablex, 203–274.

Du Bois, John W. 1981. *The Sacapultec language.* Ph.D. dissertation. Berkeley: University of California, Berkeley.

Du Bois, John W. 1985. "Competing motivations". In J. Haiman (ed.), *Iconicity in Syntax.* Amsterdam: Benjamins, 343–365.

Du Bois, John W. 1987a. "The discourse basis of ergativity". *Language* 63: 805–855.

Du Bois, John W. 1987b. "Absolutive zero: Paradigm adaptivity in Sacapultec Maya". *Lingua* 71: 203–222.

Du Bois, John W. (ed.) 2000. *Santa Barbara Corpus of Spoken American English, Part 1.* Philadelphia: Linguistic Data Consortium.

Du Bois, John W. 2003a. "Discourse and grammar". In M. Tomasello (ed.), *The New Psychology of Language: Cognitive and Functional Approaches to Language Structure, vol. 2.* Mahwah, NJ: Erlbaum, 47–87.

Du Bois, John W. (ed.) 2003b. *Santa Barbara Corpus of Spoken American English, Part 2.* Philadelphia: Linguistic Data Consortium.

Du Bois, John W., Schuetze-Coburn, Stephan, Cumming, Susanna, and Paolino, Danae. 1992. "Discourse transcription". *Santa Barbara Papers in Linguistics* 4, 1–225.

Durie, Mark. 1988. "Preferred argument structure in an active language: Arguments against the category 'intransitive subject'". *Lingua* 74: 1–25.

Durie, Mark. 1994a. "Transitivity and argument coding". In W. Bright (ed.), *International Encyclopedia of Linguistics.* New York: Oxford University Press, 176–177.

Durie, Mark. 1994b. "A case study of pragmatic linking". *Text* 14: 495–529.

Durie, Mark. 1997. "Grammatical structures in verb serialization". In A. Alsina, J. Bresnan and P. Sells (eds), *Complex Predicates.* Stanford: CSLI Publications, 289–354.

Dutra, Rosalia. 1987. "The hybrid S category in Brazilian Portuguese: Some implications for word order". *Studies in Language* 11: 163–180.

Evans, Nick. 1997. "Role or cast? Noun incorporation and complex predicates in Mayali". In A. Alsina, J. Bresnan and P. Sells (eds), *Complex Predicates.* Stanford: CSLI Publications, 397–430.

Fillmore, Charles J. 1968. "The case for case". In E. Bach and R. Harms (eds), *Universals in Linguistic Theory.* New York: Holt, 1–90.

Fillmore, Charles J. 1977a. "Topics in lexical semantics". In R. Cole (ed.), *Current Issues in Linguistic Theory.* Bloomington: Indiana University Press, 76–138.

Fillmore, Charles J. 1977b. "The case for case reopened". In P. Cole (ed.), *Syntax and semantics vol. 8: Grammatical Relations.* New York: Academic Press, 59–81.

Fillmore, Charles J. 2002. *Language Form, Meaning and Practice.* Stanford: CSLI Publications.

Fillmore, Charles J., and Baker, Collin F. 2001. "Frame semantics for text understanding". *Proceedings of WordNet and Other Lexical Resources Workshop, NAACL, Pittsburgh, June, 2001.* Pittsburgh. URL: http://framenet.icsi.berkeley.edu/~framenet/papers/FNcrime.pdf

Foley, William, and Van Valin, Robert D., Jr. 1977. "On the organization of 'subject' properties in universal grammar". *Proceedings of the Berkeley Linguistics Society* 3: 293–320.

Foley, William, and Van Valin, Robert D., Jr. 1984. *Functional Syntax and Universal Grammar.* Cambridge: Cambridge University Press.

Fox, Barbara. 1987. "The noun phrase accessibility hierarchy reinterpreted: Subject primacy or the absolutive hypothesis?" *Language* 63: 856–870.

Fox, Barbara. 1995. "The category 'S' in English conversation". In W. Abraham, T. Givón and S. A. Thompson (eds), *Discourse Grammar and Typology.* Amsterdam: Benjamins, 153–178.

Fox, Barbara, and Thompson, Sandra A. 1990. "A discourse explanation of the grammar of relative clauses in English conversation". *Language* 66: 297–316.

Frege, Gottlob. 1879 [1960]. "Begriffsschrift: A formalized language of pure thought modelled upon the language of arithmetic". In P. Geach and M. Black (eds), *Translations From the Philosphical Writings of Gottlob Frege.* Oxford: Blackwell, 1–20.

García Velasco, Daniel, and Hengeveld, Kees. 2002. "Do we need predicate frames?" In R. Mairal Usón and M. J. Pérez Quintero (eds), *New Perspectives on Argument Structure in Functional Grammar.* Berlin: Mouton de Gruyter, 95–123.

Gawron, Jean Mark. 1983. *Prepositions and the Semantics of Complementation.* Ph.D. dissertation, Linguistics Department. Berkeley: University of California, Berkeley.

Givón, Talmy. 1979. *On Understanding Grammar.* New York: Academic Press.

Givón, Talmy (ed.) 1983. *Topic Continuity in Discourse: A Quantitative Cross-Language Study.* Amsterdam: Benjamins.

Goldberg, Adele E. 1995. *Constructions: A Construction Grammar Approach to Argument Structure.* Chicago: Unversity of Chicago Press.

Goldberg, Adele E. 2001. "Patient arguments of causative verbs can be omitted: The role of information structure in argument distribution". *Language Sciences* 23: 503–524.

Goldberg, Adele E. Forthcoming. "Discourse and argument structure". In L. Horn and G. Ward (eds), *Handbook of Pragmatics.* Oxford: Blackwell.

Grimshaw, Jane. 1990. *Argument Structure.* Cambridge: MIT Press.

Guerriero, Sonia A.M., Cooper, Amy, Oshima-Takane, Yuriko, and Kuriyama, Yoko. 2001. "A discourse-pragmatic explanation for argument realization and omission in English and Japanese children's speech". In A. H.-J. Do, L. Domínguez and A. Johansen (eds), *Proceedings of the 25th Annual Boston University Conference on Language Development.* Somerville, MA: Cascadilla Press, 319–330.

Hengeveld, Kees. Forthcoming. "The architecture of Functional Discourse Grammar". In J.L. Mackenzie and M.Á. Gómez González (eds), *A New Architecture for Functional Grammar.* Berlin: Mouton de Gruyter.

Herring, Susan. 1989. "Verbless presentation and the discourse basis of ergativity". In B. Music, R. Graczyk and C. Wiltshire (eds), *Papers from the 25th Annual Regional Meeting of the Chicago Linguistic Society 25, Part 2: Parasession on Language in Context.* Chicago: Chicago Linguistics Society, 123–137.

Hopper, Paul. 1997. "Dispersed verbal predicates in vernacular written narrative". In A. Kamio (ed.), *Directions in Functional Linguistics.* Amsterdam: Benjamins, 1–18.

Hopper, Paul, and Thompson, Sandra A. 1980. "Transitivity in grammar and discourse". *Language* 56: 251–299.

Jespersen, Otto. 1924. *The Philosophy of Grammar.* London: George Allen and Unwin.

Kärkkäinen, Elise. 1996. "Preferred Argument Structure and subject role in American English conversational discourse". *Journal of Pragmatics* 25: 675–701.

Keenan, Edward L. 1976. "Towards a universal definition of "subject"". In C.N. Li (ed.), *Subject and Topic.* New York: Academic Press, 303–334.

Keenan, Edward L. 1984. "Semantic correlates of the ergative/absolutive distinction". *Linguistics* 22: 197–223.

Koenig, Jean-Pierre, and Davis, Anthony R. 2001. "Sublexical modality and the structure of lexical semantic representations". *Linguistics and Philosophy* 24: 71–124.

Kumagai, Yoshiharu. 2000. "Ergativity in English spontaneous discourse". *Mulberry: Bulletin of the Department of English, Faculty of Letters, Aichi Prefectural University* 49: 35–60.

Kumpf, Lorraine E. 1992. "Preferred Argument Structure in second language discourse: A preliminary study". *Studies in Language* 16: 369–403.

Langacker, Ronald W. 1987. *Foundations of Cognitive Grammar, vol. 1: Theoretical prerequisites.* Stanford, CA: Stanford University Press.

Langacker, Ronald W. 1991. *Foundations of Cognitive Grammar, vol. 2: Descriptive application.* Stanford, CA: Stanford University Press.

Langacker, Ronald W. 1995. "Raising and transparency". *Language* 71: 1–62.

Levin, Beth. 1993. *English verb classes and alternations.* Chicago: Unversity of Chicago Press.

Levin, Beth. 1999. "Objecthood: An event structure perspective". *CLS 35, Part I: Papers from the Main Session.* Chicago: Chicago Linguistics Society, 223–247.

Levin, Beth, and Rappaport Hovav, Malka. 1995. *Unaccusativity: At the Syntax-Lexical Semantics Interface.* Cambridge: MIT Press.

Li, Charles N., and Thompson, Sandra A. 1976. "Subject and topic: A new typology of language". In C.N. Li (ed.), *Subject and Topic.* New York: Academic Press, 457–489.

Mallinson, Graham, and Blake, Barry J. 1982. *Language typology: Cross-cultural Studies in Syntax.* Amsterdam: North-Holland.

Matsumoto, Kazuko. 1997. "NPs in Japanese conversation". *Pragmatics* 7: 163–181.

Matsumoto, Kazuko. 2000. "Intonation units, clauses and preferred argument structure in conversational Japanese". *Language Sciences* 22: 63–86.

Matsumoto, Kazuko. Forthcoming. *Intonation Units in Japanese Conversational Discourse: Syntactic, Informational, and Functional Structures.* Amsterdam: Benjamins.

McGregor, William B. 1999. "'Optional' ergative marking in Gooniyandi revisited: Implications to the theory of marking". *Leuvanse Bijdragen* 87: 491–534.

Merlan, Francesca. 1985. "Split intransitivity: Functional oppositions in intransitive inflection". In J. Nichols and A. Woodbury (eds), *Grammar Inside and Outside the Clause.* Cambridge: Cambridge University Press, 324–362.

Mithun, Marianne. 1991. "Active/agentive case marking and its motivations". *Language* 67: 510–546.

Narasimhan, Bhuvana, and Budwig, Nancy. 2001. Argument realization in Hindi child-caregiver discourse. Paper presented at *South Asian Languages Analysis Roundtable,* University of Konstanz.

Narasimhan, Bhuvana, and Budwig, Nancy, and Murty, Lalita. Forthcoming. "Argument realization in Hindi caregiver-child discourse". *Journal of Pragmatics.*

O'Dowd, Elizabeth. 1990. "Discourse pressure, genre and grammatical alignment — after Du Bois". *Studies in Language* 14: 365–403.

Partee, Barbara Hall. 1996. "The development of formal semantics in linguistic theory". In Shalom Lappin (ed), *Handbook of contemporary semantic theory.* Oxford: Blackwell, 11–38.

Payne, Doris L. 1987. "Information structuring in Papago narrative discourse". *Language* 63: 783–804.

Perlmutter, David M. 1978. "Impersonal passives and the unaccusative hypothesis". *Berkeley Linguistics Society* 4, 157–189.

Pustejovsky, James. 1995. *The Generative Lexicon.* Cambridge, MA: MIT Press.

Rappaport Hovav, Malka, and Levin, Beth. 2001. "An event structure account of English resultatives". *Language* 77: 766–797.

Schuetze-Coburn, Stephan. 1987. *Topic Management and the Lexicon: A Discourse Profile of Three-Argument Verbs in German.* Unpublished M.A. thesis, Linguistics Department. Los Angeles: UCLA.

Silverstein, Michael. 1976. "Hierarchy of features and ergativity". In R.M.W. Dixon (ed.), *Grammatical Categories in Australian Languages.* Canberra: Australian Institute of Aboriginal Studies, 112–171.

Silverstein, Michael. 1981. "Case-marking and the nature of language". *Australian Journal of Linguistics* 1: 227–246.

Silverstein, Michael. 1993. "Of nominatives and datives: Universal grammar from the botttom up". In R.D. Van Valin, Jr (ed.), *Advances in Role and Reference Grammar.* Amsterdam: Benjamins, 465–498.

Slobin, Dan I. 1996. "From 'thought and language' to 'thinking for speaking'". In J. J. Gumperz and S. C. Levinson (eds), *Rethinking Linguistic Relativity*. Cambridge: Cambridge University Press, 97–114.

Smith, Wendy. 1996. "Spoken narrative and Preferred Clause Structure: Evidence from modern Hebrew discourse". *Studies in Language* 20: 163–189.

Talmy, Leonard. 1985. "Lexicalization patterns: Semantic structure in lexical form". In T. Shopen (ed.), *Language Typology and Syntactic Description, vol. 3: Grammatical Categories and the Lexicon*. Cambridge: Cambridge University Press, 57–149.

Talmy, Leonard. 1988. "Force dynamics in language and cognition". *Cognitive Science* 12: 49–100.

Talmy, Leonard. 2000. *Toward a Cognitive Semantics*. Cambridge, MA: MIT Press.

Thompson, Sandra A. 2002. "'Object complements' and conversation: Towards a realistic account". *Studies in Language* 26: 125–163.

Thompson, Sandra A., and Hopper, Paul. 2001. "Transitivity, clause structure, and argument structure: Evidence from conversation". In J. Bybee and P. Hopper (eds), *Frequency and the Emergence of Linguistic Structure*. Amsterdam: Benjamins, 27–60.

Tomasello, Michael. 1992. *First Verbs: A Case Study of Early Grammatical Development*. Cambridge: Cambridge University Press.

Van Valin, Robert D., Jr. 1990. "Semantic parameters of split intransitivity". *Language* 66: 221–260.

Van Valin, Robert D., Jr. (ed.) 1993. *Advances in Role and Reference Grammar*. Amsterdam: Benjamins.

Van Valin, Robert D., Jr, and LaPolla, Randy J. 1997. *Syntax: Structure, Meaning, and Function*. Cambridge: Cambridge University Press.

Preferred Argument Structure across time and space

A comparative diachronic analysis of French and Spanish

William J. Ashby and Paola Bentivoglio
University of California, Santa Barbara / Universidad Central de Venezuela

Introduction

Du Bois' theory of Preferred Argument Structure relates observable discourse patterns and grammatical form, specifically the form of the "core" arguments of the verb: the subject and the direct object (Du Bois 1985, 1987a, 1987b). Du Bois first derived the theory from narratives in Sakapultek Maya, an ergative language. Because there is no unitary category of subject in Sakapultek, he follows the practice initiated by Dixon (1979) in denoting the subject of a one-argument verb as S, the subject of a two-argument verb as A, and the direct object as O.

Du Bois proposed that Preferred Argument Structure has both a grammatical dimension and a pragmatic dimension, expressed as "constraints" (i.e., measurable discourse preferences), as shown in Table 1. The grammatical dimension can be expressed by two constraints relating to the presence of full, lexical NP's in a clause. The One Lexical Argument Constraint reflects the paucity of clauses in which more than one of the core arguments is expressed as a lexical NP; any additional core arguments tend to be expressed as pronouns or as zero forms. The second grammatical constraint is the Non-lexical A Constraint. It reflects the tendency for the single lexical NP to occur either in the S or in the O role, and rarely in the A role.

Du Bois also expresses the pragmatic dimension of Preferred Argument Structure by a pair of constraints. The One New Argument Constraint reflects the tendency of clauses to contain no more than one piece of new information (see also Chafe 1994). Du Bois claims that this single piece of new information tends to appear in the O or S role, rarely in the A role; this patterning accounts for the Given A Constraint.

Table 1. Dimensions and constraints of Preferred Argument Structure

	Grammar	Pragmatics
Quantity	One Lexical Argument Constraint	One New Argument Constraint
Role	Non-lexical A Constraint	Given A Constraint

Source: Adapted from Du Bois (1987b: 829)

As is apparent in this volume, the patterns of Preferred Argument Structure first found by Du Bois in Sakapultek have been subsequently documented in a wide array of languages, both of the ergative-absolutive and of the nominative-accusative type.[1] Preferred Argument Structure has thus been rather extensively tested across space, but it has not as yet been extensively tested across time. The only studies of which we are aware that compare the manifestations of Preferred Argument Structure in the same language at different points in time are those of Bentivoglio (1994) for Spanish and of Josserand (1995) for hieroglyphic Maya. There is an obvious reason for this lacuna: namely, that the focus of Preferred Argument Structure has been on spoken language, primarily oral narratives and spontaneous conversational data. Oral data are obviously unavailable from the very distant past. Those wishing to study Preferred Argument Structure across time are thus obliged to work from written texts, preferably (for comparative purposes) with texts replete with dialogue and as reflective as possible of the spoken language of their time.

In this chapter we will test the Preferred Argument Structure hypothesis on an Old French text and an Old Spanish text, using the same methodology we have already brought to bear on the modern languages (Ashby 1995, Ashby & Bentivoglio 1993, Bentivoglio 1994, Ashby & Bentivoglio 1997).[2] We will then be able to compare the results for these different stages of French and Spanish in order to determine whether changes have occurred across both time and space: from medieval to modern France, and from Old Castile to present-day Latin America.

The medieval texts we have selected for our analysis are the *Chanson de Roland,* from late eleventh century France (Moignet 1969), and the *Cantar de Mio Çid,* from mid-twelfth century Castile (Menendez Pidal 1945). These texts are classics of the genre known as the medieval epic or *chanson de geste.* There has been considerable scholarly debate over whether the *Chanson de Roland,* and by extension other medieval epics, is the work of a single learned author or the written version of a traditional oral narrative.[3] Preferred Argument Structure theory may have something to contribute to this debate. That is, if the patterns of Preferred Argument Structure, which have been found manifested time and again in samples of spoken language, are also present in these medieval texts, this finding may provide confirmation of the essential oral quality of the epic and lend further support to the "traditionalist" viewpoint that sees this genre as oral literature. Thus, the comparison of our medieval texts with our modern spoken data may not be as far fetched as it may at first appear, although the medieval epics are obviously of a different genre than the semi-formal conversational style captured in the corpora from which our modern data derive. In part, Prefered Argument Structure is based on the assumption that there are cognitive limits on planning strategies in spoken discourse. Even though they may be essentially oral in quality, the medieval epics are surely more planned than spontaneous conversation. In any case, the medieval epics are as close as we can get to spoken language of the time.

In the first section of this chapter, we will explain the methodology adopted for our study; we will then present the results of our analysis of Old French and Old Spanish, comparing them with the results of our earlier study of Modern French and Modern Spanish.

Methodology

In order to have an equivalent amount of Old French and Old Spanish data, for each text we selected the first 800 main clauses, together with all embedded, combined and relative clauses occurring in the text from the beginning up to the eight-hundredth main clause.[4] The number of main and non-main clauses analyzed for each text is shown in Table 2.

We have followed the same methodology used in our earlier studies of the modern languages (Ashby 1995; Ashby & Bentivoglio 1993; Bentivoglio 1994; Ashby & Bentivoglio, 1997). For each corpus, every NP filling one of the core roles was coded for syntactic role, form, animacy, identifiability, and activation state, as shown in Table 3. The coded strings were then tabulated and analyzed with the help of Goldvarb 2.0 (Rand & Sankoff 1990). This program includes two applications of Sankoff's Variable Rule Program (Varbrul). One application generates probability weights for each variable, and the other selects the variables whose distributions are statistically significant.

In the Appendix, Text 1 and Text 2 give extracts of the *Chanson de Roland* and of the *Cantar de Mio Çid*, respectively, showing our coding of core arguments for syntactic role and form. Consider, for example, line 8 of Text 1, reproduced here as (1).

(1) *Vers Engletere passat li la mer salse,*
'To England crossed he the salty sea'

In (1), the transitive subject, *li* 'he', is coded as A, because it expresses the most agentive argument of the two-argument verb *passat* 'crossed' and as P, because it is a pronoun. *La mer salse* 'the salty sea' is coded as O, because it is the transitive object of *passat*, and as N, because it is a full, lexical NP.

Table 2. Distribution of clause types in the Old French and Old Spanish corpora

	Old French	Old Spanish
Main	800	800
Non-main	289	453
Total	1089	1253

Table 3. Factor groups and factors coded for each core NP token

Factor group	Factor	Definition
Syntactic role	A	Transitive Subject
	Se	Intransitive Subject, Copular
	Si	Intransitive Subject, Other
	O	Transitive Object
Form of NP	N	Lexical
	P	Pronominal
	C	Clausal
	Ø	Zero
Animacy	A	Animate
	I	Inanimate
Identifiability	I	Identifiable
	N	Non-identifable
Activation	N	New
	G	Non-new

For one-argument verbs we distinguish between the single argument of the copular verb 'to be' (coded Se), as in *Charles* in (2), and the argument of all remaining one-argument verbs (coded Si), as in *los gallos* 'the roosters' in (3).

(2) *Merveilus hom est Charles*
'Charles is a marvelous man' (Text 1, 6)

(3) *Apiessa cantan los gallos*
'The roosters were singing repetitively' (Text 2, 1)

Unlike Modern French, Old French is a "pro-drop" language, as are Old and Modern Spanish. Thus, the form of the core arguments may not only be pronominal (P) and lexical (N), as illustrated in (1), (2), and (3), but may also be zero (Ø), as with the S argument of Fr. *asemblet s'est* '(he) has joined' in (4) and the A argument of Sp. *sopieron* '(they) heard' of (5):

(4) *Asemblet s'est as sarrazins messages*
'(He) has joined with the heathen messangers' (Text 1, 2)

(5) *i sopieron el mandado*
'and (they) heard the news' (Text 2,11)

We also included the clausal form (C), as in (6), where the infinitival clause, Spanish *crebar albores* 'to break day,' is coded as the O argument of the two-argument verb *quieren*, which is C in form.

(6) *e quieren crebar albores*
'and they wanted to break day' (Text 2, 2)

The arguments within this embedded infinitival clause were also coded. Thus, two arguments of *crebar* are coded: an A argument, which takes Ø form, and an O argument, *albores*, which is expressed as an N.[5]

We also considered the complement of verbs of saying to be of C form, as in (7), where the extended quoted speech is considered the O argument of the two-argument verb *respunt* 'replies'. The arguments of each verb within the quoted speech were also coded.

(7) *Guenes respunt: "Itels est sis curages.*
'Ganelon replys: "Such is his disposition.'
Jamais n'ert hume ki encuntre lui vaille."
'Never will there be a man who measures up to him."' (Text 1, 11–12)

Results

The grammatical dimensions of Preferred Argument Structure

Table 4a and Table 4b show the distribution of NP's of lexical, non-lexical, and clausal form in the various grammatical roles (A, Si, Se, O, C) in the Old French and Old Spanish corpora, respectively. Table 4a and Table 4b show that the non-lexical form (that is, pronoun and zero taken together) predominates for all but the O role. As will be demonstrated shortly, this is because the O role is preferred for the introduction of new information, and new information must perforce take lexical form. Table 4a and Table 4b support Du Bois' Non-Lexical A Constraint insofar as it is the A role that has the lowest ratio of lexical NP's of any of the roles (26% for Old French and 16% for Old Spanish). Note that most A's are zeros (56% for Old French and 74% for Old Spanish). This finding reflects the fact that referents coded in the A role tend to be animate and continuous[6].

Figure 1 shows the distribution of lexical NP's across core syntactic roles in the Old French and Old Spanish corpora, and project a comparison of these distributions to those obtaining in our Modern French and Modern Spanish data (reported in Ashby & Bentivoglio 1993).[7] Contrary to what we would expect from the prediction of the Non-Lexical A Constraint, and contrary to what obtains in Modern French and Modern Spanish, in both Old French and Old Spanish we see a relatively high percentage of lexical NP's occuring in the A role (13% in Old French and 12% in Old Spanish, compared to 5% in Modern French and 6% in Modern Spanish).[8] We believe this relatively high ratio of lexical NP's in the A role role is specific to the epic genre and is in part the result of the frequent repetition of proper names. For example, lines 1 and 17 of Text 3, reproduced here as (8) and (9), are identical, except for the word order of the O relative to the verb, and both begin with a lexical A, *li reis Marsile* 'King Marsile'.

Table 4a. Distribution of NP's according to grammatical role and form in the Old French corpus

Role	Lexical		Pronoun		Zero		Clause		Total	
	N	(%)	N	(%)	N	(%)	N	(%)	N	(%)
A	175	(26)	126	(18)	384	(56)	0	(0)	685	(37)
Se	48	(44)	28	(26)	33	(30)	0	(0)	109	(5)
Si	139	(47)	61	(21)	95	(32)	0	(0)	480	(24)
O	403	(53)	173	(23)	5	(1)	178	(23)	730	(37)
Total	765	(41)	388	(21)	517	(28)	178	(10)	2004	

Table 4b. Distribution of NP's according to grammatical role and form in the Old Spanish corpus

Role	Lexical		Pronoun		Zero		Clause		Total	
	N	(%)	N	(%)	N	(%)	N	(%)	N	(%)
A	115	(16)	76	(11)	506	(73)	0	(0)	697	(35)
Se	27	(29)	26	(28)	40	(43)	0	(0)	93	(5)
Si	158	(33)	78	(16)	241	(50)	3	(1)	480	(24)
O	351	(48)	249	(34)	0	(0)	130	(18)	730	(37)
Total	651	(33)	42	(21)	787	(39)	133	(7)	2000	

(8) *Li reis Marsile out sun cunseill finet.*
'King M. had held his counsel.' (Text 3,1)

(9) *Li reis Marsile out finet sun cunseill.*
'King M. had held his counsel.' (Text 3,17)

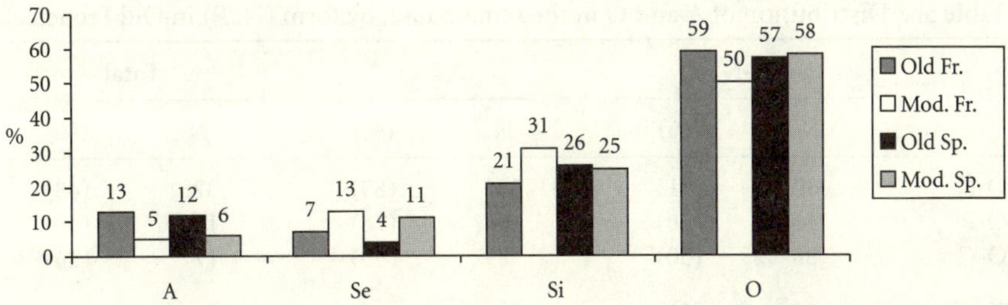

Figure 1. Comparison of lexical NP's in Old French, Modern French, Old Spanish and Modern Spanish, by syntactic role.

The second of these verses appears neither to convey new information nor to advance the story line, but it does have a certain rhetorical effect and perhaps had mnemonic value for the medieval *jongleur.* Similar repetitions occur in the Old Spanish data, as in lines 1 and 4 of Text 4, reproduced here as (10) and (11).

(10) *Mio Çid don Rodrigo a la puerta adelinyava;*
'My Çid don Rodrigo was advancing toward the door;'

(11) *Mio Çid Ruy Días por las puertas entrava…*
'Mio Çid Ruy Díaz entered through the doors…'

Here, too, it seems that the use of the second lexical S, *Mio Çid Ruy Días,* is not so much required by discourse constraints as by rhetorical or aesthetic considerations (see Martin, this volume, on the use of repetition in Mocho narrative).[9]

According to Du Bois' One Lexical Argument Constraint, it is unlikely that both the A and the O roles in a given clause will be lexical in form. This constraint is strongly supported by the Old French and Old Spanish data. Table 5a and Table 5b give the distributions of lexical and non-lexical tokens in the A and O roles in the Old French and Old Spanish corpora, respectively. These tables demonstrate that there are only 37 clauses in the Old French corpus and 27 clauses in the Old Spanish corpus that contain both a lexical A and a lexical O.

Figure 2 compares the distribution of A and O in the same clause in Old French, Modern French, Old Spanish, and Modern Spanish. The distributions shown are very similar, not only within the same language, but also between French and Spanish. In all four data sets, there is a low percentage of lexical A and lexical O in the same clause: only 7% in Old French, 5% in Modern French, 5% in Old Spanish, and 2% in Modern Spanish. We can thus affirm that both Old French and Old Spanish follow the One Lexical Argument Constraint, just as do the modern languages.

Summarizing the results of the analysis thus far, we have shown that both Old French and Old Spanish conform to the grammatical constraints of Preferred Argument Structure. Both medieval texts show that the preferred form for the A role is

Table 5a. Distribution of A and O in the same clause, by form (N, P) in Old French

	A-N		A-P*		Total	
	N	(%)	N	(%)	N	(%)
O-N	37	(11)	286	(89)	323	(48)
O-P	46	(26)	130	(74)	176	(26)
O-C	88	(50)	89	(50)	177	(26)
Total	171	(25)	505	(75)	676	

*Combines P and Ø

Table 5b. Distribution of A and O in the same clause, by form (N, P) in Old Spanish

	A-N		A-P*		Total	
	N	(%)	N	(%)	N	(%)
O-N	27	(9)	286	(91)	313	(46)
O-P	43	(17)	205	(83)	248	(36)
O-C	36	(29)	88	(71)	124	(18)
Total	106	(15)	579	(85)	676	

*Combines P and Ø

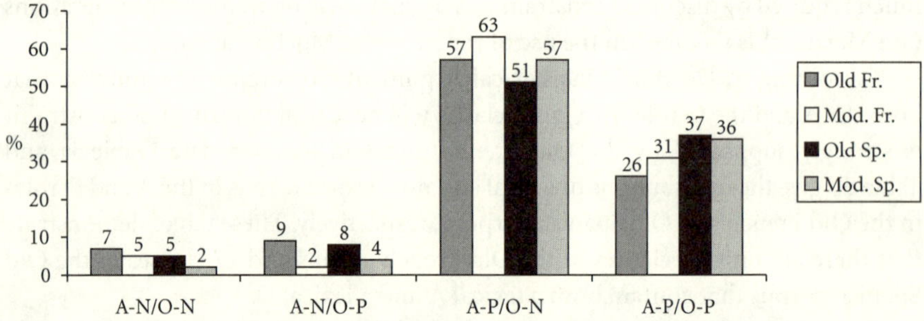

Figure 2. Distribution of lexical (N) and non-lexical (P) forms in A and O roles in same clause, in Old French, Modern French, Old Spanish, and Modern Spanish.

either pronoun or zero, thus supporting the Non-Lexical A Constraint. Both medieval texts show a low incidence of lexical NP's in both the A and O roles, thus confirming the One Lexical Argument Constraint. Despite some quantitative differences between the medieval and modern corpora — differences that seem to be genre dependent — we can affirm that both Old and Modern French, and Old and Modern Spanish exemplify the grammatical constraints of Preferred Argument Structure.

The pragmatic dimensions of Preferred Argument Structure

We now turn to the pragmatic dimensions of Preferred Argument Structure, focussing on how new and non-new information is linguistically encoded in the Old French and Old Spanish corpora. In Ashby & Bentivoglio (1993), we demonstrated that, when they encode new participants to the discourse, speakers of Modern French and Modern Spanish do not randomly choose one of the core grammatical roles, but instead give preference to the O and Si roles, avoiding not only the A role, but also the Se role. To test this hypothesis on the Old French and Old Spanish data, we set activation state (new vs. non-new) as the dependent variable for the Goldvarb analysis. The results for Old French are displayed in Table 6a and for Old Spanish in 6b. These tables also give the results for Modern French and Modern Spanish, as reported in Ashby & Bentivoglio (1993). Figure 3 presents these same distributions in graphical form.

Table 6a and Table 6b, together with Figure 3, provide dramatic confirmation of the Given A Constraint not only in the Modern French and Modern Spanish data, but in the Old French and Old Spanish data as well. In all four data sets, it is the A role that has the lowest Goldvarb probability weight for encoding referents that are new to the discourse. The weight for A in Old French is only .198; in the Modern French data reported in Ashby & Bentivoglio (1993), there were no new A's at all (hence, no probability weight is given).

Likewise in Modern Spanish, the probability of new A's was very low, only .197. In the Old Spanish data, it was higher, .415, although still the lowest of the four weights given for Old Spanish in Table 6b. It must be pointed out, however, that Goldvarb did not select role as a statistically significant factor in the analysis of the Old Spanish data; hence the probability weights given for Old Spanish in Table 6b are in brackets. (The fact that role was not selected by Goldvarb does not necessarily indicate that it is an unimportant determinant of the distribution of new vs. non-new tokens; it may simply indicate that there were simply not enough data to meet Goldvarb's test of significance.)

We also see from the data given in Table 6a, Table 6b, and Figure 3 that in all four data sets it is the O role that has by far the highest probability of encoding

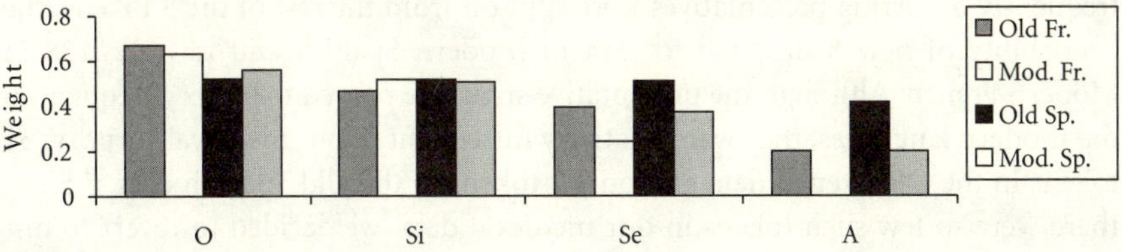

Figure 3. Distribution of new NP's in Old French, Modern French, Old Spanish, and Modern Spanish, by role.

Table 6a. Distribution of new NP's in Old French and Modern French, by role

	Old French			Modern French		
Role	Count	% New	Weight	Count	% New	Weight
O	283/403	(70)	.670	143/324	(44)	.629
Si	52/139	(37)	.465	64/203	(32)	.517
S^e	15/ 48	(31)	.393	11/87	(13)	.241
A	19/175	(11)	.198	0/32	–	–
	N = 765	Input = .460		N = 645	Input = .314	

Table 6b. Distribution of new NP's in Old Spanish and Modern Spanish, by role

	Old Spanish			Modern Spanish		
Role	Count	% New	Weight	Count	% New	Weight
O	121/351	(35)	[.520]	142/341	(42)	.558
Si	29/158	(18)	[.517]	44/150	(29)	.506
Se	5/ 27	(5)	[.509]	12/ 65	(18)	.372
A	11/115	(10)	[.415]	2/ 35	(6)	.197
	N = 651	Input = .229		N = 591	Input = .311	

referents that are new. Thus, we are confident in affirming that O favors new information and A disfavors new information, both in the Old and the Modern stages of French and Spanish.

The role of S is less clear, however. In Ashby & Bentivoglio (1993) we reported that S also appeared to be a site that favored new information, just as expected from Preferred Argument Structure theory. Thus, Si shows a weight of .517 for Modern French (Table 6a) and of .506 for Modern Spanish (Table 6b). These weights are not strong, however, being only slightly above the neutral point of .500. In Ashby & Bentivoglio (1997), we found that many of the tokens we had coded as S in Ashby & Bentivoglio (1993) were in fact arguments of the single-argument presentative structures, *il y a* (French) and *hay* (Spanish) 'there is/there are'. Once these frequently occurring presentatives were split off from the rest of the S tokens, the probability of new S dropped to .314 in Modern Spanish and to only .138 in Modern French. Although the presentative structure proved to be very frequent in the modern languages, they were relatively infrequent in our medieval corpora: 31 tokens in the Old French data and only 2 tokens in the Old Spanish data.[10] Since there were so few such tokens in our medieval data, we decided to revert to our original practice (Ashby & Bentivoglio 1993) and to group NP's occurring after these presentatives with the other Si tokens. Even so, Table 6a shows that the probability weight associated with encoding new information in the Si role in Old French is only .465; Table 6b shows that it is .517 for Old Spanish, just above the neutral point of .500. Thus, S does not appear to be a role that clearly and strongly favors the introduction of new information in any of our data sets. In all cases, however, the probability weights for Si are higher than for A, as we would expect. (We have not examined the possible role of "information pressure" [Du Bois 1987b: 836] on the variable distribution of new S in our four data sets.)

We now turn to the probability weights for Se. It was shown by Ashby & Bentivoglio (1993) that in Modern French and Modern Spanish the Se role strongly disfavors new information.[11] As reported in Table 6a, the probability weight for new Se in the Modern French corpus is only .241; Table 6b shows that it is .372 in Modern Spanish. At .393, the weight for Old French is likewise low. In Old Spanish the probability weight for new Se is higher (.509); but it is unclear whether this is meaningful, since there were so few tokens in Se in Old Spanish. (Recall that for the Old Spanish data, the distributions were not selected by Goldvarb as being statistically significant.)

We can thus arrive at the following tentative conclusions from the information given in Tables 6a and 6b:

1. In all of the data sets, A is strongly disfavored for encoding new referents; this finding provides confirmation of the Given A Constraint.
2. In all of the data sets, O is strongly preferred as the site for encoding new referents.
3. It is not obvious that S is a role that favors new referents, contra the predictions of Preferred Argument Structure. This is further evidence of the "ambivalent status of the S role" (Durie, this volume).
4. The Se role strongly disfavors new referents in all but Old Spanish. (Again, we note that Goldvarb did not select role for the Old Spanish data; moreover, there are relatively few Se tokens in Old Spanish.)

Let us now consider the pragmatic status of the arguments in the Old French and Old Spanish tokens which contain both a lexical A and a lexical O, in order to evaluate the One New Argument Constraint. Of the 37 Old French tokens, only three have *new* NP's in *both* the A and O roles. They are represented in (12), (13), and (14).

O A
(12) *Mult grand eschech en unt si chevaler*
much great booty of-it had his knights
'His knights got great booty from it' (VIII, 99)

O A
(13) *L'estreu li tint sun uncle Guinemer.*
the-stirrup DAT-3RD-SG held his uncle Guinemer
'His uncle Guinemer held the stirrup for him.'

A

(14) *Reis Almaris del regne de Belferne*
king Almaris of-the kingdom of Belferne
'King Almaris from the kingdom of Belferne'

O

Une bataille lur livrat le jur pesme.
a battle DAT-3PL delivered that day worst
'gave them a terrible battle that day.' (LXV, 813)

In none of these examples are *both* NP's "brand new" (Prince 1992), that is, both new and non-identifiable. In (12) the booty (*mult grand eschech*) can be considered both new and non-identifiable, but the knights (*sis chevalers*) are made identifiable by the possessive adjective and by schematic association with the emperor. In verses (13) and (14), one of the new arguments is a proper name, which can also be considered an indentifiable referent (see Chafe 1994: 93–107 on identifiability). Similarly, the single Old Spanish example containing new NP's in both the A and O roles, shown as (15), has referents that are identifiable, hence not brand-new.

A O

(15) *el abbat don Sancho… rezaba los matines …*
'the abbot don Sancho was reciting the morning prayers…' (I,14,237)

The small number of tokens with transitive verbs in which both arguments are new, and the total absence of tokens in which the two arguments are both new and non-identifiable constitute strong evidence in support of the One New Argument Constraint.[12]

Conclusion

Our analysis of a sample of Old French and Old Spanish must be considered a preliminary approach to the study of Preferred Argument Structure across time. It will be necessary to extend this study to other time periods and to other genres. The results obtained nevertheless validate the general hypothesis as it relates both to the grammatical and pragmatic dimensions of Preferred Argument Structure.

Our medieval and modern data sets are clearly of different genres. The modern data come from recorded conversations, where the contribution of the French and Spanish-speaking interlocutors represents discourse of an unplanned nature; consequently, it is not surprising to find that Preferred Argument Structure is followed. The medieval data, on the other hand, consist of samples of epic poetry, a genre that comes to us in written form, a genre that is surely more planned than is conversation. Nevertheless, our counts have demonstrated that Preferred

Argument Structure is manifested even in the medieval epics. This finding may support the hypothesis that the medieval epics are essentially oral in quality. In any case, we have demonstrated the robustness of Preferred Argument Structure in two very different genres. Despite this difference in genre, and despite a gap of seven centuries, we have shown that the medieval and modern forms of French and Spanish are remarkably similar in their manifestations of Preferred Argument Structure.

Notes

1. Three Romance languages have been shown to exhibit the characteristics of PAS. They are Brazilian Portuguese (Dutra 1987), French (Ashby 1995, Ashby & Bentivoglio 1993, Ashby & Bentivoglio 1997, Lambrecht 1987, Lambrecht 1988) and Spanish (Ashby & Bentivoglio 1993, Bentivoglio 1992, Bentivoglio & Ashby 1993, Ocampo 1993).

2. The Modern French data were recorded by W. J. A. in the French city of Tours in 1976. The Modern Spanish data were recorded in 1987 in Caracas, Venezuela, by university students under the direction of P. B. See Ashby & Bentivoglio (1993) for details.

3. Enders (ms.) notes "three major schools of thought" in the debate over the nature of the epic, as represented by the *Chanson de Roland.* She characterizes these schools as "the individualists, the traditionalists, and a position somewhat midway between these two". She explains the debate in the following terms:

> The individualists see the *Chanson de Roland* as the creation of one cultivated author, and argue that the epic is too well written, too near perfection to be the product of an oral literature tradition. On the other hand, the traditionalists see the *CR* as a traditional oral poem, passed down from performer to performer. The midway position attempts to reconcile these two views by claiming that a man of genius took a poem of the oral tradition and transformed it from a rude song of battle into a highly idealistic work.

As for Moignet, he is obviously of the traditionalist school (1969: 5):

> Bien que le texte des chansons que nous avons nous soit parvenu par la tradition écrite…, le genre appartient, de soi, à la littérature orale: il est créé et transmis par des *jongleurs*, à la fois auteurs, remanieurs et interprètes, qui pratiquent la récitation publique. Rien n'est plus éloigné de l'art des jongleurs que l'idée, toute moderne, d'un texte fixe, propriété littéraire d'un auteur: la matière équipe est un bien commun que chacun peut traiter à sa guise.

See also Lord (1960).

4. All clause types were included (declarative, interrogative, exclamative, exhortative). Clauses containing impersonal verbs (e.g., Sp. *mucho es huebos* 'it is very necessary') and time-indicating verbs (e.g., Sp. *Antes que anochesca* 'Before it gets dark') were not included, however.

5. The tokens of C form were not coded for animacy, identifiability, or activation state, but the NP's within these embedded clauses were coded for these factors.

6. Interestingly, the overall percentage of the null form is higher in Old Spanish than in Old French (39% for Old Spanish, only 28% for Old French). This suggests that even though Old French is considered a pro-drop language, it was already using a higher ratio of pronouns than

Old Spanish. This trend apparently continues, with the pronoun having become obligatory in Modern French, but not in Modern Spanish.

7. The tokens representing the C role, shown in Table 3a and Table 3b are not included in Figure 1, because clausal arguments were not included in our previous analysis of the modern languages.

8. Du Bois (1987a) found that 5% of A's were lexical in Sakapultek; Dutra (1987) found 8% lexical A's in Brazilian Portuguese.

9. On the other hand, proper nouns are relatively low on Ariel's "accessibility scale" (Ariel 1990), suggesting that the repetition of the proper noun may be necessary for cognitive reasons.

10. The verb on which this presentative is based is 'to have'. French *il y a* derives from Vulgar Latin *ibi habet*, literally 'there has' (*ibi* > *y* and *habet* > *a*, with the impersonal pronoun *il* added beginning in Old French). Spanish *hay* comes from *habet ibi*. Traditionally, the NP following this verb is considered the object, because in Latin it was marked for accusative case. Indeed, this NP exhibits some features of the direct object in the grammar of Modern French and Spanish (in pronominalization and in interrogation, for example). Nevertheless, in Ashby & Bentivoglio (1993), we considered it to be an S, rather than an O, because it is the sole argument of the verb. In colloquial spoken French, *il* is optional, and no other pronominal or nominal argument is possible. In Spanish, no additional argument can be used with existential *hay* (e.g., *Hay muchas muñecas* 'There are a lot of dolls', but not **Ello hay muchas muñecas*).

11. In Ashby & Bentivoglio (1993), the Se role was called X.

12. We also note in Table 6a and Table 6b that all of the referents coded as A are [+animate], and that all of the referents coded as O are [−animate].

Appendix

Text 1. Extract from the "Chanson de Roland", coded for syntactic role and form of core NP's

1 Si-N *Guenes chevalchet suz une olive halte,*
'Ganelon rides under a tall olive tree,' (XXVIII, 366)

2 Si-Ø (Ø) *Asemblet s'est as sarrazins messages;*
'(He) has joined with the heathen messangers;' (367)

3 Si-P *Mais Blancandrins **ki** envers lu s'atarguns a l'altre.*
'But (here is) Blancandrin who is lingering near.' (368)

4 Si-P *Par grant saveir parolet **li uns** a l'altre.*
'The one talks to the other with great skill.' (369)

5 A-N *Dist **Blancandrins:***
'B. says,' (370)
O-C ***"Merveilus hom … marche."***
'A marvelous man…province' (370–374)

6 Se-N *Merveilus hom est **Charles,***
'Charles is a marvelous man' (370)

7 A-P ***ki** cunquist*
'who conquered'

O-N ***Puille e trestute Calabre!***
'Apulia and Calabria!' (371)

8 A-P *Vers Engletere passat **li***
'To England he crossed'
O-N ***la mer salse,***
'the salty sea' (372)

9 A-Ø *Ad oes seint Perre en (Ø) cunquist*
'he won (the tribute) for Saint Peter'
O-N ***le chevage:***
'the tribute' (373)

10 O-P ***Que***
'What'
A-0 *nus(0) requert ça en la nostre marche?*
'does he ask of us here in our province?' (374)

11 A-N ***Guenes** respunt:*
'G. replies:'
O-C ***"Itels est sis curages…lui vaille."***
'Such is his disposition…measures up to him.' (375–376)

12 Se-N ***Itels** est sis curages.*
'Such is his disposition.' (375)

13 Se-N *Jamais n'ert **hume***
'Never will there be a man'

14 Si-P ***ki** encuntre lui vaille.*
'who measures up to him' (376)

15 A-N *Dist **Blancandrins:***
'Says B.'
O-C ***"Francs….confundent"***
'The Franks…overwhelm (him).' (XXIX, 377–379)

16 Se-N ***Francs** sunt mult gentilz home!*
'The Franks are very noble men!' (377)

17 O-N ***Mult grant mal***
'Great harm'
A-N *funt e **cil duc***
'do both these dukes'
A-N *e **cil cunte***
'and these counts' (378)

18 A-P *A lur seignur, **ki***
'to their lord, (they) who'
O-N ***tel conseill** li dunent:*
'give him such counsel:' (379)
O-P e ***altrui***
'and others'
A-Ø *(Ø) travaillent*
'(They) torment'

A-Ø *e (**0**) confundent.*"
'and (they) overwhelm' (380)

20 Si-N ***Un faldestoet** out suz l'umbre d'un pin;*
'There was a throne in the shade of a pine' (XXXI, 407)

21 Se-Ø *Envolupet (**Ø**) fut d'un palie alexandrin:*
'(It) was covered with a cloth of silk from Alexandria.' (408)

22 Si-N *La fut **li reis***
'There was the king'

23 A-P *ki*
'who'

O-N ***tute Espaigne** tint;*
'held all of Spain.' (409)

24 *Tut entur lui vint milie Sarrazins*
'Around him, twenty thousand Sarrasins.' (410)

25 Si-P N'i a *celoi*
'There are none'

26 A-P ***ki***
'who'

O-N ***mot** sunt*
'sound a word'

27 A-Ø *ne (**Ø**)*
'or (who)'

O-N *mot* tint;
'chime a word' (411)

Text 2. Extract from the "Cantar de mio Çid", coded for syntactic role and form of core NP's

1 Si-N *Apriessa cantan **los gallos***
'The roosters were singing repetitively'

2 A-Ø *e (**Ø**) quieren*
'And (they) wanted'

O-C ***crebar albores,***
'to break the day' (14, 235)

3 A-Ø *(**0**) crebar*
'to break'

O-N *albores*
'day'

4 Si-N *quando llegó a San Pero **el buen Campeador;***
'when the good *Campeador* arrived at San Pero' (236)

5 A-N *el abbat don Sancho, cristiano del Criador, rezaba*
'the abbot, Don Sancho, a Creator's Christian, was reciting' (237–238)

O-N ***los matines** abuelta de los albores.*
'the morning prayers at dawn.' (238)

6 Si-N *Y estava **doña Ximena** con çinco duenyas de pro,*
'And Doña Ximena with five good ladies was there' (239)

7 A-Ø *(Ø) rogando a San Pero e al Criador:*
'imploring Saint Peter and the Creator' (240)
O-C ***"Tú que a todos guías, val a mio Çid el Campeador."***
'You who guide everyone, protect my Cid the *Campeador*' (241)
8 A-P ***Tú que… guías***
O-P ***a todos***
9 A-Ø *(Ø) val*
O-N ***a mio Çid el Campeador***
10 Si-Ø *(Ø)Llamavan a la puerta,*
'They were knocking at the door'
11 A-Ø *i (Ø) sopieron*
'and heard'
O-N ***el mandado;***
'the news' (15, 242)
12 Se-N *Dios, qué alegre fo* ***el abbat don Sancho!***
'God, how happy the abbot Don Sancho was!" 243)
13 A-Ø *Con lumbres e con candelas al corral (Ø) dieron [salto],*
'With lights and candles (they) went out from (*lit.* gave a jump from) the court-yard' (244)
O-N *salto,*
'(a) jump'
14 A-Ø *con tan grant gozo (Ø) reçiben*
'with such great joy (they) welcome'
O-P *al [que en buena hora nasco]*
'the one [who was born happily]'
15 Si-P ***que en buena hora nasco.*** *(245)*
16 O-C ***"Gradéscolo a Dios, mio Çid…ospedalo."***
'I am grateful to God (*lit.* I accept it with pleasure to God), my Cid…hospitality.' (246–247)
A-N *dixo* ***el abat don Sancho;***
'said the abbot Don Sancho'
17 A-Ø *(Ø) gradésco[lo]*
'(I) accept with pleasure'
O-P ***lo***
'it'
18 A-Ø *"pues que aquí vos(Ø) veo,*
'because (I) see you here'
O-P ***vos***
'you'
19 A-Ø *(Ø) prendet de mí*
'take from me'
O-N ***ospedado.***
'hospitality'

Text 3. Extract from the "Chanson de Roland"

1 *Li reis Marsile out sun cunseill fenet,*
'King Marsile had held his counsel' (V, 62)
2 *Sin apelat Clarin de Blaguet,*
'He called Clarin de Balaguer,' (63)
3 *Estamarin e Eudropin, sun per,*
'Estramin and Eudropin, his peer,' (64)
4 *E Priamun e Guarlan le barbet*
'And P. and G. the bearded one' (65)
5 *E Machiner e sun uncle, Maheu,*
'And M. and his uncle, M.' (66)
6 *E Joüner e Malbien d'ultremer*
'And J. and M. from across the sea,' (67)
7 *E Blancandrins, por la raisun cunter.*
'and Blancandrin, in order to lay out his plan. (68)
8 *Des plus feluns dis en ad apelez:*
'Among the most treacherous, he called ten.' (69)
9 *"Seignurs baruns, a Carlemagnes irez.*
'Lord Barons, you will go to Charlemagne' (70)
10 *"Il est al siege a Cordres la citet.*
'He is at the siege of the city of Cordres. (71)
11 *"Branches d'olives en voz mains porterez*
'You will carry olive branches in your hands' (72)
12 *"Ço senefiet pais et humilitet.*
'This signifies peace and humility.' (73)
13 *"Par voz saveirs sem puez acorder,*
'If, by your skill, you can make an agreement between him and me,' (74)
14 *"Je vos durrai or e argent asez,*
'I will give much gold and silver,' (75)
15 *"Teres e fiez tant cum vos en vuldrez."*
'Lands and fiefdoms, as many as you wish.' (76)
16 *Dient paien: "De ço avun nus asez!"*
'The pagans reply, "With that we will be satisfied.' (77)
17 *Li reis Marsile out finet sun cunseill.*
'King M. had held his counsel.' (VI, 78)

Text 4. Extract from the "Cantar de Mio Çid"

1 *Mio Çid don Rodrigo a la puerta adelinyava;*
'Mio Çid don Rodrigo was advancing toward the door;' (23, 467)
2 *los que la tienen, quando vidieron la rebata,*
'those who hold it [the door] when they saw the sudden assult,' (468)
3 *ovieron meido e fo desenparada*
'they had fear and it [the door] was abandoned' (469)
4 *Mio Çid Ruy Días por las puertas entrava....*
'Mio Çid Ruy Díaz entered through the doors…' (470)

References

Ariel, Mira. 1990. *Accessing Noun-Phrase Antecedents.* London and New York.

Ashby, William J. 1995. "French presentational structures". In Jon Amastae et al. (eds), *Contemporary Research in Romance Linguistics.* Amsterdam & Philadelphia: Benjamins, 91–104.

Ashby, William J. and Paola Bentivoglio. 1993. "Preferred Argument Structure in spoken French and Spanish". *Language Variation and Change* 5: 61–76.

Ashby, William J. 1997. "Strategies for introducing new referents into discourse: a comparative analysis of French and Spanish presentational structures". In Robert M. Hammond and Marguerite G. MacDonald (eds), *Linguistic Studies in Honor of Bohdan Saciuk.* West Lafayette, IN: Learning Systems, Incorporated, 9–26.

Bentivoglio, Paola. 1994. "Spanish Preferred Argument Structure across time and space". *D.E.L.T.A. (Revista de Documentaçao de Estudos em Lingüística Teórica e Aplicada)* 10: 277–293.

Chafe, Wallace L. 1980. "The deployment of consciousness". In W. Chafe (ed.), *The Pear Stories: Cognitive, Cultural, and Linguistic Aspects of Narrative Production.* Norwood, NJ: Ablex, 7–40.

Chafe, Wallace L. 1994. *Discourse, Consciousness, and Time: The Flow and Displacement of Conscious Experience in Speaking and Writing.* Chicago: University of Chicago Press.

Chafe, Wallace L. 1987. "Cognitive constraints on information flow". In Russell Tomlin (ed.), *Coherence and Grounding in Discourse.* Amsterdam & Philadelphia: Benjamins, 21–51.

Dixon, Robert M. W. 1979. "Ergativity". *Language* 55: 59–138.

Du Bois, John W. 1985. "Competing motivations". In John Haiman (ed.), *Iconicity in Syntax.* Amsterdam & Philadelphia: Benjamins, 343–65.

Du Bois, John W. 1987. "The discourse basis of ergativity". *Language* 63: 805–55.

Du Bois, John W. and Sandra A. Thompson. 1991. "Dimensions of a theory of information flow". Unpublished ms., University of California, Santa Barbara.

Duggan, Joseph J. 1973. *The Song of Roland.* Berkeley: The University of California Press.

Dutra, Rosalia. 1987. "The hybrid S category in Brazilian Portuguese: Some implications for word order". *Studies in Language* 11: 163–180.

Enders, Jody. Review of Joseph J. Duggan, *The Song of Roland.* Unpublished ms, University of California, Santa Barbara.

England, Nora C. 1986. "Mamean voice: syntactic and narrative considerations". Unpublished ms. University of Iowa.

Josserand, J. Kathryn. 1995. "Participant tracking in Maya hieroglyphic texts: Who was that masked man?" *Journal of Linguistic Anthropology* 5: 65–89.

Lambrecht, Knud. 1987. "On the status of SVO sentences in French discourse". In Russell Tomlin (ed.), *Coherence and Grounding in Discourse.* Amsterdam & Philadelphia: Benjamins, 217–61.

Lambrecht, Knud. 1988. "Presentational cleft constructions in spoken French". In John Haiman and Sandra A. Thompson (eds), *Clause Combining in Grammar and Discourse.* Amsterdam & Philadelphia: Benjamins, 135–79.

Lord, Albert B. 1960. *The Singer of Tales.* Cambridge, MA: Harvard University Press.

Martin, Laura. 2002. "Narrator virtuosity and the strategic exploitation of Preferred Argument Structure in Mocho narrative: repetition and constructed speech in Mocho narrative. In John W. Du Bois et al., *Preferred Argument Structure: Grammar as Architecture for Function.* Amsterdam & Philadelphia: Benjamins.

Menéndez Pidal, Ramón (ed.). 1945. *Cantar de mio Cid. Texto, Grammática y Vocabulario.* Madrid: Espasa-Calpe.

Moignet, Gérard (ed.) 1969. *La Chanson de Roland.* Paris: Bordas.

Ocampo, Francisco. 1993. "The introduction of new referents in French and Spanish discourse: One constraint, two strategies". In William J. Ashby et al. (eds), *Linguistic Perspectives on the Romance Languages.* Amsterdam & Philadelphia: Benjamins, 351–362.

Prince, Ellen. 1992. "Subjects, definites, and information-status". In William C. Mann and Sandra A. Thompson (eds), *Discourse Description: Diverse Linguistic Analyses of a Fund-raising Text.* Amsterdam & Philadelphia: Benjamins, 295–325.

Rand, David and David Sankoff. 1990. GoldVarb 2.0 (computer program obtained from authors). Montreal: University of Montreal.

Sankoff, David. 1990. "Variable rules". In David Rand and David Sankoff, *GoldVarb Version 2: A Variable Rule Application for the Macintosh.* Montreal: University of Montreal, 1–26.

The lexicon in interaction

Developmental origins of Preferred Argument Structure in Korean*

Patricia M. Clancy
University of California, Santa Barbara

Preferred Argument Structure in development

Although Preferred Argument Structure was first analyzed in an ergative language using narrative data (Du Bois 1985, 1987), subsequent research has shown that it is a very robust crosslinguistic phenomenon (e.g. Clancy 1993, Kumpf 1992; papers in this volume). The generality and potential significance of Preferred Argument Structure raises important questions about development. Is Preferred Argument Structure characteristic of early child language? If so, how can it be accounted for? What are the developmental origins of Preferred Argument Structure in caregiver-child discourse?

In adult speech, Du Bois has proposed, Preferred Argument Structure reflects the nature of information flow. Of the three core argument roles A (subject of a transitive verb), O (direct object of a transitive verb), and S (subject of an intransitive verb), speakers tend to introduce new information primarily in S and O roles. Speakers usually introduce only one new argument per verb, with the A role being reserved for given information. This correlation between grammatical and pragmatic roles, Du Bois suggests, may reflect universal cognitive constraints on the production of spoken discourse. Introducing new referents, especially human protagonists, he proposes, "monopolizes a speaker's verbalization capacities", making it difficult to both introduce a new referent and to advance the story line in the same clause (Du Bois 1987: 833–834).

Although most research on Preferred Argument Structure has focused on adults, developmental research in a number of languages suggests that there is also a relationship between referential form and grammatical role in early child language. Assuming that children, like adults, tend to use pronominal and elliptical reference to encode given information, and lexical NP's to encode new information (e.g. Chafe 1976, 1994, Clancy 1980, Givón 1983), a variety of developmental findings can be interpreted as suggesting that children tend to present given information as subjects and new information as objects. For example, the large body of research on subject ellipsis by young children (e.g. Hyams 1986, 1991, Kim 1997, Valian 1991) may provide evidence for a tendency to place given information in subject position. Crosslinguistic research has found a higher rate of ellipsis in subject than object position (e.g. Clancy 1993, Hirakawa 1993, Wang et al. 1992). In research differentiating transitive from intransitive subjects, Ochs (1988: 105–127) presents evidence for a "two-constituent bias" in the discourse of young Samoan children and their caregivers: the typical clause type consists of a verb plus an absolutive NP (i.e. S or O), while ergative NP's (i.e. A) are much less likely to be overtly expressed. Recent research on Korean acquisition has presented evidence for the pragmatic basis of ellipsis (Clancy 1997, Kim 1997) and for the preferential distribution of pragmatically prominent referents in S and O roles (Clancy 1993). Evidence that the speech of young children, like that of adults, exhibits Preferred Argument Structure, has currently been documented for Korean (Clancy 1993), Venezuelan Spanish (Bentivoglio 1996), and Inuktitut (Allen and Schröder this volume); see Allen and Schröder (this volume) for a comparative review of these findings.

If Preferred Argument Structure can be documented for young children, we must consider what it means for them to preferentially place new information in a particular grammatical role. From a cognitive perspective, we do not have to assume that children exhibiting Preferred Argument Structure have mentally represented the grammatical roles A, O and S *per se*. Preferred Argument Structure patterns are necessarily mediated by the lexicon. As I will propose in this paper, child speakers who have learned how to introduce new information in certain argument positions with particular verbs, as well as how to use referential forms in accordance with the information status of the referent, would be quite capable of producing Preferred Argument Structure without formulating generalizations about referential form in terms of the grammatical roles A, O and S. Thus Preferred Argument Structure represents a convergence of lexical choice, referential form, and grammatical role.

The developmental questions that are raised by this convergence include the following: (1) What verbs do children use when introducing new information? (2) What is the relationship between referential form and information status? (3) In which grammatical roles do new referents appear? and (4) Why do new referents appear in these roles? In this paper I will attempt to answer these questions by examining the lexical foundations of Preferred Argument Structure. First, I will summarize quantitative data on Preferred Argument Structure in Korean acquisition, demonstrating that referential form is linked with information status and grammatical role at a very early stage. Next, I will present a qualitative analysis of certain high-frequency verbs that play a major role in the correlation between grammatical role and new information. Analysis of how these verbs are used in interaction will shed light on the reasons why they are used to introduce new information, and why that information is distributed primarily in S and O, but not A, roles. This analysis will be followed by a discussion of the underlying forces that may be postulated to account for the emergence of Preferred Argument Structure in development, and of the implications of the findings for the acquisition of grammar.

Data and methodology

The data for this paper come from longitudinal recordings of two Korean girls, Hyenswu and Wenceng, who were audio-taped for one year, beginning at 1 year, 8 months (1;8) and 1 year, 10 months (1;10) of age, respectively. Despite the small number of subjects in the case study methodology, which is common in language acquisition research, the findings are quite robust and consistent; the two children are very similar to one another and to their mothers, whose speech will not be analyzed here. The children were living in Providence, Rhode Island in a very close-knit community of Korean graduate students attending Brown University. Each child was recorded for one hour at home with her mother twice a month for one year, performing ordinary daily activities such as playing with toys, eating snacks, and reading from storybooks; one or two Korean Research Assistants also participated in these recording sessions. For this study, the transcript of one recording session per month has been analyzed, for a total of 13 hours of data for each child.

Korean is a predominantly SOV language with no agreement morphology on the verb for person, number, or gender of arguments.[1] Arguments of predicates may be freely ellipted, when appropriate in the discourse context. The grammatical case of overt NP's is marked by postpositions; whether these postpositions are used or not for subjects and direct objects has a discourse-pragmatic basis in casual speech (Lee and Thompson 1989, Clancy 1995). For the most part, Korean has nominative-accusative grammar and morphology.[2] Thus even if Preferred Argument Structure is present in Korean discourse, it has not led to the grammaticization of ergative morphosyntax.

The following examples illustrate the use of nominative and accusative casemarking in transitive sentences. Following consonants, the nominative casemarker is *-i* and the accusative casemarker is *-ul*, as in example (1); following vowels, the nominative is *-ka* and the accusative *-lul*, as in (2). (The dots indicate material omitted in order to focus on the casemarking.)[3]

(1) Wenceng, at 2;7 years old, is telling about her visit to the medical center.
... uysa sensaygnim-i i-ke[4] *son-ul po-ass-e.*
doctor teacher-NOM this-thing hand-ACC see-ANT-IE
'... the doctor looked at this hand.'

(2) Wenceng, at 2;7 years old, is describing how a playmate hit her while she was trying to draw.
... *yunco-ka* *na-lul* *ttayly-e ilehkey.*
Yunco-NOM 1SG-ACC hit-IE like.this
'... Yunco hits me like this.'

Since fewer than 10% of all clauses for each child have more than one overt core argument, and casemarking of overt arguments is not obligatory, examples such as (1) and (2), in which both casemarkers appear in a single clause, are vanishingly rare.

Each main clause having an overt verb that was both interpretable and used correctly with respect to transitivity has been included in the analysis. The core arguments (i.e. subject and, for transitive predicates, direct object) of each of these verbs have been coded for referential form and information status.[5] Three types of verbs are coded: equational, with core argument Se; existential, with core argument Sx; other intransitive, with core argument Si; and transitive, with core arguments A and O.[6] The data included a total of 4363 clauses, of which 50% were transitive, 14.4% equational, 6.5% existential, and 29.1% other intransitive, for a total of 50% intransitive clauses.

Three types of referential form are distinguished: ellipsis, pronouns, and lexical noun phrases. Personal pronouns are used by the children only for first and second person; in the third person, the deictic NP's *yo-ke* and *i-ke* 'this-thing' and *ku-ke* and *ce-ke* 'that-thing' have been treated here as pronouns, although they have more lexical weight than the first and second person pronouns *na* 'I' and *ne* 'you' (Ariel 1990:73) and, unlike first and second person pronouns, frequently encode new information. All core arguments in the database that were codable as bearing A, O, or S grammatical roles have been included in the quantitative analysis.

New information has been defined very rigidly on the basis of the single criterion of prior mention, a methodology that does not take into consideration the potential accessibility of referents via frames on their first mention (Chafe 1987). Any referent that was not mentioned previously during the recording session is coded as new. Even speaker and addressee are not treated as given information until after their first mention. Although it is likely that conversational participants had already been mentioned before the recording began, treating them as new on first mention does not affect the quantitative findings, since the number of participants in the recording sessions is so small.

Since the overall distribution of new information in the data is strongly influenced by the arguments of certain high-frequency verbs, a qualitative analysis of how these verbs function in caregiver-child interaction will shed light on the patterns found in the quantitative analysis. The qualitative analysis is based on the seven verbs that were among the ten most frequent for both children, as well as *ota* 'come', a verb of moderate frequency which has been important in previous research on Preferred Argument Structure, and which is included here in order to have two intransitive verbs in addition to the copula and the existential in this analysis. The four transitive verbs to be analyzed are *hata* 'do', *pota* 'look at/see', *mekta* 'eat', and *cwuta* 'give', which comprise 59% of Hyenswu's transitive verb tokens and 40% of Wenceng's. The four intransitive verbs include the copula *ita*, the existential *issta* 'exist', *kata* 'go', and *ota* 'come', which together account for 58% of all intransitive verb tokens for Hyenswu and 50% for Wenceng.

A quantitative analysis of Preferred Argument Structure

Quantitative analysis of referential form in A, O, and S roles reveals a distribution of forms that is consistent with previous research on Preferred Argument Structure, and quite similar in both children's speech. Figure 1 presents this distribution. As the figure shows, the percentage of ellipsis in the A role is very high (78% in Hyenswu's speech, 74% in Wenceng's speech), while the rate of lexical mentions is quite low (12%, 14%). The referential forms in the O role are dramatically different, with a much lower percentage of ellipsis (45%, 39%) and a much higher rate of lexical mentions (31%, 46%). The distribution of referential forms in the S role falls between these two extremes. The percentage of ellipsis (54%, 57%) is higher than for O but lower than for A, while the percentage of lexical reference (28%, 24%) is higher than for A in both children's speech and about the same (Hyenswu) or lower (Wenceng) than for O. Thus in accordance with Du Bois' Non-Lexical A Constraint, the A role is clearly the preferred site for ellipsis, and the O and/or S roles for lexical mentions.

The S role has the most internally diverse distribution of referential forms, since the copula and the existential are quite different from one another, and from other intransitives. Figure 2 breaks down the S role, presenting the distribution of referential forms in the children's Se, Sx, and Si arguments. The distributional patterns for each role are remarkably similar for the two children.

The core argument of equational predicates, Se, is elliptical in the majority of cases (61% for Hyenswu, 56% for Wenceng), frequently pronominal (36%, 41%), and very rarely lexical (3%, 3%). This is quite different from the distribution of referential forms for Sx. The core argument of the existential has a lower rate of ellipsis (41%, 27%), a much lower percentage of pronouns (5%, 4%), and a very much higher proportion of lexical noun phrases (53%, 69%). The core argument of the remaining intransitive verbs, Si, is similar to Se in percentage of ellipsis (55%, 62%), similar to Sx in the low rate of pronouns (12%, 9%), and has a frequency of lexical reference (32%, 28%) falling in between that of Se and Sx. Thus Sx and Si are responsible for most of the lexical mentions in the S role seen in Figure 1, while Se is responsible for most of the pronominal mentions.

Figure 3 summarizes the distribution of lexical mentions across grammatical

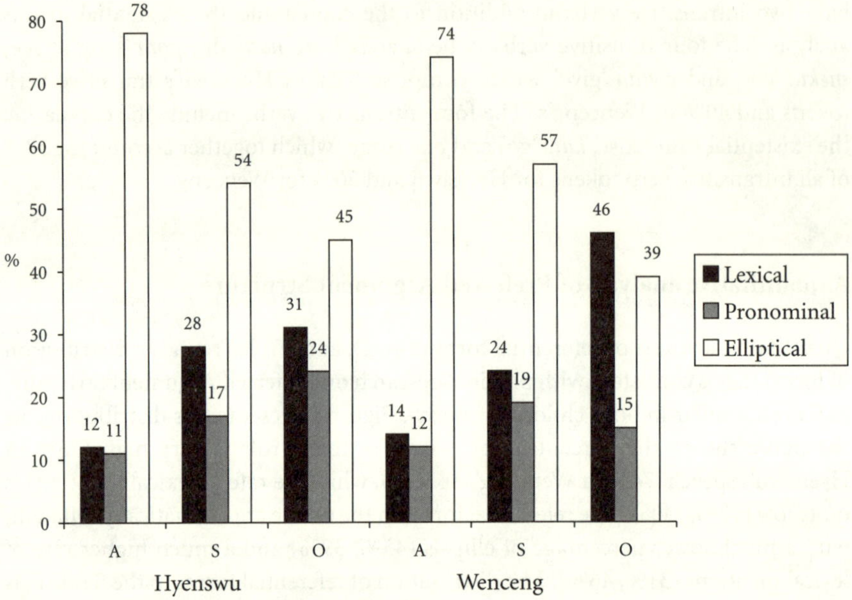

Figure 1. Distribution of referential forms in A, S, and O roles.

roles in the two children's speech. Of all lexical arguments in the data, the greatest proportion is found in the O role (44% for Hyenswu, 51% for Wenceng). The percentage of lexical mentions in the S role is slightly lower in Hyenswu's speech (39%), and much lower in Wenceng's (32%). The A role has the lowest percentage of lexical mentions (17%). As the breakdown of the S role on the right side of Figure 3 shows, Si and Sx account for most of the lexical mentions in the S role; very few occur with the copula (Se). The overall pattern of lexical mentions in A, S, and O roles is remarkably similar to Du Bois' original findings. The children also conform to the One Lexical Argument Constraint: only 4.7% of Hyenswu's transitive predicates and 5.4% of Wenceng's have two lexical arguments (including object complements as lexical raises these percentages to 5.1% for Hyenswu and 6.5% for Wenceng). Thus the grammatical dimension of Preferred Argument Structure is clearly evident in the data.

Figure 4 depicts the pragmatic dimension of Preferred Argument Structure, giving the percentage of new information in A, O, and S roles. The expected difference in the percentage of new information in A (2%, 4%) vs. O roles (38%, 38%) is apparent, while an intermediate rate of new information is found in the combined S roles (23%, 25%). Thus both children have a higher percentage of new information in the O role than in the S role. This difference between O and S did not appear in Du Bois' original study, which found very similar percentages of new information in S (22.5%) and O (24.7%) roles.

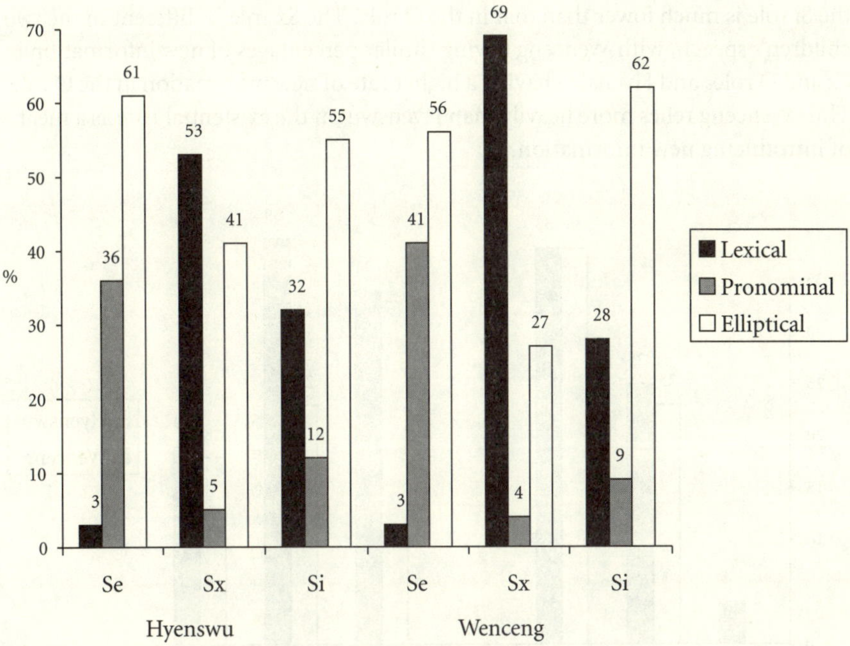

Figure 2. Distribution of referential forms in the S role.

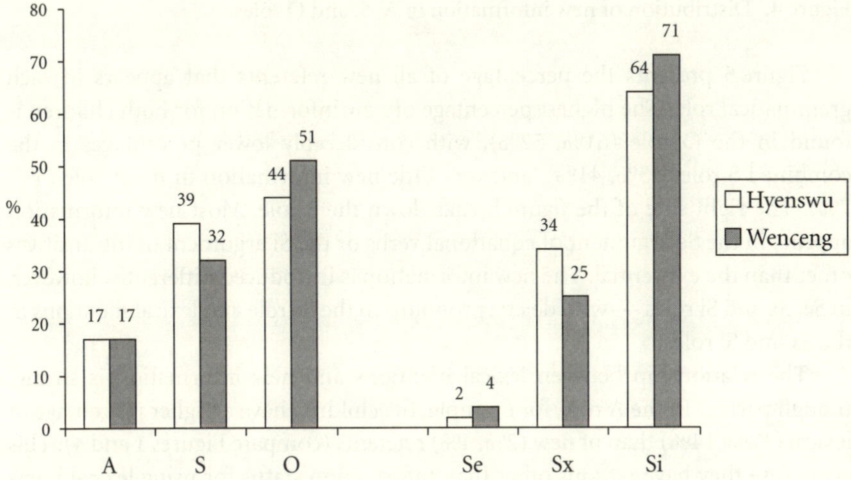

Figure 3. Distribution of lexical arguments across grammatical roles.

The right side of the Figure 4 breaks down the S role. In both children's speech the core argument of the copula (Se) has a percentage of new information that is similar to what is found in the O role, while the percentage of new information in the Si role is much lower than that in the O role. The Sx role is different in the two children's speech, with Wenceng having similar percentages of new information in Sx and O roles and Hyenswu having a higher rate of new information in the O role. Thus Wenceng relies more heavily than Hyenswu on the existential *issta* as a means of introducing new information.

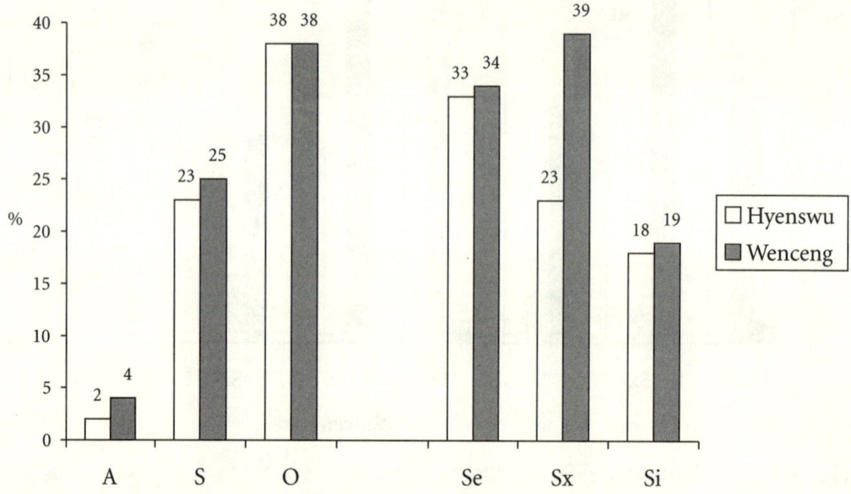

Figure 4. Distribution of new information in A, S, and O roles.

Figure 5 presents the percentage of all new referents that appears in each grammatical role. The highest percentage of new information for both children is found in the O role (61%, 52%), with considerably lower percentages in the combined S role (35%, 41%), and very little new information in the A role (4%, 7%). The right side of the figure breaks down the S role. Most new information appears in the Se argument of equational verbs or the Si argument of intransitives other than the existential. The new information is introduced differently, however, in Se, Sx and Si roles — with deictic pronouns in the Se role and lexical mentions in the Sx and Si roles.

The relationship between lexical mentions and new information is strong, though partial. In the A role, for example, the children have a higher percentage of lexical (12%, 14%) than of new (2%, 4%) referents (compare Figures 1 and 4). This is because they have reasons other than information status for using lexical mentions, such as contrast (Clancy 1993, 1997). The reverse, i.e. using ellipsis or deictic pronouns rather than lexical noun phrases to introduce new information, also occurred. Since new referents in the children's speech are typically present objects that can be indicated by gesture or eye gaze, the intended referent is often clear from the non-verbal context, even if ellipsis or deictic pronouns are used on first

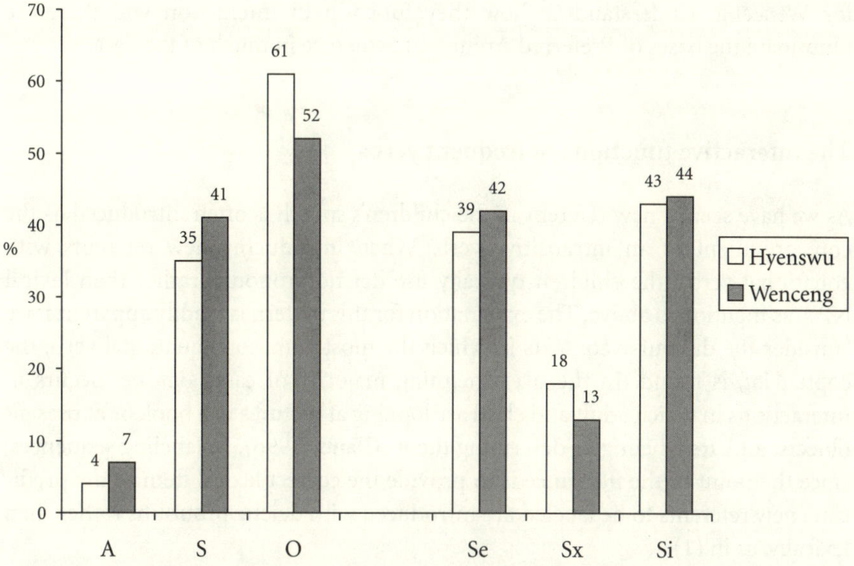

Figure 5. Distribution of new information across grammatical roles.

mention. The correlation between lexical mention and new information may therefore be weaker in the speech of very young children than in adult speech.

In sum, the two Korean children in this study exhibit Preferred Argument Structure at a very early stage of acquisition. In addition to the One Lexical Argument Constraint, they also abide by the One New Argument Constraint (Du Bois 1987:819, 826). Only 1.3% of Hyenswu's transitive verbs, and 2.2% of Wenceng's, have two new core arguments (including new object complements increases these percentages to 1.7% for Hyenswu and 3.5% for Wenceng). Du Bois' proposed constraints on lexical mention and new information in the A role are also strongly substantiated: arguments in the A role are not often lexical (Hyenswu 12%, Wenceng 14%) and very rarely new (Hyenswu 2%, Wenceng 4%). (See Allen and Schröder (this volume) for similar documentation of these constraints in the speech of Inuktitut-speaking children aged 2;0–3;6 years old.) Thus a fundamental relationship between referential form and information status is clearly evident in the speech of these Korean two-year-olds, and is already strongly linked to grammatical role.

How can this patterning be accounted for? In the qualitative analysis in the next section, I will examine how the children introduce new information with specific verbs, focusing on the S argument of *ita* 'be', *issta* 'exist', *kata* 'go', and *ota* 'come', and on the O argument of *hata* 'do', *pota* 'see', *mekta* 'eat', and *cwuta* 'give'. The four intransitive verbs account for 67% of new S arguments for Hyenswu and 56% for Wenceng; the four transitive verbs account for 65% of new O arguments for Hyenswu and 45%

for Wenceng. Understanding how they function in interaction will therefore illuminate the bases of Preferred Argument Structure in much of the data.

The interactive functions of frequent verbs

As we have seen, a new referent in the children's speech is often introduced as the core argument of an intransitive verb. When introducing new referents with equational verbs, the children typically use deictic pronouns rather than lexical NP's, as mentioned above. The explanation for this pattern is readily apparent if we consider the discourse contexts in which the most common equational verb, the copula *ita*, is found. In the overwhelming majority of cases, *ita* 'be' occurs in interactions in which adult and child are looking at pictures in a book or at present objects, and are labeling or describing them (Clancy 1996). In labeling sequences, since the point of the utterance is to provide the correct lexical item as the predicate, new referents to be labeled are introduced with deictic pronouns rather than lexically, as in (1).

(1) Wenceng (W), at 2;1 years old, and her mother (M) are looking at a Winnie the Pooh storybook.
M: *i-ke-nun aki kangaloo-lase loo-ya ilum-i.*
this-thing-TOP baby kangaroo-be:CONN Roo-be:IE name-NOM
'This one is a baby kangaroo so it's "Roo", his name (is).'
W: (pointing to Piglet)
→ *i- i-ke*
th- this-thing
'this,'
M: *ung.*
yes
'uh-huh.'
W: *twayci-ya.*
pig-be:IE
'is a pig.'

The child may also introduce a new referent to ask for its label, as in (2). (In Hyenswu's utterance, *-ntey* is a contraction of *-i-ntey*; *-i-* is the copula.)

(2) Hyenswu (H), at 2;2 years old, and Research Assistant K are drawing pictures. K has drawn a car, and H is asking about the car window.
→ H: *i-ke mwue-ntey?*
this-thing what-be:CIRCUM
'What's this?'

K: *i-ke* *yuli-chang.*
this-thing glass-window
'This (is) the window.'

When introducing a new referent with *ita*, the children also frequently used the copula to mention some important visual or social property of the referent. Wenceng pointed out a variety of properties using the copula, including possession, color, number, size, and similarity to other objects. For Hyenswu, who had a 5-year-old sister, the most common attribute described with *ita* (contracted to *-ta* following vowels) was possession. In (3), she introduces the referent, which has been focused by her action, with a deictic pronoun.

(3) Hyenswu, at 2;7 years old, points to a piece of apple that her mother is holding.
H: ***yo-ke*** *nay-ke-ya.*
this-thing my-thing-be:IE
'This one is mine.'

The two children exhibit almost identical patterns of referential forms in the Se role (see Figure 2) because virtually all Se arguments occur in the same type of interactive context: labeling or describing objects or pictures that are present in view. When the children are answering questions about referents introduced by the adult, ellipsis is common; when introducing new referents, they frequently use deictic pronouns, as in (1)–(3). Thus the referential patterns for Se arguments reflect the nature of the interactive context in which the copula *ita*, the most frequent equational verb, usually occurs.

As we have seen in Figure 2, Sx and Si arguments are much more likely than Se arguments to be lexical. The single most frequent source of arguments in the S role in the data is the existential predicate *issta* 'exist/be present/be located'. The most common context in which *issta* occurs with a new, lexical core argument is when the child is calling adult attention to a picture in a book, as in (4), or to a present object or toy, as in (5).

(4) Hyenswu, at 2;0 years old, and her mother are labeling pictures in a book, when H sees a picture of a dog.
→ H: ***mengmengi*** *iss-ta.*
doggie exist-DECL
'There's a doggie.'
M: *ung. mengmengi yeki iss-ta.*
yes doggie here exist-DECL
'Uh-huh. A doggie is here.'

H: *yeki iss-ta. yeki iss-ta.*
here exist-DECL here exist-DECL
'Here it is. Here it is.'

(5) Hyenswu, at 2;0 years old, is playing with a toy stove and refrigerator. She picks up a plastic bottle that looks like a lotion bottle.
H: ***hwacangphwum** yeki iss-ta.*
make-up here exist-DECL
'Here is make-up.'
K: (laughs)

Once the child introduces a referent with *issta* 'exist', the adult may comment, as in (4), engage in joint action on the object with the child, or simply watch the child play with the object. Focusing adult attention on a new referent with *issta* 'exist' thus serves as a way of engaging the adult in interaction and/or talk with the child.

While both children use *issta* 'exist' to focus adult attention on new objects or pictures, only Wenceng, who is more advanced linguistically, also uses *issta* to introduce characters and important props when storytelling from books, as in (6).

(6) Wenceng, at 2;5 years old, and K are reading the story of Jack and the Beanstalk.
K: *kulayse hwa-ka na-se emma-ka **khong-ul***
so:then anger-NOM arise-CONN mother-NOM bean-ACC
pak-ulo naypeli-nun-ke-ya. celen.
outdoors-toward throw.away-ATTRIB-thing-be:IE oh my
kulay-ss-te-ni keki-ey?
do:like:that-ANT-RETROS-CONN there-LOC
'So then the mother gets angry and throws the beans outdoors. Oh my! So then at that place (what happened)?'
→ W: ***namwu-ka** iss-e.*
tree-NOM exist-IE
'There's a tree.' (the beanstalk)
K: *o. keki-se namwu-ka cala-ss-kwuna.*
oh there-LOC tree-NOM grow-ANT-UNASSIM
'Oh. A tree grew up there.'

This usage integrates the attention-to-referent function illustrated in (4) and (5) into the activity of storytelling. Wenceng also uses new Si arguments with *issta* 'exist' in stories of personal experience, usually elicited by adult questions about past events, as in (7).

(7) Wenceng, at 2;8 years old, is answering her mother's questions about a visit to the Buddhist temple with her father.

M: *wencengi cel-ey appa ttala-ka po-ass-ni?*
Wenceng temple-LOC daddy follow:CONN-go:CONN try-ANT-INTERR
'Have you gone to the temple with daddy?'

W: *ung.*
yes
'Uh-huh.'

M: *ka-nikka mwue ha-tey cel-eyse?*
go-when what do-RETROS:IE temple-LOC
'When you went, what were (people) doing at the temple?'

→ W: ***pap mek-nun sunim-i*** *iss-ess-e.*
rice eat-ATTR monk-NOM exist-ANT-IE
'There were monks eating.'[7]

Individual differences can also be seen in the use of two other intransitive verbs, *ota* 'come' and *kata* 'go'. Both children use *ota* most frequently with subjects that are not new information in the imperative *ili wa* 'Come here!'. Occasionally, however, the arrival of a new person is announced with *ota*, as in (8).

(8) Hyenswu, at 2;5 years old, hears the noise of a car outside.

H: ***appa*** *o-ass-ta!*
daddy come-ANT-DECL
'Daddy has come!'

Such announcements represent the only use of *ota* 'come' with new information in Hyenswu's speech, but Wenceng also uses *ota* to introduce new characters in storybooks, either in response to adult questions or spontaneously, as in (9).

(9) Wenceng, at 2;7 years old, is reading the story of Thumbelina with her mother and K. Having incorrectly mentioned a candle, which does not actually figure in the story, Wenceng corrects herself.

W: (focusing on the page where the frog arrives)
ani, ***turtle-i*** *o-ass-e* ***turtle.***
no turtle-NOM come-ANT-IE turtle
'No, the turtle came, the turtle.'

Thus Wenceng uses both *issta* 'exist' and *ota* 'come' in comparable narrative contexts to mark the arrival of important new story referents, while Hyenswu does not.

On the other hand, Hyenswu, but not Wenceng, uses *kata* 'go' in the expression *X eti kasse?* 'Where did X go?' to guide her search for desired objects, as in (10), or to request them, as in (11).

(10) Hyenswu, at 2;8 years old, and her father are playing with her doll.
H: *kuncengi camos eti ka-ss-e?*
Kunceng pajamas where go-ANT-IE
'Where did Kunceng's pajamas go?'
F: *yo-ke camos-i-ya.*
this-thing pajamas-be-IE
'These are her pajamas.'

(11) Hyenswu, at 2;6 years old, speaks up after her sister has put the soda bottle back in the refrigerator.
H: *hyenswu soda eti ka-ss-e?*
Hyenswu soda where go-ANT-IE
'Where's my soda?' (i.e. 'a soda for me')

Since Wenceng rarely uses the expression *X eti kasse?* 'Where did X go?' to seek new referents, she has a much lower rate of new Si arguments with *kata* 'go' than Hyenswu. Thus the use of a certain verb for a particular interactive function, or the emergence of a new function for an already acquired verb, can have a powerful impact on the overall frequency of the verb and of the referential forms that its arguments take.

In sum, the high rate of new and lexical Si arguments in the data to a large extent reflects the fact that the lexical content of several intransitive verbs, such as *issta* 'exist' and *ota* 'come', is well-suited to referent introductions (Du Bois 1987:831, Cumming 1994). In terms of interactive function, the new Si arguments of *issta* 'exist', *ota* 'come', and (for Hyenswu) *kata* 'go' serve to focus adult attention on pictures and objects that the child and caregiver can talk about, objects that they can act upon, and people whom they can interact with. Wenceng's data suggest that in time this function expands to encompass the introduction of new referents in narratives with *issta* 'exist' and *ota* 'come'.

As we have seen, O is the core argument role in which new information is most frequently introduced in the children's speech. By far the most common verb in the data is the multi-functional *hata* 'do'; in its transitive uses,[8] it is the most common source of new O's in the data. New O arguments with *hata* 'do' usually refer either to new actions or to new inanimate objects upon which actions are to be performed. When the intended referent is evident from the non-verbal context, ellipsis or deictic pronouns are often used, even on first mention. In (12), for example, the intended action is apparent from the child's non-verbal behavior and the object at hand.

(12) Hyenswu, at 2;1 years old, is playing with a toy screwdriver.
H: *hyenswu mos-hay.*
Hyenswu NEG (IMPOT)-do:IE
'Hyenswu can't do (it).'

When the new O argument is an inanimate patient, however, it is often introduced lexically. Such references are frequently found in announcements of the child's intention to perform actions involving the drawing or making of new objects, as in (13).

(13) Hyenswu, at 2;2 years old, and K have been playing with a shawl.
H: *chima ha-l* *ke-ya.*[9]
skirt do-ATTR (IRREALIS) thing-be:IE
'I'll make a skirt.'

Proposals for joint activity to be initiated on new objects are also common, as in (14).

(14) Wenceng, at 2;6 years old, has been looking at a storybook with K; suddenly she picks up a toy medicine bottle.
W: *yak,* *yak,* *yak-pyeng* *ha-ca.*
medicine medicine medicine-bottle do-PRP
'Let's use (this) medicine bottle.'

New lexical O arguments also appear in imperatives telling the addressee to perform or refrain from performing an action on an inanimate object, as in (15).

(15) Hyenswu, at 2;8 years old, and her father are playing with her doll Kunceng. Hyenswu wants her father to put a rubber band with a bell on it in the doll's hair.
H: ***kuncengi pangwul** hay* *cwu-e.*
Kunceng bell do:CONN give:IE
'Do Kunceng's bell.'

As these examples show, the A argument is typically the child speaker, as in (12) and (13), the adult addressee, as in (15), or both, as in (14). The object upon which the action is to be performed serves as the new O argument, and is often expressed lexically.

The second most common transitive verb, *pota* 'look at/see', is also frequently used to initiate action involving a new object. The most common function of *pota* in the speech of both children is in imperatives addressed to present participants. The new referents appear in the O role and are introduced either lexically, as in (16), or with deictic pronouns; all are third person.

(16) Hyenswu, at 2;6 years old, had been playing with a toy mixer, a hairpin, some balls; suddenly she focuses on something new.
H: (to her mother and K)
***nay chayk** po-a*
my book look.at-IE
'Look at my book.'

The children use *pota* to urge their caregivers to look at pictures in books, at particular toys that they are playing with, and at things that they have made. Thus *pota* contributes to Preferred Argument Structure because it so frequently serves as a directive focusing the attention of co-present participants (i.e. given, second person referents) to objects that they are not currently attending to (i.e. new, third person referents). The lexical content of *pota* 'look at/see' gives the directive *X pwa* 'look at X' the same attention-focusing function as the declarative *X issta* 'X exists', providing a striking example of the potential functional similarity between S and O roles.

A different function of *pota* involves elicited narration, usually from books; it occurs mainly in Wenceng's data. In this usage, Wenceng narrates from storybooks, at first in response to adult prompts. The new information appears in the O role, while reference to Wenceng herself appears in the A role and is elliptical, as in (17).

(17) Wenceng, at 2;3 years old, has labeled a fish in a book.
M: *tongmwulwen-ey ka-se mwulkoki po-ass-e?*
zoo-LOC go-CONN fish see-ANT-IE
'Did (you) go to the zoo and see fish?'
→ W: *ung. say po-ass-ta.*
yes bird see-ANT-DECL
'Uh-huh. (I) saw birds.'

The children are virtually identical in their distribution of new information with *pota*: Hyenswu has no new A's vs. 49% new O's, while Wenceng has 1% new A's vs. 43% new O's. This skewing reflects the consistent participant roles in their verbal interactions involving *pota* 'see'. The child or addressee is the one who sees, and frequently what they see is something new.

Another common transitive[10] verb, *cwuta* 'give', also is often used primarily as a directive, especially in Hyenswu's speech. The referent in the A role is usually the addressee or the child, while virtually all of the referents in the O role are third person inanimates. The distributional skewing of new information with *cwuta* is strong: Hyenswu has 3% new A's vs. 34% new O's, while Wenceng has 9% new A's vs. 32% new O's. The single most common interactive function of *cwuta* is to tell co-present participants what to give the child, as in (18).

(18) Wenceng, at 2;3 years old, wants to comb people's hair.
W: *emma, na pis cwu-e pis.*
mommy 1SG comb give-IE comb
'Mommy, give me a comb.'

The items requested by the children are usually generic categories of food or drink, but also include specific objects, such as the child's toys and books. The desired item is not always present in view, and is typically expressed lexically; the children apparently know that explicit information will help the addressee comply with the directive.

As with her other verbs, Wenceng also sometimes uses *cwuta* 'give' in narration from storybooks, as in (19).

(19) Wenceng, at 2;7 years old, is reading the story of Jack and the Beanstalk with K, who has urged her to continue reading.
W: *ani, khong, khong,* ***khong-ul*** *hana cwu-ess-e.*
no bean bean bean-ACC one give-ANT-IE
'No, (she, i.e. Jack's mother) gave (him, i.e. Jack) one bean.'

In these cases a previously mentioned story character typically occupies the A slot, while the item that the character gives sometimes constitutes new information, as in (19).

The final transitive verb to be considered, *mekta* 'eat', differs from *pota* 'see' and *cwuta* 'give' in that it occurs much less frequently as a directive. When the referent in the O role is new, about half the time the referent in the A role is the child. The most common usage is for the child to announce her intention or wish to eat something, as in (20).

(20) Wenceng, at 1;11 years old, and her mother have been talking about headphones in a catalog; suddenly she changes the subject.
W: *emma,* ***mwul*** *mek-ullay* ***mwul.***
mommy water eat-INT water
'Mommy, (I)'ll drink water.'

Thus the child occupies the A role and the referent in the O role conveys information known only to the child, which often is being mentioned for the first time.

Another common function of *mekta* 'eat' is to tell caregivers what the child is eating or ate at an earlier time, usually in response to questions, as in (21); here the child's answer leads to adult acknowledgment through repetition.

(21) Hyenswu, at 2;5 years old, is rolling a ball with K; she has a piece of bread in her mouth.
K: *hyenswu, cikum mwue ha-ni?*
hyenswu now what do-INTERR
'Hyenswu, what are (you) doing now?'
→ H: ***ppang*** *mek-ess-e* ***ppang.***
bread eat-ANT-IE bread
'(I) ate bread.'
K: *ppang mek-ess-e.*
bread eat-ANT-IE
'(You) ate bread.'

As with other verbs, Wenceng (rarely Hyenswu) also uses *mekta* in narration from books, as in (22).

(22) Wenceng, at 1;9 years old, is reading a book with Research Assistant T; they are looking at a picture of pigs eating potatoes.

T: *twayci-ka mwue hay?*
pig-NOM what do:IE
'What are the pigs doing?'

→ W: ***pokswunga** mek-e.*
peach eat-IE
'(They're) eating peaches.'

In these cases the referent in the A role is usually a previously mentioned story character, while the O referent is sometimes new, as in (22).

In sum, the transitive verbs *hata* 'do', *pota* 'see', *cwuta* 'give', and *mekta* 'eat' are frequently used for speech acts in which first and second person participants in the interaction appear in the A role, while inanimate objects conveying new information appear in the O role. The generality of this alignment of human A vs. inanimate O is shown in Table 1, which gives the percentage of human vs. inanimate referents in A, S, and O roles. (References to actions, animals, abstractions, body parts, plants, and locations do not appear in Table 1; pseudo-human toys, such as dolls and lego people, have not been included as Human.)

Table 1. Animacy and grammatical role

	Hyenswu					Wenceng				
	Human		Inanimate		Total	Human		Inanimate		Total
	N	%	N	%		N	%	N	%	
A	1105	(99.7)	2	(0.2)	1108	942	(87.5)	15	(1.4)	1076
S	470	(46.1)	443	(43.4)	1020	443	(41.8)	455	(42.9)	1060
O	61	(5.6)	660	(60.1)	1099	67	(6.4)	645	(61.2)	1054
Se	39	(14.6)	179	(66.8)	268	49	(13.6)	206	(57.4)	359
Sx	63	(34.4)	104	(56.8)	183	24	(23.5)	53	(52.0)	102
Si	368	(64.7)	160	(28.1)	569	370	(52.9)	196	(28.0)	699

As Table 1 shows, A and O are sharply differentiated with respect to animacy: the A role is overwhelmingly occupied by human referents, while O arguments are usually inanimate. The S role, on average, falls between these extremes, with a more even distribution of human and inanimate referents. This distribution, which is supported by Allen and Schröder's findings (this volume, Table 18) for children who speak Inuktitut, provides strong evidence that the relationship between animacy and grammatical role identified by Du Bois (1987: 841–2) is characteristic of young children's speech.

As we see in Table 1, there is also systematic differentiation by animacy within the S role, as the figures below the dotted line reveal. Like O, Se shows a strong, though somewhat less extreme, skewing toward inanimates. Sx also favors inanimates but has a much higher percentage of human referents than O. The core argument of intransitive verbs other than the copula and existential, Si, shows a clear preference for human over inanimate referents.

The grammatical distribution of referents by animacy shown in Table 1 is strongly correlated with person: human A referents frequently are first or second person, while inanimate O and S referents are usually third person. Table 2 shows the distribution of first/second vs. third person referents by grammatical role. (References combining first, second, and third person are not included in Table 2.) Again, Allen and Schröder (this volume, Table 17) have found a similar skewing in the distribution of person across grammatical roles in the speech of children who speak Inuktitut.

Table 2. Person and grammatical role

	Hyenswu					Wenceng				
	First/Second		Third			First/Second		Third		
	N	%	N	%	Total	N	%	N	%	Total
A	865	(78.1)	180	(16.2)	1108	611	(56.8)	406	(37.7)	1076
S	219	(21.5)	796	(78.0)	1020	172	(14.8)	966	(83.3)	1160
O	6	(0.5)	1093	(99.5)	1099	15	(1.4)	1039	(98.6)	1054
Se	11	(4.1)	257	(95.9)	268	5	(1.4)	354	(98.6)	359
Sx	26	(14.2)	156	(85.2)	183	3	(2.9)	98	(96.1)	102
Si	182	(32.0)	383	(67.3)	569	164	(23.5)	514	(73.5)	699

As Table 2 shows, the two children are very similar in their treatment of person in O and Se roles, which are almost always third person. They differ, however, with respect to the A, Sx, and Si roles: Hyenswu has over 20% more first/second person referents in the A role and about 10% more first/second person referents in the Sx and Si roles than Wenceng. This is because Wenceng, the more advanced child linguistically, is more likely than Hyenswu to talk about third persons, including referents not present in the discourse context and characters in storybooks.

The developmental origins of Preferred Argument Structure

What do the data reveal about the developmental origins of Preferred Argument Structure in Korean? Two fundamental properties of these caregiver-child interactions emerge as the primary forces underlying the distribution of lexical NP's and new information. Both are deeply rooted in the "here-and-now" nature of early caregiver-child discourse. And both give insight into the profoundly iconic relationship between interaction and grammar in the early stages of acquisition.

The most pervasive factor underlying Preferred Argument Structure is the importance of attention management as a goal in the children's talk. Directing the attention of caregivers is a crucial function of talk at this stage, since the establishment of joint attention is an essential foundation for further talk and interaction (e.g. Ochs, Schieffelin, and Platt 1979; Bruner 1983:68–77). The children in this study have clearly learned to use the core argument slot of intransitive verbs, including the high frequency copula *ita* and existential *issta*, as well as the O argument slot of transitive verbs, to direct their caregivers' attention to new referents. (See Allen and Schröder (this volume) for additional evidence of the attention-getting function of S and O roles among children who speak Inuktitut.)

The interactions in which the children use the copula *ita* to label items in books are prime examples of what Bruner has called the "referential format", and are based on the achievement of joint attention to the pictures to be labeled (Bruner 1983:122–125). The caregiver and child look at different pictures one after another, introducing each new focus of attention, i.e. each new Se argument of *ita* 'be', with deictic pronouns and pointing. Descriptions with *ita*, while less scripted, are similar in that they serve to focus adult attention on a present object by mentioning an inherent property of the object.

New lexical mentions in the Sx role with *issta* 'exist', and in the Si role with verbs like *ota* 'come' and *kata* 'go', also direct adult attention to new props or participants. Objects thus introduced as Sx and Si arguments may figure in upcoming activity, while new characters in storybooks may become actors in the subsequent events to be narrated. New human participants arriving on the scene become potentially available for interaction with the child, as when Daddy comes home from school. Introducing new referents in the S role before going on to engage in or talk about activities is a pattern that reflects the organization of the child's interactions into an initial attention-focusing stage, followed by action and/or talk involving the new focus of attention. This is a well-documented pattern in child discourse, both with peers and with adults (e.g. Ochs and Schieffelin 1976; Ochs, Schieffelin, and Platt 1979). From a cognitive perspective, using the S role may represent the least taxing way of introducing new referents, especially important human ones, as Du Bois has proposed (1987:833–834).[11]

The attention-focusing function in child discourse has a long developmental history, from early visual orienting toward movement and change in the environment to later pointing gestures designed to focus adult attention (Bates 1976:106–109; Bruner 1983:75–76). Both children in this study sometimes use deictic pronouns, e.g. *ike* 'this', as single-word utterances to focus adult attention on new items; the adults typically respond to this by labeling the object or asking the child to do so. In other one-word utterances, they focus adult attention by labeling a present object; this is usually interpreted by adults as an invitation to talk about the object, to act upon it with the child, or to watch the child act upon it alone. Such interactional sequences socialize the child to the power of attention-focusing strategies in initiating interaction with others. We can hypothesize, for example, that the Korean child who successfully draws adult attention with a deictic pronoun or label at the one-word stage will add the copula at the two-word stage. Similarly, the child who uses *issta* 'exist' with pointing at the one-word stage to focus a new referent will add a lexical argument at the two word stage (cf. Bates 1976: 159–161; Bates and MacWhinney 1979: 190–194). Detailed longitudinal investigation could illuminate the transition from single-word attention-focusing utterances to the kinds of syntactic patterns found in these data, e.g. *ike X-ya* 'This is an X' and *X issta* 'X exists/There's an X'. The function of the S role as a locus for the introduction of new information probably emerges developmentally from earlier, non-syntactic strategies for directing adult attention.

The second force underlying Preferred Argument Structure in the data is the participant structure of the children's interactions, which is mirrored very directly in the organization of the A and O arguments of transitive predicates. At this early stage, caregiver and child typically use talk to direct and to accompany their ongoing activities. Since the children's two-participant activities generally involve human agents acting upon inanimate objects, their lexicon of transitive verbs is dominated by ones which take a human A and an inanimate O. These verbs thus participate in what Du Bois (1987: 841) has called a "lexical conspiracy" to organize the arguments of large populations of verbs so that highly topical human referents occupy the A role, while rapidly changing transient inanimate referents occupy the O role. The cast of participants in the children's interactions (i.e. potential As) generally remains the same for long stretches of interaction, while the O role is constantly changing as their actions and accompanying talk focus on a series of different objects. From a perceptual perspective, then, the A role provides the stable "ground", which can be left unspoken, against which the O role accommodates potentially changing "figures", which call for overt mention.

Thus the developmental origin of the Given A constraint (Du Bois 1987: 827) apparently lies in the tendency for early caregiver-child talk to encode the actions of present participants, who have usually already been mentioned. In contrast, the O role provides a consistent grammatical slot that can be used to focus caregivers' attention with a lexical NP, when the object acted upon represents new information. The S role affords what may be a cognitively simpler alternative: a slot that can be used to direct attention to new referents without requiring simultaneous encoding of actions involving more than one participant (Du Bois 1987: 833–834).[12]

Preferred Argument Structure, mental representation, and the acquisition of grammar

From a psycholinguistic perspective, the findings of this study raise important questions about mental representation and the potential relationship between Preferred Argument Structure and the acquisition of grammar. Statistical patterns like Preferred Argument Structure have traditionally been relegated to the domain of "use" rather than "knowledge", since violations of Preferred Argument Structure constraints are not ungrammatical (Clancy 1993). But if we assume, following Du Bois (1987:850), that "structured performance reflects — if imperfectly — structured competence", we must ask what, if anything, children know that results in such consistent adherence to Preferred Argument Structure. Are generalizations about the relationship between the grammatical roles A, S, and O and the animacy, person, and information status of referents mentally represented by young children? If so, at what level are generalizations having psychological reality formulated?

Although this is obviously a very complex question calling for further research, the present data are consistent with the hypothesis that the relevant generalizations are not formulated in terms of A, S and O *per se*. The actual percentages of referents having particular properties with respect to animacy, person, information status, and surface form vary a good deal from verb to verb in each child's speech. As a result, there is considerable diversity within each grammatical role. Moreover, the degree of internal pragmatic, semantic, and formal consistency within A, S and O roles keeps changing as new types of interaction, such as reading from storybooks, and new functions for verbs, such as introducing story characters, emerge. It therefore seems implausible that a young child would, for example, have mentally represented a grammatical O role that is defined in part in terms of a target percentage of new information.

This conclusion is consistent with Du Bois' (1985:356–357) discussion of the theoretical status of A, S, and O. These grammatical roles, he explains, do not constitute three distinct syntactic categories in most languages. We therefore should not assume that speakers mentally represent or acquire A, S, and O *per se* as categories. Instead, Du Bois proposes, A, S, and O represent a useful intermediate level of analysis at which particular clusters of semantic and discourse-pragmatic properties can be identified, such as the semantic role Agent or the information status New; these clusters of properties may serve as potential motivations for particular groupings of A, S, and O, such as the grammaticization of A and S as Subject in certain languages. Thus A, S, and O are probably best understood as slots available for performing particular semantic and pragmatic tasks, rather than as categories to be identified with particular semantic and/or pragmatic features and mentally represented in terms of those features (Du Bois 1987:833–834).

In what sense, then, can children be said to know the kind of information that underlies Preferred Argument Structure? Children's consistent use of Preferred

Argument Structure, I would like to propose, can be understood as reflecting their mental representation of linguistic information at the discourse and lexical levels. The relevant linguistic knowledge appears to be of two types: (1) generalizations about reference in discourse, i.e. knowing which linguistic forms are selected to talk about referents having a particular information status, such as New, and (2) generalizations about how particular verbs in the lexicon, and perhaps particular classes of semantically similar verbs, can be used in interaction. Discourse-level knowledge, e.g. about ways of introducing new referents, may arise at least in part from presyntactic strategies for focusing caregivers' attention, and hence will span the child's lexicon of verbs. On the other hand, when a particular verb, such as the Korean existential *issta*, is used very frequently for a particular discourse function, such as introducing new referents, children who acquire this verb may well end up storing both the interactive function and its formal correlate of lexical reference at the lexical level, i.e. as information about this particular verb. Similarly, certain high-frequency verbs such as *cwuta* 'give' or *pota* 'see' may be used so frequently as imperatives that this interactive function and its formal correlate of elliptical A and overt O would come to be mentally represented as facts about these individual verbs.

If these proposals are correct, they have at least the following two implications for the nature of mental representations: (1) the same piece of information about a particular verb, such as the propensity of one of its arguments to introduce new referents, may be mentally represented at more than one linguistic level, e.g. at both discourse and lexical levels, and (2) the types of information that are mentally represented at one linguistic level may be different for different verbs, e.g. knowledge about referent introduction may usually be represented at the discourse level, but for certain verbs may also be represented at the lexical level. Mental representations would thus be redundant, making them more robust; they would also be somewhat inconsistent, e.g. differing in content from one verb (class) to another, reflecting their frequency-driven genesis.

Finally, let us consider the potential role of Preferred Argument Structure in the acquisition of grammar. In Korean, as in many other languages, the three grammatical roles A, S, and O do not each receive distinct grammatical treatment. Instead, Korean for the most part organizes them into two grammatical categories: Subject (A and S), which receives nominative casemarking, and Direct Object (O), which receives accusative casemarking. In morphologically ergative languages like Sakapultek or Inuktitut, however, A receives ergative casemarking while S and O are both given absolutive casemarking (Du Bois 1987, Allen and Schröder this volume). Since children acquiring different languages must acquire different alignments of A, S, and O, and some languages exhibit internal inconsistencies in alignment (e.g. "split ergativity"), we must ask what relationship, if any, exists between the grammatical roles A, S, and O and children's acquisition of grammaticized categories such as Subject and Direct Object.

As the findings of this study have shown, the organization of verbs in the lexicon into classes having particular core arguments, e.g. A and O vs. S, creates systematic distributions of referents having particular clusters of semantic, discourse-pragmatic and formal properties. To the extent that referents in a particular core argument role exhibit consistent properties, e.g. animacy, person, information status, and referential form, these clusters of properties can serve as important sources of hypotheses about the potential motivations of grammatical devices such as casemarkers or word order. In the present data, for example, consistent ways of manipulating attention and organizing activities in interaction combine with the pre-existing organization of the arguments of verbs in the Korean lexicon to create a relatively limited, stable core of semantic and discourse-pragmatic properties for the referents of the children's verbs, e.g. human, given, first/second person, elliptical A's and inanimate, new, third person, lexical O's. Arguments in S role, as we have seen, generally exhibit properties falling somewhere between A and O on each of these dimensions, potentially motivating their alignment with either A or O (Du Bois 1985, 1987), depending on the language being acquired.

Such lexical and discourse patterns, which presumably motivate grammaticization historically, may also be useful in the abstraction of grammatical generalizations during acquisition. The almost categorical distinction in animacy between A and O in the Korean data could obviously be useful to the child acquiring the distinction between nominative vs. accusative casemarking.[13] Furthermore, since only overt arguments receive casemarking in Korean, the distribution of lexical arguments has potential implications for the acquisition of casemarkers. If a high percentage of lexical arguments introduce new referents, then casemarkers will be associated with this function in the child's experience and could be interpreted as markers of new information (Clancy 1996). Thus the clusters of semantic, discourse-pragmatic, and formal properties of referents organized into A, S, and O roles are available to young children as a source of hypotheses about the functional foundations of the morphosyntactically marked categories in the language being acquired. When a particular grouping of A, S, and O has not been grammaticized in the language being acquired, generalizations about the properties of arguments in these roles may remain mentally represented only at the lexical and/or discourse levels. Thus the child acquiring English may never be motivated to postulate a category linking S and O, despite their shared properties. But when a particular grouping has been grammaticized in the language being acquired, the child is forced to deal with the presence of the relevant grammatical device(s) in caregivers' speech, e.g. a particular casemarking or word order. In this case Preferred Argument Structure may be an important tool for the child, organizing clusters of semantic and discourse-pragmatic properties into observable patterns that can be correlated with the morphosyntactic device(s) to be acquired. Thus Preferred Argument Structure has an important role to play in the functional motivation of grammar during the process of acquisition as well as grammaticization.

Summary and conclusions

In sum, quantitative analysis of the distribution of lexical reference and new information across A, S, and O grammatical roles in Korean caregiver-child discourse has revealed that very young children show a clear preference for introducing new referents with lexical NP's in O, Sx, and Si roles and with deictic pronouns in the Se role, while reserving the A role for previously mentioned, elliptical referents. Qualitative analysis of the use of eight frequent verbs in interaction — *ita* 'be', *issta* 'exist', *ota* 'come', *kata* 'go', *hata* 'do', *pota* 'see', *cwuta* 'give', and *mekta* 'eat' — has suggested two functional bases for the observed distribution of new information: attention management and the participant structure of caregiver-child interaction. The intransitive verbs are used to talk about single-participant events and states; when this participant is a new referent, it receives overt mention in the single core argument slot. The transitive verbs are frequently used to talk about actions performed on objects by the child or her caregivers, who are usually left unmentioned in the A role; when the object to be acted upon is new, it typically is mentioned with a lexical NP in the O role.

Preferred Argument Structure, as a complex set of patterns involving animacy and person as well as information status and lexical reference, is an important potential source of raw material for the acquisition of grammar, as well as for the diachronic process of grammaticization. The accumulation of semantic and discourse-pragmatic similarities and differences across the arguments of verbs in the child's lexicon, and the correlation of this semantic and pragmatic content with surface expression of arguments, provides a variety of potential bases for the differentiation of A, S, and O roles. Through such role-based patterns below the level of grammaticized categories, Preferred Argument Structure creates powerful links between the lexicon (i.e. the argument structure of individual verbs) and discourse (i.e. information flow and referential form). This gives Preferred Argument Structure an important role to play in the emergence of grammatical categories such as Subject/Direct Object or Ergative/Absolutive, which link lexicon and discourse through such general grammatical devices as word order and case-marking.

Notes

* I am grateful to the participants in the 1995 conference "Preferred Argument Structure: The Next Generation" at UCSB for their helpful comments on earlier versions of this paper, especially Susanna Cumming, Pamela Downing, Jack Du Bois, Hyo Sang Lee, and Sandra Thompson. I also appreciate the help of Soonja Choi and Hyo Sang Lee, who assisted with the interpretation of the Korean. Above all, thanks are due to Jack Du Bois, who provided the original inspiration for this work, as well as constant discussion, advice, and encouragement during its development.

1. There is honorific agreement in that the suffix *-si* is attached to verbs having a subject referent to whom the speaker wishes to show deference, but the children in this sample had not yet acquired this suffix.

2. There are some interesting exceptions to nominative-accusative casemarking with certain classes of verbs that have two core arguments. Stative verbs, such as *ypputa* 'like' (A-NOM B-NOM *ippe* 'A likes B') and *issta* 'exist' (A-NOM B-NOM *issta* 'A has B'), take nominative marking on both core arguments.

3. The abbreviations used in this paper are based on Lee 1991:

ACC – accusative	LOC – locative
ANT – anterior	NEG (IMPOT) – impotential negative
ATTR – attributive	NOM – nominalizer
CIRCUM – circumstantial	PL – plural
COMM – committal	PROP – propositive
CONN – connective	SG – singular
DECL – declarative	TOP – topic
IE – informal ending	UNASSIM – unassimilated
INT – intentional	

4. This error, using i-ke *N* 'this-thing N' for *i N* 'this N', is common in Korean acquisition.

5. For this study the verbal nouns such as *kongpwu* 'study' that combine with *hata* 'do' to form predicates, i.e. *kongpwuhata* 'to study', have not been analyzed as arguments in the O role, although they can take accusative casemarking in adult speech. Since the children never casemarked these verbal nouns, they have been treated as fully incorporated into the predicate. Onomatopeic expressions such as *ho* (sound of blowing) which also combine with *hata*, i.e. *hohata* 'to blow', have also been treated as fully incorporated into the predicate. Both types of compound predicates with *hata* 'do' have been analyzed here as intransitive.

6. The stative transitive verbs that take nominative casemarking on both core arguments are analyzable as syntactically intransitive (O'Grady 1991: 99), and could therefore be treated as having two S arguments. I have not, however, included them in the quantitative analyses in this paper.

7. In Korean, *pap mekta* 'eat rice' is a collocation meaning 'eat'.

8. As mentioned in Note 6, intransitive uses of *hata* 'do' with verbal nouns and onomatopoeic expressions are not considered here.

9. For children of this age, *-l ke-ya* is probably best treated as a unitary suffix.

10. Although *cwuta* 'give' is a ditransitive verb, I will not be concerned with the indirect object here.

11. The fact that so many new referents are introduced in the O role in these data indicates that any cognitive constraint against simultaneously introducing new information and describing actions is not absolute. Rather, the constraint may be specific to human referents, which are virtually never introduced in the O role in the children's speech, even when the lexical content of the verb, e.g. *pota* 'look at/see', would readily permit this.

12. Conceptual simplicity may also favor the early acquisition of single-argument verbs in development. Tomasello (1992: 199) has hypothesized that the child's earliest verbs are conceptualized not as two-participant actions, but as single entities acting, undergoing changes of state, or being acted upon by the child.

13. Rispoli (1987) makes this point for Japanese acquisition. Having demonstrated that referents in the O role are significantly more likely to be inanimate than referents in the S role, he argues that this semantic differentiation precedes, and can serve as the basis for, the acquisition of the syntactic categorization of verbs as intransitive vs. transitive.

References

Ariel, Mira. 1990. *Accessing Noun-Phrase Antecedents.* New York: Routledge.

Bates, Elizabeth. 1976. *Language and Context: The acquisition of pragmatics.* New York: Academic.

Bates, Elizabeth and MacWhinney, Brian. 1979. "A functionalist approach to the acquisition of grammar". In Bambi B. Schieffelin and Elinor Ochs (eds), *Developmental Pragmatics.* New York: Academic, 167–211.

Bentivoglio, Paola. 1996. Acquisition of Preferred Argument Structure in Venezuelan Spanish. Paper presented at the Seventh International Congress for the Study of Child Language, Istanbul, Turkey.

Bruner, Jerome. 1983. *Child's Talk.* New York: Norton.

Chafe, Wallace L. 1976. "Givenness, contrastiveness, definiteness, subjects, topics, and point of view". In Charles N. Li (ed.), *Subject and Topic.* New York: Academic, 24–55.

Chafe, Wallace L. 1994. *Discourse, Consciousness and Time: The flow and displacement of conscious experience in speaking and writing.* Chicago: University of Chicago Press.

Chafe, Wallace L. 1987. "Coginitive contraints on information flow". In Russell S. Tomlin (ed.), Coherence and Grounding in Discourse. Amsterdam and Philadelphia: Benjamins, 21–51.

Clancy, Patricia M. 1980. "Referential choice in English and Japanese narrative discourse". In Wallace L. Chafe (ed.), *The Pear Stories: Cognitive, cultural, and linguistic aspects of narrative production.* Norwood, NJ: Ablex, 127–202.

Clancy, Patricia M. 1993. "Preferred argument structure in Korean acquisition". In Eve V. Clark (ed.), *The Proceedings of the Twenty-fifth Annual Child Language Research Forum.* Stanford, CA: CSLI Publications, 307–314.

Clancy, Patricia M. 1995. "Subject and object in Korean acquisition: Surface expression and casemarking". In Susumu Kuno, Ik-Hwan Lee, John Whitman, Joan Maling, Young-Se Kang, and Young-joo Kim (eds), *Harvard Studies in Korean Linguistics VI,* 3–17.

Clancy, Patricia M. 1996. "Referential strategies and the co-construction of argument structure in Korean acquisition". In Barbara Fox (ed.), *Studies in Anaphora.* Amsterdam and Philadelphia: Benjamins, 33–68.

Clancy, Patricia M. 1997. "Discourse motivations of referential choice in Korean acquisition". In Ho-min Sohn and John Haig (eds), *Japanese/Korean Linguistics, Vol. 6.* Stanford: CA: CSLI Publications (Distributed by Cambridge University Press), 639–659.

Cumming, Susanna. 1994. "Functional categories in the lexicon: Referent introduction in Indonesian novels". *Text* 14: 465–494.

Du Bois, John W. 1985. "Competing motivations". In John Haiman (ed.), *Iconicity in Syntax.* Amsterdam and Philadelphia: Benjamins, 343–65.

Du Bois, John W. 1987. "The discourse basis of ergativity". *Language* 63: 805–855.

Givón, Talmy. 1983. *Topic Continuity in Discourse: A quantitative cross-language study.* Amsterdam and Philadelphia: Benjamins.

Hirakawa, Makiko. 1993. "Null subjects versus null objects in an early grammar of Japanese". *McGill Working Papers in Linguistics* 9: 30–45.

Hyams, Nina. 1986. *Language Acquisition and the Theory of Parameters.* Dordrecht: Reidel.

Hyams, Nina. 1991. "A reanalysis of null subjects in child language". In Jurgen Weissenborn, Helen Goodluck and Thomas Roeper, (eds), *Theoretical Issues in Language Acquisition,* Hillsdale, NJ: Erlbaum.

Kim, Young-joo. 1997. "The acquisition of Korean". In Dan I. Slobin (ed.), *The Crosslinguistic Study of Language Acquisition, Vol. 4.* Hillsdale, NJ: Erlbaum.

Kumpf, Lorraine E. 1992. "Preferred Argument Structure in second language discourse: A preliminary study". *Studies in Language* 16: 369–403.

Lee, Hyo Sang. 1991. *Tense, Aspect, and Modality: A discourse-pragmatic analysis of verbal affixes in Korean from a typological perspective.* Unpublished doctoral dissertation, University of California at Los Angeles.

Lee, Hyo Sang and Sandra A. Thompson. 1989. "A discourse account of the Korean accusative marker". *Studies in Language* 13: 105–128.

Ochs, Elinor. 1988. *Culture and Language Development: Language acquisition and language socialization in a Samoan village.* Cambridge: Cambridge University Press.

Ochs, Elinor and Bambi B. Schieffelin. 1976. "Topic as a discourse notion". In Charles N. Li (ed.), *Subject and Topic.* New York: Academic, 337–384.

Ochs, Elinor, Schieffelin, Bambi B., and Platt, Martha L. 1979. "Propositions across utterances and speakers". In Bambi B. Schieffelin and Elinor Ochs (eds), *Developmental Pragmatics.* New York: Academic, 251–278.

O'Grady, William. 1991. *Categories and Case: The sentence structure of Korean.* Amsterdam and Philadelphia: Benjamins

Rispoli, Matthew. 1987. "The acquisition of transitive and intransitive action verb categories in Japanese". *First Language* 7: 183–200.

Tomasello, Michael. 1992. *First Verbs: A case study of early grammatical development.* Cambridge: Cambridge University Press.

Valian, Virginia. 1991. "Syntactic subjects in the early speech of American and Italian children". *Cognition* 40: 21–81.

Wang, Qi, Diane Lillo-Martin, Catherine T. Best, and Andrea Levitt. 1992. "Null subject versus null object: Some evidence from the acquisition of Chinese and English". *Language Acquisition* 2: 221–254.

Genre and Preferred Argument Structure

Sources of argument structure in classroom discourse*

Lorraine E. Kumpf
California State University, Long Beach

Introduction

This study examines the relationship between genre and argument structure in American high school science teachers' classroom discourse, specifically, in the teachers' common mode of lecturing before the class as a whole. In this context, teachers have at least the following concerns: making the content accessible to students, creating conditions for students' retention of the content, and keeping students' attention. From the standpoint of Preferred Argument Structure, we will show that the classroom setting and teachers' goals dictate discourse characteristics. Conditions such as a shared visual field for referents or their representations and the challenge of the science content are served by the use of particular argument structures and verb distributions. Thus we shall see that the argument patterns are discourse-based, the result of adaptations which relate directly to the teachers' assessments of goals and needs. The teacher applies available grammatical tools to the special needs defined by the genre.

The perspective put forth is that the architecture which the grammar provides is realized in a genre, and the genre lends overall constraints to the discourse form. The definition of genre used here is that of Miller (1984): "typified rhetorical actions based on recurrent situations". Miller's view of genre as essentially social in nature is also shared.[1] It has been shown by O'Dowd (1990) that Preferred Argument Structure is sensitive to genre; however, genre has not been regarded as fundamental in the research sparked by Du Bois' work. To the contrary, it has been shown that Preferred Argument Structure is robustly maintained across genres: even O'Dowd's otherwise divergent data did not violate Du Bois' constraints. (See, e.g., Kärkkäinen (1996) and Kumpf (1992) for comparisons of conversation and narrative.) One is led to conclude that Preferred Argument Structure is more fundamental to the discourse than the more superficial effects of genre. However, we suspect that genre drives the special architectural features of discourse. This study explores the expectation that classroom discourse manifests highly-patterned argument structures which are motivated by the teachers' goals and needs.

This study consists of two parts: an examination of the Preferred Argument Structure constraints in the classroom data and a qualitative analysis of the discourse. Before turning to the analyses, short reviews of Preferred Argument Structure, information flow, and classroom discourse are in order.

Preferred Argument Structure

In his seminal article, Du Bois (1987) shows that there is a preferred syntactic patterning of nominals in the spoken discourse of Sakapultek. Limiting the analysis to clause cores, he examined the following roles: S, the one NP of an intransitive clause; A, the most agentlike NP of a transitive clause, and O, the transitive direct object. He found that there exists a set of tendencies, or "constraints", which link the grammatical and pragmatic structure of the language. The first grammatical tendency is the One Lexical Argument Constraint, which says that no more than one lexical NP is normally present in clause core. The second grammatical tendency, the Non-Lexical A Constraint, claims that the most agentlike nominal tends to be attenuated. The roles S and O, however, accommodate lexical nouns.

There is a pragmatic congruence that goes along with this syntactic distribution of NP types. The pragmatic counterpart of the One Lexical Argument Constraint is the tendency for clause cores to be limited to one piece of new information. This is the One New Argument Constraint. The pragmatic counterpart of the Non-Lexical A Constraint is the tendency to avoid expressing new information in the A position: the Given A Constraint. An NP carrying new information tends to occur as S or O.

In addition, Du Bois (1987) introduces the notion of "information pressure". Pressure is high when a number of new protagonists are introduced within a short span of discourse; it is low when, over a long span, there are few new mentions. Du Bois found that, when information pressure is high, lexical S's are frequent.

Thus, nominals change their syntactic form to reflect their changing information status in ongoing talk. The syntactic shape of a clause in its context is largely a result of these pragmatic considerations. Furthermore, in studies of narrative and conversation in a wide array of languages, Du Bois' constraints have been upheld. (See papers and bibliography in this volume for sources on many languages.) Du Bois (1987)posits the universality of the constraints. Insights gained into grammatical and pragmatic alignments across languages have established the utility of viewing discourse in terms of Preferred Argument Structure.

Information flow

The teachers' need to make information available and to create joint attention, among other factors, affect the way they use referring expressions. In order to talk about these and other characteristics, I have adapted the work of Chafe (1980, 1987, 1994) on information flow as the conceptual base for the categories of new, given, and accessible information. Chafe asserts the necessity of defining status of information on the given-new continuum in terms of the activation state of a concept in the consciousness of the speaker. Chafe (1987) defines given information as an already active concept, one which is already in a person's focus of consciousness at a particular time. Already active or given information is generally realized in attenuated forms, such as pronouns or pronominal inflection. New information is defined as information which is "previously inactive"; information which is inactive in consciousness, and is now in the process of being activated. New information is typically realized with full lexical nouns. Information may be semi-activated, i.e., peripherally in consciousness, by virtue of the fact that it has been mentioned before, or that it is in peripheral awareness for some other reason (e.g., present in the environment at the time of talk). Semi-activated concepts are referred to as accessible information. (Additional discussions of information flow, including alternative views, are found in Chafe (1994), and Du Bois and Thompson (1991).

In this study, I will use the terms *new, given* and *accessible* to refer to information in Chafe's activation states: active, inactive, and semi-active. New information is that which the teacher assumes will be first activated in the students' consciousness when mentioned; given information is that which the teacher assumes is already active for both teacher and student; accessible information is that which is perceived by the teacher to be in peripheral consciousness. In general, these concepts are operationalized for coding in this study following Du Bois (1987); that is, mentions are *given* if they have been mentioned in near prior text, or if they represent the speaker or addressee; *new* mentions have not been mentioned previously; *accessible* mentions are evoked by a frame, pointed out in the classroom context, or reintroduced from prior text. The 'coding' section below explains and illustrates these conditions.

Classroom discourse

Classroom discourse has been studied from a number of perspectives, though grammatical characterizations of the genre are missing. The most thorough examination of classrooms has been done through ethnography, (e.g., Heath 1983), especially participant structure analysis (e.g. Philips 1985). Ethnographies have also uncovered recurring discourse patterns, notably the well-known "IRE sequence" (e.g. Mehan 1983), describing the resilient classroom formula "Initiation/Response/ Evaluation". Another major thrust of classroom discourse study is the sociological research on the ways in which teachers address students and the implications for gender and ethnicity (e.g., Swann, 1989). Classroom interaction has been examined in the sociological tradition (e.g., Wallet and Piazza 1988, Tsui 1995). Researchers have noticed that different kinds of talk may be used in the classroom, e.g. talk which presents the subject matter (content talk) and talk which manages the classroom (regulatory or control talk). More recent work on classroom language has centered on the effect on learning of attention, teacher feedback and other aspects of classroom interaction (e.g.Tomlin and Villa 1994, Lyster and Ranta 1997). All of these approaches could fruitfully examine grammatical form in the classroom, but thus far have not. See Cazden (2001) and Chaudron (1988) for overviews of classroom discourse.

Research on the classroom language of teachers has been largely centered on speech act studies; the use of questions in the classroom is the most extensive: e.g. Heath (1982), Brock (1986), Dillon (1990). Analyses of grammar in teacher talk or classroom interaction are rare. Chaudron (1985) looks at topics in classroom discourse. Field (1993) investigates small-group classroom interaction in the tradition of Conversation Analysis. Ochs et al. (1996) examines reference phenomena in a research context (physics lab) which, while far from public school classrooms, is suggestive of aspects of classroom language. This study does not touch on argument structure or grammatical distributions, however. Pritzos (1992) looks at the syntactic complexity of teacher talk, among a number of other characteristics of discourse, when comparing teachers' talk with native English-speaking versus second-language students. Kumpf (in preparation) profiles verb use in teacher talk.

It must be noted that the character of classroom discourse can vary greatly, depending on the classroom configuration, the tasks set out by the teacher, or other variables: the classroom may be organized into interacting groups of students; discussion between teacher and students and among students may be variously configured; a task may necessitate, for example, a series of imperatives from the teacher in which no response is sought from students. Thus the genre is not unified, though "teacher talk" is certainly accepted as a recognizable way of speaking (Cazden, 2001). In this study, the data were taken from classtime in which the teachers are lecturing to the whole class, resulting in a corpus that is relatively homogeneous.

The discourse examined here is fundamentally different from other forms of discourse examined through the Preferred Argument Structure perspective to date. Four main characteristics common to this genre are:

(1) a. The teacher attempts to establish joint attention with many students.
    b. The teacher uses vocal and physical gesture, visual aids and other devices as an integral part of attention-getting and attention-holding.

c. The teacher often repeats speech patterns and uses prepackaged speech that may be characteristic of classroom discourse.
d. Low information pressure is preferred; that is, the teacher tries to utilize what the students already know and render all information as accessible as possible.

To illustrate, consider the following excerpt from a high school genetics lesson. All of the terms have been mentioned in the immediate prior text, and are not therefore new information. (Throughout this study, to highlight the form of NP's in core grammatical roles, lexical nouns are in boldface and pronouns are underlined, and square brackets represent the overlap of words and physical actions.)

(2) Teacher: HOLDING UP PAIRS OF BEADS IN EACH HAND TO REPRESENT CHROMOSOME STRINGS
OK, ^here we have **the chromosomes.**
here's [let's say ^**mama's chromosomes,**]
[SHAKES LEFT HAND]
and here's [[^**papa's chromosomes.**]]
[[SHAKES RIGHT HAND]]
now **these chromosomes** [^separate,]
[DROPS ONE STRING FROM EACH HAND]
and one of [each kind goes into mama's ^egg cell,
[JOINS THE CHROMOSOME STRINGS AND HOLDS THE PAIR AGAINST THE BOARD]
and papa's ^sperm cell,
when you have ^**fertilization,**]
[[which you ^know]] from your reading yesterday,
[[TURNS TO FACE CLASS]]
you have ^**twenty-three chromosomes** from each cell. (N80)

The information in the excerpt is loosely packed in units meant to highlight each point of information, redundancy is built in, the key term 'chromosome' is repeated; the passage contains no new information, and yet is full of lexical nouns. The shared visual field is essential to the lesson. In addition to the strings of beads representing chromosomes, the teacher uses facial expression, body positioning, and vocal and physical gestures to present the material.

It is a central premise in this study that the special conditions of managing information in the classroom affect the way in which argument structures are used by the teachers. The discourse of the teachers will be analyzed for its conformity to the tendencies defined by Du Bois. These tendencies are so robust that they are expected to be upheld in the classroom data. However, the teachers' goals (e.g., establish joint attention, create optimally available information) will motivate special characteristics in the patterning of lexical arguments. It will be shown that an important link between genre and argument structure is the tendency to use certain verbs (Chafe's (1994) 'low content transitives') and recurring syntax when introducing or reintroducing referents.

To my knowledge, no prior studies have dealt with the clausal grammar of teachers' talk or given a principled view of information status in ongoing teacher discourse. A related question of interest is to what extent these discourse characteristics are under the control of the teacher, and to what extent individual teachers' skills determine architectural features of the discourse. The question will remain one of speculation, and is not a research goal here. After we have analyzed the Preferred Argument Structure in Part I, Part II will consider genre characteristics in more detail.

Part I: Preferred argument structure analysis

Hypotheses

1. The data, consisting of both science talk and regulatory talk, will conform to Bois' four constraints.
2. There will be a high degree of given and accessible information in the teachers' talk, and relatively little new information.
3. There will be a high proportion of lexical S's and O's which are given or accessible.

Hypothesis 1 expresses the tendency toward universality which has been shown for Preferred Argument Structure. Hypothesis 2 stems from the characteristic low information pressure of the discourse. Hypothesis 3 would not be predicted by Preferred Argument Structure: it says that non-new information will be expressed with lexical S's and O's to a significant degree. Note that Hypothesis 3 makes no claim about the positioning of new information; it merely suggests that the S and O slots are available for mentions that are non-new and lexical.

Method

Subjects

The subjects for this study are four teachers of high school science who were recommended by their principals because they are 'master' teachers; their teaching abilities have been recognized. I chose master teachers for two reasons: school authorities were most comfortable allowing these teachers to be taped, and as much as possible I wished to eliminate any variable concerning the quality of teaching. The question of quality is still open, of course, but I am confident that the sample represents data from well-qualified professionals whose teaching has been positively evaluated.

Four fifty-minute classes were videotaped. The teachers are teaching life science or general science, and topics are genetics, ecology, and electricity. Two are female and two male. In the samples taken, the teachers' talk dominates; the students are generally active interlocutors even if there is minimal verbalization, since the teacher is responding to non-verbal cues. This study investigates characteristics of the teachers' talk only.

Data and sampling

The data were taken from class hours in which the teachers' basic mode is lecture-discussion. That is, the teachers deliver information and direct any discussion; the students ask questions and answer teacher elicitations and prompts. All talk in each sample was analyzed, so included in the data is any regulatory talk which occurred during the lecture time.

It is obvious that talk will vary depending on the time segment of the class hour. For example, regulatory talk will predominate at the beginning of the hour, and a sample limited to the beginning would not be characteristic of the whole. Therefore, each tape was divided into ten-minute parts, and the second minute from each part was extracted for analysis: a total of five minutes of talk per teacher. In two instances, the second minute did not yield enough talk; the data were taken from a subsequent minute-piece. It can thus be claimed that he samples were characteristic of the period of talk as a whole. Science talk and regulatory talk are combined in the samples, though separately coded as such.

The twenty minutes of talk yielded the data in Table 1. The column labeled Unattached Nominals refers to NP's which occur without any grammatical relation to a proposition; they will be referred to below. Note that Patty produced considerably less speech than the other teachers in her five minute sample. The other three teachers had remarkably similar totals.

The transcription was done by intonation unit (IU). The intonation unit is defined somewhat approximately as that stretch of speech which is uttered under a single intonation contour. (See Chafe 1994 Chapter 5 for a thorough discussion of this unit.) Even though the basic unit of analysis is the clause, I transcribed in IU's

Table 1. Data

Teacher	# of full clauses	Unattached nominals	Core NP's coded
Patty	93	41	174
Nancy	132	30	258
Ron	125	43	254
Bob	134	31	256
Total	484	145	843

because the data contain partial clauses and unattached nominals. The extent and nature of this non-clausal data is of interest.

Coding

Clauses were coded for the Preferred Argument Structure analysis. Whereas Du Bois' constraints are expressed in terms of clause core (the verb with its A/O or S arguments), all nominals were coded here, including obliques and unattached nominals. Table 2 includes the coding points.

Table 2. Coding categories

1. features of the talk
   a. individual speaker identification
   b. mode of talk (science or regulatory)
2. features of the NP
   a. form (zero, pronoun, full noun, clause)
   b. grammatical role (A, O, S, indirect object, locative, temporal, other oblique, predicate nominal, other)
   c. person
   d. number
   e. activation state (given, new, accessible)
3. features of the clause
   a. type of verb (equative, action, saying, cognition, existential)
   b. speech act (declarative, interrogative, imperative, vocative, other)

Coding guidelines

Coding was done on the clause, as Preferred Argument Structure is framed in terms of the clause. Fragments of clauses that were false starts or truncated by interruption were not counted, but other incomplete clauses, usually in the form of unattached nominals, that represented a complete utterance, were counted separately.

Form of NP
NP's were coded as zero, pronoun or lexical noun. Clausal NPs were counted separately: virtually all were direct objects, particularly objects of verbs of saying. The superordinate clause was coded first, and the complement clause was coded separately. The total number of clausal NPs was very low. Because the clause was not a frequent form of NP, clausal direct objects were left out of the statistical analysis.

Grammatical role of NP was coded with the following guidelines: S was used for the single argument of intransitive verbs, including the subject of existentials. Predicate nominals were coded separately and did not figure into the analysis of core arguments.

The agent of a transitive verb was designated A, regardless of the degree of agency involved. The data show many 'low content transitives', especially HAVE, in clauses like "here we have **a diagram**" (R58), which may function as an existential. Similarly, transitive objects, designated O, were counted as they appeared, even if the objects were not object-like, as "diagram" in the example. So-called 'predicating verbs' (Du Bois and Thompson 1991), in which the object is not separate from the predication, as in 'catch a cold' were almost non-existent in the data.

Obliques were also coded. Indirect objects were considered obliques; they were very rare in the data. Unattached nominals, NPs which occur without any grammatical relation to a proposition, seemed to be relatively frequent and were tallied. Vocatives have a special regulatory function, and they were counted separately. It is clear that information in the classroom is not always delivered in full clauses.

Person and number of personal pronouns were coded.

Activation state. All nominals were coded for status as new, given or accessible, following Chafe's terminology. I use the term "Given NP" (G) for one defined as coding an 'already active concept'; "New NP" (N) for coding one which has been inactive, and is first introduced into the discourse; and "Accessible NP" (Acc) for coding one which is "semi-active" in the background, in peripheral awareness, or evoked by a frame. Accessible NP's may have popped back into the discourse after an absence.[2] Generally, I have been conservative with the use of the category "accessible" — NP's designated accessible must have a clear channel of accessibility. One channel of accessibility which is characteristic of classroom discourse is a shared visual context: if the teacher refers to an object or representation for the first time, if it is either indicated gesturally and/or clearly in view, that referent is deemed accessible.

Results

The One Lexical Argument Constraint

These data conform to the tendency for clauses to have one or fewer lexical arguments. In the data, the appearance of two lexical NP's in the clause core is extremely rare, as seen in Table 3.

Only 1.5% of clauses, (seven out of 484) have two lexical arguments. The instances of two-argument clauses occurred in both science talk and regulatory talk, respectively, in the following examples:

(3) **a conductor** allows **electricity** to pass through. (R48)

(4) **your partner** did **the right thing.** (R93)

Table 3. Occurrence of lexical NP's in the clause core

	0 Lex NP		1 Lex NP		2 Lex NP's		Total clauses
	N	%	N	%	N	%	N %
Patty	28	30	65	70	0	0	93
Nancy	59	45	73	55	0	0	132
Ron	66	53	56	45	3	2	125
Bob	75	56	55	41	4	3	134
Total	228	47	249	51.5	7	1.5	484

The salient result is that clauses with two full NP's are extremely rare. One might expect many two-argument clauses in the lecture mode of science talk, as in clauses like example (3). In fact, this is not the case, and the question of what occurs instead will be taken up in the qualitative analysis below.

The Non-Lexical A Constraint

The constraint to avoid lexical A's is likewise borne out in the data. Table 4 summarizes the form of NP category for all data. Tables for individual teachers are found in the Appendix, Tables A–D.

Table 4 shows that, out of 249 total A's, only 22 or 8% are lexical. In comparison, S's and O's are lexical to about equal degrees, and over half the time, at 60% and 52%, respectively. This is a high level of lexical S's and O's relative to both Kumpf (1992) and Kärkkäinen's (1996) results for English conversation and narrative; it is also a point of interest that the lexical percentages of S and O are so similar. Obliques have been conflated into one category here, and do not figure prominently.

Table 4. Form of argument by role

Form of NP		Zero		Pronoun		Lexical Noun		Clause		Total	
		N	%	N	%	N	%	N	%	N	%
	A	57	23	170	69	22	8	0	0	249	33
Role	S	16	8	76	37	107	52	7	3	206	27
	O	22	9	37	5	145	60	40	16	244	32
ALL	OBL	0	0	24	37	38	59	3	4	65	8
	Total	95	12	307	40	312	41	50	7	764	100

Table 5. Lexical vs. non-lexical NP's by role

	Non-Lexical NP's	Lexical NP's	Total
A	227	22	249
O + S	151	252	403

Yates corrected $\chi^2 = 37.26$; d.f. = 1 $p < .0001$

If we look at the difference in the distribution of lexical and non-lexical NP's in Table 5 we find that the distribution is non-random at a high level of significance. After Du Bois, the S and O categories are conflated; clausal NP's are omitted. Thus A's tend to be non-lexical, and S's and O's tend to be lexical.

Lexical A's, though rare, occur in both science talk and regulatory talk, and respectively in the following examples:

(5) **the symbols** mean <u>something</u> (B65)

(6) **each student** writes <u>it</u> (P23)

In the few examples found, including those above, when the A is lexical, the O tends not to be, a fact which reflects the resilience of the One Lexical Argument Constraint.

As seen in Table 4, although A is often zero, it most likely occurs as a pronoun. Zeros here are mainly the A's of imperatives. More will be said about the pronoun pattern when we consider the prevalence of certain types of transitive verbs, especially the "low content transitives" and their function in the discourse.

Thus Du Bois' grammatical constraints are straightforwardly upheld.

The One New Argument Constraint

Turning to the pragmatic constraints, the One New Argument constraint is also maintained to a striking degree. No examples of clauses were found that contained more than one new argument. In fact, only 11% of the clause cores had any new argument at all: 89% had no new arguments. This dramatic result highlights the low information pressure in these data. Table 6 shows the figures for each teacher.

The Given A Constraint

As shown in Table 7, and as predicted by Preferred Argument Structure, new A's are avoided. There are only three instances of new A's in the whole data set.

Other facts in Table 7 are more notable. First, looking across roles, we see that there is indeed very little new information in the discourse. The data are 78% given and 15% accessible: only 7% qualifies as new. Thus the second hypothesis is borne out. Note, however, that when new information does occur, it is almost always in the S or O role, which conforms to Du Bois' tendencies.

Table 6. Number of new arguments per clause

	0 New		1 New		2 New		Total	
	N	%	N	%	N	%	N	%
Patty	86	92	7	8	0	0	93	19
Nancy	114	86	18	14	0	0	132	27
Ron	113	89	12	11	0	0	125	26
Bob	121	90	13	10	0	0	134	28
Total	434	89	50	11	0	0	484	100

Table 7. Activation state by role

Activation State		Given		Accessible		New		Total	
		N	%	N	%	N	%	N	%
Role	A	235	94	11	5	3	1	249	36
	S	146	71	40	19	20	10	206	29
	O	164	67	51	21	29	12	244	35
Total		545	78	102	15	52	7	699	100

There is a remarkable similarity between the S and O profiles — they are almost identical. The profiles show that both S's and O's are given around 70% of the time. This is a very high percentage in comparison to other studies. In addition, S's and O's are accessible over 20% of the time. The remaining NP's, around 10%, are new. We know from Table 4 that S's and O's are mainly lexical; regardless of this fact, Table 7 shows that S's and O's are around 90% non-new. Thus the third hypothesis is borne out: full lexical mentions are most likely to be non-new. These results are quite different from those of studies of English narrative and conversation (Kärkkäinen 1996, Kumpf 1992) where O tends to be preferred for new information.

The analysis clearly reveals that Du Bois' constraints are upheld. Beyond this basic conformity, further results include:

1. S's and O's tend to be lexical: over half of all S's and O's are lexical.
2. While S's are often lexical, they are also often pronouns or zeros (45%), whereas O's are less likely to be pronouns.

Given Lexical NP's

In general, givenness correlates with attenuation, not with full lexical representation. However, in these data, lexical NP's that are given are fairly well-represented

Table 8. Given Lexical NP's

Frequency			
		N	(%)
Role	A	55	(30)
	S	12	(6)
	O	69	(37)
	OBL	16	(9)
	UN's	33	(18)
	Total	185	(100)

in teacher talk, with 185 instances in the role distributions (including obliques and unattached nominals) shown in Table 8.

The vast majority (89%) of the given lexical NP's are science terms. Those that were not appeared in control talk, usually as repetitions of nouns in directives. In general, the teachers made explicit mention of science terms, and, rather than using anaphoric structures, tended to repeat the terms in full. Occasionally, teachers made immediate repetitions of clauses with lexical S when talking about science concepts.

I suggest that teachers use lexical NP's that are given in order to make sure that the full referent is available to all students. Using the lexical NP is also an aid to those who may find the science content challenging. Du Bois (1987) discusses the increased use of lexical NP with higher "information pressure", that is, when the discourse is laden with relatively many new mentions. In the science teachers' discourse, however, the lexical usage takes place even when such pressure is low. The high degree of lexical NP's seems to be a trait that distinguishes the teacher's discourse from conversation or other forms of talk.

Non-core roles and unattached nominals

There were very few indirect objects, locatives, temporals or other obliques in the data: no speaker produced as many as ten tokens in these categories. Indirect objects tended to correlate with regulatory talk, as in "Hand me your lab" (NR10). In contrast with Du Bois' (1987) suggestion, oblique roles were not used as a conduit for new information.

Each speaker produced a significant number of unattached nominals (UN's). Patty, who produced the lowest number of clauses, produced the highest number of UN's (36). It is also interesting that UN's are used to convey non-new material 85% of the time, though Nancy has relatively many new mentions of this type, as we see in Table 9.

Table 9. Unattached Nominals

Activation state	Given		Accessible		New		Total	
	N	%	N	%	N	%	N	%
Patty	11	31	22	61	3	8	36	34
Nancy	5	23	9	41	8	36	22	21
Ron	2	43	14	50	2	7	28	26
Bob	9	45	8	40	3	15	20	19
Total	37	35	53	50	16	15	106	100

Regulatory talk

Recall that regulatory talk (or 'control talk') refers to the talk of classroom management, in contrast with talk about science. Relatively little of the total talk was regulatory; it averaged about 25% of the talk.[3] We would expect the structure of regulatory talk to differ from that of science talk: in fact, regulatory talk employed mostly imperatives and questions. Regulatory talk was also more attenuated than science talk, and it accounted for many of the pronouns and zeros in the data. Vocatives were counted with regulatory talk; these and unattached nominals made up many of the regulatory NP's. Here are some examples:

(7) **Anitra.**
put that away.
you can't eat that in here. (R18)

(8) **Dustin?**
read your **answer** for us. (B31)

(9) where's **your textbook.** (R11)

(10) turn **the lab** in before you leave. (N120)

In terms of information flow, both types of talk had equally high amounts of given and accessible information (over 90% for all speakers except Nancy, who had more new information than the others). Thus, though the two types of talk are clearly different, the 'non-new' characteristic is one point of similarity.

The picture of the discourse that emerges from the Preferred Argument Structure analysis is one of little new information and many lexical mentions in S and O. Whereas these generalizations do not violate Preferred Argument Structure, they would not be predicted by it. One might expect given information in this proportion to be attenuated. To explain the profile, we need to look at qualitative aspects of the discourse.

Part II: The character of the discourse

The teachers' argument patterns need to be considered in the light of the special character of classroom discourse. The first of the defining characteristics is that of attention management.[4] Attempts by the teachers to establish joint attention are central to their goals, and one can imagine that joint attention is difficult to achieve in a class of 30 or so students of about 15 years of age.

I claim that one supporting device for attention management is the use of lexical NP's for non-new entities. The teacher constantly monitors students for signs of attention and comprehension. One way to maximize salience of an entity is to mention it in full. The teachers' ability to manipulate the information flow characteristics of the discourse relates directly to attention management.

Another very important technique to gain and hold attention is the use of the visual channel. Several strategies were employed to effect visual attention, such as the use of physical gesture; the use of realia, especially in employing the students to make or use objects of significance to the science content; the use of a blackboard or whiteboard on which the teacher wrote key words, drew diagrams, and directed gesture; the use of pictures, textbook illustrations, posters, etc. Non-visual attention-getters were, for example, the use of vocal gesture and the use of idiosyncratic language meant to amuse the students. The following excerpt illustrates many of these techniques.

(11) [and I have **this ^picture**
[T PICKS UP PICTURE AND HOLDS UP, TURNING HER BODY FOR THE CLASS TO VIEW it]
I'll pass it around ^later,
here '**some people** have never seen anybody with six ^hands-
er ..^not six hands_]
[2six ^fingers.
[2T PLACES PICTURE AGAINST HER BODY AND HOLDS IT WITH HER ARMS2]
and they have [3 **an extra ^finger** on their hands.
[3T HOLDS UP RIGHT HAND AND INDICATES PLACE OF 6TH FINGER WITH LEFT HAND3]
it ^determines,
are you gonna have [**a nice beautiful Italian nose** like ^mine.]
[T. SHOWS PROFILE TO CLASS, LIFTS RIGHT HAND TO OUTLINE HER NOSE]
or are you gonna have [[**a ^Greek nose**,]]
[[T TOUCHES NOSE]]
or **an ^Irish nose**,

or ^**what kind** of nose.
we learned ^yesterday about,
are [**your** ^**earlobes** gonna be free,]
[T. GRASPS RIGHT EARLOBE, PULLING IT BACK AND FORTH]
or are they gonna be ^attached.
about ^**freckles.**
and ^**color blindness.**
[^**a=ll that information,**]
[T. PUTS DOWN PICTURE AND GOES TO BOARD]
is in [[papa's ^sperm,]]
[[T. TOUCHES BOARD WITH LEFT HAND UNDER FIGURE OF SPERM CELL]]
and [mama's ^egg.]
[T. TOUCHES BOARD WITH LEFT HAND UNDER FIGURE OF EGG CELL]
(N32)

In this excerpt, the teacher uses a picture, her own body, and chalkboard illustrations to underscore the material, particularly the nouns, she mentions. She indicates these NP's by pointing, underlining, and using other motions such as grasping her earlobe. She also uses vocal gesture (e.g., high intonation peaks at points of primary stress), and high volume. All of this adds to the salience and the redundancy of the material. We saw in example (2) above that the teacher used model representations of chromosomes, shaking them in front of her audience. Here is another example:

(12) we have **the** [^**formula,**
[T TURNS TO BOARD AND WRITES FORMULA]
^**P** equals ^VI.]
[[^**power** equals ^voltage]]times ^current.
[[T TURNS TO CLASS]]
voltage times current.
voltage times ^amperage.
it's the same ^thing.
so now we have **a** ^**cheap way** of remembering it.
[all we have to do is remember ^**VIP.**]
[T TOUCHES BOARD UNDER FORMULA]
(10 sec.)
⟨T HAS MOVED AWAY FROM BOARD, WALKS AMONG STUDENTS⟩
so ^how do we calculate **voltage**?
[we ^have **the triangle,**]
[T POINTS TO BOARD]
^see?
we don't have to go anywhere else but on the ^board now. (R58)

In (12), the teacher uses the board to direct attention initially to the formula; later he redirects attention to what he has written on it.

We have seen that non-new lexical nouns are very common in the discourse, and have speculated that redundancy and lexical noun specification may be necessary in order to insure that the whole group of students can access referents. The teacher cannot assume that all students can recognize or attend to a referent at a specific point, so he or she facilitates access by repeating lexical nouns that are already in play in the discourse (as in example (2) above).

Another motivation behind repetition of lexical nouns may lie in the nature of the science information. The teacher may assume that the material is challenging to students. He or she is responsible for gauging the extent of that challenge and constructing appropriate discourse. Special content terms like *amperage* or *chromosome* need to be reinforced in context. Terms that create relationships in a content area, such as *anomaly* or *distribution* are also challenging. Thus these terms are repeated, sometimes in structures that typify their specialized use, and sometimes in non-technical paraphrases. The teachers' model of the student and their perception of how challenging the material is are both factors that play into NP use and the form of argument structure.

Teachers also manipulate participation structures in the classroom. One goal of this manipulation is to foster inclusion in the classes. This is particularly important when the class is being addressed as a whole. A very common way of fostering inclusion is to use the verb HAVE with 'we' as in example (12), when the teacher says "we have **the formula**", as a means to put the referent 'formula' into play. A perfectly good way of doing putting a referent into play is to use the S-role, as in an existential. However, these teachers rarely used the THERE BE existential, and very commonly used WE HAVE, and sometimes also WE GOT. Here are a few examples:

(13) we have **a diagram** on page four forty. (R38)

(14) if we have **four batteries,** (R113)

(15) look at **the situation** we have. (P77)

Regulatory talk can also serve the purpose of inclusion, as in this compliment:

(16) we have some **rocket scientists** in this room. (R98)

However, HAVE and GOT are used in regulatory talk primarily in the sense of possession, and with the second person, and often addressed to individuals, as in

(17) to S1: you got **your textbook**?
to S2: you got **paper**?
to all: everybody have **paper and pencil** ready? (B5)

Thus HAVE and GOT function primarily as existentials only in science talk.

Teachers prefer HAVE in an existential reading in science talk, because, I suggest, the use of HAVE opens up the A-slot for the teachers to manipulate in some way, usually to express inclusive language. (When teachers address the full class, WE HAVE predominates, but teachers also use YOU HAVE in this sense, with both the collective and the individual student.) HAVE, as a low-content transitive, is ideal for the dual purpose of presenting a referent, and at the same time manipulating the A slot for any purpose.[5] Much less frequent, but also attested, are the following low-content transitives:

(18) SHOW ex: **the map** on the next page shows <u>that</u> (B78)

(19) FIND ex: <u>we</u> find **a different result** (R90)

(20) SEE ex: <u>we</u> see **the little t** there (N112)

I propose that the frequent use of a few such verbs explains why the number of transitives is so high, even though the nature of the discourse would seem to dictate the prevalence of S-roles (existentials and presentatives). It also helps explain why the frequency and profiles of O and S are so similar.

Information access in the classroom: Staging

If we understand that a primary goal for the teachers is one of facilitating access to science content, then many characteristics of the discourse fall into place. A good example is the repetition of lexical nouns that are not new. This pattern is probably motivated by multiple factors, of which we have seen two: the teacher attempts to make a referent clear to the whole class through lexical repetition, and the teachers assess their students' need to hear challenging material in full form.

In the Preferred Argument Structure literature, it has been verified for many languages that the S and O positions are preferred for new information. However, in these data, while it is true that lexical nouns are most often in S and O positions, we have seen that these nouns are not primarily new. I suggest that the S and O are not only prime positions for new information, but are in fact more generally the positions that are used in "staging" a referent. By "staging" I mean that this position is used to make referents more salient. The use of the term "staging" here is related to Du Bois' (1987) use of the metaphor of Absolutive as "staging area". In the classroom data, the given information that is "on stage" appears as lexical S or O.

Chafe and many other information flow researchers are careful to define given/new as relative to the speaker's assumptions about the hearer, since it is the speaker who is encoding the talk. In lecture mode described here, the teacher encodes for the sake of the wide audience; the information is "staged" for students. Also, they continually monitor and adjust modes of delivery based on perceived reception. All of these considerations undoubtedly contribute to the teachers' tendency to use lexical nouns.

Conclusion

In these data, the teachers' talk is structured to maximize accessibility, hold attention and encourage participation. The teachers stage their referents, including given ones; gain and keep attention, focus on challenging material, and create an inclusionary atmosphere. The result is a type of talk which is loosely packed and redundant, structured around the key terms of the lesson, and reinforced with a variety of visual and auditory supports. These are big generalizations that motivate the shape of the text as a whole, but also reach into the composition of every clause, the form and placement of every NP, the frequency and distribution of every verb. Although the individual teachers have quite distinct styles, in these data they seem to march along similar structural routes to reach their goal of lesson presentation.

In these data, we have once again seen the resilience of Preferred Argument Structure in supplying supporting architecture for the discourse. We cannot underestimate the importance and the apparent universality of these patterns. However, genre constrains the discourse within these broader patterns. To force the architectural metaphor, a building is more than its foundation; there are support systems working throughout. The preferences that emerged here, such as the frequency and distribution of low-content transitives and non-new lexical noun use, also provide discourse architecture, and serve to define the genre.

Notes

* I would like thank Mira Ariel, Bill Ashby, Pat Clancy, Jack Du Bois and Sandy Thompson for valuable perspectives on this analysis. I alone am responsible for any errors in it.

1. The social construction of genre, according to Miller (1984), includes the notions of typification and exigence. Typification means the reifying of a schema or template from recurrent situations, and exigence refers to mutually-construed social motives. Classroom discourse also obviously entails power differentials which typify socially-constructed situations.

2. Du Bois (1987), following guidelines from previous studies, classifies a mention as accessible if it had been mentioned previously, but more than 20 intonation units previously. This seems to be an arbitrary limit, the motivation for which is not obvious to me; fortunately, this reemergence of mention was not characteristic of these data.

3. The male teachers used more regulatory talk than the females: females averaged 82% of talk about science, and males 68%.

4. We are using the terms "attention", "joint attention" and "attention management" in a general sense, and no technical use or cognitive claim is being made. In this we follow the lead of many researchers, e.g. Clancy, this volume.

5. Kumpf (in preparation) analyzes HAVE, GOT and related verbs in similar classrooms, looking at person and number of the A pronouns, and interprets the preference for WE HAVE over THERE BE in terms of the teachers' desire to sound inclusive. THERE BE was rarely used, but tended to be used with new, abstract information, as in "There's a law we'll learn about" (N72).

Appendix

Table A. Patty — Role by activation state

Activation state		Given		Accessible		New		Total	
		N	%	N	%	N	%	N	%
Role	A	34	97	0	0	1	3	35	35
	S	35	78	5	11	5	11	45	46
	O	11	58	7	37	1	5	19	19
total		80	81	12	12	7	7	99	100

Table B. Nancy — Role by activation state

Activation state		Given		Accessible		New		Total	
		N	%	N	%	N	%	N	%
Role	A	56	92	5	8	0	0	61	35
	S	40	59	15	22	13	19	68	39
	O	27	59	11	24	8	17	46	26
total		123	70	31	18	21	12	175	10

Table C. Ron — Role by activation state

Activation state		Given		Accessible		New		Total	
		N	%	N	%	N	%	N	%
Role	A	56	92	4	7	1	2	61	35
	S	42	72	5	42	5	9	52	31
	O	42	74	9	16	6	11	57	34
total		140	82	18	11	12	7	170	100

Table D. Bob — Role by activation state

Activation state		Given		Accessible		New		Total	
		N	%	N	%	N	%	N	%
Role	A	89	97	2	2	1	1	92	45
	S	24	75	7	22	1	3	32	16
	O	55	69	15	19	10	13	80	39
total		168	82	24	12	12	6	204	100

References

Cazden, Courtney. 2001. *Classroom Discourse.* Second edition. Portsmouth, NH: Heinemann.

Chafe, Wallace. 1980. The deployment of consciousness in the production of a narrative, in W. Chafe (ed.), *The Pear Stories: Cognitive, Cultural and Linguistic Aspects of Narrative Production.* Norwood: Ablex Publishing, 9–50.

Chafe, Wallace. 1987. Cognitive constraints on information flow, in R. Tomlin, ed., *Coherence and Grounding in Discourse.* Amsterdam: J. Benjamins, 21–52.

Chafe, Wallace. 1994. *Discourse, Consciousness and Time: The Flow and Displacement of Conscious Experience in Speaking and Writing.* Chicago: University of Chicago Press.

Chaudron, Craig. 1988. *Second language classrooms.* Cambridge: Cambridge University Press.

Clancy, Patricia. 1993. Preferred argument structure in Korean Acquisition, in E. Clark, ed. *The Proceedings of the Twenty-fifth Annual Child Language Research Forum.* Stanford: Center for the Study of Language and Information. 307–314.

Dillon J. T. 1990. *The Practice of Questioning.* New York: Routledge.

Du Bois, John. W. 1987. The discourse basis for ergativity, *Language* 63(4): 805–855.

Du Bois, John. W. and Sandra Thompson. 1991. Dimensions of a theory of information flow. Unpublished ms. University of California, Santa Barbara.

Field, Margaret. 1993. A discourse analysis of small-group cooperative interaction. Masters thesis, University of California, Santa Barbara.

Green, J. L., and J. O. Harker, eds. 1988. *Multiple perspective analyses of classroom discourse.* Norwood, NJ: Ablex.

Heath, Shirley. 1982. Questioning at home and school, in Spindlier, ed. Doing the ethnography of schooling. New York: Holt, Rinehart and Winston.

Heath, Shirley. 1983. Ethnography and education: defining the essentials. In P. Gillmore, and A. Glatthorn, eds. *Children in and out of school: ethnography and education.* Washington, DC: Center for Applied Linguistics.

Kärkkäinen, Elise. 1996. Preferred argument structure and the subject role in American English conversational discourse, *Journal of pragmatics,* 25: 675–701.

Kumpf, Lorraine. 1992. Preferred argument structure in second language discourse. *Studies in language,* 16 (2): 369–403.

Kumpf, Lorraine. in preparation. A profile of HAVE and related verbs in classroom discourse. ms.

Lyster, Roy and Leila Ranta. 1997. Corrective feedback and learner uptake, *Studies in Second Language Acquisition,* 19: 37–66.

Mehan, Hugh. 1983. The structure of classroom events and their consequences for student performance. In P. Gillmore and A. Glatthorn, eds. *Children in and out of school: ethnography and education.* Washington, DC: Center for Applied Linguistics.

Miller, Carolyn R. 1984. Genres as social action. *Quarterly journal of speech,* 70: 151–67.

Ochs, Elinor, Patrick Gonzalez and Sally Jacoby, 1996. "When I come down I'm in the domain state": grammar and graphic representation in the interpretive activity of physicists, in E. Ochs, E. Schegloff and S. Thompson, eds. *Interaction and Grammar.* Cambridge: Cambridge University Press.

O'Dowd, Elizabeth. 1990. "Discourse pressure, genre, and grammatical alignment — after Du Bois", *Studies in language* 14: 365–403.

Phillips, Susan. 1985. Participant structure and communicative competence: Warm Springs children in community and classroom, in C. Cazden, et al, eds. *Functions of language in the classroom.* Prospect Heights, IL: Waveland Press.

Swann, Joan. 1989. Talk control: An illustration from the classroom of problems in analyzing male dominance in conversation, in J. Coates and D. Cameron, eds. *Women in their speech communities.* New York: Longman, 123–140.

Tomlin, Russell and Victor Villa. 1994. Attention in cognitive science and second language classrooms. *Studies in Second Language Acquisition,* 16: 183–203.

Tsui, Amy. 1995. *Introducing classroom interaction.* London: Penguin.

Wallat, Cynthia and Carolyn Piazza, 1988. The classroom and beyond: Issues in the analysis of multiple studies of communicative competence, in J. L. Green and J. O. Harker, eds. *Multiple perspective analyses of classroom discourse.* Norwood, NJ: Ablex.

Issues in the comparative argument structure analysis in Mayan narratives*

Nora C. England and Laura Martin
University of Texas at Austin / Cleveland State University

1. Introduction

Jack Du Bois, (1985, 1987a,b) has developed a set of predictions regarding information flow in discourse and its interaction with the primary noun arguments associated with verb phrases: Transitive Subject or Agent (A), Object (O), and Intransitive Subject (S). Presented as constraints on what Du Bois terms Preferred Argument Structure, these predictions may be stated as follows (from Du Bois 1987b): (1) Avoid more than One Lexical Argument per clause; and (2) Avoid Lexical Agents (A's); (3) Avoid more than One New Argument per clause; and (4) Avoid New Lexical Mentions in A role. Although Du Bois' analysis is based on narrative material from Sakapulteko, an ergative language, he generalizes his results to apply to any language. Thus, he claims, Preferred Argument Structure is not a result of ergative syntax; on the contrary, "the ergative patterning of discourse constitutes the basis…of the grammatical phenomenon of ergativity" (1987b: 806).

England (1988) analyzed the patterns of argument structure in the Mam language in order to discover whether the use of detransitivizing voices (passives and antipassives) contributes significantly to the availability of lexical and new nominals in S function, as part of the strategy of avoiding lexical or new A's. She concluded that they did not. In England (1986) the Mam results were compared with a set from Tektiteko (Teko) and it was found, contrary to expectation, that these two Mamean languages had different distributions: those in Mam appeared to be very like those reported for Sakapulteko, while those for Tektiteko seemed anamolous, especially with regard to the distribution of NP's in Object role. England tentatively concluded that Tektiteko, which otherwise showed no signs of the grammatical decay associated with language death, might indeed show the onset of linguistic decay, characterized by a reduction in grammatical options, in its Preferred Argument Structure.

However, Terrence Kaufman (personal communication) suggested that some of the shifts noted for Tektiteko might instead be attributable to language contact influences from Mocho. Mocho, a member of the Q'anjob'alan branch of the Mayan family, is noted for the fact that it maintains ergative marking only in third person, having shifted to accusative marking for first and second persons. Martin (1987) analyzed Mocho argument structure and concluded, first, that Mocho Preferred Argument Structure is more like Sakapulteko and Mam, whereas Tektiteko is aberrant; and, second, that shifts in the ergative marking pattern in Mocho have not affected its argument structure at any obvious level. England has analyzed additional texts in Tektiteko based on these results, and concludes that in certain respects Mam is in fact more aberrant than Tektiteko in its argument structure patterns.[1]

The data available to us for these analyses are somewhat different from the data that formed the basis of the Sakapulteko analysis, and the differences have provided us with a further reason for proceeding with our investigation. Du Bois' corpus consisted of eighteen "pear stories": narratives that were elicited from a group of Sakapulteko speakers after they had all seen the "pear film", a film designed by Wallace Chafe (1980) to provide a means of eliciting controlled narrative material in any language. Our data, on the other hand, consist of more or less naturally occurring narratives in several genres, primarily including folktales and accounts of personal experiences. (We say "more or less naturally occurring narrative" in that some of the texts were taped in wholly natural situations with native audiences present while others were elicited specifically for recording by the linguist or an assistant.) Because of this difference in data type, we became interested in the ways in which the genre of narrative, especially "pear stories" versus other genres, might have affected our results.

We therefore decided to increase both the Mam and Tektiteko samples of analyzed narrative material (Tektiteko data in particular being very scanty) and to add Q'anjob'al in order to have data from another language in the same branch as Mocho. As a consequence of this extended analysis we conclude that Tektiteko is not as anomalous as England first reported it to be, that both Mocho and Q'anjob'al fit the expected patterns, and that Mam continues to be anomalous in certain distributions. None of the differences in distribution in the four Mayan languages now added to the sample contradict Du Bois' predictions, and we suppose that no additional data from other Mayan languages will do so. However, the process of analyzing Preferred Argument Structure in these languages has raised a number of methodological and analytical problems which, first of all, make it worthwhile to continue to do analyses of this sort, and, second of all, are worth discussing in terms of general issues regarding the analysis of discourse.

Du Bois' analysis involves a careful tabulation of the following categories of information: (1) the percentage of transitive and intransitive clauses found in a text, (2) the percentage of clauses with no, one, or two lexical arguments, (3) the roles of all core argument lexical NP's occurring in one-argument clauses, (4) the roles assigned to all lexical new mentions, and (5) the percentage of each argument position that contains new information.

The Sakapulteko data consist of the eighteen pear stories. The Mam data (Ixtahuacán) are three folktales, one presumed to be of European origin (*Pedro*) and two creation-cycle tales (*Orphan* and *Corn*). The Tektiteko data (Mazapa de Madero) are four folktales, three of which are of European origin (*Princess, Alligator,* and *Rats/Cheese*) and one that may or may not have an indigenous source (*Coyote*). Each of the Mam and Tektiteko texts was narrated by a different person. All of the Tektiteko speakers were bilingual; two of the Mam speakers were bilingual (although much less fluent in Spanish.) The Mocho data (Motozintla) contain two recent personal narratives (*Fire,* cf. Martin 1990, and *Mule*), three non-recent personal narratives or reminisences of childhood events (*Mama, Jar,* and *Snake3,* cf. Martin 1994a), and two folktales, one a creation cycle tale (*Bird*) and the other a fairy tale of European origin (*Orphans,* cf. Martin, this volume). All the Mocho narratives represent a single, 50-year-old male speaker, fully bilingual in local Spanish. The Q'anjob'al data (Santa Eulalia) consist of four narratives: a Pedro-type *chiste* of Spanish origin (*Chewo*), an animal fable collected in written form (*Hat,* cf. Martin 1980), an incident from town history (*Tiltik,* cf. Martin 1980), and an earthowner or *dueño del cerro* tale (*Yaxkalamte*). The *chiste* and the fable were narrated by the same speaker, a young bilingual man in his mid-twenties; the other narratives reflect the speech of two elderly monolingual speakers, a man and a woman. Following Du Bois' categories (1987b), the results in the five Mayan languages under consideration are summarized in Table 1 and Figures 1–4. (Because of rounding, percentages may not add to 100%.)

In spite of several areas of variation among the languages, discussed below in Section 4, all distributions are essentially in agreement regarding (1) the relatively greater use of intransitive clauses, (2) the relatively even distribution of clauses with no or one lexical argument against the extremely low percentage of clauses with two lexical NP's, (3) the low incidence of full NP's in A role, and (4) the tiny percentage of lexical new mentions appearing in A function, whether absolutely or calculated as a percent of possible occurrences.[2] Du Bois' constraints regarding Preferred Argument Structure and its pragmatics are therefore supported by data from other Mayan languages, based on noncontrolled narrative elicitation. (See Hofling, this volume, for a sixth set of data on this point.)

2. Analytical decision making

The analyses we have made do not contribute to a new understanding of argument structure in Mayan languages or universally, except insofar as they confirm Du Bois,

Table 1. Distribution of new lexical mentions, as % of possible direct argument positions

	Sak	Mam	Tek	Mch	Q'an
A	3	4	2	3	2
N=	187	85	187	322	81
S	23	16	9	12	15
N=	258	324	304	510	272
O	25	19	17	18	15
N=	170	85	187	322	81

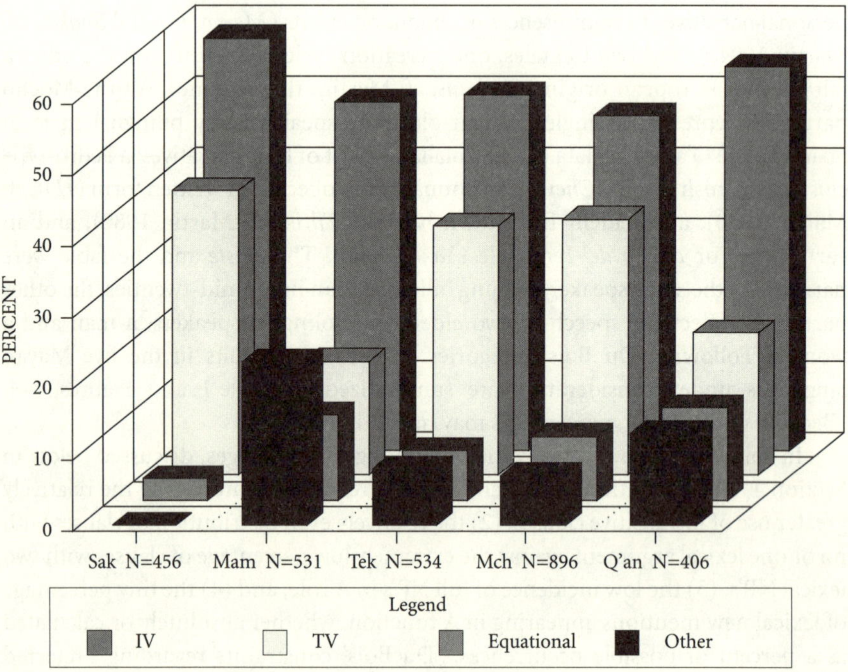

Figure 1. Distribution of clause types, as % of total clauses examined.

discount the possibility that controlled elicitation somehow skewed his data, and discount the possibility that changes in ergativity such as those that Mocho has undergone might affect the overall distributions. However, the decisions that we needed to make in order to count clause and NP types in our less controlled data are of some intrinsic interest in terms of understanding Mayan grammar and discourse. In deciding what was an NP, what role each NP filled, what was a clause,

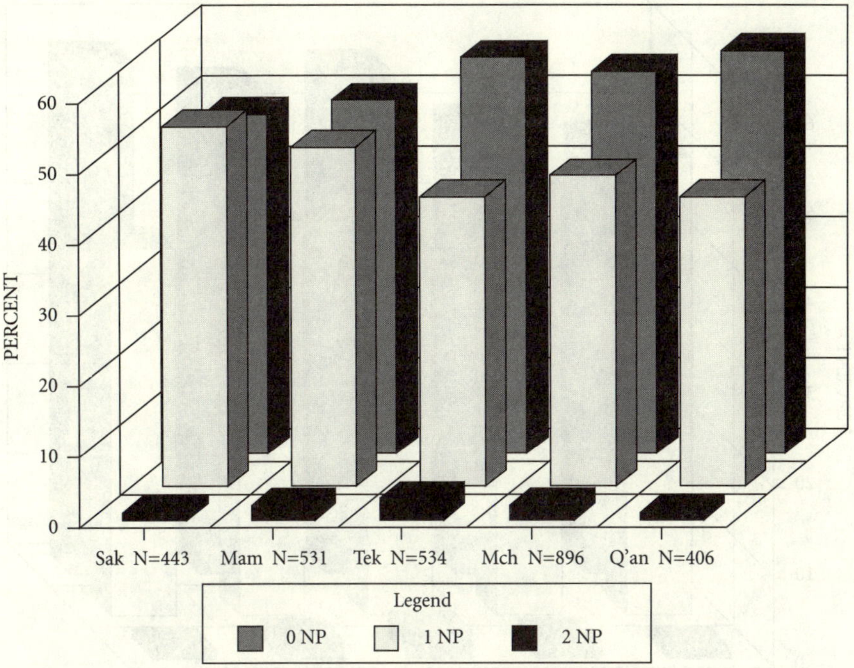

Figure 2. Distribution of clauses with no, one, and two lexical NP arguments, as % of total clauses for which clause type could be determined.

and what type of clause each instance represented, we did not always arrive at the same conclusions as each other or as Du Bois, although mostly we were in agreement. We would like to emphasize at the outset that we believe that these differences affected the percentage outcomes very little. Still, we feel it is valuable to discuss and make explicit those areas in which decisions were not readily apparent to us, because we have found them illuminating, both for their contribution to cross-language grammatical comparisons and for the insight they give us into discourse differences.[3]

2.1 What constitutes a Lexical Mention?

At first glance, determining whether a phrase constitutes a full lexical mention ought to be a simple matter. Upon attempting it, however, we found two related problems. Mayan languages have three ways to mark the core arguments of a verb phrase. First, full NP's with head nouns may occur and be cross-referenced on the verb as A (ergative) or S/O (absolutive). Next, verbal cross-referencing may occur alone. Finally, pronouns of various types may occur in addition to verbal cross-referencing. Our first problem involves the analysis of clauses with first- or second-

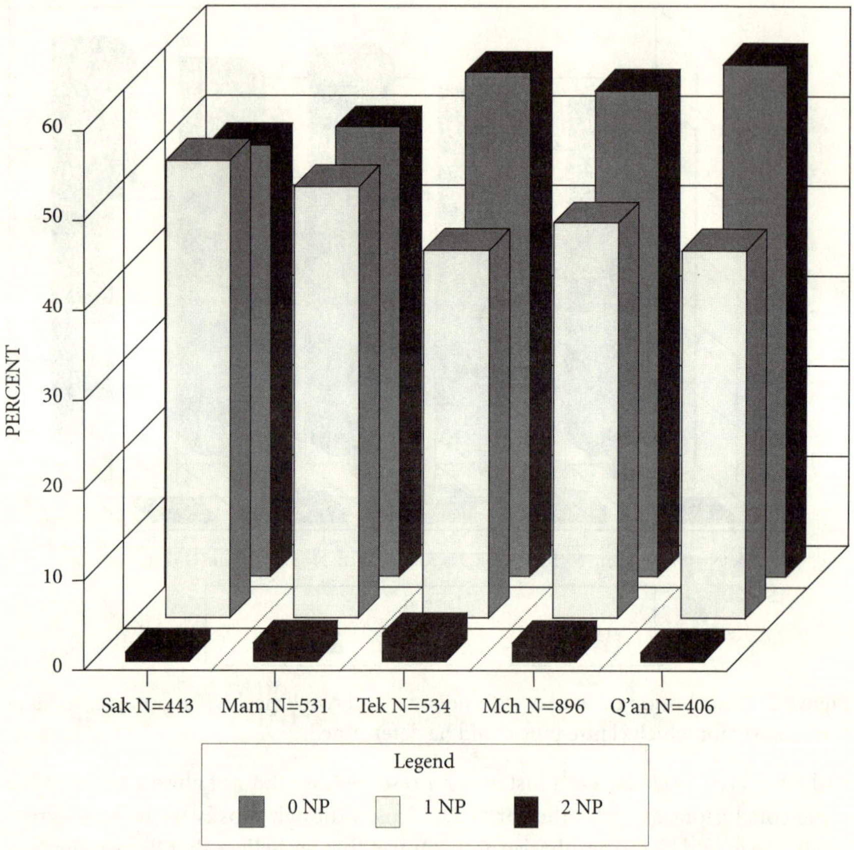

Figure 3. Roles occupied by core argument lexical NP's in clauses with one argument, as % of total one-argument clauses with lexical NP's.

person arguments as opposed to those with third-person arguments. The second problem concerns individual language differences in pronominal types.

Because of the controlled nature of the Sakapulteko narratives, Du Bois' narratives contained neither direct quotes nor any recounting of personal experiences. As a consequence, Du Bois did not have to deal with the fact that first- and second-person arguments occur with some frequency in direct quotation in many types of narratives and in conversation. These arguments do not generally have nouns as their realizations. Du Bois counted both pronouns and verbal affixes as instances of nonlexical reference, which seems a fairly obvious division when third-person arguments are being considered. However, it may be that pronouns for first- or second-person arguments, especially in languages where such pronouns are optional, ought to be considered the equivalent of the full NP representation of an

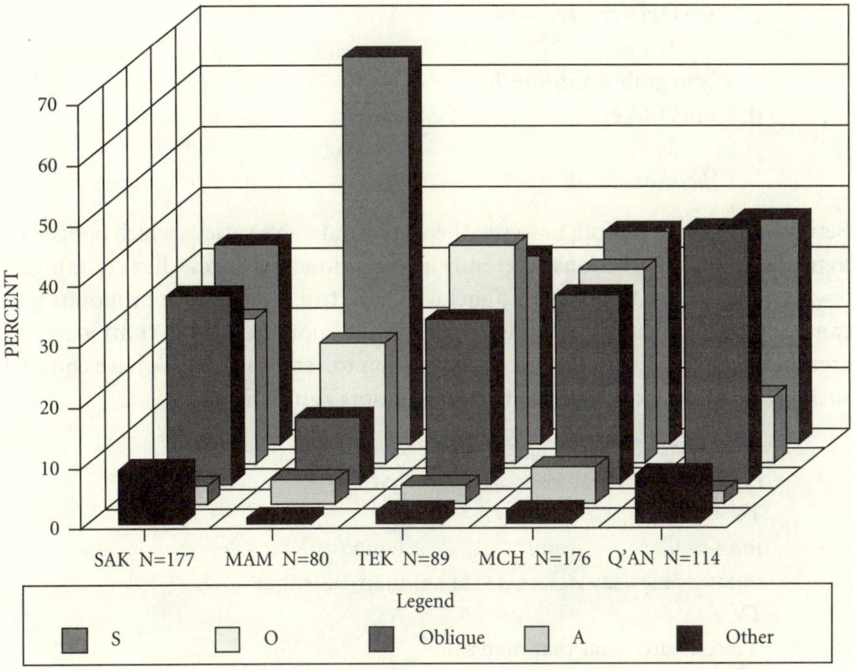

Figure 4. Distribution of new lexical mentions, as % of total new mentions.

argument in third person. Moreover, the presence of direct discourse also introduces the possibility of vocative constructions in which full NP's, namely the vocative, could be construed as arguments. Such vocative NP's appear to function as focused forms (fronted in Mayan languages), fully equivalent to third-person focused NP's. (We deal with both vocatives and direct quotation in more detail in 3.1, below.)

A related problem in deciding whether pronouns are more like affixes or more like nouns has to do with the fact that Mayan languages have different kinds of pronouns. Since all Mayan languages cross-reference direct arguments on verbs, there is no instance in which there is complete zero marking of an argument, except for third-person singular absolutive arguments without lexical or pronomial referents. Consider the Mam examples in (1).

(1) a. *ma* ***chi*** *ku'-tz* ***t****-tzyu-'n-****a***
REC 3P.ABS DIR-DIR 2S.ERG-grab-DS-2S
'***you*** grabbed ***them***'

b. *ma* ***chin*** *b'eet-****a***
REC 1S.ABS walk-1S
'***I*** walked'

c. *ma Øku'-tz t-tzyu-'n-a*
3S.ABS
'you grabbed ***it/him/her***'

d. *ma Ø-b'eet*
3S.ABS
'***he/she*** walked'

Beyond that generalization, however, there is considerable variety, which obliged us to treat similar constructions differently in the various languages when counting. A few languages, like Q'anjob'al or Kaqchikel, have true independent pronouns that can refer nonemphatically (though they may be more frequently contrastive) to arguments in any person and occur in addition to verbal affixes. We have counted such pronouns as lexical mentions. See (2) from Q'anjob'al.

(2) *max-w-ab' k'apax **ayinti** tzet*
COMP-1S.ERG-hear also I what
TV A O
max-y-al cham winaq-tu'
COMPL-3ERG-say NCL:MALE(RESP) man-DEM:that
TV A
'I also heard what that man said.'

Some languages, like Mam, have no true independent pronouns; pronouns may only be used emphatically and then they can be analyzed as functioning as the head of a stative predicate. That is, pronominal words never unemphatically repeat verbal cross-referencing, almost always occur in focus position, and otherwise have characteristics of independent stative clauses (England 1983b: 241, 283–284). Pronouns of this sort have been counted as separate clauses. (3) provides a Mam illustration. There is no unemphatic reading for (3) with *aa qiina*; the only possibility for an unemphatic version would be the structure in (4).

(3) *aa qiin-a xhin juusa-n-a*
STAT 1S.ABS-1S REC.DEP+1S.ABS burn-AP-1S
t-e chib'aj
3S-RN/PAT food
'I burned the food.'

(4) *ma chin juusa-n-a t-e chib'aj*
REC 1S ABS
'I burned the food.'

Certain languages, especially those in the Q'anjob'alan branch (but not Mocho), have noun classifiers with pronominal functions (cf. Craig 1986). We have counted these clitic-like forms as nonlexical mentions. A Q'anjob'al example is given in (5).

See also (2) above for a non-promoninal use of the same noun classifier.

(5) *max-Ø-apn-i* *cham* *b'ay*
COMP-3ABS-arrive-IV NCL:MALE(RESP) PREP:at/in
jun sapatería
one shoestore
'He arrived at the shoe store.'

Finally, many languages, like Mocho, Tektiteko, and Mam, also use the relational noun *-eet* ~ *-eetz* ~ *-ee* pronominally. Usually relational nouns can be clearly analyzed as obliques in Mayan languages. However, the pronominal uses of this particular relational, especially in Mocho, seem more like independent pronouns than like obliques, as shown in (6).

(6) *tzaani k-ii-took'-le'* *ya*
now INCOMP-1S-word-TV because
TV
q-eet-oo' *Ø-q-il-a-oo'*
POSS:1PL-RN-1PLEX COMP-1PL-see-TV-1PLEX
A TV
'Now I will tell (it) because (of how) we saw it.'

Using the model provided by Q'anjob'al independent pronouns, such Mocho forms, in first and second person, were counted as full lexical mentions.

Other problems not addressed by Du Bois also occurred in the determination of lexical mentions, but these seemed to us less serious and we dealt with them more cavalierly: the status of interrogative pronouns (not NP's), compounds (one NP), and NP's linked indivisably with a particular verb as part of an idiomatic phrase, as in the Mocho construction *lo'e' aak'u'uul* 'you're hungry' from '(lit.) your stomach is eaten' (full NP's.)

2.2 What constitutes a new mention?

Du Bois, following Chafe, recognized that there is at least one intermediate category between *new* and *given* information and called that category *accessible.* He classified a mention as accessible if "it was part of a previously evoked entity-based frame…, although previously unmentioned; or if it had been mentioned previously, but more than 20 intonation units previously…" (1987b: 816). Du Bois concluded that accessible information patterned in essentially the same way as given information. We agree and found that for our texts it was quite important to make this intermediate distinction between new and given. Each of our texts includes at least one lexical mention that on its face appears to be new in that it had not been mentioned previously, but in fact is assumed by both narrators and listeners to be part of the narrative context. As Du Bois found, such accessible nouns are not best considered as new mentions, but often special care must be taken in less controlled texts to make proper identification of accessible nouns masquerading as new mentions. Such nouns have several sources.

One source of accessible information that might turn up in recorded texts as apparent new information is the text titles and explanatory material that are sometimes given before a recording session begins. Speakers often suggest recording "the story of X, when so-and-so did Y" and then the taping begins. Although not recorded or transcribed as part of the text, X, Y and so-and-so must be considered as accessible information. That such referents are already given is clearly shown by the fact that they are often introduced into the narrative as definites (see Hofling, this volume, for a pertinent discussion of definiteness and information status.) Obviously it is advisable to note text titles and similar discourse-orienting remarks, but linguists often fail to do so.

Another source of accessible information that superficially appears to be new comes from the cultural context shared by native speakers and hearers. The texts used by Du Bois were specifically elicited to reduce the effects of such cultural associations. Our texts, on the other hand, are rich with them, some more covert than others. Some associations are nearly universally cued. It is obvious to anyone that houses imply entrances; thus doors ought not be considered as new mentions once a house has been presented within the discourse. It may not be quite as obvious that ritual implies incense or that the mention of a particular local figure implies his brother or his wife. In the Mocho narrative *Mama*, for example, the use of the verb for making tortillas at clause nine implicates a series of nouns in later clauses: dough in clause 26, griddle in 29, tortilla in 32, and tortilla container in 35. It is unlikely that for native speakers any of these nouns can properly be considered new mentions. While these implicatures are probably apparent to a Meso-americanist, other sorts of associations are more opaque, because more narrowly relevant, and tracking down the accessibility status of particular mentions can sometimes be a knotty problem if not done on the spot. This difficulty is especially exacerbated when the text involves a traditional tale whose context is known by any normal hearer or if it recounts a personal experience with elements that are partly shared with normal hearers, e.g., kin relations or property ownership. In general, linguists are simply not normal hearers, and successful interpretation of "newness" in lexical mentions is an analytical problem much impinged upon by this fact.[4]

Other problems in the proper treatment of new lexical mentions concern a category we call "ephemeral" mentions: NP's that are not strongly motivated by the narrative line itself, appearing and disappearing rapidly and providing little more than a bit of context or enrichment to the narrative. Such NP's typically are not tracked through a narrative, are not instrumental in any of the action, and may not be mentioned in a second recounting. We have used the following measure for categorizing ephemeral mentions: Any noun referent that receives fewer than three full lexical mentions per 100 clauses is ephemeral. This diagnostic is based in part on Martin's unpublished work on redundancy analysis in texts in non-Mayan languages. It obviously requires confirmation and refinement, but we have found that it successfully distinguishes the clearly important NP's within our narratives. (It removes all of the tortilla-related nouns from consideration in the *Mama* narrative, for example.) However they are eventually defined, we believe ephemeral NP's should be separated from others in examining new mentions. Doing so can reveal potentially interesting patterns in the relationship between the grammatical and discourse roles for particular lexical mentions. For example, discourse promotion processes may cause an ephemeral NP, first introduced into the narrative as an oblique, to become a participant later in the narrative. It may then be reintroduced, after several clauses of absence, in S role.

A final source of spurious, or at least controversial, new mentions derives from the exigencies of Mayan rhetorical style. Speakers of Mayan languages, as Mayan linguists know and speakers themselves recognize, are very prone to the use of repetition and semantic parallelism (cf. Du Bois, this volume, Brody 1986, 1994). One prominent feature of Mayan narrative style is the frequent use of rhetorical synonymy in successive mentions of a participant. In the Mocho *Bird* narrative, a practiced folktale, many such paired synonyms occur as couplets, as in (7).

(7) *heeni mére Ø-k'uul-a-hi we'*
when just 3ABS-made-TV-PAS DEF
mundo we' q'ach
world DEF earth
'The world, the earth had just been made.'

In a more complex example from *Fire*, the narrator reports as direct discourse the prayer of his wife to her deceased father-in-law in which she first names *wichmaal* 'my husband', then immediately *aak'aahool* 'your son'. The referent is, of course, also the narrator, present in the narrative as its main protagonist since the first clause (6), where he is introduced solely through verbal cross-reference prefixes.

We are inclined to treat referents of this sort as given rather than as new mentions, but we note that on occasion an originally synonymous mention can figure as an independent character at a later time in a text, as when *chantiil* 'wife' refers to both the first and second wives of the father in the Mocho fairy tale *Orphans*.

Moreover, there are cases where apparently synonymous reference actually serves to mark significant changes in a participant's nature. Such a strategy is the case in *Orphans* when the children are introduced as *xk'aahol — huune' iti xiip la huune' ixoq* 'his children — a little boy and a female'. They are referred to almost immediately and throughout the opening episodes also as *ch'in* 'children'. The NP's *xiip* and *ixoq* are counted as new mentions because, in spite of their synonymity, they add important information about the characters; *ch'in*, on the other hand, is counted as old information. Once the children grow up, their new maturity is signaled by *la ooki keremo' la ooki muqulo' we' ch'in kee* 'and the children became a young man and became a young woman'. Here the NP's *kerem* 'young man' and *muqul* 'young woman' are counted as new information. Throughout, by the narrator and in their reported dialogues, the characters are also called *tuun* 'brother' and *nu'ul* 'sister'. We counted these references as old information, synonymous with *k'aahool*. Finally, in the last episode, the father again appears and refers to them as *niñito*, counted again as old information (Martin, this volume).

2.3 What constitutes a clause?

There are several clause types that provide analytical problems because they limit the number of possible associated NP's. In general we suggest that if a clause type does not permit the usual arguments (S for intransitives and A and O for transitives), then it should be counted separately from other clauses, that is, placed in its own category.

Reflexives provide a case in point. Clauses with reflexive verbs cannot have independent lexical A's and O's, so a lexical argument in a reflexive clause must be counted either as a lexical A *and* O, or, somewhat arbitrarily, as just an A. Separating reflexives from other transitives avoids this problem.

Various types of complex clauses also limit arguments. The main verb, whether intransitive or transitive, can usually have lexical realizations of any argument, though there is language-specific variation on this point. For example, if the main verb is 'want', it may take an infinitival complement in some Mayan languages, such as Jakaltek (Craig 1977:315).

(8) *Ø-qan* *ha-k'ul* [*sajchoj*]
3S.ABS-3S.ERG-want 2S-stomach play-INF
'you want [to play]'

In Mam, however, 'want' never takes an infinitival complement, but instead a finite complement with full person marking, as in (9).

(9) *Ø-w-ajb'el-a* [*chin waa'-n-a*]
3S.ABS-1S.ERG-want-1S 1S.ABS eat-AP-1S
'I want [to eat]'
**Ø-w-ajb'el-a* [*waa'-l*]
-INF

Clauses with embedded infinitives do not permit core A's or S's of the infinitive verb, and may restrict core O's as well. In Mam, an infinitive by definition cannot have a direct A or S. It can have a core O, but often does not. Whether the O is core or not depends on the informational status and the contrastiveness of the O. For instance, the first sentence below places the O in an oblique phrase, where it is necessarily old information and contrastive. The second sentence has a core O, which need not be old information and is not contrastive.

(10) a. *n-chi* *ku' teen xjaal* [*belaara-l*
PROG-3P.ABS DIR be person watch-INF
t-e *jun weech*]
3S.RN/PAT one fox
'The people began [to watch the fox].'
b. *n-chi ku' teen xjaal* [*belaara-l jun weech*]
'The people began [to watch the fox].'

To resolve these conflicts in our analysis, we counted clauses with embedded infinitives as one clause, rather than two, effectively eliminating the complement verb from our counts, but we counted the O, if lexical, as either a core lexical argument or an oblique, whichever it was. Thus we sometimes counted an argument without counting its verb. We usually counted other types of complements as separate clauses, since by and large they do not restrict the types of arguments that can occur in them. We suggest that any complement that is found to restrict argument types be counted as part of the main clause, or else considered separately.

Directionals in Mayan languages present other complexities for clause identification. Generally, directionals are derived from intransitive verbs of motion and usually function in verb phrases as auxiliary verbs. They may take at least part of the verbal inflection, although there is considerable cross-language variation on this point (Zavala 1993). However, a directional verb should not necessarily be counted as an independent verb and therefore a separate clause. Consider these two cases from Mocho, which has an especially rich system of directional verbs, directional auxiliaries, and directional complements (Martin 1994b). Note that in this pair of examples, the main verb root (*onh* 'go [incomp]') of (11) appears as the directional particle *noonh* in (12) while the particle base (*ik'* 'pass by') of (11) is the main verb root in (12).

(11) *ni k-ii-'onh* *mah-oon* *chik'i*
YA INCOMP-1S-go look.for-AP DIR:around
IV(DIR) DIR COMPL
paloom te' *ti montánya*
dove here in mountain
DIR COMPL
'I'm going to go hunt doves here in the mountains.'

(12) *k-ii-'ik'-i* *noonh* *we' beha'*
INCOMP-1s-passby-IV DIR:away DEF canyon
IV(DIR) DIR COMPL
'I passed through the canyon.'

2.4 Direct quotation

The absence of direct quotation in Du Bois' narratives is most unusual, since apparently all other Mayan discourse genres potentially include direct quotation and frequently include a great deal of it (Martin 1992). Because all our narratives do include direct quotation, deciding how such passages might affect the analysis was something we, unlike Du Bois, needed to face. Three issues arose in relation to our analysis of directly quoted discourse. One is the issue of whether pronominal reference in first and second person should be considered equivalent to lexical reference in third person, discussed above in 2.1. The second issue concerns the counting of quote verbs themselves. Mayan languages have a number of different quotative verbs, some transitive and some intransitive, as in Mam.

Three Mam quotatives are illustrated in (13); the first is intransitive, the second is a passive formed from a transitive root, and the third is transitive.

(13) *xb'u'q-Ø* *per chib'aj n-Ø-b'ant*
rag-3s.ABS but meat PROG-3s.ABS-make
w-u'n-a *nyaa' ti-i'-la*
1s-RN/AGT-1s NEG what-EMPH-doubt
tqal-ta ***Ø-chi-tzan*** ***Ø-q'uun-j***
what-EMPH 3s.ABS-say:IV-well 3s.ABS-say:TV-PAS
t-e *meeb'a kyja'-w*
3s-RN orphan like this-?
Ø-Ø-ok ***t-ma-'n***
PAST.DEP-3s.ABS-DIR 3s.ERG-say:TV-DS
'"It's a rag, but I'll make it into meat, nothing else", **it is said he said,** thus the orphan **said it**.'

Mocho has an elaborate system of verbs that refer to speech, including quoted speech, but only some of them are true quotatives; the others are best handled as regular transitives (Martin 1990). Transitive quote verbs are usually used without a specific object other than the quote itself. Because the types of object are severely limited in these clauses, and in fact the S or A is also rather restricted compared to other verbs, we counted all quotative clauses separately from other types of clauses. This decision contributes in part to the large number of clauses assigned to the category Other in Figure 1, when compared to Du Bois' figures.

A third issue is the appropriate treatment for the vocatives and personal names that occur frequently in quoted material. A typical example is found in the Mocho narrative *Jar* where the principal protagonist is identified with the following sequence of unique names: "my uncle Yawo-Yawo we call him but Santiago is his real name. 'Come with us, Yawut,' said my father." One possible solution is to treat such nouns like any other appositive material and count them as nonarguments. Another possibility, however, is to treat vocatives as full lexical representations, at least in second person. We favor the latter solution, especially because of the parallelism we see between independent pronouns and vocatives that provide lexical reference for verbal cross-reference markers. Imperatives, as reflected in the Yawut clause described above, are a common environment for such double marking, as when the linguist herself is first introduced into the *Fire* narrative as a vocative agent in (14).

(14) *doña Láwra doña Láwra*
title name title name
VOC VOC (=A)
muuq-u'-Ø *we' q'ak*
look-TV-IMP DEF fire
TV (marked for A cross-reference) O
'Doña Laura, doña Laura, look at the fire!'

Vocatives, however, are also found with many non-imperatives, as in (15) again from *Jar.*

(15) *kuñada* *k-ii-kolt-a-qaa* *noonh*
sister-in-law INCOMP-1S-help-TV-2S.A DIR:away
VOC (=O) TV (marked for O cross-reference)
'Sister, I'm going to help you.'[5]

It is worth pointing out that quoted discourse also presents an extremely hospitable environment for the introduction of the synonymous NP's discussed in 2.2.

2.5 Language particular differences

Mayan languages have specific points of grammatical difference that can affect the comparative analysis of Preferred Argument Structure or, for that matter, any other gross grammatical or discourse characteristic (cf. England 1983a). Examples already addressed are the differences in the structure and syntax of pronouns in different languages and consequent difficulties in making decisions as to what constitutes a lexical mention. Other examples also provoked our interest.

One concerns clause type definition. In his analysis of clause types, Du Bois lists a low 3% in his category Equational. England, in her first analysis of the Mam material, reported a high 23%. However, fully 11% of that figure come from Mam locative/existential predicates formed on the base *at* 'exist'. These are equivalent to the Sakapulteko *k'o* predicates, which Du Bois counts as intransitives. Further, while Mam of Ixtahuacán divides equationals into two types of verbless predicates, statives and locative/existentials (as do Mocho and Q'anjob'al), other Mam dialects divide them up a little differently, always recognizing two categories (England 1990). We suggest reporting statives, locatives, and existentials separately, in whatever categories reflect the language-particular grammar. Gross counts of NP's in S function can lump these, although it is useful to indicate as well the subcategories of intransitive S, stative S, locative S, and existential S. Such detail can provide clues to interesting language-specific variation such as the contrast between Mocho detransitivized nominalizations (16) and Mam intransitives with relational noun "agents" (17).

(16) *péro heel ik'-obaal hu'm aaw-u'uuh-e'*
but if bring-NOM/RESULT paper 2S-RN/AGT-PL
'But (only) if you bring your papers' (lit. 'But (only) if brought papers by you-all')

(17) *ma Ø-jaw w-u'n-a*
ASP 3S.A-go up 1S-RN/AGT-1S
'I lifted it.' (lit. 'It went up by me.')

A second case of language-specific features that can enter into the analysis involve the basic arguments themselves. Because of the nature of Sakapulteko grammar, Du Bois was able to define two-argument clauses as strictly transitive with full agent and object NP's. Q'anjob'alan languages, however, permit two direct NP's to appear in certain formally intransitive constructions, especially those created by the antipassive or agentive focus voices (for examples, see Maxwell 1976, Zavala 1992). Neither of the NP's is marked as being in an oblique relation. Both Q'anjob'al and Mocho permit new mentions to appear as the patient in such constructions, which may, depending on the language and the specific structure, be either the S or a stranded O. There is some evidence that such mentions may only be possible for ephemeral NP's. Such a case in Mocho is illustrated in (11) above: *paloom* 'dove' is a stranded O for the antipassive verb *mahoon* 'look for'. Q'anjob'al seems to exploit constructions of this type more frequently than does Mocho, a difference that appears to apply to the use of antipassive generally. At some point, whether for examining more profoundly the subtle individual language differences that exist synchronically in argument structure patterns or for investigating the historical development of those differences, information of this sort will become crucial. Thus it seems to us that any such grammar-specific peculiarities should be fully represented in linguists' reports.

2.6 Unanalyzable residue

Inevitably, even with the most careful consideration of linguistic categories beforehand, there are always some grammatical constructions that are unanalyzable or uncategorizable. We will not pretend that it was any different for us. On occasion we simply could not tell if some construction was a verb or not, and therefore could not analyze the clause type. On other occasions we could not decide how to analyze a complex clause — as one clause or two. Some of these difficulties reflect the fact that, at the time of the analysis, some languages in the sample had been more thoroughly analyzed than others. Finally, some clauses in our narratives do not contain predicates at all. Predicateless clauses are often found in extended passages of direct quotation where conversational responses such as "Yes", "Already", and "Ah, thus!" are commonplace. These, at least, may be discardable as non-clause intonation units.

All these intractable cases were relegated to the Other category for purposes of clause type analysis and then omitted from the further counts altogether. Of course, the subcategories of Can't tell, Don't know, and Not relevant differ from one another and ought perhaps to be distinguished. Fortunately, these problems are few and have no bearing so far as we can tell on the overall picture of Preferred Argument Structure in any of our languages. If such analysis were eventually applied to even less controlled data than ours, such as conversational material, it might be expected that many more of these unanalyzable cases would surface.

3. A revised analysis

The lumping of categories, such as Du Bois established for Sakapulteko and we have followed in Table 1 and Figures 1–4, is sufficient for the basic analysis of Preferred Argument Structure. However, other questions, such as the one that England originally set out to answer regarding the contribution of voice changes to the availability of S NP's in Mam discourse, require finer distinctions. In a discussion of these issues at the 1987 Cleveland Conference on Mayan Text and Discourse, several suggestions for more detailed subcategorizations emerged. Du Bois, for example, asserted the need to reexamine information structure within the context of finer distinctions of transitivity (cf. Hopper and Thompson 1980). Terrence Kaufman summarized some of the discussion by preparing a list of categories worth distinguishing. We present that list here, with some modifications of our own.

NP categories:	Predicate categories:
Direct:	TV
A	Reflexive
S:	IV:
S IV	IV
S Passive	Passive
S Antipassive	Antipassive
O	Agentive/Focus
S Equational:	Equative
S Stative	Stative (noun/adjective)
S Locative/Existential	Locative/Existential
Not Direct:	Quotative
Oblique NP	Other
Stranded NP	
Indirect Object (if different from Oblique NP)	
Vocative	

In Tables 2–6, we give our revised analyses for Mam, Tektiteko, Mocho, and Q'anjob'al, using these new categories, where data are complete. Zero means No instance; blank means Not distinguished.

Table 2. Distribution of clause types, as % of total clauses examined

	Sak	Mam	Tek	Mch	Q'an
IV	58	38	45	47	54
IV		25	37	39	38
Passive		7	4	5	4
Antipassive		6	4	3	12
Equational	3	23	12	9	13
Stative		12	7	8	
Loc/Exist		11	5	1	
TV	40	16	35	36	20
TV		16	34		
Reflexive		< 1	1		
Quotative		12	3	5	5
Other	0	23	8	2	9
N=	456	531	534	896	405

Table 3. Distribution of clauses with one and two lexical NP arguments, as % of total clauses examined (no change from Figure 2)

	Sak	Mam	Tek	Mch	Q'an
0 NP	48	50	56	54	57
1 NP	51	48	41	44	41
2 NP	1	2	3	2	1
N=	443	531	534	874	368

Table 4. Roles occupied by core argument lexical NP's in clauses with one lexical argument, as % of total one-argument clauses with lexical NP's

	Sak	Mam	Tek	Mch	Q'an
S	58	89	56	58	74
S IV		44	34	26	
S Passive		6	3	6	
S Antipass		4	1	5	
S Equational		35	23	21	
S Stative		17	12	18	
S Loc/Exit		18	11	3	
O	37	6	32	35	21
A	5	6	11	6	4
N=	218	25	219	387	152

Table 5. Distribution of new lexical mentions, as % of total new mentions

	Sak	Mam	Tek	Mch	Q'an
A	3	4	3	6	2
S	33	64	31	36	36
S IV		23	8	14	
S Passive		6	1	3	
S Antipass		6	4	4	
S Equational		29	18	15	
S Stative		14	7	13	
S Loc/Exist		15	11	2	
O	24	20	36	26	11
Oblique NP	31	11	27	32	41
Stranded NP				2	4
Other	9	1	2	0	7
N=	177	80	89	176	118

Table 6. Distribution of new lexical mentions according to narrative importance, as % of total new lexical mentions in each role

	Mam	Tek	Mch	Q'an
A				
New	33	100	50	0
Ephemeral	67	0	50	100
N=	3	3	8	2
S				
New	31	46	31	24
Ephemeral	69	54	69	76
N=	51	28	62	42
O				
New	56	16	27	15
Ephemeral	44	84	73	85
N=	16	32	45	13
Oblique				
New	33	36	14	15
Ephemeral	67	84	86	85
N=	9	24	57	48
Other				
New	0	100		38
Ephemeral	100	0		62
N=	1	2		13
Total				
New	36	36	24	22
Ephemeral	64	64	76	88
N=	80	89	176	118

4. Variation

Beyond the consideration of overall Mayan argument structure revealed by the global analysis of more than 2300 clauses in four languages and the individual language peculiarities we discovered along the way, we also became interested in the amount and kinds of variation found across individual texts. We believe this variation also has implications for the study of argument structure specifically and discourse analysis more generally. At least three types of variation are of interest and are illustrated in our data: variation in genre, variation among speakers, and variation among topics by the same speaker.

Du Bois made several detailed predictions (1987b: 834–836) about the likely variation to be found in genres other than pear stories, and our study presents some opportunity to test these specific predictions. Overall, there is much less variation by genre than might have been expected. In discussing the relationship of genre to Preferred Argument Structure, Du Bois introduces the concept of "information pressure", which can be defined briefly as the ratio of new humans to clauses. The pear stories are very high in information pressure while conversation would generally be very low. Most of our materials seem to be intermediate on a scale of high to low information pressure. The Mocho materials in particular tend toward the relatively low end since their content was known by the narrator to be familiar to the linguist, either because they had previously been recounted in Mocho or in Spanish or because she was a participant in the reported events.

Du Bois predicts, for example, that narrative with lower information pressure could be expected to have more Zero NP clauses than the Sakapulteko pear stories. As seen in Figure 2, this prediction holds throughout our corpus, though the differences are slight: 48% in Sakapulteko vs. an average of 54% across Mam, Tektiteko, Mocho and Q'anjob'al. Du Bois has also suggested that differences in the distribution of clause types and arguments may also correlate with information pressure and, therefore, with genre. At a gross level, we found few differences across genres and Martin (1987) has shown that, in Mocho at least, practice through repeated recountings has no effect whatever on overall patterns of argument and clause distribution. We believe that genre may exert some subtle effects on the occurrence of particular clause subtypes, e.g., statives, antipassives or passives. We note that in Mocho, for example, statives seem to have a much higher incidence in folktales than in personal narratives of any type. The lack of available comparable information on Sakapulteko and Mamean genre variation makes further interpretation on this point difficult; however, Hofling (this volume) makes some related points.

It seems to us, then, that Du Bois' predictions about genre variation are generally confirmed in our data, but we want to suggest that the concept of information pressure will need refinement for appropriate application to genres with few human participants. Our work with ephemeral vs. important NP's suggests that it might be profitably defined as having to do with familiarity of content, whether through previous tellings, cultural assumptions, or the speaker or listener's personal involvement in the reported events.

Variation by speaker is not unexpected, since speakers differ both in individual style and in proficiency with particular genres. For instance, the text-by-text breakdown for Tektiteko shows considerable variation among different speakers telling different stories. Thus, the total percentage of intransitive clauses in *Princess* is almost double that of *Alligator* (59% vs. 32%). Two texts (*Coyote* and *Rats/ Cheese*) have no introductions of lexical new mentions in S role while in the other two texts S role accounts for about 14% of the total new mentions. Du Bois reports (personal communication) that he found a fair amount of variation among different speakers telling the same story in his pear corpus.

The greatest degree of variation in our materials is conditioned by narrative topic. The Mocho texts, which include narratives with great variety in topics but controlled for speaker, illustrate this strikingly. In individual Mocho narratives, the exigencies of topic can cause considerable skewing in the distribution of clause types and of lexical roles as well as in the distributions of roles utilized for new mentions. For example, *Fire* has a very high rate of intransitive clauses (60% of all clauses) when compared to *Mule*, another recent personal narrative. This distribution can be accounted for on the basis of topic. *Fire* involves few important inanimate objects and incorporates many references to motion, requiring many more intransitive verbs than counterpart personal experience narratives such as *Mule* and *Snake3*. By contrast, *Jar* and *Orphans*, representing quite different genre types (personal narrative vs. well-practiced folktale), share greater clause-type distributional similarities with each other (54% and 50% IV clauses respectively) than with their respective genre partners *Jar* and *Bird*. This degree of text-specific variation is a potential factor in the accurate evaluation of Preferred Argument Structure and other discourse investigations and emphasizes the need not only for large data sets but for diverse ones.[6]

5. Conclusions

5.1 Mam oddities

Because we originally undertook this detailed analysis in order to resolve questions raised by the appearance of aberrance in the data used for earlier work, it is worth summarizing here our conclusions about these oddities. Mam has the most unusual distributions of the Mayan languages reported here. In particular, Mam shows a low 16% of transitive clauses (as % of total clauses examined) and a high 89% of direct argument lexical NP's in S role in one-argument clauses (Tables 2 and 4). Mam also has a high distribution of equational clauses (23%, Table 2) and a similarly high use of equational S roles for lexical NP's in one-argument clauses (35%, Table 4), contributing to the high 89% of S role NP's overall.

When compared on these points, Sakapulteko, Tektiteko, and Mocho are quite consistent. Q'anjob'al is the only other language that approaches Mam distributions, although it does not have equally high or low figures. It must be emphasized that the somewhat unusual Mam distributions do not affect any of the information flow constraints proposed by Du Bois. Mam, like all languages sampled thus far, has very few clauses with two lexical arguments (2%, Table 3) and very few lexical A's (Tables 4 and 5). Nevertheless, the obvious peculiarities of the Mam figures beg for explanation.

The high proportion of equational clauses and the consequent high percentage of lexical S's might be thought to be an artifact of some aspect of Mamean grammar. In particular, Mam locative/existentials are counted as equationals (cf. Section 2.5) and focused NP's are analyzable as statives (England 1983b: 241), and these analyses might be expected to elevate the equational distributions. However, the analysis of Tektiteko in these regards is identical, but Tektiteko does not have equally high equational counts. Therefore, either Mam is not as out of line with regard to equationals as it seems to be — but then Tektiteko must be unusually low — or Mam is unusually high, and this pattern is not simply due to the facts of Mamean grammar.

There is a possible language-specific explantion for the low incidence of transitive clauses in Mam. Mam is the only Mayan language that has an incomplete set of person prefixes, either absolutive or ergative, in which second-person markers have disappeared and third-person markers have taken on both functions. A seven-way person system is completed with an additional set of person enclitics, but because only one person enclitic is possible on a verb, there can be ambiguity in A and O person/number specification on transitive verbs (England 1983b: 60ff). It seems reasonable to suppose that on occasion transitive verbs are avoided in order to reduce or eliminate such ambiguity. However, this explanation is not very persuasive because it should entail an increased use of antipassive and/or passive constructions as the most easily available detransitivizing mechanisms, and Mam figures for these clauses types are not especially high (Table 2).

England has claimed (1983a) that Mam is a strongly ergative language. A consideration of whether strong ergativity might have affected the distributions has led us, somewhat reluctantly, to the conclusion that such an explanation has little validity. If Mam showed even stronger Preferred Argument Structure Constraints than the other languages, this hypothesis would be more tenable but there is no evidence that Mam does so.

We do not, then, find a grammatical explanation for the Mam distributions. It occurs to us that the fact that Q'anjob'al approaches Mam distributions in certain regards could be due, at least in part, to the effect of the so-called "Huehuetenango sphere of influence", but we can offer no specific explanation of how such influence might work. We also wonder whether there is any sociolinguistic bias. Q'anjob'al and Mam are certainly the largest and most viable of the five Mayan languages that have been sampled. However, without much more research on the possible effects of language viability on discourse structure, we confess that such speculations are premature. We are open to further suggestions for a more refined discourse analysis that might clarify this and other potentially useful explanatory hypotheses.

5.2 Tektiteko oddities

Tektiteko figures are not odd when compared with Mocho or Sakapulteko. The original hypothesis of oddity as a possible consequence of language death processes affecting Tektiteko was made by England in 1986 based on counts of only two texts, *Coyote* and *Rats/Cheese*. These two texts include no use of S function nouns for lexical new mentions. England therefore wondered whether the constraint against new A's might have been extended to S function nouns. However, the two additional Tektiteko texts do not maintain this distribution pattern and the notion must be abandoned. We conclude that the two original texts merely exhibit coincidental text-specific distributional peculiarities, like those found in the Mocho data set. Tektiteko does show more divergence by text, (i.e. speaker), than does Mam, but the averages over four texts in Tektiteko are not at all peculiar.

5.3 Mocho oddities

It will be recalled that the original motivation for the work reported by Martin in 1987 was the suggestion that a shift from ergative to accusative marking in first and second person in Mocho might have encouraged the increased use of transitives and thus of nouns in A or O roles. A comparison of Mocho to Q'anjob'al, its nearest relative in the sample, does reveal that Mocho has a greater proportion of transitive clauses (36% vs. 20%, Table 2), more lexical mentions in O role (35% vs. 21%, Table 4), and more new mentions in A (6% vs. 2%) and O (26% vs. 11%, both Figure 4) than does Q'anjob'al. However, these Mocho figures are very close to those reported for Tektiteko and Sakapulteko, suggesting that the person system shifts in Mocho have had little effect on overall argument structure. Of course, Du Bois has reported (1987b) that Preferred Argument Structure Constraints apply across many language families, including many that are strongly accusative. It is no surprise to us then to find that Mocho obeys normal preferred argument patterns. Certain subtle differences within the Q'anjob'alan group, namely the apparently greater dependence on antipassive constructions in Q'anjob'al, hint at the usefulness of further comparisons between Mocho and the other languages of the group since those differences may in fact be related to the person system shifts in Mocho.

5.4 Summary

In sum, then, we conclude that Du Bois' analysis is fully predictive throughout the Mayan family. Certain definitions and categories must be modified in order to accommodate the differences between controlled narratives such as pear stories and the more usually collected narrative materials that linguists might want to use in applying the analysis. We also believe that it is important, as reports on this and similar topics proliferate, to specify the nature of any language-specific decisions related to assignment of structures to the categories. We doubt that any real revision of the Du Bois analysis is likely. Even so, the detailed examination of syntax and discourse that the process of doing the analysis forces upon an investigator is extremely useful in uncovering subtle aspects of grammatical structure and in stimulating new research questions in language comparison and discourse organization. We believe everyone should have the experience at least once.

Notes

* The authors wish to thank those agencies, institutions, and individuals who have contributed to the work reflected in this paper. Most of England's work on Mam, including text collection and analysis, was done, beginning in 1972, with the help of Juan Maldonado Andrés, Juan Ordoñez Domingo, and Juan Ortíz Domingo, to whom she is deeply grateful for their invaluable assistance. All the Mam research was done at the Proyecto Lingüístico Francisco Marroquín and would not have been possible without the generous support of Narciso Cojtí Macario (Director 1975–87), Martín Chacach Cutzal (Director 1987–90), and Francisco Pérez Mendoza (Director of Linguistics 1987–90). Her work was also supported during the summers of 1978, 79, and 80 by a University of Iowa summer research fellowship. The Tektiteko material was collected in 1984 with the support of a University of Iowa Faculty Scholarship. Many thanks to Herculano García Hernández and Enrique Martínez Bravo for recording or collecting the Tektiteko texts and helping with the analysis. Martin's Q'anjob'al texts were narrated or collected by Diego de Diego Antonio and Francisco Pascual in 1973 with the support of the Proyecto Lingüístico Francisco Marroquín. The larger Mocho corpus includes generous donations of data by Terrence S. Kaufman. The texts specifically considered here were collected by Martin during a 1986 field stay made possible by a Fulbright-Hayes Faculty Research Abroad fellowship. The affectionate hospitality and patient assistance extended during that time by don Juan Méndez Matías and his family are well remembered and deeply appreciated. All the Q'anjob'al and Mocho field research used here has received the support of various units of Cleveland State University: the College of Graduate Studies; the College of Arts and Sciences, especially the Office of the Dean; and the Departments of Anthropology and Modern Languages. Martin also thanks Nadine Grimm and Susan Shelangoskie for invaluable assistance at the eleventh hour.

1. This paper results from the lengthy conversations we enjoyed during the period of Martin's 1987 analysis of Mocho. At Martin's request, England counted additional Mamean materials for comparison, and at England's suggestion, we agreed to collaborate on an account of our experiences with the analyses. We prepared a detailed outline at the Cleveland Conference on Mayan Text and Discourse (October 1987). England wrote a first draft, Martin expanded it greatly, and, since then, drafts have been exchanged until we have each been satisfied. Thus the order of authorship reflects the unmarked case for a jointly written paper, that is, alphabetized.

2. The results reported in Table 1 are theoretically interesting in that speakers may be assumed to have all slots (e.g., A and O) equally available in an "all things equal" universe. They are less interesting when we consider that it was already clear that speakers do not treat A's like O's or S's. The "percentage of available slots" calculation is worth doing once in order to demonstrate that the "Avoid Lexical A's" Constraint is not a calculation artifact; however, having contrived such a calculation scheme, linguists must avoid being seduced into believing that they have learned something new by repeating it. It merely confirms patterns whose validity is already apparent.

3. Herring (1989), using data from Tamil, has suggested that Du Bois' methodology is flawed. In particular, with regard to the specific analysis of new mentions, she identifies non-arguments (Obliques and Verbless presentation) as the more important locus for introduction of new information. Since our attention has been directed at the details of decision-making and language variation in applications of Du Bois' analysis to ordinary narrative and not to the issue of new mentions specifically, we cannot address her findings in detail. We note, however, that in our sample there are rather wide variations by language on the importance of Obliques as a site for new mentions (see Figure 4). Moreover, in no case can the excluded Other category, which includes Verbless presentation, be shown to have an important function in the introduction of new NP's in our texts.

4. Accessible nouns are even more frequent in conversation than in single-speaker narratives; at least the work done so far on Mocho conversations suggests as much. Certainly, one area to which preferred argument structure analysis might be profitably extended is multi-speaker discourse.

5. Du Bois (personal communication) points out that vocatives, including some in these examples, tend to occur in separate intonation units, suggesting that they are neither arguments nor appositives.

6. Du Bois (personal communication) suggests that analysis of retellings by same speaker in the same and different languages would be useful. We agree but intend to leave that work to others.

References

Brody, [Mary] Jill. 1986. "Repetition as a rhetorical and conversation device in Tojolob'al (Maya)". *International Journal of American Linguistics.* 52(3): 255–274.

Brody, [Mary] Jill. 1994. "Multiple repetitions in Tojolob'al conversation". In Barbara Johnstone (ed.), *Repetition and Discourse, Vol. II.* Norwood, NJ: Ablex 3–14.

Chafe, Wallace (ed.). 1980. *The Pear Stories: Cognitive, Cultural, and Linguistic Aspects of Narrative Production.* Norwood, NJ: Ablex.

Craig, Colette G. 1977. *The Structure of Jacaltec.* Austin: University of Texas Press.

Craig, Colette G.. 1986. "Jacaltec noun classifiers: a study in grammaticalization". *Lingua* 70: 241–284.

DuBois, John W. 1985. "Competing motivations". In John Haiman (ed.), *Iconicity in Syntax.* (*Typological Studies in Language, Vol. 6*). Amsterdam and Philadelphia: Benjamins, 343–365.

DuBois, John W. 1987a. "Absolutive zero: paradigm adaptivity in Sacapultec Maya". In R.M.W. Dixon (ed.), *Studies in Ergativity. Lingua* 71: 203–222.

DuBois, John W. 1987b. "The discourse basis of ergativity". *Language* 63: 805–855.

England, Nora C. 1982. "The Structure of Couplets in Mam Narrative". Paper presented to the American Anthropological Association, Washington, D.C.

England, Nora C. 1983a. "Ergativity in Mamean (Mayan) languages". *International Journal of American Linguistics.* 49: 1–19.

England, Nora C. 1983b. *A Grammar of Mam, a Mayan Language.* Austin: University of Texas Press.

England, Nora C. 1986. "Mamean Voice: Syntactic and Narrative Considerations". Paper presented to the American Anthropological Association, Philadelphia.

England, Nora C. 1988. "Mam voice". In M. Shibatani (ed.), *Passives and Voice.* (*Typological Studies in Language, Vol. 16*). Amsterdam and Philadelphia: Benjamins, 525–545.

England, Nora C. 1990. "*El mam: semejanzas y diferencias regionales*". In Nora C. England and Stephen R. Elliott (eds), *Lecturas sobre la lingüística maya.* Antigua, Guatemala: Centro de Investigaciones Regionales de Mesoamérica. 221–252.

Herring, Susan C. 1989. "Verbless presentation and the discourse basis of ergativity." *Chicago Linguistic Society Parasession on Language in Context.* 123–137.

Hopper, Paul and Thompson, Sandra A. 1980. "Transitivity in grammar and discourse". *Language* 56: 251–299.

Martin, Laura. 1980. "Kanjobal texts". In Louanna Furbee (ed.), *Mayan Texts III.* (IJAL-NATS Monograph No. 5). Chicago: University of Chicago Press and University Microfilms International. 80–88.

Martin, Laura. 1987. "Information Flow in Mocho Mayan Narrative". Paper presented to the American Anthropological Association, Chicago.

Martin, Laura. 1990. "Los verbos de discurso en mochó". In Nora C. England and Stephen R. Elliott (eds), *Lecturas sobre la lingüística maya.* Antigua, Guatemala: Centro de Investigaciones Regionales de Mesoamérica. 421–443.

Martin, Laura. 1992. "Dramatic strategies, quoted speech, and narrative genres in Mocho". Unpublished ms., Cleveland State University.

Martin, Laura. 1994a. "Discourse structure and rhetorical elaboration in Mocho personal narrative". *Journal of Linguistic Anthropology* 4(2): 131–152.

Martin, Laura. 1994b. "Coming here and going there: a preliminary account of motion and direction in Mocho". *Función* (December) Nos. 15–16: 2. 119–167.

Maxwell, J[udith] M. 1976. "Chuj intransitives: or when can an intransitive verb take an object?" In Marlys McClaran (ed.), *Mayan Linguistics, Vol. I.* Los Angeles: American Indian Studies Center, University of California at Los Angeles. 128–140.

Zavala, Roberto. 1992. *El kanjobal de San Miguel Acatán.* Mexico City: Universidad Nacional Autónoma de México.

Zavala, Roberto. 1993. "Clause integration with verbs of motion in Mayan languages. Some facts without fiction". Unpublished ms., University of Oregon, Eugene.

New light on information pressure

Information conduits, "escape valves", and role alignment stretching*

Mark Durie
University of Melbourne

Motivations for grammatical form: External and local

In his seminal article, "The discourse basis of ergativity", Du Bois (1987) proposed that formal properties of ergative patterns of argument coding in languages of the world are motivated at least in part by Preferred Argument Structure. Preferred Argument Structure is a set of principles which describe empirical constraints on the informational status and coding of direct arguments in the clause. These principles, as stated by Du Bois, and using the SAO terminology of Dixon (1979) are as follows:

i. Avoid lexical A's (Non-Lexical A Constraint).[1]
ii. Avoid new A's (Given A Constraint).
iii. Avoid more than one lexical argument per clause (One Lexical Argument Constraint).
iv. Avoid more than one new argument per clause (One New Argument Constraint).

These constraints are intended to apply in the first instance to discourse: they are not strictly speaking syntactic constraints applying directly to grammar, but are language-external in nature, applying to the products of human speaking. However, it is proposed that through processes of grammaticalization, Preferred Argument Structure does over time constrain the evolution of grammars, restricting the typology of argument coding systems.

As a set of empirical generalizations, or natural laws, Preferred Argument Structure is itself in need of explanation, as is implicit in Du Bois's original discussion. At the most general level the principles can be explained in terms of what it is natural for human beings to talk about, and the cognitive costs of activating and tracking referents: it remains an important question for further research to what extent particular languages strengthen, fine-tune or entrench these "recurrent clusterings in parole" (Du Bois 1985: 357).[2] This issue is addressed to a limited extent in this paper, since it is argued that the Preferred Argument Structure constraints apply in Acehnese in a modified way which is congruent with the specific grammatical typology of the language. Certainly Du Bois (1987) predicted that the preferences could be stronger or weaker in specific local discourse contexts (see below).

Du Bois (1987: 837ff) referred to extensive empirical verification of the Preferred Argument Structure constraints which had already taken place, and he argued further that Preferred Argument Structure motivates certain well-known coding asymmetries in the typology of ergative and accusative grammatical patterns. The principal motivation for ergative coding patterns is proposed to be that:

– Ergative case gives a grammatical shape to a regular pattern of discourse by marking A as distinct from the locus of lexical arguments in discourse, S/O.

By Preferred Argument Structure constraint (i), S and O will form the locus of lexical arguments in discourse, and ergative coding, which treats these alike and distinct from A, is motivated by the natural coherence of S/O as the locus of lexical mentions in discourse.

In contrast, the empirical generalization that topics tend to be A or S (because agents are preferred topics) motivates the accusative coding pattern:

– Accusative case gives a grammatical shape to a regular pattern of discourse by marking O as distinct from the locus of expressions of high topic continuity in discourse, A/S.

The association in discourse between arguments and such factors as lexical status and topicality can be referred to as role alignment or *pragmatic linking* (Durie 1994), in contrast to the alignment between arguments and verbal semantics, which is widely referred to as *semantic linking*.

In the Du Bois model, the ergative and accusative motivations are in competition for a "limited good". This is an external motivation (Du Bois 1985: 344), where preferences of discourse patterning, being outside grammar, over time (diachronically) constrain the development of the language system, the inside of grammar.

As is generally the case with competing evolutionary processes that mediate between form and function, we must expect to find local form-function mismatches (Durie 1995). As Du Bois puts it, "A system-external functional force, once appealed to, cannot simply be turned off at will" (1985: 353). In this particular case we can expect the mismatches to be of the following kinds:

– S/O will still be the locus of lexical NP's in discourse in which argument coding is accusative in pattern.
– S/A will still be the locus of anaphoric mentions in the discourse of a language in which argument coding is ergative in pattern.

Such mismatches are anticipated by Du Bois: a mismatch of the second kind is discussed by him for Sakapulteko (1987:841).[3] What is significant in understanding these mismatches is that they tend to be locally limited, i.e., in the "ecology of grammar" (Du Bois 1985:344) there is local damage control. In this case, as in general, the *pattern* of limitation of form-function mismatch can, paradoxically, provide perhaps the most important kind of evidence for the proposed form-function relationship (Durie 1995).

We can observe that the competition between the two motivations for coding patterns sets up a linear, bidirectional tension upon the coding of arguments of intransitive predicates:

$A \leftarrow S \rightarrow O$

The Preferred Argument Structure/ergative motivation would associate S with O; the topic continuity/accusative motivation would associate S with A. This tension is sometimes resolved in favour of A, giving an accusative coding pattern, and sometimes in favour of O, giving an ergative coding pattern.

While it can be difficult to find verification for hypothesized form-function relationships (Du Bois 1985:353), accounts which appeal to competing motivations can be verified empirically, since local formal asymmetries can be predicted to correlate with local differences in relevance or strength of the respective functional motivations: the form-function mismatches are predicted to be aligned in a pattern consistent with the strength or relevance of proposed functional motivations (Malkiel 1967:1238).

In the case of the Preferred Argument Structure hypotheses, we expect to find that:

i. Ergative coding relatively more frequent for full noun phrases (lexical NP's) than for non-lexicals — since the ergative motivation is proposed to be determined by lexicality.
ii. Conversely, ergative coding is relatively less frequent for pronouns, definites, and noun phrases that will tend to have greater inherent topicality (e.g., kinship terms) — since the accusative motivation is sensitive to topicality.

The effect of these predictions is particularly marked in languages which show both ergative and accusative coding in a split-ergative system conditioned by the lexical content of the nominal expressions. There is an extensive literature, beginning with Silverstein (1976), which demonstrates it to be a robust preference that, when a language has split-ergative coding system, then the ergative coding will be associated with mentions of type (i) above.

Predictions also arise concerning the different treatment of case marking and cross-referencing. It is expected that:

iii. Ergative coding is relatively more frequent with case marking — as a property of noun phrases, including all lexical mentions — than with cross-referencing/agreement.

iv. Accusative coding is relatively more frequent with cross-referencing/agreement — as a property of anaphors, associated in discourse with argument expressions of greater topic continuity (Givón 1983) — than with case marking.

Again, the cases where a language treats case marking and cross-referencing differently are especially revealing. We find that many languages have an ergative system for case marking and an accusative system for cross-referencing, but the converse is not attested: no language is known with ergative cross-referencing and accusative case marking (Comrie 1978: 340).

Predictions can also be made concerning patterns of markedness. In the domain of case marking, as claimed above, it is the ergative and accusative cases which are *functionally* marked, rather than the nominative:[4] in particular they can be expected to be less frequent than the nominative in discourse. Consequently it rarely happens that nominative case is *formally* more marked than accusative or ergative case (Dixon 1994: 58).[5] On the other hand, in the domain of cross-referencing, the function of referent tracking would favour A and S over O to be cross-referenced, since S/A form the preferred locus of expressions of high topic continuity. Indeed languages which only cross-reference O (the accusative argument) in an accusative pattern, or only S/O (the nominative argument) in an ergative pattern are exceptional (cf. Dixon 1994: 44; Moravcsik 1978: 259). Generally, if a language cross-references O, whether in an ergative or accusative pattern, then it will also cross-reference S and A.[6] In this sense therefore, we can expect quite a different pattern of formal markedness from that which applies with case. With case, accusative and ergative can be expected to be marked; however, with cross-referencing, S/A can be expected to be no less marked than O.

These predictions are preferences, i.e., probable outcomes. Exceptions are not excluded as impossible; they are merely understood to be unlikely, and as presupposing exceptional motivation, sometimes involving idiosyncratic diachronic paths. These generalizations, first pointed to by Silverstein (1976), have been amply confirmed through two decades of research.[7]

Information pressure

In his 1987 article, Du Bois emphasized the importance of information pressure, a local variable, which affects the relevance or import of Preferred Argument Structure as a constraint upon grammatical coding choices. Intuitively the idea of information pressure is that texts of comparable size can have varying numbers of referents to be tracked. In a simple narrative, involving only a few protagonists, speakers and hearers need to keep track of only a few salient referents. In contrast a narrative of comparable size which refers to more protagonists, or a complex procedural text, could have a greater information pressure. A greater number of referents mentioned in a text of a certain size implies a greater information pressure. A helpful metaphor is that of the text as a container: more of a gas in a bottle means a greater pressure inside it. We can also note that as pressure increases in the bottle the density of the gas increases.

To measure information pressure requires reference to at least three different variables: (i) a portion of text, (ii) a class of referents mentioned in the text, and (iii) a class of tokens, associated referring expressions found in the text. The "associated referring expressions" under consideration will be mentions in the text of referents from the class of referents under consideration. The portion of text itself delimits a set of token mentions or codings of the referents under consideration — it defines a domain of coded expressions. Thus information pressure can be defined operationally as *the density of referents of a particular type in a specified domain of coded expressions* (i.e., of mentions or tokens). In this paper I use the term information *pressure* to refer to the intuitive, psychological notion, but *density* is used to refer to an operational metric applied to particular set of textual data and intended to reflect some aspect of information pressure.

As information pressure goes up, one should expect a more frequent requirement for introduction of new mentions. Du Bois predicts that the proportion of intransitive predicates used for this purpose would also consequently increase: "As information pressure rises, intransitive verbs are more often invoked for carrying out the new protagonist introductions; this results in a higher frequency of new and lexical mentions in S" (1987:836) . This should in its turn strengthen the S = O alignment — the discourse motivation for ergativity — by boosting the proportion of lexical S roles. In general, higher information pressure is expected to correlate with stronger Preferred Argument Structure alignment, according to Du Bois.

In contrast, texts with low information pressure would involve less resort to intransitive predicates with lexical arguments (e.g., fewer presentatives), and the motivation for accusativity would be comparatively stronger.

In this chapter I examine the applicability of the notion of information pressure, and test Du Bois's hypothesis that greater information pressure is compensated for through an "escape valve" of intransitive predicates. I will also consider the impact of information pressure differentials upon role alignment, and specifically whether greater information pressure is associated with a strengthening of the ergative S/O alignment pattern of the Preferred Argument Structure constraints. As a language with an active or "Split-S" coding system, Acehnese offers a special opportunity to consider this issue.

Three Acehnese texts

This chapter is based upon an analysis of pragmatic linking in three Acehnese texts, an oral narrative, a written narrative, and a conversation:

Hamzah, an excerpt from a long oral narrative *Haba Amir Hamzah* (The Tale of Amir Hamzah) recorded in its entirety in the village of Cöt Trieng, North Aceh in 1981. The total narrative extends for 15 hours but it was presented by a single narrator over three nights. The story is set in pre-Mohammedan times in the Middle East, and is a traditional Islamic story. This excerpt includes the preamble, and an initial part of the narrative. The story moves in series of events set in different scenes. One scene involves the creation of a pleasure garden for the king, the opening of the gardens, and the king's being bitten by a snake. The following scene involves attempts to heal the king, and the arrival of a traveller who succeeds and is rewarded with fortune and authority in the kingdom.

Mouse-Deer, a written folk tale *Peulandôk ngön Rimueng* (The Mouse-Deer and the Tiger), which was originally committed to writing in the Arabic script at Peudada in North Aceh, and later published in Aceh in Latin script with Indonesian translations and notes by Dr. Budiman Sulaiman of Universitas Syiah Kuala (Sulaiman 1978). This story is in the familiar genre of folk tales: the mouse-deer, favourite tiger-food, convinces a tiger that a pile of warm rhinocerous dung is really the king's dinner cooking. The tiger stirs it with a stick so it doesn't burn, while the mouse-deer makes his escape.

Conversation, an excerpt of a free-wheeling extended conversation between two male Acehnese adults, recorded in January 1991 at Geulanggang near Bireuen, North Aceh, by Mawardi Hasan. The conversation covers a variety of topics. Part of it involves sharing comments about places and events mentioned in a traditional Acehnese story (the *Hikayat Malém Diwa)*, and part involves a comparison of the old- and new-style Acehnese houses. The conversation is humorous and tongue-in-cheek: the participants are talking for their own amusement.

Referential density and Core information

In this section I introduce a metric for reporting information density. We have seen earlier that a measure of information density requires reference to three variables: (i) a portion of text, (ii) a class of referents, and (iii) a class of referring expressions. In this study, the portion of text always consists of the whole excerpt of each of the three texts under consideration.

The class of referents may be restricted in various ways. For example, it may be limited to animates, or to inanimates. It may also be restricted by properties of mentions of the referents. For example, it may consist of the class of referents which are referenced somewhere in the text as the direct argument of a verb. The class of referents may also be defined by a combination of features.

The class of expressions may also be restricted in various ways. In the maximal case one might take into account all the expressions which are mentions of a particular class of referents, or one might restrict this class, for example by counting only those expressions which are the complement of a preposition within the text.

The metric **referential density** or ρ is defined as the number r of a specified set of referents mentioned in a particular portion of text, divided by the total number m of a specified set of mentions of these referents in the portion of text.

$$\rho = \frac{r}{m}$$

The value of ρ may vary as follows:

$$1 \geq \rho > 0$$

A value of $\rho = 1$ means there is only one mention per referent, and maximal referential density. A value of ρ close to 0 means many mentions per referent, and low information density. A value of $\rho = 0.5$ means that there are twice as many mentions as referents and each referent is mentioned on average just twice.

In Du Bois (1987), information pressure is defined relative to a portion of text. However, as we shall see, there are good reasons to distinguish between different kinds of referents within a text, that is to say, between different kinds of information. In applying this metric, the class of referents may be as restricted as a single referent, or it may represent a larger class, for example all animates mentioned in a text.

Referential density is a *referent-oriented* metric in that it measures an attribute of a class of referents across a text, not properties of mentions in a local context. In this sense referential density differs significantly from such *mention-oriented* metrics as lookback and persistence (Givón 1983).

In coding nominal expressions, a primary distinction is made between expressions which can be counted as mentions, and those which are non-referring and are not mentions of some referent. In discourse not all nominal expressions can be counted as mentions of some referent. For example, predicate nominals are often non-referring, as in (1) where *barang nyang peunténg-peunténg* functions as a predicate, not as referring expression. Non-referring nominals may also appear under the scope of negation, as in (2) where *peuratah* 'bed' has no referent associated with it, and cannot be counted as a mention. They may also appear in the form of incorporated nominals, as in (3), where no particular *hikayat* is being referred to. Rather *kheun hikayat* 'recite epic poetry' refers to a kind of activity.[8]

(1) *nyan barang nyang peunténg-peunténg* Conversation
that goods REL important-important
'They are very important goods.'

(2) *dan masa jameun hana peuratah* Conversation
and time former not.exist bed
'And in the olden days there were no beds.'

(3) *di ulontuan,* Conversation
FOCUS I
atèe ji-kheun hikayat,
when 3-recite epic-poetry
lontuan-jak ho laén.
1-go whither other
'As for me, when someone was reciting poetry, I would go off somewhere else.'

Note that the notion of 'referring' I am using here is not the same as that of 'having a real-world referent'. What is crucial is the possibility of tracking by means of subsequent mentions, not the ontological status of the referent. Within the world of a text, something can be introduced and tracked through the text by subsequent mentions, without having any real-world existence. In (4), taken from a discussion of the comparative virtues of old- and new-style houses, the generic traditional owner *ureueng jameun* 'former person' of the generic traditional house is tracked through the text:

(4) A: *di ureueng jameun,* Conversation
FOCUS person former
sa-boh geu-peugöt rumoh,
ONE-CLASSIFIER 3-make house
man-mandum jeuet sinan.
all-all can there
nyan
indeed
nomor sa bunoe,
number one earlier
rumoh geu-peugot manyang.
house 3-make tall
'A traditional person, didn't he make just one house, yet everything could fit there. Indeed, and as for your first point, he built his house high [elevated off the ground on poles — MD].'

B: *jingki di yup moh.*
rice.pounder at under house
'The rice pounder would go under the house.'
A: *kön geu-peugöt manyang dilèe.*
not 3-make high formerly
'eu
yes
kön ka manyang.
not already high
'Didn't he used to make it high? Yeah, it sure was high.'

Interpretation of particular examples requires much care. Consider *I said, "Take a chocolate", and then she took one.* The NP *a chocolate* would normally be understood to have no referent. However, the subsequent expression *one* is referential, and it is a first mention, referring to the chocolate that was taken. There is a relationship of semantic continuity between *a chocolate* and *one*, but this is not an anaphoric relation.[9]

Because of the different interpretations which may be associated with the term *referential,* in this study I refer to prefer to use the term *trackable* to refer to expressions which are of the kind that can be tracked through the text (Durie 1994). This sense subsumes that of Du Bois and Thompson's *Tracking* (MS; see also Thompson MS):

> A useful definition of Tracking NP's involves a computational metaphor. Thus we can say that in using such an NP the speaker expects the listener to do something with respect to a file in his/her directory. Either a new file must be opened, or information must be added to an existing file. Thus we can think of Tracking NPs as being 'Open File NPs'. (Du Bois and Thompson MS: 11)

Trackable expressions, in my usage, include mentions which need not be associated with another mention or intended mention and need not be mentioned with the purpose of tracking, but are nevertheless of a kind that they *could* be mentioned again. Trackables include Du Bois and Thompson's *Tracking* expressions, and also their *Orienting* expressions, such as *on Christmas Day,* which are used "to set a spatial or temporal framework" (Du Bois and Thompson MS: 15). Unlike other non-tracking expressions such as predicate nominals, the reference of Orienting expressions can be maintained by a series of mentions, hence they are classed here as trackable. An example of such an Orienting trackable is the *kurusi* 'seat' of the king in the following:

(5) *Watèe raja geu-duek di ateueh kurusi,* Hamzah
when king 3-sit at TOP seat
bu cit ka teungoh di-hidang,
rice too already middle 3-serve

keubeutulan,
it.so.happened
bak gaki kurusi,
at foot seat
na sa-boh aneuk uleue,
exist one-CLASSIFIER child snake
'When the king sat down on his seat (or throne) — the food was being served — it happened that at the foot of the seat there was a small (or young) snake.'

Note that the concept of information pressure, and the associated metric of referential density, only make sense over trackable expressions. For non-trackables the notion of information pressure, as defined by Du Bois, is meaningless.[10] In principle reported events and states could be regarded as trackable. Yet in actual texts the referents of verbal expressions (together with their dependents) are typically not tracked through the text. In any case, in this study I focus on nominal expressions.

Table 1 gives the overall referential density for each text, together with the total numbers of Expressions and Referents.

Table 1. Referential density (ρ) for each text

Text	Referents	Expressions	ρ
Mouse-Deer	72	341	.21
Hamzah	164	430	.38
Conversation	187	608	.31

The Du Bois account of Preferred Argument Structure appeals to the notion of information pressure as one factor which impacts upon argument coding. However in examining information pressure we must distinguish between different kinds of information. The point can be made clearer by means of an analogy. In a film not all characters make equal demands upon the attention of the viewer. Some characters have continuity throughout the film, and the viewer is expected to be able to identify them and remember things about them on repeated appearances, to "track" them through the film. Other bit parts, such as people in a crowd scene, have no continuity and in many cases would be unlikely to be recognized if they did happen to appear more than once during the film. Indeed there may be thousands of people in a crowd scene, but the viewer is not expected to keep track of the identities of this multitude of faces. In this the camera aids and directs the viewer, as it focuses on and spotlights the principal characters which we will need to keep track of. The cognitive demands of keeping track of characters in a film generate a kind of information pressure, but not all characters which appear on the screen make a contribution to this pressure — only the foregrounded characters will contribute to this pressure, since they demand our attention in some way. In just the same way, within a particular text not all referents are equally relevant to information pressure.

Du Bois's (1987) theory of information pressure is only concerned with the impact of information pressure upon the coding of direct arguments (S, A and O). Indeed there is good reason to regard Core arguments as a specific site or conduit for tracked referents: Thompson (MS), supporting an observation of Du Bois (1980: 255), argues that a distinctive function of Core roles is the tracking of participants which occupy the focus of attention. Thus such peripherally coded referents as that of *now* in *It's quiet now* contribute nothing to information pressure. In exploring Du Bois' theory, it therefore makes sense to focus upon those referents which are made available in the text for mentions in the Core domain. Other referents, such as are coded by temporal and locative expressions — for example the expression *Uroe Seunin nyoe* 'this Sunday' in (6) — are typically not used at all in Core roles, and we can assume they contribute nothing to information pressure in the Core domain.

Within Acehnese texts we can distinguish five main grammatical types of coding sites for trackable nominal expressions: Core, Oblique, Predicate, Adnominal, and Free. Core expressions are the direct arguments of a clause predicate. Oblique expressions are peripheral elements in a clause, including complements of prepositions, and some locative, manner and temporal NP's which are not arguments. We see in (6–7) examples of Obliques, marked in bold.

(6) ***Uroe Seunin nyoe,*** Hamzah
day Sunday this,
kamoe meu-langkah
we 1EXCL-go
'This Sunday we will go…'

(7) ***nyan ban*** *di-bôh adat lé Alkas Meuntri bunoe* Hamzah
that manner 3-give law by Alkas Meuntri aforementioned
'In that way the aforementioned Alkas Meuntri laid down the law.'

(8) ***nyoe bak malam nyoe,*** Hamzah
now on night this
lôn ka trôk,
I already arrive
u Meulasah Cöt Trieng,
to Meunasah Cot Trieng
'Now on this night, I have arrived at the Meunasah of Cöt Trieng.'

The other three major grammatical types of nominal expressions are: Predicates (NP's and in PP's), Adnominals and Free expressions. Adnominals are what are often referred to as "possessive" NP's. Free expressions are extra-clausal, and thus bear no grammatical relation to a predicate or to another nominal.[11] Free expressions fulfil a variety of functions, some of which are illustrated in (9–11): the Free expressions are in bold.

(9) ***rumoh jameun*** *dilèe* Conversation
house traditional earlier
atèe ta-ék nyan bak rinyeun
when 1INCL-climb that at steps
payah ta-lôp bak pintô
must 1INCL-enter.hole at door
'A traditional house, when we climb up its steps, we have to crouch to enter.'

(10) *lôntuan kalön,* Conversation
I see
nyankeuh aleumareuhôm Nèk
really deceased Grandfather
Ali yah Apa Sén.
Ali father younger uncle Sén
geu-undang ureueng-geuh u rumoh ++ gopnyan.[12]
3-invite person-3 to house he
adak sinoe ***Teungku Muhammad Sulaiman.***
if here Teungku Muhammad Sulaiman
'I observed the deceased Grandfather Ali, father of Apa Sén. He would invite people to his house [to hear a recital]. Here [it would be] Teungku Muhammad Sulaiman.'

(11) B: *hai sabap lôntuan sendiri* Conversation
well because I myself
ka peureunah teukarang hikayat.
already ever write epic
'Well you see even I have composed an epic poem.'
A: *'eu*
yes
B: ⟨laughs⟩
A: *hikayat ~*
epic
B: ***Hikayat Raja Jeumpa***
'The Epic of The King of Jeumpa'

A: *'eu*
Hikayat Teungku Malém
'The Epic of Teungku Malém'
B: ***Hikayat Putroe Bunsu***
'The Epic of Princess Bungsu'
éh 'ö
uh yes
Hikayat Putroe Gumbak Meuh
'The Epic of Princess Golden Hair'
A: *nyö*
yes
Putroe Gumbak Meuh
'Princess Golden Hair'

In (11) note that the titles in bold are not continuations of the Undergoer of *karang* 'compose': they are a list of well-known traditional folk epics, not examples of further texts composed by A.

My central concern in this study is with Core arguments, and we shall first contrast them with Oblique expressions. Free expressions will be discussed in due course. Properties of Adnominals are not discussed here, although they deserve a careful study in their own right.

That it is necessary to distinguish Core from Oblique information is illustrated in Figure 1, which shows Core and Oblique referential density for each of our three texts.[13] Core referential density is calculated over Core mentions and the class of referents associated with them, and Oblique referential density is calculated over Oblique mentions and the class of referents associated with them. This shows the density of referents *within* each coding type: it reflects the turnover of referents within Core and Oblique domains.[14]

Figure 1 suggests that referential density values can be quite different and vary independently in Core and Oblique domains across different texts. Note firstly the consistently greater overall referential density for the Oblique referents in each text. Note furthermore that the relativity between Core and Oblique referential density is not consistent: while all three texts have roughly similar density of information in Oblique roles (referential density in the range of 0.6–0.7, implying around two mentions per referent), for the Core roles the referential density for the written narrative 'Mouse-Deer' is significantly lower: about half that of the other two texts (0.16 compared to 0.33 and 0.31).[15] Continuing our dramatic analogy, the 'Mouse-Deer' text has a variety comparable to the other texts in the props and backdrops used, but its principal actors are much fewer and more sustained throughout the text.

The question arises whether it is valid to speak of "information pressure" for Oblique expressions at all. Oblique expressions characteristically occupy a peripheral

Table 2. Referential density (ρ) for each text

Text	Referents	Expressions	ρ
Core:			
Mouse-Deer	41	250	0.16
Hamzah	112	362	0.33
Conversation	75	224	0.31
Periphery:			
Mouse-Deer	36	50	0.72
Hamzah	52	82	0.71
Conversation	49	69	0.63

degree of attention: in Thompson's (MS) study they served only minimally in tracking participants, and were much less likely than Core roles to be *Identifiable and Given.* As such they appear not to demand the same cognitive effort required by Core expressions. An Oblique expression is less likely to need to be tracked, so the cognitive file (Du Bois and Thompson MS) needed for it can be cheaply set up, and easily allowed to fade. Since it does not demand attention, it does not generate information pressure in the same way that a tracked, Core mention does. That these three texts all display higher referential density in the Oblique than in the Core domain can be taken to be a symptom of the principle that Oblique mentions are cognitively less costly, because they generally do not need to be kept track of.[16]

I therefore propose that within the clause the notion of *information pressure* is not generally valid for Oblique expressions. (We will consider the contribution of

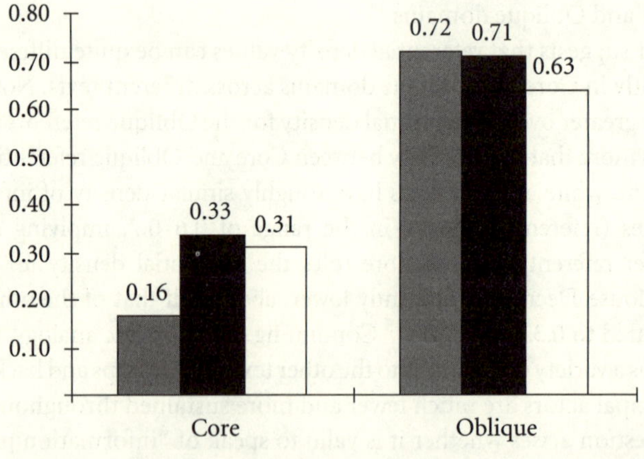

Figure 1. Referential density by text of Core referents in the domain of Core mentions, and Oblique referents in the domain of Oblique mentions.

extra-clausal mentions later.) This means that in seeking to refine Du Bois's notion of information pressure, we need to focus on Core information, and here we can take referential density as a metric of information pressure. As referential density in the Core domain goes down, information pressure is also less. Let us then further explore the difference we have observed in these texts: that "Mouse-Deer" has roughly half the referential density of "Hamzah" and "Conversation", and hence significantly less information pressure. We are now in a position to test Du Bois's hypothesis that as information pressure increases, intransitive predicates will be resorted to more frequently (Du Bois 1987:835–836), to introduce the more frequent new mentions which a higher information pressure implies. To test the correlation between information pressure and intransitivity, the percentage of intransitive verbs in each text was calculated as a proportion of all verbs. Only verbs which had at least one trackable argument were included in these counts: it is assumed that verbs with no trackable arguments play no role in relation to information pressure.[17] The results are given in Table 3. Table 4 provides similar data, but only includes those verbs with a *first mention* as a Core argument; that is, only those verbs which have a presentative function were counted for this table. (The definition of a first mention will be given more precisely in due course.) Figure 2 shows the percentages of intransitive verbs in each text, presenting the data of Tables 3 and 4 in graphic form.

Table 3. Ratio of transitive to intransitive verbs, by text

Text	Transitive verbs	Intransitive verbs	Totals
Mouse-Deer	107	74	181
Hamzah	71	81	152
Conversation	124	114	238

Table 4. Ratio of transitive to intransitive verbs which take a first mention argument, by text

Text	Transitive verbs	Intransitive verbs	Totals
Mouse-Deer	22	13	45
Hamzah	31	23	53
Conversation	35	22	57

Figure 2 shows that both "Hamzah" and "Conversation" do indeed have higher proportions of intransitive verbs than "Mouse-Deer". This would appear to support Du Bois's hypothesis.[18] Note that the proportion of intransitives is greater in "Hamzah" than in "Conversation". As we shall see later, "Conversation" uses Free mentions for important new mentions where "Hamzah" would use an intransitive verb: this may be part of the reason for the greater use of intransitives in "Hamzah".

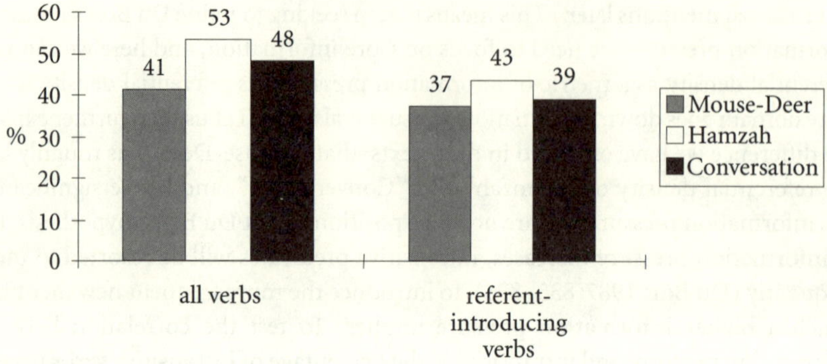

Figure 2. Proportion of intransitive verbs among all transitive and intransitive verbs: (a) for all verbs with a trackable argument; (b) for verbs which introduce as an argument the first mention of a trackable referent.

Figure 2 also shows that a verb introducing a first mention of a referent is *less* likely to be intransitive than one which is not introducing a first mention. This suggests that the greater frequency of intransitive verbs found in "Hamzah" and "Conversation" compared to "Mouse-Deer" cannot be due to the increased use of intransitive verbs to introduce new referents. In the following section I consider other possible correlates of greater information pressure in "Hamzah" and "Conversation".

Other correlates of higher information pressure

Higher Lexical Density (LD)

Higher information pressure might be expected to correlate with use of more explicitly coded mentions, all things being equal. Greater explicitness of coding might compensate for the increased cognitive demands of greater information pressure. One way of measuring this is with the metric *lexical density*: i.e., the proportion of lexical mentions among all mentions. A lexical mention in Acehnese is one which uses a nominal expression of some form, excluding zero anaphora and cross-referencing.[19] The Core lexical density of the three texts is reported in Table 5.

We do in fact find that in "Hamzah" and "Conversation" the LD metric is higher than in "Mouse-Deer". Thus, for example, in "Mouse-Deer", about one in every three Core mentions is lexical (LD = 0.33), but in "Hamzah" it is one in every two (LD = 0.52).

Non-core mentions

Another correlate of greater information pressure in the Core domain appears to be increased appearance of Core information in non-Core coding sites. Table 6 reports the density of non-Core codings of Core trackable referents, among all mentions of Core referents. Its right-hand column shows that in the text, "Mouse-Deer", referents which are somewhere coded as a Core argument are mentioned as non-Core in 16% (LD = 0.16) of instances. In the other two texts, non-Core codings of Core referents run at 25% (LD = 0.25) and 26% (LD = 0.26). Thus, it appears that the two texts with greater information pressure in the Core domain, "Hamzah" and "Conversation", also show greater *information channel overlap* of Core information in non-Core coding contexts. Of course the significance of this putative correlation needs to be explored using a larger and more diverse sample of texts.

Table 5. Core lexical density (trackable referents)

Text	Lexical Density
Mouse-Deer	0.33
Hamzah	0.52
Conversation	0.43

There are interesting differences in how non-Core mentions of Core referents are distributed within each text. Some non-Core referents are grammatically dependent upon something else within a clause or some other syntactic unit, e.g. as Obliques of various kinds, or as Adnominal expressions. Others occur *Free.* The middle two columns in Table 6 factor out the Free from dependent non-Core codings of Core referents. A comparison with the right-hand (Total) column shows that "Mouse-Deer" and "Conversation" have similar degrees of Core channel overlap amongst dependent mentions: the main difference between these two texts is that "Conversation" has a significant proportion of Free mentions of Core referents. In the oral narrative, "Hamzah", the density (or proportion) of non-Core mentions is still significantly higher than for "Mouse-Deer", even after the Free NP's are factored out. The number of tokens of Free mentions is given in Table 7.

Functional differentiation of information pressure

The handling of first mentions plays a key role in Du Bois's theory of information pressure and information flow management, because he proposes that first mentions create a demand for the use of lexical S expressions, undergirding the discourse lexical motivation for ergative coding. We have so far made a distinction between Core and Oblique information, arguing that when discussing information pressure, it is important to distinguish Core from other kinds of information,

Table 6. Proportion of non-Core mentions of Core referents, among all mentions of Core referents

Text	Free	Dependent	Total
Mouse-Deer	(<5%)	16%	16%
Hamzah	6%	21%	26%
Conversation	11%	14%	25%

Table 7. Free mentions of Core referents

Text	Tokens
Mouse-Deer	1
Hamzah	15
Conversation	52

suggesting that only Core information can be considered to generate information pressure of the kind Du Bois has referred to. The Du Bois hypothesis can be further extended by a careful differentiation of different kinds of information. The key idea is that different kinds of new information create different cognitive demands on Hearers, and in particular more important new mentions demand greater focus of attention and consequently generate more information pressure. The issue then arises of how different coding choices correlate with the pragmatic status of referents in texts. In this section I discuss the functional differentiation of roles, in terms of the kind of new mention that they are characteristically used to introduce.

Acehnese grammatical relations

Acehnese has an active grammatical typology (Durie 1985, 1987, 1988b). The two major Core grammatical relations are:

1. Actor: A of transitive and some S's of intransitive verbs (Sa).
2. Undergoer: O or transitive and some S's of intransitive verbs (So); also the argument of a non-verbal predicate (Se).

> For transitive verbs the Actor and Undergoer correspond respectively to what are usually termed transitive subject and object, and they are distinguished in the grammar by a variety of syntactic and morphological properties, as one would expect. But what is unusual about Acehnese is that intransitive verbs fall into two distinct classes: some take an argument identifiable on language-internal grounds as an Actor, and the others take what is identifiable as an Undergoer. Morpho-syntactic properties which treat transitive Actor and Undergoer differently also treat intransitive Actor and Undergoer differently… (Durie 1987: 366)

Arguments for using this particular classification of grammatical relations in Acehnese, rather than the traditional subject-object classification, are presented in detail in Durie (1987) and (1988b). The distinction is reflected most obviously in the cross-referencing system: Actors are obligatorily cross-referenced by a proclitic on the verb; in contrast verbal Undergoers are usually not cross-referenced, although verbal Undergoers and some non-verbal ones may be cross-referenced by an enclitic. Examples given below illustrate this difference.

Syntactic properties which are sensitive to Actor status in Acehnese are: control (equi), verb serialization, incorporation and formation of imperatives. Examples of properties which are sensitive to Undergoer status are: possessor ascension, resultative constructions, verb serialization and incorporation. Other important syntactic processes do not distinguish between Actors and Undergoers, including syntactic raising, topicalization and relativization.

An interesting feature of Acehnese is that Actor and Undergoer have comparatively transparent semantic linking: Actors are volitional causers or controllers of events and states, whereas Undergoers are affected, non-volitional and non-controlling participants. Consequently, one cannot say the equivalent of "the rock hit the tree" using an Acehnese transitive verb: the rock as a non-volitional causer cannot be an Actor. Consistent with the semantic linking is the fact that there are no relation-changing grammatical constructions such as passive or anti-passive in Acehnese (Durie 1986). Instead, there are lexical derivational processes that can alter grammatical relations — Actors to Undergoers and vice versa — but also necessarily change the meanings of verbs with respect to the semantics of volition. For example *döng* 'stand up, be standing' describes a controlled state or event and takes an Actor, but its derivative *teudöng* 'be upright' describes a non-volitional state: a person can 'stand' (*döng*) but a tombstone is 'upright' (*teudöng*).

In this grammatical system, transitive predicates take an Actor and an Undergoer; intransitive verbs can take an Actor or an Undergoer. The arguments of non-verbal predicates (i.e., of NP or PP predicates) generally behave like Undergoers, though they have partly distinct and not completely homogeneous grammatical properties (see Durie 1985, 1987). In the system used here, the following Core role types are distinguished:[20]

Role	**Definition**
A	Actor of transitive verb
Sa	Actor of intransitive verb
So	Undergoer of intransitive verb
Se	Undergoer of nonverbal predicate (NP or PP predicate)
O	Undergoer of transitive verb

Examples illustrating the coding of these argument types follow. As examples with Undergoer enclitics are relatively uncommon, I have taken some examples from another Mouse-Deer story, *The Mouse-Deer and the Dog* (M-DD). This story is also taken from Sulaiman (1978).

Transitive (A and O):

(12) a. *ka lheueh ro di gata* M-DD
already finished so FOCUS you
O
adak geu-peukawén-teuh?
maybe 3-marry-2
A-VERB-O
'So he has already married you off?'

b. … *makén geu-padang-kuh sit* M-DD
the.more 3-look.at-1 too
A-VERB-O
'…the more he looked at me too.'

c. *kadang ta-puwayang kèe* M-DD
maybe 2-trick I
A-VERB O
'Maybe you are tricking me.'

d. *bôh ta-buka treuk pintô …* M-DD
Do! 2-open right.away door
A-VERB O
'Open the door right away…'

Intransitive (Sa):

(13) a. *ta-teubiet treuk gata di sinan …* M-DD
2-EXIT right.away you from here
Sa-VERB Sa
'You come out of there right away …'

b. *watèe raja geu-duek di ateueh kurusi …* Hamzah
when king 3-sit on TOP chair
Sa Sa-VERB
'When the king sat down on his chair …'

Intransitive (So):

(14) a. *di gata ka rayëk-teuh …* M-DD
FOCUS you already big-2
So VERB-So
'You are already grown up …'

b. *ka* *beungèh-geuh* Conversation
already angry-3
VERB-So
'He was angry.'

c. *beungèh raja* Hamzah
angry king
VERB So
'The king was angry.'

Intransitive (Se):

(15) a. *jingki* *di yup* *moh* Conversation
rice-pounder at under house
Se PP-PRED
'The rice pounder is under the house.'

b. *di* *nanggroe Baitul Mukadé kuta Madiyan* Hamzah
at country city
PP-PRED Se
'The city of Madiyan was in the country of Baitul Mukadé.'

c. *Putroe* *Bunsu* *ureueng* *Takengön* Conversation
princess Bungsu person Takengon
Se NP-PRED
'Princess Bungsu was a Takengon person.'

Non-Core roles are functionally more diverse than Core roles. The major types as classified in the data base are as follows:

Adnom(inal)	"possessive" or Adnominal NP's
Obl(ique)	non-Core constituents of the clause, both with and without a preposition
Free	grammatically independent NP's
Pred(icate)	an NP predicate or a complement of the P in a PP predicate

In the following sections I will examine the use of these roles for coding mentions.

Use of roles for first mentions

In analysing the text, mentions were coded according to their "Givenness" (Chafe 1987, Prince 1981). For our purposes the following distinctions among trackable mentions are relevant (for further details of the coding see Durie 1994: 513–514):

Evoked: a mention whose identity can be determined on the basis of deixis, e.g., first and second pronouns, and expressions like *there, this one.*

Mentioned: a mention of something which has been previously mentioned in the text and can therefore be assumed to be in the consciousness of the Hearer.

Inferable: a mention whose identity can be grounded or inferred from context, but which has not been mentioned before and was not Evoked.
Accessible: a mention whose identity can be expected to be known by the speaker, but not because it is Evoked, Inferable or Mentioned; e.g., a place name that is assumed to be known to the Hearer.
Brand-New: a first mention whose identity is assumed not to be inferable from context (i.e. neither Evoked nor Inferable), and is not assumed to be Accessible.

For some mentions two status values might be regarded as valid; e.g., a first person pronoun referring to someone who had previously been mentioned. In such cases the coding followed the order given above: an expression was given the first applicable category in the list.[21]

First mentions comprise Inferable, Accessible and Brand-New mentions. Figure 3 presents the proportions of mentions in each role type which are also first mentions. Across the three texts there emerges a hierarchy of frequency of use or roles as a staging site for first mentions. This hierarchy can be represented as follows:

A < Sa << Adnom << So < Se << O < Obl < Free < Pred

where < indicates relative position on the hierarchy, and << indicates a relatively larger increment of difference.

Note that this hierarchy groups the Core roles, together with the Adnominal role,[22] as the set of roles with less frequent new mentions (grouped on the left of the figure). Actors (Sa, A) are sharply distinguished from other Core roles by very low rates of first mentions. Furthermore, although both So and O have more first mentions than Actors, they are also distinct from each other in their proportions of first mentions, with O manifesting the higher proportion. This is consistent with the observation made earlier that a verb introducing a first mention is *less* likely to be

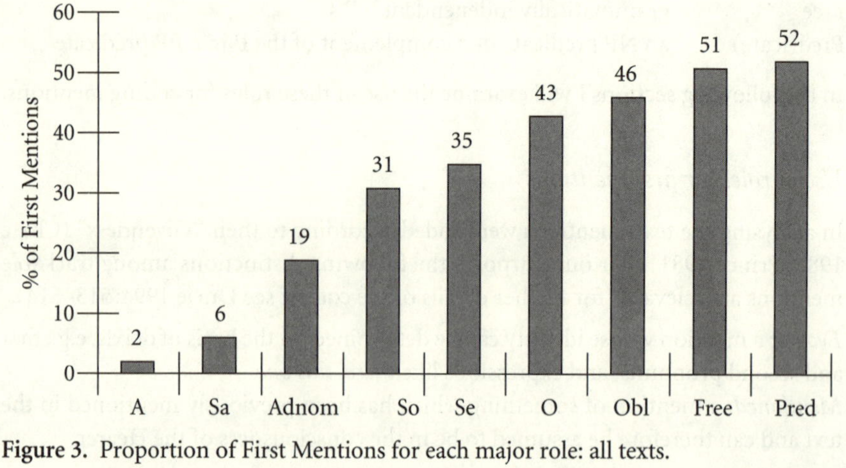

Figure 3. Proportion of First Mentions for each major role: all texts.

intransitive than one which is not introducing a first mention (Figure 2). (Another factor is that intransitive verbs are not a coherent class: those which take Sa are hardly used at all for first mentions.)

The hierarchy derived from Figure 3 could be summarized as follows, in which the S is a *pragmatically* mediate and internally heterogeneous grouping between A and O, incorporating Sa, So and Se:

$A < S[_{Sa < So < Se}] < O < \text{Obliques}$

This hierarchy, or at least that part which deals with Core Roles, provides a universal pragmatic framework for interpreting the preferred grammatical coding systems found in the languages of the world as outcomes of grammaticalization. An ergative coding pattern imposes a major coding discontinuity between A and S, thus:

A << S/O

An accusative coding pattern imposes the discontinuity between S and O, thus:

A/S << O

And an active or "Split-S" coding pattern like that found in Acehnese splits the S, in this case producing a split alignment:

A/Sa << So/(Se)/O

What is especially significant about Acehnese is that location of the larger increment of difference, so as to split the S is not just a property of the grammatical coding system: it is also reflected in pragmatic alignments of grammatical roles in texts, as we have seen in Figure 3. We can see this split alignment particularly clearly if we consider the proportions of new mentions by Core Roles in each text. Figure 3 summarizes the proportions of first mentions across all three texts; in Figure 4, the proportions are given for Core Roles only, with a breakdown by text.

Note that in "Mouse-Deer", A is very close to Sa, and So is very close to O in their proportions of First Mentions, with a difference of 1% and 2% respectively. Therefore, based on Figure 4, we can reformulate that part of the Acehnese version of the role hierarchy which deals with the Core Roles as:

A ≤ Sa << So ≤ Se ≤ O

From Figure 4 we can observe that *stretching* of the role hierarchy appears to be a correlate of greater information pressure in "Hamzah" and "Conversation". This involves a greater differentiation *within* the Actor (Sa, A) and Undergoer (So, Se, O) groups: these groups are hardly differentiated internally at all in the Mouse-Deer story. There is nevertheless no *realignment* of the Sa/A < So/Se/O distinction in favour of an ergative or accusative pattern. We will return to this observation later.

There are also significant differences between the *kinds* of new mentions which

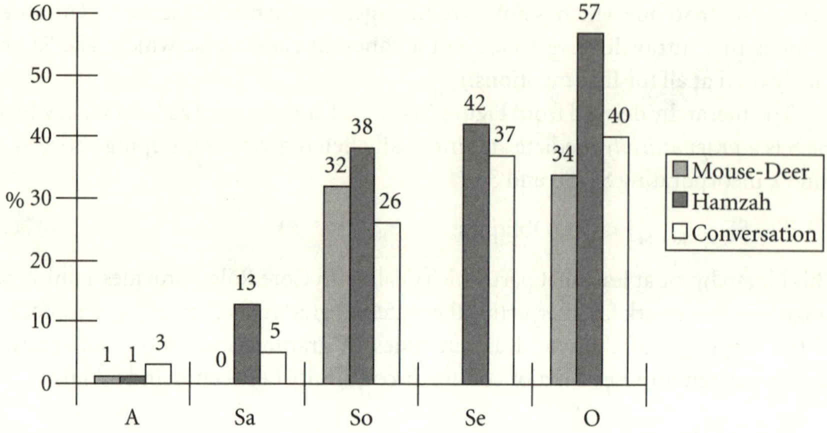

Figure 4. Proportion of First Mentions by Core role and text.[23]

are introduced into each role type. Some of these differences are discussed in the next section.

Roles as stages

Important functional differences are also found between Core roles in their value as stages for new mentions. I propose that these differences constitute differences in the conventional pragmatic profiles of roles (cf. Silverstein 1976: 152). These profiles are communicatively significant, because they constitute part of the indexical semiotic content of grammar, helping to guide the Hearer's interpretation of mentions. Different roles index differences in pragmatic status. A grammatical coding choice associated with new mentions of high activation in texts can be expected to elicit greater activation effort on the part of the Hearer, as the referent is likely to demand more attention and be more persistent and important for the ensuing text. Conversely, it is proposed that a coding choice associated with low activation will demand less activation effort on behalf of the Hearer. The notion of information pressure has to be mediated by these observations: information which needs to be kept in the active focus of attention creates more pressure than information which serves an orienting or contextualizing function and which is therefore not in the focus of attention.

A first, striking example of difference between Core roles is that when an Actor (A/Sa) does code a first mention — something which happens only rarely, as we have seen — then this will be an unimportant mention (less likely to recur than a first mention expressed in other Core roles): see Durie (1994: 520) for details. This is of course the Acehnese analogue of Chafe's "Light subject constraint" (Chafe 1994); however, it applies not to "Subjects" (A/S) in Acehnese, but to Actors (A/Sa).

(16) *Lapan plôh thôn teuk,* Hamzah
eight year after
ngön lahé Nabi Muhamat,
after born Prophet Muhammad
lahé sa-boh raja di tanöh Madiyan.
born one-CLASS king LOC country Madian
nyang geu-kheun jinoe,
REL 3-call now
'Peulastina'.
Palestine
nyang ka di-cok lé,[24]
REL already 3-take by
nyoe pue nan,
now what name
bani Israél.
tribe Israel
'Eighty years after the birth of the Prophet Muhammad, a certain king was born in the country of Madian, which is now called "Palestine", which has been taken by — what are they called — the tribe of Israel.'

In (16) the tribe of Israel, which is introduced as an At, plays no part in the story and is not mentioned again.[25] Note that this involves a kind of semiotic reversal: normally A/Sa are associated with mentions of established referents of high importance, which occur in the focus of attention. However when a first mention of a referent occurs in this staging site, the reverse inference can be drawn that this is an unimportant referent.

When something important must be introduced which might appear first in a Actor role by virtue of the ideational content of the story, then a predicate may be introduced to facilitate a non-A/Sa introduction. For example in an incident in this story this same king is bitten by a snake. This is an important incident. When the story teller introduces the snake he might have simply said "a snake was lying under his chair", but since the verb *éh* 'lie, sleep' takes an Sa argument — as seen by the proclitic in (17) — a presentative verb *na* is used so that the snake on its first appearance is presented as So:

(17) *keubeutuluan,* Hamzah
it.came.to.pass
bak gaki kurusi nyan,
at foot chair that
na sa-boh aneuk uleue,
be one-CLASS child snake

di-éh,
3-lie
'It happened that there was a small snake lying there at the foot of the chair…'

Now let us consider the pragmatic status of other roles in staging first mentions. We first need to make some distinctions between different kinds of first mentions. Of the three types of first mentions, Accessible expressions are relatively infrequent in Core roles, as Table 8 shows.

Table 8. Core First Mentions, by type and text

Text	Inferable	Accessible	Brand-New
Mouse-Deer	23	1	12
Hamzah	46	3	14
Conversation	32	12	32

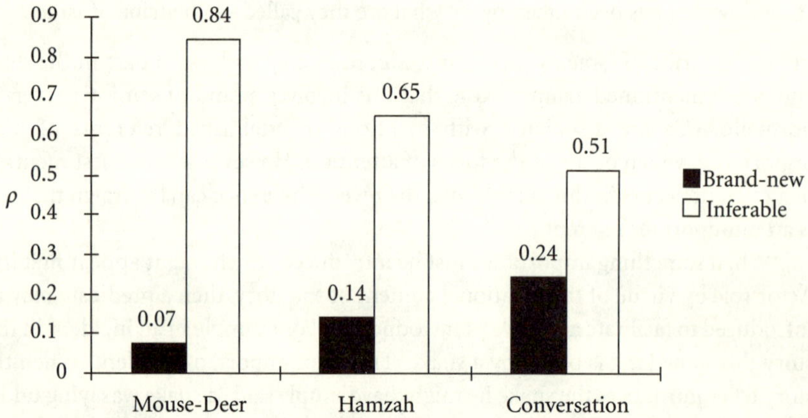

Figure 5. Referential density of referents introduced as Brand-New and Inferable, by text.

Of all first mentions, Brand-New mentions as a group have higher activation cost (Chafe 1994:73) since they have minimal grounding in context or prior knowledge. Strikingly, Brand-New mentions are also more persistent in each text than the other types of first mentions: high activation cost correlates with high importance, and an implicit high level of activation or focus of attention for the ensuing discourse. This is reflected in Figure 5, which shows that Brand-New mentions have much lower referential density (i.e., they are mentioned much more requently) than Inferables. Here referential density is the number of referents divided by the total sum of their mentions: across all three texts Brand-New mentions are mentioned again more than five times on average, while Inferables are mentioned again less than one time on average.

Note also that persistence differentials between Brand-New and Inferable mentions are most marked in the written narrative "Mouse-Deer", and least marked in the conversation: as the persistence of Brand-New first mentions rises, so does the persistence of Inferable first mentions fall. The reason for this contrast between the texts is clearly due to the planned nature of narrative in comparison to conversation. In a conversation the topics being discussed are in general not those under the exclusive control of one speaker, and they may be changed, possibly in response to those which were initially mentioned as if in passing. In contrast a narrative is presented by one speaker, who is in a position to reliably anticipate how the story-line will develop, and to tailor his text accordingly.

This difference between the texts points to the possibility of genre-specific expectations of differentials in activation status, associated with differences in initial activation cost. In other words, the reader/hearer of the written narrative might anticipate a high level of persistence for Brand-New mentions, much higher than for Inferables. However, a participant in a conversation might expect less differentiation between the persistence of Brand-New and Inferable mentions, because initial activation cost is a less reliable indicator of future persistence in conversation.

Now that we have established the high persistence of Brand-New mentions, we can consider further the functional differentiation of roles. A significant difference emerges between the text, "Conversation" and the two narratives, "Mouse-Deer" and "Hamzah" (Figure 6).

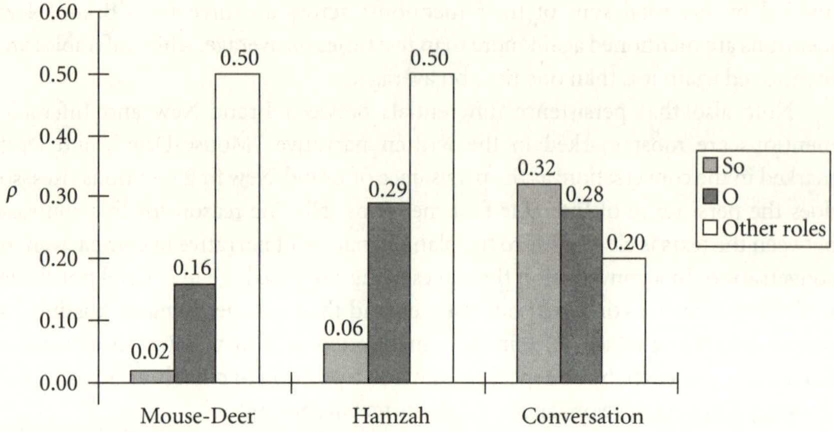

Figure 6. Referential density of referents introduced as Brand-New.

We find that in the narratives, roles more to the left of the hierarchy So < O < Oblique make Brand-New introductions which are more persistent throughout the whole text. This is reflected in lower referential density values, as shown in Figure 6: Brand-New mentions in the So role are highly continuous throughout the ensuing discourse in "Mouse-Deer" and "Hamzah", being mentioned again on average approximately 50 times ("Mouse-Deer") and approximately 16 times ("Hamzah") within each text. In contrast, Brand-New mentions in other roles are on average mentioned again only once ($\rho = 0.50$). The transitive Undergoer O occupies a more intermediate position: its Brand-New introductions are on average mentioned again between 2 and 5 times ($\rho = 0.29, 0.16$).

In the text "Conversation" there appears to be a functional reversal: the marked difference among roles in the kinds of Brand-New mentions is not apparent, but what differences there are point to Oblique Brand-New mentions having the greater ensuing continuity in "Conversation".

Why is there such a functional reversal? The key to understanding the distinctive pragmatic profiles of roles in "Conversation" lies in the use of Free NP's. In "Conversation" these form the preferred locus for *persistent* new mentions. This is demonstrated in Table 9, which shows that of all roles, the Free Brand-New first mentions are the most persistent in the text "Conversation".

As is also apparent in Table 10, this appears to have rendered redundant the use of So for important new mentions which we find in the narratives. This table shows that "Hamzah" and "Conversation" have a similar *total* proportion of Brand-New mentions in So and Free roles (38% and 41% respectively), but in the text "Conversation" many more are found in the Free role, although in "Hamzah" relatively few are Free. Thus in "Conversation", a significant number of Brand-New mentions

Table 9. Referential density of referents of Brand-New mentions in "Conversation"

Role	ρ
Free	0.14
So	0.32
O	0.28
A/Sa	0.33
Other roles	0.33

Table 10. Percentage of Brand-New mentions which fall in the So and Free roles, by text

	Mouse-Deer	Hamzah	Conversation
So	24%	34%	14%
Free	0%	4%	27%
Total: So + Free	24%	38%	41%

which might in a narrative have appeared as Undergoers of intransitive verbs are presented as unattached, Free NP's. Moreover, it is precisely the Brand-New introductions with greater ensuing persistence which have Free status (Table 9). This appears to account for the functional reversal apparent in Figure 6.

The allocation of important new mentions to a different coding site — to Free unattached mentions, rather than in intransitive clauses — may well be a distinctive feature of Acehnese conversation, in contrast to Acehnese narrative, and of conversation in general.[26] It illustrates that the use of intransitive verbs to introduce important new mentions is not in itself a direct consequence of ideational content, i.e. of what the speaker wants to say, but can be regarded as a conventional feature of narrative discourse, and as such as an adaptive response to the need for a distinct, otherwise information-poor, grammatical frame for presenting important new mentions. It is an adaptive response at the level of discourse-grammar conventions, one that is especially useful in narrative, where major new characters can be introduced into the story using verbs of movement, appearance, or coming into existence (e.g. *be born*). This suits the semiotic of presentation well, as the motion or birth reported in the story parallels and heralds the cognitive introduction into the hearer's consciousness. Example (16) above shows the use of an So mention to introduce a major Brand-New referent.

In conversations, where foci of attention are not necessarily construed in terms of a narrative world, situated in space and time, presentation by use of intransitive verbs (e.g., of motion and coming into existence) seems less pertinent. The interactional nature of a conversation favours more modular and parenthetical presentative strategies: a referent can simply be named, and thus proffered to the hearer for confirmation, independently of whatever else needs to be said. Since conversation tends to be structured in terms of turn pairs, an unattached presentation can easily be fitted as a turn into the larger turn-taking structure. An introduction can then be confirmed, rejected, or queried by the hearer, without any complications or interruptions for the flow of the rest of the interlocutor's presentation. A typical conversational introduction of this kind is shown in (18), in which *Teungku Muhammad Sulaiman* is introduced as a Free mention, followed by multiple confirmations.[27] In contrast, narrative presentations using intransitive verbs integrate the presentation into the structure of the narrative.

(18) B: *adak sinoe Teungku Muhammad Sulaiman.* Conversation
if now Title
'And now-a-days Muhammad Sulaiman
A: *nyö*
yes
B: *nyö beutôi.*
yes indeed
A: *'eu-'eu*
uh-huh
B: *nyan geu-undang ureueng u rumoh,*
he 3-invite people to house
'He invites people to his house.'

It is important to note that Free mentions are not exclusively used in the conversation for presentation of new referents. About 50% of the Free mentions in "Conversation", and about 35% in "Hamzah" have Mentioned status. We would therefore expect that other functions, such as reactivating referents and answering questions, are also significant (cf. Tao 1993). In general the function of a coding device or grammatical form can vary according to the type of the mention. The Actor roles are used for highly persistent, previously introduced referents, and also for highly non-persistent first mentions. Likewise, the Free role fulfils a number of distinct functions. What is important for our purposes is that, in the packaging of Brand-New first mentions, the text "Conversation" devotes Free expressions to the presentation of more persistent mentions.

Lexical density correlates of higher information pressure

We have seen that the notion of information pressure must be clarified in terms of what kind of information is involved. There are distinct types of information; e.g., Core and Oblique information, which are coded very differently, and which do not contribute equally to the cognitive load implied by the term *information pressure.* Furthermore, within Core information, some referents are highly persistent and make special demands on presentation, while others are more ephemeral. It has also been argued that the genre of a text can influence coding choices for managing first mentions, or more generally for managing information pressure.[28] Du Bois's hypothesis that increased use of intransitive verbs could be an escape valve for greater information pressure is confirmed by the data of this rather limited study, but the evidence suggests that increased use of intransitives for introductions of new referents is not the reason for this correlation. Other possible correlates of greater information pressure were identified: increased use of lexical mentions, and a more frequent appearance of Core information into non-Core coding sites, including into Free mentions (concerning the latter, see also Herring 1989).

Let us now return to Du Bois's hypothesis that greater information pressure is correlated with more ergative-like coding patterns in the proportions of lexical mentions (i.e., in lexical density). We have already noted an overall higher lexical density in "Hamzah" and "Conversation", the two texts with higher information pressure (Table 5). Figure 7 shows that this is still true when the lexical density figures are broken down by Core role. However, as Figure 7 also shows, we find that the greater information pressure in "Hamzah" and "Conversation" is not correlated with *realignment* towards an ergative-like coding pattern — this would involve Sa gravitating towards So, Se and O. Rather, it is correlated with *stretching* of the lexical density hierarchy, involving differentiation *within* the Actor and Undergoer roles, although in all three texts all Undergoer sub-roles still have much higher lexical density values than the Actor sub-roles. Thus the Sa = A << So = O hierarchy of "Mouse-Deer" becomes an Sa < A << So (< Se) < O hierarchy of lexical density in "Hamzah" and "Conversation". In "Hamzah", for example, where both the Actor roles (Sa, A) and the Undergoer roles (So, O, Se) encompass a spread in lexical density values, Sa does not reassociate pragmatically with So, since Sa << So remains as the largest discontinuity in the lexical density hierarchy.

For all three texts we can propose a hierarchy of lexical density as follows:

A ≤ Sa << So ≤ O ≤ Se

This is very similar — except for the placement of Se — to the hierarchy of proportions of first mentions, shown in Figure 4 above.[29]

We are now in a position to consider the effect of locating important first mentions in the Free role rather than So, as discussed above for "Conversation". The "loss" of this pragmatically salient type of lexical mention from So clearly seems to be correlated with an effect on lexical density: So is the only Core Role in "Conversation" which has lower lexical density than in "Mouse-Deer". Note also that in the other two texts, which do not have this effect, the differential from Sa to So is a massive 39% — a jump from 18% to 57% in "Mouse-Deer" and 28% to 67% in "Hamzah". However, in "Conversation" this differential is reduced to 26% — a jump from 26% to 52%.

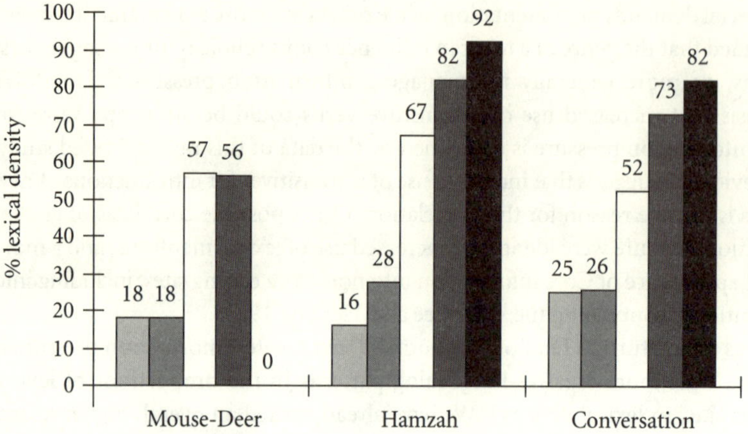

Figure 7. Lexical density by role and text.

What is especially significant is that the consequent fragmenting of the pragmatic alignments of the macro-roles of Actor and Undergoer does not amount to an ergative realignment. Note firstly that Sa and A in "Conversation" are still closely similar: if Sa is being used more for lexical expressions under conditions of greater information pressure, then so is A. Also the Undergoer roles (So, O and Se) have disassociated to a degree, encompassing a spread in referential density values ranging from 52% to 82%. What results is a blurring of the pragmatic coherence of the grammatical macro-role groupings, a stretching of the hierarchy, and at the same time an emergence or clarification of finer-grained discriminations, splitting categories that otherwise may be grouped together. This is a de-alignment effect, rather than a realignment.

Conclusions

Acehnese shows a robust split-intransitive alignment pattern — i.e., A/Sa << So/O — consistent with its morphosyntactic structure. This contrasts with the ergative A << S/O alignment reported for Sakapulteko discourse by Du Bois (1987). In this sense Preferred Argument Structure is partly language-specific: Preferred Argument Structure is tuned to the grammatical type of the language, by means of such mechanisms as language-specific preferences for the lexical selection of verbs, without losing its basic character. This basic character can be observed in the generalization that in Acehnese the O/So (Undergoer) grouping is the preferred locus of lexical mentions. This grouping is also the preferred locus for first mentions among the Core roles, as the Preferred Argument Structure account predicts.

The specific Acehnese instantiation of Preferred Argument Structure has a character which mirrors its grammatical structure. One can use the language of *negotiation* to describe this relationship. Fundamental characteristics of Preferred Argument Structure are observed to hold in Acehnese texts, but there can be a number of local compromises, in the grammar of the language — as Du Bois emphasised — but also in its discourse preferences. There is an adjustment of discourse patterns, which themselves constitute motivations of grammar, to a particular grammatical resolution of the competing motivations. Another metaphor we can use for this mutual adjustment of grammar, lexicon and pragmatics is that of *tuning*: grammar and discourse preferences are tuned to each other in a language-specific pattern, whilst still conforming to certain universal constraints.[30]

The robustness of the discourse-grammar correlations in Acehnese, which display a negotiated, language-specific character within universal constraints, suggests that emergent discourse preferences, which are constituted for a language across whole classes of texts, and established in tandem with the whole grammatical system, can in their turn impose constraints on pragmatic features of particular texts of the language. In other words, pragmatic features of texts are in part conventional and thus language-specific.

This very preliminary study also suggests that a correlate of greater Core information pressure in Acehnese is a *fragmenting* of the grammatical alignment, a stretching in the general direction of A < Sa < So < O. Here the nature of the ambivalent status of the S role is clear. However, this does not tend towards an ergative realignment as Du Bois predicted. The asymptote of greater information pressure in Acehnese is fragmentation of alignment, rather than realignment of Preferred Argument Structure to a more ergative A < S/O pattern. Yet here we still observe the robustness of the language-specific "active" pattern of alignment of grammar and discourse.

This study, in agreement with Thompson (MS), has underscored the importance of distinguishing between different kinds of information, which characteristically are channelled through different grammatical roles. Information pressure as a concept must be defined precisely in terms of the type of information being encoded. The theory of Preferred Argument Structure is primarily concerned with the treatment of "Core information": mentions of tracked referents which occupy the focus of attention, have some persistence through a text, and are encoded in the conduit of Core rather than Oblique grammatical roles.

Finally we find that the big picture of motivations for grammatical coding which Du Bois sketched in his theory of Preferred Argument Structure must be construed in any particular language out of much finer distinctions, defined against a grid of categories of reference and genre. This too is an extension rather than a contradiction of Du Bois's whole approach.

Notes

* I gratefully acknowledge the research support of the Australian Research Council through their grant "Studies Grammaticalization and Lexicalization", and to the Faculty of Arts at the University of Melbourne. Nick Nicholas provided invaluable support in helping to design the Discourse Links database system which provided all the quantitative data used in this paper. For comments on earlier draft versions, many thanks to: Judith Bishop, Bill McGregor, Nick Nicholas and also to the volume editors.

1. Lexical = not a pronoun and non-zero. For Du Bois non-lexicals include zeros, pronouns, cross-referencing affixes, and clitics. Lexicals are full NP's. "Lexical" should however be interpreted differently in different languages, depending on whether pronouns are typically used to code highly anaphoric mentions. In a language like Acehnese, with extensive zero anaphora, and in which pronouns are almost invariably stressed and often contrastive, the term could be restricted to exclude pronouns. In English it could be restricted to zeroes and *unstressed* pronouns, with stressed pronouns treated as lexical.

2. Du Bois points out that even the categories of S, A and O, "rather than being universal primitives, simply represent a convenient but fictive level of analysis" (1985: 357).

3. Herring (1989), misunderstanding the concept of motivation, regards the mismatch in Sakapulteko as a logical flaw in Du Bois's argument. A further distortion in Herring's argument derives from her demand that the grouping of S and A should involve functional specialization in terms of cognitive or semantic factors. In Du Bois's account, the cognitive/semantic motivations do not themselves *directly* impact upon coding choices, but only *proximately*, through the "recurrent clusterings in parole" (Du Bois 1985: 357) which they produce. This is of course a key difference between the Du Bois account of ergativity and more directly cognitively or semantically based approaches.

4. Here I use the term nominative to designate the case which is sometimes referred as the *absolutive* in an ergative patterning case system.

5. Dixon (1994: §3.4.3) reports a number of languages in which the accusative is formally unmarked and the nominative is formally marked. In such cases it is not always clear what the correct case analysis should be. Mel'cuk (MS) argues that in Maasai, a language which is putatively of this type, what has traditionally been called "accusative" is actually the nominative — he defines the nominative as the case of nomination (Mel'cuk 1992: 103) — and what is traditionally called "nominative" is an oblique case used to mark transitive subjects. A parallel case is Nias, which is described by Brown (MS) as having an unmarked ergative and marked absolutive (a possibility which Dixon 1994: 58 had not encountered). Here too Mel'cuk's approach would suggest that the properties of the supposed "ergative" are actually those of a nominative, and what is called an "absolutive" is in fact best regarded as an oblique case.

6. For some rare exceptions, see Dixon (1994: 44).

7. Key early developments of Silverstein's ideas are Dixon (1979) and Comrie (1978). For a more recent update and overview, see Dixon (1994). A number of different explanations for the ergative-accusative coding patterns have been proposed. Silverstein himself offered an account the subtlety of which has often been underestimated. A necessary task, which Du Bois did not attempt in his 1987 paper, and which goes beyond the scope of this paper, will be to evaluate to what extent Du Bois's account of the full range of Silverstein hierarchy effects is more satisfactory than many of the competing explanations.

8. The typology of non-referring expressions is too complex to explore here. It remains an important topic for research at the grammar-discourse interface. Impressionistically, there appear to be significant differences across languages. See Du Bois and Thompson (MS) for a categorization of some kinds of non-referring expressions in English texts.

9. Distinct from tracking relations involving multiple mentions are dependencies which are constituted by syntactic binding, including those found in relative clause constructions. Such dependencies do not constitute repeated 'mentions', since they are referentially parasitic: in themselves they do not require discourse-anaphoric identification, because their interpretation is bound to the interpretation of the head of the NP of which the relative clause is a modifier. For this reason throughout this paper I have excluded such grammatical anaphors from my counts as mentions.

10. This is not to say that non-trackables may not involve great semantic complexity. Consequently non-trackables may present processing difficulties, but not because of the pressure of referent tracking.

11. The term *Free* was introduced in Durie 1994. These are related to what Hongyin Tao calls "detached NP intonation units" (Tao 1993: Ch 8); however; it is important to distinguish prosodic attachment from syntactic dependency. It seems preferable to use the term *unattached* for prosodic separateness, and *Free* for lack of syntactic dependency. (Note that in this study, Free expressions do not include Vocatives). Also related are what Herring (1989) calls "verbless presentational utterances", although this is a somewhat infelicitous expression: unattached mentions need not be presentational, and the term "verbless" can lead to confusion in a language in which clausal predicates need not be verbs. Thus, in my classification, a predicate nominal is not Free, since it is itself the head of a clause: grammatically it is "accounted for". Neither is the subject of an NP or PP predicate a Free expression, since it is grammatically dependent upon its predicate.

12. "++" is an intonational marker. It indicates that the following material is pronounced very quickly and lightly, tacked on or cliticized to the preceding intonation unit, but without forming a distinct intonation unit of its own. This is a distinctive Acehnese intonation pattern.

13. As noted, referential density is defined only over trackable mentions.

14. Some referents may of course be both Core and Oblique, and there is thus some overlap between these two classes of referents.

15. Standard statistical tests of significance have not been applied to these data averages because the patterns of frequency of referent mentions cannot be assumed to have a normal distribution — a small number of referents have very many mentions, while most have very few. The t-test in particular cannot be used to evaluate significance.

16. Oblique material does generate some cognitive demands, such as the need to integrate locative expressions into the whole spatial deictic frame: this is a demand for establishing relational coherence between background elements. However, this is quite distinct from information pressure. One can, for example, apprehend the pattern of dots on a page, without keeping track of which dot is which.

17. In some languages it may be difficult to determine whether a particular verb used in a text is transitive or intransitive. However, in Acehnese transitivity is a clearly discriminated lexical feature of verbs: each verb is lexically transitive or intransitive. The distinction is also reflected in the use of the marker *lé* before a post-verbal Actor.

18. In an earlier paper I attempted to test Du Bois's hypothesis concerning use of intransitives in texts with greater information pressure (Durie 1994). That paper used a metric of Core trackable mentions per verb ("Expression Density per Predicate"). On the basis of that evidence I concluded

that there was not a greater resort to intransitives in "Hamzah" and "Conversation". However, my argument was flawed since this was an inadequate way of measuring transitivity: not all transitive verbs in the texts occur with two trackable referent mentions for arguments.

19. Here pronouns are counted as lexical; see note 2 above.

20. The terms in parentheses give equivalents in terms of the SAO terminology of Dixon (1979). The inventory of roles is somewhat simplified here: for a full list see Durie (1994).

21. This hierarchy is not an arbitrary construct of the researcher. Rather it reflects the formulation of definitions of the status types, and also the universal natural hierarchy manifested in languages, according to which, for example, deixis tends to override other aspects of activation status in determining the form of an anaphor, and previous mention can override accessibility or inferability. It is however important to acknowledge that these categories are merely operational approximations of cognitive distinctions involving the two distinct phenomena of activation state and identifiability (Chafe 1987, 1993; Ariel 1990; Du Bois and Thompson MS; Thompson MS).

22. Adnominals present a fascinating topic in the study of grammar and discourse. Their pragmatic profile is typically that of a Core argument, but grammatically they do not occupy the "centre stage" of Core argument status. Languages have various strategies for treating adnominals as grammatical arguments of the clause, consonant with their pragmatic status (see e.g., the studies of Chappell and McGregor 1995).

23. In "Mouse-Deer", the total number of subjects of non-verbal predicates (Se) was too small to include in the counts. Therefore this column is left blank. However, in "Mouse-Deer" the Sa column is included, because this category is well-attested: here the 0% level reflects no first mentions.

24. Despite the gloss of *lé* as 'by', this is not a passive construction, and A here is not an oblique: this can been seen from the fact that it still controls verbal cross-referencing (see Durie 1986, 1987, 1988a)

25. The appearance of *bani Israél* in an incidental relative clause also serves to de-emphasize the reference.

26. Tao 1993: 171–4 notes the important role of NP Intonation Units in introducing new referents into Mandarin Chinese conversation.

27. Indeed in the "Conversation" new introductions can be accompanied by confirmations, whatever role is used.

28. The findings of this study thus support O'Dowd's (1990) findings that a genre can employ genre-specific mechanisms for managing that pressure, no doubt partly due to the distinctive nature of different kinds of information: in her study she examined medical discourse, which involve a many body-part references.

29. Special factors may inhibit zero anaphoric realization of Se: the predicate is often nominal, giving potential for ambiguity if there is a zero anaphoric subject, and there are inhibited possibilities for enclitic cross-referencing with non-verbal predications (see Durie 1985).

30. Du Bois emphasized grammar-discourse relatedness, but of course discourse preferences and grammatical structures are also closely linked to the structure of the lexicon. The Acehnese verbal lexicon, with its sharp division between transitive and intransitive verbs, and its clear semantic contrast between Actors and Undergoers, is thoroughly implicated in this negotiated arrangement.

References

Ariel, Mira. 1990. *Accessing Noun-Phrase Antecedents.* London: Routledge.

Brown, Lea. MS. "Nominal mutation in Nias".

Chafe, Wallace. 1987. "Cognitive constraints on information flow". In R. Tomlin (ed.), *Coherence and Grounding in Discourse.* Amsterdam: Benjamins, 21–51.

Chafe, Wallace. 1994. *Discourse, Consciousness and Time.* Chicago: University of Chicago Press.

Chappell, Hilary and William McGregor (eds). 1995. *The Grammar of Inalienability: A Typological Perspective on Body Part Terms and the Part-whole Relation.* Berlin: Mouton de Gruyter.

Comrie, Bernard. 1978. "Ergativity". In W.P. Lehmann (ed.), *Syntactic Typology.* Austin: University of Texas Press, 329–394.

Dixon, Robert M.W. 1979. "Ergativity". *Language* 55: 59–138.

Dixon, Robert M.W. 1994. *Ergativity.* Cambridge: Cambridge University Press.

Du Bois, John W. 1980. "Beyond definiteness: the trace of identity in discourse". In W. Chafe (ed.), *The Pear Stories.* Norwood, New Jersey: Ablex, 9–50.

Du Bois, John W. 1985. "Competing motivations". In J. Haiman (ed.), *Iconity in Syntax.* Amsterdam: Benjamins, 343–365.

Du Bois, John W. 1987. "The discourse basis of ergativity". *Language* 63: 805–855.

Du Bois, John W. and Sandra A. Thompson. MS. Dimensions of a theory of information flow. Unpublished mansucript, June 1991.

Durie, Mark. 1985. *A Grammar of Acehnese.* Dordrecht: Foris.

Durie, Mark. 1986. "The use of passive-like strategies in Acehnese." *NUSA* 25: 19–30. *Miscellaneous Studies in Indonesian and Other Languages in Indonesia,* Part VII, Soenjono Dardjowidjojo (ed.). Lembaga Bahasa, Universitas Katolik Indonesia Atma Jaya, Jakarta.

Durie, Mark. 1987. "Grammatical relations in Acehnese". *Studies in Language* 11: 387–421.

Durie, Mark. 1988a. "The so-called passive of Acehnese." *Language* 64: 104–113.

Durie, Mark. 1988b. "Preferred Argument Structure in an active language: arguments against the category 'intransitive subject'". *Lingua* 74: 1–25.

Durie, Mark. 1994. "A case study of pragmatic linking". *TEXT* 14.4: 495–529.

Durie, Mark. 1995. "Towards an understanding of linguistic evolution and the notion 'X has a function Y'". In W. Abraham, T. Givón and S.A. Thompson (eds), *Discourse Grammar and Typology.* (Studies in Language Companion Series Vol. 27). Amsterdam: Benjamins, 275–308.

Givón, Talmy (ed.). 1983. *Topic Continuity in Discourse: A Quantitative Cross-Language Study.* Amsterdam: Benjamins.

Herring, Susan. 1989. "Verbless presentation and the discourse basis of ergativity". In B. Music, R. Graczyk and C. Wiltshire (eds), *Papers from the 25th Annual Regional Meeting of the Chicago Linguistic Society 25, Part 2: Parasession on Language in Context.* Chicago: Chicago Linguistic Society, 123–137.

Malkiel, Yakov. 1967. "Multiple versus simple causation in linguistic change". *To Honor Roman Jakobson: Essays on the occasion of his seventienth birthday.* Vol. 2. The Hague: Mouton, 1228–1246.

Mel'cuk, Igor. 1992. "Toward a logical analysis of the notion 'ergative construction'". *Studies in Language* 16: 91–138.

Mel'cuk, Igor. 1997. "Grammatical cases, basic verbal construction, and voice in Maasai: towards a better analysis of the concepts". In Wolfgang U. Dressler et al. (ed.) *Advances in Morphology.* Berlin & New York: Mouton de Gruyter, 131–170.

Moravcsik, Edith A. 1978. "On the distribution of ergative and accusative patterns". *Lingua* 45: 233–279.

O'Dowd, Elizabeth. 1990. "Discourse pressure, genre and grammatical alignment — after Du Bois". *Studies in Language* 14: 365–403.

Prince, Ellen. 1981. "Toward a typology of given-new information". In P. Cole (ed.). *Radical pragmatics.* New York: Academic Press, 223–255.

Silverstein, Michael. 1976. "Hierarchy of features and ergativity". In R.M.W. Dixon (ed.). *Grammatical Categories in Australian Languages.* (Linguistic Series No. 22, Australian Institute of Aboriginal Studies, Canberra). New Jersey: Humanities Press, 112–171.

Sulaiman, Budiman. 1978. *Haba Peulandôk.* Bireuen, Aceh: Pustaka Mahmudiyah.

Tao, Hongyin. 1993. *Units in Mandarin: Discourse and grammar.* A PhD dissertation, University of California, Santa Barbara.

Thompson, Sandra A. 1997. "Discourse motivations for the core-oblique distinction as a language universal". In Akio Kamio (ed.), *Directions in Functional Linguistics.* Amsterdam: Benjamins, 59–82.

Beyond Preferred Argument Structure

Sentences, pronouns, and given referents in Nepali*

Carol Genetti and Laura D. Crain
University of California, Santa Barbara / California State University, Channel Islands

Introduction

One of the most compelling conclusions that can be drawn from Du Bois' seminal study of Preferred Argument Structure in Sakapulteko (1987b) is that grammar and discourse are interrelated and complementary. In examining Sakapulteko discourse, Du Bois found evidence of an absolutive patterning in the appearance of lexical arguments; overwhelmingly, lexical arguments were found occurring in the S and O roles, while lexical As were extremely rare. This absolutive distribution of lexical mentions turned out to be a reflection of the pragmatics of information flow, as new mentions also appeared in absolutive contexts. Thus information-flow patterns created a preference for absolutive lexicality, which in turn motivated the ergative cross-referencing system common to Mayan languages. The notion of complementarity between grammatical and discourse patterns was further explored in Du Bois (1987a), which pointed out that the one category that is morphologically unmarked in the Mayan verbal paradigm, namely third-person absolutive, is also the same category that will appear lexically in the clause during the production of spoken discourse.

In addition to these general observations, Du Bois (1987b) made a number of specific claims, which took the form of constraints. In Du Bois' terms, constraints are preferences for a particular discourse pattern, which speakers are free to violate, but rarely do. These constraints can be deduced from the observation of patterns occurring over the aggregate of instances of language use (1987b:819). Two constraints involve the distribution of lexical mentions in discourse:

> One Lexical Argument Constraint: Avoid more than one lexical argument per clause. (Du Bois 1987b:819)

Non-lexical A Constraint: Avoid lexical A's. (Du Bois 1987b: 821)

These two constraints form the grammatical dimension of Preferred Argument Structure. It is clear that this dimension focuses predominantly on lexicality; the constraints make no mention of pronouns or "zero" mentions (unexpressed NP's). It is interesting to note that Sakapulteko is a head-marking language with extensive cross-referencing of arguments on the verb, and only the occasional use of independent pronouns (Du Bois 1987b: 814). The emphasis on lexicality is natural in a language of this type. However, other languages which are typologically distinct from Sakapulteko do use independent pronouns extensively, and so have a robust three-way system of reference (lexical, pronoun, zero). One way to build on Preferred Argument Structure research, then, is to explore languages of this type.

The two grammatical constraints proposed by Du Bois are complemented by parallel pragmatic constraints:

One New Argument Constraint: Avoid more than one new argument per clause. (Du Bois 1987b: 826)

Given A Constraint: Avoid new A's. (Du Bois 1987b: 827)

These constraints are seen as motivating the distribution of lexical mentions: since new referents are generally instantiated with lexical mentions, the occurrence of new mentions in A and S roles contributes to the overall absolutive patterning of lexical noun phrases. An interesting point, however, is that not all lexical mentions are new. Do lexical mentions which are given also occur in absolutive patterns?

The current study examines the amount and distribution of lexical, pronominal and zero mentions in Nepali, an Indo-Aryan language and the national language of Nepal. In this language, there is evidence for all four Preferred Argument Structure constraints, and it is clear that the patterns first identified by Du Bois are found. However, unlike Sakapulteko, Nepali uses independent pronouns with considerable frequency, and as a result, the number of "overt" mentions (lexical or pronominal, Du Bois 1987a) is surprisingly high. This fact is attributed to a strategy in which the sentence, as opposed to the clause, plays a pivotal role in determining the amount of overt mention. In particular, the primary pattern used by the speakers in our study was to overtly mention each referent once in a sentence, regardless of the number of times the referent functioned as a grammatical argument within that sentence.

Since Preferred Argument Structure theory focuses on lexicality, none of the constraints makes predictions regarding the distribution of frequent independent pronouns. Interestingly, the distribution of pronominal mentions appears to follow different patterns from those established for lexical mentions. In particular, pronominal mentions occur overwhelmingly in the S and A roles, hence follow a nominative, as opposed to an absolutive, pattern. Nepali thus shows evidence of a split-ergative system based on mention type (absolutive lexical mentions and nominative pronominal mentions). The nominative distribution of pronouns is clearly related to another pattern, a nominative distribution of given lexical mentions. Since pronouns in the A and S roles are primarily given, the number of given lexical mentions in these roles is correspondingly low. Thus nominative patterning is found with both pronominal and lexical mentions with given activation cost: given mentions have nominative distribution and non-given (new, accessible and non-referential mentions) have absolutive distribution. This study thus provides further evidence for the notion of competing motivations in the determination of preferred patterns of argument mention in discourse (cf. Du Bois 1985). In addition, the very different patterns which are found in Nepali are related to independent typological facts about Nepali grammar and discourse. Thus this paper provides strong support for the general claim regarding the interrelationship of grammar and discourse.

Background

Data

Data for our study were taken from three native speakers of Nepali, all from Kathmandu, and all approximately of the same age and socioeconomic class.[1] The five narratives from Mrs. Kalyāni K. C. were recorded in Nepal in 1988, while the three from Mr. Hemrāj Pahāri were recorded in Berkeley in the same year. The two narratives of Mrs. Rājeswari Bista were recorded in Santa Barbara in 1991. Nine of the ten narratives tell common folk stories or ghost stories. One of Mr. Pahāri's narratives is a first-person account of his trip to the United States. The study is based on a total of 816 clauses. Given the small size of our database, we consider our findings to be preliminary, and leave open the possibility that there may be variation based on genre, dialect, and/or sociolinguistic variables.

Relevant background on Nepali morphosyntax

Nepali is a verb-final language; the positioning of arguments and adjuncts before the verb is free, and presumably controlled by discourse factors. It is also possible for arguments or adjuncts to be postposed after the verb; this construction is marked.

Nepali may be characterized as a dependent-marking language (Nichols 1986). In particular, case distinctions are signaled by a set of suffixal casemarkers found on nouns and pronouns; the verbal agreement system is not involved in the specification of case roles. The Nepali case system is generally described as split-ergative. The primary pattern is that the ergative case suffix *-le* marks nouns in A-role in perfective contexts, while nouns in A-role in imperfective contexts carry no morphological marking. However, it is not unusual to find counter-examples to the stated pattern in natural discourse. In particular, *-le* may be found in some imperfective contexts. Thus whether or not Nepali is best characterized as split-ergative is still an open question and will require further study.

Indirect objects in Nepali are marked with the case suffix *-lāi*. This suffix also may mark direct objects. The suffix *-lāi* is also found marking experiencer subjects with certain types of predicates (Wallace 1985, Ichihashi-Nakayama 1994).

The Nepali finite verb always agrees with the person of its subject (S or A).[2] Prescriptively, it also agrees with the subject in number and gender. In actual use, however, these categories are often not instantiated (Genetti 1993). Non-finite verbs may be chaining or adverbial; they do not carry agreement morphology.

In Nepali discourse, complex sentences commonly occur, formed by combinations of clause chains, clausal complements, and adverbial clauses (Wallace 1985, Crain 1992). These sentences often consist of two to four clauses, but longer sentences of six or eight clauses are not at all unusual. These structures are highly integrated, with extensive embedding, at times causing verbs and their arguments to be separated by complete clauses or even combinations of clauses. An example of a complex structure is given in (1):[3]

(1) Rājeswari Bista
1. *timile* *lyā-eko* *khānekurā*
   2SG.ERG bring-PART food
2. *malāi*
   1SG.DAT
3. *khā-na*
   eat-PURP
4. *hatār bhaisak-yo*
   hurry be.finish-3SG.PST
   'I am in a hurry to eat the food that you brought.'

In this relatively simple example, the verb *khā-na* 'eat' in line 3 functions as the complement of the complex predicate 'be in a hurry' (line 4) which takes a dative subject (*malāi* in line 2). Interestingly, the object of 'eat' is the NP 'the food that you brought' in line 1. It is divided from its verb by the intervening *malāi*. While the subjects of the two verbs are coreferential, the dative casemarking of the pronoun in 2 clearly marks it as being the grammatical subject of 'be in a hurry', and not the grammatical subject of 'eat'. So line 1 contains the object of the verb in line 3, while line 2 contains the subject of the verb in line 4.

Somewhat more complex is the following example:

(2) Hemrāj Pahāri
1. *ma*
1SG
2. *uhā̃ pani*
3SG also
3. *sut-tāi lagā-era*
suit-tie put.on-CC
4. *āu-nuholā*
come-3SG.FUT2
5. *bhanne soc-eko thi-ẽ.*
COMP think-PART be-1SG.PST
'I had thought he would also come wearing a suit and tie.'

The first person singular pronoun in line 1 is the subject of the verb *soceko thi-ẽ* 'had thought' in line 5. The object of this verb is an embedded direct quote set off by the complementizer *bhanne*.[4] The quote consists of a two-predicate clause chain, the non-finite verb being *lagāunu* 'to put on (clothing)', and the finite verb being *āunu* 'to come'. The subject of the embedded direct quote is a third person singular referent which receives a pronominal mention in line 2. Since the pronoun is in the unmarked absolutive case, it clearly holds the subject grammatical relation with the intransitive verb *āunu* 'come' in line 4, even though the transitive clause in line 3 intervenes. The coreferential subject of the transitive clause receives a zero mention.

In addition to the interweaving of arguments and predicates, Nepali makes extensive use of direct quotation. Since most direct quotes in narrative are embedded as object complements of cognition or utterance verbs, this typological feature of the language contributes both to the length of sentences and to their complexity. Indeed, entire conversations may be embedded within a single Nepali sentence, as in the following rather straightforward example:

(3) Kalyāni K. C.
1. *tyahī kurā "ghiu ghasde"*
that.same word butter rub.IMP
2. *bhan-era*
say-CC
3. *ani tyas-pachi "la" bhan-era*
then that-after OK say-CC
4. *besmāri tyo khoṭo daldi-echa re*
forcefully that pitch rub.on-3SG.NRP EVID
'He$_i$ said the same thing "Rub on the butter" and then after that he$_j$ said "OK" and forcefully rubbed on the pitch.

Syntactic division

The narratives were transcribed and divided into sentences. Ends of sentences were identified by the presence of a non-embedded finite verb; sentence breaks were made after post-verbal particles and postposed arguments. The latter were identified by an examination of the semantic and prosodic structure of the clause. Direct quotes were not considered to be separate sentences even though they had final finite verbs; rather, they were seen as being embedded into a main clause containing a cognition or utterance verb. If no verb of quotation followed the direct quote, then the final verb of the quotation was taken to be the end of the sentence.

Sentences were then divided into clauses. This at times presented some problems due to the prolific use of clause combining in the language. Clause breaks were made after the clause-chaining suffixes and adverbial subordinators. Clausal complements were separated from their complement-taking verbs and counted as separate clauses.[5] This included complements of cognition and utterance verbs, which were ubiquitous.[6] Relative clauses were not considered to be separate clauses, but rather modifiers of NP's. They were not included in the current study.

When the data were imported into a relational database program, each clause was represented as a separate record. In cases where embedded or chained clauses intervened between verbs and their arguments and adjuncts (as in examples (1) and (2) above) the "stranded" arguments were placed in their own records and coded as "fragments"; fragments were coded as regular lexical or pronominal arguments of their verbs. In the examples given in this paper, each line of text contains one record, i.e. constitutes either a clause or a fragment.

Coding

Verbs were coded as being copular, intransitive, transitive, or ditransitive. In addition, they were coded for the number of non-complement arguments they governed (see discussion below regarding types of mention). Nominal arguments were coded for syntactic role, type of mention and activation cost. Details of the nominal coding system are given below.

Syntactic role

Each NP was coded for whether its syntactic role was A (subject of transitive or ditransitive verb), S (subject of intransitive), O (object of transitive or ditransitive), I (indirect object of ditransitive), or Obl (oblique). Dative-marked subjects were counted as S's, not as I's. Subjects of copular clauses were also counted as S's.

Types of mention

We used four types of mention in our study: lexical, pronominal, zero and verbal complement. The latter category was especially necessary due to the frequent use of quotation in Nepali. Other options to coding 'verbal complement' as a separate category would have been to exclude all complement-taking verbs or to count complements as lexical. The former would have significantly reduced the database and given an unrealistic picture of Nepali argument structure. The latter would have given inaccurate results, because complements are not generally realized as pronouns, and they are never unexpressed. We thus coded them as a separate category.

A further problem with integrating complements into a Preferred Argument Structure study is how to assess patterns of lexical and pronominal expression in clauses where one argument is a complement. For example, in a ditransitive clause with a direct quote complement, the speaker has options of zero expression only with the A and I categories; the O is necessarily a complement. If both the A and the I are represented lexically, then should this be considered an example of a ditransitive with two lexical arguments or with three? Neither of these descriptions accurately reflects the complexity of the situation. We have therefore decided to categorize verbs not only in terms of their transitivity but also in terms of the number of core non-complement arguments (NCA's) they contain. Thus some ditransitive verbs, such as those of cognition or utterance, are coded as "2-NCA" verbs, while others, such as verbs of transfer, are coded as "3-NCA" verbs. Similarly, transitive verbs with complements are "1-NCA" verbs. And intransitive verbs with subject complements are considered to be "0-NCA" verbs and thus are not counted in the tables dealing with number of expressed arguments.

Activation cost

The coding of NPs by activation cost follows Chafe (1987, 1994), who defines activation cost cognitively. *Given* referents are those which the speaker judges are already active in the mind of the listener at the point that a mention of that referent is made. In the current study, any previously mentioned referent was coded as given, since there were no referents that were reintroduced after a long hiatus of not being referred to. *Accessible* referents are those which the speaker judges the hearer to have in semi-active consciousness. Accessible referents are often invoked by schema. For example, in a stretch of text about a man butchering goats, one does not have to introduce the knife being used as a new participant; everyone in Nepalese culture knows that to butcher goats one must use a knife, so the presence of a knife will already be in the semi-active consciousness of a person listening to a discourse about butchering. Reference to a knife being used in this context would presumably not take as much cognitive effort for the listener to identify as would a knife being introduced without an appropriate schema. *New* referents are those which are newly introduced at the mention, and which the hearer must newly activate. Finally, many noun phrases are *non-referential.* In this category we included generic noun phrases (e.g., *bāhunlāi kehi nadiikana* 'by not giving something to a (any) Brahmin'), predicate nominals, referents whose identity is unrecoverable and unimportant (e.g. *sut-tāi banāuna lagāẽ* 'I had (someone) make a suit'), and universal pronouns (e.g., *sabay janā* 'everyone'). Nominals used to characterize events (e.g. *sut-tāi lagāunu* 'to wear a suit and tie') were also counted as non-referential.

Evidence for Preferred Argument Structure in Nepali

Table 1 gives the distribution of clauses by transitivity in our database.

Table 1. Number of clauses by transitivity

	N	%
Copular clauses	134	(16)
Intransitive clauses	273	(33)
Transitive clauses	285	(35)
Ditransitive clauses	124	(15)
Total	816	(100)

The majority of clauses are either simple intransitive or transitive; ditransitive and copular clauses occur about half as frequently as the other two types.

Table 2 shows the number of lexical mentions by number of non-complement arguments (NCA's) per clause. Copular clauses are not counted with the 1-NCA verbs since they clearly follow a different pattern and strongly favor lexical expression.

1-NCA verbs tend to have no lexical arguments, while 2-NCA and 3-NCA verbs tend to have no more than one. Only 41 (11%) of the 381 clauses with a valence of two or more had more than one lexical argument expressed. This follows the basic predictions of Preferred Argument Structure theory. In particular, Nepali speakers seem to follow the One Lexical Argument Constraint, although perhaps not as strongly as do Sakapulteko speakers, who have a considerably lower rate of lexical expression (Du Bois 1987b: 819).

Figure 1 shows the distribution of lexical mentions in relationship to grammatical role. Among the core arguments, lexical mentions commonly occur in the S and O roles, while lexical A's occur less frequently. Again this is the Preferred Argument Structure pattern. In this case it is the Lexical A Constraint which is in effect. Once

Table 2. Number of lexical argument mentions per clause by number of non-complement arguments

Lexical Mentions	Copular N	Copular %	1-NCA N	1-NCA %	2-NCA N	2-NCA %	3-NCA N	3-NCA %	Total
0	39	(32)	218	(77)	141	(43)	13	(24)	411
1	83	(68)	65	(23)	158	(49)	28	(51)	334
2	N/A		N/A		27	(8)	14	(25)	41
3	N/A		N/A		N/A		0		0
Total	122	(100)	283	(100)	326	(100)	55	(100)	786

more, however, it appears that the constraint may not be as strongly adhered to as in Sakapulteko. Figure 2 displays the distribution of A's with respect to mention type; 13% of A's are lexical. This percentage is somewhat higher than what is generally reported in Preferred Argument Structure studies.

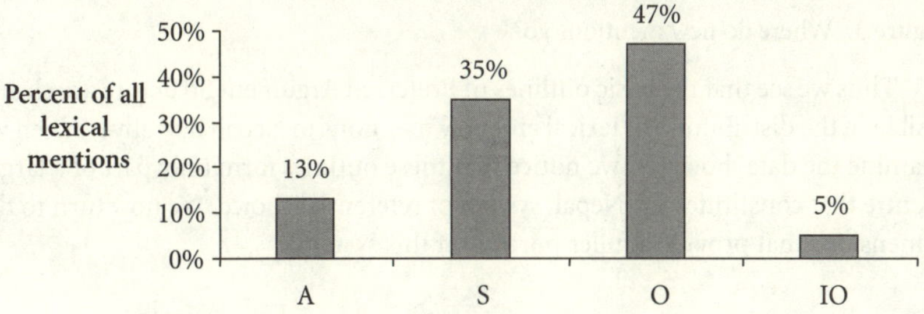

Figure 1. Where do lexical mentions occur?

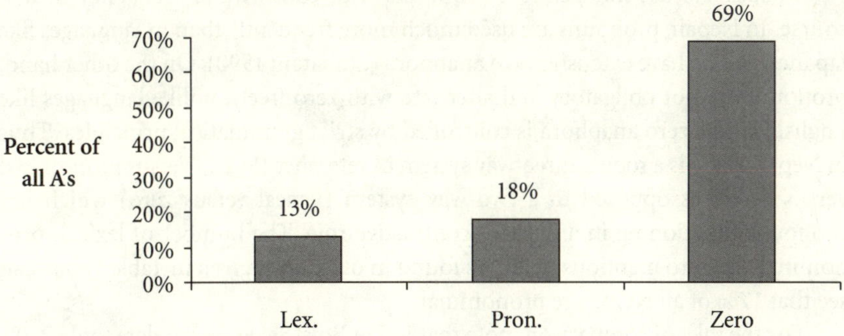

Figure 2. Distribution of A's by mention type.

Turning to the pragmatic dimensions of Preferred Argument Structure, the first interesting point to note is that the Nepali narratives have a very small number of arguments with new activation cost. Only 45 (4%) of the 1,042 core arguments are new. These new arguments, however, are clearly distributed following the patterns suggested by the One New Argument and the Given A constraints. We have no examples of two new arguments occurring in a single clause (thus the One New Argument Constraint is unviolated in our sample). And, as illustrated in Figure 3, new arguments in the A position are rare.

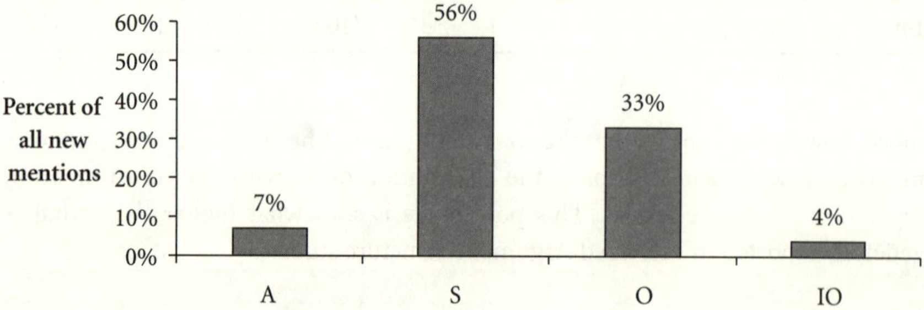

Figure 3. Where do new mentions go?

Thus we see that the basic outlines of Preferred Argument Structure are clearly visible in the distribution of lexical and new mentions in Nepali narrative. When we examine the data, however, we notice that these outlines form only part of a larger picture that constitutes the Nepali system of referential choice. We now turn to the dimensions that provide a fuller portrait of this system.

Beyond Preferred Argument Structure I: Overt mentions and the sentence

Nepali speakers use independent pronouns with considerable frequency in discourse. In Nepali, pronouns are used much more frequently than in languages like Japanese which have extensive zero anaphora (Shibatani 1990). On the other hand, pronouns are not obligatory and alternate with zero freely, unlike languages like English, where zero anaphora is controlled by strict grammatical principles. Thus in Nepali, there is a robust three-way system of reference (lexical versus pronominal versus zero), as opposed to a two-way system (lexical versus zero) which has pronouns functioning in a limited, contrastive role. The number of lexical, pronominal and zero mentions of NCA's found in our data is given in Table 3; one can see that 17% of all NCA's are pronominal.

For the sake of comparison, note that in Du Bois' Sakapulteko data, only 2.7% of argument mentions were pronominal (based on Du Bois 1987b: 822, Table 2).

Table 3. Lexical, pronominal, and zero mentions of non-complement arguments

	N	%
Lexical	415	(34)
Pronominal	213	(17)
Zero	604	(49)
Total	1232	(100)

Thus, in addition to considering the distribution of lexical as opposed to non-lexical mentions in Nepali, it is also important to examine the distribution of what we term "overt mentions", or non-zero realizations of NPs (cf. Du Bois 1987a). Table 4 shows the number of overt mentions per clause, by number of NCA's possible.

Table 4. Number of overt non-complement arguments per clause

Overt Mentions	Copular N	Copular %	1-NCA N	1-NCA %	2-NCA N	2-NCA %	3-NCA N	3-NCA %	Total
0	14	(12)	147	(52)	102	(31)	10	(18)	273
1	108	(88)	136	(48)	145	(45)	15	(27)	404
2	N/A		N/A		79	(24)	24	(44)	41
3	N/A		N/A		N/A		6	(11)	6
Total	122	(100)	283	(100)	326	(100)	55	(100)	786

When the pronominal and lexical data are combined in this way, the rates of overt expression are high: 24% of 2-NCA verbs have two overt arguments, as do 43% of 3-NCA verbs. In addition, 11% of 3-NCA verbs have all three arguments overtly expressed. If we do the parallel calculation that was done for lexical mentions, we see that 109, or 28% of the 2-NCA and 3-NCA clauses have at least two overt arguments. These percentages are strikingly high when one is accustomed to the low numbers of lexical expression commonly found in Preferred Argument Structure research.[7] This high percentage of overt mentions in narrative is a reflection of a strategy which takes the sentence, as opposed to the clause, as a crucial unit for determining when to use lexical and pronominal expressions.

Patterning in the sentence

As we examined our data in our attempts to understand the nature of Nepali Preferred Argument Structure, we were struck by the fact that certain syntactic constructions seemed to favor zero mentions, although in these constructions zero was not grammatically required, as a small number of examples could be found with lexical or pronominal mentions. Imperative constructions are an example of this type. Of our 38 imperative clauses, only 4 had pronominal mentions in the A or S roles. Other syntactic constructions which favored zero mention included the ubiquitous quotatives (the I of which was generally zero), same-subject clause chains, recapitulations (see below), and certain conjunctions used with quotative verbs.

The presence of these constructions which seemed to favor zero mention suggested that referential choice might not be entirely based on discourse and semantic properties like activation cost and animacy (following the common explanatory parameters in Preferred Argument Structure theory), or by measures such as referential distance and topic persistence (following work by Givón, e.g. 1983b, 1990, and various papers in Givón 1983a). Instead, it seemed to us that referential choice might be in part conditioned by syntactic factors. An additional insight came through a closer investigation of same-subject clause chains, in which we noticed that in such constructions the subject referent tended to have exactly one overt mention, even if the referent was a highly continuous topic, such as the protagonist of the story. The fact that Nepali discourse is organized and presented in coherent, complex and integrated sentences suggests that Nepali speakers might attend to the sentence when they make referential choices in the production of narrative.

Table 5 presents data on the number of overt mentions of arguments at the sentence level. The vertical axis represents the number of times an argument was overtly mentioned in a grammatical sentence: 0, 1, or 2 times. The horizontal axis represents the number of times a given referent was a grammatical argument of a verb in the sentence.[8] The following sentence can serve as an example of our coding system:

(4) Rājeswari Bista
bhāgawān bisnu
God Vishnu
laksmi-lāi sāth li-era
Laxmi-DAT beside take-CC
pundarik kahā̃ ā-e.
Pundarik place come-3SG.PST
'God Vishnu, taking Laxmi with him, came to Pundarik's house.'

This sentence consists of two verbs in a clause chain. The referent Vishnu is the A of the first clause and the S of the second, but is mentioned only once. The referent Laxmi is only an argument of one verb (the O of *li-era*), and also is mentioned only once. This sentence, then, would be tallied twice in Table 5, once for the referent Vishnu, which would be counted as a 1/2 (one overt mention per two argument positions), and once for the referent Laxmi, which would be counted as a 1/1 (one overt mention per one argument position).

Roughly two-thirds of the referents received one and only one overt mention in a sentence, regardless of the number of times the referent functioned as an argument (cf. the discussion of "double positive avoidance" in Du Bois 1987a). This suggests that in Nepali narrative, a constraint on the amount of overt mentions is present at the sentence level, and that Nepali speakers have a discourse preference for producing one overt mention of each referent in a sentence. This strategy thus accounts for the higher than expected numbers of overt mentions in the clause-based study. Since new referents do not appear as frequently as sentence boundaries, speakers preferring overt mention of participants in sentences are going to produce higher percentages of both lexical and pronominal NPs in all grammatical roles, including A. In addition, since this strategy is not based on activation cost, Nepali has a larger than expected number of given referents realized lexically.

In light of the previous research on Preferred Argument Structure, our sentence-based percentages of overt mention constitute a very strong finding. No previous studies that we know of have suggested levels of overt mention anywhere close to this number. These studies have all examined Preferred Argument Structure from the perspective of the clause, but it is clear that in languages like Nepali the sentence is a syntactic unit that plays a significant role in the planning and presentation of a discourse. To understand the amount and type of mentions in Nepali, one must take the sentence into account. The fact that a referent is likely to be mentioned once and only once in a sentence suggests that sentence breaks in languages like Nepali are significant discourse boundaries that speakers attend to. While further studies of this phenomenon are necessary, it appears to us that the tendency for speakers to use overt mentions for all referents in Nepali sentences is related to the fact that sentences are so beautifully complex and integrated. The overt mentions both complement the verbs, and serve as guideposts throughout the intricate and interwoven structures.

It is interesting to note that in cases where a particular referent holds argument positions in more than one clause, the overt mention of the referent is often not in the first clause, but is found later in the sentence, as in the following example:

Table 5. Number of overt mentions by number of argument positions per referent per sentence

Overt Mentions	1 arg posit		2 arg posit		3 arg posit		Total
	N	%	N	%	N	%	
0	224	(32)	37	(26)	15	(30)	276
1	465	(67)	94	(67)	29	(58)	588
2	8	(1)	9	(6)	6	(12)	23
Total	697	(100)	140	(100)	50	(100)	887

(5) Hemrāj Pahāri
yo kurā sun-dā
this talk hear-CC
bāhun chakka par-yo
Brahmin surprise feel-3SG.PST
'Hearing this, the Brahmin became surprised.'

This sentence comes from a story in which the Brahmin referred to is the protagonist. The Brahmin referent served as the subject of an imperative in the immediately preceding clause, so is a given and highly continuous topic at the time this sentence is produced. The identity of the Brahmin as the subject of both verbs in this example is unambiguous from context; no other character is available to have this response. Since the overt mention is not being used to introduce or reactivate a participant, it is not necessary to put it in the initial clause of the sentence. The speaker has options of positioning which can be exploited for other discourse or stylistic purposes.

Another interesting finding can be drawn from Table 5. This is that while speakers tend to use overt mentions for argument referents once in every sentence, they only rarely refer overtly to the same referent more than once in a sentence. Examples like the following, where the shared subject referent of three verbs receives overt mention once, are common:

(6) Kalyāni K.C.
u sādhay khānekurā lyā-era
3SG always food bring-CC
sarāsar phark-era
immediately return-CC
jān-thyo re.
go-3SG.PSTHAB EVID
'She would always bring the food and return immediately.'

Indeed, only 2.6% of referents were overtly mentioned more than once at the sentence level.[9] This second finding is evidence in support of Du Bois' (1987a) claim that double mentions of a participant are rare in actual discourse. In this paper on the status of absolutive zero in Mayan systems of ergativity, Du Bois explores the complementarity of absolutive lexical mentions and the zero marking of the third person absolutive category on the verb in Mayan languages. He draws attention to the fact that the morphological verbal paradigm and Preferred Argument Structure seem to conspire to allow one mention per argument per clause. In Nepali we see the same type of phenomenon, but the relevant domain for such a constraint is not the clause, but the sentence.

One way to conceptualize the sentence-based strategy used in Nepali is as a violable constraint, following Du Bois (1987b):

One Overt Mention Constraint: Produce one overt mention for each referent in a sentence.

The extent to which this constraint applies outside of Nepali we will leave for other researchers to explore.[10] While violations of this constraint produced by mentioning a referent more than once are very rare, violations by under-marking, where referents receive no overt mention, occur frequently, roughly one-third of the time. We now turn to discussion of this issue.

Explanation of zero mentions

Given the fact that in about one-third of the examples, a referent in a sentence received no overt mention, one wonders whether proposing the One Overt Mention Constraint is justified.. If speakers really have such a constraint, then why should they choose zero mention so often? A partial answer to this question is that the theory of Preferred Argument Structure as articulated by Du Bois (1987a,b) explicitly claims that constraints are not grammatical rules, but speaker preferences for patterns; not all speakers follow these patterns at all times. Flexibility allows speakers a wider range of expressive options.

In addition, however, there are certain regular grammatical and discourse environments where speakers strongly prefer to use zero mentions. In other words, while the One Overt Mention Constraint favors overt expression, there are competing strategies which favor zero mention. The primary environments of this type are imperative constructions, certain types of non-referentials, recapitulations and quotatives.

The tendency to delete subjects of imperatives is commonly known. In our database only 4 of the 38 imperative clauses had overt subjects. The high number of zero mentions appears to be a reflection of (presumably interactional) factors which are independent of the proposed constraints.

Among the non-referential arguments, those which are non-referential due to their universal applicability are given zero mentions in Nepali. An example is the following (the speaker is referring to the length of time it takes to drive from Texas to New York):

(7) Hemrāj Pahāri
cār pā̃c din-samma moṭar-mā jā-nu-par-cha
four five day-up.to automobile-LOC go-INF-must-3SG.PRES
'One must go for four or five days by car.'

The fact that it takes four or five days to make the drive will be true for most people. Nepali speakers consistently use zero mentions in such situations; in our database, 10 clauses had zero mentions of this type.

Recapitulation is a device commonly used in Nepali narrative. It occurs at the beginning of sentences when speakers briefly summarize the primary events of the preceding sentence. An example is the following:

(8) Kalyāni K. C.
ani bagãycā-mā yoṭā sarpa-le uslāi ṭoki-di-echa.
then garden-LOC one snake-ERG 3SG.DAT bite-give-3SG.NRP
ṭok-era
bite-CC
tyo rājkumāri mar-echa
that princess die-3SG.NRP
'Then in the garden a snake bit her. (It) having bitten her, the princess died.'

This example consists of two sentences, the first ending with the finite verb *ṭokidiecha* 'to bite'.[11] The immediately following clause contains a repetition of the verb in clause-chaining form, which thus recapitulates the primary action of the preceding sentence. As in this case, speakers commonly omit arguments when producing recapitulations. 16 of our zero mentions occurred in structures of this type.

Quotative verbs commonly involve zero mentions of three different types. To begin with, it is rare to overtly mention the indirect object of a quotative verb. At the clause level, only 9 of the 72 I's in our database occurring with quotative verbs received overt mention. This pattern may be due to a desire to avoid the redundancy that would result from a "He said to her — then she said to him" type of structure. The number of zero mentions at the sentence level is somewhat lower, due to the fact that referents that are in the I position often hold additional argument positions in complex sentences, and may receive mention accordingly. 26 I arguments never received any mention, even at the sentence level.

Zero A's are found with quotatives when direct quotes are postposed after utterance verbs. There are two positions for zero mentions of A in this construction. First, if the preceding clause contains a finite verb, and if the clause with the utterance verb begins with the conjunction *ra* and if the direct quote is postposed, then the A will receive a zero mention, as in the following example:

(9) Hemrāj Pahāri
yo kurā sun-dā
this talk hear-CC
bāhun chakka par-yo.
Brahmin surprise feel-3S.PST
ra bhan-yo.
and say-3SG.PST
'Hearing this, the Brahmin became surprised. He said...'

All 14 of our examples of this type had zero mentions of A. Also, there are times when a quote is postposed, but is still itself followed by a complementizer and another instantiation of the quotative verb:

(10) Rājeswari Bista
sudāmā-le pani bicār gar-e.
Sudāmā-ERG also think do-3SG.PST
ra bhan-e
and say-3SG.PST
"(direct quote of seven clauses in length)"
bhanera bhan-yo.
COMP say-3SG.PST
'Sudāmā thought. And he said "(direct quote)".'

When this happens, the A is commonly omitted. Of the twelve examples of such structures in our database, only one had an overt mention of the A.

Thus, of our 276 examples of referents that received no overt mention at the sentence level, 111 or 40% occur in particular constructions which favor zero mention. This leaves only 165 examples (19% of the total database) where no overt mention was made to an argument referent in a sentence, and where there were no independent motivations for the use of zero. We attribute these examples to the optionality of constraints, thus to speakers exercising their creative options in language.

Beyond Preferred Argument Structure II: Pronouns and given referents

A closer look at pronouns

At this point we have treated our pronominal arguments in two ways. In our discussion of the basic patterns of Preferred Argument Structure, we focused on lexical mentions, which resulted in the grouping of pronouns with zeros. In our discussion of the sentence, we focused on overt mentions, and so grouped pronouns with lexical NPs. A third option is to break apart these categories, and to treat pronominal mentions independently (cf. Ariel 1988, 1991, Tao 1993). Pronouns constitute an intermediate category between lexical and zero mentions, with similarities to both other types.

Similarities between pronominal and lexical mentions

The primary similarity between pronominal and lexical mentions is that both are overt, i.e., the speaker has chosen to instantiate a referent with phonological material (cf. Du Bois 1987a). This does not strike us as being a trivial property of these mention types.

While a full exploration of when speakers use pronouns is beyond the scope of this paper, we will suggest below that the use of independent pronouns in Nepali is the result of a referential strategy based on the syntactic sentence.

An additional similarity between pronominal and lexical mentions is found in reference to speech act participants. The three-way system of reference that speakers employ for third-person participants is reduced to a two-way system for first- and second-person participants, as pronouns and zeros are the only two options. Table 6 shows the number of lexical, pronominal and zero mentions for third-person as opposed to first- and second-person participants.

Table 6. Expression of 1st and 2nd versus 3rd person referents

	1st/2nd person		3rd person		Total
	N	%	N	%	
Lexical	0		560	(46)	560
Pronominal	79	(40)	161	(13)	240
Zero	117	(60)	486	(40)	603
Total	196	(100)	1207	(100)	1403

If a speaker wishes to refer overtly to a first- or second-person participant, he or she must use a pronoun. Thus a pronoun is the least reduced form available for first- and second-person reference, just as a lexical mention is the least reduced form available for third-person reference. This is another similarity between pronominal and lexical mentions. (See also Scancarelli (1985), which shows that first- and second-person pronouns share discourse functions with full NPs in Chamorro.)

Similarities between pronominal and zero mentions

Not only do pronouns share properties with lexical mentions, but third-person pronouns also share properties with zero mentions. When a third-person referent is first introduced into a narrative, a speaker must use a lexical mention. But established participants are more commonly referred to with either zero or pronominal mentions. This trend is reflected in Table 7, which displays activation cost for the three different mention types for third-person participants.

Pronominal and zero mentions have similar high rates of use with given participants. This contrasts with the clearly lower rate of lexical mentions with given participants (see below). These results are not surprising, but follow the predictions of a number of researchers (e.g. Givón 1983b, 1984, 1990, Du Bois 1987b, Chafe

Table 7. Activation costs of different types of 3rd-person mentions

	Lexical		Pronominal		Zero		Total
	N	%	N	%	N	%	
Given	228	(55)	115	(82)	427	(88)	770
Accessible	60	(14)	11	(8)	3	(1)	74
New	45	(11)	0		0		45
Nonref	82	(20)	14	(10)	57	(12)	153
Total	415	(100)	140	(100)	487	(100)	1042

1976, 1994, Fox 1987). If anything is surprising in Table 7, it is the high rate of lexical mentions with given activation cost. These issues are addressed below.

Summary

We have argued that in languages like Nepali which have a robust three-way system of reference, pronominal mentions are similar to lexical mentions in having the property of overtness, but are similar to zero mentions in being used to refer to participants with given activation cost. Therefore pronouns should not be grouped with either of the other categories, but should be seen as an independent third option in languages of this type. The theory of Preferred Argument Structure which focuses on lexicality can be enriched by studying the interaction of lexicality and pronominality.

Distribution of pronouns

We have seen that lexical mentions in Nepali occur primarily in the S and O roles, hence have the absolutive distribution commonly cited in Preferred Argument Structure studies. Interestingly, pronominal mentions in Nepali have a significantly different distribution. Consider Figure 4.

The primary categories realized by pronouns are A (35% of pronouns) and S (43% of pronouns). Only 17% of pronouns occur in the O role. Thus, while lexical mentions favor the absolutive roles, pronominal mentions favor the nominative roles.[12]

The reason for the nominative occurrence of pronominal mentions is tied to animacy. Of the 214 pronouns in the database, 197 (92%) were used with animate referents.[13] Only 4 pronouns were used with inanimate referents, and 13 were used for non-referentials (e.g. *tyo dekhera* 'seeing that happen'). Thus, while inanimates occur freely with either lexical or zero mentions, they occur only rarely with pronominal mentions. Nepali speakers seem to abide by the following constraint (cf. Corston this volume):

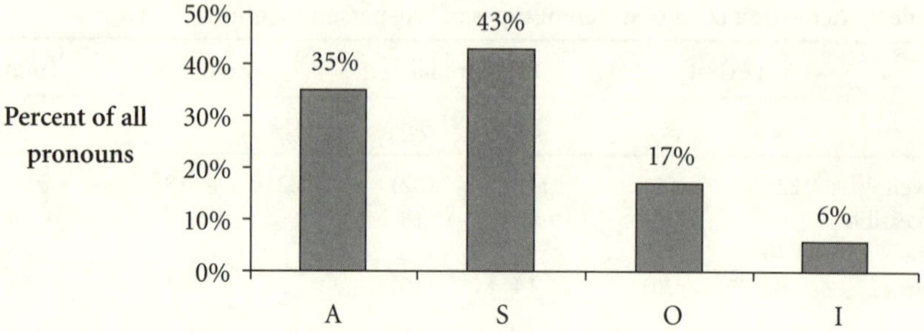

Figure 4. Where do pronouns occur?

Animate Pronoun Constraint: Avoid pronominal mentions for inanimate referents.

Again, speakers may violate this, but rarely do. This constraint is tied to the nominative distribution of pronouns, since actions tend to be instigated by animate agents and themes, and animates which are semantic patients may be cast as grammatical subjects through the passive construction.

When we characterize the overall distribution of mention types in Nepali, therefore, we may describe it as split-ergative, since it has both absolutive and nominative dimensions. This description is especially appealing when one considers that some languages (e.g. Yidin^y (Silverstein 1976, Dixon 1977, 1979. 1984)) have split-ergative casemarking patterns that follow exactly the same lines, with casemarking of lexical items being on an ergative/absolutive basis and casemarking of pronouns being on a nominative/accusative basis. This pattern is clearly related to additional patterns involving given mentions.

A closer look at given mentions

As discussed above, one way that pronouns and lexical mentions differ is that pronouns strongly favor given referents. As Table 8 shows, pronouns are never new, and are only rarely accessible or non-referential.

We may thus propose yet another constraint:

Given Pronoun Constraint: Avoid new, accessible and non-referential pronouns.

Another fact discernible from Table 8 is that among the given mentions, a clear nominative pattern is found. Non-given pronouns, however, occur in the S and O, i.e. absolutive, roles exclusively. Thus pronouns themselves appear to have split-ergative distribution, based on activation cost.

The next question is whether the split-ergative pattern found in pronouns is also present with lexical mentions. Table 9 presents the relevant data.

Consider first the non-given mentions, those which are non-referential, new or

Table 8. Activation cost by grammatical role for pronouns

	Nonref		New		Access		Given		Total
	N	%	N	%	N	%	N	%	
A	0		0		0		75	(39)	75
S	6	(43)	0		0		85	(45)	91
O	8	(57)	0		10	(100)	18	(9)	36
I	0		0		0		12	(6)	12
Total	14	(100)	0		10	(100)	190	(100)	214

Table 9. Activation cost by grammatical role for lexical mentions

	Nonref		New		Access		Given		Total
	N	%	N	%	N	%	N	%	
A	2	(2)	3	(7)	3	(5)	46	(20)	54
S	27	(33)	25	(56)	26	(43)	66	(29)	144
O	52	(63)	15	(33)	31	(51)	100	(44)	198
I	2	(2)	2	(4)	1	(2)	16	(7)	21
Total	83	(100)	45	(100)	61	(100)	228	(100)	417

accessible. These clearly cluster in an absolutive pattern, as only 8 of the 234 mentions in this category occur in the A role. We would like to propose that since A's occur rarely not only with new referents, but also with accessible referents and non-referentials, the current wording of the Given A Constraint ("Avoid new A's") be revised:

Revised Given A Constraint: Avoid new, accessible and non-referential A's.

When we observe the distribution of lexical mentions with given referents, we see that, like the given pronouns, they do not have absolutive distribution. The number of given referents in the S role is closer to the number in the A role, and thus this distribution also approximates a nominative pattern.

The nominative distribution of given lexical mentions is clearly related to the nominative distribution of pronouns. Due to the tendency for subjects to be animate, speakers usually have the option of using either a pronoun or a lexical item in the A and S roles, and, since pronouns are generally given, the number of given lexical mentions in the A and S roles decreases.[14] This point is illustrated by the data in Table 10, which illustrates the pronominal and lexical distribution of given referents in the various roles.

The high number of pronominal mentions in the A and S roles is complemented by a correspondingly low number of lexical mentions in the same roles. When we

Table 10. Mention type by grammatical role for overt given mentions

	Pronominal		Lexical		Total
	N	%	N	%	
A	75	(39)	46	(20)	121
S	85	(45)	66	(29)	151
O	18	(9)	100	(44)	118
I	12	(6)	16	(7)	28
Total	190	(100)	228	(100)	418

consider O's, we see that since pronouns rarely occur in the O role, the number of lexical O's is correspondingly high. I's which are generally human and so may also be referred to with pronouns, have distribution patterns similar to the A's and S's.

If given lexical mentions are distributed in a nominative pattern, then one may ask why the Preferred Argument Structure studies, including the illustration of basic Preferred Argument Structure patterns in Nepali given above, characterize the distribution of lexical mentions as absolutive. There are two reasons for this. One is that languages which do not have frequent use of independent pronouns are not likely to split the A and S roles between mention types, a split which results in the nominative distribution of given lexical mentions. Another reason is that not all lexical mentions are given. In our database given and non-given lexical mentions occur in roughly equal numbers (228 and 234 tokens respectively), and so the large numbers of S and O mentions in the non-given categories, together with the S and O mentions which are given, produce an overall pattern which is absolutive in nature. Pronouns, on the other hand, are overwhelmingly given, so the nominative pattern found with animate referents dominates this category, effectively obscuring the absolutive distribution of the non-given pronominal mentions. Thus the surface split-ergative pattern of absolutive lexical mentions and nominative pronominal mentions is shown to be a reflection of the deeper principles that form the true basis of the system.

Conclusions

The current paper has presented many diverse statistics on the amount and distribution of mention types in Nepali. Taken together, they present a picture of a coherent functional system. The outlines of this system may be discerned when one considers the effects of the following four interacting constraints:

One Overt Mention Constraint: Produce one overt mention for each referent in a sentence.

Animate Pronoun Constraint: Avoid pronominal mentions for inanimate referents.

Given Pronoun Constraint: Avoid new, accessible and non-referential pronouns.

Revised Given A Constraint: Avoid new, accessible and non-referential A's.

The application of the One Overt Mention Constraint results in remarkably high numbers of overt mentions in the clause-level counts. This is due to the fact that the amount and type of mentions used in Nepali are not based only on a calculation of activation cost, but also on the syntactic structuring and partitioning of the discourse. Since sentence boundaries occur more frequently than new arguments, large numbers of overt given mentions are found.

This large number of overt mentions is split between the pronominal and lexical categories. Animate referents, which generally occur in the S and A roles due to their propensity to instigate actions, may be realized either pronominally or lexically, while inanimate referents are restricted primarily to lexical mentions by the Animate Pronoun Constraint. This nominative pattern based on animacy primarily applies to given referents, due to the Given Pronoun Constraint. The interaction of these constraints results in a high number of pronominal given mentions in the A and S roles, and a correspondingly low number of lexical given mentions in these roles. Thus both the lexical and the pronominal given mentions are distributed in a nominative pattern. Non-given mentions, those whose referents are non-referential, accessible or new, cluster in an absolutive pattern, primarily due to the Revised Given A Constraint. This results in two related split-ergative patterns, one based on mention type (nominative pronouns and absolutive lexical NPs), and one based on activation cost (nominative given mentions and absolutive non-given mentions).

We have shown that all four constraints interact to produce the Nepali patterns, patterns that, when studied in detail, look somewhat different from those generally reported in Preferred Argument Structure studies. We have shown that pragmatics is only one dimension which speakers use to determine the amount and distribution of mentions in Nepali; animacy, and the role of the sentence in the partitioning and presentation of discourse are important dimensions as well. This study provides excellent support for the notion of competing motivations, as it illustrates how the syntactic, pragmatic, and discourse factors work independently to produce preferred patterns of distribution in the production of natural discourse.

In addition, this study has highlighted the fact that the amount and type of mentions which are found in natural discourse may vary with independent typological properties of the language. For example, one feature that sets off Nepali typologically from Sakapulteko is the propensity of the former for clause combining and complex sentences. In Nepali, the finite verb agrees with the subject in person, number and gender. Non-finite verbs, however, including clause-chaining forms, do not. So in complex sentences with several verbs, only one argument, the subject of the final verb, receives verbal marking. Lexical and pronominal mentions are the only options available for the phonetic instantiation of any argument other than the subject of the finite verb, so these options are exploited, resulting in percentages of overt mentions that are higher than those found in languages which have different typological properties. Independent pronouns are thus used more frequently in Nepali than in some other languages, and this use then triggers a split in the distribution of given mention types, a split that will not necessarily be found in languages with lower pronoun use (we leave this question to others). This study thus supports the general conclusion made by Du Bois (1987a, b) that grammatical patterns and discourse patterns are interrelated and complementary.

Finally, this paper has shown that the syntactic sentence may be an important factor in the determination of the amount and type of anaphoric reference one finds in natural discourse (see also Fox 1987). In Nepali, speakers use sentences extensively in the planning and implementation of discourse, and some discourse phenomena, such as the amount of overt mentions, may only be understood with an examination of this higher level. This of course leads to the larger question of the discourse function of the sentence (Clancy 1980, Chafe 1980, 1987, 1994). Obviously such a study is beyond the scope of this paper. We will say, however, that we do not expect to find a one-to-one correlation between the sentence and any particular discourse unit (such as the episode). As noted by Chafe (1980, 1987, 1994), sentences vary greatly in their length and complexity and speakers employ them for a variety of rhetorical needs. Nevertheless, a fuller understanding of how and why speakers form sentences will greatly enhance our understanding of the relationship between grammar and discourse, especially in languages like Nepali, where sentences are robust and complex. In our opinion, a true understanding of the role of the sentence in discourse will only come through the combined effort of a number of linguists studying these questions in a wide variety of languages, and a wide variety of genres.

Notes

* We would like to thank John Du Bois, Patricia Clancy, Sandra Thompson and Jim Reed for providing us with valuable discussion about this project and comments on an earlier draft. We accept full responsibility for errors and inconsistencies that remain.

1. We did find some variation among speakers in the distribution of mention type. This appears to be due to different speakers' tendencies to use different syntactic constructions, some of which favor zero mentions (see 3.1). All speakers show the same overall patterns, which are discussed here.

2. There is clear evidence for the syntactic category of subject in Nepali, despite the fact that the casemarking roughly follows a split-ergative pattern. Verb agreement is one clear diagnostic of subject in this language, as the verb agrees with the S of an intransitive clause and the A of a transitive clause. See Wallace (1985) and Kärkkäinen (1994) for further discussion of this issue.

3. Each line of text in our examples represents one record in our database, hence either a clause, or a clause fragment (see discussion of syntactic division below). Abbreviations used in grammatical glosses are as follows:

1	1st person	2	2nd person
3	3rd person	CC	clause-chaining form
COMP	complementizer	DAT	dative
ERG	ergative	EVID	evidential
FUT	future	IMP	imperative
INF	infinitive	LOC	locative
NRP	narrative past	PART	participle
PL	plural	PRES	present
PST	past	PSTHAB	past habitual
PURP	purposive non-finite form	SG	singular

4. In Nepali, as in many other languages, the complements of cognition verbs like *socnu* 'think' are arguably direct quotes, as indicated by pronominal indices, verb agreement, change in deixis and other grammatical markers.

5. The modal verb *parnu*, used to indicate obligation, is not separable from its complement verb. Therefore its behavior seems closer to that of an auxiliary than to an independent complement-taking verb. This verb was not considered to constitute a separate clause for the purposes of this study.

6. The forms of the verb 'say' *bhanne* and *bhanera* were taken to be complementizers if they were directly followed by a quotative verb, otherwise they were considered to be main verbs.

7. This is especially true in light of the fact that our narrative has low information pressure, that is, a relatively low number of new human referents. Du Bois (1987b: 834) states that in some languages, discourse with low information pressure may not show expected patterns of Preferred Argument Structure since the number of overt mentions will tend to be smaller when fewer new mentions are introduced. However, in Nepali we have found low information pressure but higher percentages of overt mentions. As we will show, the general sentence-based pattern of argument distribution in Nepali accounts for these high numbers; information pressure does not seem to be relevant.

8. An additional 9 sentences contained referents holding argument positions in four different verbs, 3 contained referents holding argument positions in five different verbs, and 3 contained referents holding argument positions in six different verbs. These categories were excluded from Table 5 due to the small number of examples in each case. For the interested reader, the numerical data are presented here:

	Number of Times Referent Mentioned			
	0	1	2	3
4 argument positions per sentence	3	3	2	1
5 argument positions per sentence	1	2		
6 argument positions per sentence	1	1		1

9. Eight of the 25 examples of double mention of a referent were in sentences where the referent held only one argument position. An example of this is the following:

a. *yoṭa gajabko mānche ā-echa re*
one strange man come-3SG.NRP EVID
ṭhulo mānche
big man
'A strange man came, a big man.'

In this case, the second repetition of the NP appears to have the function of providing further elaboration on the qualities of the man. In other cases, the function of the second mention is less clear.

10. We suspect that the results may vary with the typology of the language being studied.

11. This verb is morphologically complex, since it contains the verb *-di-* 'give' along with the root *ṭok-* 'bite'. The functions of 'give' in this construction are quite varied; see Genetti and Shakya (2000).

12. Similar patterns appear to be found in Roviana. See Corston-Oliver (this volume) Table 2.

13. Actually, the majority of the pronominal referents were human. The non-human animate referents referred to with pronouns were generally found as characters in folk narratives, where they were imbued with human attributes, such as language.

14. Of course, given mentions in the A and S role also may be unexpressed, hence coded as zero. Recall that Nepali also has the One Overt Mention Constraint, which results in a high number of overt mentions in all roles. Once a speaker has opted for an overt mention, pronominal and lexical mention are the two remaining choices.

References

Ariel, Mira. 1988. "Referring and Accessibility". *Journal of Linguistics* 24: 65–87.

Ariel, Mira. 1991. "The function of accessibility in a theory of grammar". *Journal of Pragmatics* 16: 443–463.

Chafe, Wallace. 1976. "Givenness, contrastiveness, definiteness, subjects, topics and point of view". In Charles Li (ed), *Subject and Topic.* New York: Academic Press, 25–55.

Chafe, Wallace. 1980. "The deployment of consciousness in the production of a narrative". In Wallace Chafe (ed), *The Pear Stories: Cognitive, Cultural and Linguistic Aspects of Narrative Production.* Norwood: Ablex NJ, 9–50.

Chafe, Wallace. 1987. "Cognitive constraints on information flow". In Rusell Tomlin (ed), *Coherence and Grounding in Discourse.* Amsterdam & Philadelphia: Benjamins, 21–52.

Chafe, Wallace. 1994. *Discourse, Consciousness and Time: The Flow and Displacement of Conscious Experience in Speaking and Writing.* Chicago: University of Chicago Press.

Clancy, Patricia. 1980. *The Acquisition of Narrative Discourse: A Study in Japanese.* Ph.D. dissertation, University of California, Berkeley.

Comrie, Bernard. 1978. "Ergativity". In Winfred Lehman (ed), *Studies in the Phenomenology of Language.* Austin: University of Texas Press, 329–394.

Corston-Oliver, Simon H. This volume. "Core arguments and the inversion of the nominal hierarchy in Roviana".

Crain, Laura. 1992. *Clause Chaining in Nepali Discourse.* Ph.D. dissertation, University of California, Los Angeles.

Dixon, R. M. W. 1977. *A Grammar of Yidin^y^.* Cambridge: Cambridge University Press.

Dixon, R. M. W. 1979. "Ergativity". *Language* 55(1): 59–138.

Dixon, R. M. W. 1994. *Ergativity.* (Cambridge Studies in Linguistics 69.) Cambridge: Cambridge University Press.

Du Bois, John W. 1987a. "Absolutive zero: Paradigm adaptivity in Sacapultec Maya". *Lingua* 71: 203–222.

Du Bois, John W. 1987b. "The discourse basis of ergativity". *Language* 63(4): 805–855.

Fox, Barbara. 1987. *Discourse Structure and Anaphora: Written and Conversational English.* (Cambridge Studies in Linguistics 48) Cambridge: Cambridge University Press.

Genetti, Carol. 1993. "Variation in agreement in the Nepali finite verb". *South Asian Language Review* 4(1): 90–104.

Genetti, Carol and Daya Ratna Shakya. 2000. "GIVE and the Nepali -idinu construction: A study in polysemy". Unpublished manuscript, University of California, Santa Barbara.

Givón, T. (ed) 1983a. *Topic Continuity in Discourse: Quantified Cross-language Studies.* Amsterdam & Philadelphia: Benjamins (Typological Studies in Language 3).

Givón, T. 1983b. "Topic continuity in discourse: An introduction". In T. Givón (ed), 1–42.

Givón, T. 1984. *Syntax: A Functional-Typological Introduction*, Vol. 1. Amsterdam & Philadelphia: Benjamins.

Givón, T. 1990. *Syntax: A Functional-Typological Introduction*, Vol. 2. Amsterdam & Philadelphia: Benjamins.

Ichihashi-Nakayama, Kumiko. 1994. "On dative 'subject' constructions in Nepali". In Carol Genetti (ed), *Aspects of Nepali Grammar.* Santa Barbara Papers in Linguistics, Vol. 6, 41–76.

Nichols, Johanna. 1986. "Head-marking and dependent-marking grammar". *Language* 62 (1): 56–119.

Scancarelli, Janine. 1985. "Referential strategies in Chamorro narratives: Preferred clause structure and ergativity". *Studies in Language* 9: 335–362.

Shibatani, Masayoshi. 1990. *The Languages of Japan.* Cambridge: Cambridge University Press (Cambridge Language Surveys).

Silverstein, Michael. 1976. "Hierarchy of features and ergativity". In R.M.W. Dixon (ed). *Grammatical Categories in Australian Languages.* Canberra: Australian Institute of Aboriginal Studies, 112–171.

Tao, Hongyin. 1993. *Units in Mandarin: Discourse and Grammar.* Ph.D. dissertation, University of California, Santa Barbara.

Wallace, William. 1985. *Subjects and Subjecthood in Nepali: An Analysis of Nepali Clause Structure and its Challenges to Relational Grammar and Government and Binding.* Ph.D. dissertation, University of Illinois, Urbana-Champaign.

Multiple constraints on reference form

Null, pronominal, and full reference in Mapudungun*

Jennifer E. Arnold
University of Rochester

Introduction

The issue of reference has commanded much attention in the linguistic and psycholinguistic literature, as researchers have tried to understand what factors lead people to use one form of reference over another. For example, the following example illustrates several forms which the speaker could use to refer to Professor Jones, or the people listening to Professor Jones.

(1) Professor Jones peered over the podium and examined her audience. Several students looked positively comatose. She/The professor/ Professor Jones/Jones crumpled up a piece of paper and threw it at one of the sleepers.

As a part of understanding language production and comprehension, language researchers want to know not only when it is acceptable to use, for example, a pronoun, but also when people are more likely to use one. Many scholars have suggested that the form of reference depends on the discourse status of the referent, where pronouns or null anaphors are generally used for items that are salient to the discourse, and full NPs are generally used for items that are new to the discourse or not currently in the focus of attention (among others, Ariel 1988, 1990, 1994; Du Bois, 1987, Chafe, 1976, 1994; Givón, 1983; Gundel et al., 1993; Grosz et al., 1995). However, the question of what determines "salience", or "focus of attention" has not been resolved. Furthermore, other factors have been shown to play a role as well, such as parallelism (e.g. Chambers and Smythe, 1998; Grober et al., 1998) and the One Lexical Argument Constraint (Du Bois, 1987).

The current study was conducted to investigate the constraints that affect the choice of reference form in Mapudungun. Mapudungun is the language of the

Mapuche people, who live in Chile and Argentina. Recent estimates of the Mapuche population range between 440,000 and 1,040,000 (Smeets, 1989: 3). The method of investigation was text analysis, where I analyzed over 700 clauses of narrative texts in Mapudungun. The goal of the study was to look for patterns in the form of reference, to reveal correlations between form of reference and linguistic structure. While form of reference is often thought of as a pragmatic choice, many researchers have pointed out links between sentence structure and pragmatic use (e.g., Du Bois, 1987; Grosz, Joshi, and Weinstein, 1995; Givón, 1983).

Although there are many dimensions along which structure and reference correlate, in this paper I will discuss three structural aspects which constrain the form of reference in Mapudungun. First, my data confirm that form of reference is highly sensitive to the grammatical function of both the anaphor and the antecedent. As Du Bois (1985, 1987) has suggested, grammatical positions are specialized for discourse status, so that "given", accessible referents are placed in certain positions (like subject position) more often than others. At the same time, the accessibility of a referent is partly influenced by the way in which it was last mentioned, such that referents last mentioned in subject position are usually perceived as more salient than those last mentioned in object position (e.g. Grosz et al., 1995; see Arnold, 1998 for a discussion).

Second, my data provide supporting evidence for Du Bois' (1987) proposal that there is a restriction on the number of full arguments that can appear in a given clause (the One Lexical Argument Constraint). Furthermore, I will show that this constraint appears to exist independently of accessibility, or status of givenness.

Third, I will show evidence that the relative structure of two clauses influences the form of reference. Parallel structures facilitate null reference, and nonparallel structures favor full forms of reference. In addition, I will provide evidence that parallelism effects in Mapudungun are influenced by whether the voice marking in two clauses is the same or not, and is not simply a function of the relative positions of the anaphor and its referent.

Through demonstrating that all these patterns can be simultaneously observed in the same data, I will argue for a theory of language use that allows for several constraints to simultaneously play a role. One can think of language production as a struggle between the desire to be maximally informative and the pressure to be maximally efficient (Almor, 1995, 1999). Therefore, there is not always a single preferred form of reference, and many constraints conspire to produce the output. I will present several sources of pressure on form of reference, and it will be apparent that each source operates independently, and none may be ignored in a theory of language use.

Before I describe the methods of analysis and the resulting data, I will provide a brief description of Mapudungun.

Mapudungun: Background

Mapudungun exhibits what is known as an "inverse system" (Grimes, 1985), a system which has also been observed in Algonquian languages (Rhodes, 1990; Dahlstrom, 1986), Cherokee (Scancarelli, 1987), and others (see Givón, 1994, for a thorough discussion). What an inverse system means is that the language has two verb paradigms for expressing transitive verbs: direct and inverse. The inverse form is similar to the passive voice, except that the Actor[1] argument is usually not demoted, and the choice between these two paradigms depends on which of the two arguments is "higher", or "more salient".

The identification of the more salient argument in an inverse language depends on a salience (or animacy) hierarchy, which is language-particular. The salience hierarchy for Mapudungun is presented below.

(2) 1st, 2nd person > 3rd person proximate > 3rd person obviative

While 1st and 2nd person are defined by the identity of the speaker and hearer, the difference between 3rd proximate and 3rd obviative is determined by the discourse.

The basic rule for Mapudungun is that the higher argument must be the grammatical subject (Arnold, 1994). In the Direct verbal form, the Grammatical Functions map onto the arguments in the "normal" way, such that the Actor is the subject and the Undergoer is the object. In the Inverse, on the other hand, the Actor is the object and the Undergoer is the subject.

The salience hierarchy pre-determines the verbal form for most cases, since 1st and 2nd person are *always* considered "more salient" than 3rd persons, and therefore must always be the grammatical subject. This means that whenever one chooses to express the proposition "She saw me" (for example), the inverse construction must be used. To say "I saw her", one would use the direct form of the verb. With two 3rd-person arguments, the verbal form depends on which argument is "proximate" (more salient to the discourse), and which argument is "obviative" (less salient to the discourse).[2] For a fuller description of the inverse system in Mapudungun, see Arnold (1994).

The definition of "subject" and "object" that I am using is motivated by the morphology of the language, since this analysis allows for a consistent account of the verbal morphology and word order in matrix clauses, subordinate clauses, and questions (Arnold, 1994). Because of the inverse marking in Mapudungun, the result of this assumption is that the grammatical subject is not always semantically the Actor. This definition is not a common one, and indeed is controversial (e.g., Ives Goddard, p.c.). The cross-linguistic definition of "subject" is problematic because all languages define grammatical functions in terms of syntax, semantics, and pragmatics, but not always in the same way. Some languages give more weight to one dimension, some to another. The result is that grammatical functions in

Mapudungun reflect their pragmatic function much more strongly than in English. Therefore, an alternative analysis of Mapudungun where the link between the Actor and the subject were maintained would necessitate sacrificing morphological and pragmatic consistency.

Nevertheless, it should be noted that in the data I will present, inverse verbs represent a very small proportion of the clauses, as illustrated in Table 1.

Table 1. Distribution of voice marking in analyzed clauses

Voice	% of Total (*n*=500)
active	79%
passive	16%
inverse	5%

Because inverse verbs appear so infrequently, adopting an alternative analysis where the subject were the Actor wouldn't change the majority of the claims I will be making (the exception being my claims about parallelism).[3]

Example (3), excerpted from the text "An Old Man" (published in Smeets, 1989) illustrates how the direct and inverse verbal forms are used to maintain the main character as the grammatical subject.

(3) From Smeets 1989, "An Old Man" (512)[4]

(a) 'I shall continue my story [and tell you] as far as I know this old man. First of all, his name was Joan Soñan Kinchekew.

(b) When he was a young man, he used to work around in all sorts of places as a day-laborer. — SUBJ = man

(c) *rumé weshá trem- ürki-y* — SUBJ = man
very bad grown-REP-3,SUBJ
He grew up in great misery;

(d) *kim- ürke- la- y ñi ñuke;* — SUBJ = man
know- REP- NEG- 3S,SUBJ his mother — OBJ = mother
he did not know his mother;

(e) *ñi chaw duam- ürke- la- e- y- ew;* — SUBJ = man
his father care- REP- NEG- INV- 3,SUBJ- 3,OBJ — OBJ = father
his father did not care for him;

(e)	*yall-*	*tuku-*	*rke-*	*e-*	*y-*	*ew*	SUBJ = man
	son-	beget-	REP-	INV-	3S,SUBJ-	3,OBJ	OBJ = father
	ka	*domo*	*mew*				OBL = another
	another	woman	with				woman

he begot him as an illegitimate child with another woman.'

The controversial analysis of grammatical functions in this language is important to take into account during the following discussion. When claims are made about the pragmatic specialization of grammatical functions, it is important to remember that the "subject" in Mapudungun does not mean "Actor" in all cases. This is of course also true in other languages, such as ergative languages, or languages like English which make use of the passive voice for pragmatic reasons. The difference is that the pragmatic uses of grammatical function and voice have become grammaticalized in Mapudungun, so that the voice of transitive verbs is determined by the relative prominence of the two entities. Therefore, when I demonstrate the pragmatic behavior of the "subject" in Mapudungun, I am not proposing a characteristic of subjects *per se*, but rather showing that there is a particular structural category in Mapudungun (which is called the subject and has similarities to subjects in other languages) that reflects certain pragmatic tendencies.

In sum, it should now be clear that Mapudungun is a good language for looking at the issue of reference, for several reasons. In the first place, it permits both a null subject and a null object, which allows us to look at the role of null anaphors in addition to those of pronouns and full NP's. In the second place, it has an inverse system, so correlations with grammatical function cannot be mistaken as correlations with semantic roles like agent, patient, etc. (a problem that arises in languages like English). On the other hand, grammatical function is tightly linked with pragmatic salience, as mentioned above, and this definition of grammatical function must be taken into account. However, for this reason the inverse form itself is an additional diagnostic for relative discourse salience, since every transitive verb forces a choice between the two arguments as to which one is more salient.

Methods of investigation

I conducted a text analysis of over 700 clauses from several narratives in Mapudungun. These texts were chosen because they contain primarily third-person characters. The narratives were all published in written form, although some of them had originally been spoken and transcribed (and doubtlessly edited). 1st- and 2nd-person narratives were excluded, because the salience of 1st and 2nd persons is determined by both the speech situation and the discourse structure itself. In addition, reference to 1st- and 2nd-person entities is necessarily null or pronominal.

Furthermore, when 1st and 2nd person arguments are paired with a 3rd person argument in Mapudungun, the 1st or 2nd person argument always has to be the grammatical subject, even on the rare occasions when the 3rd-person character is more salient. To avoid these complications, the 9 clauses containing 1st- or 2nd-person arguments in these texts were excluded from the final analysis.

Also excluded from the analysis were quoted material and clauses such as "it became morning". Quotes were excluded primarily to simplify the analysis, since reference in the main body of the text is unlikely to refer to something within a quote, and vice versa. For the remaining clauses, each argument was coded for form of reference (full, pronominal, or null), and for four levels of "salience". Following Du Bois (1987), each argument was also identified as either an A, S, or O, using the labels introduced by Dixon (1979) to refer to subjects of transitive clauses (A's), subjects of intransitive clauses (S's), and objects (O's).

This analysis also only includes the main clauses in the corpus. There are several types of subordinate clauses in Mapudungun, some of which allow full mention of all arguments, and other types of clauses where the subject argument is controlled by a higher clause. Since this study investigated the variation between null and full reference form, I did not want to include cases where a full NP argument was disallowed. It was beyond the scope of this study to identify which subordinate clauses allowed full subject arguments and which did not, so only references which occurred in matrix clauses were included.

The term "salience" that I am using is intentionally underspecified. Some linguists have discussed the status of discourse entities using dichotomies such as "given" and "new", "topic" and "focus", "theme" and "rheme", or "topic" and "comment" to describe differences in discourse status. At the same time, researchers in a psycholinguistic or cognitive tradition have used notions like "salience", "accessibility", or "activation" to discuss different levels of representation. These terms are not identical, but they are related: Given referents are usually more salient than new referents, and topical referents are usually more salient than non-topical referents. When information is salient, it is also usually accessible, although other factors can influence accessibility (such as competition from other salient referents (Ariel, 1990; Arnold, 1999; Clancy, 1980; Givón, 1983)). In this paper, I am using "salience" to refer to the cognitive status of particular referents, much as the terms "focus of attention" or "accessibility" have been used (e.g., Almor 1995, 1999; Ariel 1988, 1990, 1994).

Part of the purpose of this study is to better understand the factors that affect the cognitive status of discourse entities. The term "salience", as I am using it, is a general notion of cognitive status, but the salience of discourse referents is influenced by the linguistic structure. The contribution of linguistic information to discourse processing is especially apparent in narrative texts such as these, where most relevant information can be found in the texts, rather than the discourse situation itself.

For each referring form, the salience of the referent was coded in terms of two properties: (1) recency and (2) prominence, or position with which the antecedent was last mentioned. This resulted in the following four levels:

(4) Codings for the salience of discourse referents
Prev. Subj. = referent last mentioned as subject of the previous clause.
active = referent last mentioned as object of previous clause, subpart of subject or object of previous clause, or both subject and object of previous clause together.
old = referent had appeared in text previously, but not in previous clause.
new = referent is brand new to the text.

Salience is assumed to be a continuous property, where a given entity can be more or less salient, or more or less accessible. As a representation of this continuous property, these four levels are used as a tool to explore the relationship between salience and form of reference.

This coding scheme differs from that used by other researchers, most notably in that it allows us to observe multiple constraints affecting the form of reference. For example, not only does it include the notion of "givenness" (whether an entity has previously appeared or not), but it also measures differences in salience among "given" referents. Although other scholars have also identified different levels of salience for given referents, the levels have usually been measured by a single metric, such as "recency of mention" (e.g. Chafe, 1994; Givón, 1983), or "position of last reference" (e.g. Grosz et al., 1995).

For example, a commonly used scheme is the one proposed by Chafe (1994), which distinguishes between three levels: "new", "active", and "given". In Chafe's system, the difference between these three categories is how recently the entity has been mentioned in the discourse. A conceptually similar scheme, used by Givón (1983), looks at how recently an entity has been mentioned in the discourse (along with two additional measures, interference and persistence). Both of these systems suggest that the salience of a discourse entity is partly a function of recency of mention, but neither one pays attention to the position in which an entity was last mentioned.

A different framework for addressing reference form is Centering Theory (e.g., Grosz et al., 1995), which concentrates on how certain structures mark an entity as more salient, but does not look further back than one clause in order to look for effects of salience. The question of distinguishing among several entities in a clause raises the difficult issue of determining exactly which structures are indicative of heightened salience, and to what extent. Work in the framework of Centering Theory has depended on the hierarchy of grammatical functions (subject > object > oblique) as one indicator of the ranking of a clause's arguments in terms of salience (Brennan, Friedman, and Pollard, 1987), and it has also considered the role of fronting as a strategy to mark salience (Walker and Prince, 1996; Gordon et al., 1993).

Nevertheless, scholars who work in the framework of Centering Theory acknowledge that these structures are not the only ones that may play a role.

In contrast with previous studies, this study simultaneously distinguishes between both recency of mention (by comparing "Prev. Subject" and "active" with "old") and position of last reference (by comparing "Prev. Subject" with "active"). By combining under "salience" both recency of mention and the relative salience of two referents in the same clause, I am claiming that both concepts are part of the same cognitive phenomenon: the activation of an entity in the mental model of the discourse, which is reflected in the ease with which it is accessed for use. Like Centering Theory, I will use grammatical functions as an indicator of relative salience within a clause, where subjects are assumed to be more salient than objects. This generalization is particularly true for Mapudungun, which has grammaticalized the need to place the more salient characters in subject position in transitive clauses.

The view adopted here is similar to Ariel's Accessibility Theory (e.g. 1988, 1990), or the approach of Clancy (e.g. 1980), which also assume that many factors influence the accessibility of a particular entity, and consider the issue of reference from a cognitive perspective. While the factors addressed here differ slightly from those addressed by Ariel, Clancy, and others, the spirit is similar insofar as it is the mental representation of an entity which is taken as relevant to the form of reference, not the textual referent. The production of a particular reference form may be due to the interaction of these constraints within the production mechanism of the speaker, or it may be that the speaker is carefully monitoring the discourse in order to produce a text that is optimal for the hearer to comprehend. In either case, I assume that the linguistic form is the result of the cognitive status of a referent in the mental models of the speaker and hearer, and I assume that the mental models are affected in part by the prior linguistic context of the discourse.

Structural constraints on choice of reference

I will now turn to the results of this text analysis, and discuss the ways in which reference form patterns with four structural properties in Mapudungun. First, I will show that grammatical functions are pragmatically specialized, as suggested by Du Bois (1987), where entities mentioned as the subject of transitive verbs tend to be more salient than those mentioned as subjects of intransitive verbs, which are also more salient than those mentioned as objects. Second, I will show that grammatical functions also function to mark a referent as more salient for purposes of future reference. Third, I will demonstrate that there is a restriction on having more than one lexical argument in a clause, as Du Bois (1987) suggested, and furthermore that this restriction is independent from the salience of the referents in a clause. Fourth, I will show that the relative structure of two clauses influences the form of reference, where parallel structures facilitate null reference (e.g. Chambers and Smythe, 1998; Grober et al., 1978), and suggest that parallelism is not only a function of the positions of the referent and its antecedent, but also the voice marking on the verb.

Grammatical functions, salience, and reference form

The first generalization that can be drawn from the text analysis is that there is a correlation between the grammatical function of a referring form and the salience of its referent. The referents of transitive subjects (A's) tend to be more salient than those of intransitive subjects, and the referents of both transitive and intransitive subjects tend to be more salient than the referents of objects. The pattern of salience for these three positions is illustrated in Figure 1 and Table 2, which show the distribution of arguments in each position of salience for each grammatical function.

Note that A and S pattern similarly, but transitive subjects (A's) tend to be more salient than intransitive subjects (S's). The difference between these categories is significant ($\chi^2=20$, $df=6$, $p<.001$). Both transitive and intransitive subjects differ greatly from objects, which tend to be used for new entities far more than given ones.

The pragmatic specialization of grammatical functions, and particularly the difference between A's and S's, was first noticed by Du Bois (1985, 1987) in his analysis of Sakapulteko Maya. Du Bois showed that A's, S's, and O's differ in terms of reference form. The functions that are used for more salient referents also tend to be null more frequently. The tendency for grammatical functions to be specialized for pragmatic role and form of reference form two of the major tenets of Du Bois' theory of Preferred Argument Structure. The same principles have since been

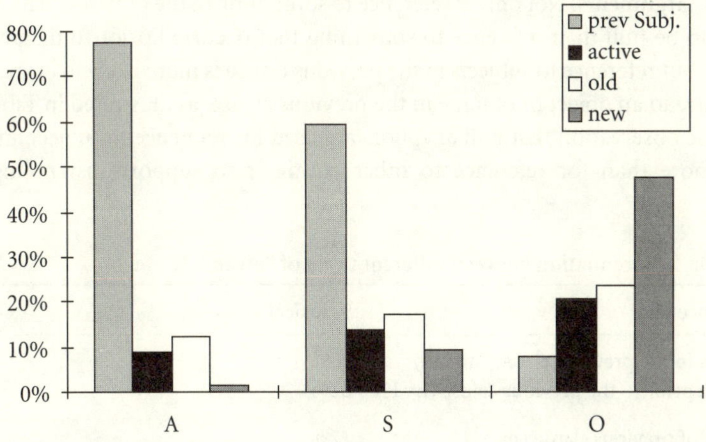

Figure 1. Percentage of referents in each category of salience, for each grammatical function.

Table 2. Number of referents in each category of salience, for each grammatical function

Grammatical function	prev. Subj.	active	old	new	total
A	125	14	20	2	161
S	202	47	58	32	339
O	13	33	38	77	161

shown to occur in many other languages as well (e.g. Clancy, 1993; Durie, 1988; Payne, 1987; Ashby and Bentivoglio, 1993; Bentivoglio, 1993).

The same pattens of referential form that Du Bois and others have found can be observed in the data from Mapudungun. Figures 2a–c show the frequency of lexical NP's for A, S, and O for each level of salience. Due to the very low numbers of pronouns, the graph conflates the categories "pronoun" and "full" under the label "lexical", since pronouns appear to function much like full NP's except that they cannot be used for a completely new entity. The distribution of lexical arguments across the four categories of salience is significant for each grammatical position ($p<.01$).

The data in Figures 2a–c reveal several distinctions which are often missed by language scholars studying reference form. First, it is not sufficient to look only at the preceding clause to determine salience, since elements that appeared previously in the narrative (but not in the preceding clause) can appear with null reference, whereas completely new elements can only be introduced with lexical terms. Second, these data show that a simple categorization of "given" and "new" does not capture the distinctions in salience that arise when we differentiate between types of "given" arguments. Not only is reference to something in the previous clause more likely to be null than reference to something that occurred prior to the previous clause, but reference to subjects in the previous clause is more likely to be null than reference to an object or oblique in the previous clause, as illustrated in Table 3.

The observation that null anaphors are used for reference to subject antecedents more than for reference to other entities also supports psycholinguistic

Table 3. Differentiation between different types of "given"

Reference to:	% lexical
Entities in the previous clause (n=434)	26%
Entities prior to the previous clause (n=116)	82%
subject of previous clause (n=341)	17%
nonsubjects of previous clause (n=94)	60%

evidence that reference to the entity denoted by the previous subject is more often pronominal than lexical (Arnold, 1998; Stevenson et al. 1994). Researchers have also found that if a repeated lexical NP is used to refer to the subject of the previous clause, comprehension can be impaired (Hudson-D'Zmura and Tanenhaus, 1998; Gordon et al., 1993).

As mentioned above, the data on Mapudungun are consistent with claims about the pragmatic specialization of grammatical functions (e.g., Du Bois, 1987).[5] Figure 3 shows the overall rates of lexical references occurring in each position. Referring forms in subject position are more likely to be null than referring forms in object position, which in turn are more likely to be null than those in oblique

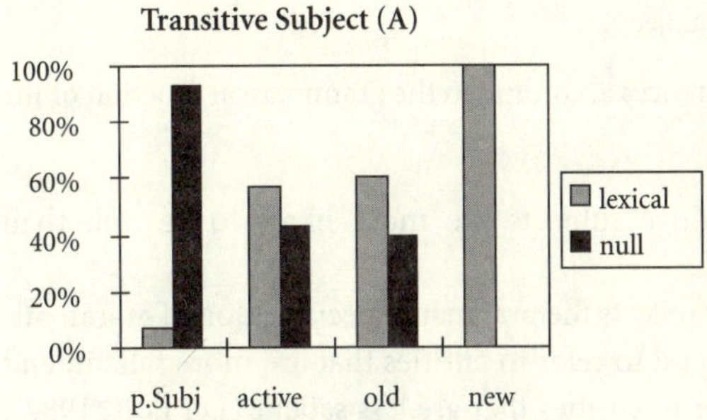

A	Prev Subj	act.	old	new
full	5	7	10	2
pro	3	1	2	0
null	117	6	8	0
total	125	14	20	2

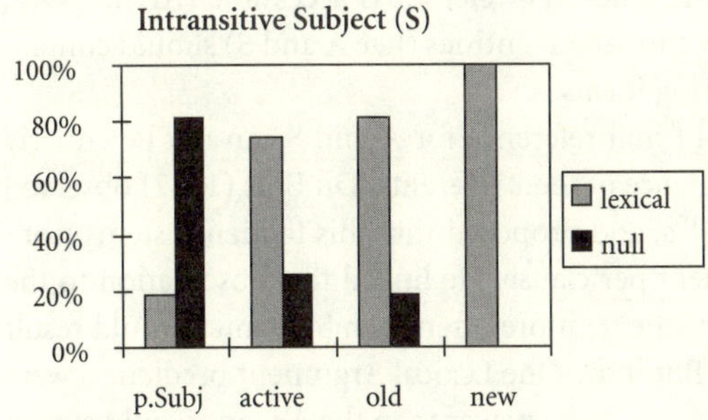

S	Prev Subj	act.	old	new
full	27	31	44	31
pro	11	4	3	1
null	164	12	11	0
total	202	47	58	32

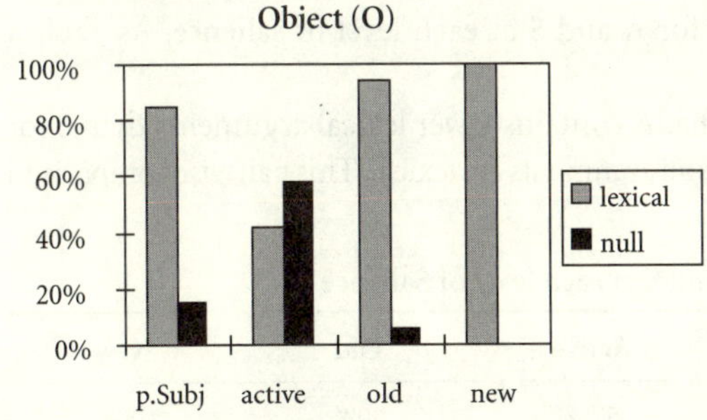

O	Prev Subj	act.	old	new
full	11	13	36	77
pro	0	1	0	0
null	2	19	2	0
total	13	33	38	77

Figure 2a–c. Discourse Salience vs. Reference: the use of lexical and null forms of reference for each level of salience and each grammatical function.

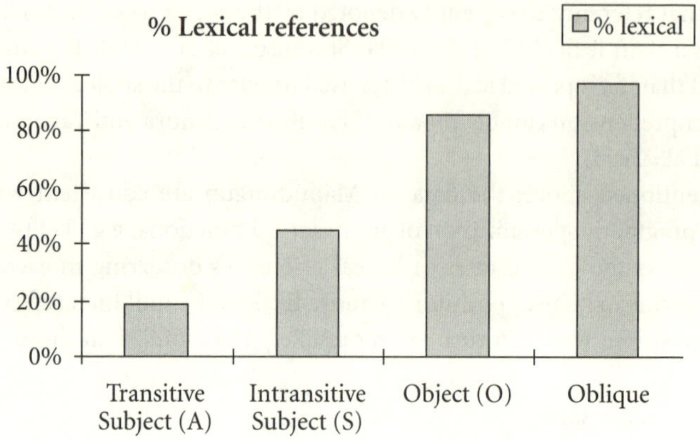

Figure 3. Percentage of lexical references according to the grammatical function of the referring form.

position. Within subjects, transitive subjects are more likely to be null than intransitive subjects.

The pattern in Figure 3 partly reflects the pragmatic specialization of grammatical functions such that subjects tend to refer to entities that are more salient, and objects and obliques tend to refer to entities that are less salient (Du Bois, 1987). Since null anaphors are used more when the referent is accessible (Ariel, 1990), positions that are used for referring to salient entities (like A and S) should contain a higher proportion of null referring forms.

However, the different rates of null reference for A and S can not be entirely attributed to different levels of salience of their referents. Du Bois (1987) observed that A's are null more often than S's, and proposed that this tendency stems from a limit to only one lexical argument per clause. He linked this observation to the tendency for A's to be "given" (or salient) more often than S's, which would result in a higher rate of null reference. But if the One Lexical Argument prediction were solely a function of the tendency for S's to be newer than the A's, one would expect similar rates of lexical reference for A and S at each level of salience. As Table 4 shows, this is not the case.

The data in this table show that A contains fewer lexical arguments than S for every category except "new", where all arguments are lexical. This pairwise comparison

Table 4. Lexical arguments for A and S at each level of Salience

	Prev Subj	Active	Old	New
A	6%	57%	60%	100%
S	19%	74%	81%	100%

is statistically significant for both the "Prev. Subj." ($p<.002$) and a combined "active/old" category ($p<.05$).

The results in Table 4 show two things. First, they support Du Bois' principle of "no more than one lexical argument per clause". Second, they suggest that it may not be possible to explain the One Lexical Argument Constraint completely in terms of the tendency for A's to be more salient than S's: when salience is held constant, lexical arguments are still used more for S than A. These data suggest that for transitive subjects, lexical arguments may be suppressed, whereas for intransitive subjects, lexical arguments may be allowed more frequently.

Parallelism effects

The curious thing about Figure 2c, repeated here, is why objects tend to be null more in the "active" category than the "Previous Subject" category. Research has shown that entities mentioned in subject position are more salient than those mentioned in object position. Given the relationship between salience and referring form (e.g., Ariel, 1990; Arnold, 1998; Du Bois, 1987), one would expect that the "Previous Subject" category should have the highest percentage of null arguments.

The high rate of null objects for the "active" category reflects an additional factor: parallelism effects. Researchers in the area of Sentence Processing have shown that often the default interpretation of a pronoun is the entity in the parallel syntactic position (e.g. Chambers and Smythe, 1998; Grober et al., 1978). For example, in the sentence "Jane called Sally before she went to the graduation", many hearers will assume that "she" refers to "Jane". The problem is that in much of this work (an exception being Chambers and Smythe, 1998), parallelism effects are demonstrated only with subjects. In these cases the effects of parallelism are confounded with the general tendency for pronouns to refer to the subject of the previous clause, regardless of the position of the pronoun.

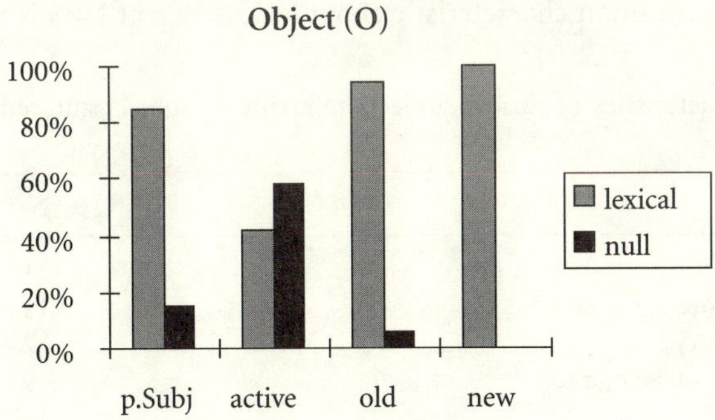

Figure 2c. Discourse Salience vs. Reference for objects.

In the text analysis done here, recall that the category "active" is a "catch-all" category, including objects of the previous clause, subparts of subject or object of previous clause, or both the subject and the object of previous clause together. To better understand the distribution of lexical reference, I divided the category "active" into the categories "previous object" and "model" (including subparts of the subject or object or both the subject and object together, categories where the referent is expected to be in the discourse model but not the textual model *per se*).

As Figure 4 clearly shows, objects tend to be null more often when they refer to the entity in the object position of the preceding clause. This observation indicates that when the referent of an anaphor is in the parallel position in the preceding utterance, null reference is more likely. By including an account of parallelism, we are also able to observe the salience of the "prev. subj" category more easily. Discounting those objects that refer to the object of the preceding clause, it is clear that the rate of lexical arguments increases monotonically from the more salient to the less salient categories, just as it does for the transitive and intransitive subjects. If the increased null reference for the category "prev. subj." had been an artifact of the parallelism between subject anaphors and antecedents, we would not expect a higher rate of null reference for objects referring to subjects as well. Therefore, the distribution of reference for objects shows evidence of both the prominence of the grammatical subject and an effect of parallelism.

Further evidence for an effect of parallelism can be found by looking at those few cases where the subject refers back to the referent of the subject of the previous clause, but contrary to expectations, the argument is lexical. If we look at Figures 2a and b above, we notice that in the highest level of salience (defined as cases where both anaphor and antecedent are subjects), the argument is far more likely to be null than lexical. Then why are there lexical subjects in this category at all? Combining the transitive and intransitive subjects, there are a total of 32 full referring forms used in subject position to refer to a subject antecedent. Each of these cases has one or more of the characteristics in Table 5, which might contribute to the speaker's choice to use a full referring form.

The most common characteristic about lexical, salient NP's is that they very

Table 5. Characteristics of lexical subjects referring to subject antecedents from the previous clause

Characteristic	N
nonrepeated NP's	31
intervening quote	14
beginning of story	2
Feimew/Fey discourse marker	9
voice change	14

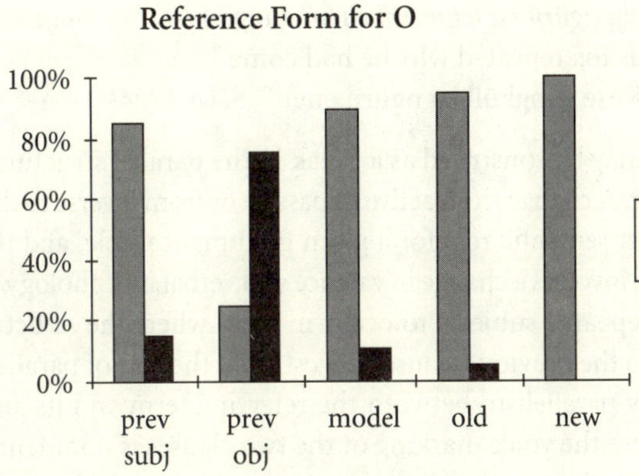

Figure 4. Discourse salience vs. Reference form for objects.

rarely involve the repetition of the same NP in two consecutive clauses, supporting the observation that repeated NP's are dispreferred and difficult to process (Almor, 1999). In 24 of these cases, lexical reference follows a null reference to the same entity, in 3 cases a lexical NP is followed by a different NP, and in 4 cases a lexical NP is followed by the same NP but with a different article (for example, "the man…. this man". In only one case out of all 32 lexical references to subject antecedents does a repeated NP occur, and in this case a quote intervenes between the anaphor and the antecedent.

Another characteristic that may increase the tendency to use a lexical form of reference is when the referent was last mentioned prior to a quote. I have discounted quotes from the analysis, considering them to belong to a different discourse segment (following Grosz and Sidner, 1986). However, interruptions in the flow of the main body of the narrative do make establishing reference more difficult, and make lexical reference more likely (Clancy, 1980; Walker, 1998; see Arnold, 1998 for a discussion). In other cases, the repeated reference occurs at the beginning of the story, so the referent may not yet be firmly established in the discourse model, or when the discourse markers "Feimew" or "Fei" indicate that a new discourse segment is beginning. Although none of these factors are sufficient for requiring the speaker to use lexical reference, they are all factors which invite future investigation.

One of the most striking characteristics of this set of clauses is that nearly half of these lexical, salient subjects occur when there is a change in voice from the previous clause. This voice change may be from passive to active/direct (n=11), from inverse to passive (n=2), or from inverse to active/direct (n=1). An example is given in (5).

(5) a. "*Chumimi am ngürü?*" *pingeparkei* *ta ngürü.*
"What's the matter, fox?" the fox was asked.

b. *Feimew chi ngürü ka feipirkefi chem dungu mew tañi amun.*
'Then this fox repeated why he had come.'[6]
(From "Kuse pangküll ka ngürü engu", Salas 1984)

This change in voice may be construed as a break in the parallel structure between one clause and another. A change from active to passive or from inverse to direct voice also involves a different semantic role for a given grammatical role, and the change from inverse to passive involves a change in valence and verbal morphology. Thus, the tendency for lexical repeated subjects to occur in cases where the structure of the clause is not parallel to the previous clause suggests that the role of parallelism may extend beyond merely parallelism between the referring term and its antecedent, and include cases where the voice marking of the two clauses is not identical.

I tested this hypothesis by examining the voice marking of all clauses which are parallel in terms of the position of the referring term and antecedent. As illustrated in Table 6, different voice marking between two adjacent clauses more than doubles the rate of lexical forms of reference.

Table 6. Voice parallelism versus referent parallelism

Case I: subjects referring to subjects ($\chi^2 = 8.46$, $df = 1$, $p < .005$)		
	% lexical	
same voice marking	10%	(n=230)
different voice marking	23%	(n=97)
Case II: objects referring to objects ($\chi^2 = 4.1$, $df = 1$, $p < .05$)		
	% lexical	
same voice marking	16%	(n=19)
different voice marking	60%	(n=5)

The effect of parallelism in voice marking may reflect a continuity of perspective on the discourse, where changing the voice marking may indicate that the speaker is taking a new perspective, or beginning a new discourse segment.

Discussion

The principal result of the study presented here is that multiple interacting factors affect the form of reference in Mapudungun. Many of these concepts have been previously introduced by researchers in the fields of functional linguistics (e.g. Ariel, 1990; Du Bois, 1985, 1987), psycholinguistics (e.g. Grober et al., 1978; Stevenson et al., 1994), and computational linguistics (e.g. Grosz et al., 1995). In this study, I not only demonstrated their applicability to Mapudungun, an inverse language, but I also demonstrated the viability of parallelism effects and the One Lexical Argument Constraint, holding other factors constant. Furthermore, I have added a new dimension to the notion that parallelism between clauses facilitates null reference by showing that parallel voice marking also affects the tendency to use null reference. In addition, this study has brought together ideas from a broad range of subdisciplines, and suggests that each generalization is relevant to the other approaches to the study of reference.

While it is certainly likely that other factors which were not investigated here also play a role, the demonstration of the independent validity of various factors provides further evidence for the growing trend to view language processing as satisfying various constraints simultaneously, as opposed to following a set of rules or principles. Even though the field of linguistics has often focused on the search for universal principles that would capture the set of possible utterances, a growing number of researchers have been moving towards an approach that allows for the simultaneous influence of "soft constraints", which can be violated on occasion. The results presented here argue strongly against an approach to the study of language that focuses on the search for one or two predictive principles, and support an approach that focuses on the interaction among various influencing factors.

The use of "soft constraints" has appeared in several linguistic theories recently, some of the earliest of which are Du Bois (1985, 1987: 819) and Ariel (1988, 1990, 1994). Another approach, Optimality Theory, is founded on the notion that constraints are ranked, and lower ranked constraints may be sacrificed as long as the higher ranked constraints are satisfied (Prince and Smolensky 1993; Grimshaw 1997). Nevertheless, the goal in Optimality theoretic accounts of formal language systems is to uniquely predict the set of grammatical outputs through the correct ranking of constraints. The type of soft constraints that I am advocating in this paper is closer to those proposed in constraint-based models of sentence processing (MacDonald et al., 1994; Trueswell and Tanenhaus, 1994), or the competing constraints of the Competition Model of language comprehension (Bates and MacWhinney, 1989). In these theories, multiple sources of information (e.g. discourse information, syntax, lexical frequencies, etc.) compete on-line and affect language production and comprehension.

In addition to simultaneously demonstrating the correlation of several factors with choice in reference, the data presented here also provide evidence for what some of these important factors may be. In the first place, these data support the many claims that grammatical function is correlated with degree of salience. Furthermore, this study distinguishes between the role of grammatical functions in establishing the salience of a discourse referent (proposed among others by Brennan, Friedman, and Pollard, 1987) and the specialization of different grammatical functions for realizing arguments of various degrees of salience, including a difference between transitive and intransitive subjects (proposed by Du Bois, 1987). Second, these data also show evidence that Du Bois' One Lexical Argument Constraint allows intransitive subjects to be lexical more often than transitive subjects, independently of their discourse status. Third, the high rate of null objects referring to the object in the previous clause points toward a role for parallelism independently of a general subject bias. In addition, the tendency for reference to be lexical when there is a change in voice suggests that choice in reference is sensitive to the structural parallelism of the entire clause, and not just parallel position of the anaphor and its referent.

In sum, the work presented here suggests that in order to account for choices in reference form, many factors must be attended to simultaneously — the search for a single predictive factor such as "parallelism", or "salience of referent" will leave much variation unexplained. The job for researchers of language processing, language production, pragmatics, and computational linguistics is to determine what these factors are, how they interact, which are the most important, and how they contribute to our ability to use language.

Notes

* Some of the data in this paper are published as a part of my Ph.D. dissertation (Stanford University, 1998). I am very grateful to the following people for their comments on drafts at various stages of development of this paper and related conference presentations: Judith Aissen, Mira Ariel, Eve Clark, Herb Clark, Maryellen MacDonald, Henriëtte deSwart, Spike Gildea, Masayo Iida, Lidia Polanyi, Peter Sells, Elizabeth Traugott, Thomas Wasow, and two anonymous reviewers.

1. I will use the general terms "Actor" and "Undergoer" to refer to the roles sometimes termed the "logical subject" and "logical object" (Foley and Van Valin, 1984).

2. The terms "proximate" and "obviative" are borrowed from the literature on Algonquian languages, where these functions are expressed in the verbal morphology. In Mapudungun, however, they are not morphological, but rather are determined by the discourse structure.

3. Note also that the frequency of constructions in Mapudungun differs from that of most inverse languages, which tend to have a higher rate of inverse than passive (Givón 1994: 11).

4. Abbreviations used in this example:

SUBJ	=	subject
OBJ	=	object
OBL	=	oblique
REP (rke)	=	reportative morpheme
NEG (la)	=	negation morpheme
INV (e)	=	inverse morpheme

For a further description of the morphology of Mapudungun, see Arnold (1994).

5. While the grammatical subject has been claimed to be a marker of salience, it is posssible that this is because of its association as a "Topic" position. This association is heightened in

Mapudungun because of the inverse verbal system. However, this distinction will not be discussed in this paper.

6. An anonymous reviewer suggested that this example may be accounted for by the fact that the story contains two foxes. However, at this point in the story, only one fox had been introduced.

References

Almor, Amit. 1995. *Noun-phrase anaphora and focus: The informational load hypothesis.* Ph.D. Dissertation, Brown University.

Almor, Amit. 1999. "Noun-Phrase Anaphora and Focus: The Informational Load Hypothesis". *Psychological Review* 106: 748–765.

Ariel, Mira. 1988. "Referring and accessibility". *Journal of Linguistics* 24: 65–87.

Ariel, Mira. 1990. *Accessing Noun-Phrase Antecedents.* London: Routledge.

Ariel, Mira. 1994. "Interpreting anaphoric expressions: A cognitive versus a pragmatic approach". *Journal of Linguistics* 30: 3–42.

Arnold, Jennifer. 1994. "Inverse voice marking in Mapudungun". In S. Gahl, A. Dolbey, & C. Johnson (eds.), *TheTwentieth Annual Meeting of the Berkeley Linguistics Society.* Berkeley: Berkeley Linguistics Society, 28–41.

Arnold, Jennifer. 1998. *Reference Form and Discourse Patterns.* Ph.D. Dissertation, Stanford University.

Arnold, Jennifer. 1999. *Marking Salience: The Similarity of Topic and Focus.* Ms, Stanford University.

Ashby, William J. and Bentivoglio, Paola. 1993. "Preferred Argument Structure in French and Spanish". *Language Variation and Change* 5: 61–76.

Bates, Elizabeth and MacWhinney, Brian. 1989. "Functionalism and the competition model". In B. MacWhinney & E. Bates (eds), *The Cross-linguistic Study of Sentence Processing.* Cambridge: Cambridge University Press, 3–96.

Bentivoglio, Paola. 1993. "Full NPs in spoken spanish: A discourse profile". In W. J. Ashby et al. (eds), *Linguistic Perspectives on the Romance Languages: Selected Papers from the XXI Linguistic Symposium on Romance Languages, Santa Barbara, February 21–24, 1991.* Amsterdam: Benjamins, 211–224.

Brennan, Susan E., Friedman, Marilyn W. and Pollard, Carl J. 1987. "A centering approach to pronouns." *Proceedings from the 25th Annual Meeting of the Association for Computational Linguistics. July 6–9, 1987.*

Chafe, Wallace L. 1976. "Givenness, contrastiveness, definiteness, subjects, topics, and point of view." In C. N. Li (ed.), *Subject and Topic.* New York: Academic Press, 25–56

Chafe, Wallace L. 1994. *Discourse, Consciousness, and Time.* Chicago: University of Chicago Press.

Chambers, Craig G. and Smythe, Ron. 1998. "Structural parallelism and discourse coherence: A test of centering theory". *Journal of Memory and Language* 39 : 593–608.

Clancy, Patricia. 1980. "Referential choice in English and Japanese narrative discourse". In W. Chafe (ed.), *The Pear Stories.* Norwood, NJ: Ablex.

Clancy, Patricia. 1993. "Preferred Argument Structure in Korean acquisition". In E. Clark (ed.), *The Proceedings of the Twenty-Fifth Annual Child Language Research Forum.* Stanford: CSLI Publications, 307–314.

Dahlstrom, Amy. 1986. *Plains Cree Morphosyntax.* Ph.D. dissertation, University of California, Berkeley.

Dixon, Robert M. W. 1979. "Ergativity". *Language* 55: 59–138.

Du Bois, John W. 1985. "Competing Motivations". In J. Haiman (ed.), *Iconicity in Syntax*, 343–65.

Du Bois, John W. 1987. "The discourse basis of ergativity". *Language* 63: 805–855.

Durie, Mark. 1988. "Preferred Argument Structure in an active language: Arguments against the category 'intransitive subject'". *Lingua: International Review of General Linguistics* 74: 1–25.

Foley, William. A. and Van Valin Jr., Robert D. 1984. *Functional Syntax and Universal Grammar.* Cambridge: Cambridge University Press.

Givón, Talmy. 1983. "Topic continuity in discourse: An introduction". In T. Givón (ed.), *Topic Continuity in Discourse: A Quantitative Cross-Language Study.* Amsterdam: Benjamins, 1–42.

Givón, Talmy. 1994. "The pragmatics of de-transitive voice". In T. Givón (ed.), *Voice and Inversion,* Amsterdam: Benjamins, 3–46.

Gordon, Peter C., Grosz, Barbara. J. and Gilliom, Laura A. 1993. "Pronouns, names, and the centering of attention in discourse". *Cognitive Science* 17: 311–347.

Grimes, Joseph E. 1985. "Topic Inflection in Mapudungun Verbs". *IJAL* 51: 141–63.

Grimshaw, Jane. 1997. "Projection, heads, and optimality." *Linguistic Inquiry* 28: 373–422.

Grober, Ellen H., Beardsley, William and Caramazza, Alfonso. 1978. "Parallel function strategy in pronoun assignment". *Cognition* 6: 117–133.

Grosz, Barbara and Sidner, Candace L. 1986. "Attention, intentions, and the structure of discourse". *Computational Linguistics* 12: 175–204.

Grosz, Barbara J., Joshi, Aravind. K. and Weinstein, Scott. 1995. "Centering: A framework for modelling the local discourse". *Computational Linguistics* 21(2): 203–225.

Gundel, Jeanette. K., Hedberg, Nancy and Zacharaski, Ron. 1993. "Cognitive Status and the form of referring expressions". *Language* 69(2): 274–307.

Hudson-D'Zmura, Susan & Tanenhaus, Michael K. 1998. "Assigning antecedents to ambiguous pronouns: The role of the center of attention as the default assignment". In M. Walker, A. Joshi, & E. Prince (eds.), *Centering Theory in Discourse.* Oxford: Oxford University Press, 199–226.

MacDonald, Maryallen. C., Pearlmutter, Neal J. and Seidenberg, Mark S. 1994. "The lexical nature of syntactic ambiguity resolution". *Psychological Review* 101: 676–703.

Payne, Doris L. 1987. "Information structuring in Papago narrative discourse". *Language* 63: 783–804.

Prince, Alan & Smolensky, Paul. 1993. *Optimality Theory: Constraint Interaction in Generative Grammar.* Ms., Rutgers University, New Brunswick, and University of Colorado, Boulder.

Rhodes, Richard A. 1990. "Obviation, inversion, and topic rank in Ojibwa". *BLS 16 Special Session*: 101–115.

Salas, Adalberto. 1984. *Textos Orales en Mapuche o Araucano del Centro-Sur de Chile.* Concepción, Chile: Editorial de la Universidad de Concepción.

Scancarelli, Janine. 1987. *Grammatical Relations and Verb Agreement in Cherokee.* Ph.D. Dissertation, University of California, Los Angeles.

Smeets, Ineke. 1989. *A Mapuche Grammar.* Leiden, Holland.

Stevenson, Rosemary J., Crawley, Rosalind A. and Kleinman, David. 1994. "Thematic roles, focus and the representation of events". *Language and Cognitive Processes* 9: 473–592.

Trueswell, John C. and Tanenhaus, Michael K. 1994. "Towards a lexicalist framework of constraint-based syntactic ambiguity resolution". In J.C. Clifton, L. Frazier, & K. Rayner (eds), *Perspectives on Sentence Processing.* Hillsdale, NJ: Erlbaum, 155–179.

Walker, Marilyn A. 1998. "Centering, anaphora resolution, and discourse structure". In M. Walker, A. Joshi, and E. Prince (eds), *Centering Theory in Discourse.* Oxford: Oxford University Press, 401–435.

Walker, Marilyn A. and Prince, Ellen F. 1996. "A bilateral approach to givenness: A hearer-status algorithm and a centering algorithm". In T. Fretheim & J.K. Gundel (eds), *Reference and Referent Accessibility.* Amsterdam: John Benjamins, 291–306.

Texts

Blanco Painequeo, Jose. 1988. "Füta peni ka kude pangküll". In *Dollümko ñi Kuyfike Nütram.* Temuco, Chile: Imprenta y Editorial Küme Dungu.

Blanco Painequeo, Jose. 1988. "Kiñe Wentru Nierkey Kiñe Kon̠a". In *Dollümko ñi Kuyfike Nütram.* Temuco, Chile: Imprenta y Editorial Küme Dungu.

Huisca-Melinao, Rosendo. 1990. "Ngülamtuwün Ti Pu Dewü". *Amuldungun*, Año V-No. 2.

"Kiñe wentru l̠an̠turkei". (traditional). In A. Salas (ed.), *Textos Orales en Mapuche o Araucano del Centro-Sur de Chile.* 1984. Concepción, Chile: Editorial de la Universidad de Concepción, 42–62.

"Kuse pangküll ngürü engu". (traditional). In A. Salas (ed.), *Textos Orales en Mapuche o Araucano del Centro-Sur de Chile.* 1984. Concepción, Chile: Editorial de la Universidad de Concepción, 62–94.

Quinchavil, Luis. 1989. "An Old Man". Transcribed and translated by I. Smeets. In *A Mapuche Grammar.* Ph.D. Dissertation, Leiden.

Quinchavil, Luis. 1989. "Missionary". Transcribed and translated by I. Smeets. In *A Mapuche Grammar.* Ph.D. Dissertation, Leiden.

Argument splits in Finnish grammar and discourse*

Marja-Liisa Helasvuo
Turku University

Introduction

Across languages, pronouns are known to exhibit coding systems that are distinct from those of full NP's. For example in English, personal pronouns realize a nominative-accusative marking system, whereas full NP's have no case marking. In some typological studies this has led to the exclusion of pronouns from the description of coding systems (see e.g. Siewierska 1994). Instead, full definite NP's are taken to exhibit the basic coding system of a language. However, pronouns are much more frequent than full NP's in spoken data. Moreover, several studies have shown that clauses with two full NP's are extremely rare in spoken discourse (see e.g. Du Bois 1985, Lambrecht 1987, Ochs 1988, D. Payne 1987). Thus, typological data that exclude clauses with pronominal arguments are severely biased from the point of view of language use.

Studies on the grammatical coding of syntactic functions have shown that classifying languages into accusative, ergative or active languages is often oversimplifying, if not misleading; instead, there are many kinds of splits in the marking systems across languages. There is a wealth of research into splits in coding systems, especially into the ways in which they manifest themselves in case marking and agreement patterns (see e.g. Silverstein 1976, Durie 1988, Mithun 1991a). However, there are fewer studies that explore the effects of these splits on word order patterns. In this paper, I would like to discuss the ways in which case marking, agreement and word order work to code syntactic functions in spoken Finnish. I am especially interested in the coding of subject. I will suggest that the key to understanding how the coding systems work is the category of person. I will show that personal pronouns behave differently with respect to case marking and agreement from other pronouns and nouns. I will further demonstrate that this split can also be seen in word order patterns. In regard to all three coding strategies, personal pronouns are the ones that are most explicitly coded when they function as subjects.

This paper is organized as follows: I will first introduce my data. Then I will discuss case marking, agreement and word order patterns with respect to the ways in which they are used to code syntactic functions, especially the subject role. The findings will then be discussed first from the viewpoint of the referential semantic features of the subject NP's and then from the point of view of the discourse functions subjects serve. Finally, I will discuss the grammaticization of the subject role by contrasting it to some borderline cases.

Data and coding

The data for this study consist of six audiotaped excerpts of multiparty conversations. The excerpts are each about 5 minutes long, together amounting to 35 minutes of transcribed data. My data are representative of conversational language only. However, I do assume that grammaticization patterns are most readily observable in conversational discourse.

Crosslinguistically, questions and clauses with negative polarity are known to function quite differently with regard to word order. So for this paper, I have excluded questions and negative clauses in the discussion on word order.

The data have been analyzed syntactically, with codings for several features of clause structure and the constituent NP's. The NP's were coded for case, syntactic structure and function. Also coded were several features of information flow described below:

Activation cost: An NP was coded as new if the referent had not been mentioned in the discourse and it was not present in the situation. Non-referential NP's, however, were not coded for activation cost.
Semantic class: A referent was coded for humanness or nonhumanness.
Tracking: An NP was coded as tracking if it was mentioned more than once in the discourse.

Du Bois and Thompson (1991) discuss the tracking function in terms of discourse referentiality. According to them, an NP is tracking if it is used to speak about an entity as such, with continuous identity over time (cf. Du Bois 1980 on referentiality). In the same spirit, Durie (1994:504) discusses the distinction *trackable* vs. *non-trackable.* He calls trackable those referents that are "of the kind that could be mentioned again". According to him, trackables require "the hearer to open a file for them". However, I find it hard to decide in the coding procedure whether a referent *could* be mentioned or not, and furthermore, if it requires the hearer to open a new file or not. Instead, I considered whether it really was mentioned again, admitting that in some cases there may be changes in plans so that something that the speaker means to track will not be mentioned again.

Case marking

If we look at personal pronouns, Finnish is a straightforward nominative-accusative language, whereas for other pronouns and full NP's the markings are more complex. In this section, I will discuss the differences in the case marking of pronouns and nouns.

When personal pronouns function as objects, they are always marked, either with the accusative (ending *-t*) or with the partitive (for a discussion on this alternation, see e.g. Heinämäki 1983 and Helasvuo 2001). The nominative (no ending) is reserved for subjects. This means that if a personal pronoun is in the nominative, it functions as a subject. Thus, personal pronouns exhibit a nominative-accusative coding system with a marked coding for objects and unmarked for subjects. Table 1a illustrates this (the inflection of the 1st person singular pronoun *minä* is given as an example).

Table 1a. Case marking of the object: personal pronouns[1]

Case marking of the O	**Singular**		**Plural**	
Personal pronouns	**Acc**	**Ptv**	**Acc**	**Ptv**
1st, 2nd and 3rd person (nominative *minä*)	-t (*minut*)	-a (*minua*)	-t (*meidät*)	-tä (*meitä*)

Interestingly enough, the 3rd person personal pronoun *hän* 'she/he' is not used very much in the colloquial language.[2] Instead, the demonstrative pronoun *se* 'it' is being used both for human and non-human 3rd person referents. It has been suggested that the Finnish *se* should be considered a personal pronoun (e.g. Karlsson 1982a, A. Hakulinen 1988). In terms of case marking, however, *se* does not pattern morphologically like other personal pronouns — inter alia, it does not take the same accusative ending as other personal pronouns, and it does not have an obligatory object marking but can stand in the unmarked form, the nominative. Instead, it lines up with other pronouns (see Table 1b). In terms of the interactional work pronouns do in discourse, there is a clear difference between the 1st and 2nd person pronouns on the one hand and the 3rd person pronoun *se* on the other: the 1st and 2nd person pronouns refer to speech act participants who are most often present and in face-to-face contact, whereas for *se*, the set of referents the pronoun can refer to is wide and varied. *Se* does not distinguish between human and non-human referents, a distinction which will be shown to be relevant in regard to word order (see below on word order).

In contrast, the marking of other pronouns and full NP's is much more varied than that of personal pronouns, as can be seen from Table 1b. (In Table 1b, Ø indicates zero ending, and blank areas indicate that the given case marking is not available as a choice in the context, e.g. nominative case is not available for object marking if there is an NP subject in the clause. The word *talo* 'house' is given as an example of the inflection pattern.)

Table 1b. *Case marking of the object. Full NPs and non-personal pronouns.*

Case marking of the O	Singular			Plural	
Non-personal pronouns & full NP's	Acc	Ptv	Nom	Ptv	Nom
– in clauses with NP subject	-n (*talon*)	-a (*taloa*)		-a (*taloja*)	-Ø (*talot*)
– in clauses without NP subject		-a (*taloa*)	-Ø (*talo*)	-a (*taloja*)	-Ø (*talot*)

Table 1b shows that for singular NP's, case marking works to distinguish the object from the subject: if there is an NP subject, the object has to be marked either with the accusative or the partitive. However, if there is no subject, the object can take the "subject case", i.e. the nominative (there are exceptions to this principle, such as arguments of infinitival constructions). Thus, the case marking system of singular full NP's and non-personal pronouns follows a principle of distinguishing the different functions only if needed.[3]

In the plural, this principle does not work. As we can see from Table 1b, case marking does not keep the subject and the object role apart in the plural since both can stand in the nominative.[4] Note, however, that the need for distinguishing the subject and the object in the plural is not so great, since it is rare to have clauses in which both the subject and the object would be plural full NP's or pronouns other than personal ones. In the data for this study, out of a total of 724 subjects, I found no instances of clauses with plural full NP subject and object, and only one instance with plural full NP object and a pronominal plural subject.

Thus, there are three subsystems in the case marking of the core roles: first, personal pronouns realize a nominative-accusative system where the nominative codes the subject, and the accusative or the partitive marks the object. Secondly, other pronouns and singular full NP's exhibit a coding system where the object is marked only if there is a need to distinguish it from the subject. Thirdly, plural pronouns and full NP's realize a neutral coding system with similar case markings both for the subject and the object. (For a discussion of the so-called "partitive subjects" in Finnish, see below.)

To summarize, Finnish case marking does not exhibit a real split system since both full NP's and personal pronouns do realize a nominative — accusative pattern (at least in the singular). However, the marking of personal pronouns is more explicit than that of other pronouns and full NP's because the subject and the object roles are strictly kept apart (subjects are marked with the nominative, objects are marked with the accusative or the partitive; there are no shared case markings). As an indicator of syntactic function, case marking is least explicit in the coding of plural NP's, since it does not distinguish between subjects and objects.

Agreement and the category of person

In Finnish, verbal agreement morphology codes the subject according to person and number. Finnish distinguishes between 1st, 2nd, and 3rd person and two grammatical numbers, singular and plural. The system is illustrated in Table 2; the inflection of the word *istuu* 'sit' is given as an example.

Table 2. Agreement system in Finnish: verbal agreement morphology

Agreement morphology	**Singular**	**Plural**	
		standard system	**colloquial system**
1st person	-n (*istun*)	-mme (*istumme*)	PASSIVE: -tVVn (*istutaan*)
2nd person	-t (*istut*)	-tte (*istutte*)	-tte (*istutte*)
3rd person	-V (*istuu*)	-vAt (*istuvat*)	-V (*istuu*)

The 1st and 2nd person markings originate in personal pronouns, whereas the 3rd person singular ending stems from a present participle ending (see e.g. L. Hakulinen 1979). The 3rd person singular is indicated through lengthening of the final vowel of the verb stem or, if the stem ends with a long vowel or dipthong, there is a zero ending. In the plural, the markings are more complicated in the colloquial language: in the plural 1st person, the old personal suffix has been replaced by a passive form, a kind of non-specific personal verb form.[5] In the 3rd person, number opposition is neutralized to a great extent, and the 3rd person singular form is used with plural subjects also. In connection with 3rd person plural subjects in my data, there were no instances with the 3rd person plural verbal suffix; instead, the 3rd person singular form was used.

In principle, the 1st and 2nd person pronoun can be omitted when functioning as subject, and the verbal suffix alone conveys the information about person (e.g. *istun* 'sit-1SG' can be used instead of *minä istun* 'I sit-1SG' to convey the meaning 'I sit/am sitting'). In the standard language, this is the preferred alternative, whereas in the colloquial language, it is rare to have the 1st or 2nd person pronoun omitted;

in my data, there were only two instances.[6] In clauses with 3rd person verb form, if there is no pronoun, the zero may be interpreted as anaphorically bound to some previous mention or as indexically open so that the reference can be co-constructed by the conversation participants (consider ex. 2 below; see Laitinen 1995b, 1996). The 1st person plural works in a parallel way: if there is no pronoun and we only have a passive verb form, the clause may be interpreted in (at least) three ways: (i) as containing zero anaphora, (ii) as a passive and, thus, having a non-specific human agent, or (iii), if the clause is verb-initial, as a suggestion (optative, e.g. *syödään* 'Let's eat'). Thus, the 1st and 2nd person singular forms are still personal forms even if the pronoun has been omitted, whereas the 3rd person and the 1st person plural may turn into forms with which the personal reference is left non-specific.

The 3rd person singular has been described as the unmarked form in the verbal person marking system (Hakulinen and Karlsson 1979) because it is the form that is used when person oppositions have become neutralized for some reason (e.g. there is no subject in the clause). Not only are the verbal markings reduced in the 3rd person, but also distinctions expressed by pronouns are neutralized as we saw in the previous section.

To sum up, agreement works to code the subject in the first and second person, whereas in the 3rd person the coding is far less explicit, since the number opposition and the opposition between human and non-human are neutralized. As we saw in the previous section, the case marking system works exactly in the same way: the codings are most explicit in 1st and 2nd person, whereas in the 3rd person, they are weaker.

Word order

Finnish word order has often been characterized as being relatively free with "very few genuinely grammatical constraints" (Vilkuna 1989: 9–10). Support for this view has been sought in the fact that syntactic permutations rarely yield ungrammatical orderings. However, if we take language use as a starting point, a very different pattern emerges. There is a clear tendency for the subject to precede the verb and for the object to occur after the verb. In Hakulinen et al.'s corpus of written Finnish, the subject preceded the verb in 61% of the clauses (Hakulinen et al. 1980: 145), and the same tendency can be seen in Huumo's data from literary fiction where the percentage lies around 77% (Huumo 1994). In my spoken data, over 90% of the subjects preceded the verb.[7] This tendency is even more robust if we look at pronominal subjects only. If we further separate pronouns referring to humans, we come fairly close to a fixed Subject — Verb pattern. In this section, I will first illustrate the overall tendency with an example. I will then give a more fine-graded analysis of the tendency.

Let us now look at example (1). In the example, Noora tells about her work mate, who went to buy some food after coming home from work. The ordering of the main constituents is given in the fourth line underneath the free translation. (Abbreviations: Subj = subject; V = predicate verb; O = object; Obl = oblique; App = apposition; COMP = complement; Q = question word; NEG = (finite) negation verb, @ = laughter. For abbreviations used in the glosses, see note 1.)

(1) Birthday party (544–557)

1 N: .. *se tuli,* .. *kerran töi-stä koti-in Kerava-lla ja,*
it came+3SG once work-ELA home-ILL K.-ADE and
'He once came home from work in Kerava (place name) and
Subj V Obl

2 .. *meni, pyyhkäs lähi-kauppa-an,*
went+3SG rushed+3SG close-store-ILL
went rushing to the closest store and,
V Obl

3 *sit se rupes katto-on et,*
then it started+3SG look-INF COMP
then he started to look
Subj V Comp

4 .. @ *mikä-s se tuolla liha-tiski-llä on,*
what-CLT it there meat-counter-ADE is
what's there at the meat counter
Q-Subj Obl V

5 *jos ei heidä-n Ville?* @
if NEG+3SG they-GEN V.
if not their Ville (name of the cat).
NegV Subj

6 All: @@@

7 N: *kissa istu siel liha-tiski-n ääressä,*
cat sat+3SG there meat-counter-GEN next.to
The cat was sitting there at the meat counter,
Subj V Obl

8 *katto silmä-t ymmyrkäis-i-nä, kano-j-a grilli-ssä*
watched+3SG eye-PL round-PL-ESS chicken-PL-PTV barbecue-INE
watching chicken in the barbecue with its eyes wide-open.'
V App O Obl

In the example, the subject precedes the verb in most of the clauses or is a zero, as in lines 2 and 8. The only exception to the Subject–Verb ordering is in line 5, where we have a negative clause. In Finnish, negation is expressed through a verbal element which has verbal suffixing morphology, such as person marking.[8] The negation element often takes 1st or 2nd position in a clause. In the clause in line 5, the subject is a full NP and it is after the negation verb. This is a point where there is a shift in the topic of the discourse.[9] There is one other full NP subject (*kissa* 'cat' in line 6) which is before the verb. All the pronominal subjects are before the verb (lines 1, 3, 4).

Our example reflects the more general constraints that guide the ordering of subject and verb in my data: pronominal subjects are almost always before the verb, whereas full NP subjects are more flexible with regard to word order. Table 3 shows how 3rd person pronominal subjects distribute themselves with respect to the verb. (N.B: Questions and clauses with negation or with zero subjects are excluded.)

Table 3. Word order in clauses with 3rd person pronominal subjects

Word order		**before verb**		**Total**
3 person pronouns		N	%	N
Human	A	42	91.3	46
	Se	27	100	27
	S	21	100	21
	Total	90	95.7	94
Non-human	A	11	91.7	12
	Se	111	93.3	119
	S	52	96.3	54
	Total	174	94.1	185

Table 3 shows that 3rd person pronominal subjects are mostly in preverbal position. There doesn't seem to be much difference between human and non-human referents in the percentages — both have percentages around 95% for subjects preceding the verb. If we look at the absolute numbers, however, we can see that the majority of non-human pronominal subjects (over 60%) are subjects of copular clauses (marked with Se in table), whereas only a few function as transitive subjects (6.3%). Table 4 looks at word order in clauses with 1st and 2nd person subjects.

Table 4 shows that over 96% of 1st and 2nd person pronouns also precede the verb when they function as subjects. So, 1st, 2nd and 3rd person pronouns work similarly for word order.

In contrast, when we look at clauses with full NP subjects, the ordering is no longer a strict Subject — Verb -order, but instead, it shows more flexibility. If we consider full NPs which refer to humans, 84% of the subjects precede the verb. For full NPs that refer to non-humans, the average is only 63% (see Table 5).

Note also the low absolute numbers for full NP's in comparison to the numbers for pronominal subjects.

Table 4. Word order in clauses with 1st or 2nd person subjects

Word order 1st and 2nd person pronouns	before verb		Total N
	N	%	
A	99	96.1	103
Se	19	100	19
S	32	94.1	34
Total	150	96.2	156

Table 5. Word order in clauses with full NP subjects

Word order Full NPs		before verb		Total N
		N	%	
Human	A	28	87.5	32
	Se	9	75.0	12
	S	10	83.3	12
	Total	47	83.9	56
Non-human	A	3	75.0	4
	Se	15	75.0	20
	S	21	55.3	38
	Total	39	62.9	62

We can see from Tables 4 and 5 that the ordering of 1st and 2nd person subjects with respect to the verb is much more constrained than that of full NP subjects. If we compare Tables 3 and 4 to Table 5, we can see that pronominal subjects are much more frequent than full NP's (83% of subjects are pronominal). Comparison of Tables 3 and 5 shows that non-human subjects are most often subjects of copular clauses. One interpretation of this could be that the subject position is usually reserved for human referents. NP's that refer to non-human referents are in the subject position if they are being characterized some way.

Figure 1 combines Tables 3–5 showing the percentage of subjects that precede the verb in each subject type. It shows a cline from the strict ordering principles of clauses with 1st and 2nd person subjects to the more variable ordering of subjects and verbs in clauses with full NP subjects.

Note, however, that Figure 1 only compares percentages. As we have seen, there are many more pronominal subjects than full NP's: 414 (82.8%) vs. 86 (17.2%). Thus, the rightmost columns represent only a small minority of the subjects. Therefore, the tendency for the subject to precede the verb is even more pervasive than Figure 1 would indicate, yielding over 90% of subjects preceding the verb.

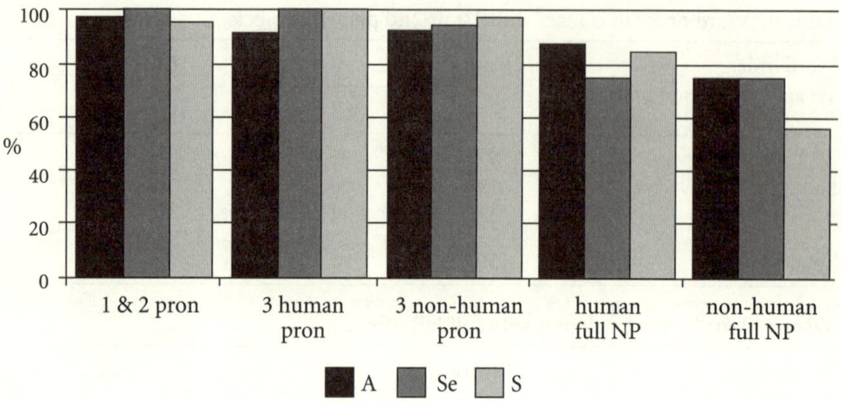

Figure 1. Percentage of subjects preceding the verb.

To summarize, I have shown that the order of subject and verb is virtually invariant in clauses with 1st and 2nd person subjects, whereas in the 3rd person, there is more variation. In clauses with 3rd person pronominal subjects, subjects precede the verb in about 95% of the clauses. In contrast, clauses with full NP subjects show a pattern which is much more flexible, especially if the NP is referring to a non-human referent. It is worth noting here that the other two coding strategies, case marking and agreement, work to single out 1st and 2nd person subjects with strict codings, whereas the 3rd person subjects have less explicit codings. Regarding word order, however, the 1st and 2nd persons pattern with the 3rd person pronominal subjects in showing fixed word order, whereas full NP subjects are much less constrained in their word order.

Inherent lexical content and grammaticization of the subject role

In his seminal article on ergative splits, Silverstein (1976) proposed that the splits are not random, but rather, correspond to a hierarchy of "inherent lexical content" of noun phrases. Personal pronouns rank highest in the hierarchy; they are followed by third person pronouns, proper nouns and kin terms, then nouns that refer to humans, then animates, then inanimates (Silverstein 1976: 122; see also Silverstein 1981). We have seen that Finnish also reflects this hierarchy in the coding of grammatical functions. In this section, I will briefly discuss the ways in which this hierarchy could be interpreted from the point of view of the grammaticization of coding systems in discourse.

According to Silverstein (1976: 113), this hierarchy expresses "the semantic naturalness for a lexically-specified noun phrase to function as agent of a true transitive verb, and inversely the naturalness of functioning as patient of such".

Silverstein thus relates the hierarchy of inherent lexical content of noun phrases to the syntactico-semantic roles A and P (in our terminology O). He speaks about a "metapragmatically based understanding of predication-perspective" according to which "language structure is grammaticalising (with characteristic asymmetry) the perspective from which a state of affairs is predicated of referents, the most 'natural' being that which grows out of the configuration of the ongoing speech event, the informational givens of which, the maximally presupposable entities, are of course of the same ordering as above [cf. the hierarchy]" (Silverstein 1981:243). Thus, the speech act participants are the most natural A's, and the least natural O's (or, in Silverstein's terminology, P's).

In addition to inherent lexical content and case relations (A, O, S), Silverstein (1976) names two additional variables that affect case marking, namely tightness of clause-linkage and reference-maintenance relations of arguments. Especially the last named of these two received a lot of research interest in the 1980's, inter alia in studies on topic continuity (see e.g. Givón 1983). In his account of coding splits, Du Bois (1985, 1987) sees them as results of different ways of managing information flow. To put it broadly, an ergative system could be seen as a way to mark new information in a consistent way, whereas a nominative-accusative system could be seen as a way to code topics consistently. These two motivations can be in competition, thus resulting in splits in the coding systems.

Let us now look how Finnish works in this regard. If we look at personal pronouns, Finnish exhibits a clear nominative-accusative system in terms of case marking, agreement, and word order. As regards case marking, 1st and 2nd person subjects are marked with the nominative, and objects with the accusative or the partitive. In the agreement system, 1st and 2nd person subjects trigger explicit codings, and with regard to word order, personal pronouns exhibit a relatively fixed Subject-Verb ordering. In contrast, the coding of full NP's in Finnish approaches a neutral coding system in some respects. Case marking of full NP's is not distinctive in the plural, nor is agreement, since oppositions are neutralized. In word order patterns, we can see a cline from the relatively fixed Subject-Verb ordering of personal pronouns and 3rd person pronouns to the more flexible ordering principles of lexical NP's. Verb-Subject order is most frequent when the subject is a full NP referring to a non-human referent.

If we compare transitive, intransitive and copular clauses, the codings exhibit a unified subject role in Finnish: subjects in these different clause types receive identical codings. The split between explicit and more flexible codings can be accounted for by referring to the inherent lexical content of the NP in question (person, human vs. non-human). However, if we look at the coding system as it is realized in actual discourse, we can see that the different coding types are not evenly distributed across clause types. Consider Figure 2.

The majority of transitive subjects (A's) are 1st and 2nd person pronouns

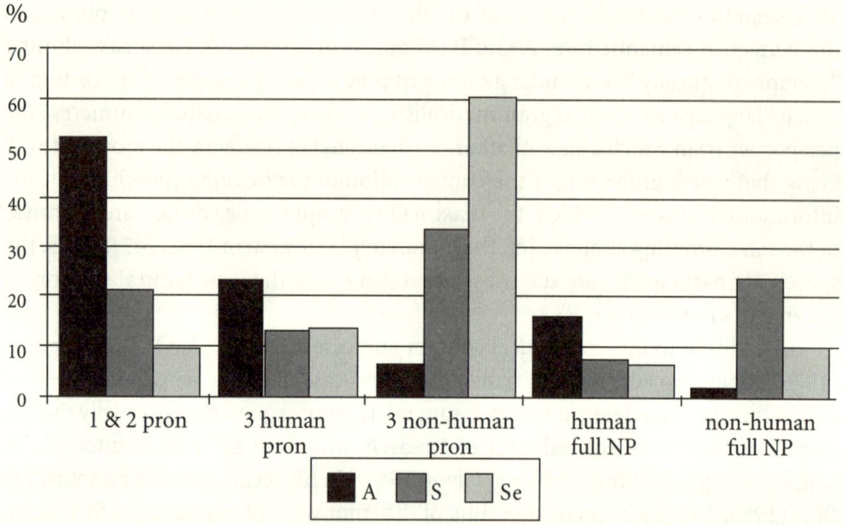

Figure 2. Type of subject NP and grammatical role.

(52.3%), whereas for subjects of intransitive (S's) and copular clauses (Se's), the largest group is formed by 3rd person pronouns which refer to non-humans (34% of S and 60.4% of Se). There are not very many full NP subjects in transitive clauses (18.2% of A), whereas in intransitive clauses, the percentage is considerably higher (31.4% of S). This is congruent with the idea of Preferred Argument Structure as proposed by Du Bois (1985, 1987), especially the Non-Lexical A Constraint according to which there is an overwhelming tendency in spoken discourse for NP's in the A role to be non-lexical.

If we interpret the findings presented in Figure 2 in terms of explicit and variable coding, we can see that those NP's which exhibit the most explicit coding when functioning as subjects (i.e. personal pronouns) appear mostly in transitive clauses. In contrast, the coding of subject is less explicit in intransitive and copular clauses, since the majority of subjects in these clause types are either pronouns referring to non-humans or full NP's. Of course, the functional load on the codings in distinguishing different functions is much greater in transitive clauses than in intransitives.

To sum up, I have shown that inherent lexical content of the NP plays an important role in the grammaticization of coding patterns. The category of person seems to be the key to understanding how the coding systems work. The role of 1st and 2nd person becomes especially important if we look at the coding systems from the viewpoint of their use in discourse, since 1st and 2nd person pronouns make almost 40% of all subjects and the majority of transitive subjects. Their role has gone underestimated in most previous work on coding systems, because studies have been based either on third person narrative or isolated sentences taken from reference grammars or elicited speech.

Information flow and the function of subject

In the previous section we have discussed the referential semantic characteristics of subjects. The question I would like to address in this section is the need for subjects in discourse. I will approach this question by discussing some information flow features that characterize subjects. I will start by discussing the relationship between introduction of new referents and the subject role. I will then discuss how the referents are treated after the introduction, i.e. whether they are tracked or dropped after the first mention. Then there will be a discussion of the subject role with respect to the semantic class of the referent. Finally, I will discuss the idea of subjects as starting points.

According to Chafe, it is typical of intonation units[10] that they contain only one piece of new information, and that the new information is not likely to reside in the subject (Chafe 1979, 1994). Chafe (1994) formulates a "light subject constraint" which entails that subjects tend to refer to referents that are either not new to the discourse or are new but of trivial importance. This is indeed what we find in the Finnish data. We have already seen in previous sections that pronominal NP's outnumber full NP's in the subject role; we would expect attenuated forms of reference such as pronouns to refer to referents that are not new. In addition, we have seen that 1st and 2nd person pronouns figure significantly in the subject role. They are of course always given, by their nature as speech act participants. Table 6 illustrates the relationship between grammatical role and activation cost in the Finnish data. (Note that in Tables 6 and 7 the category S does not include subjects of copular or existential clauses.)

Table 6. Activation cost and grammatical role

Act. cost and gramm. role	New		Total
	N	%	N
A	29	10.4	279
S	44	20.6	214
O	113	38.0	297
Obl	186	43.6	427

Table 6 shows that both transitive and intransitive subjects show low percentages of new mentions, whereas the percentages of new mentions in the object and oblique roles are considerably higher (around 40%).[11] However, subjects of transitive and intransitive clauses do not figure alike with respect to activation cost, but instead, intransitive subjects are much more likely to carry new mentions than transitive subjects (around 20% of S are new, but only 10% of A).

When studying Sakapulteko spoken narratives, Du Bois (1985, 1987) found that clauses hardly ever have more than one full NP argument and, moreover, this full NP is usually in the object or intransitive subject (S) role, but not in the transitive subject (A) role. Du Bois suggests two constraints to describe this patterning, namely the One Full NP Constraint and the Given A Constraint. In the Sakapulteko data, Du Bois finds an ergative patterning in which the A role stands out as the locus for given information, whereas the S aligns with the O role in carrying more new information. The Finnish data conform to the Given A Constraint, but the data do not suggest an outright ergative patterning. Table 6 shows a continuum from transitive subjects, which contain the least new mentions, to obliques, with the most new mentions.

It is important to note here that the continuum that can be seen in the proportion of new mentions in Table 6 hides an important difference between new mentions made in the core roles and new mentions in the oblique role: the new mentions that are made with oblique NP's differ from the ones made with NP's in the core roles in one important respect; namely, those referents that are introduced in the oblique role are hardly ever mentioned again in the discourse (18 referents of the total of 186 new oblique mentions were mentioned again, i.e. 9.7%), whereas referents that are first mentioned with NP's in the core roles are much more likely to be tracked in the discourse (for discussion, see Helasvuo 1997, 2001). Durie (1994) reports on similar findings for Acehnese discourse.

It seems, then, that the core roles do important discourse work by keeping track of participants. It is especially typical of subjects that they refer to referents which are being tracked in the discourse. Table 7 illustrates this.

Table 7. Referent tracking and grammatical role

Referent tracking and gramm. role	Tracking		Total
	N	%	N
A	250	89.6	279
S	187	87.4	214
O	232	78.1	297
Obl	30	11.9	253

From Table 7 we can see that NP's in the subject roles are mostly tracking, whereas in the object role the percentage of tracking mentions is lower. For NP's in the oblique role (adverbials), the percentage is only around 12%. Thus, NP's in the subject role contain the most tracking mentions, and NP's in the object role somewhat less, whereas in the oblique role, only a minority of the NP's is tracking (see Thompson 1997 for similar findings for English conversation).

As we have seen in the previous sections, transitive subjects typically refer to human referents (over 90% of A's are human), whereas less than half of intransitive subjects refer to human referents (about 42%; see Tables 3–5). The object role accommodates mainly non-human referents, as only 6.4% of objects are human. There is evidence from other languages that the low percentage of human referents might be characteristic of the object role even in more general terms (see Du Bois 1987 for Sakapulteko, Herring 1989 for Tamil, Ashby and Bentivoglio 1993 for French and Spanish, Nakayama and Ichihashi-Nakayama 1994 for Japanese, Kärkkäinen 1996 for English).

Chafe (1994) discusses subjects as "starting points". He states, "Each [clause] has a point of departure, a referent from which it moves to provide its own new contribution. It is this starting point referent that appears grammatically as the clause's subject." (Chafe 1994: 83; see also Chafe 1976). This is an interesting insight, especially in view of the fact that so many subjects are 1st or 2nd person pronouns: the speech act participants are quite natural starting points in interaction. In a very concrete way, we "move" from the speech act participants "to provide new contributions" (cf. also Silverstein's "predication-perspective" discussed in the previous section). In a language like English in which every clause has to have a subject, it is natural to think of the subject as grammaticizing the starting point function. In my view, however, the subject should not be thought of as the only grammaticization possibility of the starting point function. For example in Finnish, subjectless clauses are perfectly acceptable, but it would be odd to consider these clauses as having no starting point. In subjectless clauses, there is usually some constituent — most often a locative or temporal adverbial — before the verb, i.e. in the normal position for subjects (see Vilkuna 1989: 40–50). Consider ex. 2, which is an excerpt from a conversation between mother (T) and daughter (L). The mother has been complaining how tired she has been, and the daughter has suggested that she should take vitamins to cheer her up.

(2) Christmas (56–59)

1 T: *mä oo-n niin paljo syöny [vitamiine-i,]*
I be-1SG so much eaten vitamin-PL+PTV
"I have eaten so many vitamins,

[three intonation units omitted]

5 L: *nii-st saa jonku taudi.*
they-ELA get+3SG some+ACC disease+ACC
"(One/you) may get some disease from them (from eating so many vitamins)."

In example 2 line 1, the verb shows agreement with the first person pronominal subject, which appears before the verb. In contrast, in the clause in line 5, there is no subject NP, and the verb is in the 3rd person singular form with a zero subject. The reference of the zero subject is not anaphorically bound, but rather, it is open indexically. It could be interpreted as referring to the speech act participants, the mother and the daughter, or to any potential participants. The accusative NP *jonku taudi* 'some disease-ACC' is the object.[12] In the absence of an overt subject, the locative NP *niist* 'from them' appears before the verb and serves as the starting point. In some clause types, e.g. in existential and habitive clauses, the adverbial constituent has been grammaticized to the preverbal position (see Huumo 1996). Thus, the starting point function does not seem to characterize the subject role distinctively, but could rather be understood as a more general organizing principle of clause structure.

To sum up, the subject function is not so much used for bringing new referents into the discourse, but instead is well suited for keeping track of referents. Among the core roles, transitive subjects are mainly used for tracking human referents, while intransitive subjects accommodate other kinds of referents also. In the object role, mainly non-human referents are being tracked.

Grammaticization of the subject role in Finnish: Some borderline cases

In the above discussion on the coding of subject, I have argued for a definition of subject according to which only those NP's should be considered as subjects in Finnish which are in the nominative and which trigger agreement. In this section, I would like to discuss this definition from a grammaticization viewpoint and contrast it with two cases which have traditionally been considered to be subjects in Finnish linguistics, namely the so-called existential "subjects" and subjects with open quantification.

In the previous sections I have discussed the coding of grammatical relations in terms of case marking, agreement and word order. We have seen that personal pronouns realize a straight nominative-accusative system with a clearly distinguished subject role. If we look at the subject role from a grammaticization viewpoint, we could say that personal pronouns exhibit a highly grammaticized nominative-accusative coding system, and, accordingly, a clearly defined subject role. We have also seen that in terms of actual frequencies in spoken discourse, personal pronouns figure significantly in the subject role.

In contrast, the marking of full NP's is closer to a neutral alignment system. Accordingly, the coding does not clearly distinguish the subject as a distinct grammatical role, but instead, there is much overlap in the coding system. Nevertheless, full NP's can be recognized as subjects based on the model of pronominal subjects.

This paper has been based on a fairly abstract definition of subject that makes reference to case (nominative) and agreement patterns (an NP functions as a subject if it triggers agreement in the verb). I have shown that the subject thus defined shows a distinctive discourse profile (subject NP's are mainly used to track referents, but rarely used to bring new referents). It is noteworthy that this definition contains no information that would be specific to certain sets of verbs or clause types. In the next two subsections, my aim is to show that the two cases under consideration, namely "subjects" of existential clauses and "subjects" that are partially quantified, fall outside the category of subject because they only partially satisfy the criteria for subjects and, moreover, they are characterized by several features that are idiosyncratic to a certain set of verbs or to a clause type.

Existential clauses

Many researchers seem to assume that there is a special need to express existence or deny it and that languages often have a special clause type that is grammaticized to fulfil this need (see e.g. Jespersen 1924: 155, Lyons 1977: 469–470). In Finnish, existential constructions are usually formed with a locative NP together with the copular verb *olla* and an NP in the nominative or in the partitive case. Henceforth, I will refer to the latter NP as the E-NP (the so-called "existential subject" in traditional Finnish linguistics).[13] Also possible are other verbs that are existential or indicate coming into existence. The schema given in (3) represents the Finnish existential construction.

(3) LOC + V (exist.) + E-NP (nom or ptv)

The schema given in (3) reflects the preferred word order; sometimes there is no locative phrase. Habitive constructions are formed in a similar way: the possessor is in the adessive case, and the possessed is given after the copular verb in the nominative or the partitive case.

The following example illustrates how existential constructions work in Finnish discourse (for more discussion, see Helasvuo 1996a). The example is an excerpt of Veijo's story about his first visit to the home of his girlfriend Noora. Before the excerpt there has been talk about what cats can do, and this obviously brings the story to Veijo's mind.

(4) Birthday (120)

1 V: *nii-tte olohuonee-s on kangas-tapeti-t*
they-GEN livingroom-INE is fabric-wallpaper-PL
"In their living room they have wallpaper made of fabric,

2 *ja siel oli, .. seinä revi-tty sit, alaosa-sta,*
and there was wall scratch-PSS+PCP then lower side-ELA

and the wall(paper) was scratched (lit. there was wall scratched) at the bottom.

3 *näi-tte isä totes mu-lle,*
these-GEN father told+3SG I-ALL
Her father told me

4 *toss on vähän Noora-n repi-mä-ä seinä-ä.*
there is some N.-GEN scratch-PCP-PTV wall-PTV
"There is some wall that has been scratched by Noora."

5 All: @@@

6 S: *Noora saa semmos-i-a kohtauks-i-a.*
N. get+3SG such-PL-PTV attack-PL-PTV
Noora gets that kind of attacks."

In example 4, we have two existential clauses (lines 1 and 4). In both clauses, there is first a locative NP (*niitte olohuonees* 'in their living room' and *toss* 'there'). After the copula, we have NP's that refer to the entities that are being presented (*kangastapetit* 'fabric wallpaper' and *Nooran repimää seinää* 'wall scratched by Noora'). The former is in the plural, but there is no plural agreement in the verb. As was noted in the section on agreement, number agreement in the 3rd person plural is rare in the colloquial language. In existential constructions, however, number agreement is often lacking even in the formal language. In the latter clause (line 4), the E-NP *Nooran repimää seinää* is in the partitive and thus could not trigger agreement anyway, no matter what person or number it represented. The reason for having partitive case here is that the NP is quantified with the adverb *vähän* 'a little, some'.[14] In line 5, we have a partitive NP *semmosia kohtauksia* 'that kind of attacks' functioning as an object which is the most common function for partitive NP's.

We may ask, then, what the best analysis would be for the E-NP in an existential or habitive construction. It shares some of the features typically identified with subjects. Namely, it is the first argument of the verb, given that it is the only NP that is in a non-locative case. It is obligatory in the sense that the clause would not be comprehensible without it, whereas the locative NP can often be left out. However, it lacks most of the coding features discussed above. It is usually after the verb, and it does not trigger agreement. It may be in the nominative, but it may also be in the partitive. As was shown above, most subjects are pronominal, but the E-NP's are most often full NP's (97/118; 82.2%) and they mostly bring new referents into the discourse (89/118; 75.4%). They usually refer to non-humans (108/118; 91.5%), this is in striking contrast with subjects (c.f. Tables 2, 3, and 4, which show that 247 out of 553 subjects, i.e. less than 45%, refer to non-humans). Moreover, they are never agentive. Thus, they share more features with objects than with subjects.[15]

Karlsson (1982b: 109) has suggested that in existential and habitive constructions, the distinction between subject and object has been neutralized. He has proposed that the E-NP (the so-called "existential subject" in Finnish linguistics) should be called the "ject" (Finnish *jekti*; the English term *ject* has been suggested by Vilkuna 1989:156). I would like to argue here that in order to understand the grammaticization of the E-NP reference has to be made to the notion of clause type: the whole clause type has been grammaticized. In an e-clause, the case marking and position of the E-NP have been crystallized as well as the choice of the verb (*olla* 'to be' and certain other verbs) and the position and case marking of the locative NP. In contrast, the subject role as defined in this paper is characterized by syntactic features that are independent of clause type.

It has been assumed that existential clauses function to bring new referents into discourse (see e.g. Wähämäki 1975, Huumo 1996). The analysis of spoken discourse reveals that this indeed is true: the majority of E-NP's bring new referents into discourse. However, if we look at how these referents are treated in the discourse, we can note that only a few of them are tracked. Namely, only 26 of the 89 E-NP's with referents which are new to the discourse (i.e. 29%) are ever mentioned again. As was noted above, low frequency of further mentions is characteristic of oblique arguments (cf. Helasvuo 1997, 2001). It seems that although E-NP's are used to introduce new referents, these referents are not being kept track of, but instead they are dropped. In an existential clause, the new NP is presented in relation to a spatial or habitive frame. It seems that it is the frame that is the most relevant to the discourse, not the presented referent. The frame serves as the starting point of the clause. Huumo (1996:297) proposes that existential clauses function to state "a predication about the locative space by reporting its content". I would like to argue that existential clauses function to characterize the locative space by establishing a relationship between it and a new referent. The locative space may be concrete (as in ex. 4 line 1) or more abstract, as in the following example.

(5) Kids (173–176)

1 A: *oikeen si-ll on, ny semmose-t nah [ka-housu-t jala-ssa ja.]*
really it-ADE is now such-PL leather-pants-PL leg-INE and
"Really he now has leatherpants on and,

2 P: *[nii-t on erilaisi-a]*
those-PTV is different-PTV

3 *taipumuks-i-a nii-ll [ja].*
inclination-PL-PTV those-ADE and
They tend to have different kinds of inclinations.

4 A: *[ja sit] si-l on viel*
and then it-ADE is moreover

5 *kura-housu-t,*
mud-pants-PL
And then he also has rubber pants."

In example 5, four men are discussing their kids and the cost of everything they need. Aarre (speaker A) is saying of his son that he wears out his clothes so quickly. On line 1, the referent of the NP *semmoset nahkahousut* 'such leatherpants' is introduced. Pekka (P) is continuing with the more general topic, kids, on lines 2 and 3. On line 4, Aarre goes on about the son and his clothing. Thus, the leather-pants are introduced on line 1, but they are not referred to after that; instead the speaker continues with the referent of the adessive NP *sill* 'it/he-ADE', i.e. the frame. This example reflects the general pattern: existential constructions are used to introduce referents (here *nahkahousut* 'leatherpants', *kurahousut* 'rubber pants') that are not central to the discourse and, consequently, are usually not mentioned again. It is the frame that is more central, and the presented referents serve to characterize the referent of the locative NP.

We can conclude that E-NP's do not have the coding features that characterize subjects in Finnish. With their lack of coding features, they do illustrate, however, how the function of subject is built up by several features that together work to make subjects useful in grammar and in discourse for certain purposes, but not perhaps for others. Inter alia, the subject function is not well suited for introducing new referents into discourse. This is reflected in the word order patterns: the postverbal position is the preferred locus for new information in Finnish, and since subjects rarely refer to referents that are new to the discourse, they are predominantly preverbal. Furthermore, subject NP's are mainly pronominal. In contrast, the E-NP's offer a grammatical slot for introducing new non-human referents. Consequently, they are almost always full NP's and take a postverbal position.

Open quantification and the function of subject

As was noted in passing in the previous section, the partitive is mainly used to mark objects. As an object case marker, the partitive can be used to indicate open quantification or, more specifically, unbounded quantity of the referent (Heinämäki 1983, Larjavaara 1988; see above, ex. 4 line 6). This meaning potential can also be put to use in the marking of E-NP's (see ex. 4 line 4). Sometimes the partitive is used in connection with verbs that do not merely indicate existence or coming into existence, but something more, such as motion. In this section, I will discuss briefly the use of the partitive in open quantification of NP's other than object.

Example 6 below illustrates this usage. Before the segment given in ex. 6, there has been talk about a project, namely the building of a bridge in the area where Linnea's (L's) summer house is located. Because of the project, the water in the near-by bay does not flow out of the bay any more. But there are other problems too:

(6) Women (661–662)

1 L: *noi-t lannotte-i-t ku tule-e aina ni,*
those-PTV fertilizer-PL-PTV as come-3SG always so
"Because those fertilizers always get there (to the bay),

2 *se rehevöity-y nii mahrottoma-sti.*
it become eutrophic-3SG so impossible-MANNER
it (the bay) becomes so eutrophic."

In example 6 on line 1, we have the verb *tulee* 'come' which is a motion verb used to indicate that the fertilizers come to the bay from somewhere else, most probably from the farm lands adjacent to the bay. The verb does not merely state the existence of the fertilizers, but rather, it indicates motion. The partitive case marking of the NP *noit lannoitteit* 'those fertilizers-PTV' conveys that there is an unbounded (partial) quantity of the fertilizers. In the discourse, this is the first (and the last) time that the fertilizers come up.

In terms of frequencies, partitive NP's that do not function as objects are in no way central: in my data, there are 126 partitive NP's that function as objects, whereas there are only 49 non-object partitives of which 45 were in existential or habitive constructions (E-NP's). This leaves only 4 partitive NP's that are not E-NP's but arguments of some intransitive verbs.

The question is, then, whether the partitive NP *noit lannoitteit* should be analyzed as a subject or not. It bears some resemblance to the subject: inter alia, it is the first argument of a verb that usually takes a subject. However, the set of verbs with which it is possible to use the partitive is very limited (the copula or some intransitive verb; for more discussion, see Wähämäki 1975). Furthermore, the verb does not show agreement with the partitive NP. The information flow features that characterize partitive NP's are atypical of subjects. Namely, partitive NP's most often refer to non-human referents that are new to the discourse. As we have seen in previous sections, these are all features that correlate with the loss of coding. Thus, there is very little support to an analysis of partitive NP's as subjects.

Interim summary

In this section, I have discussed E-NP's (the NP being presented in an existential construction) and the so-called "partitive subjects" in Finnish. I have shown that these NP's lack most of the coding features that characterize subjects: they do not trigger agreement, and may appear in the partitive case as well as in the nominative. Regarding word order, E-NP's are always in postverbal position. We have seen that subjects are most often pronominal, whereas the majority of E-NP's and "partitive subjects" are full NP's. In terms of the discourse work NP's do, E-NP's are used for introducing new non-human referents. In subsequent discourse, however, these referents are not usually tracked, but instead are dropped. In contrast, subjects serve to track participants that have already been introduced to the discourse. The referents of subject NP's are usually human. Thus, the respective discourse profiles are completely different, and so are the coding features. We can conclude that they do not represent the same syntactic function, i.e. the subject.

Conclusions

In this paper, I have discussed the splits that can be seen in the coding systems of argument relations in Finnish. By splits I mean differences between explicit coding and more variable coding. In agreement patterns there is a split between the 1st and 2nd person on the one hand and 3rd person pronouns and full NP's on the other. With regard to word order, the split goes between pronouns and full NP's. I would like to propose that they reflect the grammaticization of the subject role in Finnish. Namely, the personal pronouns realize a highly grammaticized subject role, whereas the coding of full NP's does not provide such strong evidence for a grammaticized subject role.

This paper has highlighted the role of 1st and 2nd person pronouns in the coding system. They have a special status in discourse since they are always given, identifiable, and tracking. They are important referents as they are most often the ones that are being talked about. They are also potential agents. In grammar, they have the most explicit codings for the grammatical functions in the clause core, especially the subject role. In other words, they are best or most prototypical subjects, and they are most explicitly coded as such. In contrast, full NP's may introduce new topics but they are not usually used for keeping track of already introduced participants (Mithun 1991b). Instead of excluding personal pronouns from the description of coding systems, this paper has taken the coding of personal pronouns as its vantage point in the discussion on the coding of argument relations. I hope to have shown that it is necessary to study the personal pronouns in order to understand the grammaticization patterns in the argument structure.

Notes

* I would like to thank Wally Chafe, Auli Hakulinen, Tuomas Huumo, Anneli Kauppinen, Lea Laitinen, Sandy Thompson and the editors of this volume for insightful comments on earlier versions of this paper.

1. The following grammatical abbreviations are used in the glosses: — = morpheme boundary; + = fused morphemes; ACC = accusative; ADE = adessive; ALL = allative; ELA = elative; ESS = essive; GEN = genitive; ILL = illative; INE = inessive; PL = plural; PTV = partitive; 1SG = 1st person singular; 3SG = 3rd person singular; INF = infinitive; NEG = negation verb; PCP = participle; PSS = passive; PST = past tense; COMP = complementizer; CLT = clitic; MANNER = derivational suffix indicating manner.

2. There are dialectal differences here. In my data, there are 14 instances of *hän* or *he* 'she/he or they' 12 of which come from the same conversation between speakers of the Southwestern dialect of Finnish. In the Southwestern and Eastwestern dialects, the use of the personal pronoun *hän* is more pervasive, but in most Finnish dialects, the use of *hän* is restricted to evidential or affective contexts (for a detailed discussion, see Vilppula 1989, Laitinen 1995a). The demonstrative pronoun *se* is used elsewhere.

3. Transitive clauses with a first person plural subject make an interesting case here: the verb usually takes the passive form instead of the 1st p plural, and thus, it does not show agreement with the subject (see below section on agreement). The subject pronoun is in the nominative but so is the object, be it full NP or pronoun (personal pronouns, however, are marked with the accusative -t even in this context). I.e. the object is marked as if the clause was a real passive clause with no subject NP. Consider the following ex.:

Me ote-ta-an *toi.*
we take-PASS-PERS that
'We take that (one)'.

In the example, both *me* 'we' and *toi* 'that (one)' are in the nominative. The fact that the personal pronoun *me* 'we' is in the nominative case indicates that it cannot function as an object but rather it has to be the subject of the clause.

4. The final *-t* in the nominative plural is a plural marker, not a case ending.

5. The Finnish passive has many interesting characteristics: for example, in the passive form, there is a a person marking on the verb in the morphotactic slot for personal suffixes (the so-called "4th person"; Tuomikoski 1971). Moreover, the passive is almost exclusively used to describe actions and states that involve an unspecified human agent or patient (for a discussion of the Finnish passive, see Shore 1988).

6. Certain sequential contexts make an exception here: in a question-answer-pair, it is preferred not to repeat the subject pronoun in the answer. I am grateful to Marja-Leena Sorjonen for pointing this out to me.

7. The numbers are not fully comparable because of differences in the definition of subject. In this paper, subject is defined as the core argument of a transitive, intransitive, or copular verb that stands in the nominative case and triggers agreement. Hakulinen et al. (1980) and Huumo (1994) apply a broader definition that includes NP's in the partitive case.

8. Note, however, that the negation element is not a full verb — it does not inflect for tense for example — and in some usages it is closer to being a particle. In many dialects, even the person inflection is lacking (Savijärvi 1977). The negation element has particle-like features with regard to word order too: it seems to prefer the beginning of clause or intonation unit just like particles. (For discussion, see Lindén 1963, Dahl 1979, J. Payne 1985 and Helasvuo 1997.)

9. The shift occurs in two phases: first, the new topic is mentioned with a definite NP (l. 5 *heidän Ville* 'their Ville') in reported thought, and then it becomes the subject of the following clause (l. 7 *kissa* 'the cat'). The clue of the story is that the way the new topic is introduced (using a person name) creates an expectation that it is a person, not a cat, since Ville is not a typical cat name, but an ordinary male name. Only in line 7 does the speaker reveal that it is a cat.

10. Chafe (1987:22) defines an intonation unit as "a sequence of words combined under a single coherent intonation contour" (see also Chafe 1994: esp. 53–70).

11. Huumo (1994) reports on similar findings regarding the relationship between activation cost and the subject role based on a study on Finnish literary fiction. In his data, 14.2% of the subjects were mentions of referents new to the discourse. In comparison, the percentage of new mentions in the subject role in my data (i.e. A+S) is 14.8%. Note again the slight differences in the definition of subject; I have not included existential clauses among intransitives (for further discussion, see section on existential clauses).

12. Note that clauses with an indexically open zero subject (as exemplified in ex. 2 line 5) function against the general principle presented in Table 1b: as regards the marking of the object, the zero subject functions like NP subjects. Therefore, the object *jonku taudin* (ex. 2 line 5) receives an accusative marking (see Laitinen 1995b, 1996 for details).

13. I prefer to use the term E-NP instead of Sx which is used in the rest of this volume because I try to argue against the analysis of E-NP's as subjects.

14. The choice between nominative and partitive here is determined by quantificational distinctions (see below): the nominative expresses a bounded quantity (e.g. *kangastapetit* 'fabric wall papers'), while the partitive expresses unboundedness (e.g. *vähän Nooran repimää seinää* 'some wall scratched by Noora'). There are some further factors which may affect the choice of case (for more discussion, see Heinämäki 1983).

15. In habitive constructions, if the E-NP is a personal pronoun, it stands in the accusative form (e.g. *sinut* 'you-ACC' in *Onneksi minulla on sinut* 'Luckily I have you', lit. 'on me is you-ACC'). This could be taken to indicate that the E-NP is really an object. However, I find it quite problematic to base any broader argument on example sentences like this, because they are so very rare in discourse: the communicational pressure for expressing possession of 1st or 2nd person is not very high.

References

Ashby, William and Paola Bentivoglio. 1993. "Preferred Argument Structure in Spoken French and Spanish". *Language Variation and Change* 5: 61–76.

Chafe, Wallace L. 1976. "Givenness, contrastiveness, definiteness, subjects, topics, and point of view". In Charles N. Li (ed.), *Subject and Topic.* New York: Academic Press, 22–55.

Charles N. Li. 1979. The flow of thought and the flow of language. In Talmy Givón (ed.), *Discourse and Syntax.* New York: Academic Press.

Charles N. Li. 1994. *Discourse, Consciousness, and Time. The Flow and Displacement of Conscious Experience in Speaking and Writing.* Chicago: University of Chicago Press.

Dahl, Östen. 1979. "Typology of sentence negation". *Linguistics* 17: 79–106.

Du Bois, John W. 1980. "Beyond definiteness: the trace of identity in discourse". In Wallace Chafe (ed.), *The Pear Stories.* Norwood, NJ.: Ablex, 9–50.

Du Bois, John W. 1985. "Competing motivations". In John Haiman (ed.), *Iconicity in Syntax.* Amsterdam: John Benjamins, 343–365.

Du Bois, John W. 1987. "The discourse basis of ergativity". *Language* 63: 805–855.

Du Bois, John W. and Sandra A. Thompson. 1991. "Dimensions of a theory of information flow". Unpublished ms., University of California, Santa Barbara.

Durie, Mark. 1988. "Preferred Argument Structure in an active language: arguments against the category 'intransitive subject'". *Lingua* 74: 1–25.

Durie, Mark. 1994. "A case study of pragmatic linking". *Text* 14 (4): 495–529.

Givón, Talmy (ed.). 1983. *Topic Continuity in Discourse: A Quantitative Cross-Language Study.* Amsterdam: John Benjamins.

Hakulinen, Auli. 1988. "Miten nainen liikkuu Veijo Meren romaaneissa". In Lea Laitinen (ed.), *Isosuinen nainen.* Helsinki: Yliopistopaino, 56–70.

Hakulinen, Auli and Fred Karlsson. 1979. *Nykysuomen lauseoppia.* Helsinki: Finnish Literature Society.

Hakulinen, Auli, Fred Karlsson and Maria Vilkuna. 1980. *Suomen tekstilauseiden piirteitä.* University of Helsinki: Publications of the Department of General Linguistics, Vol. 6.

Hakulinen, Lauri. 1979. *Suomen kielen rakenne ja kehitys.* 4th, revised edition. Helsinki: Otava.

Heinämäki, Orvokki. 1983. "Aspect in Finnish". In C. de Groot and H. Tommola (eds), *Aspect bound. A voyage into the realm of Germanic, Slavonic and Finno-Ugrian aspectology.* Dordrecht: Foris, 153–177.

Helasvuo, Marja-Liisa. 1996a. "Ollako vai eikö olla — eksistentiaalilauseen subjektin kohtalonkysymys". (English summary: To be or not to be — the question of existential subject in Finnish.) *Virittäjä* 3: 340–356.

Helasvuo, Marja-Liisa. 1996b. "A discourse perspective on the grammaticization of the partitive case in Finnish". In Timo Haukioja, Marja-Liisa Helasvuo and Elise Kärkkäinen (eds), *SKY 1996.* Helsinki: Yearbook of the Linguistic Association of Finland, 7–34.

Helasvuo, Marja-Liisa. 1997. Functions of case-marking vs. non-marking in Finnish. In Anne-Marie Simon-Vandenbergen, Kristin Davidse and Dirk Noël (eds), *Reconnecting Language: Morphology and Syntax in Functional Perspectives.* Amsterdam: Benjamins.

Helasvuo, Marja-Liisa. 2001. *Syntax in the Making. The Emergence of Syntactic Units in Finnish conversation.* Studies in Discourse and Grammar 9. Amsterdam: John Benjamins.

Herring, Susan. 1989. "Verbless presentation and the discourse basis of ergativity". *Papers from the 25th Annual Regional Meeting of the Chicago Linguistic Society.* Chicago: Chicago Linguistic Society.

Huumo, Tuomas. 1994. "On the position of subject in Finnish and in Estonian". In Riitta Kataja and Kristiina Suikkari (eds), XXI Kielitieteen päivät Oulussa 6.-7.5.1994. *Acta Universitatis Ouluensis Humaniora, B 19.* Oulu: University of Oulu, 79–87.

Huumo, Tuomas. 1996. "Domain shifts and the grammaticalization of case: A Case Study of the Finnish Adessive. *Folia Linguistica Historica.*

Jespersen, Otto. 1924. *The Philosophy of Grammar.* London: Allen & Unwin.

Karlsson, Fred. 1982a. *Suomen peruskielioppi.* Helsinki: Finnish Literature Society,.

Karlsson, Fred. 1982b. "Kieliteorian relevanssi suomen kielen opetukselle". In Fred Karlsson (ed.), *Suomi vieraana kielenä.* Helsinki: WSOY, 89–114.

Kärkkäinen, Elise. 1996. "Preferred Argument Structure and subject role in American English conversational discourse. *Journal of Pragmatics* 25: 675–701.

Laitinen, Lea. 1995a. "Persoonat ja subjektit". In Pirjo Lyytikäinen (ed.), *Subjekti. Minä. Itse.* Helsinki: Finnish Literature Society, 35–79.

Laitinen, Lea. 1995b. "Nollapersoona". (English summary: The Zero Person.) *Virittäjä* 99: 337–358.

Laitinen, Lea. 1996. "Indexical site to be identified with: The case of the "Zero Person" in Finnish conversation". Paper given in the 4th International Pragmatics Conference. July 1996. Mexico City, Mexico.

Lambrecht, Knud. 1987. "On the status of SVO sentences in French discourse". In Russell Tomlin (ed.), *Coherence and Grounding in Grammar and Discourse.* Amsterdam: John Benjamins, 217–262.

Larjavaara, Matti. 1988. "Suomen kvantitatiivinen spesies". (English summary: Quantitative *spesies* in Finnish.) *Virittäjä* 92: 469–503.

Lindén, Eeva. 1963. "Kieltolauseen sanajärjestyksestä suomen kirjakielessä". *Virittäjä* 77: 214–226.

Lyons, John. 1977. *Semantics.* Vol. 2. Cambridge: Cambridge University Press.

Mithun, Marianne. 1987. "Is basic word order universal?" In Russell Tomlin (ed.), *Coherence and Grounding in Grammar and Discourse.* Amsterdam: John Benjamins, 281–328.

Mithun, Marianne. 1991a. "Active/Agentive case marking and its motivations. *Language* 67: 510–546.

Mithun, Marianne. 1991b. "The role of motivation in the emergence of grammatical categories: the grammaticization of subjects". In Elizabeth Traugott and Bernd Heine (eds), *Approaches to Grammaticalization*. Vol. 1. Amsterdam: Benjamins, 159–184.

Nakayama, Toshihide and Ichihashi-Nakayama, Kumiko. 1994. "Discourse perspective for core-oblique distinction in Japanese". *Santa Barbara Papers in Linguistics* 5: 158–177. University of California, Santa Barbara.

Ochs, Elinor. 1988. *Culture and Language Development: Language Acquisition and Language Socialization in a Samoan Village*. Cambridge: Cambridge University Press.

Payne, Doris L. 1987. "Information Structuring in Papago Narrative Discourse". *Language* 63: 783–804.

Payne, John R. 1985. "Negation". In Timothy Shopen (ed.), *Language Typology and Syntactic Description*. Vol. 1. Cambridge: Cambridge University Press, 197–242.

Savijärvi, Ilkka 1977. *Itämerensuomalaisten kielten kieltoverbi.* (English summary: The Negative Verb in the Baltic-Finnic Languages.) Helsinki: Finnish Literature Society.

Shore, Susanna. 1988. "On the so-called Finnish passive. *Word* 39: 151–176.

Siewierska, Anna. 1988. *Word Order Rules*. London: Croom Helm.

Siewierska, Anna. 1997. "The formal realization of alignment systems: a functional perspective". In Anne-Marie Simon-Vandenbergen, Kirsten Davidse and Dirk Noël (eds.), *Reconnecting Language: Morphology and Syntax in Functional Perspectives*. Current Issue in Linguistic Theory, vol. 154. Amsterdam: Benjamins, 181–210.

Silverstein, Michael. 1976. "Hierarchy of features and ergativity". In R.M.W. Dixon (ed.), *Grammatical Categories in Australian Languages*. Linguistic Series No. 22. Humanities Press, New Jersey: Australian Institute of Aboriginal Studies, Canberra, 112–171.

Thompson, Sandra A. 1978. "Modern English from a typological point of view: some implications of the function of word order". *Linguistische Berichte* 54: 19–35.

Thompson, Sandra A. 1997. "Discourse motivations for the core-oblique distinction as a language universal". In Akio Kamio (ed.), *Directions in Functional Linguistics*. Amsterdam: Benjamins, 309–341.

Thompson, Sandra A. 1998. "A discourse explanation for the cross-linguistic differences in the grammar of interrogation and negation". In Anna Siewierska and Jae Jung Song (eds), *Case, Typology, and Grammar*. Amsterdam: Benjamins, 309–341.

Tuomikoski, Risto. 1971. "Persoona, tekijä ja henkilö". (English summary: 'Person' in Finnish Grammars.) *Virittäjä* 75: 146–152.

Vilkuna, Maria. 1989. *Free Word Order in Finnish: Its Syntax and Discourse Functions*. Helsinki: Finnish Literature Society.

Vilppula, Matti. 1989. "Havaintoja hän- ja he-pronominien käytöstä suomen murteissa". (English summary: On the use of the 3rd person pronouns in Finnish dialects.) *Virittäjä* 93: 389–400.

Wähämäki, Börje. 1975. "Om finskans existentialsatser och därtill hörande problem". Licenciate's thesis. Department of Finnish, Åbo Akademi.

Core arguments and the inversion of the nominal hierarchy in Roviana*

Simon H. Corston-Oliver
Microsoft Research

Introduction

The focus of this chapter is the typologically unusual marking of core arguments in Roviana, a member of the Western Oceanic branch of Austronesian. Case marking follows an ergative-absolutive pattern, with ergative as the unmarked case and absolutive as the marked case, a typologically unusual pattern which can be traced to the development of the absolutive marker as the grammaticization of a particle used to mark new mentions in discourse. Direct object pronominal affixes on the verb are also typologically unusual. The third person plural direct object affix has zero form, whereas all other object affixes have non-zero form, a fact which is also attributable to patterns evident in Roviana discourse.

Terminological preliminaries

A few terminological preliminaries are in order before proceeding to the main body of this paper. I employ the labels A, O and S as (approximately) 'transitive subject', 'transitive object' and 'single argument of intransitive' respectively (Dixon 1994; Corston 1993, for prototype definitions of the labels applied to Roviana). By ergativity is meant a system in which S and O received the same treatment, whether in morphology, syntax or discourse, which differs from the treatment of A. Ergativity in the lexicon is not considered here. By accusativity is meant a system in which S and A receive the same treatment, which differs from O. A neutral system is one in which A, O and S are not distinguished.

S is treated as a unitary category in Roviana, there being no language internal evidence to suggest distinguishing S arguments which are like A (Sa) from those which are like O (So).

The terms "core" and "core arguments" are used to denote the set {A, S, O}, while the term "core argument" is used to denote any member of this set. Although it may be the case that a "core" vs "oblique" distinction is universally motivated (Thompson, 1997), the distinction might not be made in the same way in all languages. I therefore discuss the core-oblique distinction in Roviana in the next section.

The term "marked" is used in various senses in the literature. Trask (1979), for example, uses the term "marked" to mean that something has a mark, i.e. an overt non-zero phonological realization, and to mean that something is cross-linguistically unusual. I use the terms "marked" and "unmarked" in a Praguian sense (Trubetzkoy 1936/1969) to mean having or not having a mark respectively. This definition of markedness corresponds to Mayerthaler's (1988) terms "featured" and "featureless", in that it can be determined by an inspection of a phonological string. I employ circumlocutions like "cross-linguistically unusual" to avoid the ambiguity of using the term "marked" to also refer to the convergence of various types of evidence including diachronic change, cross-linguistic frequency, language pathology, and regularity.

Finally, the following terms are used with the meanings given (based on Dixon 1994), unless otherwise stated:

'ergative':	A
'absolutive':	{S, O}
'(direct) object':	O
'subject':	{A, S}

The core-oblique distinction in Roviana

Pronominal object suffixes and the ergative-absolutive distinction apply to subsets of the core arguments, but do not prove that the core has an overall unity, nor do they rule out the possibility that the core might include arguments other than A, S and O. However, relative clause formation, the case marking of NP's in verbal clauses and restrictions on information status provide language internal evidence that the set {A, S, O} receives a unified treatment which differs from the treatment of obliques.

Relative clause formation

Verbal relative clauses may be formed only on core arguments. Clausal nominalization is used for relativization on A, with nominal suffixes indexing the argument corresponding to O, e.g. (1) and (2), while a verbal clause type is used for relativization on absolutive, e.g. (3) and (4).

(1) *hierana sa tie sapu tupa-gu rau*[1]
this DEF man REL punch-1SG.NSUF 1SG[2]
'This is the man that punched me.'[3]

(2) *hierana sa koreo sapu tupa-na e zone*
this DEF boy REL punch-3SG.NSUF PERS John
'This is the boy that punched John.'

(3) *hierana sa tie sapu kote taloa*
this DEF man REL FUT leave
'This is the man who is going away.'

(4) *hierana sa koreo sapu tupa-i-a e zone*
this DEF boy REL punch-TR-3SG.DO PERS John
'This is the boy that John punched.'

The case marking of NP's in verbal predicates

In verbal predicates, NP's occurring without case markers are always to be interpreted as core arguments. In (5), *sa siki* 'the dog' is A, *sa koburu* 'the child' is O, and in (6), *sa siki* 'the dog' is S.

(5) *yarat-i-a sa siki sa koburu*
bite-TR-3SG.DO DEF dog DEF child
'The dog bit the child.'

(6) *taloa sa siki*
leave DEF dog
'The dog left.'

The article *sa* 'DEF' indicates the information status of the NP which it modifies, but does not indicate the NP's grammatical relation. For example, in (7), *sa* 'DEF' occurs in a prepositional phrase.

(7) *hiko pan-i-a sa tie sa buka*
steal take-TR-3SG.DO DEF man DEF book
koa sa barikalege
DIR DEF woman
'The man stole the book from the woman.'

Thus, it can be seen that zero marked NP's with verbal predicates are always to be interpreted as core arguments. However, it is not the case that all NP's which have overt marking of grammatical relation are oblique, since for example, the absolutive particle *se* indicates both grammatical relation (absolutive) and NP type (proper NP).

Information status

Core arguments can be distinguished from non-core arguments according to restrictions in information status. Core arguments must be either specific or, if non-specific, then specified as non-referential by being modified by *loketoŋa* 'nothing' and occurring in sentence initial focus position. In example (8), A is non-specific but specified as non-referential, while in examples (9) and (10), O is non-specific but specified as non-referential. Non-core arguments may be of any information status.

(8) *loketoŋa tie loke tie hiβa sapot-i-a kamhire*
nothing person NEG person want support-TR-3SG.DO now
'Nobody wants to support him now.' (Government 034)

(9) *loketoŋa ɣinua lea-di si βa-turu-i-Ø*
nothing thing good-3PL.NSUF FOC CAUS-stand-TR-3PL.DO
sa popoa kamhire
DEF country now
'He hasn't done any good things for the country.' (Government 035)

(10) *loketoŋa tiŋtoŋa si boka tate-a ɣami*
nothing thing FOC able do-3SG.DO 1PL.EXCL
'There's nothing we can do.' (Government 011)

Two constructions are important in maintaining this restriction on the information status of the core. One construction is the passive, which is always agentless, and is used in situations where the actor is not known or is generic, e.g. (11).

(11) *ba sa elo edere sapu pa batu-na*
but DEF leaf sago.palm REL LOC head-3SG.NSUF
sa βetu si lopu kagu ta-poka ɣore
DEF house FOC NEG must PASS-nail go.down
'... but the sago palm leaf, which is on top of the house, must not be nailed down.' (Leaf, 051–053)

Example (11) occurs in a discussion of the techniques for constructing a traditional leaf house. No specific agents are mentioned in the text, but rather generic builders are understood throughout.

The other construction which is important in maintaining this restriction on the information status of core arguments is the backgrounded object construction, which differs from the canonical two argument construction with the constituent order VAO in having an undergoer immediately adjacent to the verb (Corston 1993). The backgrounded object construction is obligatorily used when the undergoer is non-specific and is not being specified as non-referential, and is optionally used if the undergoer is specific but the speaker wishes to background it in the discourse. Compare (12) in which *sa talo* 'the taro' is specific and definite to (13) in which *talo* 'taro' is non-specific and therefore backgrounded, with reduced transitivity of the clause (Hopper and Thompson (1980)) reflected in the marking of *yami* '1PL.EXCL' as absolutive and in the absence of a suffix on the verb indexing O.

(12) *raro-a* *yami* *sa* *talo*
cook-3SG.DO 1PL.EXC(ERG) DEF taro
'We cooked the taro.'

(13) *raro* *talo* *si* *yami*
cook taro ABS 1PL.EXCL
'We cooked taro'/'We did some taro-cooking.'

Example (14), from a discussion of World War II, illustrates the obligatory use of the backgrounded object construction for a non-specific undergoer.

(14) *lopu βa-mate* *tie* *si* *rau*
NEG CAUS-die person ABS 1SG
'I didn't kill anybody.' (Grandpa, 018)

The text in which example (14) occurs asserts that the speaker was not involved in killing during the war, rather than asserting the non-referentiality of any undergoers.

Grammatical description

Two aspects of the grammar of Roviana are particularly relevant to the markedness of core arguments, namely ergativity in the marking of NP's and accusativity in pronominal affixes on the verb.

Ergativity

Relative clause formation in Roviana is syntactically ergative, since the selection of relative clause formation strategy is sensitive to whether the coreferent of the head noun in the matrix clause is ergative or absolutive within the relative clause. Other syntactic phenomena usually included in studies of syntactic ergativity, such as inter-clausal anaphora, show no significant preference for ergative-absolutive or nominative-accusative pivots. Rather, such phenomena appear to be pragmatically constrained, with zero anaphora permitted whenever it is possible from pragmatics or the discourse context to resolve the referent of an omitted NP (Corston 1996).

Morphological ergativity in Roviana is split according to two parameters: clause type and NP type. These two parameters are discussed in turn below. A fuller discussion of the minutiae of these splits is to be found in Corston (1996) and Corston-Oliver (2002).

Split-ergativity according to clause type

In main clauses there is ergative-absolutive patterning, whereas in subordinate clauses, there is no distinction made in the marking of core argument NP's. I term this "neutral marking", in opposition to the ergative-absolutive marking found in main clauses. Subordinate clauses are underlined in the examples in this section.

In examples (15) and (16) below, the proper NP *e zone* 'John', is O and A respectively, but does not formally distinguish the two grammatical relations.

(15) *hierana sa koreo sapu* ***tupa-na e zone***
this DEF boy REL punch-3SG.NSUF PERS John
'This is the boy that punched John.'

(16) *hierana sa koreo sapu* ***tupa-i-a e zone***
this DEF boy REL punch-TR-3SG.DO PERS John
'This is the boy that John punched.'

Examples (17) and (18) illustrate the neutral marking of pronouns in subordinate clauses. In (17), the pronoun *ri* 'they' is A, while in (18) it is S.

(17) *ke beto* ***βaɣ-i-Ø ri sarina in-aβoso***
so finish gather-TR-3PL.DO they DEF.PL NOM-know
si la buna-i-a ri sa βasina asa
FOC go bomb-TR-3SG.DO they(ERG) DEF place that
'So after they had gathered all the information, they went and bombed that place.' (Grandpa, 057–058)

(18) ***en-ene ri la hoirana***
DUP-walk they go there
si tutuβ-i-a ri se manue
FOC meet-TR-3SG.DO they(ERG) ABS Possum
'As they were walking along, they met Possum.'[4] (Animals, 016–017)

In examples (17) and (18), the same pronominal form *ri* 'they' is glossed both 'they' and 'they (ERG)'. It would be misleading to gloss such noun phrases as 'ERG' in subordinate clauses, since within that syntactic environment there is not a formal contrast between ergative and absolutive. The gloss '(ERG)' within parentheses indicates that the form is ergative, but since the ergative case is unmarked, this must be inferred from the absence of overt marking of case.

Split-ergativity according to NP type within main clauses

Within main clauses, in core argument positions, enumerated NP's (i.e. NP's containing modifiers which serve to quantify the head noun), pronouns and proper

NP's distinguish ergative-absolutive by the use of special particles and by the use of special pronominal forms, as illustrated in the following subsections.

All other NP's in core argument positions in main clauses have a neutral system of marking, as illustrated in examples (5) and (6) above, reproduced here as example (19), where the definite article *sa* occurs with *siki* 'dog' as A, *koburu* 'child' as O, and in example (20) with *siki* 'dog' as S.

(19) *yarat-i-a sa siki sa koburu*
bite-TR-3SG.DO DEF dog DEF child
'The dog bit the child.'

(20) *taloa sa siki*
leave DEF dog
'The dog left.'

Enumerated NP's

The term "enumerated NP" is used to mean a lexical NP in which there is a quantifier modifying the head noun. Enumerated NP's occurring as absolutive in main clauses are marked with the absolutive particle *si* ('ABS'), whereas enumerated NP's occurring as ergative in main clauses are zero-marked. In examples (21) and (22), the NP's preceded by *si* 'ABS' are S and O respectively. In (23), where there is an enumerated NP as A, there is no special particle preceding the NP.

(21) *turu si karua koburu*
stand ABS two child
'Two children are standing up.'

(22) *meke doyor-i-a ri si keke iyana*
and see-TR-3SG.DO they(ERG) ABS one fish
'and they saw a fish.' (Animals, 034)

(23) *seke-a karua tie sa siki*
hit-3SG.DO two man DEF dog
'Two men hit the dog.'

Pronouns

Only third person pronouns distinguish ergative vs. absolutive in the form of the pronoun. The pronouns are given in Table 1.

In main clauses, the pronouns labeled 'Ergative and neutral' occur only as A. In subordinate clauses, these same pronominal forms are used for any core argument, according to the neutral marking in subordinate clauses.

The pronouns labeled 'Focal' are used in focus, i.e. when new or prominent information is being conveyed in clause initial position or in contrastive constructions, as in example (24).

Table 1. Pronouns

Person	Absolutive	Ergative and neutral	Focal
1SG	*rau*	*rau*	*arau*
2SG	*yoi*	*yoi*	*ayoi*
3SG	*asa*	*sa*	*asa*
1PL.INC	*yita*	*yita*	*yita*
1PL.EXC	*yami*	*yami*	*yami*
2PL	*yamu*	*yamu*	*yamu*
3PL	*sarini*	*ri*	*arini*

(24) *arau oβia hola yinoroi*
1SG hungry extremely today
'I was really hungry today.' (Day, 004)

As Table 1 shows, the 3SG ABS pronoun (*asa*) has more phonological weight than the 3SG ERG pronoun (*sa*), and the 3PL ABS (*sarini*) pronoun has more phonological weight than the 3PL ERG pronoun (*ri*). In Corston (1996) I argue that, etymologically, the 3SG ABS *asa* consists of an article *a*- plus *sa*, which was formerly a 3SG pronoun unmarked for case, while the 3PL ABS *sarini* '3PL.ABS' results historically from the phonological coalescence of the sequence '*si arini*' ('FOC + 3PL.FOC', later reanalyzed as 'ABS + 3PL.FOC'), a point to which I return in when discussing the discourse basis for marked absolutive vs zero-marked ergative below.

First and second person pronouns have the same form for absolutive and ergative. Thus, in no person or number is the ergative pronominal form more marked than the corresponding absolutive form.

The ergative-absolutive distinction is indicated with pronouns in a further way. With the exception of *sarini* '3PL.ABS' (which already includes the particle *si* 'ABS', see above), pronouns occurring as absolutive are introduced by the particle *si* 'ABS'. See for example (25) and (26)

In contrast to non-3PL absolutive pronouns, pronouns occurring as ergative are not introduced by special particles. In examples (25) and (26) below, *si* 'ABS' introduces pronouns in S and O respectively. In (26), *rau* '1SG' is A, but is not introduced by any special particles. It is glossed with 'ERG' in parentheses to indicate the fact that the ergative is zero marked. Example (26) also illustrates the typologically unusual double marking of the absolutive in the case of 3SG, since the 3SG absolutive has both a special form (*asa*) and is introduced by the ABS particle *si* (see the discussion of markedness further concerning the "markedness" of ergative and absolutive).

(25) *la pa 'cafeteria' si yami*
go LOC cafeteria ABS 1PL.EXC
'We went to the cafeteria.' (Day, 023)

(26) *doɣor-i-a rau si asa*
see-TR-3SG.DO 1SG(ERG) ABS 3SG.ABS
'I saw him.'

Independent pronouns rarely occur in Roviana discourse as O. An example such as (26), in which there is multiple marking of the referent 'him' — by the use of an independent pronoun, a special pronominal form for absolutive, the particle *si* 'ABS', and a coreferential verbal suffix (*-a* '3SG.DO') — is therefore extremely uncommon in Roviana discourse, and so pragmatically special when it does occur.

Examples (27) and (28) illustrate the fact that *sarini* '3PL.ABS' occurs without *si* 'ABS'.

(27) *kote arina tie mae mayu-i-Ø sarini*
FUT PL man come carve-TR-3PL.DO 3PL.ABS[5]
'The men will come and carve them up.' (Feast, 016)

(28) *kote la sarini pa soloso*
FUT go 3PL.ABS LOC jungle
'They will go into the jungle.' (Feast, 003)

Proper NP's

Proper NP's occurring as absolutive are preceded by the ABS article *se*, whereas those occurring as ergative are zero marked, as illustrated in examples (29)–(32).

(29) *seke-i-a (e) zima se maepeza*
hit-TR-3SG.DO PERS(ERG) Zima ABS Maepeza
'Zima hit Maepeza.'

(30) *seke-i-a (e) maepeza se zima*
hit-TR-3SG.DO PERS(ERG) Maepeza ABS Zima
'Maepeza hit Zima.'

(31) *moho se zima*
sick ABS Zima
'Zima is sick.'

(32) *taloa se zima*
leave ABS Zima
'Zima left.'

The personal article *e* is optional in all contexts,[6] but the absolutive article *se* is obligatory with proper NP's in absolutive. It must be emphasized that the personal article *e* does not mark ergative case. For example, this article occurs with proper NP's in non-absolutive contexts, as illustrated in examples (33)–(36).

(33) *hol-holu-ni-a* *rau* *sa* *boko* *ko* *e* *zima*
DUP-sell-VAL-3SG.DO 1SG(ERG) DEF pig DIR PERS Zima
'I sold the pig to Zima.'

(34) *ka-made sarina pati βasina*
ORD-four DEF.PL party place
Alliance Party United Party amm Labor Party
Alliance Party United Party um Labor Party
me ɣina isa e Liberal Party
and maybe that.SG PERS[7] Liberal Party
'There are four parties there, the Alliance Party, the United Party, um, the Labor Party and maybe the Liberal Party.' (Government 026–027)

(35) *kamahire e solomone mamaloni si korapa Prime Minister*
now PERS Solomon Mamaloni FOC still Prime Minister
'At the moment Solomon Mamaloni is still Prime Minister.' (Government 001)

(36) *esei poza-mu si aɣoi e saimone?*
who name-2SG.NSUF FOC 2SG.FOC PERS Simon
'Who are you? Simon?' (Day 001)

Additional evidence for considering *e* to be a personal article rather than a case marker comes from the fact that *e* occurs in subordinate clauses, where there is a neutral system of case marking, marking the core arguments A, S and O, e.g. in example (16), reproduced here as example (37), *e* occurs with O, while in example (15), reproduced here as example (38), *e* occurs with A.

(37) hierana sa *koreo* *sapu tupa-na e zone*
this DEF boy REL punch-3SG.NSUF PERS John
'This is the boy that punched John.'

(38) *hierana sa koreo* *sapu tupa-i-a e zone*
this DEF boy REL punch-TR-3SG.DO PERS John
'This is the boy that John punched.'

Since *e* does not mark ergative case, but only the fact that the NP is a proper NP with a human referent, the fact that an NP is A must be inferred from the absence of any other indication of case, e.g. *se* or a preposition indicating an oblique role. I therefore differ from Corston (1993) in glossing *e* as 'PERS (ERG)' rather than 'ERG'.

Native speakers reject the use of *se* for anything other than marking absolutive. For example, in (36) above, *se saimone* as an independent appellation is rejected as ungrammatical. The fact that the personal article *e* occurs instead does not imply that the ergative is the citation form. Rather, citation forms involve zero marking, and the ergative involves zero marking.

Accusativity

O is the only grammatical relation which is indexed on the verb. Considering core arguments, this therefore constitutes a nominative-accusative pattern, in which A and S are treated alike by not being indexed, whereas O is treated differently, by being indexed. Table 2 illustrates the direct object pronominal suffixes. The 1SG form *-u* occurs after /i/, while the form *-au* occurs elsewhere.

Table 2. Direct object pronominal suffixes

Person	Suffix	Independent Pronoun
1SG	*-u, -au*	*rau*
2SG	*-yo*	*yoi*
3SG	*-a*	*asa, sa*
1PL.INC	*-yita*	*yita*
1PL.EXC	*-yami*	*yami*
2PL	*-yamu*	*yamu*
3PL	-Ø	*ri, arini, sarini*

Ross (1988: 242–243) refers to these suffixes as "pronominal enclitics of the verb phrase" in viewing Roviana from a diachronic perspective and comparing it with a number of related languages. In the synchronic grammar of Roviana, however, there does not appear to be any evidence for considering these elements to be anything other than pronominal suffixes. Ross (1988) also claims that these elements are coreferential with the absolutive NP. While this is true in transitive clauses, where they are coreferential with O, e.g. (39), they do not occur in intransitives as coreferential with S, e.g. (40).

(39) *seke-i-a rau sa siki*
hit-TR-3SG.DO 1SG(ERG) DEF dog
'I hit the dog.'

(40) *mae se zima*
come ABS Zima
'Zima came.'

The direct object pronominal suffixes can occur even if there is not an overt object NP in the same clause, e.g. (41) and (42), suggesting that they have independent referring potential, and do not just copy features from NP's in the clause.

(41) *ai lul-i-u mo*
INTJ follow-TR-1SG.DO DT
'Hey! Follow me.' (Animals, 011)

(42) *e* *saimone sa* *tie* *he-heyere* *hoirana*
PERS Simon DEF man DUP-laugh there
'That's Simon, the man who's laughing over there.'
aβos-i-a *yoi?*
hear-TR-3SG.DO you(ERG)
'Do you hear him?' (Day, 029–030)

In Roviana, direct objects must be specific or, if non-specific, then specified as non-referential, and must not be backgrounded in the discourse. To say that the direct objects are not backgrounded, however, is not to imply that they are being given special prominence by being foregrounded. There is a cline of foregroundedness according to the prominence given in discourse to the referent of the object NP which corresponds to a variety of syntactic possibilities from the constituent order VAO (low prominence) to preverbal and clause initial positions (which do not always coincide, but which indicate higher degrees of prominence). A full account of pragmatic possibilities awaits further study, and in any case lies outside the scope of the present study. For the present study, what is germane is the fact that the referent of a pronominal object suffix is always specific or specified as non-referential. This fact is important in considering the typological peculiarity of the fact that it is the third person plural object suffix alone which is unmarked.

As Table 2 illustrates, the majority of the object suffixes are clearly cognate with independent pronouns. The 3SG is perhaps cognate with **ia* a 3SG pronoun reconstructed for Proto Oceanic (Ross 1988). In the following section I consider the development of the object suffixes, and a discourse based explanation for the zero 3PL form.

Discussion of markedness

The discussion in this section is based on the analysis of a small heterogeneous corpus of spoken Roviana consisting primarily of monologic texts. Texts in various genres are represented, with narratives, procedural texts, discussions of the politics and economy of the Solomon Islands, and so on.

The term "mention" is used to mean an independent pronoun, a lexical NP, an object affix occurring without an overt NP, or a zero mention where the referent is recoverable from the discourse context and clearly required by the valence of the verb.

The discussion of the discourse basis for marked absolutive vs zero-marked ergative below is a summary presentation of Corston (1996) while the discussion of the 3PL object suffix in the next section is based on a slightly larger sample than the one examined in Corston (1996).

The discourse basis for the zero-marked 3PL object suffix

It is uncontroversial for Oceanic languages that the bound object affixes attested have developed historically from independent pronouns according to the following schema (see e.g. Ross 1988): Independent Pronoun → Clitic → Affix. This path of development would certainly account for the evident cognacy observable between the independent pronouns and the non-3PL object suffixes (Table 2). However, since Roviana has third person plural independent pronouns, the fact that the 3PL object suffix has zero form requires an explanation. Two possibilities suggest themselves:

i. Roviana had a non-zero 3PL.DO suffix but has since lost it.
ii. Roviana never developed a 3PL.DO suffix.

I propose that patterns observable in the discourse of Roviana support (ii).

The first thing which must be noted about independent pronouns in Roviana is that they rarely have non-human referents, as illustrated in Table 3.

Table 3. Animacy of referents of independent pronouns

Animacy of referent	**Number**
Human	218
Non-human animate	2
Inanimate	14
Total	234

As Table 3 shows, a total of 16 out of 234, or 6.8% of all independent pronouns in the data have non-human referents. The small number of independent pronouns with non-human referents is not, however, simply a reflection of a small number of mentions of non-human referents in the texts analyzed. For example, there are 228 mentions of inanimates out of a total of 675 mentions, i.e. inanimate mentions constitute 33.8%, or a little over a third of all mentions in the corpus.

Table 4 and Figure 1 below illustrate the distribution of various kinds of mention in syntactic positions. A zero mention in the case of O means an affix occurring with a zero NP. We see that mentions of independent pronouns in O are rare (7 out of 675, or approximately 1.0% of all mentions), although mentions in O are not rare (151 out of 675, or 22.4% of all mentions). Since the object affixes can occur in the absence of an overt object NP, it would appear that they have independent reference, and that independent pronouns are used as O in the contemporary grammar of Roviana only under very marked circumstances.

It is instructive to compare the distribution of mentions of A and O in Table 4, since the total number of tokens is exactly the same. Independent pronouns occur with great frequency in A. It does not seem to be the case, therefore, that pronouns are rare in all syntactic positions in Roviana.

Table 4. Distribution of types of mention

	Zero	Lexical NP	Independent Pronoun	Total
A	30	19	102	151
S	66	50	115	231
O	72	72	7	151
Obl	–	65	0	65
Other	–	67	10	77
Total	168	273	234	675

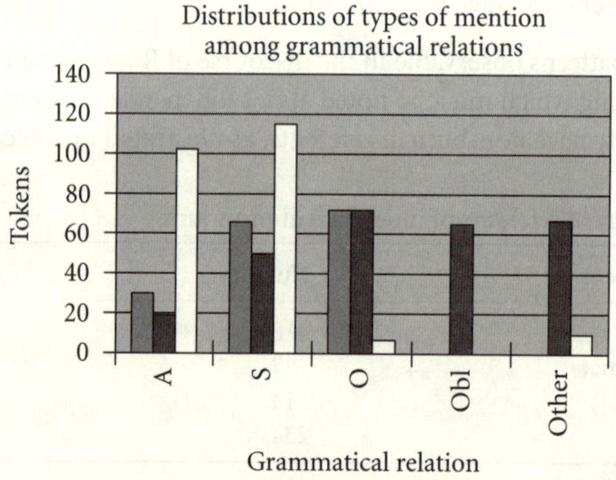

Figure 1. Distribution of types of mention.

Since independent pronouns occur so infrequently as O in the corpus, it is necessary to consider all mentions of 3PL in O in considering the 3PL DO suffix.

As Table 5 shows, there are no instances of 3PL non-human animate mentions as O in the corpus, although this would appear to be an artifact of the corpus examined, there being no mentions of 3PL non-human animates.

It can be seen from Table 5 that mentions of 3PL as O are rare (a total of 36 out of 675 mentions, or 5.3% of all mentions), and that mentions of 3PL humans as O

Table 5. Mentions of 3PL as O

	Zero	Lexical NP	Independent Pronoun	Total
Human	6	1	7	14
Non-human animate	0	0	0	0
Inanimate	7	1	14	22
Total	13	2	21	36

are especially rare (a total of 14 out of 675 mentions, or 2.1% of all mentions). It is not the case that 3PL humans are mentioned extremely rarely. As Table 6 shows, there are 75 mentions (11.1% of all mentions) of 3PL human referents.

Table 6. Mentions of 3PL humans

Position	Number
A	36
S	24
O	14
Obl	4
Other	7
Total	75

Since it is common for Oceanic languages to largely limit the use of independent pronouns to human referents, it is not unreasonable to assume that the preference for human referents for independent pronouns observed in contemporary Roviana would have been true at an earlier stage in the language's history.

Applying a similar uniformitarian assumption, 3PL human mentions would have been rare as O, whether the mentions were achieved by pronouns, lexical NP's or by zero. Since only a portion of 3PL mentions are achieved by independent pronouns, 3PL human mentions as independent pronouns would have been extremely uncommon.

I therefore propose that the 3PL DO suffix in Roviana has zero form because the 3PL independent pronoun which would have occurred as O did not occur with sufficient text frequency to be grammaticized as a bound affix. Givón (1979) for example has suggested that there is a statistical threshold below which grammaticization does not take place. While it is not the case that things which occur frequently will necessarily be grammaticized, it may be the case that things which occur infrequently will not provide the impetus to motivate their grammaticization. The quantification of such thresholds remains a matter for future study. Interestingly, however, 3SG mentions as O occur approximately 2.5 times as often as 3PL (95 versus 36). The 3SG.DO affix has been grammaticized (*-a*, apparently cognate with an erstwhile 3SG independent pronoun **ia*, reconstructed for Proto Oceanic (Ross 1988)).

3PL human and non-human mentions are marked on the verb with zero, although as I argue, this is historically simply a matter of no affixal marking. In the case of 3SG *-a*, however, both human and non-human mentions receive the same marking, possibly representing a generalization of the marker used with humans to non-human referents after the affix had become bound. The difference in affixal marking between 3PL and 3SG is not simply a difference in referentiality, since both

3SG and 3PL DO have the same restrictions on information status.

It follows from the above line of argumentation that independent pronouns may develop historically into clitics and then into affixes on a case by case basis, perhaps with the most frequent items leading, and with less frequent items developing later. In some cases infrequent items may eventually succumb to the pressure of structural symmetry, although in Roviana this has not happened. The net result of this case by case grammaticization may well be a change in an entire category, but this is not to say that it is the category of independent pronouns as a whole which is being grammaticized.

The discourse basis for marked absolutive vs. zero-marked ergative

Roviana is typologically unusual in that it is the absolutive which is marked, while ergative is unmarked. In many languages, including Roviana, new mentions show a preference for {S, O} and a strong dispreference for A (Du Bois 1987, Corston 1996). In Corston (1996) I argue that the forms which mark absolutive in Roviana are cognate with erstwhile markers of new mentions, and have been reanalyzed as markers of absolutive according to this discourse tendency for new mentions to occur in {S, O}. In the discussion below I summarize the discussion in Corston (1996) concerning the development of ergative-absolutive marking in Roviana.

Since Roviana only distinguishes ergative versus absolutive in verbal predicates, I first examine the number of new arguments which occur in transitive (two argument) clauses and intransitive (single argument) clauses. As Table 7, illustrated in Figure 2, shows, there is not a single clause in the corpus examined which contains two new mentions in core argument positions. This fact is not attributable to a low frequency of transitive clauses, however, since 139 out of the total of 339 clauses, or 41.0%, are transitive.

The distribution of new mentions is Table 8 (illustrated in Figure 3). New mentions strongly disfavor A. Although an almost equal number of new mentions occur in core and non-core positions (54 versus 55), among the core positions both S and O are favored over A by a factor of at least four to one.

Table 7. Transitivity and number of new arguments in clause

	0 new core args		1 new core arg		2 new core args		Total
	n	%	n	%	n	%	n
Trans	105	(75.5)	34	(24.5)	0	(0.0)	139
Intr	181	(90.5)	19	(9.5)	–	–	200
	285	(84.4)	54	(15.6)	0	(0.0)	339

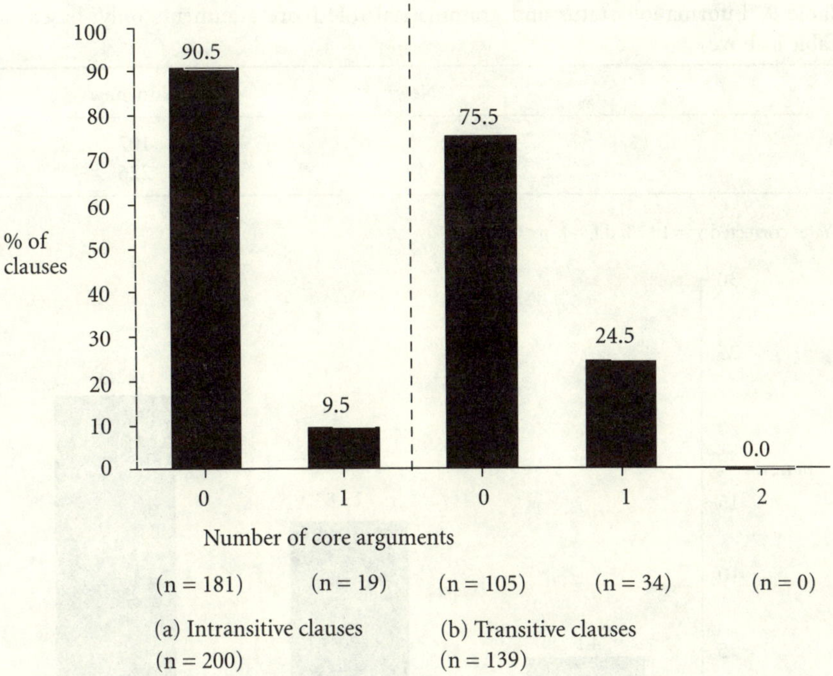

Figure 2. Frequency of clauses with zero, one, and two new arguments (intransitive vs. transitive clauses).

Table 8. Grammatical role and information status of mentions

	New		Given		Total
	n	%	n	%	n
A	5	(4.5)	107	(95.5)	112
S	20	(13.8)	125	(86.2)	145
O	29	(22.3)	101	(77.7)	130
Obl	33	(66.0)	17	(34.0)	50
Other	22	(47.8)	24	(52.2)	46
Total	109	(22.6)	374	(77.4)	483

($\chi^2 = 98.17$, d.f. $= 4$, $p < 0.001$)

New mentions tend not to occur in A, but prefer {S, O} out of the core argument roles. Moreover, A is less likely than either S or O to contain new mentions, as illustrated in Figure 4. This tendency is statistically significant, as shown in Table 9.

Table 9. Information status and grammatical role (core arguments only; based on Table 8 above)

	New	Non-new
A	5	107
S+O	49	226

(Yates corrected $\chi^2 = 10.73$, d.f. = 1, $p < 0.005$)

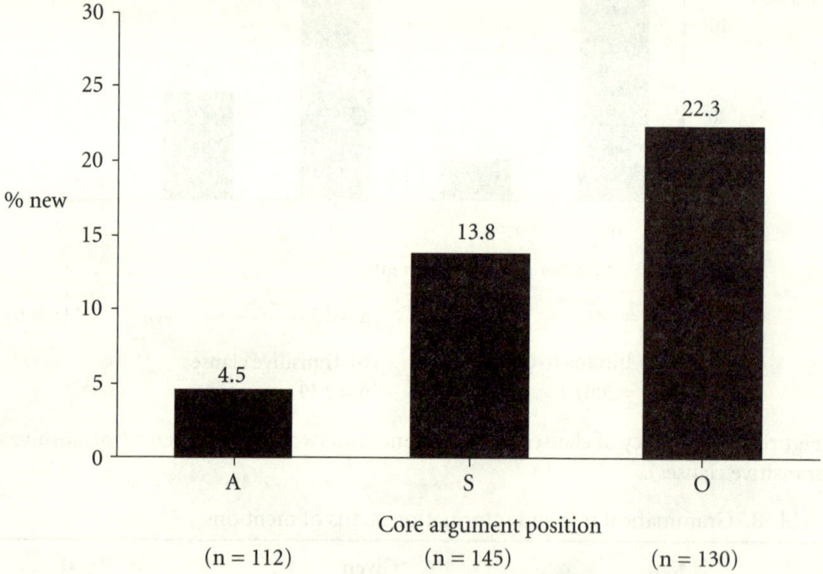

Figure 3. Proportion of each core argument position which is new ($n = 387$).

The marking of NP's

The particle *si* 'ABS' used with enumerated NP's in absolutive and with non 3PL pronouns in absolutive is cognate with a particle which used to mark 'focus', i.e. new mentions in discourse (Ross 1988, Corston 1996). The particle se 'ABS' used with proper NP's in absolutive is etymologically the phonological coalescence of the sequence *si e* 'FOC' + 'PERS' (Waterhouse 1928, 1946; Ross 1988; Corston 1996).

It must be emphasized from Table 8 that not all mentions in S and O are new. However, what was once a marker used for new mentions has become grammaticized as a marker of absolutive by the tendency observed in discourse for new mentions to occur in S and O, and is now applied to all appropriate types of NP in absolutive, irrespective of whether or not they are new.

As in the discussion of the zero-marked 3PL object suffix above, the question arises of how frequently a pattern must occur before grammaticization is motivated. As Table 8 and Figure 3 show, although the distribution of new and given mentions is statistically significant, only a small percentage of mentions in absolutive are actually new. However, the particle *si* 'ABS' occurs only with overt NP's, not with zero mentions. If non-zero mentions are examined with respect to their information status, then the tendencies observed here become clearer. I examined the information status of mentions in the corpus examined in the discussion of the zero-marked 3PL object suffix.

Considering all mentions, including zero mentions, the results obtained were fairly similar to those in Figure 3. Table 10 presents the results, disregarding the heterogeneous "Other" category.[8]

Table 10. Grammatical role and information status of all mentions

	New		Given (including zero mentions)		Total
	n	%	n	%	n
A	7	(4.6)	144	(95.4)	151
S	20	(9.2)	198	(90.8)	218
O	30	(20.3)	118	(79.7)	148
Obl	45	(69.2)	20	(30.8)	65
Total	102	(17.5)	480	(82.5)	582

If zero mentions are excluded, then the percentage of S and O which is new increases, as seen in Table 11.

Table 11. Grammatical role and information status of non-zero mentions

Given (excluding zero mentions)		Total		New	
n	%		n	%	n
114	(94.2)	A	7	(5.8)	121
139	(87.4)	S	20	(12.6)	159
51	(63.0)	O	30	(37.0)	81
20	(30.8)	Obl	45	(69.2)	65
374	(76.1)	Total	102	(23.9)	426

Since oblique mentions are never zero in Roviana, the percentage of obliques remains the same. The tendency for S and O to contain new mentions becomes much clearer. 12.6% of the non-zero mentions in S are new, and 37.0% of the non-zero mentions in O are new. It may well be the case that in other genres, or in longer texts with greater continuity of referent mentions, this tendency would be even more striking.

Since the majority of oblique mentions are new, we must ask why they are not also marked by the particles *si* and *se* and why the 3PL absolutive pronoun *sarini* does not occur in oblique positions. The answer may lie in the distinction between core and oblique arguments. Du Bois (1980: 225) notes that "the peripheral syntactic (and semantic) status of the [oblique] noun phrase is accompanied by a peripheral degree of attention". Similarly, Thompson (1997) notes that core arguments tend to be discourse referential, whereas non-core arguments tend not to be discourse referential. Finally, Mithun (1994) notes that in Kapampangan, a Western Austronesian language, the discourse topicality of a referent is an important factor in deciding whether it will occur in the core or in an oblique role. It may be the case that in Roviana the particle *si* was used to mark referents which were not only new, but were also salient, or were intended to be discourse referential. By virtue of their salience or because they were intended to be discourse referential, such referents would exhibit a greater affinity for core argument positions than for oblique roles. Within the core, such referents would, if new, favor {S, O} over A.

Third person pronouns

The special third person absolutive pronouns have more phonological weight than the non-absolutive counterparts. If absolutive in Roviana represents the grammaticization of a category of new information, then this is not surprising, since new information in discourse tends to receive heavier coding, being maximally discontinuous and therefore cognitively relatively difficult to process (Givón 1983).

Split-ergativity according to clause type

The split-ergative pattern conditioned by clause type, by which main clauses have ergative-absolutive marking for certain kinds of NP, while subordinate clauses do not formally distinguish core arguments, is also founded on observed tendencies in Roviana discourse. As Table 12 illustrates, new mentions do not occur in core argument positions in subordinate clauses in Roviana. Roviana therefore conforms to the cross-linguistic tendency for subordinate clauses to contain discourse presupposed material (Givón 1979).

The absolutive particle *si*, which is postulated to have developed from the reanalysis of a particle marking new information would therefore not have occurred with new mentions in core argument positions in subordinate clauses, and so would not have been grammaticized as a marker of absolutive in that syntactic environment. Similarly, the fact that the particle *se*, which occurs with proper NP's in absolutive, and the 3PL ABS pronoun *sarini* do not occur in subordinate clauses

Table 12. Grammatical role and information status of mentions in subordinate clauses

	New		Given		Total
	n	%	n	%	n
A	0	(0.0)	13	(100.0)	13
S	0	(0.0)	26	(100.0)	26
O	0	(0.0)	23	(100.0)	23
Obl	4	(50.0)	4	(50.0)	8
Other	0	(0.0)	2	(100.0)	2
Total	4	(5.6)	68	(94.4)	72

reflects the fact that *si*, which is etymologically included in both of these forms, would not have occurred with core arguments in subordinate clauses. The existence of a handful of new mentions in oblique position in subordinate clauses does not contradict this claim, since obliques do not participate in the ergative-absolutive distinction made in the core, but perhaps serve as a "safety valve for extra information in the clause" (Du Bois 1987: 833).

The nominal hierarchy and typological considerations

Dixon claims that, "All languages which use an S/O pivot, to any degree, show some ergativity." While this is true for Roviana, which has an S/O pivot in relative clause formation and ergative-absolutive marking on noun phrases, in Roviana the S/O pivot does not coincide with morphological ergativity. In relative clauses, where the S/O pivot occurs, the marking of core arguments does not distinguish A/S/O, while in main clauses where the marking on noun phrases does distinguish ergative-absolutive, there is no evidence of an S/O pivot (Corston 1996).

It has been claimed (e.g. Trask 1979; Dixon 1979, 1994; *inter alia*) that in most if not all languages with morphological ergativity, ergativity is not applied to all core argument NP's in all syntactic environments. Certainly, Roviana is no exception, having ergative-absolutive marking only for certain kinds of NP and only in main clauses. However, where Roviana does not conform to such generalizations is in the fact that ergative-absolutive marking alternates with a neutral system of case marking, rather than with an accusative system. Trask (1979: 387) for example claims that in languages with split-ergativity, ergative-absolutive marking always alternates with accusative, while such an assumption underlies Dixon's (1979, 1994) discussion of split-ergativity conditioned by NP type. Similarly, Silverstein (1976: 112) notes:

> Data for all ergative languages show a distinction between at least two complementary configurations for indicating the grammatical function of the principal noun phrases in a sentence. … We find one kind of two-way distinction usually called 'nominative-accusative', another two-way distinction which we can call 'ergative-absolutive' (or 'ergative-nominative'), and sometimes three way distinctions which we can call 'objective-agentive-subjective'.

Based on observed cross-linguistic patterns in such splits in case marking, Silverstein proposed a hierarchy of noun phrase types based on "inherent lexical content" (Silverstein 1976: 113). This is essentially the following Nominal Hierarchy presented by Dixon (1994).

				Common nouns		
		Demonstratives				
1st person pronouns	2nd person pronouns	3rd person pronouns	Proper nouns	Human	Animate[9]	Inanimate

←

more likely to be in A than O function

Figure 4. The Nominal Hierarchy (Dixon 1994: 85).

The Nominal Hierarchy presented in Figure 5 is often used to represent splits in case marking where ergative marking is applied to NP's to the right of the hierarchy, and accusative marking to NP's to the left, with the exact cut off point being peculiar to a given language. In some languages, there is an area of overlap rather than a sharp cut-off in the transition from ergative to accusative marking (Dixon 1994: 87).

At first, Roviana would appear to challenge the universality of this hierarchy for the representation of split ergativity. The NP's in Roviana which mark ergative-absolutive are to the left of this hierarchy, namely pronouns (including demonstratives) and proper NP's, while common nouns have neutral marking. Thus, Roviana appears to employ an inverted Nominal Hierarchy.

A possible way to avoid this challenge is to say that the Nominal Hierarchy is really best suited for splits between ergative and accusative marking. However, Wierzbicka (1981) has demonstrated that the same hierarchy can be used to represent splits in case marking in Latin, where masculine and feminine common nouns distinguish nominative and accusative, whereas neuter common nouns do not. Furthermore, it is possible that other languages which have been described as having ergative and accusative morphology in conformity with the Nominal Hierarchy really have ergative and neutral morphology.

Demonstratives					
1st person pronouns	2nd person pronouns	3rd person pronouns	Proper nouns	Enumerated common NP's	Common NP's
Ergative-absolutive					Neutral

Figure 5. Revised nominal hierarchy for Roviana main clauses.

A further problem is that the Nominal Hierarchy lacks a position needed for a full account of Roviana, namely enumerated NP's. Enumerated NP's whose heads are pronouns do not require special treatment, since the ergative-absolutive marking which they display is captured by the position of pronouns in the hierarchy. Enumerated NP's with proper nouns as heads are not attested in my data, leaving only enumerated NP's with common nouns as heads. I propose adding a position to the Nominal Hierarchy for Roviana between proper NP's and common NP's. Since all common NP's, regardless of the animacy of their referents, pattern the same in Roviana, this position effectively captures both the similarity in marking to NP's to the left and the commonality with common NP's to the right. The addition of such a position is motivated by evidence from Tongan, where Broschart (n.d. ms.) observes that enumerated NP's with numeral classifiers in Tongan exhibit an affinity in discourse for absolutive.

The Revised Nominal Hierarchy for Roviana Main Clauses is presented in Figure 5, where the NP's to the left of the vertical line receive ergative-absolutive marking, while those to the right receive neutral marking.

In Figure 5, the fact that 3SG and 3PL pronouns distinguish ergative vs absolutive is represented by the position for 3rd person pronouns in the revised hierarchy. The fact that 3PL pronouns make this distinction only in the form of the pronoun, whereas 3SG has both a special form of the pronoun and the article *si* 'ABS' and NP's other than 3rd person pronouns make this distinction only by the use of the articles *si* 'ABS' and *se* 'ABS' is not represented.

The basis of the Nominal Hierarchy

Concerning the Nominal Hierarchy, Silverstein (1976: 113) proposes "This hierarchy expresses the semantic naturalness for a lexically-specified noun phrase to function as the agent of a true transitive verb, and inversely the naturalness of functioning as the patient of such." Dixon (1979: 85) likewise interprets the animacy hierarchy as corresponding to the "potentiality of agency" or the "likelihood of functioning as transitive agent", where the speaker is the quintessential agent, with the next most likely agent being the addressee, and so on.

What is not clear from the discussion of Silverstein (1976) and Dixon (1979) is why there should be any ordering amongst lexical NP's distinct from the ordering of pronouns. Surely, the potentiality for agency is a characteristic of the referent of an NP rather than of the NP itself. A mention of a referent as a pronoun ought therefore to exhibit the same potentiality for agency as a mention as a proper NP or common NP.

In fact, it would appear that animacy per se is not what underlies this hierarchy. Wierzbicka (1981), for example, studies novels and plays, looking at clauses in which there is both a human agent and a human patient, and finds that the first person does not display a greater tendency to appear as the agent. She calls in to question the notion of the speaker as quintessential agent reflecting an ego-centric orientation of humans in discourse.

Dixon (1994: 84–85) presents a modified view in which the positions to the left of the Nominal Hierarchy are more likely to occur as A than as O. His discussion, however, essentially continues the "potentiality for agency" idea.

In order to test the hypothesis that this nominal hierarchy corresponds to the likelihood of various kinds of NP to occur as A rather than O, I examined the texts on which the present study is based. The findings are presented in Table 13. Mentions of O which are achieved by means of a verbal affix alone are counted together with independent pronouns occurring as O.

From Table 13 it does appear that first and second person pronouns are more likely to occur as A than they are to occur as O, while other types of NP occur in O with approximately equal frequency as A (in the case of human common NP's) or with much greater frequency than A.[10] Since the expected values of animate common NP's are less than five, it is necessary to collapse animate non-human and inanimate mentions together, in order to perform a χ^2 test for significance in the distribution of A and O, yielding Table 14.

First and second person pronouns, which are more likely to occur as A than O are also amongst those which have marked absolutive contrasted with unmarked ergative. Since A in Roviana overwhelmingly contains given mentions (Corston

Table 13. Various types of NP in core argument positions

					Common NP			
	1 pron	2 pron	3 pron/dem.	Proper NP	human	animate	inanimate	Total
A	45	24	33	2	13	1	3	121
O	18	2	59	6	12	2	52	151
S	58	24	33	13	12	2	23	165
Total	121	50	125	21	37	5	78	437

Table 14. Various types of NP in A and O

	1 pron	2 pron	3 pron/dem.	Proper NP	Common NP human	Common NP animate	Common NP inanimate	Total
A	45	24	33	2	13	1	3	121
O	18	2	59	6	12	2	52	151
Total	63	26	92	8	25	3	55	272

$\chi^2 > 50000$, $p < 0.001$, d.f. = 10

1996 reports that 95.5% of all mentions in A are given), it is difficult to see why an erstwhile marker of new information which has been grammaticized as an absolutive marker should come to be associated with first and second person pronouns at all. I suggest two possibilities as avenues for future research.

i. The pattern used for certain lexical NP's and for 3rd person has been generalized to 1st and 2nd pronouns.
ii. The particle *si* which used to mark new mentions also marked focus of contrast. These two functions are often performed by the same morpheme in Oceanic languages, including Roviana (Corston 1996).

Wierzbicka (1981) proposes that the Nominal Hierarchy corresponds to the relative topic-worthiness of participants in discourse. It may be that factors such as topic-worthiness motivated the marking of only certain kinds of NP in Roviana as new information and only in core argument position, and that subsequently only the marking on such NP's was amenable to grammaticization as ergative-absolutive marking.

Finally, why should proper NP's be ranked above common NP's in Roviana? Based on the texts analyzed to date, it would appear that one possible reason is that named individuals in core argument positions in Roviana are always discourse referential, whereas common NP mentions of individuals in core argument positions may or may not be discourse referential. At present, however, I have too few tokens of proper NP's to be able to test this proposal.

Conclusion

As we have seen in this chapter, the marking of core arguments in Roviana, a member of the Western Oceanic branch of Austronesian, is typologically unusual in a number of ways.

There is an ergative-absolutive distinction made in pronouns and in the marking of certain kinds of lexical noun phrases. This ergative-absolutive distinction, however, is perhaps unique amongst ergative languages studied to date in that it is the ergative which has zero marking, while the absolutive is marked. The marked absolutive has been shown to have developed historically from the grammaticization of a particle which occurred marking new mentions in discourse, where new mentions favor absolutive {S, O} over A.

Split-ergativity in Roviana is conditioned by clause type (main vs subordinate) and noun phrase type. Split-ergativity according to clause type is typologically unusual in that ergativity occurs in main clauses but not in subordinate clauses, unlike the more widely attested split according to clause type in which main clauses are accusative while some or all subordinate clauses are ergative (Dixon 1994: 101–104). Split ergativity according to noun phrase type is unusual in that it is noun phrase types to the left of the Nominal Hierarchy of Dixon (1979, 1994) rather than those to the right which receive ergative-absolutive marking.

There are direct object pronominal affixes on the verb which distinguish person, number, inclusive vs exclusive, and which indicate by their mere presence that the direct object is specific and not backgrounded. Although there are direct object pronominal affixes in Roviana, there are no affixes on the verb indicating any other grammatical relation. The object pronominal affixes are also unusual since it is the third person plural which has zero form, whereas all other object affixes have non-zero form.

While the contemporary grammar of Roviana appears typologically unusual in the marking of core arguments, I hope to have demonstrated that these peculiarities are based on tendencies observable in discourse. By considering the patterns of language use and how these mold grammar, we find functional explanations for grammatical patterning.

Notes

* My thanks go to Marianne Mithun and the members of the Fall 1995 graduate seminar on Case, Voice and Grammatical Relations, University of California, Santa Barbara, and to the participants in the conference on Preferred Argument Structure: The next generation, held at the University of California, Santa Barbara, 12–14 May 1995, for their comments on earlier drafts of this paper. Naturally, none of these people are to blame for any remaining imperfections.

1. The orthography introduced in Corston (1993) has been modified. /β/ replaces /v/ to represent a voiced bilabial fricative, /g/ replaces /q/ to represent a pre-nasalized velar stop, /ŋ/ replaces /ñ/ to represent a velar nasal, and /ɣ/ replaces /g/ to represent a voiced velar fricative.

2. The following abbreviations are used in this paper: 1 = first person; 2 = second person; 3 = third person; ABS = absolutive; CAUS = causative; DEF = definite; DEM = demonstrative; DIR = directional; DO = direct object; DT = downtoner (a kind of modal); ERG = ergative; EXC = exclusive; INC = inclusive; INTJ = interjection; k.o. = kind of; NOM = nominalizer; NSUF = noun suffix; PERS = personal article (replacing the gloss 'ART' of Corston (1993)); PL = plural; REL = relative clause marker; SG = singular.

3. All examples are taken from my own field notes.

4. This example is taken from a story in which animals act like people, and have proper names such as 'Possum' and 'Rat'. The absolutive article *se* is therefore used with the name *manue* 'Possum'.

5. Note that in example (27) *sarini* '3PL.ABS' is being used to refer to the pigs in the feast being described, not to the men carving the meat.

6. Some speakers apparently treat *e* as obligatory, others routinely omit it (Corston 1993).

7. Proper NP's denoting political parties, which consist of human members, appear to be marked with the personal article. Other proper NP's occurring in my data without human reference do not occur with the personal article.

8. The totals in Table 3 differ slightly from those in the discussion of the zero-marked 3PL object suffix due to the way an NP intermediate between a lexical NP and a pronominal NP is counted. There is a special NP type in Roviana consisting of a reference to the speaker and a proper NP (Corston 1993). This kind of NP is counted as both a pronominal mention (of the speaker) and a lexical NP mention (of the named referent). For the purposes of information flow, however, the information status is that of the pair of individuals as a single discourse referent.

9. 'Animate' is used here to mean 'non-human animate'.

10. It is a curious quirk of this corpus that there are exactly as many second and third person pronouns in A and S.

References

Broschart, J. n.d. ms. "Local classifiers in Tongan."

Corston, Simon H. 1996. *Ergativity in Roviana, Solomon Islands.* Pacific Linguistics Series B-113. Canberra: ANU Printing Service.

Corston, Simon H. 2002. "Roviana". In Lynch, John, Ross, Malcolm and Crowley, Terry (eds.). *The Oceanic Languages.* Surrey: Curzon Press.

Dixon, R.M.W. 1979. "Ergativity". *Language* 55: 59–138.

Dixon, R.M.W. 1994. *Ergativity.* Cambridge Studies in Linguistics 69. Cambridge: Cambridge University Press.

Du Bois, John W. 1980. "Beyond definiteness: the trace of identity in discourse". In Chafe, Wallace (ed.). *The Pear Stories: Cognitive, Cultural, and Linguistic Aspects of Narrative Production.* Norwood, NJ: Ablex. 9–50.

Du Bois, John W. 1987. "The discourse basis of ergativity". *Language* 63: 805–855.

Givón, Talmy. 1979. *On understanding grammar.* NY: Academic Press.

Givón, Talmy. 1983. *Topic continuity in discourse: A quantitative cross-language study.* Amsterdam and Philadelphia: John Benjamins Publ. Co.

Hopper, Paul J. and Thompson, Sandra A. 1980. "Transitivity in grammar and discourse". *Language* 56: 251–299.

Mayerthaler, Willi. 1988. *Morphological naturalness.* (Original German edition: *Morphologische Natürlichkeit,* 1981, Wiesbadem: Akademische Verlagsgesellschaft Athenaion). Linguistica Extranea, Studia 17. Ann Arbor: Karoma Publ. Inc.

Mithun, Marianne. 1994. "The implications of ergativity for a Philippine voice system". In Fox, Barbara and Hopper, Paul J. (eds.). 1994. *Voice: Form and function.* Amsterdam and Philadelphia: John Benjamins Publ. Co. 247–277.

Ross, Malcolm D. 1988. *Proto Oceanic and the Austronesian languages of Western Melanesia.* Pacific Linguistics Series C, No. 98. Canberra: ANU Printing Service.

Silverstein, Michael. 1976. "Hierarchy of features and ergativity". in R.M.W. Dixon (ed.) *Grammatical categories in Australian Languages.* Linguistic Series No. 22, Australian Institute of Aboriginal Studies, Canberra. 112–171

Thompson, Sandra A. 1997. "Discourse motivations for the core-oblique distinction as a language universal". In Akio Kamio (ed.). *Functionalism in Linguistics.* Berlin: Mouton de Gruyter, 59–82.

Trask, R.L. 1979. "On the origins of ergativity". In Plank, Frans (ed.). *Ergativity: Towards a theory of grammatical relations.* New York: Academic Press. 385–404.

Trubetzkoy, N.S. 1969. *Principles of Phonology.* Orig. 1936, *Grundzüge der Phonologie.* English translated by C. Baltaxe. Berkeley: University of California Press.

Waterhouse, J.H.L. 1928. *A Roviana and English dictionary, with English-Roviana index and a list of natural history objects.* Guadalcanal: Melanesian Mission Press.

Waterhouse, J.H.L. 1949. *A Roviana and English Dictionary with English-Roviana index, list of natural history objects and appendix of old customs.* (Reprint of Waterhouse 1928, revised and enlarged by L.M. Jones). Sydney: Epworth Printing and Publishing House.

Wierzbicka, Anna. 1981. "Case marking and human nature". *Australian Journal of Linguistics* 1: 43–80.

Preferred Argument Structure in early Inuktitut spontaneous speech data*

Shanley E. M. Allen and Heike Schröder
Boston University

Introduction

It is well known that speakers tend to represent nominal referents in their speech in each of the different morphological forms permitted in their language, according to a variety of discourse properties associated with the referent in question (Chafe 1976, 1987, Li & Thompson 1979, Clancy 1980, Givón 1983). Thus, a referent which has not been previously mentioned in the discourse is more likely to be represented as a lexical NP, while a referent which has just been mentioned in the previous clause is more likely to be represented as a pronominal, or only through a verbal cross-referencing affix or not at all if the language in question permits the latter two options. Work by Du Bois (1985, 1987) further illuminates these patterns of referential choice by showing that grammatical role strongly correlates with the distribution of referring expressions both in relation to their discourse properties and in relation to the morphological form in which they are represented.[1] Thus, referring expressions which are full lexical NPs and referring expressions representing new referents tend to appear relatively frequently in the S and O roles, but relatively infrequently in the A role. Du Bois refers to this pattern as Preferred Argument Structure, and discusses at some length the pragmatic and grammatical tendencies associated with it.

The central notions of Preferred Argument Structure can be expressed in the form of four constraints, as shown in Table 1. These constraints illustrate the correlation between grammatical role, pragmatic information and morphological form of arguments, as observed in data from Sakapulteko Maya adult narratives in the original instance (Du Bois 1985, 1987), and in several other languages of varying typologies. It has also been shown to provide an accurate description of referential choice in certain instances of both first and second language acquisition (Kumpf 1992, Clancy 1993, this volume, Bentivoglio 1996).

Table 1. Dimensions and constraints of Preferred Argument Structure

	Grammar	Pragmatics
Quantity	One Lexical Argument Constraint: Avoid more than one lexical argument per clause.	One New Argument Constraint: Avoid more than one new argument per clause.
Role	Non-Lexical A Constraint: Avoid lexical A's.	Given A Constraint: Avoid new A's.

(Source: Adapted from Du Bois 1987: 829)

The present paper seeks to describe and explain the patterns of distribution of morphological forms of arguments in a set of spontaneous speech data taken from four Inuktitut-speaking children aged 2;0 through 3;6. Inuktitut is a morphologically ergative language with rich verbal morphology in which arguments tend to be represented solely through verbal cross-referencing affixes, and thus it provides an interesting parallel with Sakapulteko which has similar characteristics (Du Bois, 1987). As far as we are aware, there is only one other study of Preferred Argument Structure in an Eskimo language (Rubino 1996), focussed on oral narratives. In addition, only two languages have been investigated specifically in terms of Preferred Argument Structure in child language: Korean spontaneous speech data from children aged 1;8–2;10 (Clancy 1993, 1995, 1996, 1997, this volume) and Venezuelan Spanish oral narrative data from children aged 3–6 years (Bentivoglio 1996). Thus, the present paper offers useful elaboration in both these areas.

Results indicate that each of the constraints in Table 1 hold in the Inuktitut data examined here, such that a strong relationship is observed between morphological form and grammatical role, between morphological form and recency of mention, and between recency of mention and grammatical role. In order to help address the universality of the constraints proposed by the Preferred Argument Structure framework, Inuktitut child data are compared with three other data sets following the dimensions noted above: adult Sakapulteko narratives (Du Bois 1987), adult Yup'ik narratives (Rubino 1996), and child Korean spontaneous speech (Clancy 1993, this volume). Inuktitut data are consistent with data from these three languages in terms of the four constraints. However, comparisons reveal a substantially lower percentage of lexical arguments and transitive clauses in Inuktitut than in the other languages. Potential reasons for these differences are explored in the discussion section.

Inuktitut structure

Inuktitut is a language of the Eskimo-Aleut family spoken in parts of northeastern Canada; the dialect discussed here (Tarramiut) is spoken in northern Quebec. It is a polysynthetic language which is generally considered morphologically ergative, and which has basic SOV word order. Various aspects of its grammar encode person and number; 4 persons (1, 2, 3 coreferent, 3 disjoint) and 3 numbers (singular, dual, plural) are normally differentiated. Inuktitut also has a rich system of both nominal case-marking affixes and verbal cross-referencing affixes. Two aspects of Inuktitut structure essential to the paper are elaborated further below.

Morphological form of arguments

The morphological form of arguments in Inuktitut involves two components: verbal cross-referencing affixes on the one hand and independent lexical or demonstrative NPs on the other. Verbal cross-referencing affixes are obligatory (except in restricted situations in colloquial speech), while independent NPs are optional.

The system of verbal cross-referencing affixes in Inuktitut is particularly rich.[2] Subjects of grammatically intransitive clauses (1) and both subjects and objects of grammatically transitive clauses (2) are reflected in portmanteau affixes on the verb, which provide information about verbal modality as well as about both the person and the number of the subject and object. While these portmanteau affixes were undoubtedly originally formed from distinct component parts, these parts are no longer reliably distinguishable in a systematic way. Apart from this difference, Inuktitut morphology is similar to that of Sakapulteko in terms of the information coded on the verb (Du Bois 1987), and hence provides a useful comparison.

(1) a. *Arqarama.*
arqa-gama
get.down-CSV.1sS[3]
'I'm getting down.' (Paul 2;6)[4]

b. *Qailangannginavit.*
qai-langa-nngit-gavit
come-FUT-NEG-CSV.2sS
'You aren't going to come.' (Louisa 3;6)

(2) a. *Qukisigakkit.*
qukiq-si-gakkit
shoot-PRSP-CSV.1sS.2sO
'I'm shooting you.' (Paul 3;3)

b. *Aanninaravinga.*
aanniq-naq-gavinga
hurt-CAUS-CSV.2sS.1sO
'You're hurting me.' (Elijah 2;5)

Independent lexical or demonstrative representation of arguments apart from the portmanteau affix is not required in Inuktitut. However, third person arguments may be represented in the form of either independent lexical NPs or independent demonstratives in addition to verbal cross-referencing affixes. Note that there are no third person pronominals in Inuktitut, but rather a rich system of demonstratives which convey information about the number, relative location, and motion of the referent. Thus, third person arguments may appear in three possible morphological forms: lexical (lexical NP plus verbal affix), demonstrative (demonstrative plus verbal affix), and affixal (verbal affix only). The examples in (3) show simple active intransitive sentences based on the verbal root *sinik-* 'sleep', with third person subjects represented as lexical (3a), demonstrative (3b), and affixal (3c).

(3) a. *Panik, piarait sinisijuq.*
panik piaraq-it sinik-si-juq
daughter baby-ABS.2S.SG sleep-PRSP-PAR.3sS
'Daughter, your baby is sleeping.' (Paul 3;3)

b. *Una sinisimmat.*
u-na sinik-si-mmat
this.one-ABS.SG sleep-PRSP-CSV.3sS
'This one is sleeping.' (Lizzie 2;10)

c. *Sinilirmat.*
sinik-liq-mmat
sleep-INCP-CSV.3sS
'He/she is sleeping.' (Elijah 2;9)

First and second person arguments are virtually never represented lexically or pronominally, even for emphasis, but rather only through verbal cross-referencing affixes (this is true both in the language in general and in the data discussed in this paper).[5, 6] While first and second person pronouns do exist in Inuktitut, they are used primarily in single word utterances as arguments of ellipted verbs (4b) and to indicate possession (5b), and in equational structures (6). Note that ergative, absolutive and possessive pronouns are homophonous.

(4) a. *Maqailanganngitualu?*
maqaiq-langa-nngit-juq-aluk
hunt-FUT-NEG-PAR.3sS-EMPH
'He won't go hunting?' (Mother)

b. *Aaa, ivvit.*
aaa ivvit
yes you/your/yours
'Right, you (will)' (Elijah 2;0)

(5) a. *Kinaup paisikuunga?*
kina-up paisikuuq-nga
who-ERG.SG bicycle-ABS.3S.SG
'Whose bicycle is this?' (Mother)

b. *Uvanga.*
uvanga
I/me/my/mine
'Mine.' (Paul 3;3)

(6) a. *Una ivvit.*
u-na ivvit
this.one-ABS.SG you/your/yours
'This one is yours.' (Lizzie 3;3)

b. *Uvangaunngimat.*
uvanga-u-nngit-mmat
I/me/my/mine-be-NEG-CSV.3sS
'It's not me.' (referring to a person in a photo) (Paul 2;11)

For emphasis or contrast involving first and second person arguments, a number of strategies may be used including intonational emphasis on the cross-referencing affix, use of the word-internal morpheme *-mi-* 'also', use of the word-internal morpheme *-ngaaq-* 'instead', use of the reflexive *imminik* 'my/your/him/herself', and use of a first or second person pronoun in a single word utterance. However, use of pronouns as arguments in verbal clauses is considered ungrammatical in such instances.

Ergativity

Inuktitut is generally classified as a morphologically ergative language. Ergativity is no longer clearly visible for the most part in the verbal affixation system due to the conflation of component parts of the portmanteau verbal affixes noted above. However, ergativity is reflected through the nominal case marking system. Arguments in S (subject of intransitive) and O (object of transitive) grammatical roles are both marked with absolutive case (7a,b) while arguments in the A (subject of transitive) role are marked with ergative case (7c).

(7) a. *Qimmiapik qialirtuq.*
qimmiq-apik-ø qia-liq-juq
dog-DIM-ABS.SG cry-INCP-PAR.3sS
'The cute little dog is crying.' (Louisa 3;2)

b. *Miaji takulaunngitait.*
Miaji-ø taku-lauq-nngit-jait
Mary-ABS.SG see-PAST-NEG-PAR.2sS.3sO
'You didn't see Mary.' (Lizzie 2;10)

c. *Kinaup pijanga.*
kina-up pi-janga
who-ERG.SG do-PAR.3sS.3sO
'Who is doing this?' (Elijah 2;5)

The case marking paradigm for nouns and demonstratives which have no possessor is given in Table 2. Note that the ergative and absolutive forms are identical for dual and plural, and only differ for the singular. In addition, the absolutive, by far the more frequent of the two cases, is not phonetically realized in the singular form. Thus it may appear that the ergative-absolutive patterning in Inuktitut is rather spurious. However, the patterning becomes much more evident in the paradigms for nominals which have a possessor. The paradigm for singular nominals possessed by a singular possessor is given in Table 3. The examples in (8) illustrate this paradigm for the nominal *ataata* 'father', possessed by a first person singular entity.

Table 2. Case marking paradigm for Inuktitut non-possessed nominals

	Ergative		Absolutive	
	Case	Demonstrative	Case	Demonstrative
Singular	*-up*	*uuma*	*-ø*	*una*
Dual	*-Vk*	*ukua*	*-Vk*	*ukua*
Plural	*-it*	*ukua*	*-it*	*ukua*

Table 3. Case-marking paradigm for singular nouns possessed by singular possessors

	Ergative	Absolutive
my singular item	*-(m)ma*	*-ga*
your (SG) singular item	*-ppit/-vit*	*-it*
his/her/its singular item	*-ngata*	*-nga*

(8) a. *Ataataga itirtuq.*
ataata-ga itiq-juq
father-ABS.1S.SG enter-PAR.3sS
'My father is coming in.' (Lizzie 2;6)

b. *Ataataga siniqunngilauruk.*
ataata-ga sinik-qu-nngit-lauq-guk
father-ABS.1S.SG sleep-tell-NEG-POL-IMP.2sS.3sO
'Tell my father not to sleep.' (Elijah 2;5)

c. *Ataatamma kaivaluakainnatanga.*
ataata-mma kaivalua-kainnaq-janga
father-ERG.1S.SG turn-PAST-PAR.3sS.3sO
'My father spun it.' (Elijah 2;9)

Having described the basic relevant features of the structure of Inuktitut, we turn now to the methodology used in this paper.

Method

Subjects

Data used in this paper are taken from the spontaneous speech of four Inuit children — Elijah, Lizzie, Louisa and Paul[7] — aged 2;0, 2;6, 2;10 and 2;6 respectively at the outset of data collection. Elijah was adopted by his grandparents and lived in an extended family with these grandparents, his birth mother, and his siblings by adoption. His grandmother did not work outside the home, and served as his primary caretaker. Each of the other subjects lived in nuclear families in which both parents worked outside the home; the children were cared for during the day by members of their extended families. Elijah, Louisa and Paul were the youngest siblings in their respective families, while Lizzie was the oldest. One baby was born in Elijah's family during the duration of the data collection period. (See Allen 1996 for more details about the subjects.)

All of these children lived in the same functionally monolingual Inuit community of some 200 inhabitants in arctic Quebec. All Inuit in this community (some 97% of the permanent population) are native and fluent speakers of Inuktitut (Tarramiut dialect), though most between the ages of about eight and forty are also fluent to varying degrees in English and/or French.

Data collection and preparation

The children were each videotaped by the first author, 4 hours per month for nine months, in naturalistic communication situations with their friends and families. Approximately one half of the data (two hours per child per month) were selected for transcription on the basis of relative frequency of utterances of the subject and potential ease of transcription of the tape. These data were then transcribed by native speakers of Inuktitut and entered into computer following the CHAT transcription conventions of the CHILDES project (MacWhinney & Snow, 1990). Transcripts of the first, middle and last months of taping for each child were chosen for intensive analysis. These transcripts were checked for accuracy by the first author in consultation with native speakers of Inuktitut, and then coded for various morphological, syntactic and discourse features including those described below.

Data analysis was conducted using the CLAN programs (MacWhinney & Snow, 1990). Only utterances which were fully intelligible and complete from the point of view of the child's intonation, and which were not comprised solely of routines (e.g., songs, alphabet), were included in the data set to be analyzed. Note that utterances comprised of partial and complete imitations of previous speakers and self-repetitions were included in the analysis.

Following Du Bois (1987) and other work involving Preferred Argument Structure, the unit of analysis considered for this paper is the verbal clause. Thus, verbal utterances in the data were divided into individual verbal clauses, each containing a verb or verbal element and its arguments. All intransitive and transitive clauses with verb roots and cross-referencing affixes were analyzed.[8] Intransitive clauses (9) include those which are simple actives, passives, antipassives, noun incorporation structures, and complex actives (e.g. want to V). Transitive clauses (10) include those which are simple actives, causatives, noun incorporation structures, and complex actives (e.g. want to V). Verbal clauses lacking either a verb root (11a) or cross-referencing affix (11b) or both (11c), but containing other verbal affixes (e.g. secondary verb, tense, aspect, or negation), were also included in the analysis as intransitive or transitive clauses. Such clauses are considered colloquially appropriate in adult and child Inuktitut, and the root and affix information is recoverable from context (Swift & Allen 2002a, 2002b).

(9) a. *Qupanuarulu qailangammat.*
qupanuaq-guluk-ø qai-langa-mmat
bird-dim-abs.sg come-fut-csv.3sS
'The little bird is going to come.' (Lizzie 2;11)

b. *Maunaasijunga.*
ma-una-aq-si-junga
here-via-go-prsp-par.1sS
'I'm going through here.' (Paul 2;6)

(10) a. *Una aturtara.*
u-na atuq-jara
this.one-abs.sg use-par.1sS.3sO
'I'm using this one.' (Elijah 2;5)

b. *Ijukkatilauruk.*
ijukkaq-tit-lauq-guk
fall-caus-pol-imp.2sS.3sO
'Make it fall.' (Louisa 3;2)

(11) a. *Tilauruk.* [= *Itsivatilauruk.*]
tit-lauq-guk [= itsiva-tit-lauq-guk]
caus-pol-imp.2sS.3sO [= sit-caus-pol-imp.2sS.3sO]
'Make it do X.' [= 'Make it sit down.'] (Lizzie 2;6)
(asking her mother to help her make a doll sit down)

b. *Paisikunnguaq.* [= *Paisikunnguatuq.*]
paisikuq-nnguaq [= paisikuq-nnguaq-juq]
bicycle-pretend [= bicycle-pretend-par.3sS]
'Pretending to bicycle.' [= 'He's pretending to bicycle.'] (Paul 2;6)
(explaining that a cartoon character is pretending to bicycle)

c. *Gumanngit.* [= *Atjiliuqtaugumannginama.*]
guma-nngit [= atjiliuq-jau-guma-nngit-gama]
want-neg [= film-pass-want-neg-csv.1sS]
'Don't want to.' [= 'I don't want to be filmed.'] (Elijah 2;0)
(telling his mother that he doesn't want to be videotaped)

In addition, all clauses with overt copular verbs were analyzed, including equational clauses (12a) and existential clauses (12b).[9]

(12) a. *Piarautsutiit?*
piaraq-u-tsutit
baby-be-ctm.2sS
'When you were a baby?' (Louisa 3;6)

b. *Haakirutialu silamiituq.*
haakiq-guti-aluk-ø sila-mi-it-juq
hockey-used.for-emph-abs.sg outside-loc-be-par.3sS
'The hockey stick is outside.' (Elijah 2;0)

Equational and existential clauses without overt copular verbs (13) were not included in the analysis, although they are perfectly grammatical in Inuktitut. This was done in order to make the Inuktitut data maximally comparable with that from other languages, since most other analyses of Preferred Argument Structure include only clauses with overt verbs.

(13) a. *Una arnaq.*
u-na arnaq-ø
this.one-abs.sg woman-abs.sg
'This (is a) woman.' (Paul 3;3)

b. *Piipili?*
piipi-li
baby-where
'Where (is the) baby?' (Lizzie 2;6)

The final data set used for analysis in this paper, then, contains a total of 2588 clauses: 1633 intransitive clauses, 617 transitive clauses, 164 equational clauses, and 174 existential clauses.[10] The quantitative details of the data set are summarized in Table 4.

Data were also divided into 3 groups of increasing grammatical complexity for purposes of assessing any developmental changes. The mean number of morphemes per utterance was calculated for all utterances of each child at each age which contained a verbal element (verb root, verbal cross-referencing affix, or other verbal affix), and which were complete, intelligible, non-repetitive and non-imitative. Most acquisition literature assumes that children's mean length of utterance (MLU) will increase as their grammatical complexity increases, since producing structures of increased complexity usually involves adding a morpheme to the structure (Brown 1973). Previous work showed that calculating MLU over only verbal utterances rather than over all eligible utterances in the data set provided a better characterization of increasing complexity for the utterances in this data set (Allen 1996). Groups are given in Table 5.

Table 4. Data analyzed

Child	Age	No. intransitive clauses	No. transitive clauses	No. equational clauses	No. existential clauses	Total
Elijah	2;0	151	41	12	10	214
	2;5	187	89	25	11	312
	2;9	219	42	11	24	296
Lizzie	2;6	45	40	5	6	96
	2;10	216	79	11	16	322
	3;3	72	20	14	21	127
Louisa	2;10	62	33	15	1	111
	3;2	230	118	22	10	380
	3;6	162	65	20	53	300
Paul	2;6	66	22	8	13	109
	2;11	49	29	5	7	90
	3;3	174	39	16	2	231
Total		1633	617	164	174	2588

Table 5. Data grouped by verbal MLU

Group	Verbal MLU	Data included
1	3.25–3.99	Louisa 2;10, Louisa 3;2, Paul 2;6
2	4.00–4.74	Elijah 2;0, Lizzie 2;6, Lizzie 2;10, Louisa 3;6, Paul 2;11, Paul 3;3
3	4.75–5.49	Elijah 2;5, Elijah 2;9, Lizzie 3;3

(Source: Adapted from Allen 1996:48)

Coding

All clauses under analysis were coded as either grammatically intransitive (verbal cross-referencing affix for subject only) or grammatically transitive (verbal cross-referencing affix for both subject and object).[11] All nominal referring expressions in the data were coded for grammatical role. Arguments of verbal clauses were coded as either subjects of grammatically intransitive clauses (Si), subjects of grammatically transitive clauses (A), or objects of grammatically transitive clauses (O). Subjects of copular clauses were coded as either equational (Se) or existential (Sx). In addition, all referential obliques were coded (Obl), including those marked as modalis (patient of antipassive, second object of causative or double object construction), allative (including agent of passive), ablative, locative, and vialis.

All nominal referring expressions were also coded for morphological form (lexical, demonstrative, affixal), person of referent (first, second, third), animacy (human, animal, inanimate), recency of mention of referent in discourse (new, non-new), physical presence of referent in context (absent, present), and contrastiveness of referent in discourse (contrast, no contrast), following Clancy (1993, 1997). Referring expressions were coded as new if the referent which they denoted had not been mentioned in the preceding 20 clauses or was newly introduced to the discourse, and as non-new if the referent had been mentioned one or more times in the preceding 20 clauses.[12] First and second person arguments were all classified as non-new, following Chafe (1976) and Du Bois (1987).

Results

The four constraints of Preferred Argument Structure, presented in Table 1 above, have been found to provide an accurate representation of tendencies in the distribution of lexical and new arguments across a variety of language typologies and data types. In this section, we assess their validity for the child Inuktitut spontaneous speech data outlined above. Inuktitut results are also compared to results from Sakapulteko adult narratives (Du Bois 1987), Yup'ik adult narratives (Rubino 1996) and Korean child spontaneous speech (Clancy 1993, this volume).

Quantity constraints

The quantity constraints of Preferred Argument Structure involve the number of lexical and new arguments per clause. Du Bois (1987) shows that clauses involving either two lexical arguments or two new arguments are dispreferred in discourse.

The One Lexical Argument Constraint is fully supported in Inuktitut child language, in that only 0.04% of all clauses (0.2% of transitive clauses) have two lexical arguments. Results for all quantities are shown in Table 6. The percentage of clauses with two lexical arguments in Inuktitut is consistent with figures for adult Sakapulteko (1.1% of all clauses; 2.8% of transitive clauses (Du Bois 1987: 819)), adult Yup'ik (1% of all clauses (Rubino 1996: 144)), and child Korean (4.7%-5.4% of transitive clauses[13] (Clancy this volume)).

Table 6. Transitivity and number of lexical arguments per clause

	No lexical arguments		One lexical argument		Two lexical arguments		Total	
	n	%	n	%	n	%	n	%
Transitive	574	93.3	42	6.5	1	0.2	617	100.0
Intransitive	1544	94.5	89	5.5	–	–	1633	100.0
Equational	157	95.7	7	4.3	–	–	164	100.0
Existential	151	86.8	23	13.2	–	–	174	100.0
Total	2426	93.7	161	6.2	1	0.04	2588	100.0

Two differences between the Inuktitut data and data from other languages are quite striking, however. First, the percentage of clauses with one lexical argument in Inuktitut (6.2%) is very different from figures for Sakapulteko (52.6%), Yup'ik (32%) and Korean (28.2–30.3% (Clancy p.c.)). In fact, only 7.8% of referring expressions in the Inuktitut corpus are represented lexically (5.1% of arguments and 77.6% of obliques), compared with some 44.2% in Sakapulteko (Du Bois 1987: 819). As this factor is also relevant for the other constraints, we will return to it in the discussion below.

Second, the ratio between the number of intransitive and transitive clauses is quite different in Inuktitut (27.4% transitive) than in Sakapulteko (40.4% transitive (Du Bois 1987: 819)) and Korean (50% transitive (Clancy this volume). Figures for Yup'ik narratives vary from 26.0% transitives for a retelling of a true incident to 37.7% for the pear story and 40.5% for a retelling of a mythological tale (Rubino 1996: 147–147). The variation in figures for Yup'ik depending on the type of narrative told may indicate that discourse which is more personal (child interaction, retelling a personal story) may yield a lower percentage of transitives than that which is less personal (pear story, mythological tale). We return to the issue of differences in the number of transitive and intransitive clauses in the discussion below.

Du Bois's One New Argument Constraint is also supported by Inuktitut child data. Only 0.04% of all clauses (0.2% of transitive clauses) have two new arguments, as shown in Table 7.[14] Clancy (this volume) reports that between 1.3% and 2.2% of transitive predicates in her data from child Korean have two new arguments, while Du Bois (1987: 826) reports 0% for his Sakapulteko narrative data (Rubino (1996) does not give figures for this constraint in Yup'ik). Thus, the Inuktitut child data fit with the pattern suggested by other languages.

Note that the Inuktitut figures for both two lexical arguments and two new arguments represent only one utterance, from the final session of Elijah which contains the most grammatically advanced data in the present corpus, as given in (14). Interestingly, all examples of lexical A's in the data, as well as half of the examples of new A's, are also found in data from Elijah.

(14) *Anaanangata Jaaniup aarqirataakainnatanga niiniganngguara.*
anaana-ngata Jaani-up aarqik-rataaq-kainnaq-janga
mother-ERG.3S.SG Johnny-ERG.SG fix-just-PAST-PAR.3sS.3sO
niinigaq-nnguaq-ga
organ-toy-ABS.1S.SG
'Johnny's mother just fixed my toy organ.' (Elijah 2;9)

Table 7. Transitivity and number of new arguments per clause

	No new arguments		One new argument		Two new arguments		Total	
	n	%	n	%	n	%	n	%
Transitive	437	73.9	153	25.9	1	0.2	591	100.0
Intransitive	1361	88.9	170	11.1	–	–	1531	100.0
Equational	130	83.3	26	16.7	–	–	156	100.0
Existential	124	73.8	44	26.2	–	–	168	100.0
Total	2052	83.9	393	16.1	1	0.04	2446	100.0

In sum, the percentage of clauses both with two lexical arguments and with two new arguments is relatively very small in Inuktitut, like in Sakapulteko, Yup'ik, and Korean. However, the distribution of the number of clauses containing only one and no lexical arguments differs substantially across these four languages.

Role constraints

The role constraints of Preferred Argument Structure involve the relative distribution of arguments across the grammatical roles available within a clause. Du Bois (1987) shows that the placement of either lexical or new arguments in the A role is dispreferred in discourse.

Du Bois's Non-Lexical A Constraint is supported by Inuktitut child language data since only 1.1% of all arguments in the A role are lexical. In addition, all seven tokens of lexical A's are from the same child, Elijah, whose data is the most grammatically advanced of the 4 subjects. Table 8 gives the data for all morphological forms in each grammatical role, including non-argument roles.[15]

The pattern observed here is similar to that in other languages in that there is a relatively small percentage of lexical arguments in the A role compared to the other roles. Du Bois (1987: 822) reports 6.1% lexical A's in adult Sakapulteko narratives (vs. 48.1% lexical S's and 45.9% lexical O's), Rubino (1996: 145) reports 0% lexical A's in adult Yup'ik narratives, and Clancy (this volume) reports 12–14% lexical A's in child Korean spontaneous speech (vs. 3% lexical Se's, 53–68% lexical Sx's, 28–32% lexical Si's, and 30–42% lexical O's). Although the percentage differences between the number of lexical arguments in the A role vs. the other roles do not look as striking in Inuktitut as in the other languages, it is nevertheless the case that lexical arguments in Inuktitut occur about twelve times more often in the Si role and five times more often in the O role than they do in the A role, as shown in Table 9.

Table 8. Distribution of morphological forms within grammatical roles

	Lexical		Demonstrative		Affixal		Total	
	n	%	n	%	n	%	n	%
A	7	1.1	0	0.0	610	98.9	617	100.0
Se	7	4.3	16	9.8	141	86.0	164	100.0
Sx	23	13.2	40	23.0	111	63.8	174	100.0
Si	89	5.5	119	7.3	1425	87.3	1633	100.0
O	37	6.0	149	24.1	431	69.9	617	100.0
Obl	97	77.6	28	22.4	–	–	125	100.0
Total	260	7.8	352	10.6	2718	81.6	3330	100.0

It remains, however, that the overall percentage of lexical arguments in Si and O roles in Inuktitut is relatively low compared to the other languages discussed here. We return to this issue in the discussion below.

We turn finally to Du Bois's Given A Constraint, which is also supported by Inuktitut child data since only 0.7% of arguments in A position represent new referents. Table 10 gives the data for the number of both new and non-new referents represented in each grammatical role, including non-argument roles.[16]

The pattern of distribution of arguments representing new and non-new referents in the A role, as well as the proportion of difference between the percentage of arguments representing new referents in the A role compared with the S and O roles, is similar to that found for other languages. Some 3.2% of arguments in the

Table 9. Distribution of lexical referring expressions across grammatical roles

	Lexical referring expressions	
	n	%
A	7	2.7
Se	7	2.7
Sx	23	8.8
Si	89	34.3
O	37	14.2
Obl	97	37.3
Total	260	100.0

A role in adult Sakapulteko narrative represent new referents (Du Bois 1987:826; compared to 22.5% in S and 24.7% in O), while 2–4% of arguments in the A role in child Korean spontaneous speech represent new referents (Clancy this volume; compared to 33–34% in Se, 22–38% in Sx, 18% in Si, and 35–37% in O) (Rubino (1996) does not give comparable figures for this constraint in Yup'ik). The difference in number of new arguments in S vs. O roles is similar to that in Korean, though different from that in Sakapulteko.

Table 10. Distribution of recency of mention within grammatical roles

	New		Non-new		Total	
	n	%	n	%	n	%
A	4	0.7	609	99.3	613	100.0
Se	26	16.7	130	83.3	156	100.0
Sx	44	26.2	124	73.8	168	100.0
Si	170	11.1	1361	88.9	1531	100.0
O	163	27.0	440	73.0	603	100.0
Obl	52	44.4	65	55.6	117	100.0
Total	459	14.4	2729	85.6	3188	100.0

This is likely the result of the difference in narrative vs. spontaneous speech data. The distribution across grammatical roles of all referring expressions representing new referents is shown in Table 11.

In sum, the role constraints of Preferred Argument Structure are supported in child Inuktitut spontaneous speech data since only a very small percentage of the referring expressions appearing in the A role are either lexical or new. Interestingly,

Table 11. Distribution of referring expressions representing new referents across grammatical roles

	Referring expressions representing new referents	
	n	%
A	4	0.9
Se	26	5.7
Sx	44	9.6
Si	170	37.0
O	163	35.5
Obl	52	11.3
Total	459	100.0

however, the number of lexical referring expressions in the O role, and to a lesser extent in the Si role, is substantially lower than in the other languages considered. We return to this issue in the discussion below.

Relationship between morphological form and recency of mention

The results for each of the four constraints above certainly suggest that there is strong correlation between grammatical and pragmatic information in determining the distribution of referring expressions across grammatical roles in Inuktitut child speech. It is evident that both lexical and new referring expressions tend to avoid appearing in the A role, and it is rare to find two lexical or two new arguments in the same clause. Further investigation shows more clearly the direct relationship between recency of mention and morphological form. Table 12 illustrates that referring expressions are more likely to be represented as lexical (or demonstrative) when they denote new referents than when they do not. Table 13 illustrates that a lexical (or demonstrative) form is more likely to represent a new referent than is an affixal form. In addition, it is interesting to note that 50% of all arguments in the A role representing new referents are lexical, compared with 15.4% in Se, 29.5% in Sx, 23.5% in Si, and 10.4% in O. We return in the discussion below to the relatively low percentage of new O's which are lexical.

Use of first and second person pronominal arguments

Although first and second person pronouns are not considered grammatical in argument positions, the children in this data set did occasionally use them. The complete set of utterances with verbs in which they were produced is given in (15).

Table 12. Morphological form across categories of recency of mention

	New		Non-new		Total	
	n	%	n	%	n	%
Lexical	112	24.5	125	4.6	237	7.4
Demonstrative	165	36.1	181	6.6	346	10.9
Affixal	180	39.4	2425	88.8	2605	81.7
Total	457	100.0	2731	100.0	3188	100.0

Table 13. Categories of recency of mention across morphological form

	New		Non-new		Total	
	n	%	n	%	n	%
Lexical	112	47.3	125	52.7	237	100.0
Demonstrative	165	47.7	181	52.3	346	100.0
Affixal	180	6.9	2425	93.1	2605	100.0
Total	457	14.3	2731	85.7	3188	100.0

(15) a. *Uvanga maaniikainnatuq!*
uvanga ma-ani-it-kainnaq-juq
I/me/my/mine here-LOC-be-PAST-PAR.3sS
'I was here!' (Lizzie 3;3)
(trying to reclaim the place where she was previously standing, now taken by someone else)

b. *Uvanga inutuulunga.*
uvanga inutu-u-lunga
I/me/my/mine single.person-be-ICM.1sS
'I'll be alone.' (Lizzie 3;3)
(wanting to stand on the bed alone, without her friends who are currently on the bed)

c. *Uvagut sinilangagunnaiqugut?*
uvagut sinik-langa-gunnaiq-vugut
we/us/our/ours sleep-FUT-not.be.permitted.to-IND.1pS
'Are we not permitted to sleep?' (Elijah 2;9)
(asking his mother whether he and his companions are permitted to go to sleep, probably since he knows he should stay awake while being videotaped)

In (15a–b), the pronouns used serve a specific function of contrast and emphasis, in that Lizzie is trying to assert her right to stand in a certain spot instead of her friend, or be on the bed by herself instead of her friends also being there. The pronoun in (15c) does not seem to have a contrast function, since Elijah does not seem to be contrasting his right to sleep with anyone else's. However, it is possible that he is contrasting his right with that of the videographer, or of a character on television, and that this contrast does not come across explicitly on the videotape. An interesting feature of the utterance in (15a) is the use of the third person verbal cross-referencing affix when the utterance is clearly talking about first person subjects. It may be that Lizzie's awareness that pronouns are prohibited in combination with first person affixes prompts her in this case to alter the affix in order to feel comfortable using the pronoun.

In addition, a few equational utterances without verbs contained first and second person pronouns, as shown in (16) (note that these utterances were not included in the analysis, but are shown here to further the argumentation above). Each of these utterances was used to identify the make-believe play roles of the speakers or their playmates.

(16) a. *Uvanga Raapa.*
uvanga Raapa
I/me/my/mine Raapa
'I'm Raapa.' (Paul 3;3)

b. *Ivvit Taksisaan.*
ivvit Taksisaan
you/your/yours Taksisaan
'You're Taksisaan.' (Paul 3;3)

c. *Inuppaalu uvanga.*
inupaaluk uvanga
giant I/me/my/mine
'I'm a giant.' (Louisa 3;6)

d. *Uvanga anaana.*
uvanga anaana
I/me/my/mine mother
'I'm a mother.' (Paul 3;3)

The pronouns in these utterances also all serve a contrastive function, since in each case the child in question is contrasting the make-believe role specified in the utterance with the make-believe role of another child. While these utterances would most likely be expressed as equationals with a copular verb in adult language, they are not as strongly dispreferred as the utterances in (15).

A word about ergativity

One of the main points made by Du Bois (1987) with respect to Preferred Argument Structure is that the distribution of arguments he observed provides a potential discourse basis for an ergative case system and an ergative pattern of information flow in discourse. In Sakapulteko, the roles which take absolutive case (Si and O) are preferred for introducing new referents in discourse. Thus, Du Bois (1987:834) states that "…the absolutive syntactic position constitutes a sort of grammatically defined 'staging area' — reserved for accommodating the process, apparently relatively demanding, of activating a previously inactive entity concept".

Since Inuktitut is an ergative language, it is interesting to speculate whether this may also be true for Inuktitut. Table 11 above, in fact, reveals that the same two roles (Si and O) share about equally the burden of representing new referents in discourse in the Inuktitut data considered here. Thus, the pattern in Inuktitut is comparable to that in Sakapulteko. It is interesting that Rubino (1996) did not find this pattern in his corpus of Yup'ik narratives, since Yup'ik is a member of the same language family as Inuktitut. Rubino rather found that obliques were the preferred role for introducing new referents in his data: 62.7% of all new referents appeared in Obl, in comparison with 13.7% in Si and 7.8% in O.

This completes the review of the results of our investigation of the adequacy of the Preferred Argument Structure constraints in adequately accounting for the distribution of arguments in Inuktitut child speech. In the following sections, we discuss in more detail two issues arising from these results.

Discussion

Several issues of interest arise from the investigation of the Preferred Argument Structure constraints in Inuktitut child speech. Although these constraints were overall shown to hold in Inuktitut, two main differences were found from the typical pattern of argument distribution in other languages. First, child Inuktitut evidences a relatively low percentage of lexical arguments overall in comparison with the other languages under review, and particularly in the Si and O roles. Second, the percentage of transitive clauses in the Inuktitut corpus is much lower than the percentage of intransitive clauses, and the ratio between these two is substantially different from Sakapulteko, Korean and, to a lesser extent, Yup'ik. In this discussion section, we consider various hypotheses to explain these two differences.

Overall lack of lexical referring expressions

One of the most noticeable characteristics of the Inuktitut child language in the present corpus is the overall lack of lexical referring expressions — a mere 7.8% of all referring expressions (only 5.1% of arguments) in the data set. This stands in contrast to some 44.2% lexical referring expressions in Sakapulteko adult narratives. In addition, the number of lexical Si's (5.5%) and lexical O's (6.0%) is quite low in comparison with other languages (48.1% lexical S and 45.9% lexical O in Sakapulteko; 3% lexical Se, 53–68% lexical Sx, 28–32% lexical Si and 30–42% lexical O in Korean). We present here four possible reasons for this phenomenon in Inuktitut.

Data type and information pressure

The first hypothesis involves the types of data under study and the relative information pressure associated with them. Recall that the Inuktitut data treated in this paper all derive from spontaneous speech, while Du Bois's work on Sakapulteko derives from oral narrative data. It is well known that the type of data used, and the situation in which it is collected, has some effect on choice of morphological form. Thus, data from oral narratives collected in situations in which the narrator is telling a story to a stranger exhibit high information pressure. Neither the details of the story nor the background experiences of the two participants are shared, and none of the referents are in the current physical context of the discourse, so a high percentage of the information must be made explicit, often in the form of lexical NPs. On the other hand, data from spontaneous conversations between friends and family members exhibit relatively low information pressure. The participants share some degree of common background and often some degree of familiarity with the topic of conversation, so much of the information does not need to be made explicit and a higher percentage of pronominal or affixal forms are expected. This may be particularly true in conversation involving young children where most of the conversation concerns objects and activities present in the physical context. In addition, there is likely to be a much higher percentage of first and second person forms in spontaneous speech data than in narrative data recounting the story of a film.

Du Bois (1987) particularly chose situations of high information pressure within which to conduct his study in order to have the maximum potential occurrence of lexical NPs. The Information Pressure Quotient of his corpus, defined as the ratio of new humans to clauses, is .153 or an average of an introduction of a new human referent every 6.6 clauses (Du Bois 1987: 834). The Information Pressure Quotient of our Inuktitut corpus is .025 (62 new humans in 2446 clauses), or an average of an introduction of a new human referent every 39.5 clauses. Since the Inuktitut corpus analyzed here is of relatively low information pressure, we would expect it to manifest a lower percentage of lexical NPs.[17]

To test this hypothesis, we first examined the distribution of first, second and third person referring expressions in the data. We found that only 48.6% of all referring expressions in the data set are third person (see Table 18), leaving 51.4% which are first and second person and therefore cannot be lexical. Of those third person referring expressions, only 16.1% are lexical. Interestingly, 39.6% of lexical third person referring expressions denote referents that are absent from the physical context of the discourse, and 43.9% denote referents that are new (note that these two categories overlap substantially). By comparison, only 9.1% of non-lexical third person referring expressions denote absent referents, and 28.2% denote new referents.

These results indicate that person of the referent, presence of the referent in the physical context of the discourse, and to a lesser degree newness of the referent, are key factors in determining the morphological form of the referring expression. Since these are all important components of determining information pressure, it is not surprising that the percentage of lexical referring expressions differs substantially between the Inuktitut data set on the one hand and the Sakapulteko set on the other. However, this factor of information pressure cannot explain the difference in lexical forms between the Inuktitut and Korean data sets, since both these are presumably of low information pressure. It also does not explain the lack of lexical O's and Si's in comparison with the number of lexical forms in other grammatical roles.

Development and increase of lexical uses with age

A second possible explanation for the relatively low number of lexical referring expressions in the Inuktitut data may have to do with the relative grammatical complexity of the language of the subjects. When the Inuktitut data samples are broken down into three groups of increasing grammatical complexity as listed in Table 5 above, it is clear that more lexical referring expressions are used at the more advanced stages.[18] These figures are shown in Table 14. This is also true for lexical forms in the Si and O roles specifically. The number of lexical forms in the Si role increases from 2.3% in group 1 to 9.9% in group 3, and those in the O role increase from 2.9% to 9.9%.

In addition, the number of clauses with one lexical argument increases from 7.1% (2.9% of transitive) in group 1 to 15.3% (11.8% of transitive) in group 3, as shown in Table 15. Note also that the only instance of a clause with two lexical arguments (shown in (14)) is from the grammatically most advanced data. Study underway of Preferred Argument Structure in Inuit adult spontaneous speech data will undoubtedly shed further light on the hypothesis that the number of lexical forms increases in tandem with an increase in overall grammatical complexity. Once again, however, this hypothesis explains the difference between Inuktitut and Sakapulteko data, but not between Inuktitut and Korean data. Since the Korean subjects are slightly younger than the Inuit subjects, they would not be expected to produce more lexical forms than the Inuit under this hypothesis.

The role of pronominals and demonstratives

A third possible explanation for the relatively low number of lexical referring expressions involves the role of pronominals and demonstratives in Inuktitut compared to Sakapulteko and Korean. Inuktitut is not typical of many of the languages in which Preferred Argument Structure has been studied so far in that it does not normally permit pronominals in argument roles in any person. However, demonstratives are permitted as third person arguments. While it is not clear from other literature on Preferred Argument Structure how demonstratives are treated, this issue comes into clear focus in Inuktitut. Demonstratives in Inuktitut are similar to pronominals in other languages in that they do not give all the information contained in a lexical NP. However, they are dissimilar in that they have more lexical weight than does the typical pronominal (Ariel 1990:73), including giving information about relative location and dynamicity of motion.[19] In terms of function, demonstratives in Inuktitut seem to function in some cases like lexical forms in other languages, such as in introducing new referents (17a), in some cases like demonstratives, such as in differentiating one item from other similar items (17b), and in some cases like pronominal or affixal forms, such as in referring to non-new referents.

Table 14. Morphological form of referring expressions by groups

	Lexical		Demonstrative		Affixal		Total	
	n	%	n	%	n	%	n	%
Group 1	21	2.7	73	9.3	689	88.0	783	100.0
Group 2	102	6.4	179	11.2	1323	82.5	1604	100.0
Group 3	137	14.5	100	10.6	706	74.9	943	100.0
Total	260	7.8	352	10.6	2718	81.6	3330	100.0

Table 15. Number of lexical arguments per clause by groups

	No lexical arguments		One lexical argument		Two lexical arguments		Total	
	n	%	n	%	n	%	n	%
Group 1	585	97.5	15	2.5	0	0.0	600	100.0
Group 2	1192	95.1	61	4.9	0	0.0	1253	100.0
Group 3	649	88.3	85	11.6	1	0.1	735	100.0
Total	2426	93.7	161	6.2	1	0.0	2588	100.0

(17) a. *Una ukkuali?*
u-na ukkuaq-li
this.one-ABS.SG close-IMP.3sS
'Shall this one be closed?' (Lizzie 2;6)
(referring to a door which has not been mentioned yet in discourse and is not related to the conversation at hand)

b. *Uvani una sinilangajuq.*
uv-ani u-na sinik-langa-juq
here-LOC this.one-ABS.SG sleep-FUT-PAR.3sS
'This one will sleep here.' (Louisa 3;6)
(referring to one doll among the set of dolls she is playing with)

c. *Una atulanganngitara.*
u-na atuq-langa-nngit-jara
this.one-ABS.SG use-FUT-NEG-PAR.1sS.3sO
'I'm not going to use this one.' (Elijah 2;5)
(referring to a spoon which has already been mentioned several times in the preceding utterances and which is not being differentiated from any other spoon)

Thus, it is not clear whether arguments represented by demonstratives should in some instances be grouped with those represented by lexical NPs or with those represented only by verbal cross-referencing affixes in order to provide results more comparable to other languages.

Let us take the One Lexical Argument Constraint as an example. If we were to assume that demonstratives function mostly like lexical forms in Inuktitut, and thus grouped demonstrative and lexical forms together, figures for the one non-affixal argument category would be considerably higher than those for the one lexical argument category in Table 6, as shown in Table 16. These figures are much more similar to Sakapulteko, Korean and Yup'ik data than figures for lexical arguments alone, though they are still substantially lower.

This hypothesis would also help to explain the low percentages of lexical forms in Si and O roles.[20] Demonstrative forms serve an important function in representing referents particularly in the O role, as shown in Table 8 above. This function, across both O and Si roles, seems to be primarily drawing attention to referents in the physical context which have not yet entered into discourse, as in (17a) above, and distinguishing referents from other potential similar referents in the physical context, as in (17b) above (see Clancy (this volume) for more detailed treatment of these functions in Korean child language). Not surprisingly, such uses of demonstrative forms are most often also accompanied by a pointing or touching gesture indicating the referent in question. As one quantitative example of the important role of demonstratives, Table 17 gives the percentages of new referents represented by the three morphological forms for all roles as well as for Si and O roles individually.

Table 16. Transitivity and number of non-affixal arguments per clause

	No non-affixal arguments		One non-affixal argument		Two non-affixal arguments		Total	
	n	%	n	%	n	%	n	%
Transitive	428	69.4	185	30.0	4	0.6	617	100.0
Intransitive	1425	87.3	208	12.7	–	–	1633	100.0
Equational	141	86.0	23	14.0	–	–	164	100.0
Existential	111	63.8	63	36.2	–	–	174	100.0
Total	2105	81.3	479	18.5	4	0.2	2588	100.0

Table 17. Morphological forms used to represent new referents

	Lexical		Demonstrative		Affixal		Total	
	n	%	n	%	n	%	n	%
Si	40	23.5	44	25.9	86	50.6	170	100.0
O	17	10.4	75	46.0	71	43.6	163	100.0
All roles	112	24.5	165	36.1	180	39.4	457	100.0

Further research would be very fruitful in uncovering in more detail the exact nature of the function of demonstratives in Inuktitut, and in comparing them with the function of different morphological forms in other languages. Until then, however, it is certainly important to bear in mind that this is a factor that must be taken into account in assessment of the use of lexical forms in Inuktitut.

The role of verbal cross-referencing affixes

A final hypothesis that may explain the difference between Inuktitut and Korean data with regard to percentage of lexical forms involves the role of verbal cross-referencing affixes in each of these languages. Inuktitut has a rich system of verbal cross-referencing affixes for both subject and object, while Korean has no verbal cross-referencing affixes at all. Since arguments in Inuktitut are always represented affixally, the need for an additional lexical item in the form of a lexical NP or demonstrative may well be decreased to only those instances which crucially require it, such as to denote a contrastive referent, a new referent or a referent which is not in the physical context of discourse. In Korean, however, there is no verbal cross-referencing inflection so lexical and pronominal arguments are the only ways to indicate any features of the referent. It may well be, then, that the lack of affixal forms in Korean leads to more cases than in Inuktitut in which the referent would be unclear without either a lexical or pronominal specification of the referent, and that lexical NPs would be used more than pronominals for this purpose. However, note that this hypothesis would not explain differences between Inuktitut and Sakapulteko data since the latter also has a rich system of verbal cross-referencing affixes. In any event, this hypothesis merits further investigation with other languages of typologies which vary in this respect.

Summary
In the above section, we have raised four possible hypotheses to explain the lower percentage of lexical forms in Inuktitut data than in Sakapulteko and Korean. These include the type of data involved and the resulting information pressure associated with it, the increase in use of lexical forms with increase in grammatical complexity in language, the relative role of pronominals and demonstratives across the three languages, and the role of verbal cross-referencing affixes in Inuktitut and Korean. Each of these undoubtedly plays some part in the differences across languages, depending on the structural typology and information packaging patterns of the languages in question. These four factors, as well as the interaction between them, likely account for most of the reason for the overall low number of lexical forms in the Inuktitut data. The low number of lexical Si's and O's is likely related both to the relative grammatical complexity of the data set and to the function of demonstrative forms in comparison with lexical forms in these roles.

Ratio of transitive to intransitive clauses

A second interesting feature of these data in contrast with data from other languages is that there is a substantially higher proportion of intransitive than transitive clauses. Our Inuktitut corpus contains 27.4% transitive clauses, while Du Bois's (1987:819) Sakapulteko corpus contains 40.4% transitive clauses, Clancy's (this volume) Korean corpus contains 50% transitive clauses, and Rubino's (1996:146–147) Yup'ik narratives vary from 26.0% transitives for a retelling of a true incident to 37.7% for the pear story and 40.5% for a retelling of a mythological tale. We briefly discussed the possibility above that this difference might be due to the type of data analyzed. We consider below the possibility that this difference also reflects the frequent use of detransitivizing processes in Inuktitut and the role played by the animacy hierarchy in the distribution of agents and patients across the four different constructions in Inuktitut that permit both agent and patient to be expressed.

Detransitivizing processes
Inuktitut offers three possible detransitivizing processes through which to represent clauses containing both agent and patient: passive, antipassive, and noun incorporation. While a full treatment of the different discourse functions of these processes is beyond the scope of this paper, we describe each briefly as relevant for our purposes.[21]

The passive in Inuktitut, like in other languages, serves to promote the patient from O to S while demoting the agent from S to Obl, in accompaniment with certain morphology on the verb. Most of the passive clauses in the present data are basic passives without overt subjects or agentive phrases, as in (18a). However, eleven of the passives have overt agentive phrases, as in (18b), and nine have overt subjects, as in (18c). There are 62 passive clauses in the Inuktitut corpus.

(18) a. *Kiijautsaruarama.*
kii-jau-tsaruaq-gama
bite-PASS-might-CSV.1sS
'I might really get bitten.' (Elijah 2;0)

b. *Itsumunga aijaugavit.*
itsu-munga ai-jau-gavit
that.one-ALL.SG get-PASS-CSV.2sS
'You will be brought by that one.' (Louisa 2;10)

c. *Tigujaunngituq Pita?*
tigu-jau-nngit-juq Pita-ø
take-PASS-NEG-PAR.3sS Peter-ABS.SG
'Peter won't be taken away?' (Lizzie 3;3)

In contrast, the antipassive serves to demote the agent from A to S, and to demote the patient from O to Obl, also in accompaniment with certain verbal morphology. The antipassive morpheme on the verb in Inuktitut may take a small number of phonetic forms or may not be phonetically overt. Patients in the oblique role, if overtly expressed, take modalis case. Thus, antipassives may be indicated either through phonetically overt antipassive affixation on the verb (19a), through modalis case marking on the patient nominal (19b), through both these means (19c), or through neither of them. In the latter case, the contextual situation or verb semantics usually indicates presence of an antipassive patient, often through analogy with an adjacent parallel utterance (20b), though of course the identification of such patients is open to interpretation. There are 155 antipassive clauses in the Inuktitut corpus (32 with an antipassive morpheme on the verb, 61 with an lexical or demonstrative patient, 16 with both a verbal morpheme and an overt patient, and 41 with neither).[22]

(19) a. *Qaitsigit!*
qai-tsi-git
give-ATP-IMP.2sS
'Give me some!' (wants a can of soda) (Louisa 3;2)

b. *Piarakkanik atjiliurama.*
piaraq-kkanik atjiliuq-ø-gama
baby-MOD.1S.PL film-ATP-CSV.1sS
'I took a picture of my babies.' (referring to dolls) (Paul 3;3)

c. *Piganik aitsilaurlanga?*
pi-ganik ai-tsi-lauq-langa
thing-MOD.1S.SG get-ATP-POL-IMP.1sS
'Shall I get my thing?' (referring to her sunglasses) (Lizzie 3;3)

(20) a. *Taatsuminga takulaarqit?*
ta-u-minga taku-ø-laaq-vit
ANAPHORIC-this.one-MOD.SG see-ATP-FUT-INT.2sS
'Will you see this one?' (Mother)

b. *Takulaannginama.*
taku-ø-laaq-nngit-gama
see-ATP-FUT-NEG-CSV.1sS
'I won't see (her).' (Elijah 2;5)

In noun incorporation, the patient of the verb appears as part of the verbal word. The patient serves as a nominal base, which then becomes verbal through affixation of a verbalizing morpheme and the appropriate verbal cross-referencing affix. In Inuktitut the verbalizing morphemes involved in noun incorporation may only serve as affixes, in contrast with languages such as Mohawk in which the forms which serve to verbalize nominal bases may also serve as independent verbs (Mithun 1984). Thus, noun incorporation in Inuktitut is not as free as passivization or antipassivization to serve as host to all the agent-patient pairs in the discourse since it is limited to use with only a small number of possible verbs (17 in this data set), which typically cannot be expressed using other constructions (e.g., transitive) since these verbs appear in the language only as affixes, without counterpart or equivalent independent verbs. Noun incorporation clauses mostly appear in this data set without lexical or demonstrative subjects, as in (21a), but 5 do appear with demonstrative subjects, as in (21b), and 12 appear with lexical subjects, as in (21c). There are 166 noun incorporation clauses in the Inuktitut corpus.

(21) a. *Nasaqanngituq.*
nasaq-qaq-nngit-juq
hat-have-NEG-PAR.3sS
'He doesn't have a hat.' (Louisa 3;6)

b. *Uquqsiurialangajualuguna.*
uquuqu-siuq-giaq-langa-juq-aluk-u-na
animal-look.for-begin.to-FUT-PAR.3sS-EMPH-this.one-ABS.SG
'This (person) is going to go look for an animal.' (Elijah 2;0)

c. *Ataataga kuapaliasijuq?*
ataata-ga kuapaq-liaq-si-juq
father-ABS.1S.SG coop-go.to-PRSP-PAR.3sS
'Is my father going to the co-op?' (Louisa 3;2)

The clauses containing these three types of detransitivizing processes together number 384, and make up 23.5% of the intransitive clauses in the present data set. Note that two-argument structures all together make up 44.5% of the total clauses (excluding equational and existential clauses) in the data set, a figure similar to that for Sakapulteko, Korean, and Yup'ik.

Agents and patients in paired relationships are distributed across clauses of the three detransitivizing types as well as transitive clauses in a pattern that respects the animacy hierarchy. We first describe briefly the animacy hierarchy, and then present the distribution of data across the various types of agent-patient clauses.

Animacy hierarchy

It has long been noticed in the literature (e.g., Dixon 1979, Comrie 1989) that the property of animacy inherent to nominals plays an important part in the structural relationship between nominals in discourse. Most discourse is oriented first to the speaker, then to the addressee, and then to third persons and inanimates, along the lines of the hierarchy proposed by Dixon (1979:85):

1 > 2 > 3 pronoun > demonstrative	3 proper noun >	3 common noun human > animate > inanimate

Since speakers tend to think in terms of what they do to others rather than what is done to them, the first person pronoun is more likely than any other constituent to be in the A role rather than the O role. Next most likely is the second person pronoun, and so on down the hierarchy. Comrie (1989:128) notes that there is a strong tendency for information flow from A to O to correlate with information flow from more to less animate, such that the most natural kind of transitive construction is one in which A is high in animacy and O is lower than A in animacy. In general, the argument in the lower position in a clause should not outrank the argument in the higher position. This hierarchy predicts, then, that A will be a dispreferred site for third person arguments, and especially for inanimate third person arguments. In agent-patient pairs in which the patient ranks higher than the agent, several strategies can be used to avoid violating the animacy hierarchy. For example, a passive construction is often used to promote the patient to a role (S) higher than the agent (demoted to Obl). We discuss below how the animacy hierarchy affects the distribution of person and animacy characteristics across grammatical roles in the present data. Note that both Du Bois (1987:840–844) and Clancy (this volume) find effects of both person and animacy of referent in their respective data sets.

Non-third-person and animate A constraints

There is a strong relationship in Inuktitut data between the person and animacy of arguments and their morphological form and recency of mention. As previously found in both Sakapulteko and Korean, the placement of third person arguments and inanimate arguments in the A role in Inuktitut is strongly dispreferred. Figures for person are shown in Table 18. Recall that first and second person arguments in Inuktitut may not normally be represented by other morphological forms than verbal cross-referencing affixes. Also, by definition, first and second person arguments are never new. The observed pattern, then, suggests the obvious: that one will only find lexical and/or new arguments where one also finds third person arguments.[23] Note that the predominance of first and second person A's is clearly a feature of spontaneous speech data that would not be expected in narratives which do not involve talk about the speaker or hearer.

It is interesting to note that all the clauses with third person A's respect the animacy hierarchy: one human A with human O, five inanimate A's with inanimate O's, and ten human A's with inanimate O's. All the clauses with lexical A's are of the latter type. All the clauses with inanimate A's are cases of doll play in which the doll is the A in question. Depending on one's coding preferences, one might choose to call these cases ones of human A's since the doll is essentially being treated as human in these instances. Examples are given in (22) through (24) respectively. Examples (7c), (8c) and (14) above also show the pattern indicated in (24).

(22) Human A, Human O
Sauniapirlaalu aipparikainnatanga.
sauniq-apik-aluk-ø aippaq-gi-kainnaq-janga
namesake-DIM-EMPH-ABS.SG companion-have.as-PAST-PAR.3sS.3sO
'His big namesake was with him.' (Elijah 2;9)
[lit. 'He had his big namesake as a companion.']
(talking about the relationship between two men who visited earlier)

(23) Inanimate A, Inanimate O
Una atukallarulu. [= *Una atutillugu.*]
u-na atuq-kallaq-guluk [atuq-tit-lugu]
this.one-ABS.SG use-DIM-DIM [use-SW.REF-ICM.3sS.3sO]
'She'll use this one.' (Lizzie 2;10)
(talking about a piece of clothing that a doll will wear)

(24) Human A, Inanimate O
Qaakainnatanga.
qaaq-kainnaq-janga
burst-PAST-PAR.3sS.3sO
'He burst it.' (Paul 3;3)
(talking about his brother bursting a balloon)

Table 18. Distribution of persons across grammatical roles

	First person		Second person		Third person		Total	
	n	%	n	%	n	%	n	%
A	328	53.2	273	44.2	16	2.6	617	100.0
Se	25	15.2	51	31.1	88	53.7	164	100.0
Sx	27	15.5	22	12.6	125	71.8	174	100.0
Si	616	37.7	281	17.2	736	45.1	1633	100.0
O	49	7.9	39	6.3	529	85.7	617	100.0
Obl	0	0.0	0	0.0	124	100.0	124	100.0
Total	1045	31.4	666	20.0	1618	48.6	3329	100.0

Table 19. Distribution of animacy categories across grammatical roles

	Human		Animal		Inanimate		Total	
	n	%	n	%	n	%	n	%
A	610	99.0	0	0.0	6	1.0	616	100.0
Se	102	65.4	6	3.8	48	30.8	156	100.0
Sx	62	36.7	4	2.4	103	60.9	169	100.0
Si	1072	69.9	37	2.4	425	27.7	1534	100.0
O	117	19.3	11	1.8	478	78.9	606	100.0
Obl	27	22.3	10	8.3	84	69.4	121	100.0
Total	1990	62.1	68	2.1	1144	35.7	3202	100.0

There is also a very strong constraint in the data against inanimate A's, as indicated in Table 19. Even the six instances of inanimate A's indicated in the table are somewhat misleading since they are all cases in which the A in question is a doll being treated as a human. One example is given in (23) above; another is given in (25). These data in combination indicate that the animacy hierarchy is being fully respected in relations between A and O in transitive clauses. The A role is predominantly filled by first and second person animates, while the O role is predominantly filled by third person inanimates. No violations of the animacy hierarchy occur in the present data set. Note that animacy data for Korean child language (Clancy this volume) are strikingly similar to the Inuktitut data.

(25) *Ainngitait.*
ai-nngit-jait
get-NEG-PAR.2sS.3sO
'You won't get it.' (Lizzie 2;10)
(telling the doll she's playing with that she won't get the paper Lizzie is holding)

Distribution of argument characteristics across agent and patient roles

The data in Tables 18 and 19 leave open the question of how relationships between third person agents and first, second and third person patients are expressed within one clause. We hypothesize that the frequent use of the three detransitivizing processes in Inuktitut described above may provide an answer to this question, since these offer alternative ways to express agents and patients in the same clause. We therefore investigated the distribution of four characteristics of nominal referents (person, animacy, recency of mention, and morphological form) in agents and patients across the four structures which permit expression of both agent and patient (transitive, antipassive, passive, noun incorporation). The distribution of agent characteristics is summarized in Table 20, while the distribution of patient characteristics is summarized in Table 21.

Several interesting patterns arise from the figures in these tables. First, as already discussed, the A role is filled almost exclusively by first and second person, animate, non-new arguments. Third person agents appear in each of the three other

Table 20. Distribution of characteristics of nominals in agent roles

	Transitive subject		Antipassive subject		Passive agentive		Noun incorporation		Total	
	n	%	n	%	n	%	n	%	n	%
PERSON										
1/2	601	97.4	102	68.0	0	0.0	97	58.4	801	84.1
3	16	2.6	48	32.0	11	100.0	69	41.6	152	15.9
Total	617	100.0	150	100.0	11	100.0	166	100.0	953	100.0
ANIMACY										
Animate	610	99.0	133	91.1	9	81.8	125	86.8	886	95.7
Inanimate	6	1.0	13	8.9	2	18.2	19	13.2	40	4.3
Total	616	100.0	146	100.0	11	100.0	144	100.0	926	100.0
RECENCY										
Non-new	609	99.3	133	91.7	4	50.0	131	92.3	877	96.6
New	4	0.7	12	8.3	4	50.0	11	7.7	31	3.4
Total	613	100.0	145	100.0	8	100.0	142	100.0	908	100.0
FORM										
Affixal	610	98.9	136	90.7	0	0.0	149	89.8	904	94.9
Demonst	0	0.0	4	2.7	3	27.3	5	3.0	12	1.2
Lexical	7	1.1	10	6.6	8	72.7	12	7.2	37	3.9
Total	617	100.0	150	100.0	11	100.0	166	100.0	953	100.0

Table 21. Distribution of argument characteristics within patient roles

	Transitive object		Antipassive patient		Passive subject		Total	
	n	%	n	%	n	%	n	%
PERSON								
1/2	88	14.3	0	0.0	40	64.5	131	15.8
3	529	85.7	80	100.0	22	35.5	697	84.2
Total	617	100.0	80	100.0	62	100.0	828	100.0
ANIMACY								
Animate	128	21.1	17	22.1	51	85.0	206	25.5
Inanimate	478	78.9	60	77.9	9	15.0	601	74.5
Total	606	100.0	77	100.0	60	100.0	807	100.0
RECENCY								
Non-new	440	73.0	38	53.5	55	91.7	583	73.1
New	163	27.0	33	46.5	5	8.3	215	26.9
Total	603	100.0	71	100.0	60	100.0	798	100.0
FORM								
Affixal	431	69.9	0	0.0	53	85.5	553	66.8
Demonst	149	24.1	18	22.5	4	6.5	171	20.7
Lexical	37	6.0	62	77.5	5	8.0	104	12.5
Total	617	100.0	80	100.0	62	100.0	828	100.0

possible agent positions, with the passive agentive role filled exclusively by third person forms. All four agent positions are filled almost exclusively by animate and non-new referents; most of the inanimate agents appear in the subject position of noun incorporation clauses.

Complementary patterns are found in the distribution of patients across the three argument structure types. The O role, as already noted, tends to be filled with third person, inanimate, non-new referents, though about 20% of O positions are filled by the alternative option in each case. Most of the passive subjects are first and second person, animate, non-new patients. Antipassive patients are exclusively third person and mostly inanimate.

While it is undoubtedly true that a number of factors affect the distribution of agents and patients across these four clause types in Inuktitut, the animacy hierarchy certainly seems to be one of these factors. Almost all the agents in this data set are human, so violations of inanimates ranked above animates is not an issue. The main shifting patterns, then, seem to follow the distribution of person. Third person agents almost never appear in the A role, but rather in the less highly ranked Si or

Obl roles, as subject of antipassive or noun incorporation clauses, or in the agentive phrase of passive clauses. First and second person patients which would outrank third person agents almost all appear in the passive subject position, so that they are in a higher position (Si) than the agents which are demoted to Obl.

Summary
Since the use of detransitivizing processes is so frequent in Inuktitut, at least partly in order to avoid violations of the animacy hierarchy, there are less transitive clauses in Inuktitut than there might be in other languages which do not use detransitivization processes so frequently. It would be most interesting to investigate the use of detransitivizing processes in Sakapulteko, Yup'ik and Korean for purposes of comparison with the Inuktitut data.[24]

Conclusion

This paper has explored the distribution of arguments across grammatical roles with respect to their morphological form and degree of recency of mention in spontaneous speech data from four Inuit children aged 2;0 through 3;6. The investigation detailed herein reveals that these children uniformly follow the statistical patterns of Preferred Argument Structure described by Du Bois (1985, 1987). Thus, Inuit children produce maximally one lexical and/or new argument per clause, and tend not to place lexical or new arguments in the A role. In fact, the factors of morphological form and recency of mention are not independent, since arguments are more likely to be represented as lexical when they denote new referents. In addition, the ergative pattern of information flow found by Du Bois is replicated in these Inuktitut data.

Two main issues of interest arise in contrasting the Inuktitut data with data from Sakapulteko (Du Bois 1987), Yup'ik (Rubino 1996), and Korean (Clancy this volume). First, the Inuktitut data show a much lower percentage of lexical forms than do data from the other languages. Several reasons for this are explored, including the type of data investigated and the resulting information pressure, the relative grammatical complexity of the language of the subjects, the relative role of demonstratives across these languages, and the role played by the presence of verbal cross-referencing affixes. Each of these factors seems to contribute to the relatively low number of lexical forms in Inuktitut.

Second, the Inuktitut data show a lower percentage of transitive clauses than do data for the other languages. The difference in type of data investigated is likely one contributor to this discrepancy. Another main contributor is the frequent use of detransitivizing processes in Inuktitut (passive, antipassive, noun incorporation). Further investigation of the latter reveals that the animacy hierarchy has an important role in Inuktitut in determining the distribution of agents and patients across clause types that allow expression of both these referents. Since third person referents and inanimate referents almost never appear in the A role, the use of detransitivizing processes serves in part to accommodate placement of third person and inanimate agents, especially in combination with first or second person animate patients.

The data presented here add information to the growing body of research on Preferred Argument Structure from an age range of subjects and a language family which have had relatively little treatment with respect to Preferred Argument Structure.

Notes

* We wish to thank Pat Clancy, Jack Du Bois, Michael Fortescue, Lorraine Kumpf, Marianne Mithun, Carl Rubino, and Tony Woodbury for helpful comments and discussions on an earlier version of this paper. Data collection for this study was funded by grants from the Kativik School Board and the Social Sciences and Humanities Research Council of Canada, for which we are most grateful. Our greatest debt is to the subjects of this study and their families for allowing themselves to be videotaped, and to the many Inuit who patiently transcribed and checked and discussed the data.

1. Terminology used is as follows. The term *referent* is used to denote the object in the real world that is being represented linguistically. The term *referring expression* is used to denote the nominal expression that is used to represent the referent linguistically. The term *argument* is used to denote that referring expression which is required by any given verb as a subject or object of that verb.

2. The term *verbal cross-referencing affix* is used here to denote the affix on the verb which indicates information about the subject and object of the verb. This affix has been called "verbal inflection", "verbal agreement" and "pronominal argument" among other things, depending on the theoretical persuasion of the writer. One issue relevant to appropriate terminology is whether the verbal cross-referencing affix is actually the argument itself, with independent (lexical, demonstrative or pronominal) representations of the relevant referent serving as adjuncts, or whether the verbal cross-referencing affix is really an agreement marker, while independent representations of the relevant referent are the true arguments. This issue has not been resolved for Inuktitut, and thus a relatively neutral terminology is used here.

3. The following grammatical abbreviations are used in glosses:
Nominal case: ABS=absolutive; ALL = allative; CTM = contemporative; ERG = ergative; ICM = incontemporative; LOC = locative; MOD = modalis; VIA = vialis.
Verbal modality: CSV = causative; IMP = imperative; IND = indicative; INT = interrogative; PAR = participial (functionally equivalent to indicative in Tarramiut).
Word-internal morphology: ATP = antipassive; CAUS = causative; DIM = diminutive; EMPH = emphatic; FUT = future; INCP = inceptive aspect; NEG = negative; PASS = passive; PAST = past; POL = politeness (preceding imperative); PRSP = prospective aspect; SW.REF = switch reference.
Verbal inflection (e.g. PAR.3sS): 1 = first person; 2 = second person; 3 = third person; s=singular; p=plural; S=subject; O=object
Nominal inflection (e.g. ABS.SG): SG=singular
Possessed nominal inflection (e.g. ERG.3S.SG): 1 = first person possessor; 2 = second person possessor; 3 = third person possessor; S = singular possessor; SG = singular possessum; PL = plural possessum.

4. Attributions for each example give the name of the subject who produced the utterance cited and their age in the format years;months (rounded to the closest month). Attributions for adults do not include age information.

5. Frequent use of first and second person pronouns in argument position has been observed in one specifically language impaired Inuktitut-speaking child aged 5;0 (Crago & Allen 1996). Her family found this practise so unusual that they nicknamed her *ivvit-uvangaraapik* 'cute little I-you'.

6. Note that Yup'ik does permit use of first and second person pronouns in argument position (Jacobsen 1984).

7. These and all other names used in this chapter are pseudonyms used to protect the identity of the subjects.

8. Note that clauses whose main verbal component is a word which begins with a verbal root but ends as a nominalized construction were not included in the analysis.

9. Inuktitut has a large number of predicative verbs, such as *angi-* 'be big' and *kavaq-* 'be sad'. Clauses containing these verbs were treated as intransitives rather than equationals, since they share the same structure as intransitives in Inuktitut.

10. Of these, 282 intransitive (17%), 159 transitive (26%), and 11 equational clauses (7%) were missing either a verb root or cross-referencing affix or both.

11. Each clause was also coded for clause type, including simple active, complex active, passive, antipassive, causative, and noun incorporation. Results differing by clause type are not discussed in detail in this paper since numbers of some clause types are too small to reach any sound conclusions. In general, however, results for all clause types taken together did not differ substantially from those for only simple active clauses.

12. Note that Du Bois (1987) limited the category *new* only to referring expressions mentioned for the first time in the narrative. He considered all referring expressions mentioned more than 20 utterances previously in the narrative as accessible, and grouped them for analysis with the given referring expressions. However, he also noted that very few referring expressions fell into the accessible category. While this classification seemed appropriate for time limited adult narratives, it seemed too free for child spontaneous speech occurring in chunks of up to two hours. Therefore, we defined 20 utterances as the cutoff point between new and non-new for our data.

13. Clancy gives separate figures for each of the two children in her study; we represent both figures rather than averaging them.

14. The total number of clauses analyzed for this and several subsequent tables is slightly smaller than the total number of clauses overall since clauses which contain arguments which are not identifiable for the feature being analyzed are omitted from the analysis.

15. Note that there are no affixal obliques, since obliques are not marked in the verbal cross-referencing affix, and since we conservatively did not code any obliques which were not phonetically overt, even when they were indicated by the argument structure of the clause (e.g., patient of antipassive, agent of passive, second object of causative or double object construction).

16. Totals for A and O in this table differ slightly from totals in Table 7 since some instances occurred in which either A or O was not identifiable as to recency of mention. For instance, we did not code for recency of mention for WH-question words in such utterances as the equivalent of *Who ate the cake?* For a clause to appear in Table 7, both arguments had to be identifiable in this regard.

17. Preliminary results of eliciting narratives based on picture books in Inuktitut show this to be true. Children age 8 use a significantly higher proportion of lexical NPs in telling the frog story (Mayer 1969) than do the present children, age 2;0–3;6, in spontaneous speech. This effect seems to be primarily a result of modality of talk, and not of age difference.

18. The increase in use of lexical forms by group is much larger for referring expressions which represent new referents (12.4% in group 1 vs. 32.5% in group 3), inanimate referents (4.1% vs. 24.9%), and third person referents (6.3% vs. 28.3%) (Allen 1998).

19. On the other hand, it is worth noting that some 93% of demonstrative arguments used in the child Inuktitut data are ones which denote a relatively close and static referent. In these data, then, the children are not making use of the wide variety of possible demonstratives available in their language, partly because they are mostly talking about referents that are close by and partly because they have not yet learned the full range of demonstrative options available. This evidence may be taken to indicate that demonstratives do not give any more information than pronouns for these children, and thus should be treated as pronominals in analysis of Preferred Argument Structure constraints.

20. Patricia Clancy (personal communication) suggests that there may be various other reasons for the higher rate of lexical A's in Korean than in Inuktitut. She notes that one of her subjects frequently imitated adult utterances and tended to preserve lexical subjects even when they had just been mentioned. Additionally, she notes that contrast was common with agents since many of them were making clear who would get to perform some desired action, etc. It would clearly be fruitful to compare Inuktitut and Korean data in more detail, taking such factors into account. Note that none of the Inuktitut-speaking children in this study referred to themselves in the third person, as often happens with English-speaking children, and as was the case with Clancy's childrens' contrasts.

21. See Allen (1996) for a detailed discussion of the acquisition of passives and noun incorporation in Inuktitut.

22. Note that only antipassive obliques which are phonetically overt are included in the counts in this paper. This includes 80 of the 150 total antipassive clauses in the data set.

23. Patricia Clancy (personal communication) points out two counterexamples to this claim for Korean (and Japanese). First, as already mentioned above, Korean children often use their own name rather than a first person pronoun in situations of contrast. Second, Korean (and Japanese) children and adults typically use kin terms for self-reference to family members of lower status (e.g. *mommy* instead of *I*), and use the child's name (children use the adult's kin term) for second person reference (e.g. *Hyenswu* or *mommy* instead of *you*). Indeed, Clancy notes that first and especially second person pronouns can only be used in specific social contexts and/or relationships in both Korean and Japanese.

24. One might expect the frequency of detransitivizing processes to be the same in Yup'ik and Inuktitut since both are Eskimo-Aleut languages. However, Tony Woodbury (personal communication) reports that Yup'ik does not have as high a frequency of use of detransitivizing processes as in these Inuktitut data, and that passive constructions are rarely used in Yup'ik though they are possible syntactically.

References

Allen, Shanley E.M. 1996. *Aspects of Argument Structure Acquisition in Inuktitut.* Amsterdam: Benjamins.

Allen, Shanley E.M. 1998. "Learning about argument realization in Inuktitut and English: Gradual development in the use of non-ellipsed forms." Paper presented at the Workshop on Cross-linguistic Perspectives on Argument Structure: Implications for Learnability, Max Planck Institute for Psycholinguistics, Nijmegen, Netherlands.

Ariel, Mira. 1990. *Accessing NP Antecedents.* London: Routledge.
Bentivoglio, Paola. 1996. "Acquisition of Preferred Argument Structure in Venezuelan Spanish." Paper presented at the Seventh International Congress for the Study of Child Language, Istanbul, Turkey.
Brown, Roger. 1973. *A First Language.* Cambridge, MA: Harvard University Press.
Chafe, Wallace L. 1976. "Givenness, contrastiveness, definiteness, subjects, topics and point of view." In C.N. Li (ed.), *Subject and Topic.* New York: Academic Press, 25–55.
Chafe, Wallace L. 1987. "Cognitive constraints on information flow." In R. Tomlin (ed.), *Coherence and Grounding in Discourse.* Amsterdam: Benjamins, 21–51.
Clancy, Patricia. 1980. "Referential choice in English and Japanese narrative discourse." In W.L. Chafe (ed.), *The Pear Stories: Cognitive, Cultural, and Linguistic Aspects of Narrative Production.* Norwood, NJ: Ablex, 127–202.
Clancy, Patricia. 1993. "Preferred argument structure in Korean acquisition." In E.V. Clark (ed.), *Proceedings of the 25th Annual Child Language Research Forum.* Stanford, CA: CSLI, 307–314.
Clancy, Patricia. 1995. "Subject and object in Korean acquisition: Surface expression and case-marking." In S. Kuno, I.-H. Lee, J. Whitman, J. Maling, Y.-S. Kang and Y. Kim (eds), *Harvard Studies in Korean Linguistics*, VI, 3–17.
Clancy, Patricia. 1996. "Referential strategies and the co-construction of argument structure in Korean acquisition." In B. Fox (ed.), *Studies in Anaphora.* Amsterdam: Benjamins, 33–68.
Clancy, Patricia. 1997. "Discourse motivations of referential choice in Korean acquisition." In H. Sohn and J. Haig (eds), *Japanese/Korean Linguistics* 6. Stanford: CSLI Publications, 639–659.
Clancy, Patricia. This volume. "The lexicon in interaction: Developmental origins of Preferred Argument Structure in Korean." In J.W. Du Bois, L.E. Kumpf and W.J. Ashby (eds), *Preferred Argument Structure: Grammar as Architecture for Function.* Amsterdam: Benjamins.
Comrie, Bernard. 1989. *Language Universals and Linguistic Typology* (2nd edition). Chicago: University of Chicago Press.
Crago, Martha B. and Allen, Shanley E.M. 1996. "Building the case for impairment in linguistic representation." In M.L. Rice (ed.), *Toward a Genetics of Language.* Mahwah, NJ: Erlbaum, 261–289.
Dixon, Robert M.W. 1979. "Ergativity." *Language* 55: 59–183.
Du Bois, John W. 1985. "Competing motivations." In J. Haiman (ed.), *Iconicity in Syntax.* Amsterdam: Benjamins, 343–365.
Du Bois, John W. 1987. "The discourse basis of ergativity." *Language* 63: 805–855.
Givón, Talmy. 1983. "Introduction." In T. Givón (ed.), *Topic Continuity in Discourse: A Quantitative Cross-language study.* Amsterdam: Benjamins, 1–41.
Jacobsen, Steven A. 1984. *Yup'ik Eskimo Dictionary.* Fairbanks, AK: Alaska Native Language Center.
Kumpf, Lorraine E. 1992. "Preferred argument structure in second language discourse: A preliminary study." *Studies in Language* 16: 369–403.
Li, Charles and Thompson, Sandra. 1979. "Pronouns and zero-anaphora in Chinese discourse." In T. Givón (ed.), *Discourse and Syntax.* New York: Academic Press, 311–335.
MacWhinney, Brian and Snow, Catherine. 1990. "The Child Language Data Exchange System: An update." *Journal of Child Language* 17: 457–472.
Mayer, Mercer. 1969. *Frog, Where Are You?* New York: Penguin.
Mithun, Marianne. 1984. "The evolution of noun incorporation." *Language* 60: 847–893.
Rubino, Carl. 1996. "The introduction of new information and Preferred Argument Structure in Central Alaskan Yup'ik narratives." In M. Mithun (ed.), *Santa Barbara Papers in Linguistics Volume 7: Prosody, Grammar, and Discourse in Central Alaskan Yup'ik.* Santa Barbara: Linguistics Department, University of California at Santa Barbara, 139–153.

Swift, Mary D. and and Allen, Shanley E M. 2002a. "Contexts of verbal inflection dropping in Inuktitut child speech." In B. Skarabela, S. A. Fish & A. H.-J. Do (eds.), *Proceedings of the 26th Annual Boston University Conference on Language Development*. Somerville, MA: Cascadilla Press, 689–700.

Swift, M. D. & Allen, S. E. M. 2002b. "Verb base ellipsis in Inuktitut conversational discourse." *International Journal of American Linguistics* 68: 133–156.

The role of Preferred Argument Structure for understanding aphasic sentence planning*

Susan E. Kohn and Ana Cragnolino

Introduction

Over the past several decades, researchers have increasingly focused on the performance of aphasic speakers (i.e., adults with neurologically-induced language deficits) as a window into the intact language processing system. Neurological damage, particularly following stroke, allows one to examine the language processing system when specific components are no longer functioning properly. By determining the ways in which particular language components fail, one can then deduce structural and functional properties of the intact system.

The use of pronouns is one such example. Aphasic speakers classified as *agrammatic* tend to omit and substitute free-standing grammatical morphemes (e.g., pronouns, determiners, auxiliaries), as well as inflections (Caramazza and Berndt, 1985; Schwartz, Fink and Saffran 1995). In a recent study (Kohn, Cragnolino, and Pustejovksy 1996), we used the normal pattern of performance on a Sentence Generation task to examine pronoun production in a group of agrammatic aphasics. The purpose for this study was to further understand the nature of the aphasics' sentence production difficulty. However, as will be seen below, the normal pattern of performance, in conjunction with the ways that aphasic speakers depart from the normal pattern, has implications for understanding basic properties of the intact sentence planning system.

In the Kohn et al. (1996) study, sentence production was examined with a task that presents single transitive verbs in an uninflected form for the construction of isolated sentences. Normal speakers typically produced pronouns in subject position and produced noun phrases (NPs) with specific semantic content in direct object (DO) position, as in the following examples (target words are capitalized):

I BORROW sugar from my neighbor.
Please BORROW the book.

I plan to DECORATE my living room.
I DECORATED my house last year.
We are going to DECORATE the tree.

This distribution of NP types permitted us to identify three abnormal patterns of pronoun use in the agrammatic speakers: (a) greater than normal pronoun production, signaling word-finding difficulty; (b) moderate pronoun avoidance, associated with the substitution of "general nouns" (e.g., 'woman,' 'person'); and (c) severe pronoun avoidance, associated with the substitution of semantically specific NPs (e.g., 'teacher').

While this study was based on sentences produced in isolation, and without the typical kinds of discourse constraints, it was argued that the normal pattern could be seen as consistent with a long tradition in linguistics that argues for semantic asymmetries between subject and object NPs. Such work suggests tighter semantic ties between verbs and their DOs than verbs and their subjects (Marantz 1984, Sapir 1921). The current study was motivated by the surface similarities between the normal pattern of lexicalization on our Sentence Generation test and the theory of Preferred Argument Structure (Du Bois 1987). Because this functional theory of linguistics focuses explicitly on the flow of information across the arguments of an utterance, it seemed particularly well-suited for guiding further examination of the normal Sentence Generation data, and for leading to better understanding of the aphasic data. The tendency for normal speakers to select pronominal subjects and semantically specific DOs when planning a transitive sentence out of context conforms to the two basic constraints of the theory:

(1) *One Lexical Argument Constraint*: Avoid more than one lexical argument per clause.[1]
(2) *Non-lexical A Constraint*: Avoid lexical A's.[2]

The conformity of the normal Sentence Generation data with the constraints of Preferred Argument Structure has potential implications for models of sentence planning. Preferred Argument Structure evolved largely from observations about discourse, such as narrations of the *Pear Tree* film (Chafe 1980), across a variety of different languages. The constraints have been viewed as reflecting universal properties of discourse in relation to grammar. By our finding similar patterns in a set of isolated sentences, it appears that the Preferred Argument Structure constraints apply even when there are virtually no prior discourse or other contextual conditions. One could argue, then, that these constraints are somehow built into the language processing system at an early stage of sentence planning. The potentially rudimentary nature of Preferred Argument Structure is supported by recent data that show that the basic tenets of Preferred Argument Structure appear to constrain the speech of autistic children (Weber, this volume) and patterns of language acquisition in Korean speakers (Clancy, this volume). Thus the constraints of Preferred Argument Structure may not only capture universal properties of language, but may operate in real time as a component of the language processing system.

This reasoning prompted the current study, which represents a more systematic analysis of the extent to which the sentences of normal and aphasic speakers adhere to the constraints of Preferred Argument Structure. We again used the Sentence Generation task, but now with a larger number of subjects than examined in our earlier study on pronoun production (Kohn et al., 1996). The number of control subjects was increased from 20 to 30, and the number of aphasic subjects was increased from 9 to 13, now including some fluent, as well as nonfluent agrammatic, aphasics.

The approach taken for analyzing the data with respect to Preferred Argument Structure constraints was influenced by the patterns of pronoun substitution in the aphasic performance observed in the prior study, as mentioned above. Patterns of pronoun avoidance took two forms: Substituting what we called *General Nouns* (e.g., 'man,' 'woman,' 'something') and/or substituting *Specific NPs* (see *Methods* for formal definitions). In our earlier study, we had not restricted analysis to transitive sentences. We had also analyzed sentences without DOs if they included a prepositional phrase that functioned as an argument of the verb (e.g., "gaze at the *moon*"). Nevertheless, a majority of the trials elicited transitive constructions, as planned. In order to conduct a cleaner test of Preferred Argument Structure with the present corpus, we restricted analysis to responses that involved transitive constructions, or where the NP following the verb was always a direct object.[3]

Responses were classified into one of nine possible patterns, or templates, based on the type of transitive Subject (A) and Direct Object (O) NP:

A/O:

1. Pronoun/Specific NP
2. Pronoun/Pronoun
3. Pronoun/General Noun
4. General Noun/Specific NP
5. General Noun/Pronoun
6. General Noun/General Noun
7. Specific NP/Specific NP
8. Specific NP/Pronoun
9. Specific NP/General Noun

The first 3 templates preserve Preferred Argument Structure constraints, in that there is no more than one lexical argument and, if present, the lexical argument is in the DO position. The next 3 templates can be viewed as consistent with Preferred Argument Structure constraints, if General Nouns are considered to be acceptable substitution terms for Pronouns (Kohn et al., 1996). The last 3 templates clearly violate Preferred Argument Structure constraints. We analyzed the Sentence Generation performance for the distribution of these templates to determine to what extent the normal and aphasic subjects' performance conformed to Preferred Argument Structure or appeared to be in violation of this linguistic theory of information flow. In this way, we were able to test more precisely to what extent Preferred Argument Structure might capture parameters of early sentence planning and provide insight into aphasic sentence planning deficits.

Methodology

Subjects

Control subjects

Thirty normal, native speakers of English were tested, matched for age and education to the aphasic subjects. There were 20 women and 10 men; all but one were right handed. Subjects' mean age was 61 (SD = 13.8), and mean years of education was 14 (SD = 2).

Aphasic subjects

Thirteen aphasic subjects were tested. There were 8 men and 5 women; all but one were right handed. Subjects' mean age was 60 (SD = 9.2), and mean years of education was 13.4 (SD = 1.8). Each had suffered a single left middle cerebral artery stroke that resulted in a nonfluent, agrammatic aphasia and right hemiparesis in 11 cases and a fluent aphasia in two cases. The speech articulation of the agrammatic aphasics was labored, with some phonetic distortions. At least acutely, their speech displayed classic signs of agrammatism, such as the omission of inflections and free standing grammatical morphemes. See the Appendix for a sample of agrammatic discourse. At the time of experimental testing, the agrammatic aphasic subjects were from 2 to 18 years post onset. In some cases, their conversational speech had evolved to the simple, yet often correct syntactic form associated with "recovered" agrammatism. One fluent aphasic was diagnosed as a conduction aphasic (HB) and the other was a recovered Wernicke's aphasic (TW; see Table 1 for details).

Stimuli and procedures

The Sentence Generation task involved 90 transitive verbs that were presented individually in an uninflected form for constructing a sentence. Only verbs whose word frequency according to Frances and Kucera (1982) was more frequent in the verb than noun reading were selected. So that the verbs represented a range of constraint on noun selection in sentences, they were chosen to equally reflect three

Table 1. Subject background information

Aphasics	Age	Gender	Education	Aphasia Type	Hemiplegia
AF	47	M	13	nonfluent, agrammatic	yes
BM	64	F	16	nonfluent, agrammatic	yes
JW	58	M	12	nonfluent, agrammatic	yes
JS	51	M	12	nonfluent, agrammatic	yes
PJ	56	F	12	nonfluent, agrammatic	yes
FO	62	M	16	nonfluent, agrammatic	yes
GG	51	M	14	nonfluent, agrammatic	yes
PW	45	F	15	nonfluent, agrammatic	yes
GR	66	M	12	nonfluent, agrammatic	yes
AM	62	F	12	nonfluent, agrammatic	yes
LF	79	M	16	nonfluent, agrammatic	yes
HB	65	F	12	Conduction	no
TW	58	M	12	recovered Wernicke's	no
mean	60		13.4		
SD	9.2		1.8		
Controls (10M:20F)					
mean	61		14.0		
SD	13.8		2.0		

levels of selectional restriction on possible nouns in sentences, following methodology described in Kohn and Pustejovsky (1994). This was determined by examining the definitions of verbs in *the Longman Dictionary of Contemporary English* (Procter 1978), which reflect three levels of constraint on arguments: none, minimal, and maximal. Thirty verbs from each level were selected so that the three levels were matched for word frequency and number of syllables.

The procedure for the Sentence Generation task was identical to that employed in Kohn, Lorch, and Pearson (1989). The examiner presented a single verb on a card and read it. The subject was instructed to orally produce a sentence that contained the target word. The examiner trained subjects by first modeling some sample responses to given verbs in which the subject NP was varied among the 3 categories of interest for the original study: pronoun, General Noun, Specific NP (Kohn et al., 1996). An unintended consequence of the training paradigm was that some models violated Preferred Argument Structure constraints. This makes the degree of conformity to Preferred Argument Structure in both the normal and aphasic performance all the more striking (see below). Subjects were encouraged to produce complete sentences. Performance was tape recorded for later transcription.

Results and discussion

Recall that the analysis focused on transitive sentences. In determining the corpus for analysis, we removed performance involving 11 of the original 90 target verbs, which consistently elicited either intransitive constructions or were used typically as nouns. Sentences in which the target verb occurred in the infinitive form were included (see below). If more than one attempt was provided, only the final, complete attempt was considered. The control subjects produced a mean of 51.9/79 (SD = 8.5) transitive sentences (total n = 1558). The aphasic subjects produced a mean of 49.8/79 (SD = 9.8) transitive sentences (total n = 620). These data were examined for the distribution of the 9 templates based on the 3 categories of NP types by grammatical position, as described in the Introduction.

We begin by examining the frequency of sentences produced by the control subjects that conformed to the first template, A: Pronoun/O: Specific NP, as in the following examples:

She KNITS nice sweaters.
I like to ESTABLISH good relationships.
They FORFEITED the game.

These responses represent the most prototypical application of both Preferred Argument Structure constraints, because only one argument is lexical and the lexical argument is located in object position.

Figure 1 displays the relative frequency of sentences that conformed to the template A: Pronoun/O: Specific NP (i.e., the black portion of each vertical bar). The first bar represents the normal mean performance. The region within the dashed horizontal lines represents two standard deviations above and below the normal mean. The remaining bars correspond to the performance of individual aphasic subjects, which will be discussed below. Figure 1 shows that, on average, the control performance conformed to this template reflecting adherence to Preferred Argument Structure 60% of the time. This is rather high, considering that there were 8 other patterns identified.

To assess the Sentence Generation of the aphasic subjects, we considered performance that fell within two SDs of the normal mean as representing "within normal performance". Seven of the 13 aphasic subjects used the A: Pronoun/O: Specific NP template at a rate that fell within the normal range; one aphasic subject actually exceeded the normal tendency (see Figure 1).

Figure 1 also displays the relative proportion of sentences involving the template A: General Noun/O: Specific NP, depicted by the gray portion of each bar. While the normal, control subjects rarely selected a General Noun as a transitive subject, as discussed earlier, it was quite common for certain aphasics. If we consider General Nouns as acceptable alternates to pronouns in this context (see

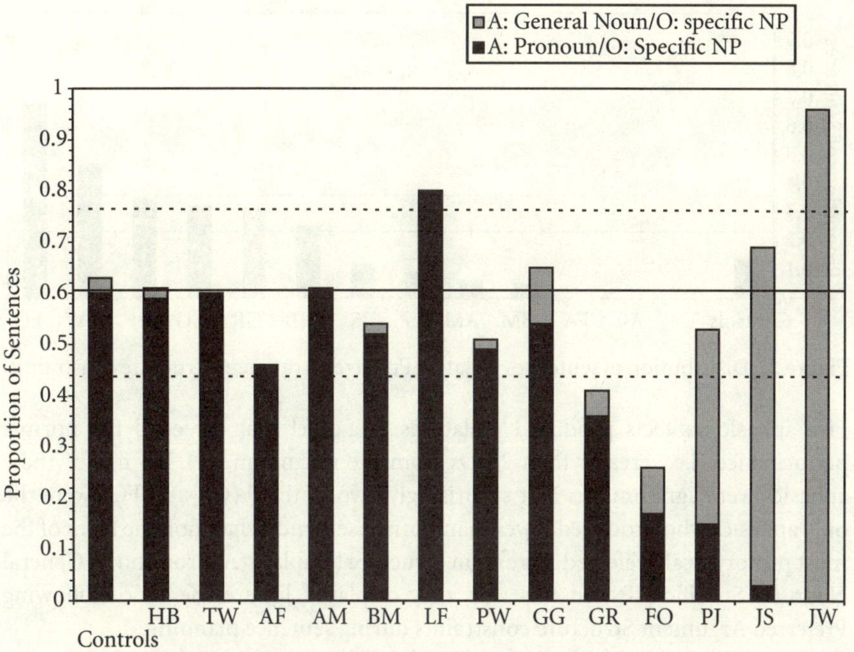

Figure 1. Distribution of sentences conforming to the prototypical Preferred Argument Structure constraints.

introduction), then all but two of the aphasic subjects can be viewed as employing at normal rates the most prototypical sentence template based on Preferred Argument Structure constraints (see Figure 1). Thus despite the presence of grammatical errors in the aphasic performance (which will be focused on below), the normal tendency to "lexicalize" only the direct object, which reflects adherence to the constraints of Preferred Argument Structure, was generally preserved.

To determine which other types of templates were being used, we turn now to the templates that violate Preferred Argument Structure constraints. Recall that there were three of them: A: Specific NP/O: Pronoun, A: Specific NP/O: General Noun, A: Specific NP/O: Specific NP. Collapsing across these 3 templates, the distribution of the frequency of violations is presented in Figure 2. On average, the control subjects violated Preferred Argument Structure constraints only about 13% of the time. The following are some examples:

An analysis of the fingerprints VINDICATED him.
The crowd HECKLED the man.
The teacher DETAINS the students.

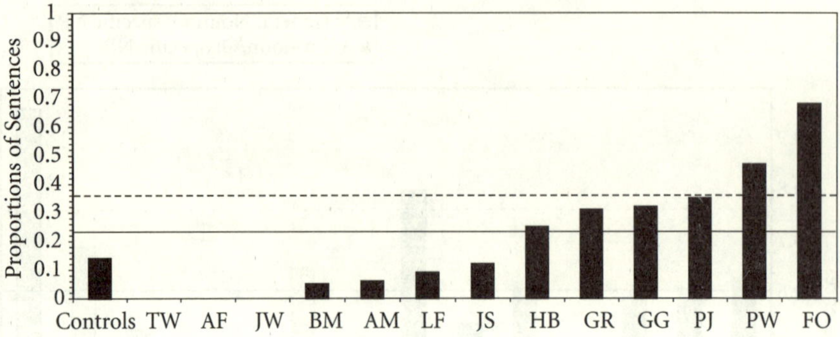

Figure 2. Distribution of sentences violating Preferred Argument Structure constraints.

Five aphasic subjects produced violations at a level that exceeded the normal performance (i.e., greater than 2 SDs from the normal mean). All five of these aphasics were agrammatic. Not surprisingly, two of the 5 (GR and FO) were the only aphasics who produced fewer than normal sentences that took the form of the most prototypical Preferred Argument Structure template (A: Pronoun or General Noun/O: Specific NP). In this way, they displayed little evidence of following Preferred Argument Structure constraints during sentence planning.

The following are typical examples of the sentences with Preferred Argument Structure violations produced by the 5 aphasics with above normal tendency to do so:

FO: Genghis Khan CAPTURE villa.
GG: The sister is CHEATING the test.
PJ: My daughter is DECORATE apartment.
GR: My wife ASSIST me everywhere I go.
PW: The Christmas time the DECORATED the tree.

As displayed in these aphasic examples, Preferred Argument Structure violations often occurred in sentences that contained errors that generally seemed to be of a grammatical nature. This was to be expected, given that these aphasic subjects were tested because of their sentence planning difficulties. In examining the above examples, it is important to recall that analyses were restricted to transitive constructions. In determining whether an anomalous response met this criterion, we considered the surface structure. So, in GG's sentence involving CHEAT (above), the fact that a well-formed sentence would be created by inserting the word 'on' after the verb was not considered. An unambiguous reconstruction was often not possible, especially when one considers that even the target verb is sometimes substituted by these subjects. What if GG had intended to say "The sister is TAKING the test"?

In our earlier Sentence Generation study (Kohn et al., 1996), we had observed that the aphasics who produced the most transitive subjects with Specific NPs produced the most sentences that could be considered "anomalous" (i.e., contained mostly unambiguous syntactic errors, but sometimes possible errors in lexical selection). This association between Specific NP subjects and sentence anomalies was somewhat perplexing. Recall from the Introduction that this study was focusing on patterns of pronoun avoidance, and that some aphasics avoided pronouns as transitive subjects by using Specific NPs, while other aphasics opted for General Nouns. The latter pattern was associated with greater pronoun avoidance, while the former pattern was associated with more anomalous sentences. Thus there was not a direct association between the degree of pronoun avoidance and sentence errors. To understand this pattern, we noted that the aphasics who frequently selected General Nouns as transitive subjects also tended to produce sentences whose structure was quite invariant, or perseverative. Their sentences typically took the form: Det. + General Noun + *is* + Verb-*ing* + Specific NP, as in "The children is disturbing the man." We argued that the use of invariant sentence structures by these aphasics led to fewer errors, because the sentence template served as a strategy for reducing the number of on-line decisions required about sentence structure (cf. Kolk and Heeschen 1990).

The relationship between sentence anomalies and Preferred Argument Structure violations has the potential to add some clarity to this apparent association between the presence of Specific NP subjects and sentence anomalies. It stands to reason that if Preferred Argument Structure constraints reflect basic, early decisions about a sentence plan, then violation of these constraints would be related to a severe breakdown in the sentence planning process. To test this hypothesis, we performed a correlation for all aphasic subjects between their proportion of sentences with Preferred Argument Structure violations and proportion of sentences that were anomalous (again, most errors were unambiguously syntactic). There was a strong correlation between these two measures (Spearman Rank Correlation $r=.681$, $p<.02$; see Figure 3). This finding suggests that when Preferred Argument Structure constraints no longer consistently guide the sentence planning process, there is a reduction in well-formed output. This relationship between anomaly and violations of Preferred Argument Structure, then, supports the proposal that Preferred Argument Structure constraints are driving forces of the early sentence planning system.

We can gain more insight into the way(s) in which Preferred Argument Structure constraints are violated in aphasia, by examining the types of violations produced by the 5 aphasics with an above normal proportion of Preferred Argument Structure violations. For these aphasics, as well as the control subjects, most violations were due to producing sentences of the form A: Specific NP/O: Specific NP, where a lexicalized subject *and* direct object were included (see Figure 4).

There are two possible interpretations of the A: Specific NP/O: Specific NP template with respect to Preferred Argument Structure constraints. To facilitate discussion, the two constraints are repeated below:

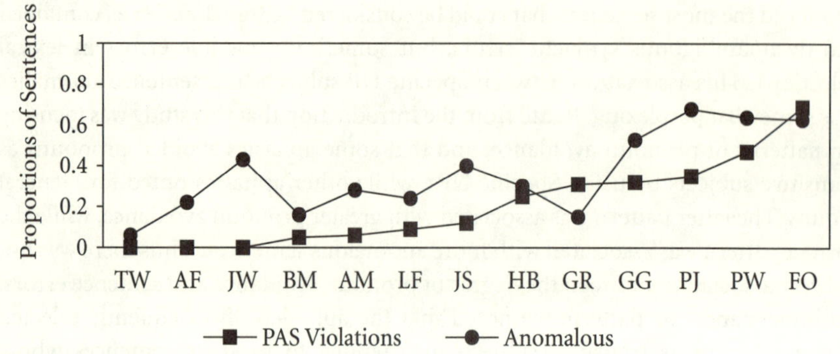

Figure 3. Relationship in the aphasic performance between sentences with anomalous structure and violations of Preferred Argument Structure constraints.

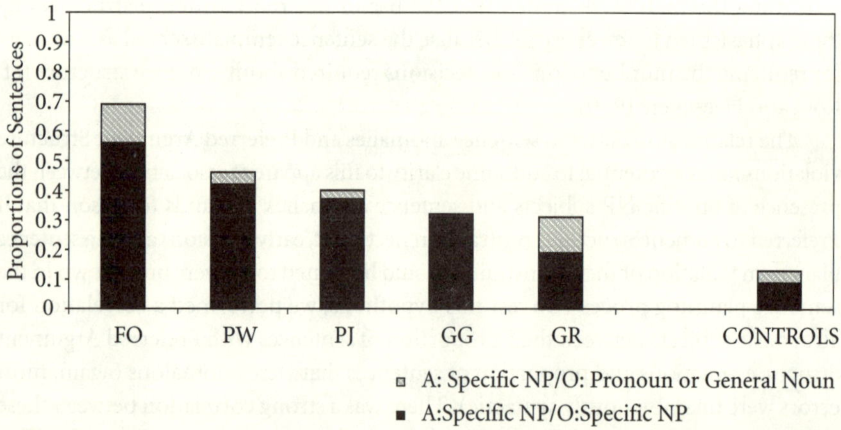

Figure 4. Distribution of sentences according to types of Preferred Argument Structure constraint violation, for aphasic subjects with above-normal proportion of violations.

(1) *One Lexical Argument Constraint*: Avoid more than one lexical argument per clause.

(2) *Non-lexical A Constraint*: Avoid lexical A's.

At first pass, it appears that both constraints are violated with sentences containing both a specific subject and direct object. With this sentence template, there is more than one lexical argument, violating the One Lexical Argument Constraint, and the subject is lexical, violating the Non-lexical A Constraint. However, a different interpretation emerges when a few facts are considered. First, a violation of constraint 1 will subsume a violation of constraint 2, because when the transitive subject and DO are lexical, constraint 2 will also be in violation. By contrast, a violation of constraint 2 alone is possible, reflected by the templates A: Specific NP/O: General Noun and A: Specific NP/O: Pronoun. However, as shown in Figure 4, these templates were rarely used. Given the rarity of sentences that violate only the second constraint, the more conservative interpretation of the aphasic performance involving an above normal proportion of sentences with specific transitive Subjects and DOs is that they reflect violation of constraint 1 only, with a preserved knowledge that the DO is typically lexicalized. This is consistent with the fact that 3 of the 5 aphasic subjects with above normal violations, nevertheless, also employed the templates reflecting adherence to Preferred Argument Structure constraints at normal rates. At a more general level, this interpretation suggests that the constraint to avoid lexical A's is stronger than the constraint to avoid more than one lexical argument, at least when planning sentences out of context.

Conclusions

While the theory of Preferred Argument Structure has been developed to account for lexicalization patterns in discourse, the current study explored the possibility that the constraints of this theory play a role even in decontextualized situations. The simple rules of lexicalization put forth in Preferred Argument Structure could operate as a component of the cognitive system for sentence planning. The constraints could serve as unmarked templates for setting up the basic structure of intended utterances.

The purpose of the current study was to test whether the constraints of Preferred Argument Structure operate at an early level of the cognitive system for planning transitive sentences. A corpus of transitive sentences was created by asking normal and aphasic speakers to produce sentences based on individual, uninflected verbs. Performance was examined for the relative status of the One Lexical Argument and Non-lexical A constraints. Several results support the role of these constraints during the planning of sentences in isolation. First, a majority of the sentences produced by the normal, control speakers conformed to the Preferred Argument Structure constraints. That is, typically only one argument was lexicalized, and this argument tended to involve O's, not A's (i.e., direct objects, not transitive subjects). In addition, most of the aphasic subjects obeyed the constraints within normal limits. Finally, there was a strong association between the degree to which aphasic subjects violated Preferred Argument Structure constraints and their tendency to produce sentence errors that were mainly of a grammatical nature.

An examination of the sentences produced by the 5 aphasics with above normal tendency to violate Preferred Argument Structure constraints suggested that one constraint may be more basic than the other. Sentences that only violated the Non-lexical A constraint were rare, indicating that violations were due to the willingness to produce more than one lexical argument. This led us to suggest that the most basic principle for sentence planning derived from Preferred Argument Structure may be to lexicalize the direct object. To follow up these conclusions, one must now examine to what extent Preferred Argument Structure is preserved in the isolated intransitive sentences of aphasic speakers, as well as explore their adherence to these constraints in discourse context.

Notes

* This paper is based on a presentation given at the conference entitled "Preferred Argument Structure: The Next Generation", at UC, Santa Barbara, May 12–14, 1995. The authors wish to thank Dr. Nancy Hildebrandt for introducing us to Preferred Argument Structure. This study was supported by NIH Grant DC01371.

1. A *lexical* NP is "filled" with a full noun phrase, rather than ellipted (zero) or realized as a pronoun.

2. *A* refers to the subject of a transitive sentence.

3. Note that the current corpus did not present us with the opportunity to examine Preferred Argument Structure constraints in the context of intransitive sentences. The prediction would be that the lexical NPs in the S role (or intransitive subject) would be less constrained than the lexical NPs in the A (or transitive subject) role. As it stands, a transitive-verb-only study cannot distinguish between the merits of the Given A Constraint (Du Bois 1987) versus the Light Subject Constraint (Chafe 1994), since it is compatible with both.

Appendix

Agrammatic Discourse Sample: The Story of Cinderella, as told by Subject PW

The story is Cinderella… the, ah, mother… two sisters, stepsister… and a Cinderella… were all the time… and sit down the… the sisters, ok, sisters, the mother sit down, ok… ok… but… the Cinderella… and a wish… the, the, the, the, ah, ahm, wish, ok, ahm… ok, so… the, the, the, castle… the..is the two sis-, two sisters and the mo-, mother… the Cinderella had no clothes… but surprise… the… the good wi-wi- … witch, ahm… good witch… and the… the, the, wand… and the… cause the Cinder was so… the gown… and the slippers… and the, the, the… coach, and the, the, the, ahm, this, ok, the wand and the Cinderella… the castle… but the deadline… twelve o'clock.,..and run Cinderella to… ready for the curfew… cause change mind… and… fled… the castle… once one the slippers, forgot the slippers… meanwhile, the… ahm same… same Cinderella same thing same housework… the prince.. .whole wide world… to find the slippers… the mother… two sisters… too big… and, ok, very, very important find the slipper the whole wide world… and, ahm, the prince… the… and the … knocked on the door… the… get… the whole, the whole… two, two sisters and find the… that fits… so they happy… see, ah, Cinderella, Cinderella and the prince is far, far away and happy.

References

Caramazza, Alfonso and Berndt, Rita S. 1985. "A multicomponent deficit view of agrammatic Broca's aphasia". In Mary Louise Kean (ed.), *Agrammatism.* NY: Academic Press, 27–63.

Chafe, Wallace (ed.). 1980. *The Pear Stories: Cognitive, Cultural, and Linguistic Aspects of Narrative Production.* Norwood, NJ: Ablex.

Chafe, Wallace. 1994. *Discourse, Consciousness, and Time.* Chicago and London: University of Chicago Press.

Clancy, Patricia M. This volume. "Preferred Argument Structure and the lexicon: some evidence from Korean acquisition".

Du Bois, John. 1987. "The discourse basis of ergativity". *Language,* 63, 805–855.

Francis, W. Nelson and Kucera, Henry. 1982. *Frequency Analysis of English Usage. Lexicon and Grammar.* Boston: Houghton Mifflin Co.

Kohn, Susan E., Lorch, Majorie P., and Pearson, Dawn M. 1989. "Verb finding difficulty in aphasia". *Cortex* 25, 57–70.

Kohn, Susan E., Cragnolino, Ana, and Pustejovsky, James. 1995. "Pronoun production in agrammatic speakers: Patterns of use and avoidance in context neutral sentences". *Aphasiology,* forthcoming.

Kohn, Susan E. and Pustejovsky, James. 1994. *Asymmetries in Semantic Typing for Sentence Generation.* Unpublished manuscript.

Kolk, Herman and Heeschen, Claus. 1990. "Adaptation symptoms and impairment symptoms in Broca's aphasia". *Aphasiology* 4, 221–232.

Marantz, Alec. 1984. *On the Nature of Grammatical Relations.* Cambridge, MA: MIT Press.

Procter, P. 1978. *Longman Dictionary of Contemporary English.* Harlow, UK: Longman.

Sapir, Edward. 1921. *Language. An Introduction to the Study of Speech.* New York: Harcourt, Brace and World, Inc.

Schwartz, Myrna F., Fink, Ruth B., and Saffran, Eleanor M. 1995. "The modular treatment of agrammatism". *Neuropsychological Rehabilitation* 5, 93–127.

Weber, Elizabeth G. This volume. "Nominal information flow in the talk of two boys with a diagnosis of Autism".

Nominal information flow in the talk of two boys with autism

Elizabeth G. Weber
California State University, Northridge

Introduction

This paper examines patterns of information flow (Chafe 1987, 1992, 1993, 1994) exhibited by noun phrases (NP's) in the talk of two brothers who have a diagnosis of autistic disorder. Particular attention will be paid to core arguments of verbs following the hypothesis of Preferred Argument Structure developed by Du Bois (1985, 1987). According to Chafe, information flow involves the way speakers package their message for their recipients. Factors relevant to patterns of information flow include the morphosyntactic shape used to realize new and continuing referents in the talk, the distribution of new and continuing referents across grammatical roles, and the rate at which new information comes into the discourse.

Competent management of information flow in discourse requires speakers to "not only take account of the changing activation states of information in their own minds, but also attempt to appreciate the parallel changes that are taking place in the minds of their listeners" (Chafe 1994: 54). A speaker's belief about activation states in other minds affects the form in which language is produced. Speakers make judgments about what is active and inactive in the listener's consciousness and then linguistically code that information as given or new accordingly. In fact, it is impossible to understand the distinction between given and new information without taking consciousness into account (Chafe 1974, 1976, 1994). This dimension of information flow in discourse makes it especially relevant for study in the population of persons with autism because it has been hypothesized that these persons are deficient in a theory of mind, i.e., it is suggested that they are unable to infer the mental states of others.

The ability of persons with autism to infer the mental states of others has been shown to be deficient on a variety of tasks. Children with autism have been shown to be unable to predict the false beliefs of others (Baron-Cohen, Leslie and Frith

1985, 1986). This type of first-order belief task requires an understanding of the relationship between another person's belief and reality. Children with autism have also been shown to be unable to pass second-order belief tasks which require an understanding of one person's beliefs about another person's beliefs about reality (what someone thinks someone else thinks about something) (Baron-Cohen 1989; Ozonoff, Rogers and Pennington 1991). The theory of mind deficit account of autism suggests that communication, socialization and imagination handicaps of individuals with autism result from their inability to infer the mental states of others (Frith 1989a; Leslie 1987; Leslie and Frith 1988). Tasks which require the listener's thoughts and feelings to be taken into account have been shown to be the most impaired (Frith 1989a, 1989b; Tager-Flusberg 1993, as cited in Frith and Happé 1994).

Given the claims in the literature that theory of mind deficits are central to autism and are reflected in the communication problems of this population, it is relevant to examine the discourse of autistic persons to see if their use of language reveals the same kind of perspective taking difficulties which the experimental research has found to exist. Baltaxe and D'Angiola (1992) examined discourse cohesion in the talk of young normal, specifically language impaired, and autistic children. They found that the children with autism had the lowest frequency of correct use of cohesive ties. Difficulty understanding speaker-hearer presuppositions and differentiating old and new information were suggested as possible explanatory factors for the subjects' problems producing cohesive texts. Fine, Bartolucci, Szatmari, and Ginsberg (1994) also looked at the use of cohesive links in the conversation of children with high-functioning autism, Asperger Syndrome, and children with nonspecific social problems. Individuals with Asperger Syndrome do not experience significant early language delay, but in other respects resemble highly verbal individuals with autism. The authors examined the phoricity of nominal groups and found that the high-functioning autistic subjects used fewer endophoric references than the other two groups. The Asperger group made more unclear references; they coded new information as given, "expecting the listener to add information to the conversation for it to make sense" (p. 324). It was suggested that the Asperger subjects failed to monitor what information was needed by the listener.

Baltaxe (1977) observed that some persons with autism have difficulty distinguishing between new and old information, as reflected in their failure to use anaphora for previously mentioned referents in discourse. Their overuse of full NP's gives the discourse "a sense of pedantic literalness and redundancy" (p. 179).

The literature states, and clinical observation confirms, that the discourse of children with autism may be characterized by tangential, out of context remarks, irrelevant remarks, and abrupt switches of topic without sufficient background information to contextualize the topic (Baltaxe 1977, 1987; Baltaxe and Simmons 1983; Adams and Bishop 1989; Minshew, Goldstein and Siegel 1995; Church and Coplan 1995). These behaviors suggest that the speaker is not taking into account what the listener knows; the speaker does not adapt his/her talk to the listener's needs. Consequently the listener has difficulty interpreting the discourse as coherent.

Few studies of interactional discourse of autistic children and adolescents have been done (Baltaxe and D'Angiola 1992; Sudhalter, Cohen, Silverman and Wolf-Schien 1990; Adams and Bishop, 1989; Bishop and Adams 1989; Landry and Loveland 1989; Oshima-Takane and Benaroya 1989; Fine, 1988; Fine, Bartolucci, Ginsberg and Szatmari 1991; Prizant and Wetherby 1987; Baltaxe and Simmons 1975; Baltaxe 1977). Among these studies, interview, game playing or semi-structured play situations have generally been employed. Adult interviewers or play partners have been involved in the interaction. The discourse genre of this study is a play interaction. The interaction was entirely spontaneous and self-directed by the participants; no adults were involved. The type of self-directed play interaction which constitutes the database for this study has not previously been examined with respect to the discourse of persons with autism.

An examination of how information flow is managed by the boys in this study will add another dimension to our general understanding of the discourse of children with autism. Because discourse analysis of the narratives of family members of high-functioning autistic persons have revealed language disorders, it has been suggested that studying the interactions of highly verbal autistic persons from a discourse perspective might reveal further aspects of their language abnormalities (Landa, Folstein and Isaacs 1991). Specific patterns of use will be examined to see if they add to the disordered quality of the boys' discourse. I will first consider how information is managed across NP's of all grammatical roles, both arguments and nonarguments. Secondly, I will examine whether or not the language in this study conforms to Preferred Argument Structure constraints. Thirdly, I will consider to what extent an examination of nominal information flow and Preferred Argument Structure illuminate the social communication deviance demonstrated in the interaction. Finally, I will consider whether or not the patterns of information flow exhibited by the speakers are explained by theory of mind deficits.

The second goal of this paper is to examine whether or not these data conform to the four constraints of Preferred Argument Structure. The first grammatical constraint is the One Lexical Argument Constraint. This constraint reflects the statistical discourse preference for only one core argument of the verb to be realized by a full lexical NP. The second grammatical constraint is the Nonlexical A Constraint. This reflects the statistical discourse preference for the single lexical NP core argument to be realized as the subject of an intransitive verb (S) or as an object (O), not as the subject of a transitive verb (A).

The first pragmatic constraint is the One New Argument Constraint. This constraint is reflected in the statistical discourse preference for there to be only one new argument in a clause. The second pragmatic constraint is the Given A Constraint. This constraint is reflected in the statistical discourse preference for new information in an argument role to be realized as the subject of an intransitive verb (S) or as an object (O), not as the subject of a transitive verb (A).

The grammatical and pragmatic constraints of Preferred Argument Structure are related insofar as cross-linguistic studies have revealed that there is a strong correlation between NP shape, activation state, and grammatical role. New or previously inactive information tends to be realized by full NP's, while given or currently active information tends to be realized by attenuated forms, e.g., by pronouns.

This paper differs from other work on Preferred Argument Structure in that it looks at talk produced by individuals with a diagnosed disorder associated with language deficits (but see also Kohn, this volume). Fine, Bartolucci, Szatmari, and Ginzberg (1994) suggest that although it is common knowledge that social communication deficits are exhibited when persons with autism talk with others, there is as yet no clear understanding of the mechanism of the breakdown. Because a number of studies of Preferred Argument Structure in English have been published to date, it will be possible to compare the way information flow is managed by speakers with autism to typical speakers. Differences which might exist in the management of information by speakers with autism will be examined with respect to whether or not such differences add to the speakers' communication deficits.

The discourse genre examined in this paper, play interaction, has not been previously studied with respect to Preferred Argument Structure. In addition, the speakers in this study are school-aged children, whereas most previous studies of Preferred Argument Structure in English have looked at the talk of adults (but see Clancy 1993 and this volume). This paper, then, expands the study of Preferred Argument Structure across the dimensions of genre, chronological age and atypical language. When interpreting the results of this study, it should be kept in mind that Preferred Argument Structure may differ markedly from one discourse genre to another, as well as among different parts of an instance of any discourse genre (Kärkkäinen 1996; O'Dowd 1990). Since language used in play among English-speaking middle class school-aged children has not been previously examined with respect to Preferred Argument Structure, we cannot be sure to what extent the results of this study reflect the constraints of the discourse genre versus language use characteristic of children with autism.

Data

The database for this study is a completely spontaneous play interaction between two brothers videotaping themselves making a movie. There are no adults involved in the situation. Glen is the younger brother and was 9 years old when the videotape was made in January of 1994. To the extent that we can generalize, we can say that Glen's language performance and other behaviors are typical for highly verbal children with a diagnosis of autism. Evan is the elder brother and was almost 11 years old when the videotape was made. He presents as more language/learning disabled than autistic with respect to both his language and interactions. Evan has a history of astrocytomas or brain tumors and has had several brain surgeries. He exhibits some neurological symptoms as a result of this. His word finding problems and dysfluencies have undoubtedly been increased as a result of his medical condition. Both boys have scored within the range of average on cognitive tests.

Speech and language deficits associated with the syndrome of autism

Autism is an organic brain disorder which significantly affects thinking, behavior and language (Rimland 1964; Rutter 1978; Rutter and Schopler 1987; Coe and Matson 1989; American Psychiatric Association 1980). The *Diagnostic and Statistical Manual of Mental Disorders*, fourth edition's (DSM-IV; American Psychiatric Association 1994) criteria for a diagnosis of autism include three categories in which deficits must be manifested: social interaction, communication, and restricted, repetitive and stereotyped patterns of behavior, interests and activities. Note that language deficits are criterial for a diagnosis of autism. Persons with autism relate to others atypically. It has been hypothesized that a deficit in social interaction itself leads to the communication and behavior disorders associated with autism. Koegel, Valdez-Menchaca, and Kogel (1993: 166) state that "impairment in the use and processing of social stimulation may constitute the common lone characteristic of autism" with the interaction between degree of social impairment and other abilities, including cognitive level, accounting for the wide range of variation found among individuals with the disorder. Young children with autism do not play spontaneously with others (Lord and Hopkins 1986; Howlin 1986; McHale 1983; Strain and Cooke 1976; Hingston and Trost 1966) and fail to develop friendships as they grow older (Mesibov 1992; McHale 1983; Wing 1983; Rumsey). Their limited social experience further disadvantages children and adolescents with autism insofar as they do not have the opportunity to learn the social conventions of their speech communities in the course of ordinary, everyday interaction.

Within the deficit category of communication, children with autism may be mute or very delayed in acquiring spoken language; they do not employ compensating communicative gesture to the extent typically-developing children do. Among individuals with good phonology and morphosyntax, there is difficulty initiating or sustaining a conversation with others. Language may be stereotyped, repetitive or idiosyncratic. There is a lack of varied, spontaneous make-believe play or social imitative play appropriate to developmental level.

Although so-called high-functioning autistic children may have fluent speech after the preschool years, they are reported to exhibit difficulties with the social use of language. They often produce irrelevant or out-of-context comments, and are uncommunicative and repetitive in conversation (Garfin and Lord 1986; Lord and O'Neill 1983; Szatmari, Bartolucci and Bremmer 1989; Szatmari, Bremmer and Nagy 1989). Problems with communication among this population may be based in part on a variety of language and social communication deficits, including semantic paraphasias such as are reported for aphasics, poor syntax, word finding problems, echolalia, processing delays, oddities of word choice and phrasing, abnormalities in prosody, difficulty interpreting complex or abstract and metaphoric language including humor, problems with turn taking, difficulty maintaining topics, inadequate repair initiation, inadequate responses to requests for clarification, restriction of language content to a narrow range of interests, and difficulty taking the appropriate speaker or listener role in conversation with respect to managing information (Baltaxe 1977, 1987; Baltaxe and Simmons 1983; Adams and Bishop 1989; Minshew, Goldstein, and Siegel 1995; Church and Coplan 1995).

The language competence of the subjects of this study is relatively high, although their productions are characterized by significant phonological, morphosyntactic and semantic deficits, as well as problems with fluent language production and the social use of language. In the following section, examples of disordered productions will be given across these different parts of language. It should be noted, however, that none of the following examples by itself makes a person's language disordered. In fact, many of the difficulties exemplified may be found in typical language. A diagnosis of expressive language disorder requires the frequent production of such problematic productions to the extent that there is "a significant deficit relative to environmental expectations" (Paul 1995: 4). In addition, according to the *Diagnostic and Statistical Manual of Mental Disorders*, fourth edition (DSM-IV; American Psychiatric Association 1994) and the International Code of Diseases (ICD-10; World Health Organization 1992), a diagnosis of child language disorder must also be based on below average performance on standardized language tests. It should also be noted that the examples demonstrating morphosyntactic problems, formulation problems, and fluency problems are not only typical of the language productions of persons with autism; rather, these types of problematic forms can be found across the language productions of a variety of diagnostic populations. The examples exhibiting problems in the social use of language, however, are more typically associated with the interactions of persons with autism. The word finding problems of the boys are also demonstrated in these examples.

These examples are taken from a play interaction in which the boys are making a movie in which they are in a ship at sea. The data have been transcribed according to the conventions of Du Bois, Schuetze-Coburn, Paolino, and Cumming (1992). Examples (1) through (3) demonstrate morphosyntactic errors.

(1) GLEN: u=h.\
Well I've got a ⟨F whopper F⟩ here.\

EVAN: Whop- —
Oh,_
how big.\ ((STRUMMING UKELELE))
→ GLEN: **About a size of two 'fishies,**
Come on,_
help me [pull it],_

In this example, Glen uses an indefinite article in place of the required definite article. NOTE: The indefinite article is clearly hearable as [ʌ], not as a flap [D].

In example (2), Glen exhibits the incorrect use of a preposition, substituting the preposition *in* for *for* in the intended phrase *for lunch.*

(2) GLEN: Oh._
Hm.\
→ **Well I'm still fishing.. in lunch,_**

Example (3) demonstrates difficulty with verb forms.

(3) GLEN: That landlubber —
lubber ha- —
→ **... hasn't 〈F came F〉 .. yet,_**

In this example, Glen is not able to produce the past participial form of the verb *come.*

Semantic deficits are typically associated with the language of children with autism. In the following, Glen does not correctly interpret the meaning of *too fast* in the emergent interaction.

(4) EVAN: Whoa whoa whoa!_
GLEN: 〈F Oh watch out F〉,_
〈F Ooh ooh ouch jeez ow ooh ooh F〉!_
EVAN: What's wro=ng,_
Going too fast,_
GLEN: No.\
→ **We 〈MRC went full blast MRC〉._**
EVAN: That's what .. I .. asked .. wh- —
That's what too fast i=s!_

This example demonstrates that Glen has semantic problems insofar as he lacked the semantic flexibility to recognize the similarity of meaning between *going too fast* and *going full blast.*

In example (5), Glen's use of *just* in the phrase *sailing off just for a long time* reveals subtle incompetence. The use of the word *just* in the frame *just for a* followed by a temporal term conveys the interpretation of a limited period of time, for example *I fell asleep just for a minute,* or *I studied abroad just for a year.* The use of the temporal term *for a long time* is not compatible with the limiting meaning of *just.*

(5)	GLEN:	We're gonna be —
	EVAN:	Hey.\
→	GLEN:	**... sailing off,**
→		**⟨X just for a long time X⟩.**

In the following, Glen's use of the verb *heard* in connection with a newspaper is semantically anomalous.

(6)	GLEN:	**I heard that in the newspaper this morning.**

Persons with autism typically demonstrate deficits with the social use of language. Examples (7), (8), and (9) all exhibit instances of a nonrelevant response to a prior utterance.

(7)	EVAN:	⟨MRC Guess what MRC⟩.\
→	GLEN:	**Me matey.**
→		**⟨%Come on in%⟩.**
(8)	GLEN:	Oh .. by the way,_
		don't [⟨F forget a solar-powered phone F⟩,_
	EVAN:	[Here .. here's a fishing pole].\ (COUGHING)
	GLEN:	Don't forget the solar-powered phone,_
→	EVAN:	**Here's a —**
	GLEN:	Here's what.\
→	EVAN:	**A fishing pole.\\ (COUGHING)**
(9)	EVAN:	.. where were you born.\
→	GLEN:	**...(7.4) Lookit.**
		((MAKES RINGING SOUNDS PLAYING TELEPHONE))

Example (10) demonstrates nonresponsiveness to a prior utterance.

(10)	EVAN:	Do you hear my guitar?/
		...(4.5) Do you hear my guitar?/
		...(9.4) Did you hear my guitar?/
		...(2.5) While you were all the way over the .. wa- um,_
		... do you hear% .. hear my guitar?/
	GLEN:	Uh yes,_
		I did.\

In example (11), Evan attempts to initiate a new imaginative theme pertaining to the story world of the play situation. Glen responds with a next turn repair initiator (Schegloff, Jefferson and Sacks 1977), attempting to clarify the referent of *father*. Although in the story world Glen and Evan do not have the same father, Glen appears to interpret Evan's remarks as referring to their real father. Glen is unable to interpret Evan's reference as relevant to the story world.

(11) EVAN: ⟨P Maui P⟩.\
Wait a minute.\
My father was born there.\
My father was born there.\
→ GLEN: **Father was?/**
EVAN: Yeah,_
my father,_

Glen's syntactic reformulation in example (12) is evidence of his problem with language formulation, i. e., expressing his communicative intent in a timely, fluent way.

(12) GLEN: ((MAKES PHONE RINGING NOISE 2X))
Hello,_
...Yes.\
...Okay.\
...I'll get there right this minute.\
→ **Says the I'm- —**
→ **... (2.0) they're still marooned —**
... ⟨X marooned X⟩ on the .. island.\

In addition to the types of deficit exemplified above, the speakers' talk was characterized by perseveration on themes and a lack of focus on story world participants versus nonhuman elements, e. g., islands. Perseveration on themes is characteristic of the language of some children with autism. They sometimes have a limited repertoire of topics about which they will talk and they may obsess on these topics. It has also been noted that children with autism show more interest in objects than persons (Kanner 1943). This has been observed in the earliest stages of development in which these children prefer to play with objects rather than with other children. This interest in objects over people is exhibited in older children in their topics of conversation. They may perseverate on a narrow range of inanimate topics (maps, flags, weather, addresses, birthdays, insects).

Methodology

The data consist of 485 intelligible NP's produced during a thirty minute spontaneous play interaction. A small number of partially unintelligible NP's were excluded from the data. NP's were coded for syntactic, pragmatic and semantic factors, including grammatical roles, morphosyntactic shape, activation state, and animacy (Chafe 1987, 1993, 1994; Du Bois 1980, 1985, 1987; Du Bois and Thompson 1991; Thompson 1997; Dutra 1987; Bentivoglio 1989; Ashby and Bentivoglio 1993). These factors were chosen to illuminate the way the speakers manage information flow in the discourse. The relation between the way the speakers package information (morphosyntactic form across grammatical roles) and the information status of the referents (given, accessible, new across grammatical roles) reflects the speakers' judgment of the needs of the listener in following the talk. An examination of this packaging with respect to core arguments of the verb demonstrates whether or not the speakers with autism conform to the Preferred Argument Structure which has been demonstrated for English discourse (O'Dowd 1990; Kumpf 1992; Kärkkäinen 1996; Thompson 1997) as well as cross-linguistically (Ashby and Bentivoglio 1993; Du Bois 1987; Payne 1987; Scancarelli 1987). An examination of the semantic feature animacy reveals the distribution of animate vs. nonanimate referents, a potential area of difference between typical language and the language of persons with autism. Together, these factors will be interpreted with respect to whether or not they illuminate the disordered aspects of the discourse and add to the discussion of theory of mind deficits in autism.

In this study, core arguments of the verb were labeled A, S, and O as proposed by Comrie (1978) and Dixon (1979), and Se as proposed by Dutra (1987) and Bentivoglio (1989, 1992). The category S includes all subjects of intransitives. Se refers to subjects of copulas, while Si refers to all other subjects of intransitives. These labels indicate the grammatical role of the NP. Although the labels A, S, and O were not initially conceived as a classification schema, coding NP's for their grammatical role has been shown to illuminate patterns of information flow in discourse.

Recent work on Preferred Argument Structure has made the distinction between NP's which are core arguments of the verb and predicating NP's which are not arguments of the verb (Thompson 1997). Predicating NP's have a predicating function; they are part of the naming of a type of event, activity, or situation (*I have hair*). The distinction between objects and predicating NP's is relevant for coding because subjects of clauses with predicating NP's are labeled S and not A. In other words, the verb is analyzed as intransitive rather than transitive. In the utterance *I have hair*, the subject *I* was coded as S and the NP *hair* was coded as a predicating NP. This can be contrasted with the utterance *I cut his hair*, in which the NP *hair* would be coded as an O and, consequently, the subject *I* would be coded as A.

Additional grammatical roles which label nonargument NP's in the data include obliques (obl), predicate nominals (pred NOM) of copular verbs, nonclausal or free NP's, vocatives, and formulaic NP's. A noun was labeled nonclausal if it was not realized as part of a complete clause. A noun was labeled formulaic if it appeared in an idiomatic or formulaic phrase (*by the way, of course, just a minute*).

The second grammatical factor which was coded in this study is noun phrase shape. All noun phrases were coded as clause, lexical NP, pronoun, or zero. A small number of grammatical subjects *it* (*because it's hot*) and *there* (*there seems to be an SO mes-... S message*) were coded separately as dummy subjects.

The pragmatic factor of activation was also coded. Activation state refers to the status of information in the recipient's focus of consciousness. If information had been previously activated, the NP which realizes the information was coded as given. In other words, an NP is given if it refers to a concept already active in the recipient's consciousness. If information had not been previously activated in the recipient's focus of consciousness, the NP which realizes the information was coded as new. In other words, an NP is new if it refers to a concept not active in the recipient's consciousness. An NP was coded as accessible if it refers to a concept which is accessible to the recipient's focus of consciousness by virtue of a previous mention which has faded from consciousness, the environment, the situation, or a semantic frame. NP's were coded as given if they had previously been mentioned in the discourse or referred to the participants (*I, you*). NP's were coded as new if there was no previous mention of the referent in the discourse. A small number of NP's were coded as accessible, primarily those which had not been previously mentioned but were given in the environment (*here, take these glasses*).

In regard to the semantic factor of animacy, subjects were coded as being animate versus inanimate.

Table 1. Distribution of all NP's by Argument vs. Nonargument role

Arguments	273	56%
Nonarguments	212	44%
	n=485	100%

The results of this study will be compared to previous English Preferred Argument Structure studies to the extent that the relevant information is retrievable. O'Dowd (1990) looked at three discontinuous segments of lecture and instructional dialogue, each lasting 3 to 4 minutes. Both core and oblique arguments were examined. Kumpf (1992) looked at four native English speakers in the context of her examination of Preferred Argument Structure in the talk of second language speakers. Two of her speakers narrated the events of a short movie (The Pear Film, Chafe 1980), and two were engaged in conversation. Core and oblique arguments were examined. Kärkkäinen (1996) examined 3 to 5 minute segments from three different conversations. Both core and oblique arguments were examined; results for all subtypes of obliques were presented separately. Thompson (1997) looked at a 10 minute conversation among three speakers. Both core and oblique arguments were examined.

Results

Clause structure

When looking at disordered language, it is always relevant to determine to what extent the speaker is utilizing syntactic form in the way of clause structure. The talk of speakers with significant language disorder may be characterized primarily by nonclausal forms in those communicative situations in which clause structure would be more appropriate. Such speakers may have difficulty formulating utterances with clause structure for a variety of reasons, for example, because of a motor speech disorders such as apraxia, because of word finding problems or problems with syntactic competence. An examination of all the NP's in these data revealed that slightly more than half of the NP's were realized as core arguments of the verb, while slightly less than half of the NP's were realized as nonarguments, as shown in Table 1.

This table demonstrates that the speakers with a diagnosis of autism were using argument structure in their talk. The distribution of arguments vs. nonarguments differs from previous studies by Kumpf (1992) and Kärkkäinen (1996), however, in that these data show a greater percentage of nonargument NP's than in the texts reported in these previous studies. In these data, 44% of NP's are nonarguments compared to Kumpf's data in which only 19% are nonarguments and Kärkkäinen's data in which 28% are nonarguments.

Grammatical role

NP's in these data distributed across grammatical roles as shown in Table 2. Among nonarguments, obliques and nonclausal NP's appear most frequently. Nonclausal or free NP's are not associated with a verb and its arguments. As noted in Table 1, these data reveal an increased percentage of nonarguments when compared to previous studies. The frequent production of nonclausal NP's is an important contributing factor to the high percentage of nonargument NP's.

We may ask why there are so many nonclausal NP's in the data. Are they the result of speaker or genre features? In other words, does this distribution reflect the speakers' language disorder or is it perhaps consequential to the discourse genre — a play interaction constituted by the participants acting out a scenario they intend to be a movie or TV show. An example of how these NP's are functioning in the discourse is necessary to begin to answer this question. The function of nonclausal NP's will be analyzed below in the context of the discussion of the morphosyntactic shape of these nonclausal forms.

Table 2. Distribution of all NP's by grammatical role

A	51	10%	obl	66	14%
X	71	15%	pred NOM	26	5%
S	100	21%	predicating NP	25	5%
it	8	2%	nonclausal	57	12%
there	1	0%	vocative	10	2%
obj	42	8%	formulaic	28	6%
	n=273	56%		*n*=212	44%

Morphosyntactic shape

Baltaxe (1977) has noted that some persons with autism overuse lexical NP's, i.e., they produce a full NP when a pronoun would be more appropriate for the discourse context, as demonstrated in the following example (p. 179).

(13) Examiner: have you ever seen a lovely lady
that you thought you might like to have as your wife
Subject: No
I haven't seen a lovely lady like that
but I am going to keep meeting lots of nice looking nice lovely ladies
close to my age hopefully

The difficulty with doing referencing exemplified in the above example is associated with the language of some persons with autism. The relation of full NP's to pronouns in the discourse, then, is a relevant area for examination.

In these data, when the distribution of all NP's by morphosyntactic shape is considered, lexical NP's are somewhat less frequent than pronouns and zeros, as shown in Table 3.

The .89 ratio of lexical NP's to pronouns revealed in this table compares well to Kumpf's for native speakers (Kumpf 1992: 388). In Kärkkäinen's data, lexical NP's are relatively less frequent, consisting of 33% of all mentions. On its face, then, the

Table 3. Distribution of all NP's by morphosyntactic shape

Clausal NP's	7	1%
Lexical NP's	214	44%
Pronouns	240	50%
Zero	24	5%
	n=485	100%

Table 4. Distribution of arguments by morphosyntactic shape and grammatical role

A	lexical	1	51	2%	
	pronoun	41		80%	
	zero	9		18%	100%
X	lexical	14	71	20%	
	pronoun	57		80%	
	zero	0			100%
S	lexical	11	100	11%	
	pronoun	77		77%	
	zero	12		12%	100%
it	pronoun	8			100%
there	lexical	1			100%
obj	clause	4	42	9%	
	lexical	18		43%	
	pronoun	20		48%	
	zero	0			100%

distribution of lexical NP's and pronouns in these data does not suggest an obviously atypical ratio of lexical NP's to pronouns. When the distribution of arguments by morphosyntactic shape and grammatical role is examined, a clear difference between subjects and objects becomes apparent, as shown in Table 4. Subjects (A, S) are overwhelmingly zeros or pronouns. A's are 2% lexical, Si and Se subjects combined are lexical 15% of the time, and objects are lexical 53% of the time. When compared to Kumpf's and Kärkkäinen's studies, arguments in these data are similar with respect to morphosyntactic shape. This distribution demonstrates that speakers in these data are not overusing lexical NP's in argument positions from a numerical perspective. Though the distribution is typical, it is necessary to analyze lexical NP's in their discourse context to see if a lexical form is appropriate in each instance, or if in fact a pronominal form would have been more felicitous given the information status of the referent. This will be discussed below in the context of nonclausal lexical NP's and the percentage of inactive NP's in the data.

In regard to the morphosyntactic shape of nonarguments, these data are realized by high frequencies of lexical NP's, as shown in Table 5. As predicted by Thompson (1997), nonarguments are realized more frequently than arguments with lexical NP's. In these data, obliques are lexical 82% of the time, while other nonargument NP's are lexical 81% of the time.

When compared with previous studies, the speakers with autism fall between the speakers in Kumpf's and Kärkkäinen's data with respect to the lexical realization of nonarguments. Taken together, the results of Tables 1 and 5 demonstrate that the

Table 5. Distribution of nonarguments by morphosyntactic shape and grammatical role

obl	lexical	54	66	82%	
	pronoun	12		18%	100%
predicating NP	lexical	24	25	96%	
	pronoun	1		4%	100%
predicate NOM	clause	3	26	12%	
	lexical	19		73%	
	pronoun	4		15%	100%
nonclausal	lexical	51	57	89%	
	pronoun	6		11%	100%
vocative	lexical	9	10	90%	
	pronoun	1		10%	100%
formulaic	lexical	12	28	43%	
	pronoun	13		46%	
	zero	3		11%	100%

speakers in these data are producing a high frequency of nonargument NP's and that a high percentage of them are lexical. As shown in Table 2, among nonarguments there is a high percentage of nonclausal NP's. The question was raised above as to whether the number of nonclausal NP's in the data reflected the type of interaction, a play situation, or whether perhaps this pattern was a manifestation of the speakers' language disorder. For example, the possiblility was raised that some lexical NP's might be reflecting a failure to use conventional rules of pronominalization. In order to determine if the high proportion of nonclausal lexical NP's are adding to the disordered quality of the talk, it is necessary to examine them on a case by case basis to see how they are functioning in the discourse. Only such a functional analysis will reveal if these NP's are following a typical or atypical pattern.

Many of the nonclausal lexical NP's are, in fact, functioning typically. Some are questions (line 9), answers to questions (line 10), or third turn receipts of information (line 11), as exemplified in the following.

(14) 1 GLEN: Yep./
2 There 'seems to be an ^SO mes .. S message.\
3 It's from far ^island.\
4 EVAN: Oh what ^is [it]?/
5 GLEN: [^Some] 'people,_
6 who are ^trapped on a 'boat.\
7 EVAN: Oh.

8 Um, _
→ 9 **^what .. what islands?/**
→ 10 GLEN: **Can- .. Canary Islands.**
→ 11 EVAN: **Canary.**
12 Cane_/can*/-\

Many of the nonclausal lexical NP's in the data are functioning as an element in a repair sequence (Schegloff, Jefferson and Sacks 1977). The NP's are functioning to initiate repair in the next turn after the trouble source (NTRI's), or they are responses to NTRI's. Example (15) exhibits an NTRI (line 4) and its response (line 5).

(15) 1 GLEN: [mm=,]
2 hm
3 twelve.\
→ 4 EVAN: **Twelve** [**o'clock?**]
→ 5 GLEN: [**Lunchtime (/luntʃitaim/)!**]
((SING SONG))

Nonclausal lexical NP's also function as repairs produced by listeners to a speaker's self-initiated word search, as shown in the following.

(16) EVAN: I'll swi- —
.. I'll ‘swim (/swÁ/) into shore to get a ^swimming —
... to get eh .. eh .. um —
Akk!
What is it?
Um.
→ GLEN: **Skateboards?**
→ **⟨MRC No surfboards MRC⟩.**
EVAN: Good.
Yeah.
Surfboards and other —
.. well —

Self-initiated repetition repairs are found in the data, as are transition space repairs, as in examples (17) and (18).

(17) GLEN: Hi!
[Hi dude].\
EVAN: [Who are you].\
Who are you.\
→ GLEN: **Surfer —**
→ **... (1.3) surfer ⟨XmanX⟩.**

(18) GLEN: [Don't forget a phone.\ ]
EVAN: (COUGHING)
→ GLEN: **A sol- .. [olar-powered] —**
EVAN: [⟨F A phone! F⟩]
→ GLEN: **^Solar-powered phone.**

Nonclausal forms not implicated in repair phenomena include repetitions and nonclausal comments, as exemplified in (19) and (20).

(19) EVAN: Oh good.\
→ **The SS Monica,_**
((SINGING WHILE STRUMMING UKELELE))
→ **The SS Monica.**
((SINGING WHILE STRUMMING UKELELE))
(20) EVAN: …( ) ‘Oh my ^ha=t,\
((AS HAT BLOWS AWAY))

The functions of nonclausal forms exemplified above are found in typical language. In these data, however, the frequency and functions of the repair sequences give the talk a flavor of difference from typical talk, if not a disordered quality. Because repair sequences disrupt the projected flow of the talk, however minimally, the frequency of the repair sequences in these data give the conversation a somewhat disjointed quality. Even more significantly, however, the repair sequences are reflected troubles in the talk which are associated with a diagnosis of language disorder. In these data, self-initiated repair sequences are reflecting word finding problems, motor planning problems, and processing delays associated with language formulation. Next turn repair initiators are reflecting auditory processing deficits and semantic interpretation problems.

There are a number of instances of nonclausal lexical NP's which reflect disordered language production, specifically, difficulty formulating language. Example (21) is an instance of self-initiated repair which would be clinically judged as demonstrating language formulation problems.

(21) EVAN: ⟨H Oh H⟩,_
You know what?/
The ^surfer I ^sawed .. looks 'just 'like you.\
GLEN: Yeah,_
^that was my 'brother.\
EVAN: Oh your ^brother.\
No wonder i- .. ^why he 'looked like 'you.\
GLEN: Yeah./
EVAN: Anyway,
you like [surfing too]?/

GLEN: [He bought] —
… uh .. uh —
^ski 'shoes.\
I- .. It was about —
EVAN: ⟨H ^He ^has the 'same 'thing H⟩.\
GLEN: And —
→ EVAN: **And we even just .. us —**
GLEN: [Except 'my shoes have ^rocket 'boos-] —
→ EVAN: **[we .. us .. ^water 'shoes].**
GLEN: have ^rocket 'boosters [on 'em].\
EVAN: [Oh].\
^That must be 'crazy,

There are also a number of NP's which appear without complete clause structure and seem to demonstrate incomplete form for their position in the discourse.

(22) GLEN: Yep./
There 'seems to be an ^SO mes .. S message.\
It's from far ^island.\
EVAN: Oh what ^is [it]?/
→ GLEN: **[^Some] 'people,_**
→ **who are ^trapped on a 'boat.**
EVAN: Oh.
(23) GLEN: Hm.\
Where ^was the 'island again,
EVAN: Those were for —
GLEN: ⟨F The ^island's 'here. F⟩\
EVAN: The islands —
The ^islands,
I don't 'see them.\
? ahh
GLEN: @ They're not ^on this 'map.\
EVAN: Hm.\
Interesting.\
GLEN: Floated off in —
EVAN: [XX]
→ GLEN: **[⟨X then actually X⟩] tons of erosion. **
EVAN: ⟨X See. X⟩\
GLEN: ⟨X Thousands X⟩ of .. sand and rocks .. came —
EVAN: (0) Hm.\

GLEN: ⟨X came ^up X⟩ to it,\
and 'made the island 'bigger,\
er,
... until .. it was ^attached to the 'ocean 'floor.\

When the nonclausal lexical NP's in these data are considered on a case by case basis, it becomes apparent that many of these NP's are contributing to the disordered quality of the talk by virtue of their frequency and function in the discourse, e. g., repair implicated NP's. Other nonclausal lexical NP's reflect the use of incomplete structure in an atypical way. An examination of the data has shown, however, that nonclausal lexical NP's are not contributing to the disordered quality of the talk because they are appearing in positions where a nonlexical form would be more appropriate.

Activation state

In Table 6, the distribution of arguments by activation state and grammatical role is examined. As this table shows, subjects are rarely new, while objects are somewhat more so. These results compare well with other studies. In O'Dowd's data, the percentage of new A's is reported as 4%, 3% and 6% across three texts. S subjects are new 23%, 8% and 17%. Objects are new 45%, 70%, and 41%, showing a greater range of variability. In Kumpf's data, no A's are new. S subjects are new 16% of the time, while objects are new 22% of the time.

In Kärkkäinen's data, similar patterns are observed. A subjects are 1% new, S subjects are 4% new, and objects are 39% new. Thompson reports that A subjects in her data are new 11% of the time and S subjects are 35% new, as are objects.

In my data, A's are never new, while Si subjects are new 3% of the time, as are Se subjects. Objects are new 11% of the time. These results demonstrate that the speakers with the diagnosis of autism are not using A and S roles to introduce new NP's into the discourse. Although S roles are positions which accommodate the introduction of new information into the discourse, these data show a low percentage of new NP's in S roles. A and S roles are functioning similarly in these data in regard to new NP's entering the data. From a numerical perspective, then, the distribution of new information in A and S roles does not suggest that the speakers are introducing new and possibly out of context NP's into their talk in these positions.

In order to determine if any NP, given or new, is tangential, out of context or irrelevant in its discourse context, NP's must be examined on a case by case basis. An examination of these data reveals that there are no obvious instances of tangential, out of context or irrelevant NP's in argument positions.

In Table 7, the distribution of new NP's is examined across all NP's in these data to determine more specifically which nonargument roles are positions in which

Table 6. Distribution of arguments by activation state

A	active	51	51		100%
	semiactive	0			
	inactive	0			100%
X	active	61	7	86%	
	semiactive	8		11%	
	inactive	2		13%	100%
S	active	94	100	94%	
	semiactive	3		3%	
	inactive	3		3%	100%
obj	active	27	37	73%	
	semiactive	6		16%	
	inactive	4		11%	100%

Note: This excludes 4 clausal obj complements and 1 nonapplicable NP.

Table 7. Percentage of inactive NP's by argument and nonargument role

A	0	0%	
X	2	3%	
S	3	5%	
obj	4	6%	14%
obl	19	29%	
predicating NP	11	17%	
pred NOM	6	9%	
nonclausal	9	14%	
vocative	1	2%	
formulaic	11	17%	86%
	n=66		100%

new information is introduced. We have seen that new information is generally not coming into the discourse in argument roles. In these data, 14% of all NP's code new information. Of these new NP's, 14% were realized as a core arguments of the verb, while 86% were realized as nonarguments of the verb. This contrasts to the distribution of new NP's in O'Dowd's and Kärkkäinen's data. In O'Dowd's texts, the object role is the most frequent slot for new NP's (45%, 58% 61% across three texts), with new NP's appearing in oblique roles less frequently (35%, 34%, 21% across three texts). Kärkkäinen's data show similar results. New NP's appear most frequently in the object role (56%), with new NP's appearing in oblique roles less frequently (34%). The classification of predicating NP's in the object role in O'Dowd's and Kärkkäinen's data may be inflating their percentage of new objects somewhat. As discussed above, a new NP coded as a predicating NP would be classified as appearing in a nonargument position, whereas the same NP coded as an object would be considered a core argument, thus increasing the number of new NP's realized as arguments of the verb. In these data, when formulaic NP's and vocatives were excluded from the data, the percentage of new NP's in the oblique role increased to 35%, predicating NP's to 20%, and the remaining categories by 2 or 3 percentage points. The most frequent slots for new NP's in these data, then, are in non-argument roles. As in the case of NP's in argument positions, there are no obvious instances of tangential, out of context or irrelevant NP's in nonargument positions.

We have seen in Table 7 that nonclausal NP's are generally given. We have also seen that nonclausal lexical NP's are not being used in place of more appropriate pronominal forms. When all remaining given lexical NP's are examined to determine whether or not the speakers are overusing lexical NP's by failing to use anaphora when it is appropriate to do so, these data reveal that given lexical NP's are not used inappropriately. There were no clear instances where the use of a pronominal form would have been more felicitous than one of these given lexical NP's.

In the talk of children with language disorder, including those with a diagnosis of autism, a frequent difficulty with using NP's to manage information in the discourse is manifested not in the overuse of lexical NP's in place of pronouns but rather in their underuse. Many kinds of disordered discourse are characterized by the production of pronouns in instances where lexical NP's would be more appropriate. This deficit is frequently observed in narratives. Brand new referents are treated as given and pronominalized. These NP's are not interpretable by the listener. The listener becomes confused, loses the thread of the story, and may even experience the talk as incoherent. This kind of difficulty with coding new referents, however, is not reflected in a violation of the four constraints of Preferred Argument Structure mentioned above.

The following is an example from a 16 year-old young man with a diagnosis of autism. A pronoun is used when a lexical NP would be more appropriate.

The speaker is talking about his two younger siblings.

(24) J: I was like very young when they were born
when Kelly was born
and I was like the oldest of —
I was older though —
I was like —
well
uh
how I was saying when Kelly was born
I was like only one years old
and I didn't know who the heck that thing was

		my Mom recalls that when I first saw Kelly
		I I I was terrible cause I tried
→		**to hit her with it**
	Clinician:	with a what
	J:	with a book
	Clinician:	a book
	J:	yeah
		a hard cover
		((laughter))
→		**...she grabbed my arm**

In this example, the referent of *it*, a book, is new information. The listener is unable to determine the referent with this pronominal reference. The use of *she* in line 20 is interpretable as the speaker's mother, given the context of the prior talk, although a lexical NP might have been more appropriate. In the discourse examined in this study, the speakers did not use pronouns when lexical NP's would have been more appropriate.

Animacy

When examining the discourse of persons with autism, it is relevant to consider if the speakers are talking about animate as well as inanimate referents since it has been noted in the literature, and observed clinically, that children with autism prefer objects to people in their play and may obsess about inanimate topics. Table 8 examines the feature of animacy to determine if a preoccupation with inanimate NP's is reflected in the discourse.

A and Si subjects are more animate than objects; Se subjects are overwhelmingly inanimate, however, resembling objects. In a study of declarative clause questions in English conversation, Weber (1995) found the same relations to hold among A, Se, and Si subjects. It may be that the Se role is a locus for inanimate subjects in English conversation. With the exception of vocatives, all nonarguments are overwhelmingly inanimate. These results correlate well with O'Dowd's and Kärkkäinen's data. This distribution, on the face of it, does not reflect an atypical pattern. When the discourse is examined qualitatively, however, the play themes developed in the discourse focus more on islands and natural events than on participants. One theme involves people marooned on an island. After their initial mention, however, these participants are barely mentioned.

(25)	GLEN:	Yep./
		There 'seems to be an ^SO mes .. S message.\
		It's from far ^island.\
	EVAN:	Oh what ^is [it]?/

Table 8. Distribution of arguments and nonarguments by animacy

A	animate	51	51	100%	100%
	inanimate	0			
X	animate	14	71	20%	
	inanimate	57		80%	100%
S	animate	83	100	83%	
	inanimate	17		17%	100%
it+there	*n*=9				
obj	animate	9	37	24%	
	inanimate	28		76%	100%
obl	animate	4	66	6%	
	inanimate	62		94%	100%
pred nom	animate	3	26	12%	
	inanimate	20		77%	
	nonapplicable	3		12%	100%
predicating NP	animate	2	25	8%	
	inanimate	23		92%	100%
nonclausal	animate	12	57	21%	
	inanimate	45		79%	100%
vocative	animate	10	10		
	inanimate	0			100%

GLEN: [^Some] 'people,_
who are ^trapped on a 'boat.\
EVAN: Oh.
Um, _
^what .. what islands?/
GLEN: Can- .. Canary Islands.\
EVAN: Canary.1 Cane_/can*/-\
GLEN: …(6.5) Actually [the] ^Hawaiian_(/h^Wwain/) 'Islands.\
EVAN: [I don't see] —
(0) The Hawaiian.\
Which island?
GLEN: …(4.7) Mm,
… 'marooned [on] the 'beaches of^Waikiki _(/h^waikiki/).\

EVAN: [X]
Waikiki (/h^wakiki/).\
I know but —
isn't Maui —
GLEN: Maui.\
EVAN: Okay.\
Maui —
Mau=i! ((PITCH BREAK))
GLEN: Yep.\
EVAN: ⟨P Maui P⟩.\

This theme is picked up again later as follows.

(26) ((MAKES RINGING SOUNDS))
EVAN: X
GLEN: Hello?
…(1.5) Oh?/
…(2.2) We need to get …(2.2) to a v —
… to a ^marooned 'island which —
.. which broke up from a ^big 'earthquake which happened in the 'Hawaii.\
Hm.
Okay.
EVAN: Okay
[what is] —
GLEN: [What they're] ^marooned ⟨Xon itX⟩?/
Okay.\
EVAN: Let's see,
is it ⟨X Hawa- X⟩_(/hwA/) —
is it —
…(1.5) is it —
GLEN: It's a ^broken up 'island which —
EVAN: (0) Is it
it's ca- —
Is it .. at this island?
GLEN: …(3.4) No.\
EVAN: Is it X …⟨X ca- X⟩_(/K*/ —
GLEN: No.\
EVAN: Wait wait.\
GLEN: [No].\
EVAN: [No],_

GLEN: it goes ^that —
an island —
it's the XX —
at 'that ^latitude and the 'longitude.\
EVAN: Wait that's —
^that's degrees?/
GLEN: ⟨X This X⟩.\
EVAN: Wait
what degrees.\
[It's about] —
GLEN: [Thirty.]\
EVAN: That's thirty,\
wh=ere —
GLEN: Actually ⟨Xit'sX⟩ between thir- wirtdy_(/w^rdi)
between thirty
EVAN: (COUGH)
we're off the 'coast of Santa ^Monica.\
GLEN: Fifteen.\
EVAN: No no no no.\
GLEN: Okay!
EVAN: (0) Wait wait wait.\
when i-
.. where was the ^⟨XislandsX⟩ again.\
^island again.\
GLEN: Hm.\
Where ^was the 'island again,
EVAN: Those were for —
GLEN: ⟨F The ^island's 'here. F⟩\
EVAN: The islands —
The ^islands,
I don't 'see them.\
? ahh
GLEN: @ They're not ^on this 'map.\
EVAN: Hm.\
Interesting.\
GLEN: Floated off in —
EVAN: [XX]
GLEN: [⟨X then actually X⟩] tons of erosion. \
EVAN: ⟨X See. X⟩\
GLEN: ⟨X Thousands X⟩ of .. sand and rocks .. came —
EVAN: (0) Hm.\

GLEN: ⟨X came ^up X⟩ to it,\
and 'made the island 'bigger,\
er,
... until .. it was ^attached to the 'ocean 'floor.\

These examples demonstrate that although a dramatic situation involving human participants is initially set up, a dramatic scenario involving the characters is never developed. The play focuses on talk about islands and locations. Rather than dramatically connecting to the human participants, however, this talk marginalizes them.

Conclusions

When NP's in these data are examined with respect to the morphosyntactic, pragmatic and semantic factors described above, typical patterns of information flow are revealed. These data do differ from others, however, in that there are more NP's in nonargument vs. argument positions. Nonargument NP's, specifically obliques, predicating NP's, and nonclausal NP's are frequently realized lexically; new information is realized more frequently by nonarguments than in other studies. An examination of the discourse context reveals that many of the nonclausal lexical NP's in nonargument positions are involved in self-initiated or other-initiated repair. Some nonclausal lexical NP's which are instances of self-initiated repair are indicative of clinically significant language formulation problems.

When these data are examined with respect to Preferred Argument Structure constraints, it is revealed that the discourse conforms to the one lexical argument constraint 100%. There is no clause with two lexical arguments. There are three clauses with lexical subjects with lexical predicating NP's. These subjects were coded as S, since predicating NP's are not considered to be arguments of the verb (Du Bois & Thompson 1991, Thompson 1997).

With respect to the nonlexical A constraint, there is only one clause with an A realized as an NP; it is part of a compound subject (*me and the captain.*)

With respect to the pragmatic dimension of Preferred Argument Structure, there is no clause with more than one new argument. Among A role NP's, all A's are given. There are few new Se and Si NP's, only 3% respectively. Only 11% of objects are new.

For the clauses in these data, Se and Si subjects pattern like A subjects with respect to NP shape and activation state. Se subjects differ from A and Si subjects with respect to the animacy of subjects. Se subjects have significantly more inanimate subjects than A and Si subjects.

The speakers' compliance with Preferred Argument Structure constraints may seem surprising, given their obvious and significant problems with turn taking, with responsiveness, with producing relevant responses, and with the ability to create and interpret references and events within a story world. In fact, it is accurate to say that, among all developmental disabilities, autism results in the most disordered communication because the social aspects of interaction are atypical. The ability to manage information appropriately is certainly a fundamental aspect of competence in the social use of language. The difficulties that Glen and Evan may have in discourse, however, are not reflected in the way they realize argument structure. Violating Preferred Argument Structure constraints is not a way in which Glen and Evan's deviance in the social use of language is manifested. To the extent that Preferred Argument Structure is an epiphenomenon of discourse organization, the speakers are demonstrating a basic discourse-pragmatic competence.

An examination of information flow does reveal that the speakers had an increased frequency of nonclausal NP's in comparison to other Preferred Argument Structure studies of English. When these NP's were examined in their discourse context, it became apparent that many of these NP's were involved in repair. The frequency of repair in the talk is clinically significant and is suggestive of a number of language problems including comprehension problems, processing delays, motor planning production problems, word finding problems, incomplete structures and language formulation difficulties. As has been noted above, other areas of deficit which require an examination of the discourse contexts of NP's include anaphora, coherence, responsiveness, perseveration, and fluency.

An examination of how the speakers manage information flow in the discourse does not reveal problems which would be predicted by theory of mind deficits. The theory of mind predicts that the speakers would have difficulty inferring each other's mental state with respect to the activation state of information. If that were the case, we would expect to see some atypical patterns of information flow or the overuse or underuse of lexical NP's. The patterns of Preferred Argument Structure in these data, however, were not atypical. Additionally, there were no obvious instances in which referents were coded with the inappropriate morphosyntactic shape with respect to information status. No instance of the use of a lexical NP in place of a more appropriate pronominal form was found. Conversely, pronouns were not used to code new information, for example, pronouns were not found in instances when the use of a lexical NP would have been necessary for the listener to follow the talk. In these data, then, patterns of information flow do not reveal the same difficulties with inferring the mental states of others which have been demonstrated among persons with autism in experimental tasks.

These results are an interesting addition to the literature on the language of persons with autism because they reveal a previously unidentified discourse competence. It has been recognized that the discourse of persons with autism is different from that of typical speakers with respect to both content and coherence. These data show that speakers who exhibit some patterns of atypical discourse nonetheless are conforming to the basic constraints of information flow as realized in Preferred Argument Structure. These results suggest a nonexperimental area of research to further explore the theory of mind deficit of autism.

In regard to Preferred Argument Structure literature, these results are an interesting addition insofar as they demonstrate that the phenomenon appears robust even among the most discourse-disordered population — speakers with a diagnosis of autism.

References

Adams, C. and Dorothy V.M. Bishop. 1989. "Conversational characteristics of children with semantic-pragmatic disorder. I: Exchange structure, turntaking, repairs and cohesion". *British Journal of Disorder of Communication* 24: 211–239.

American Psychiatric Association. 1994. *Diagnostic and Statistical Manual of Mental Disorders* (4th ed.). Washington D.C.: American Psychiatric Association.

American Psychiatric Association. 1980. *Diagnostic and Statistical Manual of Mental Disorders* (3rd ed.). Washington D.C.: American Psychiatric Association.

Ashby, William J. and Paola Bentivoglio. 1993. "Preferred Argument Structure in spoken French and Spanish". *Language Variation and Change* 5: 61–76.

Baltaxe, Christiane A.M. 1977. "Pragmatic deficits in the language of autistic adolescents". *Journal of Pediatric Psychology* 2: 176–180.

Baltaxe, Christiane A.M. and D. Guthrie. 1987. "The use of primary sentence stress by normal, aphasic, and autistic children". *Journal of Autism and Developmental Disorders* 17: 255–271.

Baltaxe, Christiane A.M. and Nora D'Angiola. 1992. "Cohesion in the discourse interaction of autistic, specifically language-impaired, and normal children". *Journal of Autism and Developmental Disorders* 22: 1–21.

Baltaxe, Christiane A.M. and James Q. Simmons. 1975. "Language in childhood psychosis: A review". *Journal of Speech and Hearing Disorders* 40: 439–458.

Baltaxe, Christiane A.M. and James Q. Simmons. 1983. "Communication deficits in the adolescent and adult autistic". *Seminars in Speech and Language* 4: 27–42.

Barron-Cohen, Simon. 1989. "The autistic child's theory of mind: A case of specific developmental delay". *Journal of Child Psychology and Psychiatry* 30: 285–297.

Barron-Cohen, Simon, Alan M. Leslie, and Uta Frith. 1985. "Does the autistic child have a 'theory of mind'?". *Cognition* 21: 37–46.

Barron-Cohen, Simon. 1986. "Mechanical, behavioral and intentional understanding of picture stories in autistic children". *British Journal of Developmental Psychology* 4: 113–125.

Bentivoglio, Paola. 1989. "La posición del sujeto en las cláusulas copulativas en el español de Caracas". *Actas del VII Congreso Internacional, Asociación de Lingüística y Filolgía de la America Latina* [ALFAL], tomo II. Santo Domingo, RD: ALFAL, Filial Dominicana, 173–196.

Bentivoglio, Paola. 1992. "Linguistic correlations between subjects of one-argument verbs and subjects of more-than-one-argument verbs in spoken Spanish". In Paul Hirschbuhler and Konrad Koener (eds), *Romance Languages and Modern Linguistic Theory.* Amsterdam: Benjamins, 11–24.

Bishop, Dorothy V.M. and C. Adams. 1989. "Conversational characteristics of children with semantic-pragmatic disorder. II: What features lead to a judgment of inappropriacy?" *British Journal of Disorders of Communication* 24: 241–263.

Chafe, Wallace. 1974. "Language and consciousness". *Language* 50: 111–133.

Chafe, Wallace. 1976. "Givenness, contrastiveness, definiteness, subjects, topics, and point of view". In Charles N. Li (ed.), *Subject and Topic.* New York: Academic Press, 25–56.

Chafe, Wallace. 1980. "The deployment of consciousness in the production of a narrative". In Wallace Chafe (ed.), *The Pear Stories: Cognitive, Cultural, and Linguistic Aspects of Narrative Production.* Norwood, N. J.: Ablex, 9–50.

Chafe, Wallace. 1987. "Cognitive constraints on information flow". In Russell Tomlin (ed.), *Coherence and Grounding in Discourse.* Amsterdam: Benjamins, 21–51.

Chafe, Wallace. 1992. "Information flow". *Oxford International Encyclopedia of Linguistics.* Oxford: Oxford University Press, 215–218.

Chafe, Wallace. 1993. "Prosodic and functional units of language". In Jane A. Edwards and Martin D. Lampert (eds), *Talking Data: Transcription and Coding Methods for Language Research.* Hillsdale, NJ: Lawrence Erlbaum, 33–43.

Chafe, Wallace. 1994. *Discourse, Consciousness, and Time: The Flow and Displacement of Conscious Experience in Speaking and Writing.* Chicago: University of Chicago Press.

Church, Catharine Critz and James Coplan. 1995. "The high-functioning autistic experience: Birth to preteen years". *Journal of Pediatric Health Care* 9: 22–29.

Clancy, Patricia M. 1993 "Preferred Argument Structure in Korean Acquisition". In Eve V. Clark (ed.), *The Proceedings of the Twenty-Fifth Annual Child Language Research Forum.* Stanford: CSLI Publications, 307–314.

Coe, David and Johnny L. Matson. 1989. "Etiology, incidence, and prevalence of chronic schizophrenia and adult autism". In Johnny L. Matson (ed.), *Chronic Schizophrenia and Adult Autism.* New York: Springer, 53–88.

Comrie, Bernard. 1978. "Ergativity". In Winfred Lehmann (ed.), *Syntactic Typology.* Austin, Texas: Unversity of Texas, 329–394.

Dixon, Robert M. W. 1979. "Ergativity". *Language* 55: 59–138.

Du Bois, John W. 1980. "Beyond definiteness: The trace of identity in discourse." In Wallace Chafe (ed.), *The Pear Stories: Cognitive, Cultural, and Linguistic Aspects of Narrative Production.* Norwood, NJ: Ablex, 203–274.

Du Bois, John W. 1985. "Competing motivations". In John Haiman (ed.), *Iconicity and Syntax.* Amsterdam: Benjamins, 343–365.

Du Bois, John W. 1987. "The discourse basis of ergativity". *Language* 63: 805–855.

Du Bois, John W. and Sandra Thompson. 1991. *Dimensions of a Theory of Information Flow.* Unpublished manuscript, University of California, Santa Barbara.

Du Bois, John W., Stephan Schuetze-Coburn, Susanna Cumming, and Danae Paolino. 1992. "Discourse transcription". *Santa Barbara Papers in Linguistics* 4: 1–225

Dutra, Rosalia. 1987. "The hybrid S category in Brazilian Portuguese: Some implications for word order". *Studies in Language* 11: 163–180.

Fine, Jonathan. 1988. "Cognitive processes in context: A systemic approach to problems in oral language use". In Erich Steiner and Robert Veltman (eds), *Pragmatics, Discourse and Text: Some systemically-inspired Approaches.* Norwood, NJ: Ablex Publishing Corporation, 171–182.

Fine, Jonathan, Giampiero Bartolucci, Peter Szatmari, and Gary Ginsberg. 1994. "Cohesive discourse in pervasive developmental disorders". *Journal of Autism and Developmental Disorders* 24: 315–329.

Fine, Jonathan, Giampiero Bartolucci, Gary Ginsberg, and Peter Szatmari. 1991. "The use of intonation to communicate in pervasive developmental disorders". *Journal of Child Psychology and Psychiatry* 32: 771–782.

Frith, Uta. 1989a. *Autism: Explaining the Enigma.* Oxford: Blackwell.

Frith, Uta. 1989b. "A new look at language and communication in autism". *British Journal of Disorder of Communication* 24: 123–150.

Frith, Uta and Francesca Happé. 1994. "Language and communication in autistic disorders". *Philosophical Transactions. Royal Society of London* 346: 97–104.

Garfin, Deborah G. and Catherine Lord. 1986. "Communication as a social problem in autism". In Eric Scholpler and Gary B. Mesibov (eds). *Social Behavior in Autism.* New York: Plenum Press, 133–151.

Hingston, Joseph N. and Frank C. Trost Jr. 1966. "Shaping cooperative responses in early childhood schizophrenics: II. Reinforcement of mutual physical contact and vocal responses". In Robert Ulrich, Thomas Stachnik, and John Mabry (eds), *Control of Human Behavior.* Glenview, Illinois: Scott Foresman, 110–114.

Howlin, Patricia. 1986. "An overview of social behavior in autism". In Eric Scholpler and Gary B. Mesibov (eds). *Social Behavior in Autism.* New York: Plenum Press, 103–131.

Kanner, Leo. 1943. "Autistic disturbances of affective contact". *Nervous Child* 2: 217–250.

Kärkkäinen, Elise. 1996. "Preferred Argument Structure and subject role in American English conversational discourse". *Journal of Pragmatics* 25: 675–702.

Koegel, Lynn Kern, Marta C. Valdez-Menchaca, and Robert L. Koegel. 1993. "Autism: Social communication difficulties and related behaviors". In Michel Hersen and Vincent B. Van Hasselt (eds). *Advanced Abnormal Psychology.* New York: Plenum Press, 165–187.

Kumpf, Lorraine, E. 1992. "Preferred argument in second language discourse: A preliminary study". *Studies in Language* 16: 369–403.

Landa, Rebecca, Susan E. Folstein, and Crystal Isaacs. 1991. "Spontaneous narrative discourse performance of parents of autistic individuals". *Journal of Speech and Hearing Research* 34: 1339–1345.

Landry, Susan H. and Katherine A. Loveland. 1989. "The effect of social context on the functional communication skills of autistic children". *Journal of Autism and Developmental Disorders* 19: 283–299.

Leslie, Alan M. 1987. "Pretense and representation: The origins of 'theory of mind'". *Psychological Review* 94: 412–426.

Leslie, Alan M. and Uta Frith. 1988. "Autistic children's understanding of seeing, knowing and believing". *British Journal of Developmental Psychology* 6: 315–324.

Lord, Catherine and Patricia J. O'Neill. 1983. "Language and communication needs of adolescents with autism". In Eric Scholpler and Gary B. Mesibov (eds). *Autism in Adolescents and Adults.* New York: Plenum Press, 57–77.

Lord, Catherine and J. Michael Hopkins. 1986. "The social behavior of autistic children with younger and same-age nonhandicapped peers". *Journal of Autism and Developmental Disorders* 16: 249–262.

McHale, Susan M. 1983. "Social interactions of autistic and nonhandicapped children during free play". *American Journal of Orthopsychiatry* 53: 81–91.

Mesibov, Gary B. 1992. "Treatment issues with high-functioning adolescents and adults with autism". In Eric Schopler and Gary B. Mesibov (eds). *High-functioning Individuals with Autism.* New York: Plenum Press, 143–155.

Minshew, Nancy J., Gerald Goldstein, and Don J. Siegel. 1995. "Speech and language in high-functioning autistic individuals". *Neuropsychology* 9: 255–261.

O'Dowd, Elizabeth. 1990. "Discourse pressure, genre and grammatical alignment-After Du Bois". *Studies in Language* 14: 365–403.

Oshima-Takane, Yuriko and Sigmund Benaroya. 1989. "An alternative view of pronomial errors in autistic children". *Journal of Autism and Developmental Disorders* 19: 73–85.

Ozonoff, Sally, Sally J. Rogers, and Bruce F. Pennington. 1991. "Asperger's syndrome: Evidence of an empirical distinction from high-functioning autism". *Journal of Child Psychology and Psychiatry* 32: 1107–1122.

Paul, Rhea. 1995. *Language Disorders from Infancy through Adolescence: Assessment and Intervention.* St. Louis: Mosby.

Payne, Doris. 1987. "Information structuring in Papago narrative discourse. *Language* 63: 783–804.

Prizant, Barry and Amy M. Wetherby. 1987. Communicative intent: A framework for understanding social-communicative behavior in autism". *Journal of the American Academy of Child and Adolescent Psychiatry* 26: 472–479.

Rimland, Bernard. 1964. *Infantile Autism: The Syndrome and its Implications for a Neural Theory of Behavior.* New York: Appleton-Century-Croft.

Rutter, Michael. 1978. "Diagnosis and definition". In Michael Rutter and Eric Scholpler (eds). *Autism: A Reappraisal of Concepts and Treatment.* New York: Plenum Press, 1–25.

Rutter, Michael and Eric Schopler. 1987. "Autism and pervasive developmental disorders: Concepts and diagnostic issues". *Journal of Autism and Developmental Disorders* 17: 159–186.

Rumsey, Judith M., Judith L. Rapoport, and Walter R. Sceery. 1985. "Autistic children as adults: Psychiatric, social, and behavioral outcomes". *Journal of the American Academy of Child Psychiatry* 24: 465–473.

Scancarelli, Janine. 1985. "Referential strategies in Chamorro narratives". *Studies in Language* 9: 335–362.

Schegloff, Emanuel, Gail Jefferson and Harvey Sacks. 1977. "The preference for self-correction in the organization of repair in conversation". *Language* 53: 61–82.

Strain, Philip S. and Thomas P. Cooke,. 1976. "An observational investigation of two elementary-age autistic children during free-play". *Psychology in the Schools* 13: 82–91.

Sudhalter, Vicki, Ira L. Cohen, Wayne Silverman, and Enid G. Wolf-Schein, 1990. "Conversational analyses of males with fragile X, Down syndrome, and autism: Comparison of the emergence of deviant language". *American Journal on Mental Retardation* 94: 431–441.

Szatmari, Peter, Giampiero Bartolucci, and Rebecca Bremner. 1989. "Asperger's syndrome and autism: Comparisons on early history and outcome". *Developmental Medicine and Child Neurology* 31: 709–720.

Szatmari, Peter, Rebecca Bremner, and Joan Nagy. 1989. "Asperger's syndrome: a review of clinical features". *Canadian Journal of Psychiatry* 34: 554–560.

Tager-Flusberg, Helen. 1993. "What language reveals about the understanding of minds in children with autism". In Simon Baron-Cohen, Helen Tager-Flusberg, and Donald Cohen, *Understanding Other Minds: Perspectives from Autism.* Oxford: Oxford University Press, 138–157.

Thompson, Sandra A. 1997. "Discourse motivations for the core-oblique distinction as a language universal". In Akio Kamio (ed.) *Directions in Functional Linguistics.* Amsterdam: Benjamins, 59–82.

Weber, Elizabeth G. 1995. "Nominal information flow in declarative questions". Paper presented at the 1995 Annual Conference of the American Association for Applied Linguistics, Long Beach Hilton Hotel, Long Beach, California, March 26.

Wing, Lorna. 1983. "Social and interpersonal needs". In Eric Scholpler and Gary B. Mesibov (eds), *Autism in adolescents and adults.* New York: Plenum Press, 337–353.

World Health Organization. 1992. *ICD-10. Classification of Mental and Behavioral Disorders. Clinical Description and Diagnostic Guidelines.* Geneva: World Health Organization.

Tracking the deer

Nominal reference, parallelism and Preferred Argument Structure in Itzaj Maya narrative genres*

Charles Andrew Hofling
Southern Illinois University at Carbondale

Introduction

Work by Du Bois and others on Preferred Argument Structure and information flow in Mayan narrative suggests general constraints on clause structure with important implications for text structure and the marking of nominal reference in texts (Du Bois 1985, 1987; England 1986, 1988; England and Martin, this volume; Martin 1987, this volume). With regard to the core arguments, transitive subject (A), intransitive subject (S), and transitive object (O), Preferred Argument Structure posits two grammatical constraints: (1) avoid more than one core lexical argument per clause and (2) avoid lexical A's. That is, there is a strong tendency for lexical arguments to appear in S or O roles rather than in A role. The corresponding pragmatic constraints of Preferred Argument Structure are that no more than one new argument be introduced per clause and that the A role be restricted to given, not new, information. On these bases, the S and O case roles are aligned in contrast to the A role, corresponding to an ergative pattern. On the other hand, the distributions of human mentions and topic continuity show a preference for S and A roles, in contrast to O, in a nominative pattern.

In this paper I examine nominal reference in Itzaj Maya mythic and personal narrative in light of Preferred Argument Structure. Itzaj Maya is an endangered member of the Yucatecan branch of the Mayan family spoken in Petén, Guatemala and has a split-ergative verbal cross-referencing system (Hofling 1991, 1997, 2000). I will pay particular attention to the morphosyntactic marking of nominal mention and its discourse function. In addition to the core arguments A, S, and O, I consider indirect object (I), possessor-possessed, and locative relations in an attempt to offer a general account of how information is introduced into Itzaj narrative discourse, and if it is maintained, how subsequent references are marked to reflect discourse highlighting and cohesion.

The texts analyzed are a personal narrative about a recent deer-hunting expedition (Text 1) and a mythic tale of a deer hunter's encounter with the Lord of the Deer (Text 2), both recounted by Fernando Tesucún, a native speaker of Itzaj who also assisted in their analysis.[1] This pair of texts, both featuring deer hunting, provide an interesting contrast between the narrative genres of personal narrative, which is a relatively spontaneous genre featuring the narrator in the first person, and mythic narrative, the retelling of a traditional tale.

Split-ergative person marking

Itzaj Maya has a split-ergative cross-referencing system on the verb in which A's are always marked by one set of person marker prefixes (Set A), O's are always marked by a different set of person marker suffixes (Set B) and S's are marked like A's in the incompletive status in a nominative system, but like O's in the completive and dependent statuses in an ergative system (Hofling 1991, 1997, 2000). The differences in S marking are shown in (1) where the second person S of an incompletive verb is marked by a Set A prefix (1b), but the second person S of a completive verb is marked by a Set B suffix (2b).[2]

(1) Incompletive Aspect: Nominative–Accusative System
 a. *k-a-mäch-ik-en*
 INC-2A-grab-ITS-1SG.B
 'you grab me'
 b. *k-a-tal*
 INC-2A-come
 'you come'

(2) Completive Aspect: Ergative–Absolutive System
 a. *t-in-mäch-aj-ech*
 COM-1SG.A-grab-CTS-2SG.B
 'I grabbed you'
 b. *tal-eech*
 come-2SG.B
 'you came'

Preferred Argument Structure and the introduction of new information

Table 1 presents the results of an analysis of the two texts according to the general clause types distinguished by Du Bois (1987). (See below and England and Martin, this volume, for discussion of finer distinctions among clause types.)

Transitive clauses are subdivided according to whether they have 0, 1, or 2 core

Table 1. Distribution of clause types (Text 1 $n=81$; Text 2 $n=191$; Total $n=272$)

	Total		0 NP			1 NP: S			1 NP: A			1 NP: O			2 NP		
	T1	T2	T1	T2	Total	T1	T2	Total	T1	T2	Total	T1	T2	Total	T1	T2	Total
Transitive	37	71	25	32	57				0	10	10	12	24	36	0	5	5
Intransitive	31	86	26	69	95	5	17	22									
Equational	12	29	3	9	12	9	20	29									
Other	1	6															

lexical arguments, and if they have 1, according to its case role. Non-transitive clauses are subdivided into intransitive and equational clauses. There is a small residue of "other" clauses.

The results presented above are quite similar in most respects to those reported for other Mayan languages (cf. England and Martin, this volume). Two-argument clauses are rare (1.8%) and when lexical arguments appear, they are most commonly in S or O role, rather than A role. An interesting difference between the two texts is the degree to which these tendencies are in evidence. In the personal narrative no two-argument clauses appear, nor are there any examples of NP's in A role, while in the mythic text a rather higher than expected number of both appears. As will be elaborated below, this reflects the greater importance of deictic pronouns (rather than lexical arguments) for nominal reference in personal narrative and the need to disambiguate third person human protagonists in mythic narrative.

According to Preferred Argument Structure, one would expect new information to be introduced by lexical mentions in non-A case roles, and this pattern is generally confirmed through a count of first nominal mentions. The first occurrence of a form in a text was counted even if it was coreferential (but not synonymous) to a previously introduced nominal. For example, in the second text the main protagonist is first referred to by the noun *winik*, 'man' (2:2) and later by *ajtz'on*, 'the hunter' (2:39) (references to the texts are indicated by text number followed by line number). In a few cases, forms that had appeared previously, but were later used for new referents, were also counted. An example, also from the second text, is the use of the noun *ba'alche'*, 'animal' with different referents (2:41; 2:85). The elimination of these borderline types of first mentions would not substantially change the distributions presented in Table 2. (See England and Martin, this volume, for additional discussion of what constitutes a new mention.)

The distribution of first nominal mentions is similar in the two texts and comparable to that reported by Du Bois (1987). These results confirm the Preferred Argument Structure constraint that new information tends to enter discourse in non-A case roles. However, first mention is not an exact indicator of new informational status, as the presence of possessed forms and forms marked with the determiner in

Table 2. Case role and form of first lexical mentions (Text 1 $n=33$; Text 2 $n=40$)

	A		Si		Se		O		I		LOC		POSR		OTHER	
	T1	T2	T1	T2	T1	T2	T1	T2	T1	T2	T1	T2	T1	T2	T1	T2
Inanimate (56)																
NUM CLS N						5					1		1	2		
(ADJ) N								4			1	1			1	2
PPR N			4	2	4	5	2	3			3	5				
DET (ADJ) N					1		3				3	1	1			
PN											1					
Animate (18)																
NUM CLS N					1	2										
(ADJ) N					2		1	1					1			
PPR N		3						1	1					1		
DET (ADJ) N				1				1					1	1		
Totals:	0	3	4	3	8	12	6	10	1	0	9	7	4	4	1	2

Table 2 suggests. Thus, even on first mention the majority of nouns are marked as definite. Along the gradient of given to new, much information is introduced in a contextualized form that relates it to other elements of the discourse or to general cultural knowledge, and is not entirely new (cf. Ariel 1990, Chafe 1994).

Table 2 also reflects differences in the ways that animate and inanimate nominals are introduced into discourse. While both rely heavily on the S case role, inanimates are frequently introduced in the O and locative case roles, while the animate nouns are never locative and are infrequently Os, but do appear in A, I and possessor roles. This difference in case roles between animate and inanimate NPs reflects a topic accession hierarchy (Givón 1984: 139) according to which animate NPs occur more frequently as topics than do inanimates.

Morphosyntactic form and discourse maintenance

Inanimate nominal reference

While most first lexical mentions are inanimate (56 of 74), most of these do not become discourse topics and none are major characters in either narrative. Instead, most inanimate first mentions are "peripheral" (England and Martin, this volume) and are quickly dropped from the discourse. Furthermore, the relationship between morphosyntactic marking and definiteness of inanimate NPs is different from that of animate NPs. It has been widely noted that topical information introduced into a discourse is often marked indefinitely, but after introduction is marked definitely, either anaphorically or by other topic markers (Du Bois 1980; Brown and Yule 1983; Givón 1983, 1984). However, inanimate NPs, which may become minor topics at best (as measured by frequency of mention), are frequently marked definitely on their introduction, and rarely treated anaphorically if they are maintained at all.

Table 3. Inventory of inanimate lexical mentions (Text 1 *n*=39; Text 2 *n*=79; Total *n*=118)

	Si		Se		O		LOC		POSR		OTHER	
	T1	T2	T1	T2	T1	T2	T1	T2	T1	T2	T1	T2
NUM CLS N		1		6	1		1		1	2	1	1
(ADJ) N				1		4	1	2			1	2
PPR N	4	4	4	4	3	12	3	12	1			1
DET (ADJ) N		2	1	3	4	3	7	6	4	5		
IPR				7	1	1	1					
Totals:	4	7	5	21	9	20	13	20	6	7	2	4

Table 3 summarizes the total inventory of inanimate lexical NPs in these texts. It shows that the distribution for all inanimate mentions is similar to that of first mentions. Most inanimate nouns are simply mentioned once and not maintained or reintroduced into the discourse. They never occur in A or I roles, and as with first mentions, most references are in S, O, or LOC case relations. With regard to morphosyntactic form, Table 3 reflects an increase in modification by determiners, as one would expect for previously mentioned information, and in the appearance of independent pronouns, although low in frequency when compared to animate nouns (see Table 4 below).

The reference chains of inanimate nouns are usually short indeed, as the following examples of the most frequently mentioned inanimate nouns in the personal narrative about hunting (Text 1) indicate.

(3) *bej*, 'road'
1:2 *B'in-o'on tulakal t-a' **noj b'ej***
go-1PL.B all on-DET big way
'We went all the way on the big road
1:3 *k-u-b'el tak Sik'u'-ej*
INC-3A-go to PN-TOP
that goes up to La Trinidad.'

1:5 *Ka' nak'-o'on t-a' yax kol-oo'*
then climb-1PL.B to-DET first milpa-PL
'Then we climbed to the first milpas
1:6 *yan t-u-chi' a' noj b'ej-ej.*
EXIST on-3A-edge DET big way-TOP
that are on the edge of the road.'

In line 1:2 *b'ej* is introduced in a locative expression. It is modified by a determiner and followed by a relative clause that provides the information necessary to identify it. That is, it is definite on first mention by virtue of the context provided in the relative clause. (Note that the noun *kol* 'milpa' is similarly marked on its introduction in 1:5.) On its second and third mentions (1:6, 1:29) *b'ej* is modified by the determiner without a relative clause and is then definite by virtue of prior mention, but does not become a significant discourse topic. In line 1:6 *b'ej* appears as the possessor in a construction of the type [PPR-Possessed NP + Possessor NP], where the Set A possessive pronoun (PPR) agrees with the Possessor NP. This construction is typical of inanimate part/whole and locative relations and appears with considerable frequency as shown in Table 3. In contrast, when the possessor is human, it generally constitutes given information referenced by the Set A PPR alone, as in the following example.

(4) ***k'aak'***, 'fire, light'
1:9 "*Ko'ox kiw-utz-kin-t-ej* ***ki-k'aak'***
let's 1PL.A-good-CAUS-TRN-DTS 1PL.A-fire
'"Let's fix our light'
1:14 "*Tz'-aj tulakal a' b'ateriiya ma'lo' t-a'* ***fok-ej***
give/IMP all DET battery good in-DET flashlight-TOP
'"Put all the good batteries in the flashlight
1:15 *ii yok' u-sas-i(l)-tal uy-ich a'* ***k'aak'-ej***
and so 3A-bright-ADJ-INCH 3A-eye DET fire-TOP
(and) so that the light's bulb is bright."'

In 1:9 the noun *k'aak'*, 'light', is introduced as a possessed O, but the possessor NP is human, given, and referenced only by the possessive pronoun. The synonym *fok*, 'flashlight', appears as the next mention in 1:14, marked by a determiner and topic marker, signalling its status as given information known from previous discourse context. In 1:15 *a' k'aak'ej* appears in a possessor relation providing context for the newly introduced possessed NP, *uyich*, 'its bulb', in the inanimate possessive construction noted above. It also occurs as a humanly possessed object in 1:18. On every mention a noun appears, i.e., *k'aak'* is not referred to anaphorically.

Indefinite marking with a numeral and numeral classifier is uncommon with inanimate nouns and need not signal the introduction of important discourse information. For example, the two initial indefinite mentions recorded for Text 1 in Table 2 in locative and possessor case roles are the only mentions for those NPs in the text. Numeral and classifier can mark definite NPs as in the next example.

(5) *b'a'al*, 'thing, bullet'

1:62 *Ii a' b'a'ax uch-ij to'on-ej*
and DET thing happen-3SG.B 1PL.IOPR-TOP
'And the thing that happened to us

1:63 *kee* ***u-b'a'al*** *in-tz'on-ej*
that 3A-bullet 1SG.A-gun-TOP
is that the bullet of my gun

1:64 *ma' wak'-ij.*
NEG explode-3SG.B
didn't explode.

1:65 ***Ka'=p'eel u-b'a'al*** *t-in-tz'-aj ich-il*
two=INAM 3A-bullet COM-1SG.A-put-CTS in-POS
Two bullets I put inside

1:66 *I ma' wak'-ij* ***t-u-ka'=p'eel-il***
and NEG explode-3SG.B in-3A-two=INAM-POS
and it didn't fire on the two.'

As in previous examples, *b'a'al* is introduced in a possessive construction with the possessor NP following. Unlike the nouns in previous examples, *b'a'al* is briefly a highlighted constituent. After its introduction as a subject, it appears as a focused O in 1:65 without the presence of the following possessor NP. Focus is marked by preverbal position and the absence of the topic marker. (See Hofling 1982, 1984, 1991, 2000 for discussion of word order and highlighting in Itzaj.) In its last mention in 1:66 it appears obliquely and is marked anaphorically by the numeral and numeral classifier alone.

The function of inanimate nouns in the mythic text is much the same. They provide context and background for the actions of the major protagonists and they are for the most part of quite limited occurrence. However, certain images and concepts do gain the status of secondary topics as in the following examples. These images include blood, eyes, caves, hills, and the passage of time.

(6) *k'ik'*, 'blood'

2:44 *t-u-pul-aj* ***yaab' k'ik'.***
COM-3A-throw-CTS much blood
'(the animal) lost a lot of blood.

2:45 *I tan-u-b'el*
and DUR-3A-go
And he (the hunter) is going,

2:46 *k-uy-il-ik*
INC-3A-see-ITS
he sees
2:47 *tu'ux k-u-b'el a' k'ik'-ej*
where INC-3A-go DET blood-TOP
where the blood goes,'
2:58 *K-uy-il-ik-ej*
INC-3A-see-ITS-TOP
'He (the hunter) sees
2:59 *ke a' k'ik'-ej*
that DET blood-TOP
that the blood
2:60 *ok-ij ich a' aktun-ej.*
enter-3SG.B in DET cave-TOP
entered in the cave.'

Blood is and has been a powerful image among the Maya (cf. Schele and Miller 1986) and becomes a focus of attention in the narration after the mythic hunter wounds a deer. In example (6), *k'ik'*, 'blood', is introduced in 2:44 as an indefinite O and then appears as a definite S in 2:47 in a parallelism with line 2:45. It is reintroduced preverbally as a topical S in 2:59, and appears later in the text as a definite O in 2:74 and again as a possessed S in 2:94. It is typical of inanimates that they are referred to lexically on each mention but *k'ik'* is unusual in the number and prominence of its mentions.

The repetition of inanimate mentions is an element of the pervasive parallelism evident in Mayan texts (Brody 1986, 1994; England 1982; Martin 1990, 1994, this volume; Hofling 1989, 1993, 2000) and is striking in the following example built on the word *'ich*, 'eye'.

(7) *'ich*, 'eye'
2:134 *"Pero yan a-mutz'-ik aw-ich"*
but OBLIG 2A-shut-ITS 2A-eye
'"But you have to shut your eyes",
2:135 *ki b'in ti'ij.*
said REPORT 3IOPR
they say he said to him.
2:136 *I a' winik-ej*
and DET man-TOP
And the man,
2:137 *aj-tz'on-ej*
MASC-shoot-TOP
the hunter,

2:138 *ka' t-u-mutz'-aj uy-ich.*
then COM-3A-shut-CTS 3A-eye
then he shut his eyes.
2:139 *"asta inw-a'al-ik tech*
until 1SG.A-say-ITS 2SG.IOPR
"(Not) until I tell you
2:140 *ke k-a-jeb'-e' aw-ich-ej*
that that-2A-open-DTS 2A-eye-TOP
that you open your eyes
2:141 *k-a-jeb'-ik"*
INC-2A-open-ITS
do you open them",
2:142 *ki b'in a' chämach ti'ij-ej.*
QUOT REPORT DET old.man 3IOPR-TOP
they say the old man said to him.'

Only once in this listing of mentions of opening and shutting eyes does *'ich* fail to appear in these parallel structures as a post-verbal possessed O (2:141). All of the examples of lexical repetition occur in parallelisms involving direct quotation followed by a shift to narrative description (cf. Martin 1992, 1994, Hofling 1996, 2000), a device that continues for another half dozen lines in the text after the passage given in (7).

The sacred nature of the home of the Lord of the Deer in a cave at the foot of a mound is suggested by its prominence in the text. Caves have provided entrance to the Maya underworld since pre-Classic times (Schele and Miller 1986). Note the elaborate introduction of the cave in the examples below.

(8) ***aktun***, 'cave', and ***witz,*** 'hill'
2:54 *k'och-ij* ***t-u-chun jun=kuul witz"***
arrive-3SG.B at-3A-base one=round hill
'he arrived at the base of a hill
2:55 *i* *t-u-chun* ***a' witz-ej***
and at-3A-base DET hill-TOP
and at the base of the hill
2:56 *yan* ***jun=p'eel noj aktun***
EXIST one=INAM big cave
was a big cave,
2:57 *b'ay u-jol* ***jun=kuul naj-ej.***
like 3A-door one=round house-TOP
like the door of a house.'

The noun *witz*, 'hill', is introduced as an indefinitely marked possessor in 2:54 and is definite on its next mention (2:55). *Aktun*, 'cave', is introduced as an indefinitely marked S of the existential *yan* (2:56) and is likewise marked definitely on its next mention in 2:63. The cave at the foot of the hill is prominent both as the hunter enters it and when he departs, whereupon it disappears.

(9) ***aktun***, 'cave'

2:63	"***A'aktun je'-la'-ej***	
	DET-cave OST-PROX-TOP	
	'"As for this cave,	
2:64	*wa'ye' ok-ij a' b'a'al=che'-ej.*	
	here enter-3SG.B DET animal-TOP	
	here the animal entered.	
2:66	***A' aktun-ej***	
	DET cave-TOP	
	The cave,	
2:67	*sas-il u-jol*	
	bright-ADJ 3A-entrance	
	its entrance is bright,	
2:68	*chik-a'an kooch ich-il."*	
	appear-PART wide in-POS	
	it appears wide inside."	

As is evident from its extensive repetition in parallel structures, the cave is an important image in the text, and its prominence is marked morphosyntactically by demonstratives (2:63; 2:163), by sentence-initial topic position (2:63; 2:66), and by interclausal linkages other than lexical mentions including dependent pronominal references and locatives (2:63–64; 2:66–68; 2:70–72; 2:163–164).

In addition to the magical aura of the cave and its disappearance, the supernatural nature of the hunter's encounter with the Lord of the Deer is marked by a focus on time and on ambiguities of temporal reference and time's passage (cf. Hofling 1993). Until he returns home, the hunter believes that all of his experiences have occurred in a single day. On his arrival, his wife tearfully informs him that he has been absent three months. This contradiction and uncertainty is highlighted in the text.

(10) ***k'in***, 'day'

2:200	*La'ayti'-ej*
	3IPR-TOP
	'As for him,
2:201	*t-u-t'an-ej*
	in-3A-thought-TOP
	he was thinking

2:202 *wa la'ayt(i') a' k'in je'-lo'*
if 3IPR DET day OST-DIST
it was that day

2:203 *t-u-tz'on-aj a' keej-ej*
COM-3A-shoot-CTS DET deer-TOP
that he shot the deer,

2:204 *la'ayti' a' miismo k'in je'-lo'*
3IPR DET same day OST-DIST
it was that same day

2:205 *sut-k'-aj-ij-ej.*
return-CELER-DETR-3SG.B-TOP
he returned.

2:206 *I ke si la'ayti'*
and that if 3IPR
And that if he

2:207 *xan-aj-ij ox=p'e mes*
delay-CIS-3SG.B three=INAM month
delayed three months,

2:208 *sat-ij ox=p'e mes*
lose-3SG.B three=INAM month
he was lost three months,'

Again lexical repetition contributes to parallelism. The temporal contrast is repeatedly marked in focus constructions with the independent pronoun *la'ayti'* and the demonstrative *je'-lo'* (2:202; 2:204; 2:214). The ambiguity of time reference is also subtly echoed in the text by the use of the temporal deictic *b'a(je')la'*, 'now', to refer to the day the hunter experienced (2:107), to the day he returned three months later (2:192), and to the day the story was told (2:223).

Animate nominal reference

Unlike inanimate referents, which tend to be mentioned lexically, the bulk of animate reference is accomplished pronominally. As shown in Table 1, a majority of both transitive and intransitive clauses lack overt core lexical arguments, and, for transitives, two-argument clauses are extremely rare. Thus, the verbal person marking system, which obligatorily indexes S, A, and O with dependent pronouns of Sets A and B, plays a major role in nominal reference. No other mention of an argument need appear when reference is unambiguously signalled deictically (first and second person) or anaphorically (third person) by person markers. Once a discourse topic is established, stretches of discourse of considerable length can occur without the discourse topic being mentioned lexically. However, both nominal and independent pronominal mentions do occur with considerable frequency to signal discourse highlighting. As England and Martin note (this volume), independent pronouns may function like other lexical mentions and, like lexical arguments, they are cross-referenced on the verb by dependent pronouns. The paradigm of independent pronoun forms is given in (11).

(11) Independent Pronouns[3]

	Singular	Plural
1st person	*(in-)ten*	excl. (*in-*)to'on
		incl. *(in-)to'on-e'ex*
2nd person	*(in-)tech*	*(in-)te'ex*
3rd person	*la'ayti', ti'ij* (I)	*la'ayti'-oo', ti'ij-oo'* (I)

Discourse examples of these pronouns appear in the examples below.

Table 4 presents an inventory of animate nominal references for the Itzaj texts. Comparisons of Table 4 with Tables 2 and 3 indicate a number of distributional differences. There is a much greater proportion of A, Si, and I mentions in the total inventory of animate NPs (Table 4) as compared with first mentions (Table 2). Independent pronouns, which do not appear as first mentions, play a major role in later references, especially I mentions. There is also an expected greater occurence of mentions modified by the definite determiner, especially prominent in A and S roles.

After initial mention, there are more subsequent lexical mentions of animates than of inanimates in both texts. However, lexical and mentions are proportionally more numerous in the mythic text than in the personal narrative. In the personal narrative there were 26 initial lexical mentions for inanimates and 7 initial lexical mentions for animates. Subsequently, there were 13 more inanimate mentions and 18 more animate mentions. In the mythic narrative there were 30 inanimate and 11 animate initial mentions, with an additional 49 inanimate mentions and 90 animate mentions. Allowing for differences in the lengths of texts (81 clauses in Text 1, the personal narrative vs. 191 clauses in Text 2, the mythic narrative), subsequent animate mentions are far more numerous in the mythic text. This pattern reflects differences in discourse pragmatics between the genres. In personal narrative, the primary discourse topic is first person and dependent pronouns unambiguously mark first person reference. In mythic narrative, the primary topics are third person and lexical mentions serve a disambiguating function. (There are, of course, shifting first and second person references in quoted speech in many kinds of narrative genres.)

Animate reference in personal narrative

In the first deer hunting story, the major characters are the narrator, his companion, and a deer. Table 5 presents a tabulation of the mentions of each.

The distribution in Table 5 reflects relationships of features of animacy and

Table 4. Inventory of animate lexical mentions (Text 1 n=25, Text 2 n=101, Total n=126)

	A		Si		Se		O		I		LOC		POSR		OTHER	
	T1	T2	T1	T2	T1	T2	T1	T2	T1	T2	T1	T2	T1	T2	T1	T2
NUM CLS N					1	2										
(ADJ) N					3		1			4			1			
PPR N		3		2					2	1		1				1
DET (ADJ) N		14	1	1		10		6		5		1	2	2		2
IPR	1	4	1	19	1	7		9	7	3	2		2	3		1
Totals:	1	21	2	22	5	19	1	15	9	13	2	2	5	5	0	4

Table 5. Major character mentions in Text 1 (n=92)

	A	Si	Se	O	I	LOC	POSR
1 plural							
IPR	1	1	1		1	2	
DPR	12	16	1				1
1 singular							
IPR					3		2
DPR	19	4					5
companion							
PPR N					2		
IPR	1				2		
DPR	6	2					
deer							
(NUM CLS) N			2				
DET N		1					1
DPR		2		2			2
Totals:	39	26	4	2	8	2	11

topicality to the form and case role of mention. First person references, which are most topical and highest in animacy (Givón 1984), tend to be marked primarily by dependent pronouns, while the companion and deer, which are lower in topicality and animacy, have more lexical references. Relatedly, first person figures prominently as A or S, but not O, while the deer never appears as an A, but in the less topical case roles of S and O.

As shown in (12), first person plural is introduced at the beginning of the story by an S dependent pronoun in line 1:1. It remains the uninterrupted topic in S or

A role until 1.8 where the narrator (first person singular) is distinguished from his companion to introduce quoted speech. Conversational turns are frequently marked as narrative discourse units. (See Martin 1992 for general discussion of quotation in Mayan discourse with particular references to Itzaj discourse and Hofling 1996, 2000.) In line 1:8, the shift from first person plural to singular is marked by a dependent pronominal person marking while the companion is introduced with a lexical mention in IO case role.

(12) 1:1 *Akä'-aj-ij* *b'in-o'on ti tz'on.*
night-CIS-3SG.B go-1PL to shoot
'Last night we went to hunt.'
1:8 *k-inw-a'l-ik* ***t-inw-et'ok-ej:***
INC-1SG.A-say-ITS to-1SG.A-friend-TOP
'I say to my friend:'

In 1:12 the companion speaks, and this shift of speaker is marked by the conjunction *i*, 'and', followed by a contrastive focus construction with a pre-verbal independent pronoun. As in this case, constructions with conjunctions and independent pronominal or lexical mentions frequently mark initial boundaries of units of discourse (Brody 1987; Hofling 1989, 2000).

(13) 1:12 *I* ***la'ayti'*** *k-uy-a'al-ik* ***ten-ej:***
and 3IPR INC-3A-say-ITS 1SG.IOPR
'And he says to me:'

After a brief passage of direct quotation (1:13–15), first person plural referring to the narrator and his companion is resumed as topic, marked by an S dependent pronoun. It continues in S or A role with a sprinkling of 1SG references (1:18, 1:23, 1:31) until 1:35, where 1SG becomes primary topic. Two mentions of the 1PL independent pronoun occur in this passage (1:22, 1:26) contrasting the speaker's party to another group of hunters they hear in the fields.

Initial conjunctions continue to appear with shifts of scene and of topic, including shifts to and from direct quotation and between 1SG and 1PL, as in the examples in (14). In these minor shifts, the topic may be marked simply by dependent pronominal person markers.

(14) 1:23 *Ij* ***k-inw-a'al-ik*** *ti'ij-ej:*
and INC-1SG.A-say-ITS 3IOPR-TOP
'And I said to him:'
1:33 *I* *ka'* ***nak'-o'on.***
and then climb-1PL.B
'And then we climbed.'

1:35 *ka' kap-een in-tich'=k'ak'-t-ej*
then begin-1SG.B 1SG.A-illuminate-TRN-DTS
'then I began to illuminate it.'

The clause in 1:23 introduces direct quotation and a shift from 1PL to 1SG; 1:33 marks a shift from quotation to description, and 1:35 signals a shift from 1PL to 1SG within the narrative. The shift to 1SG begins with S and A 1SG dependent pronouns in 1:35, and is established in 1:37, where the 1SG independent pronoun appears initially as topic in a possessor role.

(15) 1:37 *in-ten-ej yan in-b'en-il*
EMP-1SG.IPR-TOP EXIST 1SG.A-path-POS
'Me, I have my path'

1SG continues as topic in S or A role marked by dependent pronouns until 1:42, where a minor shift to 1PL is signaled with the conjunction *ka'*, 'then'. *Ka'* also marks the shift back to 1SG in 1:44.

(16) 1:42 *Ka' k'och-o'on-ej*
when arrive-1PL.B-TOP
'Then we arrived.'
1:44 *ka' kap-een in-tich'=k'ak'-t-ej tulakal*
then begin-1SG.B 1SG.A-illuminate-TRN-DTS all
then I began to illuminate it all'

In 1:47, the quarry is introduced as an indefinite NP in a stative construction. Immediately after introducing the deer, 1SG is again marked as topic by an independent pronoun in a possessor role following a conjunction in 1:48.

(17) 1:47 *te' chil-a'an jun=tuul keej-i'ij...*
LOC lie-PART ONE=ANIM deer-SCOPE
'there was lying a deer
1:48 *ii in-ten-ej*
and EMP-1SG.IPR-TOP
And I,
1:49 *t-in-t'an-ej wa b'alum...*
in-1SG.A-thought-TOP if jaguar
I thought it might be a jaguar.'

A shift to 1PL in Se case role is marked by a conjunction and independent pronoun in 1:53. A couplet (1:54–55) precedes the dramatic peak, which is marked by direct quotation where the narrator tells his companion that he has spotted a deer in 1:56–58. The shift back to the narrative is again signalled by the conjunction *ka'* and the 1SG S dependent pronoun in 1:59.

(18) 1:56 *I ka' t-inw-a'al-aj t-inw-et'ok-ej*
and then COM-1SG.A-say-CTS to-1SG.A-friend-TOP
And then I said to my friend:
1:57 *"Ma a-b'el ti t'an*
NEG 2A-go to speak
"Don't go speaking,
1:58 *a'-laj keej."*
DET-PROX deer
this is a deer."'

A phenomenon related to the Preferred Argument Structure constraint against new information appearing in A role is also reflected in the case roles of topic shift. With the exception of the quotative verb *'a'l* 'to say' (which England and Martin, this volume, suggest be considered apart from other transitive verbs; cf. Munro 1982), shifted topics tend not to appear in the A role, as is evident in all of the examples mentioned above. That is, the constraint against new/lexical information in A role extends to include topic shift (see Clancy, this volume).

After attempting to shoot the deer (1:59–61), the hunter suffers the misfortune of having faulty shells which fail to explode, and there is a shift to the bullets as topic with first person mentioned obliquely in 1:62–63, again with a conjunction (see example [5] above). Direct quotation is dramatically introduced in 1:67, where the speech event is a contrastively focused object referenced by preverbal independent pronouns.

(19) 1:67 *I la'ayt(i)' a'-lo'*
and 3IPR DET-DIST
'And it is this
1:68 *k-inw-a'l-ik ti'ij-ej:*
INC-1SG-say-PM 3IOPR-REL
I say to him:'

Following the conversation, there is a rapid series of shifts back to narration (1:73), to the deer as topic, lexically mentioned in 1:75, back to a 1PL topic in 1:78, marked by the independent pronoun. First person plural continues as topic to the end, where the deer is again mentioned in the coda (1:85–86).

To summarize the topic flow in the personal narrative, 1PL is prominent at the beginning of the text when the hunters set out and at the end of the text when they return. 1SG dominates the middle of the text with brief shifts to the companion and the deer. Major topic shifts are marked by conjunctions and independent pronouns or, in the case of the deer, by nouns, while minor shifts are typically signalled by conjunctions and dependent pronouns. Topic shift frequently involves movements to and from direct discourse.

Animate reference in mythic narrative

In the mythic text, the major characters are a hunter, a deer, and the Lord of the Deer, while minor characters include the hunter's family and the narrator's family. Mentions of the major characters appear in Table 6.

Table 6. Major character mentions in Text 2 ($n=246$)

	A	Si	Se	O	I	LOC	POSR	OTHER
hunter								
NUM CLS N			1					
PPR N				1				
DET N	6	3	2		1	1	1	
IPR	3	6	3		13		2	
DPR	46	44	4	4			26	
deer								
DET N	2	4	1	1			2	
DPR	4	10	3	7		4		
Lord of Deer								
NUM CLS N			1					
DET N	5	2	3	1				2
IPR	1		1		2			
DPR	12	5	4	1			1	
Totals:	79	74	23	15	16	5	32	2

The hunter is introduced at the beginning of the text as an indefinite NP in a formulaic existential construction typical of the traditional Mayan narrative genre shown in (20).

(20) 2:1 *Uch-ij* *b'in-ej*
happen-3SG.B REPORT-TOP
'Long ago, they say
2:2 *yan-aj-ij* *jun=tuul* *winik*
EXIST-CIS-3SG.B one=ANIM man
there was a man'

The hunter continues as topic in S or A role through 2:14, marked by dependent pronouns and one independent pronoun (2:13) signalling a narrative shift from hunting to selling meat, which is highlighted in contrastive focus constuctions in 2:15–16. The fateful day of his encounter with the deer and its owner is introduced with a conjunction in 2:17 and the hunter is referenced by a topicalized independent pronoun in 2:18. It is not certain why the deer is introduced as a definite rather than an indefinite O in 2:19, but this marking suggests that the speaker judged that the audience knew which animal he was talking about by virtue of prior knowledge of this traditional tale.

(21) 2:17 *Pero yan-aj-ij b'in jun=p'e k'in …*
but EXIST-CIS-3SG.B REPORT one=INAM day
'But there was, they say, one day
2:18 *la'ayti'-ej*
3IPR-TOP
he,
2:19 *t-uy-il-aj aj-noj b'a'al=che'*
COM-3A-see-CTS MASC-big animal
he saw the big animal'

The first major topic shift is to the deer and occurs in 2:22–23. The sentence begins with conjunctions (*i a'-ka'* 'and when'), a feature of topic shift noted above, and the topicalized noun appears in 2:23. Note that in both clauses the major characters are in possessor case roles producing a vivid parallelism of the explosion of the gun and the leap of the deer.

(22) 2:22 *I a'-ka' wak'-ij u-tz'on-ej*
and DET-when explode-3SG.B 3A-gun-TOP
'And when his gun fired,
2:23 *a' keej-ej*
DET deer-TOP
the deer
2:24 *wak'-ij u-siit'.*
explode-3SG.B 3A-jump
made his leap.'

The deer continues as topic through 2:29, where the man is mentioned lexically as an oblique NP. A rare example where a non-human is in agent case role in an object focus OVA construction occurs in 2:26.

(23) 2:25 *Ma' lub'-ij.*
NEG fall-3SG.B
'It didn't fall,
2:26 *A' b'a'ax t-u-b'et-aj a' keej-ej*
DET thing COM-3A-do-CTS DET deer-TOP
What the deer did
2:27 *ka' tal-ij*
that come-3SG.B
was that it came

2:28 *tun-siit'*
DUR/3A-jump
jumping
2:29 *yok' a' winik-ej.*
over DET man-TOP
over the man.
2:30 *I a' winik-ej*
and DET man-TOP
And the man
2:31 *t-u-ka'=tz'on-aj.*
COM-3A-REPET-shoot-CTS
he shot it again.
2:32 *I a'-ka' ti' wak'-ij u-tz'on-ej*
and DET-when to explode-3SG.B 3A-gun-TOP
And when his gun fired,
2:33 *a' b'a'al=che'-ej*
DET animal-TOP
the animal …

After his oblique mention in 2:29, the topic shifts to the man in 2:30, where he is again lexically mentioned after a conjunction, only to shift back to the deer in 2:32–33 in a construction rigidly parallel to that seen above in 2:22–24. In contrast to the topic shifts in the personal narrative, these shifts involve topicalized nouns, not independent pronouns, and the possible ambiguity of pronominal reference is avoided. In fact, the deer is never referred to by an independent pronoun.

The deer remains topic from 2:33 until another topic shift to the man in 2:39 where the man is first referred to as *ajtz'onej* 'the hunter'. After a brief shift to the deer (2:43–44), again lexically mentioned, the man resumes as topic in 2:45 and remains the main topic in S or A role until 2:82. In this passage (2:45–82) the cave is introduced and becomes topic twice in quoted speech (2:63, 2:66; see examples [8] and [9] above and their discussion). One example of an independent pronoun referring to the hunter occurs in direct quotation between the topical mentions of the cave (2:65), where he he emphatically refers to himself and his determination to enter the cave, but otherwise all references to him are by dependent pronouns in S or A role.

The Lord of the Deer is introduced in a stative construction (2:77) and again appears in statives within a relative clause (2:82) and as topic (2:83–84).

(24) 2:77 *te' wa'an jun=tuul nojoch winik-i'ij*
LOC stand/PART one=ANIM old man-SCOPE
'there is standing an old man.

2:82 *a' -tu'ux yan-il a' chämach-ej*
DET-where EXIST-FOC DET old man-TOP
where the old man was.

2:83 *I la'ayti'-ej*
and 3IPR-TOP
And as for him,

2:84 *wa'an a' chämach-ej*
stand/PART DET man-TOP
the old man is standing

2:85 *tun-tz'ik u-jan-al u-b'a'al=che'-oo'.*
DUR/3A-give/ITS 3A-food-NOM 3A-animal-PL
giving his animals food.'

As expected, the old man is marked indefinitely when introduced (2:77), but definitely thereafter. After a definite lexical mention in 2:82, the Lord of the Deer becomes primary topic, marked by a topicalized independent pronoun after a conjunction in 2:83. After appearing as a stative subject (Se) marked by the independent pronoun in 2:83 and the definite mention in 2:84, the old man functions as A in 2:85, marked by a Set A person marker prefix on the verb.

Two new lexical mentions appear as possessed nouns in a possessed-possessor construction in 2:85 (*ujanal ub'a'alche'oo'* 'the food of his animals') where the possessor noun (*b'a'alche'oo'*) is also in an I role as recipient. The possessor noun *b'a'alche'oo'* is itself possessed by the old man, but since he is given information, possession is marked simply by the possessive (Set A) pronoun, again reflecting the discourse pattern noted above that for prototypical and least marked possessed nouns, the possessor is human and given information. This pattern provides motivation for the ergative marking of possessive pronouns, because prototypical As, like possessors, are human and given (cf. Du Bois 1987; Hofling 1990).

After a brief rise in prominence of the deer the old man is feeding (2:85–87), there is a rapid series of lexically marked topic shifts back to the the old man (2:88), to the deer the hunter shot (2:91) and back to the old man (2:96), before a passage of quoted speech in which the hunter becomes topic (2:97). Passages of quoted speech are bounded initially and finally by formulae in which the old man is referenced lexically as an A and the hunter by an indirect object pronoun (the old man does all of the talking) as in the opening in 2:95–96 and the closing in 2:110. (The same quotative formulae appear in 2:119, 130, 142, and 145).

(25) 2:95 *i k-uy-a'al-ik b'in*
and INC-3A-say-ITS REPORT
'and the old man says, they say,

2:96 *a' nojoch winik ti'ij-ej:*
DET old man 3IOPR-TOP
to him:
2:97 *"Kon ke tech aj-tz'on-ech-ej*
with that 2SG IPR MASC-shoot-2SG.B-TOP
"Since you are the hunter,
2:98 *in-tech a' winik-ech*
EMP-2SG.IPR DET man-2SG.B
you are the man
2:99 *k-a-senkech=tz'on-ik a' im-b'a'al=che'-oo'-ej.*
INC-2A-much=shoot-ITS DET 1SGA-animal-PL-TOP
that so often shoots the animals.'
2:110 *ki b'in a' nooch winik ti'ij-ej.*
QUOT REPORT DET old man 3IOPR-TOP
'they say the old man said to him.'

After introducing the hunter as topic in a couplet with both independent pronouns and lexical mentions (2:97–98), the hunter is marked as A by dependent pronouns, and the animals as O (99–104). The animals are first referred to lexically in the unmarked post-verbal position (2:99–100), but are highlighted as a sentence-initial topic in 2:102–103, where they are modified both by a demonstrative and a relative clause.

The usual pattern of topic shift with a conjunction and topicalized independent pronoun occurs to signal the old man as topic within the quoted passage in 2:105. Outside of quotation, lexical mentions signal the hunter as topic in 2:111, 2:128, 2:136–137, and 148–49. Elsewhere, he is referred to primarily by S and A dependent pronouns both in and out of quotation.

By 2:147 the hunter is alone outside of the cave and lexical references to the hunter virtually disappear until the summary closings at the end of the text (2:217, 2:228–29). Highlighting of the hunter is marked by third person independent pronouns in 2:158, 2:165, 2:180, 2:200, 2:206, and 2:211 and by deictic first or second person independent pronouns inside quotation in 2:187 and 2:198. That is, when the danger of ambiguity decreases after he has left the cave, independent pronominal usage increases.

After the hunter arrives home (2:169), members of his family are atypically introduced as topic (2:170).

(26) 2:169 *ka' k'och-ij t-uy-otoch-ej.*
then arrive-3SG.B at-3A-home-TOP
'then he arrived at his home.
2:170 *Uy-ätan i tulakal u-mejen paal-oo'-ej*
3A-wife and all 3A-small child-PL-TOP
his wife and all of his small children,

2:171 *a'-ka'* *t-uy-il-aj-oo'*
DET-when COM-3A-see-CTS-PL
when they saw...'

As noted previously, information does not ordinarily enter discourse as a topic (or as A). This example may be accounted for on the basis that, *otoch*, 'home', (vs. *naj*, 'house') evokes a constellation of shared cultural meanings including the family and therefore family members are not new information in this context (cf. England and Martin, this volume). In describing the interaction with family members (2:170–199), topic shifts occur among them in expected ways. The story proper winds down with the hunter as topic, thinking about his confusing experience until the standard closing in (27).

(27) 2:216 *B'aay-lo b'in uch-ij*
thus-DIST REPORT happen-3SG.B
Thus, they say, it happened
2:217 *a' winik jach (u)y-ojel=tz'on-ej.*
DET man much 3A-know=shoot-TOP
to the man who really knew hunting.

The text continues with a brief afterword in which the story itself is topic, as the narrator explains how he learned the story, and ends with an echo of the standard closing.

Summary and conclusions

Analysis of Itzaj Maya narrative texts indicates that the constraints of Preferred Argument Structure generally hold. Transitive clauses with two lexical arguments are rare, and new lexical mentions are unlikely to occur in A role. A detailed examination of how different kinds of information are introduced in narrative discourse and what happens after their introduction reveals several general patterns in the relations of case role, animacy, topicality, and morphosyntactic form and some differences between mythic and personal narrative. Inanimate NPs do not ever occur in A role. They are introduced (in order of frequency) in S, LOC and O case roles and are later mentioned lexically in these same case roles if they are maintained. They do not tend to become topics and are rarely referred to anaphorically. They are frequently marked as definite on first mention, either as possessed nouns or by the determiner in relative constructions. If the possessor is also inanimate, as in locative expressions, it too is mentioned lexically.

Animate nouns are introduced in every case role except LOC with the S role preferred for major characters. Later mentions are most frequently in A, I, and S case roles marked both lexically and pronominally. Animate (particularly human)

Table 7. Summary of inanimate and inanimate lexical mentions

	A	Si	Se	O	I	LOC	POSR	OTHER
INANIMATE	0	11	26	29	0	33	13	6
ANIMATE	22	24	24	15	22	4	10	4

NPs become major topics. It was also observed that nouns are repeated for rhetorical effects in parallelisms, especially couplets.

The general difference between animate and inanimate mentions is summarized in Table 7.

A difference was noted between the marking of topics in personal narrative and in mythic narrative. In personal narrative, deictic dependent pronouns predominate and major topic shift is marked by conjunctions and independent pronouns. Independent pronouns reflect highlighting of their referents and are often contrastive. In mythic narrative, anaphoric pronouns predominate, and topic shift is marked by conjunctions and definite lexical mentions, avoiding possible ambiguities of pronominal reference. Genre distinctions are marked by different frequencies of a constellation of features, rather than absolutely. The genre differences in mentions of major characters are summarized in Table 8.

Equative (stative) constructions with indefinitely marked NPs are an important mechanism for introducing major characters into a discourse. Topics are overwhelmingly in S or A roles, and it was observed that in topic shift, topical NPs tend to appear first in non-A roles. Topical human NPs are frequently Is when not topics. Human referents are also frequently marked as possessors, and it was noted that the ergative marking of the A role and the possessor role in the dependent pronominal system is motivated by the fact that both tend to be human, given information.

This analysis highlights the fundamental difference in nominal reference between the marking of topical humans and the inanimate environment in which they act. The dimensions of frequency of occurence, morphosyntactic form, and case role of mentions reflect this difference in predictable ways.

Nominal reference is crucial to discourse structure and interacts with a variety of other syntactic and rhetorical devices to signal the highlighting and backgrounding

Table 8. Mentions of major characters by genre

	Personal narrative	Myth
NOUN	6	40
IPR	14	31
DPR	72	175

of information, to mark boundaries of syntactic units, and to maintain discourse flow. Discourse highlighting, often signalled by lexical repetition and parallelism, reveals not only what is salient in a particular tale to a particular narrator, but also major cultural symbols. At the same time nominal reference helps signal boundaries of discourse units as changes of topic signal changes of scene, shifts to and from direct quotation, and change of deictic center, including change of speaker. Nominal reference not only signals shifts in point of view from the narrator to the protagonists and back, but reflects changes in the discourse universe, from that of personal experience to that of the mythic past. Nominal reference thus plays a major role in defining larger discourse structures and the cultural universe in which they operate.

Notes

* I am grateful to Jill Brody, and Laura Martin for their many helpful comments on earlier drafts of this paper and to John Du Bois and the other volume editors for helpful suggestions near the end.

1. Complete and more detailed transcriptions of these texts appear in Hofling 1991 as text 11. Hunting with a Friend, pp. 92–99; and text 15. The Lord of the Deer, pp. 136–153.

2. Itzaj Maya is written in the practical orthography approved by the Academia de Lenguas Mays de Guatemala (see Hofling 1997). Special abbreviations used in this paper include the following:

A	Set A person marker
ABIL	abilitive aspect
ANIM	animate
B	Set B person marker
CAUS	causative
CELER	celeritive
CIS	completive intransitive status
CLS	numeral classifier
COM	completive aspect
CTS	completive transitive status
DET	determiner
DETR	detransitve
DPR	dependent pronoun
DIST	distal deictic marker
DTS	dependent transitive status
DUR	durative aspect
EMP	emphatic
EXIST	existential
FOC	focus
IMP	imperative
INAM	inanimate
INC	incompletive aspect
INCH	inchoative
IOPR	indirect object pronoun

IPR	independent pronoun
ITS	incompletive transitive status
MASC	masculine
NUM	numeral
OBLIG	obligative aspect
OST	ostensive marker
PART	participle
PN	proper name
POS	possessive
PPR	possessive pronoun
PROX	proximal deictic marker
QUOT	quotative
REPET	repetitive
REPORT	reportative
TOP	topic
TRN	transitive

3. The parenthetic prefix *in-* is an optional emphatic marker that may appear with first and second person independent pronouns (Hofling 1991: 19).

References

Ariel, Mira. 1990. *Accessing Noun-Phrase Antecedents.* London: Routledge.

Brody, Jill. 1986. "Repetition as a Rhetorical and Conversational Device in Tojolobal (Maya)". *International Journal of American Linguistics* 52 (3): 255–74.

Brody, Jill. 1994. "Multiple Repetitions in Tojolab'al Conversation". In Barbara Johnstone (ed.), *Repetition in Discourse, Vol. II.* Norwood, NJ: Ablex, 3–14.

Brown, Gillian and George Yule. 1983. *Discourse Analysis.* Cambridge, Massachusetts: Cambridge University Press.

Chafe, Wallace. 1994. *Discourse, Consciousness, and Time: The Flow and Displacement of Conscious Experience in Speaking and Writing.* Chicago: University of Chicago Press.

Du Bois, John W. 1980. "Beyond Definiteness: The Trace of Identity in Discourse". In Wallace Chafe (ed.), *The Pear Stories: Cognitive, Cultural and Linguistic Aspects of Narrative Production.* Norwood, NJ: Ablex, 203–74.

Du Bois, John W. 1985. "Competing motivations". In John Haiman (ed.), *Iconicity in Syntax.* Amsterdam: John Benjamins, 343–365.

Du Bois, John W. 1987. "The discourse basis of ergativity". *Language* 63: 805–55.

England, Nora C. 1982. "The Structure of Couplets in Mam Narrative". Paper presented to the American Anthropological Association, Washington D.C.

England, Nora C. 1986. "Mamean Voice: Syntactic and Narrative Considerations". Paper presented to American Anthropological Association, Philadelphia.

England, Nora C. 1988. "Mam voice". In M. Shibatani (ed.), *Passives and Voice.* Amsterdam: John Benjamins, 525–45.

Givón, Talmy (ed.). 1983. *Topic Continuity in Discourse: A Quantitative Cross-Language Study.* Amsterdam: John Benjamins.

Givón, Talmy. 1984. *Syntax: A Functional-Typological Introduction. Vol. 1.* Amsterdam: John Benjamins.

Hofling, Charles Andrew. 1982. Itzá Maya Morphosyntax from a Discourse Perspective. Ph.D. dissertation, Washington University.

Hofling, Charles Andrew. 1984. "On Proto-Mayan Word Order". *Journal of Mayan Linguistics* 4(2): 35–64.

Hofling, Charles Andrew. [1989]. "Discourse Framing in Itzá Maya Narrative". *Anthropological Linguistics* 29(1987): 4: 478–88.

Hofling, Charles Andrew. 1990. "Possession and Ergativity in Itzá Maya". *International Journal of American Linguistics* 56(4): 542–60.

Hofling, Charles Andrew. 1991. *Itzá Maya Texts with a Grammatical Overview.* Salt Lake City, Utah: University of Utah Press.

Hofling, Charles Andrew. 1993. "Marking Time and Space in Itzaj Narrative". *Journal of Linguistic Anthropology,* 3(2): 164–84.

Hofling, Charles Andrew. 1996 "Dialogic Repetition in Mayan Discourse". Paper presented to the American Antrhopological Association, San Francisco.

Hofling, Charles Andrew (with Félix Fernando Tesucún). 1997. *Itzaj Maya–Spanish–English Dictionary.* Salt Lake City: University of Utah Press.

Hofling, Charles Andrew. 2000. *Itzaj Maya Grammar.* Salt Lake City: University of Utah Press.

Martin, Laura. 1987. "Information Flow in Mocho Mayan Narrative". Paper presented to the American Anthropological Association, Chicago.

Martin, Laura. 1990. Parsing Parallelism in Mocho. Kentucky Foreign Language Conference, Lexington.

Martin, Laura. 1992. "Dramatic Strategies, Quoted Speech and Narrative Discourse in Mocho". Ms.

Martin, Laura. 1994. "Discourse Structure and Rhetorical Elaboration in Mocho Personal Narrative". *Journal of Linguistic Anthropology* 4(2): 131–52.

Munro, Pamela. 1982. "On the transitivity of 'say' verbs". In P. Hopper and S. Thompson (eds), *Syntax and Semantics. Volume 15: Studies in Transitivity.* New York: Academic, 301–18.

Schele, Linda and Mary E. Miller. 1986. *The Blood of the Kings: Dynasty and Ritual in Maya Art.* Fort Worth: Kimbell Art Museum.

Narrator virtuosity and the strategic exploitation of Preferred Argument Structure in Mocho

Repetition and constructed speech in Mocho narrative*

Laura Martin
Cleveland State University

Introduction

This work is part of the on-going investigation into the organization and structure of conversation and narrative in Mocho, a moribund Mayan language spoken in southeastern Mexico.[1] Three aspects of Mocho discourse have emerged as particularly salient in all genres: the patterning and role of repetition and parallelism; the functions of constructed (quoted) speech; and the management of ambiguity. Repetition and constructed speech are extremely frequent, and each performs important discourse structuring roles. Each reinforces the other, and both are highly valued in the aesthetic system. And both devices are implicated in the ways narrators enhance or resolve ambiguity. Given these attributes, it is not surprising that both repetition and constructed speech interact with Preferred Argument Structure patterns (Du Bois 1985, 1987). In fact, they provide a most hospitable environment for close examination of such patterns.

Moreover, these familiar devices present special problems for Preferred Argument Structure analysis, producing some of the most difficult cases for investigator decision-making. The proper categorization of repeated elements, and in particular the matter of lexical co-reference, becomes crucial in a language like Mocho in which repetition is ubiquitous and rhetorically significant. The transitivity status of discourse verbs and the appropriate analysis of patterns within the quoted material itself are perplexing. Because both repetition and constructed talk are universal discourse features, this closer look at Preferred Argument Structure in Mocho narrative has implications for the wider study of discourse patterns as well.

Using a series of extended examples from a Mocho folktale, I hope to show how these features of discourse construction interact with the distribution of lexical nominals, agency, and other aspects of information flow as characterized by Preferred Argument Structure as well as illustrate the subtle intricacy with which a skilled narrator manipulates them as resources in his aesthetic program.

The data

The examples used here come from a single lengthy Mocho folk tale known as *The Little Orphans.* Although of European origin and clearly derived from the tale of Hansel and Gretel, the story has been drastically altered as it has been adapted to fit Mocho and Mayan cultural interests and narrative patterns. It is one of the favorite stories of my principal Mocho consultant, don Juan Méndez Matías of Barrio Guadalupe, Motozintla, Chiapas. Don Juan, like all Mocho speakers, is over fifty and bilingual since late childhood in the local variety of Spanish. Don Juan is a skilled and stylish narrator and conversationalist and is highly regarded locally as a good speaker of Mocho. He and his wife Victoria Echeverría use the language daily in their home, although their interlocutors are confined mostly to relatives and friends of their own age since their children (and now grandchildren and great-grandchildren) speak only Spanish.

In don Juan's story, two nameless children, a boy and a girl, are abandoned in the woods by their widowed father, at the behest of a woman who wants to be his second wife. Although the children manage to return home the first time the father tries to lose them, he is successful on his second try. The two attempts are recounted in the first two story Episodes. In the third Episode, darkness falls, and they climb a tree to find safety from wild animals. They spend a frightening night being threatened by a tiger and protected by a lion. The animals fight, the tiger is killed, and the starving children come down in the morning when the lion leaves.

Hearing a rooster's crow, they follow the sound to a house. The fourth Episode describes their experiences there where they are captured by an old woman who turns out to be a *chahwaal witz* (literally, 'owner of the mountain'). Known in Spanish as the *dueño del cerro,* this traditional Mayan supernatural has a dual nature. It is responsible for the animal spirit companions that accompany each human soul, but a *dueño* is also capable of kidnapping, often subjecting its victims to years of servitude. The old woman in this story feeds the children, but keeps them captive with clear cannibalistic intentions once she has fattened them up. When she asks to feel their fingers, they trick her by offering her the tail from a rat they have killed. Once they are strong enough, they show their real fingers, and she prepares a big pot of boiling water to cook them. They manage to trick her again by persuading her to demonstrate how to cross the plank that leads to the pot. They push her into the water, and she dies. Now in possession of her house and her great wealth of animals, the children grow to maturity.

In Episode 5, the story's Peak, the girl finds a boyfriend who convinces her to kill her older brother so they can marry. She places a sharpened bone under her brother's pillow, expecting it to pierce his throat when he throws himself on the bed. But he is too clever and discovers the bone in time. Criticizing and then punishing her for turning on him after all they've been through together, he says he will allow her to marry if her boyfriend asks for her properly. The Episode closes with her marriage. In the brief final episode, the now remorseful father returns to the woods, looking for his long-abandoned children. When he asks at the old woman's house, they first say they haven't seen any lost children, but then, chiding him for his unfatherly behavior, they kill him. The story doesn't say whether they lived happily ever after.[2]

As in many other Mocho narratives, the didactic purpose of *The Little Orphans* concerns being a proper adult. Since Mayan adult roles are heavily constrained by gender, such a message intimately concerns the acquisition of adult gender roles within family organization, roles that change over time as individuals take on the identities of child, sibling, spouse, and parent. In this story, the cultural concerns with sibling competition, appropriate ritual behavior associated with courtship and marriage, and the proper fulfillment of gender role expectations are all exhibited and resolved narratively (Martin 1997).

Repetition and constructed discourse in Mayan languages

In Mocho, as elsewhere in the Mayan family, repetition serves as a rhetorical device at the lexical and sentential levels, producing couplets and other types of parallelism. Such parallelism has been widely described and is recognized for its importance in ritual and other forms of stylized language use (see, e.g., Gossen 1974, 1975; Norman 1980; Tedlock 1983; 1996). However, repetition and the resulting parallelism it produces are just as important in ordinary talk, both narration and conversation. A frequent device for constructing repetition is, of course, lexical synonymy, the use of multiple forms with the same or very similar meanings.

England and I (this volume) have discussed at some length the issues involved in determining first mention and newness status in the context of so much lexical repetition and the extensive use of synonymous reference for rhetorical purposes. We particularly pointed to shared cultural knowledge as an important resource for interpretation of newness as well as to the need for further specification of the category of givenness. This latter problem has also engaged the attention of investigators of other languages, including many contributors to this volume, and many of the proposed subcategories now in use — e.g., invocable, inferable, accessible, etc. (Durie 1994) — seem to allow for the necessary subtypes. Still, as the Mocho examples discussed here suggest, many dimensions of the interaction between lexical repetition and information flow factors remain to be addressed.

Repetition is a structural as well as rhetorical device since it is one of the mechanisms by which discourse unit boundaries are constructed in Mocho, as in other Mayan languages. Lengthy exchanges of repetitions are a characteristic mark of topic termination or change in conversation (cf. Brody 1986), and repetition of temporal and/or locative information usually signals an episode boundary transition zone in narrative (see Hofling this volume). A commonly observed pattern in Mocho is the multiple repetition of events or episodes within a narration for aesthetic effect. There is no rhetorical validity in Mocho to notions of suspense or "punch lines". Instead, important plot points may be presented three or four times, with subtle variations in organization or content, producing cyclic patterns in narrative flow.

Don Juan's account of the events surrounding the children's attempt to leave a trail of corn grains to guide themselves home from the woods is a typical example. The first time the children are abandoned by their father, the boy cleverly carries along some corn, dropping grains along the way. Following these signs, the children are able to return home. In the second Episode, the boy again drops corn grains, but this time birds eat them, and the children become hopelessly lost. In some familiar European traditions of dramatic tension, the discovery that the grains have been eaten would constitute the peak moment of this part of the narrative. A competent narrator in this tradition would hold the information for dramatic revelation. Don Juan Méndez, an unusually competent Mocho narrator, instead reveals the information repeatedly. Aesthetic pleasure is derived from each repetition of the event as the characters discover it for themselves. One especially fruitful mechanism for accomplishing such aesthetically and structurally pleasing repetition is by presenting material in both narrative and constructed discourse forms.

In all Mayan languages, direct quotation plays an extremely important discourse role although it has been less often studied. Mocho discourse structural and aesthetic ideals require narrators and co-conversationalists, regardless of genre, to construct direct speech, that is, the apparently quoted talk of other speakers. This ideal is so strong that in retelling stories, a narrator may invent opportunities to construct discourse. Even in the narration of events where little opportunity exists for quotable talk, for example when there is only a single narrative participant, narrators use internal speech, quote animal participants, or include a narrated retelling to an interactive audience as strategies for incorporating the valued constructed discourse (see Martin 1994 for an example). This power of constructed speech as a dramatic narrative tool has of course been noted for many languages, among them English (Tannen 1989, Johnstone 1996).

I now turn to a detailed analysis of specific cases in the story where repetition and constructed discourse interact with the expected Preferred Argument Structure patterns. The first two cases illustrate patterns of discourse patterning that seem responsive to argument status and referentiality. The next two consider the ways in which repeated lexical mentions or lexical co-reference interfere with clear definition of "given" or "new" status. In all these cases, the narrator appears to strategically manipulate the inherent ambiguities produced by his lexical choices. Finally, the fifth case illustrates how patterning of unique lexical mentions systematically construct a pattern of "newness" that is discourse-driven, and not merely a product of grammatical factors.

*Case 1: Patterning by argument status (References to **ixi'm** 'corn')*

The first example presents a case where, within the confines of Preferred Argument Structure patterns, don Juan appears to manipulate argument status itself for rhetorical ends, using repetition and constructed speech to do so. The text includes the two story segments (one each from Episodes 1 and 2) in which corn, a key plot prop, appears.[3]

Episode 1

46 And given that those little kids, they had carried along
a little bit of **corn**,
*la kómo kutaq ch'in‿he, ø-ch-ik'-a-qe' noonh naalanh **ixi'm**,* O
and as little child‿DPT CMP-3E-carry-TV-PL DIR:going half corn

47 they went along spreading it on the road.
x-puq-sa-qe' choonh ti beeh. Ø = O
3E-scattered (P)-CAU-PL DIR:going PRP road

48 And the little boy says:

49 "But as for me, when we came,

50 I spread **corn** coming on the road.
*ø-ii-puq-sa' chaki **ixi'm** ti beeh.* O
CMP-1S-scattered (P)-CAU DIR:coming corn PRP road

51 That one is what we went along carrying."
ha'n q-ik'-a' choonh‿bi'."
FOC 1P-carry-TV DIR:going‿DPT

52 "Well, let's go then."

53 And they went off, so it is said.

54 They returned.

55 And they looked for the little **corn** in the road as they went.
*la ø-x-mah-a-qe' choonh kutaq **ixi'm** ti beeh.* O
and CMP-3E-look.for-TV-PL DIR:going little corn PRP road

56 They found the little **corn** in the road as they went.
ø-x-sah-a-qe' choonh kutaq ***ixi'm*** *ti beeh.* O
CMP-3E-find-TV-PL DIR:going little corn PRP road
57 They went off.
58 "Right here we passed,
59 here's the **corn**",
na' te' ***ixi'm****",* S-ext
just here corn
60 they said, so it is said.

Episode 2

80 And the little children, well, again they went along carrying a little bit of **corn**.
la kutaq ch'in‿he, ø -ch-ik'-a noonh poxo naalanh ***ixi'm****.* O
and little child‿DPT CMP-3E-carry-TV DIR:going half corn
81 They went along spreading it in handfuls,
ø-x-puq-sa' choonh, Ø = O
CMP-3E-scattered (P)-CAU DIR:going
82 right along wherever they passed by as before.
83 And the **corn**, what he went along spreading, well,
la we' ***ixi'm****, abi ø-x-puq-sa' choonh‿he,* **fronted O (focus)**
and DEF corn REL CMP-3E-scattered (P)-CAU DIR:going‿DPT
84 it's said it was eaten by doves.
ø-lo'-e' ab cho paloom. **Ø = S (Preferred Argument Structure)**
3A-eat-PAS REP by dove

...

100 "We carried the **corn** along
"ø-q-ik'-a choonh we' ***ixi'm*** O
CMP-1P-carry-TV DIR:going DEF corn
101 right where I left it scattered again."
yo ø-ii-puq-sa' kene' poxo‿a." Ø = O
where CMP-1S-scattered (P)-CAU DIR:remaining again‿DPT
102 "Let's go."
103 And they came back again, so it is said.
104 They came along looking for **corn**.
ø-x-mah-a-qe' chaki ***ixi'm*** O
CMP-3E-look.for-TV-PL DIR:coming corn
105 And that **corn** he went along scattering by handfuls, well,
la [?] ***ixi'm*** *ø-x-puq-sa' choonh‿he,* **fronted O (focus)**
and [?] corn CMP-3E-scattered (P)-CAU DIR:going‿DPT

106 right where he went along dropping it, Ø = O
yo ø-x-q'eb-a choonh‿a,
where CMP-3E-drop-TV DIR:going‿DPT
107 it's said it had been eaten by doves
ø-lo'-e' ab cho paloom. Ø = S
(**Preferred Argument Structure**)
3A-eat (TV)-PAS REP by dove
108 And they came along looking for it,
la x-mah-a-qe' chaki. Ø = O
and 3E-look.for-TV-PL DIR:coming
109 they came along looking for it.
x-mah-a-qe' chaki, Ø = O
3E-look.for-TV-PL DIR:coming
110 And it's said it never did appear for them.
muu ni ab ø-istaw-i ch-u'uuh-e'. Ø = S
NEG already REP 3A-appear-IV 3-RN:with-PL
111 "Now already we are lost -
112 the corn that I caused to be left
abi ixi'm ø-ii-ken-sa'-ø **fronted O (focus)**
REL corn CMP-1S-remain (IV)-CAU-3E
113 maybe it has already been eaten by animals.
ni ma' ø-lo'-e' cho animál. Ø = S
already perhaps 3A-eat (TV)-PAS by animal
114 Because, well, there isn't any."
ya moocho' xin." Ø = S
because NEG well

It can be seen that in some cases, reference to corn is made by lexical mention of the common noun *ix'im* and in others by cross-referencing the verb with a zero-marked 3SG Absolutive. No lexical synonyms are used. Note especially how quoted speech is matched to narrated material, as in lines 46–47, which present material immediately repeated in quoted speech by the children in lines 50–51. (The reversal in the order of the verb phrases in these two passages is typical of don Juan's narrative style and reflects the power of repetition to create variation.)

Analysis of the lexical references to corn in terms of Preferred Argument Structure reveals that the nominal mentions consistently pattern by argument status. Most references are in O status, but some are in S status and these account for all nominal S's in the segment. Subject status seems to be used when the narrative focus is centered on the point of greatest plot significance: the actual presence or absence of the corn as in lines 59, 84, 107, 110, 113, 114. This focus on the corn as Subject is congruent with other tactics involving transitivity relations within these lines. On balance, for example, the summary or concluding section (lines 103–114) shows a tendancy for lines expressed in the narrator's voice to emphasize transitive actions: scattering/spreading (*puq-* 'scattered (P) + *-sa*' 'causative', line 105), dropping (*q'eb* 'drop (TV)', line 106), and looking (*mah* 'look for (TV)', lines 104, 108, 109). Lines representing the children's own speech, on the other hand, tend to emphasize intransitive consequences: being lost (line 111), being eaten (*lo'* 'to eat' + *-e'* 'passive', line 113), and being absent (line 114).[4]

Line 112, a transitive in the character's voice, is therefore somewhat unusual. Its emphatic syntax (see below) highlights agency to contrast the character's intention (reflected in the transitive verb), with the outcome foreshadowed by the narrator's paired reportative intransitives in lines 107 and 110, that frame the doubly stated transitive references to the vain searching for grains that cannot appear.

Deliberate manipulation of narrator and character perspective works in other ways as well. The consequence that follows from the narrator's knowledge that the doves have eaten the corn (lines 84 and 107) is expressed in line 110 via a shift in perspective from narrator's total knowledge to the children's more limited knowledge. All the children really know is that the corn does not appear. This contrast of narrator and character knowledge is clearest in the replacement of the specific *paloom* 'dove' in the narrator's voice by the more generic label *animál* when the children repeat the conclusion that the corn has been eaten in line 113. Each of these references co-occurs with a focused lexical mention of corn in identical syntactic constructions, a fronted O in an appositive phrase (lines 83, 105, 112). The extreme parallelism created by this pattern of morphosyntactic repetition underscores the identity of these lines as members of a "triplet under construction", a relation extending across thirty lines.

Another contrast between narrator and character knowledge occurs in relation to the corn-scattering action. The character uses the directional-locational root *kene'* 'to remain' when referring to his corn-scattering in line 101, where it is a particle, and in line 112, where it is the main verb. When the narrator refers to the same action, he uses instead the directional particle *choonh* 'going' (lines 105, 106). *Choonh* is much less permanent in its implications than *kene'*. Its selection may reflect the narrator's consciousness that the grains will not long stay in their place.

In the case of *ix'im*, then, we can see the narrator's use of a single lexical item in contrasting argument status to emphasize a narratively significant point, a point he also emphasizes by other manipulations, including changes in transitivity or indications of permanence and in the alternation of narrative and constructed speech. In the next example, also without synonyms, we find that repeated mentions of another important plot prop, the rat and its tail, pattern according to reference status and activation state.

*Case 2: Patterning by reference status (References to **ch'oohon** 'rat')*

Example 2 presents a continuous segment from Episode 3, beginning at the point where the rat tail is first introduced. Like the corn, the rat does not undergo any significant transition in the course of the story. The narrator marks this stability by not using any synonyms.

218 And they spoke together,
219 "We're not sticking our finger right out there now.
220 That is why I already stuck out the tail of the rat",
ch-u'uuh to‿he niø- ii-ch'ixbe' neel
[x-nheeh we' ch'oohon]", **definite = Poss**
3-RN:with still‿DPT already CMP-1S-show (TV)
DIR:out.from.speaker [3-tail DEF rat]
221 he said, so they say.
222 Because given they had perhaps grabbed a little rat
in the house,
*ya kómo ø-x-lok-o-qe' ma' [**huune' iti ch'oohon**]* **indefinite = O**
x-k'uul nhaah
because as CMP-3E-grab-TV-PL perhaps [one DIM rat] 3-inside house
223 A little rat, really tiny, this small. (gesture)
*[**huune' iti ch'oohon**] iti nu'ya', inde' tzapan.* **Indefinite = free**
[one DIM rat] one small thus small
224 Perhaps they saw
225 that rat running past, well,
*ø-q'iiluun ik'i [**we' ch'oohon**]‿he,* **definite = S**
3A-run (IV) DIR:passing [DEF rat]‿DPT
226 they went by to grab it
ø-ik'-i x-lok-o-ø -qe' **Ø = O**
CMP-PASS-IV 3E-grab-TV-3A-PL
227 and they killed the little rat.
*la ø-x-poch'-oø-qe' [**iti ch'oohon**].* **definite = O**
and CMP-3E-kill-TV-3A-PL [little rat]
228 "This one is what we're showing, this one,
*"**ha'n** ch-qa-ch'ixbe' te'* **foregrounded (= *iti*)**
FOC INC-1P-show (TV) DEM
229 as if we are not eating",
230 he said, so they say.
231 And they were asked,
232 "Stick out your fingers, the biggest one of your fingers."

233 "Okay", — he brought out the little rat,
"ee" — ø-ch-ik'-a taa [*iti* ***ch'oohon***], **definite = O**
okay CMP-3E-carry-TV DIR:toward [little rat]
234 He showed the little rat's tail.
ø-[*x*]*-ch'ixbe'* [*iti x-nheeh* ***ch'oohon***]. **definite = Poss**
CMP-3E-show [little 3-tail rat]

In this passage, don Juan mentions the word *ch'oohon* 'rat' lexically seven times, sometimes in reference to the animal itself and sometimes as a Possessor. It is cross-referenced much less frequently, once by a focus demonstrative, *ha'n* 'this (one)' in line 228, and once by zero anaphor on the verb *lok-o'* 'to grab (tv)' in line 226. In the occurences of *ch'oohon,* we can again see the manipulation of perspective through the manipulation of lexical mentions, but in this case the patterning seems to be sensitive to a noun's reference status.

The first mention of the rat in line 220 is unusual in that it is fully definite, occurring as Possessor and accompanied by *we'*, a marker of definiteness and specificity. In the subsequent series of mentions, though, the usual Preferred Argument Structure pattern emerges. First, the noun appears in an indefinite phrase (marked by the indefinite *huune'* 'one') functioning as O (line 222). Next, it appears in line 223 in an appositive phrase, still marked as indefinite. It then appears as the definite and more agentive S of *q'iil-uun* 'to run (iv)' in line 225. Finally, in line 226, it is cross-referenced on the verb and not mentioned lexically at all. We can account for the peculiar initial introduction in definite status by observing that the noun is originally introduced in direct discourse by a character. In the character's world, the rat is already specifically definite. It is only in the narrator's (and audience's world) that Preferred Argument Structure patterns need be observed. The sequence in lines 222–227 in which they are followed is in fact the narrator's flashback explanation of how the rat came to be definite for the characters in line 220.

The diminutive element *iti* is another element that interacts with definiteness and reference status. It is first used in association with the rat's narrative appearance: *huune' iti ch'oohon* 'a little rat' (line 222). In the explanatory appositive utterance in line 223, *iti* is given special prominence. First, the original context phrase from line 222 is repeated exactly. Then *iti* is elaborated by being coupled with the synonymous lexical item *nu'ya* 'really small'. Finally, a second synonym, *tzap-an* 'short,' is given emphasis by means of an accompanying gesture. Here the parallelism creates first an identical couplet in lines 222 and 223, then a triplet in which the third expected occurrence of *iti* is replaced by the deictic *inde* 'thus' and gesture.

The contrast between lines 225 and 227 establishes the substitution of *iti* for the definite marker. It is in line 227 that *iti* finally takes on definite status. The fragment of constructed discourse in lines 228–229 gives a character's-eye view of the plot relevance of this emphasized attribute. Because the rat's tail is so small, the children can use it to substitute for their fingers and "prove" that they are not yet fat enough to eat. By this ruse, they can escape their intended fate. At the end of the sequence, when they show the tail to the witch, *iti* is first associated with the rat (line 233) and then transfers its meaning and its definiteness from the rat to the tail (line 234). Overall, this pattern of explicit mention and association with adjacent modifiers produces a highly repetitive structure in which individual elements nevertheless move around to create variety.

The delicacy with which don Juan seems to attend to reference and argument status as part of the crucial material in repetitions is illustrated by re-examining the first and last lexical mentions of the rat in lines 220 and 234. In both cases the nominal occurs as a Possessor, and this syntactic role is limited to just these two lines. It thus brackets the entire sequence in which the rat appears. While both mentions are definite, the definite particle *we'* only occurs in line 220, where character knowledge is being portrayed. (The attributive *iti*, established as alternating with *we'* in intervening lines 225 and 227, substitutes for it in line 233.) At its final mention, in line 234, the rat is subordinated to its tail, not taking either the definite or *iti*, whose content has been transferred to the tail. In spite of their semantic and partial syntactic parallelism, lines 220 and 234 specifically contrast in the reference status of the rat, a difference highlighted by the fact that line 220 is a constructed discourse rendition of the content of line 234.

The Preferred Argument Structure perspective highlights for us the ways in which argument status, reference status, repetition, constructed discourse, and the pressure toward parallelism all interact to produce aesthetically satisfactory narrations. In the first two examples, a closer look at the patterns of semantic role and syntactic environment have been enough to unravel the subtle exploitation to which a single repeated lexical item can be subjected by a talented narrator. In the next example, attention to information flow along with patterns of parallelism helps, but is not fully adequate, to uncover the ways in which a repeated word represents, or not, a repeated entity or semantic concept.

Case 3: Incremental "Newness" (References to **animál** *'animal')*

The lexical item *animál* appears frequently in the first three Episodes of *The Little Orphans.* Although it is repeated lexically a number of times, the contexts of contrast for each mention re-orient the hearer, altering the domain of reference within which the word is to be interpreted. That is to say, each utterance of the same lexical item actually refers to different entitites or to different features of an entity. Each use defines a new semantic class from which the item is to be selected.

Episode 1

30 And it's said the man went off,
31 He went to lose his children.
32 And it's said he arrived in the woods.
33 "Wait here, my child,
34 I'll come right back.
35 I'm going looking around for doves here in the woods.
ni k-ii'-onh mah-oon chik'i ***paloom*** *te' ti montánya.* = O
already FUT-1s-go look.for-AP DIR:passing dove here PRP mountain
36 You two wait a while",
37 and he went away, so it is said.

Episode 2

77 "You two stay waiting here — on one side of this hill.
78 As for me, I am going looking for doves there on that side
ha'ni w-eet k-ii'-onh muq-uun ***paloom*** *te' ti ládo te' la',* = l. 35
FOC 1-RN:self FUT-1s-go look.at-AP dove DEM PRP side DEM FAR
79 or if not, then animals. =
moo no, ***animál.***" **huntable animal ≠ paloom**
NEG NEG animal

…

83 And the corn, what he went along spreading, well,
84 it's said it was eaten by doves.
ø-lo'-e' ab cho ***paloom*** **given in l. 78**
3A-eat (TV)-PAS REP by dove

…

105 And that corn he went along scattering by handfuls, well,
106 right where he went along dropping it,
107 it's said it had been eaten by doves. = l. 84
ø-lo'-e' ab cho ***paloom.***
3A-eat (TV)-PAS REP by dove

…

111 "Now already we are lost -
112 the corn I left
113 maybe it was already eaten by animals.
ni ma' ø-lo'-e' cho ***animál.*** = grain-eaters (= paloom)
already perhaps 3A-eat (TV)-PAS by animal
114 Because, well, there isn't any."

Episode 3

124 "And now then, what will we do?
125 because there are animals here.
ya te'te' hi' ***animál.*** = **(dangerous?) animals**
because dem here exist animal
126 Better what we'll do,
127 what we'll do now then,
128 we'll go climb up to the tree top
129 so we won't be eaten by animals right here.
ya cho muu qa-lo'-e' cho ***animál‿a.*** = **carnivores**
because by NEG 1p-eat (TV)-PAS by animal‿DPT
130 Because here there are big animals."
ya te'te' hi' maq ti ***animál.*** = **large animals**
because DEM here exist large PRP animal
131 "Okay", said the little girl, or so they say.
132 It's said they went up to the tree top.
133 It's said they slept right there.
134 And in the night, well, about midnight perhaps, it's said
a **lion** arrived. = **O**
135 It's said he began to howl around the tree.
136 And perhaps he was looking up at the children.
137 "*Haa'w, haa'w*", he said, so they say.
138 "Now then we are going to be food.
139 But don't you cry about it
140 because if not, we will immediately be eaten
by this animal.
ya moo no, tzaa qa-lo'-e' cho te' ***animál.*** = **lion.**
because NEG NEG FUT 1P-eat (TV)-PAS by DEM animal

The text presents all the contexts for *animál* in the story and displays how the incremental recasting of its meaning is accomplished. In the sequence from Episode 2, examined earlier, *animál* occurs in a triplet with *paloom* 'dove'. The parallelism heightens the commonality of the two entities as *animál* is made structurally equivalent to *paloom* in a dove/dove/like-dove set (lines 84, 107, 113). With the prior context in view, however, we can see that this triplet is actually part of a larger-scale structure of contrast. The very first mention of the doves occurs in Episode 1 in line 35, whose content and narrative position is identical with that of the second mention in Episode 2 in line 78, except for a locative distinction between near and far. In lines 78–79, *animál* is also paired with *paloom,* but here the entities are contrasted. The similarity produced by the partial repetition of lines 35 and 78 sets up a pattern of congruence and opposition that is further developed in line 79 to produce a triplet of references in which *animál* becomes the third element in a dove/dove/not-dove set. The long-range triplet in lines 84, 107, 113 (Example 1) must thus be seen as embedded within a frame that includes an earlier triplet (lines 35, 78–79). This larger-scale structural pattern of two triplets allows an ambiguity of identity for the referent of *animál* to emerge, a context that adds tension to the interpretation of *animál*. Is *animál* to be understood as passive and harmless, like a dove? Or is it distinctly *not* like that? The deliberate manipulation of ambiguous reference is characteristic of don Juan's narrative style (cf. Martin 1994).[5]

When *animál* is reintroduced in Episode 3, line 125, we might well ask whether this third lexical mention is given or new. The word is old, but the concept seems clearly new. Previous mentions may linger in memory and form a background against which the series of increasingly explicit references can resonate. This context suggests reference to animals of a threatening type, not just any sort of animal. It is unlikely to be a reference to a category that includes doves, which the previous mention did. At the next mention in line 129, an additional specification further expands the threat. Members of the *animál* category are even more explicitly contrasted to doves. Here *animál* refers to people-eaters, not grain-eaters. In line 130 we learn that they are large, in a syntactic construction that parallels line 125 and explicitly redefines the danger implied there. At each mention, the word's meaning is developed incrementally. How can we accommodate each mention's partial givenness and partial newness within the Preferred Argument Structure categories? Is the rhetorical pressure toward parallelism enough to explain these patterns of lexical repetition? Or does the slight but significant change in meaning account for the narrator's disinclination to pronominalize or otherwise de-emphasize the lexical form, as Preferred Argument Structure patterns would predict, in, lines 129 or 130, for example?

At line 134 a specific and individualized animal arrives: *chaawi ab huune' lyónh* 'it arrived, they say, a lion'. A few lines further on, in line 140, the last mention of *animál* occurs as a synonym for *lyónh*, which is emphatically defined as carnivorous. An old word now has a completely new referent. This mention is the first referential use of the word. For most Preferred Argument Structure purposes, this one is the mention that would attract the greatest analytic attention. However, if the non-referential cases are not also examined with care, something significant about the information flow in this segment of the story is lost. Don Juan's repetition of a single lexical item creates an expanding profile of the potential referent so that in one sense *lyónh* is "less new" when it finally arrives, while each occasion of *animál* is "more new" than we might at first realize. A Preferred Argument Structure analyst's classification decisions on this point may not have much impact on the overall statistical profile of the segment or text, but careful inspection of the context of each of the narrator's mentions in sequence reveals fascinating insights into his stylistic virtuosity.

Case 4: Lexical co-referentiality and decremental "givenness"

The corn, the rat, and the other animals serve limited, though important, narrative purposes. Each is confined to a single Episode and is changeless in character, a fact reflected in the lack of any lexical synonymy in references to them. Within the context of the entire story, each one has only temporary relevance, perhaps is even "ephemeral" (cf. England and Martin, this volume). The orphan protagonists, on the other hand, are actors in all six story Episodes. In the course of the story, they undergo significant change and receive multiple nominal references. The distribution of these co-referential mentions marks the maturational stages and the accompanying role shifts as experienced by the children in the course of the narrative. These shifts are reflected in a pattern of lexical mentions that, as the story progresses, maintain co-reference while manipulating key "given" components of the referents' identity. The patterns of lexical reference by which don Juan refers to the children as they work through the conflicts and challenges of the various Episodes is shown in Table 1.

Table 1. References to the children

		Ep. 1–2 (l.5–131) **Being lost**	Ep. 3–4 (l.132–297) **Being threatened**	Ep. 5 (l.298–353) **Growing up**	Ep. 6 (l.354–375) **Being avenged**
k'aahol	'man's child'	14			3
xiip	'male'	2	3		
ixoq	'female/woman'	3		4	
ch'in	'child'	7	15	1	1
kereem	'young man'			3	1
muqul	'young woman'			3	
tuun	'older brother'			10	
nu'ul	'younger sister'			1	
niñito	'little child'				1

It is easy to see how the various family relationships that are key to the didactic purpose of the story are highlighted by the narrator's changing forms of reference. The principal form of reference in each section of the story identifies the maturational stage to which the protagonists belong and demarcates the grouping of Episodes by family type. Episodes 1 and 2 describe the father's two attempts to lose his children. Here they are referred to overwhelmingly by a Mocho term that specifies a father-child familial relationship: *k'aahol* 'a man's child'. Once they have been abandoned, the children are outside the structure of any family. In Episodes 3 and 4, which describe their frightening night in the woods and their captivity by the witch, the narrator places them outside kin networks by no longer referring to them by any kin terms or relationship nouns. He focuses reference on their youth and vulnerability by his nearly exclusive use of the generic term *ch'in* '(young) child,' undifferentiated by gender or kin relation.

To achieve the cultural purpose of the story, the children must reconstitute a kin network of family relations as they mature. The account of this maturing process and the now grown children's struggle to re-establish appropriate familial roles (always associated with appropriate ritual behavior in Mocho storyworlds) is told in Episode 5. It is thus in Episode 5 that the children become individuated as adults with gender-linked social roles. Here all but one lexical reference to the protagonists specifies gender and most specify kinship relations as well. The single use of *ch'in* 'child' occurs early and is specifically identified as their former state. The emphasis is on the conflicted sibling relationship, marked by the frequent use of *tuun* 'older brother'. The resolution of the sibling conflict is found as the two orphans assume the proper adult roles of "male head of household", the person with the authority to negotiate a betrothal, and "wife". The sister's submission to the will of her older brother and her integration into a new mature family relationship through marriage are events that satisfy the Mocho world view and leave conditions in the Storyworld in harmony.

Although the final Episode, when the father returns, has a certain afterthought quality, its patterns of nominal reference suggest that even here the conventions of reference within the Storyworld are scrupulously observed. Not used since Episodes 1 and 2, *k'aahol* 'man's child' occurs here only in constructed speech between the father and the children; like the single use of *niñito* 'little child', it is first introduced by the father. Both nouns reflect the characters' prior states and relationships. The narrator's perspective is revealed in a single use of *ch'in* 'child,' a sign of the extra-familial status in Episodes 3 and 4. At the moment of the father's death, the son is referred to as *kerem* 'young man,' a sign of his adult authority in Episode 5. Thus, in Episode 6, the distribution of lexical reference thoroughly recapitulates the relationships of the previous Episodes, just as its narrative content partially recapitulates earlier plot points.

Case 5: Lexical uniqueness and augmented "newness" (references to the boyfriend)

In late 1995, I had occasion to revisit this story with don Juan, and I asked him why he thought the children had killed their father when he came to them full of remorse. After thinking about it for a moment, don Juan said that they were just taking revenge because the father had tried to kill them. Perhaps they were not quite human, he thought, because they were living in an enchanted house *(casa de encanto)*. Since they were so far away from other people, he suggested, they couldn't have proper pity for their father. "They almost turned into enchanters themselves", he said. What was striking in our discussion was his focus on human relationships as the context for appropriate role behaviors and for interpreting this story. This theme is consistent with the analysis of *The Little Orphans* as primarily concerned with the transition into proper adult gender and kin roles. The sort of close analysis that the Preferred Argument Structure framework encourages reveals how this theme is worked out, even at the level of individual lexical choice.

A particularly striking example of don Juan's manipulation of lexical reference to highlight the changing role expectations is seen in the final example, the distribution of terms used to the refer to the boyfriend. Episode 5 is presented in its entirety.

Episode 5

298 And he became a young man (**kereem**)
299 and she became a young woman (**muqul**), those former children (**ch'in**).
300 And here comes the young woman, well,
301 it's said he appeared, a, a wooer for her perhaps.
*ø-ø-istaw-i ab huune', huune' **x-miik-een** ma'an.* — **talker = courter**
CMP-3A-appear-IV REP one one 3-talk (TV)-NOM perhaps
302 She was being spoken to by a man.
*x-mik-e' cho huune' **winaq*** — **man**
3A-talk (TV)-PAS by one man
303 And it's said her brother heard nothing —
304 in secret perhaps she was being courted.
305 And here he comes,
306 the one who was speaking to that woman, well, — **talker = courter**
***abi we' k'ooyo ch-ø -mik-oon** we' ixoq‿he,*
REL DEF who INC-3A-talk (TV)-AP DEF woman‿DPT
307 "You will kill your brother,
308 so I can take you away",
309 said that man, so they say. — **man**
*xki ab we' **winaq**.*
QUO REP DEF man
310 "But how will I kill my brother then,
311 because my brother also suffered with me.
312 Together we suffered with him.
313 Therefore, I will not kill my brother like that."
314 "But if it is your desire
315 to go with me,
316 better kill your brother."

317 And here comes that man, well, **man**
*la ø-aki taa we' **winaq‿he,***
and 3A-come DIR:toward DEF man‿DPT
318 "with this you will kill him" —
"toh te' k-aa-poch'-o-ø"
with DEM FUT-2s-kill-TV-3A
319 it was a huge bone.
320 Really pointed at its tip.
321 It's said (s)he left it right there —
322 in the bed of her brother.
323 At the time her brother goes to lie down, well,
324 they say it will go immediately into her brother's neck.
325 "With this he will die",
"toh te' tzaa x-kam-i"
with DEM FUT 3E-die-IV
326 said that boyfriend of that woman, so they say.
*xki ab we' **x-nóbyo** we' ixoq.* **"intended"**
QUO REP DEF 3-boyfriend DEF woman
327 And perhaps still it was not for him, that, that young man.
328 It's said he looked at his bed
329 and it's said he lifted his pillow.
330 "Who is it who put this down here then?"
331 "Whoever knows!"
332 "It's certain it was you
333 because maybe you have a lover.
*ya hi' ma' **aa-nha'iil.*** **lover**
because EXT perhaps 2s-lover
334 That's why you just about killed me."
335 And here comes that young man, well,
336 it's said he began to beat his sister
337 because he saw the bone
338 located in the head of his bed.
339 "Well, then, how nice!
340 We already suffered,
341 and we already suffered here.
342 The way we grew up —
343 and you're gonna kill me?
344 But maybe it's the fault of your, your husband.
*péro x-muul ma' we' [aa-] **aaw-ichmaal.*** **husband**
but 3-fault perhaps DEF [2s-] 2s-husband
345 That's why you are saying you will kill me.

346 But if that is the way it is, well, better you tell him
347 to petition for you.
348 I will give you to him too.
349 But not if you're gonna kill me."
350 "Okay", said that young woman, so they say.
351 And the woman was petitioned for, from the woman's
brother.
352 And she was given, so they say.
353 They married, so they say.
354 And there they lived.

The Episode contains a total of seven lexical mentions of the boyfriend, four of them unique. The only repeated term is generic *winaq* 'man' (line 302, 309, and 317). The four synonyms fall along a continuum on which we can track the progress of role shift and the development of socially appropriate relationships for the boyfriend, and, by implication, the two orphans. The references begin with a "sweet-talking stranger", the *miikeen* 'one who talks' of line 301. The verb base *mik* 'to speak' refers particularly to the type of flirting talk by which a man courts a woman. It is used as a main verb in line 302, and repeated in line 304. An additional pronomial mention of the boyfriend is accomplished by a relative pronoun and a detransitivized form of this same verb, *x-mik-oon*, in line 306. With four mentions using a shared root, don Juan gives extra emphaisis to the starting point on the continuum: a dangerous intruder into the family network, one whose talk disrupts and alters social relationships.

The remaining three unique mentions define the boyfriend as he passes through various stages of intimacy with the girl. First, in line 326, he is her *nóbyo*. This term, a borrowing of Spanish *novio* 'groom,' a reference in modern usage to a boyfriend with whom a girl is exclusively associated and with whom she may behave in intimate ways. It suggests a transitional moment in a relationship where an understanding may exist between the two young people but not yet have the sanction of the family. Next, don Juan uses the native term *nha'iil* 'lover,' a term that implies sexual maturity. Finally, the boyfriend achieves the culturally significant, ritually sanctioned role of *-ichmaal* 'husband,' an obligatorily possessed kin term. After that point, the man is not even mentioned obliquely until he appears, now fully incorporated into the family, as a member of the anaphoric 'they' in lines 353–354.[6] I take the slight disfluency represented by pausing and hesitation phenomena at the beginning and end points of the continuum of reference (lines 301 and 344) as evidence that don Juan is deliberately manipulating these mentions in order to highlight the transformation toward proper adult role through proper ritual behavior.

The number and uniqueness of lexical mentions of the boyfriend serves the story's social and didactic purposes, tracking the progress of this character's development toward husband-hood. As in the text of Case 3, what seems at issue here is not degrees of "givenness" but rather components of "newness" being added to a character's evolving identity. A similar motivation seems to characterize the first mention of the girl in the sibling kin relation *nu'ul* 'sister,' which appears in Object role in line 336. Almost certainly, from a Preferred Argument Structure point of view, this mention is not "new", but from a rhetorical point of view and from the point of view of the culturally-relevant goals of this narrative, the kin relation becomes "newly" significant at this point in the narrative.

Two subsections of this segment are of special interest for the way in which the multiple strategies of repetition, quotation, and agency are employed. First, consider the sequence of lines 317 to 326, a pivotal moment in the Episode. Here, the narrator introduces a key plot prop, the sharpened bone intended as a murder weapon. An outer frame is formed by the formulaic phrases typically associated with direct discourse segments (lines 317 and 326). *la aki taa NP…* 'And here comes NP…' opens them by presenting new speakers, while *xki ab NP* 'said NP, so they say' closes them by ending that speaker's speech. In each line, lexical mention is made of the boyfriend, pairing the generic *winaq* with the specific *nóbyo*. An inner frame is created by single quoted lines that exhibit a high degree of syntactic and lexical parallelism (line 318, 325). Each quote refers to the attempted assasination of the girl's older brother, but reverses the argument structure: transitive with second-person agent marking (*aa-)* in line 318 and intransitive with third- person subject marking (*x-)* in line 325.[7] The narrative section in lines 319–324 is thus doubly framed and highlighted. This pattern of reversing transitivity in parallel lines is one of don Juan's most common rhetorical devices.

Similar patterns distinguish the segment in lines 346–352. Here the culturally appropriate bride petition is described in constructed discourse and set in future time (lines 346–348). Then, on the pivot of a repeated reference to the attempted murder in line 349 (cf. line 343) and the young woman's assent in line 350, the same events are narrated in the past (lines 351–353). As seen elsewhere, quoted (predictive) material is paired with a narrative (completed) account. Line 347 is specifically paired to line 351 through repetition of the verb root *q'an-a* 'to ask for (tv)'. Line 348 is similarly associated with line 352. Don Juan attends closely to issues of agency here, as he has in other contexts. In the direct discourse half, the verbs are transitive: he will ask for you; I will give you to him. In the narrative half the verbs are detransitivized as passives or transformed into passive verbal nouns. The intricate structure seen in these two subsections and in Episode 5 as a whole is the source of much aesthetic pleasure for the Mocho storyteller and his audience. Similar attentiveness by the discourse analyst is equally rewarding in what it tells us about the degree of control that may be exerted over the patterns we identify as Preferred Argument Structure.

Conclusion

What does this closer look at Mocho narrative suggest about the directions in which we might take Preferred Argument Structure work? What we observe in well-practiced tales such as *The Little Orphans* is likely to be the result of narrator experimentation over time, experimentation that seeks compromise among the conflicting aspects of discourse production: the cognitive and cultural requirements on narrative. The optimal implementation of Preferred Argument Structure strategies must be balanced with the demands of aesthetic evaluation and didactic purpose. The examples presented here suggest that constructed discourse can be a site for the negotiation of transitivity relations as well as a convenient mechanism for creating opportunities for repetition, and that lexical repetition can serve structural, rhetorical, and cultural purposes that cannot be divorced from — but are not the same as — the local contexts and motivations that produce Preferred Argument Structure patterns. To the extent that a speaker manages this tension in spontaneous production and attends to the kinds of details illustrated here, the more he or she is liable to be identified as a "good" storyteller or a "stylish" conversationalist. It would be interesting to know more about the intersection of external evaluation of narratives and the internal manipulations to which their creators subject them. For this reason, increased analyst attention to retellings could be especially useful.

Another conclusion we can draw from this brief anlaysis concerns the importance of local variations within larger narrative units. Examination of subunits within larger complex texts can reveal much about a narrator's balancing of cognitive and creative pressures. While the overall Preferred Argument Structure figures for a complex text may be quite ordinary, attention to subunits can reveal apparently strategic manipulations of, for example, transitivity status, for specific discourse purposes. In *The Little Orphans* there are significant differences in the number of transitive verbs used in the Episodes about the animals and boyfriend, even though they occupy similar positions and roles in the overall narrative structure, are quite self-contained, and are about the same length. Total counts for *The Little Orphans* do not vary much from what we expect from an application of Du Bois' axioms.[8] However, a more local perspective reveals patterns that are not predicted by Preferred Argument Structure, but instead surrender to an analysis responsive to culturally situated standards of rhetorical style. As shown in other work in this volume, examination of complex texts will in every case produce results consonant with Du Bois' analysis of preferred patterns. Perhaps it is time to move beneath that surface similarity to focus attention on the smaller chunks within such texts where individual speakers perform individually creative discourse moves.

The issue of how much practice makes a practiced narrative is also still problematic. Tactics such as the reassignment of verbs to another transitivity status, the selection among lexical alternates, and the manipulation of narrative vs. quoted contexts are all available to speakers as "real time" devices for revisions in discourse production. How much practice is really required to reach the optimal balance between rhetorical elegance and information flow practicality? If something interesting happens on my way to the office, I might recount it to the first colleague I run into. Later, I may retell the story to a group around the lunch table. (Not the same group, of course, since in general my colleagues tolerate such story repetition much less easily than Mocho speakers!) Still later, perhaps before a committee meeting, I might find a new audience for my story. At each telling, attending to the background knowledge of my audience and to such elements as elaboration or reduction of agency, clarity in participant presentation, or the need to beef up the punch line by making it more dramatic, I make changes in, for example, transitivity, number and types of lexical mention and order, and the deployment of constructed discourse to improve my narrative. By monitoring audience reactions to these changes, I can tell whether my narrative is well received — a good exemplar of its type — and whether I am being counted as a stylish narator. This evaluation may affect my strategies in later tellings, just as it does in drafting revisions to memos or grant proposals. Since I know that I, with relative degrees of consciousness in different circumstances, behave in this way, I believe others, including Mocho speakers, do as well. Preferred Argument Structure research has not, so far, incorporated much data on the application of speaker control to Preferred Argument Structure patterns for rhetorical purposes. In the analyses I present here, for example, it is only the analyst's criteria that are considered, even when taking "context" into account. Cultural knowledge and local context are specific keys to interpretation, but so are the speaker's introspection and the listener's interpretation. We need more studies on language users' receptive interpretation, not just analysts' interpretation. We need studies that foreground the speaker, rather than the discourse linguist. Profitable contexts for such studies might again include retellings, of which constructed discourse and patterned repetition are themselves, of course, special subtypes. Perhaps by soliciting speaker comment on the motivations for specific choices and by studying listener construals of specific contexts, we may be able to learn more about the processes of discourse interpretation.

Certainly, not every informant is equally adept at introspection on these points, but in making the inquiry we can improve our methods. It must be possible to find ways to inquire of speakers why they select particular options in discourse design and of hearers how they interpret those variants. The construction of quasi-experimental contexts might be useful in this endeavor, just as they were in Du Bois' original Preferred Argument Structure work. In any case, as usual, close attention to language data, for whatever purposes and in whatever framework, unexpectedly illuminates aspects of discourse structure that may at first seem unrelated. Such attention, perhaps no longer unexpectedly, also inevitably raises new questions. As was the case in my earlier more quantitative attempt with England to apply a Preferred Argument Structure framework to narrative, so again here I find those new questions to be the most important outcome of all.

Notes

* The data on which this paper is based has been collected and analyzed with the gratefully accepted support of a grant from the National Endowment for the Humanities (RL-21845–91), a 1986 Fulbright-Hays Faculty Research Abroad award, and the Cleveland State University College of Graduate Studies and Research. I am also grateful for the 1995 CSU Faculty Professional Development Leave that gave me time to work on this particular analysis. I thank the organizers of the Preferred Argument Structure conference for one of the most enjoyable professional meetings I have ever attended. As a conference organizer myself, I know at what cost such seemingly effortless events take place, and I thank Lorraine Kumpf especially for her role in it. As always I acknowledge with deepest thanks the hospitality, affection, and assistance of the Méndez-Echeverría family.

1. Mocho is spoken primarily in the neighborhoods surrounding the town of Motozintla de Mendoza, in Chiapas near the Guatemalan border. Fluent speakers now number well under one hundred. Key linguistic sources include Kaufman (1967, 1969), Campbell (1988), and, for ethnolinguistic details, Petrich (1985, 1986) as well as my own discourse-based work (especially Martin 1989, 1990, 1994, 1997, 2000.)

2. For further details about Mocho narrative organization, consult Martin 1994. The Mocho version of *The Little Orphans* is to be included in my forthcoming collection of texts and commentary, Martin Forthcoming.

3. In the Examples, only the lines with the relevant nominal references are presented in Mocho. The reference is given in boldface. Argument status and other analytic glossing is highlighted along the right margin. Necessary morphological information is provided in the body of the paper, but morphological glosses are included in the example texts as well. Abbreviations used are 1, 2, 3 = verbal person and nominal possessor; A = absolutive; AP = antipassive; CAU = causative; CMP = completive; DEF = definite marker; DEM = demonstrative; DIM = diminutive; DIR = directional particle; DPT = discourse particle; E = ergative; EXT = existential; FOC = focus; FUT = future; INC = incompletive aspect; IV = intransitive formative; RN = relational noun; NEG = negative; NOM = nominalizer; P = positional root; PAS = passive; PL = plural; PRP = preposition; QUO = quotative; REL = relative marker; REP = reportative; S/P = singular/plural person; TV = transitive formative. (Zeros are not marked on VP's cross-referenced by full lexical NP's.)

4. Such distributions of transitivity have been identified elsewhere in don Juan's narratives, including in personal narratives about fighting a fire (Martin 1990) and hunting a mule who strayed from home. Moreover, manipulations of this type have also been seen in narratives by other speakers. One such is Juan Matías Pérez, a generation older than don Juan, who uses them both in a personal narrative about a trip and in a community history. All these texts are to be included in Martin Forthcoming.

5. Andy Hofling has reminded me of the relatedness of this episode to the Mayan mythic narrative of the Hero Twins bird-hunting, a story that still survives in contemporary Itzaj.

6. Thanks to Andy Hofling for directing my attention to this nuance.

7. The future *tzaa* interpretation triggers split ergative verbal marking in line 325 so that third Absolutive, normally zero, is given as *x*-, normally the marker of Agent.

8. For example, 54% of the clauses in the story have no lexical NP in core roles, 44.3% have only one lexical NP, and only 1.6% have two, in spite of the fact that fully 36.4% of all clauses are transitive. In clauses with one lexical core argument, 34.3% are O's, 15.8% are S's, and only 1.4% are A's.

References

Brody, Jill. 1986. "Repetition as a rhetorical and conversational device in Tojolobal (Mayan)". *International Journal of American Linguistics* 52: 255–274.

Campbell, Lyle. 1988. The linguistics of Southeast Chiapas, Mexico. New World Archeological Foundation Paper 50. Provo, UT: Brigham Young University.

Du Bois, John W. 1985. "Competing motivations". In John Haiman (ed.), *Iconicity in Syntax.* Amsterdam and Philadelphia: Benjamins, 343–365.

Du Bois, John W. 1987. "The discourse basis of ergativity". *Language* 63: 805–855.

Durie, Mark. 1994. "A case study of pragmatic linking". *Text* 14(4): 495–529.

Gossen, Gary. 1974. *Chamulas in the World of the Sun: Time and Space in Maya Oral Ttradition.* Cambridge, MA: Harvard University Press.

Gossen, Gary. 1975. "To speak with a heated heart: Chamula canons of style and good performance". In Richard Bauman and Joel Sherzer (eds.), *Explorations in the Ethnography of Speaking.* Cambridge: Cambridge University Press, 389–413.

Hofling, Charles A. 1993. "Marking time and space in Itzaj narrative". *Journal of Linguistic Anthropology* 3: 164–184.

Johnstone, Barbara. 1996. *The Linguistic Individual: Self-Expression in Language and Linguistics.* New York: Oxford University Press.

Kaufman, Terrence S. 1967. "Preliminary Mocho vocabulary". (Working Paper Number 5.) Berkeley: University of California Laboratory for Language-Behavior Research.

Kaufman, Terrence S. 1969. "Teco — A new Mayan language". *International Journal of American Linguistics* 35: 154–174.

Martin, Laura. 1989. "The interdependence of language and culture in the Mocho Bear Story". *Anthropological Linguistics* Winter 1987: 533–558. (Special issue edited by Brian J. Stross).

Martin, Laura. 1990. "Los verbos de discurso en mochó". In Stephen R. Elliott and Nora C. England (eds.), *Lecturas en la lingüística maya.* Antigua, Guatemala: Centro de Investigaciones Regionales de Mesoamérica (CIRMA). 421–443.

Martin, Laura. 1994. "Rhetorical elaboration and discourse structure in Mocho". *Journal of Linguistic Anthropology* 4: 2 (Dec.): 131–152.

Martin, Laura. 1997. "La historia de los huerfanitos en casa de los Mochos: Variación y cultura en el cuento de Hansel and Gretel". In Guillermina Herrera et al. (eds), *Procedimientos del Segundo Congreso de Estudios Mayas, 1997.* Guatemala: Universidad Landivar, 39–53.

Martin, Laura. 2000. "Parallelism and the spontaneous ritualization of ordinary talk: Three Mocho friends discuss a volcano". In Kay Sammons and Joel Sherzer (eds), *Translating Native Latin American Verbal Art: Ethnopoetics and Ethnography of Speaking.* Washington, DC: Smithsonian Institution Press, 104–124.

Martin, Laura. Forthcoming. *Hunne to'k' huune tz'a'ik — hun to to'k' hun to tz'a'ik: The Everyday Words of Mocho.* Austin: University of Texas Press.

Norman, William M. 1980. “Grammatical parallelism in Quiche ritual language”. *Berkeley Linguistic Society* 6: 387–399.

Petrich, Perla. 1985. *La alimentación mochó: acto y palabra.* (Estudio etnolingüístico). Serie Monografía 1. Centro de Estudios Indígenas. San Cristóbal de las Casas, México: Universidad Nacional Autónoma de Chiapas.

Petrich, Perla. 1986. “La semántica del maíz entre los mochó”. *Chanteirs Amerindia* No. 11, Supplément 1. Paris: Asociación de Etnolingüística Amerindia.

Tannen, Deborah. 1989. *Talking Voices: Repetition, Dialogue, and Imagery in Conversational Discourse.* Cambridge: Cambridge University Press.

Tedlock, Dennis. 1983. *The Spoken Word and the Work of Interpretation.* Philadelphia: University of Pennsylvania Press.

Tedlock, Dennis. 1996. *Popol Vuh: The Mayan Book of the Dawn of Life.* Revised and expanded edition. New York: Simon and Shuster.

Preferred Argument Structure Bibliography

This bibliography represents works relating to the specific theory and claims of Preferred Argument Structure in a significant way. The works cited range from full-fledged studies evaluating the claims of Preferred Argument Structure based on a body of discourse data, to works which comment critically on some significant aspect of the theory. (Works which merely cite an article on Preferred Argument Structure are not thereby included.)

Abracado, Jussara. 2001. "The adjacency principle and the degrees of integration between verb and object". *Revista de Documentação de Estudos em Lingüística Teórica e Aplicada (DELTA)* 17: 323–336.

Allen, Shanley E. M. 1997a. "A discourse-pragmatic explanation for the subject-object asymmetry in early null arguments: The Principle of Informativeness revisited". In A. Sorace, C. Heycock and R. Shillcock (eds), *Proceedings of the GALA '97 Conference on Language Acquisition.* Edinburgh: University of Edinburgh, 10–15.

Allen, Shanley E. M. 1997b. "Towards a discourse-pragmatic explanation for the subject-object asymmetry in early null arguments". In A. Baker, C. Blankenstijn, M. Roelofs and A. Scheper (eds), *Proceedings of the Ninth Netwerk Eerste Taalverwerving Symposium.* Amsterdam: Leerstoelgroep Psycholinguïstiek en Taalpathologie, University of Amsterdam, 1–16.

Allen, Shanley E. M. 2000. "A discourse pragmatic explanation for argument representation in child Inuktitut". *Linguistics* 38: 483–521.

Allen, Shanley E. M. and Schröder, Heike. 2003. "Preferred Argument Structure in early Inuktitut spontaneous speech data". In John W. Du Bois, Lorraine E. Kumpf and William J. Ashby (eds), *Preferred Argument Structure: Grammar as Architecture for Function.* Amsterdam: Benjamins, 301–338.

Antonio, Juliano Desiderato, and Panta, Maria Regina. 2000. "Preferred Argument Structure in oral and written Portugese". *Acta Scientiarum* 22: 15–23.

Arnold, Jennifer E. 1998. *Reference Form and Discourse Patterns.* Ph.D. dissertation, Stanford University.

Arnold, Jennifer E. 2003. "Multiple constraints on reference form: Null, pronominal, and full reference in Mapudungun" In John W. Du Bois, Lorraine E. Kumpf and William J. Ashby (eds), *Preferred Argument Structure: Grammar as Architecture for Function.* Amsterdam: Benjamins, 225–245.

Ashby, William J. 1995. "French presentational structures". In Jon Amastae et al. (eds), *Contemporary Research in Romance Linguistics,* Amsterdam: Benjamins, 91–104.

Ashby, William J. and Bentivoglio, Paola. 1993. "Preferred Argument Structure in spoken French and Spanish". *Language Variation and Change* 5: 61–76.

Ashby, William J. and Bentivoglio, Paola. 1997. "Strategies for introducing new referents into discourse: A comparative analysis of French and Spanish presentational structures". In Robert M. Hammond and Marguerite B. MacDonald (eds), *Linguistic Studies in Honor of Bohdan Saciuk.* West Lafayette, IN: Learning Systems Incorporated, 9–25.

Ashby, William J. and Bentivoglio, Paola. 2003. "Preferred Argument Structure across time and space: A comparative diachronic analysis of French and Spanish". In John W. Du Bois, Lorraine E. Kumpf and William J. Ashby (eds), *Preferred Argument Structure: Grammar as Architecture for Function.* Amsterdam: Benjamins, 61–80.

Assayag, Nurit. 1999. "Subject selection in discourse: Cognitive constraints and genre effect". Thesis, Linguistics Department, Tel Aviv University.

Augst, Alexander. 2000. "Mönster i valet av nominalfras i svenskt talspråk". Thesis, Uppsala University. URL: http://home.student.uu.se/aler5283/monster.htm.

Bellver, Phyllis. 1993. "Ergative is as ergative does". Unpublished ms., Linguistics Department, University of Colorado.

Bellver, Phyllis and Michaelis, Laura A. 2000. "What is the information structure-syntax interface in Basque?" In Steve S. Chang, Lily Liaw and Josef Ruppenhofer (eds), *Proceedings of the Twenty-Fifth Annual Meeting of the Berkeley Linguistics Society, February 12–15, 1999* (General Session and Parasession on Loan Word Phenomena). Berkeley: Berkeley Linguistics Society, 26–37.

Bentivoglio, Paola. 1990. "Los sujetos del tipo 'S' en el español hablado en Caracas". Paper presented at the X Congreso Internacional de la ALFAL. Universidade Estadual de Campinas, SP, Brazil, August 1990.

Bentivoglio, Paola. 1992. "Linguistic correlations between subjects of one-argument verbs and subjects of more-than-one-argument verbs in Spanish spoken discourse". In Paul Hirschbüler and Konrad Koerner (eds), *Romance Languages and Modern Linguistic Theory: Papers from the XX Linguistic Symposium on Romance Languages, Ottawa, 10–14 April 1990.* Amsterdam: Benjamins, 11–24.

Bentivoglio, Paola. 1993. "Full NPs in spoken Spanish: A discourse profile". In William J. Ashby, Marianne Mithun, Giorgio Perissinotto, and Eduardo Raposo (eds), *Linguistic Perspectives on the Romance Languages: Selected Papers from the 21st Linguistic Symposium on Romance Languages (LSRL XXI), Santa Barbara, California, 21–24 February 1991.* Amsterdam: Benjamins, 211–224.

Bentivoglio, Paola. 1994. "Spanish Preferred Argument Structure across time and space". *Revista de Documentação de Estudos em Lingüística Teórica e Aplicada (DELTA)* 10: 227–93.

Bentivoglio, Paola. 1995a. "Frases nominales plenas en el español de Caracas: Un análisis semántico-pragmático". In Alfredo Matus et al. (eds), *Actas del IV Congreso Internacional de "El espanol de América"*, vol. I. Santiago de Chile: Pontifica Universidad Católica de Chile, 595–603.

Bentivoglio, Paola. 1995b. "La estructura argumental preferida del español moderno". In María Vaquero and Amparo Morales (eds), *Homenaje a Humberto López Morales.* Madrid: Arco/Libros, 107–120.

Bentivoglio, Paola. 1998. "The late acquisition of Preferred Argument Structure in Venezuelan spoken Spanish". In Bernard Caron (ed), *Proceedings of the XVIth International Congress of Linguists.* CD-ROM. Amsterdam: Elsevier.

Bentivoglio, Paula and Ashby, William J. 1995. "Estrategias para introducir información nueva en el discurso: Un análisis comparativo español–francés". *Anuario de Lingüística Hispánica* 11: 41–53.

Biq, Yung-o. 2000. "Recent developments in discourse-and-grammar". *Chinese Studies* 18: 357–394. URL: http://ccs.ncl.edu.tw/Chinese_studies_18_s/18_s_16.pdf.

Brito, Célia Maria Coélho. 1996. *A Transitividade Verbal na Língua Portuguesa: Uma Investigaçao de Base Funcionalista.* São Paulo: Araraquara.

Brown, Penelope. 1998. "Early Tzeltal verbs: Argument structure and argument representation". *Proceedings of the Annual Child Language Research Forum*, 29: 129–140.

Chafe, Wallace L. and Mithun, Marianne. 1999. "What are S, A, and O?" *Studies in Language* 23: 569–596.

Chui, Ka-Wai. 1992. "Preferred Argument Structure for discourse understanding". *COLING-92: Proceedings of the 15th International Conference on Computational Linguistics/Nantes, 23–28/8/1992.* Nantes, France, 1142–1146. http://acl.ldc.upenn.edu/C/C92/C92-4180.pdf.

Chui, Ka-Wai. 1994. *Information Flow in Mandarin Chinese discourse.* Ph.D. dissertation, National Taiwan University.

Chui, Ka-Wai. 1996. *Topic continuity in spoken Chinese.* Taipei.

Clancy, Patricia M. 1993. "Preferred Argument Structure in Korean acquisition". In Eve V. Clark (ed), *The Proceedings of the Twenty-Fifth Annual Child Language Research Forum.* Stanford: CSLI Publications, 307–314.

Clancy, Patricia M. 1996. "Referential strategies and the co-construction of argument structure in Korean acquisition". In Barbara Fox (ed), *Studies in Anaphora.* Amsterdam: Benjamins, 33–68.

Clancy, Patricia M. 1997. "Discourse motivations of referential choice in Korean acquisition". In Ho-min Sohn and John Haig (eds), *Japanese/Korean Linguistics.* Stanford: CSLI Publications, 639–659.

Clancy, Patricia M. 2003. "The lexicon in interaction: Developmental origins of Preferred Argument Structure". In John W. Du Bois, Lorraine E. Kumpf and William J. Ashby, *Preferred Argument Structure: Grammar as Architecture for Function.* Amsterdam: Benjamins, 81–108.

Cooper, Amy, Guerriero, Sonia A. M. and Oshima-Takane, Yuriko. 2000. "An explanation for the null argument phenomenon in child language". Paper presented at McGill Research Day, Department of Psychology, McGill University. URL: http://psych.mcgill.ca/perpg/stds/posters/lastyearposters/poster46.html.

Corston, Simon H. 1993. "Ergativity in Roviana". M.A. thesis, Auckland University.

Corston, Simon H. 1996. *Ergativity in Roviana, Solomon Islands* (*Pacific Linguistics*, Series B-113). Canberra: Australia National University Press.

Corston-Oliver, Simon H. 2000. "Using decision trees to select the grammatical relation of a noun phrase". Paper presented at Sigdial Workshop: Theme Session On Principles for Dialogue System Evaluation. ACL-2000: The 38th Annual Meeting of the Association for Computational Linguistics, Hong Kong. URL: http://www.sigdial.org/sigdialworkshop/proceedings/corston-oliver.pdf.

Corston-Oliver, Simon H. 2003. "Core arguments and the inversion of the nominal hierarchy". In John W. Du Bois, Lorraine E. Kumpf and William J. Ashby (eds), *Preferred Argument Structure: Grammar as Architecture for Function.* Amsterdam: Benjamins, 273–300.

Crago, Martha B. and Allen, Shanley E. M. 1999. "Acquiring Inuktitut". In Orlando L. Taylor and Lawrence Leonard (eds), *Language Acquisition across North America: Cross-cultural and Cross-Linguistic Perspectives.* San Diego: Singular Publishing Group, 245–279.

Craig, Colette Grinevald. 1987. "The Rama language: A text with grammatical notes". *Journal of Chibchan Studies* 5.

Croft, William. 1990. *Typology and Universals.* Cambridge: Cambridge University Press.

Cumming, Susanna. 1994. "Functional categories in the lexicon: Referent introduction in Indonesian novels". *Text* 14: 465–94.

Cumming, Susanna and Wouk, Fay. 1987. "Is there 'discourse ergativity' in Austronesian languages?" *Lingua* 71: 271–296.

Davison, Alice. 1999. "Ergativity: functional and formal issues". In Michael Darnell, Edith Moravcsik, Frederick Newmeyer, Michael Noonan and Kathleen Wheatley (eds), *Functionalism and Formalism in Linguistics.* Amsterdam: Benjamins, 177–208.

De Leon, Lourdes. 1999. "Verbs in Tzotzil (Mayan) early syntactic development". *International Journal of Bilingualism* 3: 219–239.

Dixon, Robert M. W. (ed). 1987. *Studies in Ergativity.* Amsterdam: North-Holland.

Dixon, Robert M. W. 1994. *Ergativity.* Cambridge: Cambridge University Press.

Downing, Pamela. 1993. "Pragmatic and semantic constraints on numeral quantifier position in Japanese". *Journal of Linguistics* 29: 65–93.

Du Bois, John W. 1981a. "Ergativity and Preferred Argument Structure in Sacapultec discourse". Unpublished ms., University of California, Santa Barbara.

Du Bois, John W. 1981b. *The Sacapultec Language.* Ph.D. dissertation, University of California, Berkeley.

Du Bois, John W. 1985. "Competing motivations". In John Haiman (ed), *Iconicity in Syntax.* Amsterdam: Benjamins, 343–65.

Du Bois, John W. 1987a. "The discourse basis of ergativity". *Language* 63: 805–55.

Du Bois, John W. 1987b. "Absolutive zero: Paradigm adaptivity in Sacapultec Maya". *Lingua* 71: 203–222.

Du Bois, John W. 1987c. "Absolutive zero: Paradigm adaptivity in Sacapultec Maya". In Robert M. W. Dixon (ed), *Studies in Ergativity.* Amsterdam: North-Holland, 203–222. [Republication of Du Bois 1987b]

Du Bois, John W. 1990. "El zero absolutivo: Adaptación paradigmático en Sacapulteco. In Nora C. England and Stephen R. Elliott (eds), *Lecturas en Lingüística mayanse.* Antigua, Guatemala: Centro de Investigaciones Regionales de Mesoamérica, 473–86. [Translation of Du Bois 1987b]

Du Bois, John W. 2003a. "Argument structure: Grammar in use". In John W. Du Bois, Lorraine E. Kumpf and William J. Ashby (eds), *Preferred Argument Structure: Grammar as Architecture for Function.* Amsterdam: Benjamins, 11–60.

Du Bois, John W. 2003b. "Discourse and grammar". In Michael Tomasello (ed), *The New Psychology of Language: Cognitive and Functional Approaches to Language Structure.* Mahwah, NJ: Erlbaum, 47–87.

Du Bois, John W., Kumpf, Lorraine E. and Ashby., William J. 2003. "Introduction." In John W. Du Bois, Lorraine E. Kumpf and William J. Ashby (eds), *Preferred Argument Structure: Grammar as Architecture for Function.* Amsterdam: Benjamins, 1–10.

Du Bois, John W. Forthcoming. "The Pear Story in Sakapulteko Maya: A case study of information flow and argument structure". In Mercedes Sedano, Adriana Bolívar and Martha Shiro (eds), *Estuidios lingüísticos: Homenaje a Paolo Bentivoglio.* Caracas: Universidad Central de Venezuela.

Duranti, Alessandro. 1990. "Genitive constructions and agency in Samoan discourse". *Studies in Language* 14: 1–23.

Duranti, Alessandro and Ochs, Elinor. 1989. "Acquisition of genitive agents in Samoan". *Papers & Reports on Child Language Development, Stanford University*, 28.

Durie, Mark. 1988. "Preferred argument structure in an active language: Arguments against the category 'intransitive subject'". *Lingua* 74: 1–25.

Durie, Mark. 1994. "A case study of pragmatic linking". *Text* 14: 495–529.

Dutra, Rosalia. 1987. "The hybrid S category in Brazilian Portuguese: Some implications for word order". *Studies in Language* 11: 163–180.

Edmonson, Barbara. 1999. "The couple who were turned into raccoons". Unpublished ms., Department of Anthropology, Tulane University, New Orleans.

England, Nora C. 1986. "Mamaen voice: Syntactic and narrative considerations". Paper presented at *Annual Meeting of the American Anthropological Association*, Philadephia

England, Nora C. 1988. "Mam voice". In M. Shibatani (ed), *Passives and Voice.* (*Typological Studies in Language, Vol. 16*). Amsterdam and Philadelphia: Benjamins, 525–545.

England, Nora C. and Martin, Laura. 2003. "Issues in comparative argument structure analysis in Mayan narratives". In John W. Du Bois, Lorraine E. Kumpf and William J. Ashby (eds), *Preferred Argument Structure: Grammar as Architecture for Function.* Amsterdam: Benjamins, 131–157.

Fox, Barbara. 1987. "The noun phrase accessibility hierarchy reinterpreted: Subject primacy or the absolutive hypothesis?" *Language* 63: 856–870.

Fox, Barbara. 1995. "The category 'S' in English conversation". In Werner Abraham, T. Givón and Sandra A. Thompson (eds), *Discourse Grammar and Typology.* Amsterdam: Benjamins, 153–178.

Fox, Barbara and Thompson, Sandra A. 1990a. "A discourse explanation of the grammar of relative clauses in English conversation". *Language* 66: 297–316.

Fox, Barbara and Thompson, Sandra A. 1990b. "On formulating reference: An interactional approach to relative clauses in English conversation". *IPrA Papers in Pragmatics* 4: 183–196.

Francis, Hartwell S., Gregory, Michelle L. and Michaelis, Laura A. 1999. "Are lexical subjects deviant?" ? *Papers from the Thirty-Fifth Regional Meeting of the Chicago Linguistics Society.* Chicago: Chicago Linguistics Society, 85–97.

García-Miguel, José María. 1998. "La expresión de actantes centrales en español (romance) y bribri (chibcha): Tipología, discurso y cognicíon". Paper presented at *Primero Encontro de Lingüística Cognitiva*, Porto. http://www.uvigo.es/webs/h06/weba575/jmgm/public/porto98.pdf.

Genetti, Carol and Crain, Laura. 2003. "Beyond Preferred Argument Structure: Sentences, pronouns, and given referents in Nepali". In John W. Du Bois, Lorraine E. Kumpf and William J. Ashby (eds), *Preferred Argument Structure: Grammar as Architecture for Function.* Amsterdam: Benjamins, 197–223.

Gildea, Spike. 2000. "On the lack of a function for ergativity". Paper given at Linguistics Department colloquium. Houston, TX: Rice University.

Goldberg, Adele E. Forthcoming. "Discourse and argument structure". In Larry Horn and Gregory Ward (eds), *Handbook of Pragmatics.* Oxford: Blackwell.

Goldin-Meadow, Susan and Mylander, Carolyn. 1998. "Spontaneous gesture systems created by deaf children in two cultures". *Nature* 391: 279–281.

Goldin-Meadow, Susan, Yalabik, Elif and Gershkoff-Stowe, Lisa. 2000. "The resilience of ergative structure in language created by children and by adults". In S.C. Howell, S.A. Fish and T. Keith-Lucas (eds), *Proceedings of the 24th Annual Boston University Conference on Language Development,* Vol. 1. Sommerville, MA: Cascadilla Press, 343–353.

Guerriero, Sonia A.M., Cooper, Amy, Oshima-Takane, Yuriko and Kuriyama, Yoko. 2001. "A discourse-pragmatic explanation for argument realization and omission in English and Japanese children's speech". In Anna H.-J. Do, Laura Dominguez and Aimee Johansen (eds), *Proceedings of the 25th Annual Boston University Conference on Language Development,* vol. 1. Somerville, MA.: Cascadilla Press, 319–330.

Harris, Alice C. and Campbell, Lyle. 1995. *Historical Syntax in Cross-Linguistic Perspective.* Cambridge: Cambridge University Press.

Helasvuo, Marja-Liisa. 1997. *When Discourse Becomes Syntax: Noun phrases and Clauses as Emergent Syntactic Units in Finnish Conversational Discourse.* Ph.D. dissertation, University of California, Santa Barbara.

Helasvuo, Marja-Liisa. 2001. *Syntax in the Making: The Emergence of Syntactic Units in Finnish Conversation.* Amsterdam: Benjamins.

Helasvuo, Marja-Liisa. 2003. "Argument splits in Finnish grammar and discourse". In John W. Du Bois, Lorraine E. Kumpf and William J. Ashby (eds), *Preferred Argument Structure: Grammar as Architecture for Function.* Amsterdam: Benjamins, 247–272.

Herring, Susan. 1989. "Verbless presentation and the discourse basis of ergativity". In Bradley Music, Randolph Graczyk and Caroline Wiltshire, *Papers from the 25th Annual Regional Meeting of the Chicago Linguistic Society 25, Part 2: Parasession on Language in Context.* Chicago: Chicago Linguistics Society, 123–137.

Hofling, Charles A. 1990. "Possession and ergativity in Itzá Maya". *International Journal of American Linguistics* 56: 542–60.

Hofling, Charles A. 1991. *Itzá Maya Texts with a Grammatical Overview.* Salt Lake City: University of Utah Press.

Hofling, Charles A. 2000. *Itzaj Maya Grammar.* Salt Lake City: University of Utah Press.

Hofling, Charles A. 2003. "Tracking the deer: Nominal reference, parallelism and Preferred Argument Structure in Itzaj Maya narrative genres". In John W. Du Bois, Lorraine E. Kumpf and William J. Ashby, *Preferred Argument Structure: Grammar as Architecture for Function.* Amsterdam: Benjamins, 385–410.

Hopper, Paul. 1988. "How ergative is Malay?" In Richard McGinn (ed), *Studies in Austronesian Linguistics.* Athens, Ohio: Ohio University Press, 441–454.

Huang, Shuanfan and Chui, Ka-Wai. 1997. "Is Chinese a pragmatic ordering language?" *Chinese languages and linguistics IV, Typological studies of languages in China.* Taipei: Academia Sinica, Institute of History and Philology, 51–79.

Iwasaki, Shoichi. 1985. "The 'Given A Constraint' and the Japanese particle *ga.*" In Scott DeLancy and Russell S. Tomlin (eds), *Proceedings of the First Annual Meeting of the Pacific Linguistic Conference.* Eugene, OR: Department of Linguistics, University of Oregon, 152–167.

Josserand, Kathryn. 1995. "Participant tracking in Maya hieroglyphic texts: Who was that masked man?" *Journal of Linguistic Anthropology* 5: 65–89.

Kärkkäinen, Elise. 1996. "Preferred Argument Structure and subject role in American English conversational discourse". *Journal of Pragmatics* 25: 675–701.

Kelly, Barbara F. 1999, "Language acquisition and Preferred Argument Structure". Paper presented at *International Association for the Study of Child Language, 5th Annual Meeting,* San Sebatian, Spain.

Klomp, H. 1993. "The structure of discourse and preferred argument structure". *University of Melbourne Working Papers in Linguistics* 13: 47–61.

Kohn, Susan E. and Cragnolino, Ana. 2003. "The role of Preferred Argument Structure for understanding aphasic sentence planning". In John W. Du Bois, Lorraine E. Kumpf and William J. Ashby (eds), *Preferred Argument Structure: Grammar as Architecture for Function.* Amsterdam: Benjamins, 339–351.

Kohn, Susan E., Cragnolino, Ana and Pustejovsky, James. 1997. "Pronoun production in agrammatic speakers: Patterns of use and avoidance in context neutral sentences". *Aphasiology* 11: 157–175.

Kumagai, Yoshiharu. 2000. "Ergativity in English spontaneous discourse". *Mulberry: Bulletin of the Department of English, Faculty of Letters, Aichi Prefectural University,* 49: 35–60.

Kumagai, Yoshiharu. 2001a. "An analysis of English Pear Film narratives". *Bulletin of the Faculty of Letters, Aichi Prefectural University,* 49: 97–109.

Kumagai, Yoshiharu. 2001b. "Preferred Argument Structure and discourse ergativity in English". *Mulberry: Bulletin of the Department of English, Faculty of Letters, Aichi Prefectural University,* 50: 77–90.

Kumagai, Yoshiharu. 2001c. "Danwa shiryou ga shimesu eigo no noukakusei" [Ergativity in English as revealed in discourse]. In Spoken Language Working Group (ed), *Bunpou to Onsei* [Speech and Grammar]. Tokyo: Kurioso Publishers, 241–261.

Kumpf, Lorraine E. 1992. "Preferred Argument Structure in second language discourse: A preliminary study". *Studies in Language* 16: 369–403.

Kumpf, Lorraine E. 2003. "Genre and Preferred Argument Structure: Sources of argument structure in classroom discourse". In John W. Du Bois, Lorraine E. Kumpf and William J. Ashby (eds), *Preferred Argument Structure: Grammar as Architecture for Function.* Amsterdam: Benjamins, 109–130.

Lambrecht, Knud. 1987. "On the status of SVO sentences in French discourse". In Russell S. Tomlin (ed), *Coherence and Grounding in Discourse.* Amsterdam: Benjamins, 217–261.

Lambrecht, Knud. 1988. "Presentational cleft constructions in spoken French". In John Haiman and Sandra A. Thompson (eds), *Clause Combining in Grammar and Discourse.* Amsterdam: Benjamins, 135–79.

Langacker, Ronald W. 2001. "Discourse in Cognitive Grammar". *Cognitive Linguistics* 12: 143–188.

Larsen, Thomas W. 1981. "Functional correlates of ergativity in Aguacatec". *Proceedings of the Annual Meeting of the Berkeley Linguistics Society* 7: 136–153.

Larsen, Thomas W. 1982. "The cognitive bases of case marking and ergativity". Unpublished ms., Linguistics Department, University of California, Berkeley.

Laury, Ritva. 1997. *Demonstratives in Interaction: The Emergence of a Definitive Article in Finnish.* Amsterdam: Benjamins.

Lichtenberk, František. 1996. "Patterns of anaphora in To'aba'ita discourse". In Barbara A. Fox (ed), *Studies in Anaphora.* Amsterdam: Benjamins, 379–411.

Long, Zhihua. 1990. "The Preferred Argument Structure in Mandarin Chinese and its cogintive implications". *Colorado Research in Linguistics* 11: 42–59.

Martin, Laura. 2003. "Narrator virtuosity and the strategic exploitation of Preferred Argument Structure: Repetition and constructed speech in Mochó narrative". In John W. Du Bois, Lorraine E. Kumpf and William J. Ashby (eds), *Preferred Argument Structure: Grammar as Architecture for Function.* Amsterdam: Benjamins, 411–435.

Matsumoto, Kazuko. 1997. "NPs in Japanese conversation". *Pragmatics* 7: 163–181.

Matsumoto, Kazuko. 1998. "On the 'one new NP per unit' constraint in spoken Japanese". *The Bulletin of Aichi University of Education* 47: 17–25.

Matsumoto, Kazuko. 1999. "Intonation units and functional composition in Japanese conversational discourse". *Functions of Language* 6: 163–194.

Matsumoto, Kazuko. 2000a. "Intonation units, clauses and preferred argument structure in conversational Japanese". *Language Sciences* 22: 63–86.

Matsumoto, Kazuko. 2000b. "Japanese intonation units and syntactic structure". *Studies in Language* 24: 515–564.

Matsumoto, Kazuko. Forthcoming. *Intonation Units in Japanese Conversational Discourse: Syntactic, Informational, and Functional Structures.* Amsterdam: Benjamins.

McGregor, William B. 1989. "Discourse basis of ergative marking in Gooniyandi". *La Trobe University Working Papers in Linguistics* 2: 127–158.

McGregor, William B. 1992. "The semantics of ergative marking in Gooniyandi". *Linguistics* 30: 275–318.

McGregor, William B. 1999. "'Optional' ergative marking in Gooniyandi revisited: Implications to the theory of marking". *Leuvanse Bijdragen* 87: 491–534.

Mirzayan, Armik. 2002. "Information structure in Lakhota narratives". Paper presented at Linguistic Society of America Annual Meeting, San Francisco.

Mora-Marín, David F. 2002. "The Preferred Argument Structure of Classic Lowland Mayan texts". Paper presented at *Society for the Study of the Indigenous Languages of the Americas*, San Francisco.

Mora-Marín, David F. Forthcoming. *Discourse Structure and Coordinate Constructions in Classic Lowland Mayan texts*, Albany, NY. Anthropology Department, SUNY Albany.

Nakayama, Toshihide and Ichihashi-Nakayama, Kumiko. 1994. "Discourse perspective for core-oblique distinction in Japanese". *Santa Barbara Papers in Linguistics* 5: 158–177.

Narasimhan, Bhuvana and Budwig, Nancy. 2001. "Argument realization in Hindi child-caregiver discourse". Paper presented at South Asian Languages Analysis Roundtable, University of Konstanz.

Narasimhan, Bhuvana, Budwig, Nancy and Murty, Lalita. Forthcoming. "Argument realization in Hindi caregiver-child discourse". Journal of Pragmatics.

Neves, Maria Helena de Moura. 1994. "Estrutura Argumental Preferida do portugués falado culto do Brasil em Inquéritos do NURC". Unpublished ms., São Paulo.

O'Dowd, Elizabeth. 1990. "Discourse pressure, genre and grammatical alignment—after Du Bois". *Studies in Language* 14: 365–403.

Payne, Doris L. 1987. "Information structuring in Papago narrative discourse". *Language* 63: 783–804.

Rubino, Carl. 1995. "Preferred Argument Structure in Central Alaskan Yup'ik". *Santa Barbara Papers in Linguistics*: 7: 139–152.

Sasaki, Miyuki. 1997, "Topic continuity in Japanese-English interlanguage". *International Review of Applied Linguistics in Language Teaching (IRAL)* 35: 1–21.

Scancarelli, Janine. 1985. "Referential strategies in Chamorro narratives: Preferred Clause Structure and ergativity". *Studies in Language* 9: 335–362.

Schuetze-Coburn, Stephan. 1987. "Topic management and the lexicon: A discourse profile of three-argument verbs in German". M.A. thesis, University of California, Los Angeles.

Schuetze-Coburn, Stephan. 1994. *Prosody, Syntax, and Discourse Pragmatics: Assessing Information Flow in German Conversation.* Ph.D. dissertation, University of California, Los Angeles.

Shibasaki, Reijirou. 2003. "Diachronic aspects of Preferred Argument Structure and broader implications". *Proceedings of the Annual Meeting of the Berkeley Linguistics Society* 28.

Skarabela, B. and Allen, Shanley E.M. 2002. "The role of joint attention in argument realization in child Inuktitut". In B. Skarabela, S.A. Fish and Anna H.-J. Do (eds), *Proceedings of the 26th Annual Boston University Conference on Language Development.* Somerville, MA: Cascadilla Press, 620–30.

Smith, Wendy. 1996. "Spoken narrative and Preferred Clause Structure: Evidence from modern Hebrew discourse". *Studies in Language* 20: 163–189.

Tao, Hongyin. 1996. *Units in Mandarin Conversation: Prosody, Discourse, and Grammar.* Amsterdam: Benjamins.

Tao, Hongyin and Thompson, Sandra A. 1994. "The discourse and grammar interface: The preferred clause structure in Mandarin conversational discourse". *Journal of Chinese Language Teacher's Association* 29: 1–34.

Thompson, Sandra A. 1997. "Discourse motivations for the core-oblique distinction as a language universal". In Akio Kamio (ed), *Directions in Functional Linguistics.* Amsterdam: Benjamins, 59–82.

Uziel-Karl, Sigal. 2001. "A development model for the acquisition of verb argument structure". Paper presented at *Conference on acquisition of verb grammar and verb argument structure [ZAS], Berlin.*

Weber, Elizabeth. 2003. "Nominal information flow in the talk of two boys with autism". In John W. Du Bois, Lorraine E. Kumpf and William J. Ashby (eds), *Preferred Argument Structure: Grammar as Architecture for Function.* Amsterdam: Benjamins, 353–383.

Wieselman Schulman, Bari, Mylander, Carolyn and Goldin-Meadow, Susan. 2001. “Ergative structure at sentence and discourse levels in a self-generated communication system”. In Anna H.-J. Do, Laura Dominguez and Aimee Johansen (eds), *Proceedings of the 25th Annual Boston University Conference on Language Development*, vol. 2. Somerville, MA: Cascadilla Press, 815–824.

Name index

A

Ariel, M. 6, 37, 41, 74, 84, 213, 225, 230, 232, 236, 237, 240, 241, 322, 388

Ashby, W. 3, 38, 39, 62, 63, 66, 69–71, 234, 261, 361, 362

B

Baltaxe, C. 354, 355, 358, 365

Bentivoglio, P. 3, 38, 39, 43, 62, 63, 66, 69–71, 82, 234, 261, 301, 302, 361, 362

Börjars, K. 33

Bresnan, J. 18, 19, 21, 50

Brody, J. 141, 392, 398, 414

Butt, M. 34, 43, 50

C

Cazden, C. 112

Chafe, W. 8, 19, 23, 26, 30, 37, 39, 40, 44, 49, 61, 72, 81, 84, 111, 114, 115, 117, 126, 132, 139, 179, 182, 184, 194, 203, 214, 220, 225, 231, 259, 261, 269, 301, 311, 340, 350, 353, 361, 363, 388

Clancy, P. 3, 4, 7, 39, 56, 81, 82, 83, 88, 90, 102, 104, 107, 220, 230, 232, 234, 239, 301, 302, 311–315, 323, 325, 328, 330, 333, 335, 336, 341, 356, 400, 439

Clark, E. 8, 242, 243, 337, 381, 439

Comrie, B. 23, 30, 162, 192, 328, 362

Corston, S. (Corston-Oliver, S.) 7, 39, 215, 222, 273, 277, 280, 282, 284, 288, 290, 293, 296, 297, 298

Cumming, S. 44, 94, 358

D

Davis, A. 22, 24, 26, 44, 50, 52, 54

Dixon, R. 6, 7, 30–32, 51, 159, 162, 192, 194, 230, 243, 273, 274, 293–296, 298, 328, 362,

Du Bois, J. 1–3, 5, 15, 19, 30, 32, 33, 40, 41, 43, 44, 46, 51, 53, 54, 61, 62, 61, 62, 65, 67, 74, 81, 85, 86, 89, 94, 98, 100, 101–104, 107, 109–111, 113, 116, 117, 119–121, 126, 135, 136, 139–141, 144–147, 150–152, 154–156, 159–163, 165, 167, 168, 169, 172, 173, 175, 176, 189–194, 204, 206, 207, 209–211, 213, 214, 221, 225, 226, 230, 232–237, 240–242, 247, 248, 257, 258, 260, 261, 288, 292, 293, 301, 302, 301–303, 308, 311–315, 319, 320, 325, 328, 333, 335, 385, 386, 387, 389, 404, 411, 431, 432

Duranti, A. 7

Durie, M. 5, 21, 31–33, 39–41, 43, 50, 54, 71, 159–161, 167, 176, 177, 179, 182, 193, 194, 234, 247, 248, 260, 414

Dutra, R. 39, 54, 73, 74, 361, 362

E

England, N. 4, 5, 131, 132, 138, 145–147, 385–388, 392, 396, 400, 406, 413, 425, 433

F

Fillmore, C. 21, 23–27, 29, 42, 44, 49, 51, 54

Fine, J. 352, 355, 356

Foley, W. 26, 28, 31, 32, 49, 242
Fox, B. 32, 39, 43, 44, 54, 143, 215, 220
Frege, G. 15–18, 25, 51

G
Gawron, J. 26
Givón, T. 23, 32, 81, 162, 165, 208, 214, 225–227, 230, 231, 242, 257, 287, 292, 301, 388, 389, 397
Goldberg, A. 19, 24, 42, 43, 50, 52, 54

H
Herring, S. 40, 155, 189, 192, 193, 261
Hofling, A. 9, 133, 140, 151, 385, 386, 391–394, 398, 404, 408, 409, 414
Hopper, P. 21, 26, 44, 49, 50, 147, 277

K
Kärkkäinen, E. 39, 109, 118, 120, 220, 261, 271, 356, 362–366, 371–374, 382
Keenan, E. 26, 30, 32
King, T. 34, 43, 50, 170, 178, 179, 183
Koenig, J.-P. 22, 58
Kumpf, L. 4, 39, 81, 109, 112, 118, 120, 127, 301, 362–366, 371

L
Langacker, R. 26, 44, 49–51
Levin, B. 18, 21, 23, 25, 33, 44, 50

M
Martin, L. 4, 5, 9, 67, 131–133, 141–144, 151, 154, 155, 385, 386, 387, 388, 392, 393, 396, 398, 400, 406, 413, 414, 424, 425, 433
Matsumoto, K. 39, 54
Mayerthaler, W. 274
Mel'cuk, I. 192
Miller, C. 109, 127, 392, 393
Mithun, M. 21, 30, 32, 33, 39, 41, 247, 268, 292, 327
Montague, R. 17

O
O'Dowd, E. 40, 109, 194, 356, 362, 363, 371, 372, 374
Ochs, E. 7, 82, 100, 112, 247

P
Partee, B. 17
Paul, R. 358

R
Ross, M. 283–285, 287, 290

S
Silverstein, M. 6, 7, 30–32, 41, 51, 161, 162, 182, 192, 216, 247, 256, 257, 261, 293–296
Slobin, D. 49

T
Talmy, L. 25, 49, 50
Tao, H. 188, 193, 194
Thompson, S. 21, 23, 26, 39, 43, 44, 49, 50, 83, 111, 117, 147, 167, 169, 172, 191, 193, 194, 248, 261, 274, 277, 292, 301, 361–363, 366, 371, 378
Tomasello, M. 42, 106
Trask, R. 274, 293
Trubetzkoy, N. 274

V
Van Valin, R. 21, 26, 28, 31, 32, 41, 49, 57, 242
Vincent, N. 33

W
Waterhouse, J. 290
Wierzbicka, A. 294, 296, 297

Language index

A
Acehnese 5, 39, 54, 159–196, 260

D
Dyirbal 30

E
English 17, 20, 21, 23, 25, 33–35, 37, 39, 42, 53, 54, 104, 112, 118, 120, 192, 193, 206, 228, 229, 243, 247, 261, 265, 307, 342, 362, 363, 374, 379
Eskimo-Aleut 303, 336

F
Finnish 6, 244–270
French 3, 37, 39, 38, 61–67, 61–74
  Old French 61–78

G
Gooniyandi 35

H
Hebrew 35, 37, 39

I
Inuktitut 301–336
Itzaj Maya (see 'Maya') 9, 385–409

J
Jakaltek 142
Japanese 37, 39, 106, 206, 261, 336

K
Kapampangan 292
Kaqchikel 138
Korean 3, 7, 39, 56, 81–106, 302, 311–315, 319–325, 328–330, 333, 336, 341

L
Latin 74, 294

M
Mam 4, 131–134, 137–139, 142, 144–149, 151, 409
Mapuche 226
Mapudungun 6, 225–243
Maya/Mayan 33, 51, 61, 131–156, 197, 210, 301, 385, 387, 392, 398, 401, 411–414, 433
Mocho 9, 67, 132–134, 138–141, 143–146, 148, 151–156, 411–434

N
Nepali 5, 197–222
Nias 192

O
Oceanic 273, 284, 285, 287, 297

P
Papago 35, 37
Portugese, Brazilian 39, 54, 73, 74

Q
Q'anjob'al 132, 133, 138, 139, 146, 148, 151–154

R
Roviana 7, 222, 273–298

S
Sakapultek/Sakapulteko 4, 7, 33, 35, 37, 39, 51, 61, 62, 74, 103, 110, 131–136, 146, 147, 151–154, 161, 190, 192, 197, 198, 204–206, 219, 233, 260, 301–303, 311–315, 319, 320–325, 328, 329, 333
Spanish 3, 37–39, 61–74, 82, 133, 151, 261, 302
  Old Spanish 61–78

T
Teko/Tektiteko 131–133, 139, 148, 151–154
Tongan 295

Y
Yup'ik 302, 311–315, 319, 323, 325, 328, 333, 335, 336

Subject index

A
A role 15, 20, 21, 30, 32–41, 46, 61, 63–65, 72, 81–89, 95–99, 101–105,110, 118–119, 142, 152–154, 159–162,176–178, 180–183, 189–191, 198–200, 204–209, 212–213, 215–219, 233–237, 254–261, 273, 276, 282, 283, 285–291, 293–294, 296–297, 313–316, 328–333, 341, 344–345, 348–349, 365–367, 371–372, 374–375, 378, 386–389, 397, 398, 401, 403, 406, 407
absolutive 14, 30, 32, 40, 41, 46, 103, 126, 199, 215–219, 273–275, 277–284, 288, 290–298, 306, 319, 334, 386, 417, 433
accessibility/accessible (see 'salience') 37, 38 41, 44, 46, 84, 111, 114, 117, 120, 139, 140, 156, 180, 184, 203, 215–217, 219, 226, 230–232, 236, 363
accessibility theory 6, 232
accusative 74, 83, 104, 132, 154, 160–162, 181, 192, 216, 247, 249–251, 262, 268, 270, 283, 294, 298
activation 69, 73, 111, 117, 182, 184, 185, 194, 199, 203, 209, 216, 217, 219, 230, 232, 353, 356, 363, 371–372, 378–379, 418
activation cost 184, 185, 199, 202, 203, 206, 248, 259, 260
active 32, 33, 41, 111, 181, 191, 228, 231, 232, 234–240, 247, 270, 272, 304, 308, 335, 353, 356, 363, 371–372
actor 5, 20, 33, 176, 177, 181, 182, 183, 188–190, 227–229, 242
actor-undergoer 5, 14, 33
adaptation/adaptive 45, 187
adnominal 169, 175, 179, 180
agency/agent (see 'A role') 18, 20–23, 28, 29, 31, 32, 47, 117, 131, 145, 146, 252, 256, 268, 295–296, 325–328, 331, 332, 334–335, 402, 418
agent-patient 327, 328
agentive 31–33, 41, 63, 146, 264, 294, 326, 331, 332, 333, 420
anaphora 13, 206, 252, 277
animacy/animate 31, 32, 65, 98, 99, 102, 105, 215, 216, 217–219, 222, 285, 286, 295–298, 311, 328–334, 356, 361–363, 374, 375, 378, 388–390, 394–397, 401, 406–407
animacy hierarchy 295, 325, 328–333
antipassive 146, 153, 154, 326, 331–333
aphasia 342–343, 347
architecture/architectural 13, 15, 18, 29, 44, 47, 109, 110, 127
argument selection 16–18, 22–30, 32, 33, 41, 47, 49
argument status 194, 415, 417, 418, 421
argument structure 19, 22–23, 27, 29, 30, 32–35, 38, 42, 43–46, 48–53, 54, 105, 109, 110, 129, 131, 132, 133, 146, 150, 151, 154, 203, 233, 258, 268, 301, 302, 309, 311, 313, 315, 322, 332, 333, 340–350, 356, 362, 363, 364, 373, 378–380,

385–387, 400, 406, 411, 412, 415, 420, 421, 424, 427, 430–433
Asperger syndrome 354
attention 16, 47, 92, 94, 96, 100, 101, 103–104, 109, 111, 112, 113, 123, 125, 127, 130, 169, 172, 176, 182, 183, 184, 187, 191, 230, 421
joint attention 4, 100, 111–113, 123, 127
autism/autistic 353–362, 364–366, 371, 373, 374, 379, 380

C
Cantar de Mio Cid 62
case grammar 24
case marking 162, 247–252, 256, 257, 265–267, 282, 293, 294, 305, 306
Chanson de Roland 62
classifier 138, 390, 391
co-argument 12, 26, 27, 42, 49, 50
co-argument effects 15, 26, 27, 42, 49–51
cognition 12, 48
cognitive constraints 81, 106
cognitive processes 12
cognitive verbs 221
competing motivations 161, 191, 199, 219
competition model 241, 243
complement/complementation 19, 43, 65, 86, 89, 116, 142, 143, 165, 169, 200, 202–204, 221
complexity 42, 44, 47, 50–52, 310, 321, 325
computational linguistics 39, 241, 242
construal 26, 44, 49
constructed speech 411, 413–415, 418, 426
construction 11, 12, 14, 36, 40, 42, 43, 44, 47, 50, 52, 54, 147, 177, 220, 222, 223, 263, 264, 276, 277, 327, 328, 390, 391, 395, 398, 399, 412, 418, 424
contrast 13, 37, 40, 88, 138, 143, 192, 194, 278, 297, 305, 311, 318, 385, 386, 395, 398, 401, 418, 421, 423
copula 64, 85–87, 90, 91, 99–101, 202, 204, 254, 257–258, 264, 267, 309, 318
core argument 18, 25, 34, 35, 37, 38, 46, 49, 61, 63, 64, 63, 64, 65, 69, 81, 84, 85, 87, 90, 91, 94, 99, 100, 104, 105, 106, 110, 113, 116–119, 133–135, 142, 143, 149, 164, 169, 171–176, 179–182, 188–191, 193, 194, 203, 204, 206, 260, 268, 273–79, 283, 288–290, 292, 293, 296–298, 355, 362–364, 372–373
core-oblique 272, 274
cross-linguistic 18, 30, 33, 46, 274, 292, 294
cross-referencing 7, 46, 135, 138, 161, 162, 174, 177, 192, 194, 197, 198, 301–305, 308, 318, 323–325, 327, 329, 333

D
deficit 351, 354, 357, 358, 361, 373, 379
definite/definiteness 26, 38, 140, 247, 359, 388, 390, 391, 392, 394, 396, 419–421
deixis/deictic 84, 88, 90, 91, 94, 95, 100, 101, 105, 179, 193, 221, 395, 407–408, 420
demonstrative 306, 314, 316, 317, 322–328, 333, 336
density, referential (see 'referential density')
detransitivizing processes 131, 154, 325, 327–328, 331–334
development 160, 273, 285, 288, 361
child language development 81–108
diachronic processes 28, 61, 105, 162, 283
directive 96, 97
discourse pragmatics/discourse pragmatic (see 'pragmatics')

12–15, 23, 25, 43, 47, 48, 52, 83, 102, 104, 105, 379, 396
discourse profile 40, 42–44, 50–51, 263
disorder 353, 356–358, 364, 367, 369, 373, 379–380
ditransitive 19, 28, 36, 38, 42, 44, 50, 51, 106, 202–204
double positive 209

E
Ellipsis/eliptical 81, 82, 84, 85, 88, 91, 94–96, 103–105
E-NP (see 'existential') 263–267
epic (see 'mythic narrative') 62, 63, 66, 72, 73
equational 84, 85, 88, 90, 91, 145, 148, 152, 153, 304, 309, 310–313, 318, 324, 328, 387
ergative-absolutive 14, 32, 33, 41, 62, 105, 273, 274, 277, 278, 279, 280, 288, 292–295, 297, 298, 306
ergativity/ergative 14, 15, 29–33, 40, 41, 44, 51, 56–59, 61, 62, 79, 81–83, 103, 107, 129, 131, 132, 134, 135, 153, 156, 159–163, 175, 181, 189–192, 195, 196–200, 210, 216, 222, 223, 229, 256, 257, 260, 273, 274, 277–282, 288, 292–298, 302–306, 319, 333, 385, 386, 404, 407
event 12, 13, 17, 19–21, 23–26, 28, 40, 44, 46, 47, 49, 52, 53, 177, 257
existential (see 'E-NP') 74, 84, 85, 88, 91, 99, 100, 103, 117, 125, 146, 262–267, 270, 271, 309–316, 324, 328, 394, 401, 408

F
first mention 37, 38, 84, 89, 94, 167, 173, 174, 179–183, 259, 387, 388, 390, 406, 413, 420, 423, 430
focus 92, 94, 100, 138, 146, 169, 173, 176, 182, 183, 184, 191, 276, 279, 290, 297, 391, 392, 395, 398, 401, 402, 416, 417, 420
free NP 175, 186, 187, 362, 364
frequency 35, 82, 85, 94, 100, 103, 126, 127, 180, 193, 234, 285–289, 296, 307, 342, 343–345, 367, 369, 371, 379, 389, 390
full NP (see 'lexical NP') 118, 133, 135–137, 192, 229, 230, 234, 249, 250, 251, 254–260, 262, 266–268, 354–356, 365
function/functional 11, 13, 14, 17, 18, 19, 23, 24, 25, 27–31, 33, 36, 40, 41, 44–49, 51, 53, 54, 90–91, 92, 94–97, 100, 101, 103, 104, 133, 137, 160, 162, 226–229, 231–236, 240, 241, 247–248, 251, 254, 256, 258, 259, 261, 262, 264–269, 294, 295, 297–298, 318, 322–325, 339, 340, 362, 364, 367–369, 371, 385, 391, 396

G
genre 63, 66, 68, 73, 109–130, 132, 150–152, 185, 189, 191, 194, 355, 356, 364, 386, 396, 401, 407
Given A Constraint 61, 62, 69, 71, 101, 110, 119–120, 159, 198, 206, 217, 219, 302, 314, 355
given information/given 1, 45, 46, 81, 82, 84, 111, 114, 117, 119–121, 126, 139, 141, 172, 198–199, 213–220, 226, 230, 231, 233, 234, 236, 237, 259, 260, 268, 289, 291, 293, 296, 297, 353–356, 362, 363, 371, 373, 374, 378, 385, 388, 390, 404, 407, 411, 415, 424, 425
grammar in use 11–15, 29, 33, 40, 48, 49, 51, 53
grammatical categories 103, 105, 223
grammatical dimension 31, 34, 61, 65, 86, 198
grammatical structures 2, 6, 11, 47, 57
grammaticalization/grammaticization 2, 6, 7, 13, 14, 19, 23, 28, 29, 33, 40, 45–47, 53, 83, 102, 104, 105, 159, 181, 192, 256, 258, 261, 262,

265, 268, 273, 287, 288, 290, 291, 292, 297, 298

H
hierarchy 16, 26, 30, 32, 180, 181, 186, 189, 194, 227, 231, 256, 257, 273, 293–298, 325, 328–330, 332, 333, 388
human 6, 21, 31, 40, 81, 98–101, 104, 106, 151, 218, 222, 249, 252, 254, 255–258, 261, 262, 264, 266, 267, 268, 282, 285–287, 294, 296, 297, 320, 328–330, 332, 385, 387, 390, 402, 404, 406, 407, 412

I
imperative 93, 103, 112, 116, 208, 210, 211, 221, 222
inanimate 4, 9, 94, 95, 98, 99, 101, 104, 106, 215, 219, 285, 286, 294, 296, 297, 311, 328–332, 334, 363, 374, 375, 378, 388–392, 395, 396, 406, 407
incorporated nominals 165
indefinite 26, 359, 390–392, 419, 420
information flow 52, 81, 111, 122, 126, 131, 152, 175, 197, 257, 259, 267, 319, 328, 333, 353, 355, 356, 361, 362, 378, 379
information management 9, 37, 40, 43, 47, 49
information pressure 5, 110, 113, 114, 119, 121, 151, 158–195, 221, 320, 321, 325, 333
intonation unit 19, 39, 115, 193
intransitive 15, 20, 21, 28, 30, 39, 42, 43, 50, 82, 84, 85, 89, 93, 94, 99, 100, 105, 133, 142–144, 146, 163, 173, 174, 173, 174, 187, 188–190, 230, 232, 233, 236–238, 242, 257, 258, 259–262, 267, 288, 289, 303–305, 308, 310–313, 319, 324, 325, 328, 344, 350, 387, 395, 418, 430
inverse 29, 227–229, 239–241

L
labeling 90, 91, 101
language acquisition 39, 83, 107, 108, 129, 340
language use 1, 3, 9, 13, 34, 41, 47, 51, 53, 226, 247, 252, 298, 356, 413
lexical 16–22, 50, 52–53, 64, 126, 149, 151, 152, 154, 155, 159, 160, 161, 163, 177, 192, 193, 194, 197–199, 202–205, 204–210, 213–215, 214–218, 217–220, 222, 225, 232, 234–242, 256–258, 279, 284, 286, 287, 294, 296, 297, 302–304, 312–317, 319–333, 340–350, 365–369, 371, 373, 374, 378, 379, 387, 388, 389, 393–398, 403–404, 405- 408, 412–415, 417, 418, 420, 421, 424–427, 429–432
  lexical A 41, 71, 118, 119, 152, 205, 257–258, 313–315, 320, 366
  lexical density 174–175, 188–190, 320
  lexical NP (see 'full NP') 6, 8, 34, 35–38, 44, 61, 66, 84, 85–94, 100, 103, 104, 111, 113, 117, 120, 121, 125, 135–139, 142, 160, 161, 192, 199, 203–207, 217–219, 234–237, 257, 279, 284, 286, 287, 296–297, 302, 304, 312–315, 320, 322, 365–369, 378–379
  lexical O 71, 95, 104, 114, 118, 218, 239, 314–315, 320, 366
  lexical S 67, 100, 110, 114, 118, 121, 122, 131, 152, 163, 175, 257–258, 314–315, 320, 366
  lexical semantics 24, 54
lexicality 161, 197, 198, 215
light subject constraint 182, 259, 350
linking 12, 15, 17, 18, 24, 26, 27, 28–30, 32, 40, 41, 43, 49, 104, 160, 164, 177
logic 16, 18, 29, 44
lookback 165
low content transitive verbs 4, 114, 117, 119, 126, 127

M
machine learning 39
management
classroom management 122, 127
management of attention 16, 100, 105, 123, 353, 356
management of information (see 'information flow') 8, 9, 37, 40, 43, 47, 49, 175
mapping (see 'linking') 12, 17, 19, 23
mental representation 102, 103, 232
morphosyntax 31, 54, 83, 199
motivation 6, 38, 41, 44, 45, 104, 125, 160, 161, 162, 163, 192, 404, 430
mythic narrative (see 'epic') 9, 386, 387, 396, 401, 407

N
names (see 'proper nouns') 32, 53, 66, 144, 145, 281–282
narration 96, 97, 392, 400, 413, 414
narrative 92, 104, 109, 110, 118, 120, 140, 141, 152, 162, 164, 171, 185, 186, 187, 188, 201, 206–209, 212, 214, 226, 229, 230, 234, 259, 272, 311–315, 319–320, 325, 329, 355, 373, 385–389, 393, 396, 398–403, 406–408, 411–414, 417, 418, 423–426, 430–433
personal narrative 9, 152, 385, 386, 387, 389, 396, 400, 403, 406, 407, 410, 433
negation 22, 165, 253, 254, 268
new information/new 4, 7, 12, 34, 38, 40, 42, 44–47, 49, 50, 53, 64, 65, 69–71, 74, 81–84, 86, 87, 88, 89, 88, 89, 92, 93, 94, 96, 97, 98, 100–102, 103–106, 100, 110, 111, 113, 114, 119, 120–122, 126, 131, 133, 140, 142, 155, 166, 176, 180, 184,186, 187, 204, 225, 230, 231, 233, 234, 235, 236, 237, 239–241, 248, 257, 259–269, 273, 279, 288–293, 297, 298, 300, 301, 311–317, 319–324, 329, 331–333, 353–356, 362, 363, 371, 372, 373, 374, 378, 379, 386–388, 400, 404, 406, 415, 421, 424, 426, 430
nominal hierarchy (see 'hierarchy') 273, 293–298
nominative 14, 20, 21, 32, 41, 62, 103, 104, 106, 162, 198, 199, 215–219, 247, 249–251, 257, 262, 263, 264, 267, 283, 294
nominative-accusative 5, 6, 14, 21, 41, 83, 106, 247, 249, 250, 257, 262, 283, 294
Non-Lexical A Constraint 8, 61, 65, 66, 68, 85, 110, 118–119, 159, 198, 258, 314, 340, 348, 349
non-new (see 'given') 38, 64, 69, 114, 120, 121, 122, 123, 125, 127, 290, 314, 315, 317, 322, 331, 332
non-referential 165, 193, 199, 204, 211, 216, 217, 219, 276, 277, 284, 424
null (see 'zero') 73, 225, 226, 229, 230, 233, 235, 234–239, 241, 242
null anaphor 225, 229, 234, 236

O
O role 15, 20, 30, 32, 35, 36, 37–41, 46, 51, 61, 65–70, 81, 82, 83–89, 92–106, 110, 114, 116–119, 120, 122, 126, 131, 135, 142, 143, 146, 153, 154, 155, 160–163, 169, 171, 176, 180, 181, 186, 189–192, 194, 197, 202, 203, 204, 215, 217, 216, 218, 234, 233, 234, 236–239, 249, 250, 257, 259, 260, 273–283, 285–294, 296–298, 311, 314–316, 319–321, 323–330, 332, 341, 344–349, 362, 363, 385–393, 397, 401, 405–407, 415–420
Object, direct 6, 7, 15–17, 20–35, 51, 61, 74, 81–84, 87–96, 98, 100, 101, 105, 110, 116, 117, 121, 122, 123, 144, 146, 152, 173, 200–203, 273, 284–285, 298, 339, 341, 345, 347–348, 350

Object, indirect (I-role) 24, 37, 57, 116, 117, 121, 148, 200, 202, 212, 385, 388, 396–397,401, 406–407
oblique 116, 117, 118, 121, 141, 143, 149, 169, 171, 172, 175, 181, 186, 188, 191, 202, 234–236, 260, 261, 265, 274, 275, 291–293, 312, 319, 326, 363–364, 372, 373, 379
old information (see 'given information') 40, 142, 143
One Lexical Argument Constraint 6, 8, 61, 67, 68, 86, 117–118, 119, 204, 226, 237, 241, 242, 312, 323, 348, 355, 378
One New Argument Constraint 61–62, 71–72, 89, 119, 198, 206, 313
one overt mention 208, 209, 211, 218, 219, 222
one-place predicates 36, 38, 44
Optimality Theory 41, 241
oral literature 62, 73
orienting expressions 167
overt mention 5, 83, 84, 101, 103–105, 198, 206–213, 219, 220–222, 262, 274, 275, 278, 283–285, 291, 309, 326, 335–336

P

parallelism/parallel 6, 9, 36, 141, 145, 225, 226, 228, 233, 237, 238, 240–243, 385, 392–395, 402, 403, 408, 410, 411, 413, 418, 420, 421, 423, 424, 430, 434, 435, 442
participant structure 101, 105, 111
passive 144, 148, 149, 153, 177, 216, 227–229, 239, 240, 251, 252, 276, 325, 326, 328, 331–333, 430
patient 4, 17, 20–23, 31, 32, 95, 146, 295, 296, 325–328, 331, 332, 334
persistence 165, 185, 187, 191, 208, 231
person 7, 9, 31, 83, 84, 95, 96, 98, 99, 102, 104, 117, 125, 127, 132, 136–139, 142–145, 153, 154, 197, 199–201, 203, 210, 214, 215, 219, 227, 230, 247, 249–259, 261, 268, 273, 279, 280, 283–285, 292, 294–298, 303–306, 316–318, 320–322, 331–336, 358, 386, 387, 395–398, 400, 405, 430
perspective 9, 11, 240, 257, 261, 354, 355, 366, 418, 420, 426
pragmatic dimension of Preferred Argument Structure 31, 34, 38, 47, 61, 69–72, 86, 206
pragmatic linking 57, 160, 164, 195
pragmatics 7, 19, 23, 26, 28, 31, 37, 38, 40–52, 61, 81, 82, 83, 86, 102, 104, 105, 110, 119, 133, 176, 181, 182, 184, 186, 190, 191, 194, 197, 198, 219, 226, 228, 229, 232, 233, 235, 236, 316, 355, 356, 361, 363
predicate nominals 36, 117, 165, 167, 193, 204
pronoun/pronominal v, 5, 6, 8, 12, 20, 21, 31, 35–38, 45, 54, 61, 64, 73, 74, 81, 84, 85, 88, 90, 91, 94, 95, 100, 105, 113, 117, 119, 120, 122, 127, 135–139, 138, 139, 144, 145, 161, 179, 192, 194, 197–199, 201–204, 206–209, 213–220, 214–219, 222, 225, 229, 230, 234, 235, 237, 247–249, 250, 251, 252, 254, 255, 256–259, 261–262, 264, 266, 267–268, 273, 274, 277–281, 283–288, 290, 292, 294–297, 298, 304, 305, 316, 318, 320, 322, 324, 325, 328, 339–341, 343–347, 349, 356, 365–367, 373, 374, 379, 387, 389, 390, 394, 395–407, 409
pronoun avoidance 340, 341, 347
proper nouns (see 'names') 74, 281–282
proto-agent 17, 29
proto-patient 17, 29, 32
proto-role 29

Q

quantifier floating 39
quantity constraint 34, 35, 38
quotation/quoted speech 65, 136, 144–145, 147, 157, 201, 202, 203,

393, 396, 398–400, 403- 405, 408, 414
quotative 144–148, 208, 212, 213, 221, 400, 404

R
ranking 24, 26–28, 49, 231, 241
realization 23, 27, 28, 34–38, 40, 43, 49, 52
reference/referential 8, 9, 12, 26, 28, 31, 46, 47, 50, 56, 81, 84–86, 89, 91, 94, 96, 100, 104, 105, 107, 112, 136, 137, 141, 145, 162, 193, 198, 199, 206, 211, 214–220, 225, 226, 229–233, 235, 234, 235–239, 238–242, 252, 257, 259, 262, 263, 265, 276, 284, 285, 292, 297, 336, 374, 385, 387, 388, 389, 394–396, 401, 403, 407, 408, 413, 415, 417, 418–421, 424–427, 429, 430
  reference status 418–421
  referential density 5, 163–175, 184–190, 193
  referential form 6, 9, 38, 46, 81, 82, 84, 85, 89, 91, 94 104, 105, 234
relative clause 44, 63, 274, 277, 293, 390, 406
relativization 39, 54, 177, 274
repair 358, 360, 368, 369, 371, 378, 379
repetition 66, 67, 74, 97, 121, 125, 126, 141, 212, 222, 239, 368–369, 392–395, 408, 411, 413–415, 417, 418, 421, 423, 424, 430–432
role constraint 34, 36, 38

S
S role 5, 7, 15, 20, 21, 30, 32, 33, 35–46, 51, 61, 64, 67, 70, 71, 74, 81–96, 98–106, 110, 114, 116, 118–124, 126, 128, 129, 131, 135, 137, 141, 142, 146–154, 160–163, 169, 175, 176, 181–183, 190–192, 197–208, 115–220, 233–37, 254–256, 258–260, 273, 280, 283, 286–93, 296, 298, 314–315, 320, 326, 365–366, 371–372, 375, 378, 386–388, 396–398, 406, 407, 417
  Sa 176, 177, 180, 181–183, 189–191
  Se 69, 71, 84–88, 91, 92, 96, 98, 99, 100, 102, 105, 176, 177, 180, 181, 189, 190, 254–256, 258, 314–316, 320, 330, 366, 371, 374, 378, 388, 389, 397, 399, 401, 404, 407
  Si 64–66, 69–71, 84, 85, 86, 88, 91, 92, 94, 100, 105, 314, 315, 314–316, 319–321, 323–325, 330, 332, 333, 371, 374, 378, 388, 389, 396–397, 401, 407
  So 176, 177, 180, 181
  Sx 84–86, 88, 91, 98–100, 105, 314–316, 320, 330, 377
salience 123, 124–225, 227, 229–235, 236–239, 241–242, 292
scene 23–25, 28, 49, 54, 100, 164, 168
semantic analysis 12
semantic features 12, 26
semantic linking 160, 177
semantic structure 12, 14, 60
semantics 12, 14, 17–19, 29, 33, 40, 47–49, 52, 160, 177
sentence 5, 8, 13, 14, 20, 39, 237, 405
  in Nepali 197–223
  sentence planning, aphasic 339–350
  sentence production 8, 339
sign function 46
soft constraints 34, 41, 241
split ergativity 6, 15, 21, 30–32, 41, 51, 70, 103, 161, 198–200, 216, 218–220, 277–283, 288–294, 385, 386
split intransitivity 21, 59, 60
split S role in Acehnese 165, 181
splits, arguments, in Finnish 247–268
staging 126, 180, 183, 184, 319
subject (see S role) 6, 7, 12, 16, 17, 20–32, 35, 36, 52, 54, 61, 82–84, 93, 102, 103, 105, 117, 176, 177, 182, 200, 201–203, 208, 210, 211, 216, 217, 219, 220, 227–242, 247–268,

304–305, 318, 321, 324, 326–327, 331–333, 340–341, 346–349, 362–363, 366, 371, 374, 378, 417
subject selection 15, 16, 22, 25, 27, 29, 55
synonymy 141, 413, 425
syntax
and argument structure 1, 2, 12, 13, 17–19, 29, 44, 53, 114
and discourse 12, 114, 357–358, 418
of pronouns 145

T
targeting 27–29, 49
theory of mind 8, 353–355, 362, 379, 380
three-place predicates 28, 36, 42
token selection 34, 43, 64, 163
token aggregate 43
topic/topicality 9, 13, 14, 18, 31–32, 52, 160–162, 208, 210, 230, 254, 257, 266, 268, 292, 297, 354, 385, 388–391, 394, 395, 396–408, 414
topic continuity 31, 32, 58, 107, 160, 161, 162, 195, 223, 257, 385
topic shift 400, 402, 403, 405, 407
tracking vi, 9, 12, 46, 47, 49, 79, 140, 159, 162, 166, 167–169, 172–175, 179, 193, 194, 248, 260–262, 268
transitivity/transitive ix, 4, 5, 8, 12, 15, 19, 20, 21, 26, 28–31, 34, 35, 41–44, 50, 57, 58, 60, 63, 64, 72, 81–86, 89, 94, 95, 97, 98, 100, 101, 105, 106, 108, 110, 117, 119, 126, 131, 132, 142, 144, 146, 147, 152–154, 157, 173, 174, 176, 177, 178, 186, 192–194, 201–204, 220, 229, 230, 232, 233, 235–238, 242, 254, 256, 257, 258–262, 277, 283, 288, 289, 295, 302, 303, 305, 308, 310–313, 319, 321, 324, 325, 327, 328, 330–333, 339–342, 344, 346–350, 362, 386, 387, 395, 400, 406, 417–418, 430–432
two-place predicates 34, 35, 38, 41
typology/typological 5–7, 12, 14, 15, 30–33, 51, 53, 56, 57, 59, 60, 159, 160, 222, 247, 284, 293, 409

U
unaccusative 21
undergoer (see 'actor-undergoer') 5, 176, 177, 181, 186, 189, 190, 227, 276, 277
unergative 21
ungrammaticality 34, 41
universals 12, 32, 53
use 1–5, 8–15, 19, 25, 29, 33, 34, 40–42, 48, 51, 53, 102, 105, 109, 112, 114, 121, 123, 125, 131, 225–226, 232, 235, 238, 239, 241, 242, 247, 252, 258, 266, 267, 277, 279, 282, 287, 293, 298, 305, 316, 323–325, 331, 333–334, 339, 340, 347, 354–360, 367, 371, 373, 374, 413, 414, 421, 424

V
variation 27, 33, 133, 142, 143, 150–151, 199, 220, 230, 242, 256, 312, 357, 417, 431
verb serialization 177
violation of Preferred Argument Structure constraints 8, 102, 211, 330, 332, 333, 342, 345–349, 373

W
word order 6, 66, 104, 105, 247–249, 252, 254–257, 262, 263, 266, 267–268
written language 39, 62, 63, 164, 171, 185

Z
zero (see 'null') 5, 46, 61, 64, 65, 68, 116, 119, 137, 151, 192, 198, 201, 203, 206–208, 211–215, 220, 250–254, 262, 273–275, 277, 279–282, 284–286, 285–291, 298, 362, 365–367
zero anaphora (see 'null anaphora') 174, 194, 206, 252, 277

In the series STUDIES IN DISCOURSE AND GRAMMAR (SiDaG) the following titles have been published:

1. GELUYKENS, Ronald: *From Discourse Process to Grammatical Construction: On Left-Dislocation in English.* Amsterdam/Philadelphia, 1992.
2. IWASAKI, Shoichi: *Subjectivity in Grammar and Discourse: Theoretical Considerations and a Case Study of Japanese Spoken Discourse.* Amsterdam/Philadelphia, 1993.
3. WEBER, Elizabeth G.: *Varieties of Questions in English Conversation.* Amsterdam/ Philadelphia, 1993.
4. DOWNING, Pamela: *Numerical Classifier Systems: The Case of Japanese.* Amsterdam/Philadelphia, 1996.
5. TAO, Hongyin: *Units in Mandarin Conversation: Prosody, Discourse, and Grammar.* Amsterdam/Philadelphia, 1996.
6. DORGELOH, Heidrun: *Inversion in Modern English: Form and function.* Amsterdam/ Philadelphia, 1997.
7. LAURY, Ritva: *Demonstratives in Interaction. The emergence of a definite article in Finnish.* Amsterdam/Philadelphia, 1997.
8. MORI, Junko: *Negotiating Agreement and Disagreement in Japanese. Connective expressions and turn construction.* Amsterdam/Philadelphia, 1999.
9. HELASVUO, Marja-Liisa: *Syntax in the making: The emergence of syntactic units in Finnish conversation.* Amsterdam/Philadelpia, 2001.
10. SELTING, Margret and Elizabeth COUPER-KUHLEN (eds.): *Studies in Interactional Linguistics.* Amsterdam/Philadelpia, 2001.
11. SCHEIBMAN, Joanne: *Point of View and Grammar. Structural patterns of subjectivity in American English conversation.* Amsterdam/Philadelpia, 2002.
12. HAYASHI, Makoto: *Joint Utterance Construction in Japanese Conversation.* Amsterdam/Philadelpia, 2003.
13. ENGLEBRETSON, ROBERT: *Searching for Structure. The problem of complementation in colloquial Indonesian conversation.* Amsterdam/Philadelpia, 2003.
14. DU BOIS, John W., Lorraine E. KUMPF and William J. ASHBY (eds.): *Preferred Argument Structure. Grammar as architecture for function.* Amsterdam/Philadelpia, 2003.